*Major Problems in
the History of the
Italian Renaissance*

Major Problems in European History Series

Major Problems in the History of the Italian Renaissance

Edited by

Benjamin G. Kohl
Vassar College

Alison Andrews Smith
Wagner College

D. C. Heath and Company
Lexington, Massachusetts   Toronto

Address editorial correspondence to:

D. C. Heath and Company
125 Spring Street
Lexington, MA 02173

Acquisitions Editor: James Miller
Developmental Editor: David Light
Managing Editor: Sylvia Mallory
Production Editor: Rachel D'Angelo Wimberly
Photo Researcher: Sue McDermott
Art Editor: Gary Crespo
Production Coordinator: Charles Dutton
Permissions Editor: Margaret Roll

Cover: *Celebration of a Wedding* by Domenico (Scuola) Ghirlandaio
S. Martino dei Buonomini, Florence
Scala/Art Resource, New York

Credits:

Part Opener Photographs: p. 1 The Bridgeman Art Library/National Gallery, London; p. 33 Scala/Art Resource, New York; p. 117 The Bridgeman Art Library/ Galleria Degli Uffizi, Florence; p. 213 The Bridgeman Art Library/Ognissanti, Florence; p. 315 Giraudon/The Bridgeman Art Library.

Published simultaneously in Canada.

Printed in the United States of America.

International Standard Book Number: 0–669–28002–X

Library of Congress Catalog Number: 94–76841

10 9 8 7 6 5 4 3

Preface

The Renaissance occupies an ambiguous position, both chronologically and geographically, between the Middle Ages and the modern era. The idea of a "rebirth" of ancient culture was used by Italian intellectuals of the fifteenth century to describe their new, intense fascination with the literature and values of classical antiquity and to distinguish themselves from their immediate predecessors, largely the scholastics of the medieval university and rhetoricians of medieval courts and chanceries. These intellectuals later developed the term "Middle Ages (*Medium Aevum*)" to describe the centuries that separated the glory of ancient Rome from its rebirth in their own day. Historians of northern Europe, on the other hand, tend to use "early modern" to describe the period of transition from medieval to modern and often disagree on when that transition occurred. In the north, this is further complicated by the political and spiritual impact of the Reformation, which was nearly contemporaneous with the arrival of Renaissance culture. Thus when "Renaissance" is used for northern Europe, it tends to describe intellectual and artistic developments that were deeply influenced by Italian models.

Few would disagree that Italy witnessed extraordinary cultural, political, and social change between 1350 and 1550. First and foremost, perhaps, was the recovery of the classical literary tradition by the intellectual elite and its rapid application as an educational program that was eminently suited to the secular needs of the ruling class of the Italian cities. This political elite, moreover, lived in a world of intense economic and political competition where status was achieved as much through individual talent and determination as it was through birth and membership in traditional hierarchies. Indeed, those with artistic and literary talent were often rewarded by powerful patrons in their own efforts to create emblems of their new social status. The art and architecture produced in this period—still a major portion of the artistic canon of the West—was almost always created with reference to classical forms.

The Italian Renaissance was a distinctly urban phenomenon, which developed mainly in the cities of northern and central Italy that had forged the commercial revolution of the High Middle Ages. Although the growth of cities that began in the Middle Ages continued to be the motor for all of Europe's commercial expansion and political development, the urbanization of Italy occurred much earlier and more intensively that it did north of the Alps. Moreover, thriving, crowded, fiercely independent Italian cities managed to survive the appalling loss of population caused by repeated episodes of plague from 1348 onwards to create "Renaissance culture." By the end of the fifteenth century, the Italian peninsula included some of the most prestigious and powerful regional states (including the papacy) in all of Europe as well as the wealthiest and most advanced merchant class. In 1494 the French invaded the Italian states, and in the decades thereafter control of the Italian peninsula was contested by the French Valois dynasty and the Habsburgs of Spain and the Holy Roman Empire; each power strove to capture some of Italy's extraordinary wealth and refinement, as well as to dominate particular regional states such as Milan and Naples. The brutal sack of Rome by Imperial troops in 1527, viewed by many contemporaries as an unprecedented catastrophe, has often been adopted as the traditional date for the end of the Italian Renaissance.

The essays and documents in this volume, organized according to broad historical problems or themes, are designed to stimulate critical thinking and class discussion in college and university courses on the Renaissance. After an introductory chapter on the "Renaissance problem," the text continues with an examination of the material context of the early Renaissance cities and the economies of city and countryside just before and after the Black Death. Part Two begins by examining the emergence of political structures, such as the commune and guild government, that often had their roots in the medieval cities but flowered in the fourteenth and fifteenth centuries. It then moves on to treat the growth of the dynastic state, culminating with analyses of the meaning of Machiavelli's thought, born of the chaos of the Valois-Habsburg struggle for domination of the peninsula. Part Three focuses on the birth of humanism in Petrarch's conflicting ideals, the service of humanists in the defense of the politics and values of their city-states, and the role of the "new learning" in education and philosophical debate. The final section of the book, on society and culture in the fifteenth and sixteenth centuries, shows the intellectual, artistic and social power of Renaissance culture when it was embraced by wealthy urban elites. The final chapter addresses the historiographical problem of when— and why—the cultural movement we call "the Renaissance" came to an end in Italy. Due to limitations of space, this book does not examine the later translation of a distinctly Italian culture of the Renaissance to the local aristocracies, royal courts and urban elites of northern Europe.

Our volume reflects the cross-disciplinary quality of much of the best in recent Italian Renaissance scholarship and incorporates the subdisciplines of economic, social, political, cultural, literary, and intellectual history, along with the history of art, philosophy, religion and gender. It further mirrors the conviction that, with the exception of older historical classics, the work of recent historians tends to be better history. Except for the excerpts from Burckhardt, virtually all of the essays in this volume were written in the second half of the twentieth century, reflecting a variety of approaches and methodologies by major contemporary students of the Italian Renaissance. The selections also demonstrate a strong awareness of gender as a major category of historical analysis, not by isolating it in a chapter of its own, but by incorporating topics related to women, family and private life throughout the readings. Finally, the readings and documents are not limited to the standard Florence-Venice dyad found in so many brief treatments of the Italian Renaissance, but range more widely to include developments in smaller cities.

Within the urban matrix, the achievements of Renaissance culture belonged mainly to the wealthy elite and usually had little to do with the daily lives of artisans, servants, the lower clergy, peasants, or the poor. For example, powerful preachers like San Bernardino of Siena and Girolamo Savonarola clearly had much more to say to ordinary city-dwellers than did the humanists. Yet the written historical record for Italian cities in this period is so much more detailed than it is for most of northern Europe that scholars of "non-elites" are also being drawn to the study of

Italy—and several examples of their work are included in this book. Rich materials for the study of popular culture, lay spirituality, and labor history, for example, have been unearthed by historians who are beginning to demonstrate that the experience of the Italian city and countryside had much in common with trends in northern Europe during the period. Thus the history of Italy during the Renaissance centuries is increasingly becoming part of the mainstream of early modern European history, while retaining its claim to the unique achievement of the Renaissance itself.

The concept of this book was born several years ago in discussions between James Miller and Benjamin Kohl one spring day in Swift Hall, the history building at Vassar College. Alison Smith soon joined the project as co-editor, and the selections and shape of the volume are very much a product of our continuing discussions and mutual criticism. In general, Benjamin Kohl has been responsible for documents freshly translated from Latin and Paduan dialect, while Alison Smith has translated documents and essays from the Italian; but here again our work has profited from mutual criticism and review. We are much indebted to Robert Norton, chair of Vassar's German department, for his revisions of Middlemore's late Victorian translation of Burckhardt's *Kultur der Renaissance in Italien*, and to Brad Williams of Vassar's French department for translating Elisabeth Carpentier's depiction of the Black Death in Orvieto from the French. For suggestions for readings and documents, not always heeded, we wish to thank John Law, Laurie Nussdorfer, Dennis Romano, Nancy G. Siraisi, Charles Trinkaus, and Ronald Witt. The reviewers commissioned by D. C. Heath made many helpful suggestions, and caused us to rethink, for the better we hope, several selections and approaches in the book. We thank them: Stanley Chojnacki, Michigan State University; Anthony Grafton, Princeton University; Charles Hamilton, Simon Fraser University; Paul Knoll, the University of Southern California; John Najemy, Cornell University; Philip Niles, Carleton College; Donald Nugent, the University of Kentucky; Virginia Reinberg, Boston College; Sally Scully, San Francisco State University; and James Tracy, the University of Minnesota. At Vassar College Michael Rambadt did much of the work of photocopying, while at Wagner College Myra Farrell, Secretary of the History and Political Science department, provided indispensable assistance in preparing the manuscript for publication. The administrative assistant of Vassar's Department of History, Norma Torney, read much of the final proofs and saved us from several errors. Last but not least, we wish to thank the staff of the publisher, D. C. Heath, for their care and patience in helping us to bring this book into print, especially James Miller, David Light, and Rachel D'Angelo Wimberly.

We dedicate this book, with affection, to our children, once and future students of the Renaissance: For Benjamin G. Kohl, Jr. and Laura Kohl Ball, and for Helena C. and Julia A. Anrather.

B.G.K
A.A.S

FURTHER READING (for the entire Italian Renaissance)

Kenneth L. Bartlett, ed., *The Civilization of the Italian Renaissance: A Sourcebook* (1992)

Thomas A. Brady, Jr., et al., eds. *Handbook of European History, 1400–1600*. 2 vols. (1994–1995)

Peter Burke, *The Italian Renaissance: Culture and Society in Renaissance Italy* (1987)

Ernst Cassirer, et al., eds., *The Renaissance Philosophy of Man* (1948)

W. K. Ferguson, *Europe in Transition, 1300–1520* (1962)

Eugenio Garin, ed., *Renaissance Characters* (1991)

Myron P. Gilmore, *The World of Humanism, 1453–1517* (1952)

J. R. Hale, *The Civilization of Europe in the Renaissance* (1994)

——, *Renaissance Europe: The Individual and Society, 1480–1520* (1972)

——, ed., *A Concise Encyclopaedia of the Italian Renaissance* (1977)

Denys Hay, *The Italian Renaissance in Its Historical Background* (2d ed., 1977)

Denys Hay and John Law, *Italy in the Age of the Renaissance, 1380–1530* (1989)

Benjamin G. Kohl and Ronald G. Witt, eds., *The Earthly Republic: Italian Humanists on Government and Society* (1978)

Lauro Martines, *Power and Imagination: City-States in Renaissance Italy* (1979)

New Cambridge Modern History, Vol. 1, *The Renaissance, 1493–1520* (1957)

Eugene F. Rice, Jr., with Anthony Grafton, *The Foundations of Early Modern Europe, 1460–1559* (2d ed., 1994)

Quentin Skinner, *The Foundations of Modern Political Thought* 2 vols. (1978)

John Stephens, *The Italian Renaissance: The Origins of Intellectual and Artistic Change Before the Reformation* (1990)

Contents

DOCUMENTS

ITALY c. 1500

0   50   100   150   200 Miles
0   50   100   150   200 Kilometers

DUCHY
OF
MILAN

DUCHY
OF SAVOY-
PIEDMONT
Turin

Milan

MARQUISATE
OF
SALUZZO

MONTFERRAT

LIGURIA

Genoa

Verona

Treviso

VENETIAN

Padua

Venice

Aquileia

ISTRIA

N

MARQUISATE
OF MANTUA

Parma

DUCHY
DE FERRARA

DUCHY OF MODENA

Bologna

Rimini

REPUBLIC

DALMATIA

Lucca

Florence

Urbino

Pisa

REPUBLIC
OF
FLORENCE

THE MARCHES

Adriatic Sea

REPUBLIC
OF
SIENA

PAPAL

CORSICA

Orvieto

UMBRIA

STATE

ABRUZZI

Rome

KINGDOM

CAPITANATA

OF

SARDINIA

Tyrrhenian Sea

CAMPANIA

Naples

NAPLES

APULIA

Bari

BASILICATA

MEDITERRANEAN

CALABRIA

Palermo

Messina

SICILY

SEA

PART **I**

The Renaissance Problem

Costa, *A Concert* (early 16th century)
Music-making among men and women was a
hallmark of aristocratic style in Italian cities.

CHAPTER **1**

The Renaissance Problem

Well over a century ago, the Swiss historian Jacob Burckhardt published his famous essay defining the Renaissance in Italy as a major historical period, distinct from the Middle Ages that preceded it and anticipating the culture, values, and institutions of modern times. At the heart of most interpretations of the Renaissance lie the rise of the individual and a new acceptance of secular culture and values, especially those derived from antiquity. The new appreciation of individual achievement meant a society open to talent, especially in war, culture, and the arts. Thus the Renaissance marked a shift from hierarchical rural medieval society, where status was handed down according to birth, to the highly competitive societies of the cities of fourteenth- and fifteenth-century Italy, where status was linked to achievement. Most of all, the Renaissance is seen as the recovery of classical antiquity made for the first time the subject of scholarly study. The critical tools for the scholarly study of the ancient past—archaeology, epigraphy (the study of inscriptions), and textual criticism—were developed during this era. At the same time, painting, sculpture, and especially architecture took on "classicizing aspects," re-creating such features of Roman buildings as the dome and the colonnade. Not all sectors of the population participated equally in Renaissance culture, which was produced by an educated and privileged elite. Left out were the poor, peasants and workers, and especially women. Increasingly, then, scholars are viewing the Renaissance not as a widespread and thorough transformation of society but as initiating only a few aspects of modernity: monumental change in scholarship, secular values, and aesthetics.

ESSAYS

The essays reprinted here offer two classic approaches to the Renaissance problem. Jacob Burckhardt (1818–1897) saw the Italian Renaissance as a herald of the modern age. For him the "state as work of art" marked the beginnings of modern bureaucratic governments. Medieval governments had been founded on feudal custom, divine right, and conventional morality, but the despots of fifteenth-century Italy based their rule on statecraft, reason, and ruthless calculation. Burckhardt viewed the rise of the individual, with talent, achievement, and genius respected and rewarded, as the key element in the flourishing of Renaissance culture.

A generation ago Joan Kelly (1928–1982), who spent most of her career teaching women's history at the City College of New York and Sarah Lawrence College, introduced gender into the periodization and definition of the Renaissance with a provocative question: Did women have a Renaissance? Her answer, in the second selection, drawing on the intellectual traditions of Marxism and modern feminism, was no. Women's lives were "privatized"—that is, removed from public life—in the patriarchal societies of the commercial cities of Renaissance Italy. Capitalism placed wealth and power in the marketplace dominated by men, while the court cultures of the minor centers, such as Ferrara and Urbino, reduced women to mere ornaments in a new aristocratic society. Kelly's fresh perspective has opened Renaissance scholarship to numerous studies exploring the role of women in early modern society.

The Culture of the Italian Renaissance

JACOB BURCKHARDT

THE STATE AS A WORK OF ART

During the fifteenth century despotism exhibited a different character from that of the previous period. Many of the petty tyrants, as well as some of the greater ones such as the Scala and the Carrara, had disappeared while the powerful tyrants enlarged their fortunes and cultivated themselves in increasingly individualized ways. The new Aragonese dynasty put Naples, for instance, on a more powerful course. The most characteristic aspect of this century, however, were the efforts of the *condottiere* to achieve independent power, indeed to acquire crowns. It represented a further step on the path marked out by recognizing the brute realities for what they were, and it meant that the greatest gains went both to talent as well as to wickedness. In order to secure support for themselves, the petty despots eagerly entered the service of the larger states and became their *condottieri*, for which, in return, they received some money and probably impunity for many of their misdeeds as well, and perhaps even an increase of their own land. In general, both the great rulers and the small tyrants had to act with greater prudence and calculation, and they had to refrain from too many atrocities; they could afford to commit as many crimes as could be proven to serve their immediate purposes—they were allowed that much, but no more, by the popular opinion of disinterested observers. We see no hint here of that store of pious loyalty that was of such use to the legitimate princely families of Europe; at most they enjoyed a kind of metropolitan popularity. Talent and cool calculation were the only instrument that aided Italy's princes in their bids for advancement. A character like that of Charles the Bold, who was consumed by a furious passion to pursue his completely impractical plans, was a total enigma to the Italians.

From Jacob Burckhardt, "The Culture of the Renaissance in Italy," trans. S. G. W. Middlemore (1878), revised by Robert Norton.

[As a Milanese ambassador reported,] "The Swiss were, after all, nothing but peasants, and even if one would kill them all, that would still give no satisfaction to the Burgundian nobles who might fall in battle! Even if the duke took possession of all of Switzerland without encountering resistance, his annual income would still not increase even by 5000 ducats." The medieval aspects of character, his chivalrous fantasies, or rather ideals, had long ceased to be comprehensible to the Italians. The diplomats from the South gave him up for lost when they saw him slap his subordinate officers and yet keep them in his service, when he mistreated his troops as a means of punishing them for a defeat, and then expose his privy councilors to ridicule before his troops. Louis XI, however, who outdid the Italian Princes in their own way of conducting politics, and who above all confessed to being an admirer of Francesco Sforza, was far inferior to Italian rulers regarding culture and learning because of his vulgar nature.

In the Italian states of the fifteenth century, good and evil became intertwined in a very peculiar mixture. The personality of the ruler became so fully formed, it was often so deeply significant in itself and so characteristic of his station and task, that it is difficult to form an appropriate moral judgment.

The root and base of power were and remained illegitimate, and a curse rested on it that refused to be removed. Expressions of imperial consent and investitures made no difference, since the people paid no attention to announcements that their ruler had bought a piece of parchment in some strange land or from some foreigner passing through his territory. If the emperors had been good for something—thus went the logic of ignorant common sense—they should not have let tyrants rise in the first place. Ever since the Roman expedition of Charles IV, the emperors had only *sanctioned* despotic reigns that had arisen in Italy without their aid, but they could not in any way *guarantee* them except by issuing charters. The spectacle of Charles in Italy was one of the most disgraceful political comedies ever witnessed. One can read in Matteo Villani how the Visconti showed him around their territory, and finally escorted him out of it; how he ran around like a salesman in order to turn his wares (namely privileges) into money as quickly as possible; how he made a pitiful appearance in Rome; and how, in the end, without even having had to draw his sword, he retreated back over the Alps with his money-bags full.

Sigismund came to Italy, at least the first time (1414), with the good intention of persuading John XXIII to participate in his council. It was on that occasion, as the pope and the emperor were enjoying the panorama of Lombardy from the high tower of Cremona, that their host, the local tyrant Gabrino Fondolo, was seized with the desire to throw them both over the side. The second time Sigismund came solely as an adventurer; he subsequently sat for more than half a year locked up in Siena, as if he were in a debtors' prison, and was afterwards just barely able to get to Rome for his coronation.

And what should one think of Frederick III? His visits in Italy leave the impression of being holiday trips or recreational jaunts undertaken at the expense of those who wanted him to confirm their claims by charter, or who were flattered by being able to entertain an emperor with sufficient pomp. Such was the case with Alfonso of Naples, who spent 150,000 gold florins on such an imperial visit. Once, in Ferrara, while returning from Rome for the second time (1469), Frederick did nothing but distribute titles all day—the number came to eighty—without ever leaving his room; he created knights, counts, doctors, notaries—and counts, no less, of as many different degrees as needs dictated: counts palatine, count[s] with the right to create doctors, even to create up to five doctors, counts with the right to legitimatize bastards, to appoint notaries, to declare dishonest notaries to be honest, and so forth. His chancellor, however, demanded in return for drawing up the necessary deeds a favor that was thought to be rather excessive at Ferrara. It is not mentioned what Duke Borso thought to himself as his imperial patron so freely distributed diplomas and everyone at the little court was supplied with a title. The humanists, who were the chief spokesmen of the age, were divided in their opinion on the matter according to their interests. Whereas some of them greeted the emperor with conventional acclamations they borrowed from the poets of imperial Rome, Poggio said that he no longer knew what the coronation was actually supposed to mean. In antiquity, he wrote, only the victorious Imperator was crowned, and only with a laurel wreath at that. . . .

Connected with the political illegitimacy of the dynasties of the fifteenth century was the indifference to legitimate birth, a carelessness that struck foreigners such as Comines so forcefully. One might say, however, that the one presupposed the other. Whereas in the North, such as in the house of Burgundy, bastard children received their own, clearly defined appanages, for example bishoprics and the like, and in Portugal a bastard line preserved its place on the throne only through the most strenuous efforts, there was no longer a princely house in Italy that did not have, and even calmly accept, some illegitimate descendants in its blood lines. The Aragonese rulers of Naples represented the bastard line of the house, for the brother of Alfonso I had inherited Aragon itself. Indeed, the great Frederick of Urbino was perhaps not even a Montefeltro at all. When Pius II traveled to the Congress of Mantua (1459), eight bastards of the house of Este rode to receive him at Ferrara, among them the reigning duke Borso himself and two illegitimate sons of his equally illegitimate brother and predecessor Leonello. The latter had also had a lawful wife, who was an illegitimate daughter of Alfonso I of Naples by an African woman. Bastards were so frequently admitted into the line because the lawful children were often minors and the dangers of the situation were pressing. A kind of seniority system became instituted that paid no attention to pure or impure birth. Opportunism, the perception of the individual and of his talent, were more powerful here than the laws and customs that were otherwise familiar on the Continent. It was, one must remember, the age in which the sons of the popes founded principalities! . . .

Installing a mercenary general such as a ruler of an area could also occur without usurpation, such as when his master paid him off with a gift of land when he was short of gold or men. In any case, even if he temporarily dismissed most of his men, the *condottiere* still needed a secure place where he could set up camp for the winter and store the most crucial provisions. The first example of a captain who was established in this fashion was John Hawkwood, who received Bagnacavallo and Contignola from Pope Gregory XI. Even at the end of the fifteenth century, a Sienese writer thought he was one of the worst of his kind, comparable with the devil. But when Italian armies and leaders appeared on the scene with Alberigo da Varviano, the opportunities also increased of acquiring a principality, or, if the *condottiere* was already a tyrant somewhere, of enlarging what he had already inherited. The first great bacchanalian rite of this military desire for power and domination was celebrated in the duchy of Milan after the death of Giangaleazzo (1402). The government of his two sons was primarily aimed at the annihilation of these warlike tyrants, and the greatest of them, Facino Cane, was assimilated into the house together with his widow, as well as a series of cities and 400,000 gold florins; in addition, Beatrice di Tenda brought the soldiers of her first husband with her. From then on, the thoroughly immoral relationship between governments and their *condottieri*, which was characteristic of the fifteenth century, grew increasingly intimate. An old anecdote, one of those that are not precisely, yet profoundly true, describes the same matter approximately as follows: The citizens of a city—it is supposed to be Siena—once had a general who had liberated them from hostile oppression; every day they deliberated about how to repay him, and they concluded that no reward within their means would be great enough, not even if they made him lord of the city. At last someone rose and said, "Let us kill him and then worship him as our patron saint." And that is precisely what they did with him, more or less what the Roman senate did with Romulus.

Indeed, the *condottieri* never had to be as much on their guard as with their employers; if they fought successfully, then they were dangerous, and they vanished from the face of the earth, like Roberto Malatesta just after the victory he had won for Sixtus IV (1482); at first loss, however, vengeance was often taken out on them, which is what the Venetians did with Carmagnola (1432). The moral level of the situation can be measured by the fact that the *condottieri* often had to give their wives and children as hostages, and yet they still neither enjoyed nor inspired confidence. They would have had to be heroes of resignation, characters such as Belisarius himself, if the most profound hatred had not collected within them; only the most perfect inner goodness could have prevented them from becoming absolutely wicked. But we get to know many of them as fitting this description, full of disdain for all sacred things, full of cruelty and treachery toward human beings, almost all of them indifferent to whether they died excommunicated from the church or not. Yet, simultaneously, many developed their personality and their talents to the highest level of virtuosity and they were acknowledged and admired by their soldiers for this reason; these were the first armies in modern history in which the personal charisma of the leader, apart from any other consideration, was the motivating force. This is perfectly demonstrated, for example, by the life of Francesco Sforza; there we find no prejudice of birth that could have hindered him from gaining the greatest possible personal popularity, or from using it appropriately in difficult moments. It even happened on occasion that his enemies laid down their weapons at the sight of him, greeting him reverently with bare heads because everyone considered him to be the common "father of military men."

This Sforza family deserves particular attention because chroniclers believed that one could see the preparations for assuming power glimmering through all their actions from the very beginning. The great fecundity of the family provided the foundation of its fortune; Francesco's famous father, Jacopo, had twenty siblings, all raised under harsh circumstances in Contignola, near Faenza, under the impress of those endless Romagnol vendettas between them and the house of the Pasolini. The entire house was nothing more than arsenal and guard-room, and even the mother and daughters were completely accustomed to war. At age thirteen, Jacopo secretly rode away, at first to Panicale and to the papal *condottiere* Boldrino—the man who even in death continued to lead his troops, with the word of order being given from a tent surrounded by banners in which the embalmed body lay, until a worthy successor was found. Jacopo, after he had gradually grown in stature and repute in the service of various *condottieri*, sent for his family members, and he received through them the same advantages that a prince derives from a numerous dynasty. It was these relations who kept the army together when he remained a captive in the Castel dell'Uovo at Naples; his sister took the royal negotiators prisoner with her own hands and saved his life by using them as a security.

It was already an indication of the long-range nature of his plans that Jacopo was extremely reliable in money matters, and for that reason he found credit with bankers even after defeats. His intentions also emerge from his careful protection of peasants against the licence of his troops, and they can be seen in his reluctance to destroy conquered cities. They appear above all, however, in that he gave away his favorite concubine, Lucia (the mother of Francesco), to someone else in order to remain available himself for a princely marriage alliance. The weddings of his relatives also occurred according to a certain plan. He avoided the impious and profligate life of his colleagues, and the three rules with which he sent his son Francesco into the world were as follows: "Do not touch another man's wife; do not strike any of your followers, or if that happens, send him far away; finally, do not ride a hard-mouthed horse, or one that frequently throws a shoe." But, above all, he possessed the personality if not of a great general, then at least of a great soldier; he had a powerful, fully developed body, a familiar peasant face, and a truly astonishing memory that retained and recalled the names of all of his soldiers, their horses, and their pay rates even after many years. His education was purely Italian, but he devoted his leisure to studying history, and he had Greek and Latin authors translated for his use.

It was clear from the beginning that his still more famous son, Francesco, strove to acquire enormous power, and through brilliant military leadership and unhesitating treachery he indeed took mighty Milan (1447–50). His example caught on. Aeneas Sylvius wrote around this time: "In our Italy, in which we love change and where no ancient dynasty exists, slaves can easily become kings." One man above all others, however, who called himself "the man of Fortuna," occupied the imagination of the whole country: Giacomo Piccinino, the son of Niccolò. It was an open and burning question whether he, too, would succeed in founding a principality. The greater states had an obvious interest in preventing it, and Francesco Sforza also thought it would be advantageous if the number of mercenary leaders who became sovereigns ceased with himself. But the troops and captains that were sent against Piccinino when he wanted to take Siena for himself, for instance, recognized their own interest in supporting him, thinking: "If he were defeated here, we would have to return to farming our fields." While besieging him at Orbetello, they simultaneously supplied him with provisions; and he thus got out of this tight spot in the most honorable fashion. But in the end he did not escape his fate after all. All of Italy was betting on what would happen when he travelled (1465) to King Ferrante in Naples after a visit to Sforza at Milan. In spite of all guarantees and his high connections, King Ferrante, with the agreement of Sforza, had him murdered in the Castel Nuovo. . . .

THE DEVELOPMENT OF THE INDIVIDUAL

In the character of these states, the republics as well as the tyrannies, is found the most persuasive reason, though it is certainly not the only one, for the early development of the Italian into what we recognize as modern man. This point is decisive in seeing why he was destined to become the first-born among the sons of present-day Europe.

During the Middle Ages both directions of consciousness—the one facing the external world and the other turned toward the inner, human realm itself—lay, as if under a common veil, dreaming or half awake. The veil was woven with faith, childish prejudice, and illusion; viewed through it, the world and all of history appeared in magical colors, and human beings recognized themselves only as members of a race, people, party, corporation or family, or in some other form of general category. It first happened in Italy that this veil was lifted by the winds of change; there awakened an *objective* perception and management of the state and of everything else in the world. At the same time, however, a sense of the subjective arose with all its force, and human beings became intellectual *individuals*, and recognized themselves as such. In a similar fashion, the Greeks had once opposed themselves to barbarians, and the individualistic Arabs distinguished themselves from other Asiatics whom they considered merely as members of a race. It will not be difficult to demonstrate that political circumstances made the greatest contribution to bringing this change about.

Even in much earlier times one can occasionally recognize the development of a totally independent personality, which did not occur at the same time in the North or did not reveal itself in the same manner. The circle of powerful and vicious criminals in the tenth century, whom Liudprand described—some of the contemporaries of Gregory VII (for example, Benzo of Alba), and several opponents of the first Hohenstaufen—display physiognomies of this kind. But with the waning of the thirteenth century Italy suddenly began to swarm with people who had distinct personalities; the ban that had lain on individuality was now completely lifted, and, freed of all constraints, a thousand separate faces assumed specialized features. Dante's great poetry would have been impossible in any other country for the very reason that the rest of Europe still lay under that same category of race. Precisely because of this wealth of individuality, the sublime poet became the most national herald of the time for Italy. . . . This portrayal of the rich diversity of human nature in literature and art—this multi-faceted, descriptive characterization— . . . enters history fully formed and with complete resolution. In the fourteenth century, Italians knew little of false modesty or of any kind of hypocrisy; not a single person was afraid of attracting attention by being, or seeming to be, different from others.

Despotism, as we have already seen, allowed the tyrant, the *condottiere* himself, to develop his individuality to the highest degree; then the same happened to those whose talents he fostered, but also ruthlessly exploited—the private secretary, the official, the poet, and courtier. These people found themselves forced to become familiar with all the inward resources of their minds, their permanent capacities as well as those that were more of the moment; even their enjoyment of life was heightened and concentrated by intellectual means, all in order to give the greatest possible value and meaning to what was perhaps a very short period of power and influence.

Yet even the subjects of these sovereigns did not completely lack an experience of a similar drive. We will not include in our investigation those whose lives were consumed by secret resistance, by conspiracies, and will merely consider those who were resigned to their station, that is, to remaining purely private people, for example, most of the urban population of the Byzantine Empire and of the Islamic States. It must certainly have often been difficult enough for the subjects, say, of the Visconti to maintain the dignity of their house and person, and through their servitude countless numbers of people were forced to compromise their moral character. Not so, however, with regard to what one calls individual character: for it is precisely in the midst of political importance that the different aims and endeavors of private life flourish with all the more vitality and variety. Wealth and personal cultivation, in so far as they were able to be exhibited and enter into competition with others, combined with a still considerable municipal freedom and with the existence of a Church that, unlike that of the Byzantine or of the Muslim world, was not identical with the state—all of these elements together undoubtedly favored the emergence of individual ways of thinking, and precisely the absence of party conflicts provided the necessary leisure for them to develop. . . .

Now, in these very cities the conditions were also favorable for the development of individual character, but in yet another way. The more frequently the ruling party changed, the greater the need of each new ruler to consolidate the exercise and enjoyment of power. Thus, especially in Florentine history, statesman and popular leaders acquired such a recognizable personal character that, exceptionally, virtually no one in the entire world could be compared with them, not even Jacob von Artevelde.

But the members of defeated parties often came into position similar to that of the subjects of the despotic states, with the difference that the freedom or power that they had once already tasted gave greater animation to their sense of individuality, and perhaps even the hope of recovering what they had lost encouraged this sense as well. It is in fact among these men of involuntary leisure that we find, for instance, an Agnolo Pandolfini (d. 1446), whose work *Della famiglia* [now attributed to Alberti] is the first program of a fully formed and cultivated private existence. His account of the duties of the individual as opposed to the uncertain and thankless nature of public service can be called, in its way, a true monument to its time.

But banishment in particular possesses the quality that it either wears the exiled down or cultivates them to the highest extent. "In all of our more populous cities," says Giovanni Pontano, "we see a lot of people who have voluntarily left their homeland: after all, one takes one's virtues wherever one goes." In fact, it was by no means the case that these people only included those who had literally been exiled, but rather thousands who had left their native city without having been asked to do so because its political or economic condition had become unbearable. The Florentine emigrants in Ferrara, the Lucchese in Venice, and others formed whole colonies by themselves.

The cosmopolitanism that developed among the most intellectually active and talented emigrants represented one of the highest stages of individualism. Dante, as had already been mentioned, found a new homeland in the language and culture of Italy, but he went beyond even this in the words, "My country is the world itself." And when he was offered the chance to return to Florence if he met certain unworthy conditions, he wrote back: "Can I not see the light of the sun and the stars everywhere? Can I not everywhere meditate on the noblest truths, without therefore appearing ingloriously, indeed shamefully before the people and the city? I will not even miss my bread." With proud defiance, other artists now placed a special emphasis on their freedom from being tied to a single place. "Only the person who has learned everything," Ghiberti said, "will never be a stranger anywhere in the world; even if one is robbed of one's fortune and is without friends, that person is nevertheless the citizen of every city and can despise the changes of fortune without fear." An exiled humanist similarly wrote: "Wherever a learned man establishes residence, there is a good home."

A very acute eye practiced in reading cultural history might be able to trace, step by step, the increase in the number of completely cultivated people during the fifteenth century. Whether these people undertook this harmonious perfecting of their intellectual and material existence as a conscious and explicit goal is difficult to say; but many of them did achieve it, in as much as it was possible to do so in view of the patent imperfection of everything in this world. Even if one chooses not to consider the role that luck, talent, and character played, for example, in the overall success of Lorenzo the Magnificent, then one can look instead at an individual such as Ariosto, especially as he expressed himself in his satires. What a harmonious euphony he attained there in balancing the pride of the man and the poet, the irony toward his own desires, the most biting derision and the deepest benevolence!

When this drive to attain the highest cultivation of personality was combined with a truly powerful and, at the same time, varied culture, one that has mastered all of the elements of contemporary culture, then that was when the "universal human being" came into existence—the *l'uomo universale,* who belonged exclusively to Italy. People of encyclopedic knowledge had lived in various countries throughout the Middle Ages, since this knowledge was narrowly circumscribed; similarly, even well into the twelfth century, universal artists still appeared because the problems of architecture were relatively simple and uniform, and in sculpture and painting, the respective object of representation predominated over form. In Renaissance Italy, on the other hand, we find certain artists who created nothing but new and, of their kind, perfect works in every field simultaneously, and who also made the most profound impact as human beings. There were also other universal minds who, although outside of the sphere of the visual arts, were likewise active within an enormously wide circle of intellectual endeavors.

Even Dante, who in his lifetime was called by some a poet, by others a philosopher, and by still others a theologian, produced an abundance of compelling personal power in all of his writings, to which the reader feels forced to submit, even disregarding the subject itself. What willpower is presupposed by the steady, regular composition of the *Divine Comedy?* But if one considers its content, then one also sees that there is hardly a single important subject in the whole intellectual or material world that he had not thoroughly explored and about which his statements—often no more than a few words—would not be the most significant of that time. For the formative arts he was a primary text—but for more important things than the few lines he wrote referring to contemporary artists, he soon himself became a source of inspiration.

The fifteenth century is, above all, the age of multi-talented human beings *par excellence*. There is not a single biography that does not mention important activities that transcend the other, merely dilettantish pursuits of the person being described. Florentine merchants and statesmen were frequently also scholars of both Latin and Greek; they had the most famous humanists read Aristotle's *Ethics* and *Politics* to them and their sons; the daughters of the house were also exposed to high culture. And, in general, it is in these spheres that one finds the beginnings of private education. The humanist, for his part, was obliged to acquire the greatest versatility since his philological learning was not limited, as it is now, to the theoretical knowledge of classical antiquity, but had to serve the practical application to real life. Next to his studies of Pliny, for example, he collected natural artifacts; he used ancient geography to become a modern geographer; following the model of their historiography he wrote contemporary chronicles; as a translator of Plautus's comedies he probably also acted as the director when they were performed; he imitated as best as he could every effective form of ancient literature down to the dialogues of Lucian; and in addition to all of this he also served as notary and diplomat—not always to his own benefit.

But high above these merely versatile men tower some truly universal ones. . . . We . . . consider here, on the threshold of the fifteenth century, the figure of one of these powerful giants—Leon Battista Alberti. His biography, which is only a fragment, very rarely speaks of him as an artist and never mentions his great importance in the history of architecture at all. Let us see what he was without this particular source of fame.

In everything that wins praise Leon Battista was, from his earliest childhood, always the first. Incredible things are told of his many physical feats and gymnastic skills: how, with his feet together, he could jump over people's shoulders; how, in the cathedral, he threw a coin into the air until one heard it ring against the distant cupola; how the wildest horses trembled and shook under him. For Alberti wanted to appear faultless to others in three things: in walking, in riding, and in speaking. He learned music without a master, and yet professional musicians admired his compositions. Under the pressure of poverty, he studied both civil and canonical law for many years, until exhaustion brought on a severe illness. In his twenty-fourth year, when he found his memory for words weakened, but his sense for things unimpaired, he applied himself to physics and mathematics, meanwhile learning every kind of skill imaginable by asking artists, scholars, and artisans of all sorts, including shoemakers, about their secrets and experiences. He learned painting and modelling on the side, and he especially acquired a reputation for making extremely good likenesses, even from memory. His mysterious *camera obscura* excited particular admiration, a device in which he sometimes showed the stars and the evening moon rising over rocky hills, at others he revealed wide landscapes with mountains and ocean gulfs receding into the misty distance, and with advancing fleets in the brilliant sun or under the shade of clouds. But what other people created, he acknowledged with pleasure, and in general he thought that every human achievement that in some way followed the law of beauty was almost something divine. There are, in addition, literary works, first of all those about art itself, which are the landmarks and chief documents of Renaissance form, especially in architecture; then there are his Latin prose writings—novellas and so on—some of which have even been thought to be from antiquity, including his elegies, eclogues and humorous dinner-speeches. He also wrote an Italian treatise *On the Family* in four books; and even a funeral oration for his dog. His serious and witty sayings were significant enough to have been collected; examples of them, running many columns, are quoted in the afore-mentioned biography. And everything that he possessed and knew he shared, as truly rich natures always do, without the slightest reservation and he gave away his greatest discoveries for free. But here we finally come to the deepest source of his being—an extremely sympathetic experience, pitched at an almost nervous intensity, of everything in and around himself. At the sight of magnificent trees and of the fields before the harvest he felt the urge to weep; he venerated handsome, dignified old men as a "delight of nature," and he could never look at them long enough. Even animals of great beauty enjoyed his benevolence because he thought they were especially favored by nature; and more than once, when he was sick, the sight of a beautiful landscape made him well. No wonder that those who got to know him in this mysteriously close communion with the world ascribed to him the gift of prophecy. He was said to have correctly foretold a bloody crisis in the family of Este, the fate of Florence, and the death of the popes many years before they occurred, and to be able to read the faces and the hearts of people whenever he so desired. It goes without saying that an extremely intense power of will pervaded and sustained this whole personality; like all of the great figures of the Renaissance, he also said: "Human beings can do anything as soon as they apply their will to it."

And Alberti stood in relation to Leonardo da Vinci as the beginning to its culmination, as the dilettante to the master. If only Vasari's work had also been supplemented by a description [of Leonardo] like the one he gave Alberti. The great contours of Leonardo's character can never be more than faintly imagined.

THE REVIVAL OF ANTIQUITY

Having reached this point in our cultural-historical overview, we must consider classical antiquity, the "rebirth" of which has become the one-sided designation for this period in general. The conditions that have been described thus far would have shaken and matured Italy even without antiquity. . . . Yet, both the preceding historical circumstances, as well as those to come, are variously colored by the ancient world, and even in those cases in which the essence of things would be clear and comprehensible without it, it is still true that they actually manifest themselves only in and through classical forms. The Renaissance would not have had its great inevitability in world history that it had if one could abstract from it so easily. But we must insist . . . that it was not this revival alone, but rather its close connection with the spirit of the Italian people that fed it, that conquered the Western world. The freedom that this popular spirit maintained for itself is not always and everywhere the same, and it often seems, if one considers neo-Latin literature, for example, that it was negligible. But in the visual arts and in several other spheres this freedom is remarkably great, and the alliance between two disparate cultural epochs of the same people proved to be justifiable and fruitful because it was largely based on the autonomy of each.

The rest of Europe had to decide whether it was going to resist the powerful impulse coming from Italy, or to appropriate it either in part or in its entirety. Where the latter occurred, one should not lament the early demise of our medieval cultural forms and ideas. If they had been able to defend themselves, they would still be with us. If those elegiac souls who yearn for that past would spend even a single hour in its midst, they would quickly feel the powerful urge to breathe modern air again. The historical fact that in great processes of this kind many noble flowers of exquisite beauty perish without having been immortalized in tradition or poetry is undoubtedly true; nevertheless, one cannot wish for the great final result not to have happened. This final result consists in the establishment of a new intellectual milieu that, next to the Church—which until then, but not for very much longer, had held Europe together—spread out over the West from Italy and became the vital atmosphere for all of the more highly cultivated Europeans. The sharpest criticism that can be made of this process concerns its lack of popular content, the emerging division between the cultivated and uncultivated in all of Europe that was now inevitable. But this criticism appears entirely meaningless as soon as one admits that the situation, even though recognizable, cannot be altered. Moreover, this division is by no means as sharp and inexorable in Italy as is elsewhere the case. The works of its greatest poet, Tasso, are, after all, even in the hands of Italy's poorest inhabitants.

Greek and Roman antiquity—which affected Italian life so powerfully ever since the fourteenth century as the support and source of culture, as the goal and ideal of existence, and also partly as a conscious act of opposition—this antiquity had already partially influenced every country during the Middle Ages, including those other than Italy. The culture that Charlemagne represented was essentially a Renaissance in opposition to the barbarism of the seventh and eighth centuries, and it could not have been otherwise. Just as, subsequently, remarkably pure antique forms insinuated themselves into Northern Romanesque architecture—that is, apart from the general formal principles that were inherited from antiquity—so, too, all of monastic scholarship gradually absorbed an enormous amount of material from Roman writers, and after Einhard even their style did not remain free of imitation.

But antiquity reawakened differently in Italy than it did in the North. As soon as barbarism had ceased in Italy, the awareness of its ancient past arose in the people who were still half living in antiquity; they celebrated that age and wished to reproduce it. Outside of Italy it was a matter of scholarly, reflective adoption of individual elements of antiquity; in Italy it concerned a scholarly and yet also popular partisanship for the ancient world as a whole, for it commemorated their own greatness. The easy accessibility of Latin and the numerous extant memorials and monuments energetically fostered this development. Out of this and out of the counter-force exerted by popular spirit—which had of course changed in the meantime—by the political institutions imported by the Lombards from Germany, by European chivalry and other nothern cultural influences, by religion and the Church—out of all this grew the new, whole entity: the modern Italian spirit that was destined to become the decisive model for the Western world.

Did Women Have a Renaissance?

JOAN KELLY

One of the tasks of women's history is to call into question accepted schemes of periodization. To take the emancipation of women as a vantage point is to discover that events that further the historical development of men, liberating them from natural, social, or ideological constraints, have quite different, even opposite, effects upon women. The Renaissance is a good case in point. Italy was well in advance of the rest of Europe from roughly 1350 to 1530 because of its early consolidation of genuine states, the mercantile and manufacturing economy that supported them, and its working out of postfeudal and even postguild social relations. These developments reorganized Italian society along modern lines and opened the possibilities for the social and cultural expression for which the age is known. Yet precisely these developments affected women adversely, so much so that there was no renaissance for women—at least, not during the Renaissance. The state, early capitalism, and the social relations formed by them impinged on the lives of Renaissance women in different ways according to their different positions in society. But the startling fact is that women as a group, especially among the classes that dominated Italian urban life, experienced a contraction of social and personal options that men of their classes either did not, as was the case with the bourgeoisie, or did not experience as markedly, as was the case with the nobility.

Before demonstrating this point, which contradicts the widely held notion of the equality of Renaissance women with men, we need to consider how to establish, let alone measure, loss or gain with respect to the liberty of women. I found the following criteria most useful for gauging the relative contraction (or expansion) of the powers of Renaissance women and for determining the quality of their historical experience: 1) the regulation of *female sexuality* as compared with male sexuality; 2) women's *economic* and *political roles*, i.e., the kind of work they performed as compared with men, and their access to property, political power, and the education or training necessary for work, property, and power; 3) the *cultural roles* of women in shaping the outlook of their society, and access to the education and/or institutions necessary for this; 4) *ideology* about women, in particular the sex-role system displayed or advocated in the symbolic products of the society, its art, literature, and philosophy. Two points should be made about this ideological index. One is its rich inferential value. The literature, art, and philosophy of a society, which give us direct knowledge of the attitudes of the dominant sector of that society toward women, also yield indirect knowledge about our other criteria: namely, the sexual, economic, political, and cultural activities of women. Insofar as images of women relate to what really goes on, we can infer from them something about that social reality. But, second, the relations between the ideology of sex roles and the reality we want to get at are complex and difficult to establish. Such views may be prescriptive rather than descriptive; they may describe a situation that no longer prevails; or they may use the relation of the sexes symbolically and not refer primarily to women and sex roles at all. Hence, to assess the historical significance of changes in sex-role conception, we must bring such changes into connection with all we know about general developments in the society at large.

This essay examines changes in sex-role conception, particularly with respect to sexuality, for what they tell us about Renaissance society and women's place in it. At first glance, Renaissance thought presents a problem in this regard because it cannot be simply categorized. Ideas about the relation of the sexes range from a relatively complementary sense of sex roles in literature dealing with courtly manners, love, and education, to patriarchal conceptions in writings on marriage and the family, to a fairly equal presentation of sex roles in early Utopian social theory. Such diversity need not baffle the attempt to reconstruct a history of sex-role conceptions, however, and to relate its course to the actual situation of women. Toward this end, one needs to sort out this material in terms of the social groups to which it responds: to courtly society in the first case, the nobility of the petty despotic states of Italy; to the patrician bourgeoisie in the second, particularly of republics such as Florence. In the third case, the relatively equal position accorded women in Utopian thought (and in those lower-class movements of the radical Reformation analogous to it) results from a larger critique of early modern society and all the relations of domination that flow from private ownership and control of property. Once distinguished, each of these groups of sources tells the same story. Each discloses in its own way certain new constraints suffered by Renaissance women as the family and political life were restructured in the great transition from medieval feudal society to the early modern state. The sources that represent the interests of the nobility and the bourgeoisie point to this fact by a telling, double index. Almost all such works—with certain notable exceptions, such as Boccaccio and Ariosto—establish chastity as the female norm and restructure the relation of the sexes to one of female dependency and male domination.

The bourgeois writings on education, domestic life, and society constitute the extreme in this denial of women's independence. Suffice it to say that they sharply distinguish an inferior domestic realm of women from the superior public realm of men, achieving a veritable "renaissance" of the outlook and practices of classical Athens, with its domestic imprisonment of citizen wives. The courtly Renaissance literature we will consider was more gracious. But even here, by analyzing a few of the representative works of this genre, we find a new repression of the noblewoman's affective experience, in contrast to the latitude afforded her by medieval literature, and some of the social and cultural reasons for it. Dante and Castiglione, who continued a literary tradition that began with the courtly love literature of eleventh- and twelfth-century Provence, transformed medieval conceptions of love and nobility. In the love ideal they formed, we can discern the inferior position the Renaissance noblewoman held in the relation of the sexes by comparison with her male counterpart and with her medieval predecessor as well. . . .

The kind of economic and political power that supported the cultural activity of feudal noblewomen in the eleventh and twelfth centuries had no counterpart in Renaissance Italy. By the fourteen[th] century, the political units of Italy were mostly sovereign states that regardless of legal claims, recognized no overlords and supported no feudatories. Their nobility held property but no seigniorial power, estates but not jurisdiction. Indeed, in northern and central Italy, a nobility in the European sense hardly existed at all. Down to the coronation of Charles V as Holy Roman Emperor in 1530, there was no Italian king to safe-guard the interests of (and thereby limit and control) a "legitimate" nobility that maintained by inheritance traditional prerogatives. Hence, where the urban bourgeoisie did not overthrow the claims of nobility, a despot did, usually in the name of nobility but always for himself. These *signorie*, unlike the bourgeois republics, continued to maintain a landed, military "class" with noble pretensions, but its members increasingly became merely the warriors and ornaments of a court. Hence, the Renaissance aristocrat, who enjoyed neither the independent political powers of feudal jurisdiction nor legally guaranteed status in the ruling estate, either served a despot or became one.

In this sociopolitical context, the exercise of political power by women was far more rare than under feudalism or even under the traditional kind of monarchical state that developed out of feudalism. The two Giovannas of Naples, both queens in their own right, exemplify this latter type of rule. The first, who began her reign in 1343 over Naples and Provence, became in 1356 queen of Sicily as well. Her grandfather, King Robert of Naples—of the same house of Anjou and Provence that hearkens back to Eleanor and to Henry Plantagenet—could and did designate Giovanna as his heir. Similarly, in 1414, Giovanna II became queen of Naples upon the death of her brother. In Naples, in short, women of the ruling house could assume power, not because of their abilities alone, but because the principle of legitimacy continued in force along with the feudal tradition of inheritance by women.

In northern Italy, by contrast, Caterina Sforza ruled her petty principality in typical Renaissance fashion, supported only by the Machiavellian principles of *fortuna* and *virtù* (historical situation and will). Her career, like that of her family, follows the Renaissance pattern of personal and political illegitimacy. Born in 1462, she was an illegitimate daughter of Galeazzo Maria Sforza, heir to the Duchy of Milan. The ducal power of the Sforzas was very recent, dating only from 1450, when Francesco Sforza, illegitimate son of a condottiere and a great condottiere himself, assumed control of the duchy. When his son and heir, Caterina's father, was assassinated after ten years of tyrannous rule, another son, Lodovico, took control of the duchy, first as regent for his nephew (Caterina's half brother), then as outright usurper. Lodovico promoted Caterina's interests for the sake of his own. He married her off at fifteen to a nephew of Pope Sixtus IV, thereby strengthening the alliance between the Sforzas and the Riario family, who now controlled the papacy. The pope carved a state out of papal domains for Caterina's husband, making him Count of Forlì as well as the Lord of Imola, which Caterina brought to the marriage. But the pope died in 1484, her husband died by assassination four years later—and Caterina made the choice to defy the peculiar obstacles posed by Renaissance Italy to a woman's assumption of power.

Once before, with her husband seriously ill at Imola, she had ridden hard to Forlì to quell an incipient coup a day before giving birth. Now at twenty-six, after the assassination of her husband, she and a loyal castellan held the citadel at Forlì against her enemies until Lodovico sent her aid from Milan. Caterina won; she faced down her opponents, who held her six children hostage, then took command as regent for her young son. But her title to rule as regent was inconsequential. Caterina ruled because she mustered superior force and exercised it personally, and to the end she had to exert repeatedly the skill, forcefulness, and ruthless ambition that brought her to power. However, even her martial spirit did not suffice. In the despotisms of Renaissance Italy, where assassinations, coups, and invasions were the order of the day, power stayed closely bound to military force. In 1500, deprived of Milan's support by her uncle Lodovico's deposition, Caterina succumbed to the overwhelming forces of Cesare Borgia and was divested of power after a heroic defense of Forlì. . . .

[Women's] access to power was indirect and provisional, and was expected to be so. In his handbook for the nobility, Baldassare Castiglione's description of the lady of the court makes this difference in sex roles quite clear. One notable consequence of the Renaissance lady's need to charm is that Castiglione called upon her to give up certain "unbecoming" physical activities such as riding and handling weapons. Granted, he concerned himself with the court lady, as he says, not a queen who may be called upon to rule. But his aestheticizing of the lady's role, his conception of her femaleness as centered in charm, meant that activities such as riding and skill in weaponry would seem unbecoming to women of the ruling families, too. Elisabetta Gonzaga, the idealized duchess of Castiglione's *Courtier*, came close in real life to his normative portrayal of her type. Riding and skill in weaponry had, in fact, no significance for her. The heir to her Duchy of Urbino was decided upon during the lifetime of her husband, and it was this adoptive heir—not the widow of thirty-seven with no children to compete for her care and attention—who assumed power in 1508. Removed from any direct exercise of power, Elisabetta also disregarded the pursuits and pleasures associated with it. Her letters express none of the sense of freedom and daring Caterina Sforza and Beatrice d'Este experienced in riding and the hunt. Altogether, she lacks spirit. Her correspondence shows her to be as docile in adulthood as her early teachers trained her to be. She met adversity, marital and political, with fortitude but never opposed it. She placated father, brother, and husband, and even in Castiglione's depiction of her court, she complied with rather than shaped its conventions.

The differences between Elisabetta Gonzaga and Caterina Sforza are great, yet both personalities were responding to the Renaissance situation of emerging statehood and social mobility. Elisabetta, neither personally illegitimate nor springing from a freebooting condottiere family, was schooled, as Castiglione would have it, away from the martial attitudes and skills requisite for despotic rule. She would not be a prince, she would marry one. Hence, her education, like that of most of the daughters of the ruling families, directed her toward the cultural and social functions of the court. The lady who married a Renaissance prince became a patron. She commissioned works of art and gave gifts for literary works dedicated to her; she drew to her artists and literati. But the court they came to ornament was her husband's, and the culture they represented magnified his princely being, especially when his origins could not. Thus, the Renaissance lady may play an aesthetically significant role in Castiglione's idealized Court of Urbino of 1508, but even he clearly removed her from that equal, to say nothing of superior, position in social discourse that medieval courtly literature had granted her. To the fifteen or so male members of the court whose names he carefully listed, Castiglione admitted only four women to the evening conversations that were the second major occupation at court (the profession of arms, from which he completely excluded women, being the first). Of the four, he distinguished only two women as participants. The Duchess Elisabetta and her companion, Emilia Pia, at least speak, whereas the other two only do a dance. Yet they speak in order to moderate and "direct" discussion by proposing questions and games. They do not themselves contribute to the discussions, and at one point Castiglione relieves them even of their negligible role:

> When signor Gasparo had spoken thus, signora Emilia made a sign to madam Costanza Fregosa, as she sat next in order, that she should speak; and she was making ready to do so, when suddenly the Duchess said: "Since signora Emilia does not choose to go to the trouble of devising a game, it would be quite right for the other ladies to share in this ease, and thus be exempt from such a burden this evening, especially since there are so many men here that we risk no lack of games."

The men, in short, do all the talking; and the ensuing dialogue on manners and love, as we might expect, is not only developed by men but directed toward their interests.

The contradiction between the professed parity of noblewomen and men in *The Courtier* and the merely decorative role Castiglione unwittingly assigned the lady proclaims an important educational and cultural change as well as a political one. Not only did a male ruler preside over the courts of Renaissance Italy, but the court no longer served as arbiter of the cultural functions it did retain. Although restricted to a cultural and social role, she lost dominance in that role as secular education came to require special skills which were claimed as the prerogative of a class of professional teachers. The sons of the Renaissance nobility still pursued their military and diplomatic training in the service of some great lord, but as youths, they transferred their nonmilitary training from the lady to the humanistic tutor or boarding school. In a sense, humanism represented an advance for women as well as for the culture at large. It brought Latin literacy and classical learning to daughters as well as sons of the nobility. But this very development, usually taken as an index of the equality of Renaissance (noble) women with men, spelled a further decline in the lady's influence over courtly society. It placed her as well as her brothers under male cultural authority. The girl of the medieval aristocracy, although unschooled, was brought up at the court of some great lady. Now her brothers' tutors shaped her outlook, male educators who, as humanists, suppressed romance and chivalry to further classical culture, with all its patriarchal and misogynous bias.

The humanistic education of the Renaissance noblewoman helps explain why she cannot compare with her medieval predecessors in shaping a culture responsive to her own interests. In accordance with the new cultural values, the patronage of the Este, Sforza, Gonzaga, and Montefeltro women extended far beyond the literature and art of love and manners, but the works they commissioned, bought, or had dedicated to them do not show any consistent correspondence to their concerns as women. They did not even give noticeable support to women's education, with the single important exception of Battista da Montefeltro, to whom one of the few treatises advocating a humanistic education for women was dedicated. Adopting the universalistic outlook of their humanist teachers, the noblewomen of Renaissance Italy seem to have lost all consciousness of their particular interests as women, while male authors such as Castiglione, who articulated the mores of the Renaissance aristocracy, wrote their works for men. Cultural and political dependency thus combined in Italy to reverse the roles of women and men in developing the new noble code. Medieval courtesy, as set forth in the earliest etiquette books, romances, and rules of love, shaped the man primarily to please the lady. In the thirteenth and fourteenth centuries, rules for women, and strongly patriarchal ones at that, entered French and Italian etiquette books, but not until the Renaissance reformulation of courtly manners and love is it evident how the ways of the lady came to be determined by men in the context of the early modern state. The relation of the sexes here assumed its modern form, and nowhere is this made more visible than in the love relation. . . .

Interest even in [a] shadowy kind of romance dropped off markedly as the work of Dante, Petrarch, and Boccaccio led into the fifteenth-century renaissance of Graeco-Roman art and letters. The Florentine humanists in particular appropriated only the classical side of their predecessors' thought, the side that served public concerns. They rejected the dominance of love in human life, along with the inwardness and seclusion of the religious, the scholar, and the lovesick poet. Dante, for example, figured primarily as a citizen to his biographer, Lionardo Bruni, who, as humanist chancellor of Florence, made him out as a modern Socrates, at once a political figure, a family man, and a rhetor: an exemplar for the new polis.[1] Only in relation to the institution of the family did Florentine civic humanism take up questions of love and sexuality. In this context, they developed the bourgeois sex-role system, placing man in the public sphere and the patrician woman in the home, requiring social virtues from him and chastity and motherhood from her. In bourgeois Florence, the humanists would have nothing to do with the old aristocratic tradition of relative social and sexual parity. In the petty Italian despotisms, however, and even in Florence under the princely Lorenzo de' Medici late in the fifteenth century, the traditions and culture of the nobility remained meaningful. Castiglione's *Courtier*, and the corpus of Renaissance works it heads, took up the themes of love and courtesy for this courtly society, adapting them to contemporary social and cultural needs. Yet in this milieu, too, within the very tradition of courtly literature, new constraints upon female sexuality emerged. Castiglione, the single most important spokesman of Renaissance

---

1. David Thompson and Alan F. Nagel, eds. and trans., *The Three Crowns of Florence: Humanist Assessments of Dante, Petrarca, and Boccaccio* (New York: Harper & Row, 1972).

love and manners, retained in his love theory Dante's two basic features: the detachment of love from sexuality and the allegorization of the love theme. Moreover, he introduced into the aristocratic conception of sex roles some of the patriarchal notions of women's confinement to the family that bourgeois humanists had been restoring.

Overtly, as we saw, Castiglione and his class supported a complementary conception of sex roles, in part because a nobility that did no work at all gave little thought to a sexual division of labor. He could thus take up the late medieval *querelle des femmes* set off by the *Romance of the Rose* and debate the question of women's dignity much to their favor. Castiglione places Aristotle's (and Aquinas's) notion of woman as a defective man in the mouth of an aggrieved misogynist, Gasparo; he criticizes Plato's low regard for women, even though he did permit them to govern in *The Republic*; he rejects Ovid's theory of love as not "gentle" enough. Most significantly, he opposes Gasparo's bourgeois notion of women's exclusively domestic role. Yet for all this, Castiglione established in *The Courtier* a fateful bond between love and marriage. One index of a heightened patriarchal outlook among the Renaissance nobility is that love in the usual emotional and sexual sense must lead to marriage and be confined to it—for women, that is.

The issue gets couched, like all others in the book, in the form of a debate. There are pros and cons; but the prevailing view is unmistakable. If the ideal court lady loves, she should love someone whom she can marry. If married, and the mishap befalls her "that her husband's hate or another's love should bring her to love, I would have her give her lover a spiritual love only; nor must she ever give him any sure sign of her love, either by word or gesture or by other means that can make him certain of it." *The Courtier* thus takes a strange, transitional position on the relations among love, sex, and marriage, which bourgeois Europe would later fuse into one familial whole. Responding to a situation of general female dependency among the nobility, and to the restoration of patriarchal family values, at once classical and bourgeois, Castiglione, like Renaissance love theorists in general, connected love and marriage. But facing the same realities of political marriage and clerical celibacy that beset the medieval aristocracy, he still focused upon the love that takes place outside it. On this point, too, however, he broke with the courtly love tradition. He proposed on the one hand a Neo-Platonic notion of spiritual love, and on the other, the double standard.

Castiglione's image of the lover is interesting in this regard. Did he think his suppression of female sexual love would be more justifiable if he had a churchman, Pietro Bembo (elevated to cardinal in 1539), enunciate the new theory and had him discourse upon the love of an aging courtier rather than that of a young knight? In any case, adopting the Platonic definition of love as desire to enjoy beauty, Bembo located this lover in a metaphysical and physical hierarchy between sense ("below") and intellect ("above"). As reason mediates between the physical and the spiritual, so man, aroused by the visible beauty of his beloved, may direct his desire beyond her to the true, intelligible source of her beauty. He may, however, also turn toward sense. Young men fall into this error, and we should expect it of them, Bembo explains in the Neo-Platonic language of the Florentine philosopher Marsilio Ficino. "For finding itself deep in an earthly prison, and deprived of spiritual contemplation in exercising its office of governing the body, the soul of itself cannot clearly perceive the truth; wherefore, in order to have knowledge, it is obliged to turn to the senses . . . and so it believes them . . . and lets itself be guided by them, especially when they have so much vigor that they almost force it." A misdirection of the soul leads to sexual union (though obviously not with the court lady). The preferred kind of union, achieved by way of ascent, uses love of the lady as a step toward love of universal beauty. The lover here ascends from awareness of his own human spirit, which responds to beauty, to awareness of that universal intellect that comprehends universal beauty. Then, "transformed into an angel," his soul finds supreme happiness in divine love. Love may hereby soar to an ontologically noble end, and the beauty of the woman who inspires such ascent may acquire metaphysical status and dignity. But Love, Beauty, Woman, aestheticized as Botticelli's Venus and given cosmic import, were in effect denatured, robbed of body, sex, and passion by this elevation. The simple kiss of love-service became a rarefied kiss of the soul: "A man delights in joining his mouth to that of his beloved in a kiss, not in order to bring himself to any unseemly desire, but because he feels that that bond is the opening of mutual access to their souls." And instead of initiating love, the kiss now terminated physical contact, at least for the churchman and/or aging courtier who sought an ennobling experience—and for the woman obliged to play her role as lady.

Responsive as he still was to medieval views of love, Castiglione at least debated the issue of the double standard. His spokesmen point out that men make the rules permitting themselves and not women sexual freedom, and that concern for legitimacy does not justify this inequality. Since these same men claim to be more virtuous than women, they could more easily restrain themselves. In that case, "there would be neither more nor less certainty about offspring, for even if women were unchaste, they could in no way bear children of themselves . . . provided men were continent and did not take part in the unchastity of women." But for all this, the book supplies an excess of hortatory tales about female chastity, and in the section of the dialogue granting young men indulgence in sensual love, no one speaks for young women, who ought to be doubly "prone," as youths and as women, according to the views of the time.

This is theory, of course. But one thinks of the examples: Eleanor of Aquitaine changing bedmates in the midst of a crusade; Elisabetta Gonzaga, so constrained by the conventions of her own court that she would not take a lover even though her husband was impotent. She, needless to say, figures as Castiglione's prime exemplar: "Our Duchess who has lived with her husband for fifteen years like a widow." Bembo, on the other hand, in the years before he became cardinal, lived with and had three children by Donna Morosina. But however they actually lived, in the new ideology a spiritualized noble love *supplemented* the experience of men while it *defined* extramarital experience for the lady. For women, chastity had become the convention of the Renaissance courts, signaling the twofold fact that the dominant institutions of sixteenth-century Italian society would not support the adulterous sexuality of courtly love, and that women, suffering a relative loss of power within these institutions, could not at first make them responsive to their needs. Legitimacy is a significant factor here. Even courtly love had paid some deference to it (and to the desire of women to avoid conception) by restraining intercourse while promoting romantic and sexual play. But now, with cultural and political power held almost entirely by men, the norm of female chastity came to express the concerns of Renaissance noblemen as they moved into a new situation of a hereditary, dependent class.

This changed situation of the aristocracy accounts both for Castiglione's widespread appeal and for his telling transformation of the love relation. Because *The Courtier* created a mannered way of life that could give to a dependent nobility a sense of self-sufficiency, of inner power and control, which they had lost in a real economic and political sense, the book's popularity spread from Italy through Europe at large in the sixteenth and seventeenth centuries. Although set in the Urbino court of 1508, it was actually begun some ten years after that and published in 1528—after the sack of Rome, and at a time when the princely states of Italy and Europe were coming to resemble each other more closely than they had in the fourteenth and fifteenth centuries. The monarchs of Europe, consolidating and centralizing their states, were at once protecting the privileges of their nobility and suppressing feudal power.[2] Likewise in Italy, as the entire country fell under the hegemony of Charles V, the nobility began to be stabilized. Throughout sixteenth-century Italy, new laws began to limit and regulate membership in a hereditary aristocratic class, prompting a new concern with legitimacy and purity of the blood. Castiglione's demand for female chastity in part responds to this particular concern. His theory of love as a whole responds to the general situation of the Renaissance nobility. In the discourse on love for which he made Bembo the spokesman, he brought to the love relation the same psychic attitudes with which he confronted the political situation. Indeed, he used the love relation as a symbol to convey his sense of political relations.

The changed times to which Castiglione refers in his introduction he experienced as a condition of servitude. The dominant problem of the sixteenth-century Italian nobility, like that of the English nobility under the Tudors, had become one of obedience. As one of Castiglione's courtiers expressed it, God had better grant them "good masters, for, once we have them, we have to endure them as they are." It is this transformation of aristocratic service to statism, which gave rise to Castiglione's leading idea of nobility as courtiers, that shaped his theory of love as well. Bembo's aging courtier, passionless in his rational love, sums up the theme of the entire book: how to maintain by detachment the sense of self now threatened by the loss of independent power. The soul in its earthly prison, the courtier in his social one, renounce the power of self-determination that has in fact been denied them. They renounce *wanting* such power; "If the flame is extinguished, the danger is also extinguished." In love, as in service, the courtier preserves independence by avoiding desire for real love, real power. He does not touch or allow himself to be touched by either. "To enjoy beauty without suffering, the Courtier, aided by reason, must turn his desire entirely away from the body and to beauty alone, [to] contemplate it in its simple and pure self." He may gaze at the object of his love-service, he may listen, but

---

2. Fernand Braudel, *The Mediterranean World* (London: Routledge & Kegan Paul, 1973); A. Ventura, *Nobiltà e popolo nella società Veneta* (Bari: Laterza, 1964); Lawrence Stone, *The Crisis of the Aristocracy, 1558–1641* (Oxford: Clarendon Press, 1965).

there he reaches the limits of the actual physical relation and transforms her beauty, or the prince's power, into a pure idea. "Spared the bitterness and calamities" of thwarted passion thereby, he loves and serves an image only. The courtier gives obeisance, but only to a reality of his own making: "for he will always carry his precious treasure with him, shut up in his heart, and will also, by the force of his own imagination, make her beauty [or the prince's power] much more beautiful than in reality it is."

Thus, the courtier can serve and not serve, love and not love. He can even attain the relief of surrender by making use of this inner love-service "as a step" to mount to a more sublime sense of service. Contemplation of the idea the courtier has discovered within his own soul excites a purified desire to love, to serve, to unite with intellectual beauty (or power). Just as love guided his soul from the particular beauty of his beloved to the universal concept, love of that intelligible beauty (or power) glimpsed within transports the soul from the self, the particular intellect, to the universal intellect. Aflame with an utterly spiritual love (or a spiritualized sense of service), the soul then "understands all things intelligible, and without any veil or cloud views the wide sea of pure divine beauty, and receives it into itself, enjoying that supreme happiness of which the senses are incapable." What does this semimystical discourse teach but that by "true" service, the courtier may break out of his citadel of independence, his inner aloofness, to rise and surrender to the pure idea of Power? What does his service become but a freely chosen Obedience, which he can construe as the supreme virtue? In both its sublimated acceptance or resignation and its inner detachment from the actual, Bembo's discourse on love exemplifies the relation between subject and state, obedience and power, that runs through the entire book. Indeed, Castiglione regarded the monarch's power exactly as he had Bembo present the lady's beauty, as symbolic of God: "As in the heavens the sun and the moon and the other stars exhibit to the world a certain likeness of God, so on earth a much liker image of God is seen in . . . princes." Clearly, if "men have been put by God under princes," if they have been placed under princes as under His image, what end can be higher than service in virtue, than the purified experience of Service?

The likeness of the lady to the prince in this theory, her elevation to the pedestal of Neo-Platonic love, both masks and expresses the new dependency of the Renaissance noblewoman. In a structured hierarchy of superior and inferior, she seems to be served by the courtier. But this love theory really made her serve—and stand as a symbol of how the relation of domination may be reversed, so that the prince could be made to serve the interests of the courtier. The Renaissance lady is not desired, not loved for herself. Rendered passive and chaste, she merely mediates the courtier's safe transcendence of an otherwise demeaning necessity. On the plane of symbolism, Castiglione thus had the courtier dominate both her and the prince; and on the plane of reality, he indirectly acknowledged the courtier's actual domination of the lady by having him adopt "woman's ways" in his relations to the prince. Castiglione had to defend against effeminacy in the courtier, both the charge of it and the actuality of faces "soft and feminine as many attempt to have who not only curl their hair and pluck their eyebrows, but preen themselves . . . and appear so tender and languid . . . and utter their words so limply." Yet the close-fitting costume of the Renaissance nobleman displayed the courtier exactly as Castiglione would have him, "well built and shapely of limb." His clothes set off his grace, as did his nonchalant ease, the new manner of those "who seem in words, laughter, in posture not to care." To be attractive, accomplished, and seem not to care; to charm and do so coolly—how concerned with impression, how masked the true self. And how manipulative: petitioning his lord, the courtier knows to be "discreet in choosing the occasion, and will ask things that are proper and reasonable; and he will so frame his request, omitting those parts that he knows can cause displeasure, and will skillfully make easy the difficult points so that his lord will always grant it." In short, how like a woman—or a dependent, for that is the root of the simile.

The accommodation of the sixteenth- and seventeenth-century courtier to the ways and dress of women in no way bespeaks a greater parity between them. It reflects, rather, that general restructuring of social relations that entailed for the Renaissance noblewoman a greater dependency upon men as feudal independence and reciprocity yielded to the state. In this new situation, the entire nobility suffered a loss. Hence, the courtier's posture of dependency, his concern with the pleasing impression, his resolve "to perceive what his prince likes, and . . . to bend himself to this." But as the state overrode aristocratic power, the lady suffered a double loss. Deprived of the possibility of independent power that the combined interests of kinship and feudalism guaranteed some women in the Middle Ages, and that the states of early modern Europe would preserve in part, the Italian noblewoman in particular entered a relation of almost universal dependence upon her family and her husband. And she experienced this dependency at the same time as she lost her commanding position with respect to the secular culture of her society.

Hence, the love theory of the Italian courts developed in ways as indifferent to the interests of women as the courtier, in his self-sufficiency, was indifferent as a lover. It accepted, as medieval courtly love did not, the double standard. It bound the lady to chastity, to the merely procreative sex of political marriage, just as her weighty and costly costume came to conceal and constrain her body while it displayed her husband's noble rank. Indeed, the person of the woman became so inconsequential to this love relation that one doubted whether she could love at all. The question that emerges at the end of The Courtier as to "whether or not women are as capable of divine love as men" belongs to a love theory structured by mediation rather than mutuality. Woman's beauty inspired love but the lover, the agent, was man. And the question stands unresolved at the end of The Courtier—because at heart the spokesmen for Renaissance love were not really concerned about women or love at all. . . .

In sum, a new division between personal and public life made itself felt as the state came to organize Renaissance society, and with that division the modern relation of the sexes made its appearance, even among the Renaissance nobility. Noblewomen, too, were increasingly removed from public concerns—economic, political, and cultural—and although they did not disappear into a private realm of family and domestic concerns as fully as their sisters in the patrician bourgeoisie, their loss of public power made itself felt in new constraints placed upon their personal as well as their social lives. Renaissance ideas on love and manners, more classical than medieval, and almost exclusively a male product, expressed this new subordination of women to the interests of husbands and male-dominated kin groups and served to justify the removal of women from an "unladylike" position of power and erotic independence. All the advances of Renaissance Italy, its protocapitalist economy, its states, and its humanistic culture, worked to mold the noblewoman into an aesthetic object: decorous, chaste, and doubly dependent—on her husband as well as the prince.

DOCUMENTS

Self-awareness has long been a criterion in the definition of the Renaissance. In the first selection reprinted here, the early Italian humanist Leonardo Bruni (1370–1444) cites Francesco Petrarca as the key figure in rekindling a new interest in and appreciation of the literature and culture of antiquity, which he came to define as the humanities. Next, the Italian humanist, architect, and theorist Leon Battista Alberti (1404–1472) insists that Renaissance artists were capable of achieving the same level of excellence as had the artists of classical antiquity. Born in Venice but brought up in Paris, Christine de Pizan (1364–1430) recorded the exploits and importance of women in her biography, known as *The Book of the City of the Ladies*. Christine is a nearly unique example of a learned woman who wrote for publication and in the preface to this work, which is reprinted as the final document, she conveys the massive scholarly and contemporary consensus that women were greatly inferior to men and inclined to vice.

| Leonardo Bruni Praises Petrarch's | Rekindling of Antiquity, 1404

[Niccolò Niccoli says] "Now since I have said, I think, enough about Dante, let us say a few things about our Petrarca, although the excellence of such a man would not be satisfied with a few praises. But I beg that you listen to me as to a man insufficiently suited for speaking, especially since, as you all see, I must speak extemporaneously and completely without any consideration beforehand." Pietro replied: "Proceed, Niccolò. We are not unacquainted with your ability, which we have just experienced in your commendation and defence of Dante, for you omitted no topic of praise." Niccolò proceeded: "When, as I said before, I had traveled to Padua to transcribe the books of our Petrarca, not many years after his death, I often met those men who were his good friends while he was alive. From them I obtained such an acquaintance with his character that it was almost as if I had seen him myself— although previously I had heard the same from the very venerable and learned theologian, Luigi. They all, then, declared that in Petrarca there had been many things worthy of praise, but three especially; for they said he had been very handsome, and wise, and the most learned man of his age. All these things they attested with

"Bruni on Petrarch's Rekindling of Antiquity" in L. Bruni, "Dialogue to Pier Paolo Vergerio" in D. Thompson and A. Nagel, eds. *Three Crowns of Florence: Humanist Assessment of Dante, Petrarca and Boccaccio*, Harper Torch, 1972, pp. 48–51. Reprinted by permission of the editors.

witnesses and reasoned arguments. But let us say nothing of his good looks and wisdom, since they regard his personal life. I do not suppose you have failed to hear of his dignity, moderation, integrity, moral purity and other outstanding virtues; but as I say, let us pass over these as private matters. However, since he left it for us all let us consider his learning and the reasoning by which they showed that our Petrarca excelled in this as well. When they praised his learning, then, they said that Francesco Petrarca was to be set before all the poets who preceded him. Beginning with Ennius and Lucretius they ran on to our own times in such a way that whatever poet they adduced was shown to have been brilliant in some one genre. The work of Ennius, Lucretius, Pacuvius and Accius consisted of poems, but none of them wrote any prose worth being praised. Petrarca, though, left beautiful poems in elegant verse, and many books in prose. So great was his genius that he equaled the best poets with his poetry and the most learned orators with his prose. When they had shown me his poems—heroic, bucolic, familiar—they brought forth as testimony to his prose many books and epistles; they showed me exhortations to virtue, censures of vice, and many things which he wrote about cherishing friendship, about loving one's country, about the ordering of states, about disdaining fortune, about the correction of character. From this it was easy to perceive that he had abundant learning. Moreover, his genius was so accommodated to every type of composition that he did not refrain from the popular sort of writing; in this, as in the others, he appears most elegant and eloquent.

"When they had shown me this they asked me if I had anyone from all antiquity who could prove a match for such praises, to bring him forward; but if I could not do so, and had no one equally proficient in every genre, I should not hesitate to set my fellow citizen before all the most learned men up to this day.

"I do not know how it seems to you, but I have now touched upon just about all the points they used to establish Petrarca's cause. Since their arguments struck me as excellent I agreed with them and persuaded myself that such was the case. But will those foreigners think this way, while we are cooler in praise of our fellow citizen? Shall we not venture to honor him for his merits, especially when this man restored liberal studies, which had been extinguished, and opened the way for us to be able to learn? And perhaps he was the first to bring the laurel to our city. *But the book to which he most applied himself is not much approved.* Who is so severe a critic as not to approve it? I should like him to be asked on what grounds he does this; although if there were anything in the book which could be condemned, that would be because death had prevented Petrarca's polishing it thoroughly. *But his bucolics have no pastoral flavor.* I do not think so, however; for I see everything stuffed with shepherds and flocks—when I see you."

When everyone laughed at this, Niccolò added: "I am speaking because I heard some people making such charges against Petrarca: don't think I have any part in them. But since I had heard them from certain people, I repeated them to you yesterday, for the reason you now know. And so now it pleases me to rebut not myself—since I was pretending—but the silly fools who really thought that. What they say, about preferring one poem of Virgil's and one epistle of Cicero's to all the works of Petrarca, I often turn around this way: I say that I far prefer an oration of Petrarca's to all the epistles of Virgil, and the poems of Petrarca to all the poems of Cicero. . . .

Leon Battista Alberti on the Value of Contemporary Painting, 1435

I used to marvel and at the same time to grieve that so many excellent and superior arts and sciences from our most vigorous antique past could now seem lacking and almost wholly lost. We know from [remaining] works and through references to them that they were once widespread. Painters, sculptors, architects, musicians, geometricians, rhetoricians, seers and similar noble and amazing intellects are very rarely found today and there are few to praise them. Thus I believed, as many said, that Nature, the mistress of things, had grown old and tired. She no longer produced either geniuses or giants which in her more youthful and more glorious days she had produced so marvellously and abundantly.

Since then, I have been brought back here [to Florence]—from the long exile in which we Alberti have grown old—into this our city, adorned above all others. I have come to understand that in many men, but especially in you, Filippo [Brunelleschi], and in our close friend Donat[ell]o the sculptor and in others like Nencio, Luca and Masaccio, there is a genius for [accomplishing] every praiseworthy thing. For this they should not be slighted in favour of anyone famous in antiquity in these arts. Therefore, I believe the power of acquiring wide fame in any art or science lies in our industry and diligence more than in the times or in the gifts of nature. It must be admitted that it was less difficult for the Ancients—because they had models to imitate and from which they could learn—to come to a knowledge of those supreme arts which today are most difficult for us. Our fame ought to be much greater, then, if we discover unheard-of and never-before-seen arts and sciences without teachers or without any model whatsoever. Who could ever be hard or envious enough to fail to praise Pippo the architect on seeing here such a large structure, rising above the skies, ample to cover with its shadow all the Tuscan people, and constructed without the aid of centering or great quantity of wood? Since this work seems impossible of execution in our time, if I judge rightly, it was probably unknown and unthought of among the Ancients. But there will be other places, Filippo, to tell of your fame, of the virtues of our Donato, and of the others who are most pleasing to me by their deeds.

As you work from day to day, you presevere in discovering things through which your extraordinary genius acquires perpetual fame. If you find the leisure, it would please me if you should look again at this my little work On Painting which I set into Tuscan for your renown. You will see three books; the first, all mathematics, concerning the roots in nature which are the source of this delightful and most noble art. The second book puts the art in the hand of the artist, distinguishing its parts and demonstrating all. The third introduces the artist to the means and the end, the ability and the desire of acquiring perfect skill and knowledge in painting. May it

"Alberti on Painting" by Leon Battista Alberti from On Painting by Leon Battista Alberti, trans. by Jonathan Spencer, pp. 39–40. Copyright © 1966 Yale University Press. Reprinted by permission of the publisher.

please you, then, to read me with diligence. If anything here seems to you to need emending, correct me. There was never a writer so learned to whom erudite friends were not useful. I in particular desire to be corrected by you in order not to be pecked at by detractors. . . .

Christine de Pizan Explains *The Book of the City of Ladies,* 1405

One day as I was sitting alone in my study surrounded by books on all kinds of subjects, devoting myself to literary studies, my usual habit, my mind dwelt at length on the weighty opinions of various authors whom I had studied for a long time. I looked up from my book, having decided to leave such subtle questions in peace and to relax by reading some light poetry. With this in mind, I searched for some small book. By chance a strange volume came into my hands, not one of my own, but one which had been given to me along with some others. When I held it open and saw from its title page that it was by Mathéolus, I smiled, for though I had never seen it before, I had often heard that like other books it discussed respect for women. I thought I would browse through it to amuse myself. I had not been reading for very long when my good mother called me to refresh myself with some supper, for it was evening. Intending to look at it the next day, I put it down. The next morning, again seated in my study as was my habit, I remembered wanting to examine this book by Mathéolus. I started to read it and went on for a little while. Because the subject seemed to me not very pleasant for people who do not enjoy lies, and of no use in developing virtue or manners, given its lack of integrity in diction and theme, and after browsing here and there and reading the end, I put it down in order to turn my attention to more elevated and useful study. But just the sight of this book, even though it was of no authority, made me wonder how it happened that so many different men—and learned men among them—have been and are so inclined to express both in speaking and in their treatises and writings so many wicked insults about women and their behavior. Not only one or two and not even just this Mathéolus (for this book had a bad name anyway and was intended as a satire) but, more generally, judging from the treatises of all philosophers and poets and from all the orators—it would take too long to mention their names—it seems that they all speak from one and the same mouth. They all concur in one conclusion: that the behavior of women is inclined to and full of every vice. Thinking deeply about these matters, I began to examine my character and conduct as a natural woman and, similarly, I considered other women whose company I frequently kept, princesses, great ladies, women of the middle and lower classes, who had graciously told me of their most private and intimate thoughts, hoping that I could judge impartially and in good

"Preface" from *The Book of the City of Ladies* by Christine de Pizan, trans. By Earl Jeffrey Richards, copyright © 1982 by Persea Books, pp. 3–5. Reprinted by permission of Persea Books Inc.

conscience whether the testimony of so many notable men could be true. To the best of my knowledge, no matter how long I confronted or dissected the problem, I could not see or realize how their claims could be true when compared to the natural behavior and character of women. Yet I still argued vehemently against women, saying that it would be impossible that so many famous men—such solemn scholars, possessed of such deep and great understanding, so clear-sighted in all things, as it seemed—could have spoken falsely on so many occasions that I could hardly find a book on morals where, even before I had read it in its entirety, I did not find several chapters or certain sections attacking women, no matter who the author was. This reason alone, in short, made me conclude that, although my intellect did not perceive my own great faults and, likewise, those of other women because of its simpleness and ignorance, it was however truly fitting that such was the case. And so I relied more on the judgment of others than on what I myself felt and knew. I was so transfixed in this line of thinking for such a long time that it seemed as if I were in a stupor. Like a gushing fountain, a series of authorities, whom I recalled one after another, came to mind, along with their opinions on this topic. And I finally decided that God formed a vile creature when He made woman, and I wondered how such a worthy artisan could have deigned to make such an abominable work which, from what they say, is the vessel as well as the refuge and abode of every evil and vice. As I was thinking this, a great unhappiness and sadness welled up in my heart, for I detested myself and the entire feminine sex, as though we were monstrosities in nature. And in my lament I spoke these words:

"Oh, God, how can this be? For unless I stray from my faith, I must never doubt that Your infinite wisdom and most perfect goodness ever created anything which was not good. Did You yourself not create woman in a very special way and since that time did You not give her all those inclinations which it pleased You for her to have? And how could it be that You could go wrong in anything? Yet look at all these accusations which have been judged, decided, and concluded against women. I do not know how to understand this repugnance. If it is so, fair Lord God, that in fact so many abominations abound in the female sex, for You Yourself say that the testimony of two or three witnesses lends credence, why shall I not doubt that this is true? Alas, God, why did You not let me be born in the world as a man, so that all my inclinations would be to serve You better, and so that I would not stray in anything and would be as perfect as a man is said to be? But since Your kindness has not been extended to me, then forgive my negligence in Your service, most fair Lord God, and may it not displease You, for the servant who receives fewer gifts from his lord is less obliged in his service." I spoke these words to God in my lament and a great deal more for a very long time in sad reflection, and in my folly I considered myself most unfortunate because God had made me inhabit a female body in this world.

FURTHER READING

Marvin B. Becker, "Individualism in the Early Italian Renaissance: Burden and Blessing," *Studies in the Renaissance* 19 (1972), 273–297

_____, "Towards a Renaissance Historiography in Florence," in *Renaissance Studies in Honor of Hans Baron* (1971), 141–172

William J. Bouwsma, *A Usable Past: Essays in European Cultural History* (1990)

Jacob Burckhardt, *The Civilization of the Renaissance in Italy*, trans. S. G. C. Middlemore, intro. P. Burke (1990)

Wallace K. Ferguson, *The Renaissance in Historical Thought* (1948)

Peter Gay, "Burckhardt's Renaissance: Between Responsibility and Power," in *The Responsibility of Power*, eds. L. Krieger and F. Stern (1968), 198–214

Felix Gilbert, *History: Politics or Culture? Reflections on Ranke and Burckhardt* (1990)

M. A. Holly, *Panofsky and the Foundations of Art History* (1984)

Joan Kelly, *Women, History, and Theory* (1984)

William Kerrigan and Gordon Braden, *The Idea of the Renaissance* (1989)

Erwin Panofsky, *Renaissance and Renascences in Western Art* (1971)

Mary Beth Rose, ed., *Women in the Middle Ages and the Renaissance* (1986)

Susan Stuard, ed., *Women in Medieval History and Historiography* (1987)

B. L. Ullman, "Renaissance, the Word and Underlying Concept," *Studies in the Italian Renaissance* (1973), 11–26

P A R T   II

The Material World

Pietro, "Bankers". Detail from *The Life of San Matteo* (late 14th century) in Prato. Bankers and money-changers conducted their business in elegant open air stalls in the marketplace.

C H A P T E R **2**

The Plague and Public Health

I n the middle of the fourteenth century the Mediterranean basin and western Europe suffered the worst demographic collapse in history. The Black Death, which would probably be diagnosed as bubonic plague today, killed between one-quarter and one-third of the population. The nature and effects of the plague on medieval Europe have been a matter of great scholarly debate. Certainly the most immediate effect was enormous social and economic dislocation and psychological trauma. The long-term impact included a rise in wages (due to chronic labor shortages), economic consolidation, heightened popular piety, disillusionment with the established church, and, according to some historians, increased emphasis among the wealthy on amassing private wealth. Repeated epidemics of the plague continued through the sixteenth century to reduce the population and impede recovery. Moralists and theologians wrote about preserving and protecting the family unit (see, for example, the comments of Francesco Barbaro on marriage in Chapter 9), and medical professors, concerned with the need to replenish the population, turned their attention to the problem of ensuring conception.

E S S A Y S

In the first essay, French historian Elisabeth Carpentier, of École des Hautes Études in Paris, examines the effects of the plague in one small Italian city, Orvieto, just north of Rome. She describes the immediate dislocation of government, economy, and social relations arising from the Black Death, despite strenuous efforts of city fathers, physicians, and clergy to cope with the catastrophe. In the second essay, Nancy G. Siraisi, who has taught the history of medieval medicine and science at Hunter College and the Graduate Center of the City University of New York for many years, examines the changes in popular attitudes toward medical professors caused by the Black Death. While admitting that physicians met increasing criticism and some reduction in status because of their inability to cure or even mitigate the ravages of plague, Siraisi concludes that the medical profession, and science generally, recovered much of its prestige in the fifteenth century. In the third essay, two French historians of medicine and sexuality, Danielle Jacquart and Claude Thomasett, trace the ongoing preoccupation of the medical profession in promoting conception as a Christian duty in order to replenish a drastically reduced population. In promoting a higher birthrate, medical practitioners relied mainly on Avicenna's two-

seed theory, which held that both men and women emitted seeds at the moment of conception.

The Plague Strikes Orvieto

Elisabeth Carpentier

In the wake of the plague, in September of 1348, Orvieto was a lamentable sight to
be seen. The *Discorso historico* and the *Riformagioni* send clear messages, or, rather,
show clear symptoms. Let us analyze the impressions which are to be gleaned from a
reading of the chronicle. First of all, there is a feeling of unprecedented demographic
catastrophe: nine tenths of the population are said to have disappeared. Although
the proportions may seem excessively high, examination of the lists of the Council
of Seven (according to which six out of thirteen people died every two months) and
the lists of the Council of Twelve (according to which four out of twelve people died
every month) prove that at least half of the population must have perished. There is,
therefore, reason to speak of a demographic catastrophe. The consequences for both
the physical composition of the city as well as for the behavior of its inhabitants are
mirrored in the *Discorso:* the survivors were terrorized. They probably kept count of
each other and sought each other out, like the survivors of bombings during the last
war. They had suffered a psychological shock which would take a long time to forget.
The *Discorso* even speaks of a physiological shock: "The survivors stayed sick." Are
we thus to understand that those who had been afflicted with the plague, and who
had managed to survive, recovered only partially? Or rather, and more likely than
not, that the population, after years of famine and that year of death and mourning,
remained weakened? The text seems to include the entire population. Who knows,
moreover, whether the pulmonary after-effects of the plague did not take years to
disappear?

The number of abandoned homes constitute a clear indication of the devastation which had struck the city and of the confusion which reigned among the survivors. The text notes two causes for their being abandoned: the deaths of all the inhabitants of a single dwelling (we know this to have occurred; the *Discorso* clearly
states that entire families were swept away), and the flight of those who didn't dare
return to homes that seemed cursed. Uninhabited, and abandoned, these homes ran
a high risk of falling little by little into decay or of becoming the object of devasta-
tions and pillage, all of which only aggravated the plague of 1346 and 1347. In fact,
on October 18, 1348, the city council reminded all of its officers of a long-standing
interdict to destroy houses; at the same time, the council added that it was also forbidden to enter houses so as to remove either shingles or slates, stones, wood or any

From Elisabeth Carpentier, "The Plague Strikes Orvieto," trans. Brad Williams, from *Une ville devant la
peste noire. Orvieto et la Peste noire de 1348* (Paris:SEVPEN, 1962), pp. 150–157.

other building materials. The sight of those decaying, abandoned, or half-pillaged homes must have been a bit disconcerting and was in itself sufficient to maintain an atmosphere of desolation—unbecoming to the betterment of the public morale. Statutes of the *Riformagioni* state very clearly: "The citizens of Orvieto interested in good living as well [as] the city's foreign merchants were revolted by this sight." These signs of misery did not please the wealthy, nor were they good for the poor. The undeniable material, moral and physiological ruin made it imperative to develop an entire program of reconstruction. Orvieto's city council had already begun outlining that program in the last months of 1348. Within a few weeks, the council had articulated the bases for a political, demographic, economic, social and psychological renewal. An examination of those attempts at reconstruction permits an evaluation of the immediate consequences of the plague; as a result, destruction and reconstruction will necessarily remain closely linked.

At first glance, it may seem strange that Orvieto's reconstruction was based on a platform of political reform; yet, this is not surprising when one recalls the events which immediately preceded the epidemic. Orvieto had, more or less completely, given itself over to Perugia. Whenever a medieval city managed to secure control of a city of lesser importance, the stronger city attempted to force the new subject city to remodel its institutions according to its own. Let us also remember that for several years, Orvieto had been shaken by a political and economic crisis which its traditional institutions had not managed to resolve: if one recalls the discussion of March 12 which gave rise to a decision to revise certain municipal statutes, one might rightfully note with surprise that the closely knit alliance with Perugia was not followed more rapidly by an internal reform. In reality, only the plague can explain the delay. During those trying months, the magistrates of the city could neither read, correct nor prepare legal texts. However, as soon as the epidemic was over, things started happening rapidly. While for several months, only the Seven and the Twelve were meeting with regularity and the Capitano del Popolo was constantly absent or replaced by a vicar, September 19 marked a change. The Capitano del Popolo called for "a general and extraordinary council of the nobles and people of Orvieto" to meet under his auspices and under his presidency. This had to have brought together an unusually large constituency, for at the end of the meeting, some 327 votes had been registered; to that need be added those persons who did not have suffrage and those who had abstained. Consequently, [this was] an impressive assembly, like those that are called together under exceptional circumstances or for very important decisions. This was indeed such an instance: at issue, the reform of the city, of the "*contado*, of the people and of the commune." It was decided by a vote of 317 to 10 to assign the reform to the Seven and to a commission of twelve, named by them and by the Capitano del Popolo (The Twelve, named September 7, subsequently disappear after having only served for twelve days . . .). This was not an unusual procedure during the Middle Ages: The decision at large was made by a large assembly, designed to represent the will of all the citizens, while application was confided to a small commission with sizable powers. Let us stop for a moment to listen to the terms in which the Perugian Capitano del Popolo proposes the reform: "Orvieto, its *contado* and its district, which had been plagued by terrible wars and by cruel distress and oppression, hurled to the ground and trampled at the brutal feet of tyrants, is now resting, thanks be to God, in sweet peace." The positive results of its submission to Perugia! But also, relief at the end of a series of long crises capped by the plague.

Without delay, the next day, September 20, the Seven and the Capitano del Popolo proceeded to name the Twelve. Their first working session convened September 21. Its first decision: all discussions of the council, as it thus stood, were to be secret. The reform of the city began with that first session. Important measures were taken, which could not have been improvised. On the contrary, they had to have been the product of much work: a general council and the Council of Twelve were the product of a well prepared staging, which probably did not fool anyone. September 21, it was decided to give new statutes to the Seven for a duration of three or four years and to create for the same period of time a Council of Twenty-four Citizens to replace the former Council of Forty Nobles and Citizens; the latter's tenure was to be renewed every six months and from their ranks were to be chosen the four captains of the Guelf alliance. Finally, the essential legislative powers were to be confided to the larger Council of Two-Hundred Citizens, where a quorum of seventy members was sufficient to make applicable decisions. It is important to note that, as of the first day of the reform, no roll is given to the nobles, who, at the beginning of the year, had been represented in the Council of Forty Nobles and Citizens. The intention of the reformers became clearer when they decided, at the end of the meeting, to refuse entry to the Palace of the Commune to all members of the Monaldeschi, Filippeschi, Ranieri families, both legitimate and illegitimate, unless they were to have special authorization, valid for only one day. Are we thus witnessing, in the wake of the plague, a reaction of the people? Let us not forget that Perugia was then in the midst of a period of democratic government and confrontation with nobles whose names were literally nailed to the *pilori* in the famous *Red Book*. Moreover, it was, indeed, the nobles of Orvieto who called upon Perugia for assistance. But, after a few months, the undertaking seems to have clearly turned to their disadvantage. The imitation of Perugia became flagrant when September 21, the office of the Seven and the office of the Standard-bearer were replaced by an office of eight citizens called the Priors, just like in Perugia. They maintained, moreover, the same attributes and the same salary as the former Seven.

Analogous measures were being taken every day. As of September 24, the members of the Council of Twenty-four Citizens were named for three months, while from among their numbers four captains of the alliance were chosen. The anti-noble reaction was perhaps not as deep as one might have thought, for at the same time, twenty-five nobles thought to have been popular were selected to meet during six months with the Twenty-five and would furnish five other captains of the Guelf alliance: the mystery of reforms and of compromises. . . . Moreover, two days later, two measures were adopted that were clearly hostile to the noble cause. The first of the two doubled all the fines incurred by both legitimate and illegitimate nobles, as well as the fines of their familiars, of which they were obliged to furnish an exact list. The second list revoked all the powers which may have been conceded to nobles and to magnates as well as to any other persons. While attempting to limit the abuses committed by the nobility, Orvieto did not attempt to make outlaws of them. The same prudence and caution were noticeable September 27 in a statute which called back to life the *Massa del Popolo*, an old Orvietan institution which had fallen into disuse. It foresaw the meeting of four hundred citizens, with or without arms, at the call of the Capitano del Popolo and the Priors, in order to protect the public order. At their head, four standard-bearers, one per quarter. The text served as a reminder that in the case of unrest, nobles were not authorized to leave their homes without the permission of the Capitano del Popolo or of the Podestà. In the case of troubles, all private citizens were also forbidden to bring into Orvieto unauthorized members of the "contado" or foreigners. These interdicts demonstrated quite clearly the manner in which "troubles" were handled in Orvieto.

With the Priors (the first of which were named September 24 before assuming their functions November 1), the Council of the Twenty-four Citizens, the Council of Two hundred Citizens and the Massa del Popolo, the characteristic organisms of Orvieto's new constitution were hence in place. The quality of the latter remains difficult to judge; it had to function in very difficult and troubled times. These difficulties included a year of internal and external political strife between noble families and where the Monaldeschi family had been particularly prominent, the recent Perugian alliance, months of turmoil in the aftermath of the plague (which led to a crippling of political institutions and to limited activity within the councils) and the fatigue of the population after so many trials. Which of these factors was determining? Or was any one of them determining? It would be fruitless to try to ascribe solely to the plague a political reform of this type. It suffices to remark that in the wake of the epidemic, the popular party of Orvieto sought to take back control of a dominance which it had tended to abandon to the nobility in preceding years. And, that the nobles do not seem to have offered much resistance. Had the social climate perhaps changed? . . .

The reform of internal policy accompanied an attempt to reorganize the *contado*, . . . which had been, especially affected by the epidemic. It had already been ruined by bad harvests, totally disrupted by the war, and was running an ever greater risk of escaping Orvieto's sphere of influence. That had already happened in certain frontier areas, particularly, in the regions under the domination of Benedetto de Bonconte. The summer of 1348 was, however, not marked by any military undertaking: a major novelty when compared with 1346 and 1347, and undoubtedly due to the plague.

The same famine led a Pistoian chronicler to note that in 1347 "neither king nor lord undertook war." In Orvieto, famine was not sufficient reason to bring a halt to armed confrontation, but the plague managed to do so, and the commune attempted to profit from the calamity in order to regain control of a compromised situation. When on September 22, the Seven and the Twelve organized the city's reform, they became very concerned with the salary of the castellan holding Collelungo under the auspices of Orvieto. The same concern surfaced September 26 and involved the castellan holding Cetona: two key strategic outposts for the control of the explosive northern and eastern sectors. The problems associated with the protection of those two posts were, moreover, often discussed during the following months. At the same time, Orvieto got Paterno back. On October 14, tensions rose: the commune reminded all of the counts, barons, nobles, magnates, lands, communes and communities of the *contado* of their yearly obligations to Orvieto. Many of the city's subjects had profited from the anarchy born out of the wars and aggravated by the plague and had neglected their obligations in 1348. Orvieto insisted emphatically that those obligations were the same then as they had been in the past. At the same time, the city attempted to show clemency. On October 24, the city encouraged the people of Cetona, Sarteano, Chianciano, Pian Castagniao and of Abbey of S. Salvatore—all former rebels—to surrender in all serenity in Orvieto: amnesty was granted until January 1 (this act of generosity went, needless to say, hand in hand with the city's economic imperatives . . .). Always seemingly motivated by the cause of peace, Orvieto went so far as to forbid its subjects to become involved in internal quarrels in the commune of Todi. Only the counts of Montemarte, because of personal territorial litigation with Todi, were allowed to intervene. Orvieto, however, did not want to be drawn into any new adventures.

Medical Reputations and the Black Death

NANCY G. SIRAISI

As a learned discipline, medicine had secured a position of distinction in Italy by the middle of the fourteenth century. The sources of medical learning were ancient, and its twelfth- and thirteenth-century expansion and development had been part of a European intellectual movement that was in no way peculiar to Italy. Nevertheless, two generations of Italian physicians (flourishing approximately from 1265 to 1325) had succeeded in bringing renown to north and central Italian seats of learning, most notably Bologna and Padua, as centers for the study of medicine in a university setting and in developing a regional tradition of preeminence in the interpretation of medical texts. Furthermore, as is well known, an important local surgical tradition was at least partially incorporated into the university curriculum, and some development of anatomical study took place. From the thirteenth century, too, medicine and surgery came to play a recognized role in Italian civic life. As a group, physicians probably never enjoyed the prestige of lawyers. Nonetheless, medical guilds and colleges of physicians were formed in a number of cities, and their members included influential leading citizens, some of whom from time to time played a significant role in political life. Moreover, urban governments both appointed *medici* under long term contract to treat the citizenry and called upon physicians and surgeons for professional opinions as juridical occasion arose. In short, both in terms of development of an academic discipline and in terms of the growth of an organized and socially influential occupational group (the word profession is unavoidable but should perhaps be used with caution), the record of medicine in Italy

"The Physician's Task: Medical Reputations in Humanist Collective Biographies" by Nancy G. Siraisi from *The Rational Arts of Living*, A. C. Crombie and Nancy Siraisi, eds., Smith College Studies in History, Vol. 50, 1987, pp. 108–123, 128–133. Reprinted by permission of the publisher.

in the late thirteenth and early fourteenth century is one of rather remarkable success.

This thriving medical profession was soon faced with one of the most dramatic medical calamities in human history, the catastrophic plague outbreak of 1348. Yet although the scale of the disaster was unprecedented, the helplessness of the physician before the onset of major, life-threatening disease could not have been a new discovery. Whatever disillusionment with the medical profession may have occurred at that time does not seem to have been general or prolonged. Subsequent generations, familiarized with plague by recurrent serious but lesser outbreaks, continued to support a medical profession essentially unchanged in organization and approach. Indeed, it has been argued that plague crises, by increasing anxiety about disease, may even have heightened dependence upon the advice of doctors about general regimen for health. From the standpoint of the careers and reputations of individual physicians, it would certainly be difficult to demonstrate that, for example, Marsiglio Santa Sofia, Giacomo da Forli, and Ugo Benzi, all of whom flourished in the late fourteenth and early fifteenth century, represented any significant break with late thirteen-/early fourteenth-century Italian medical tradition, or enjoyed renown and esteem either notably less or much different in kind from that of, say, Dino del Garbo and Gentile da Foligno in the years before the Black Death.

The experience of plague did, however, unquestionably play a part in shaping the views of certain highly articulate critics of medicine, filled with a sense of the uselessness of human science in the face of the judgment of God. As an example, one may cite the Florentine chronicler Matteo Villani "Concerning this pestiferous infirmity the physicians in every part of the world had neither explanation nor cure through natural philosophy, or through medicine, or through astrology. Some of them, for the sake of making a profit, paid visits and gave their explanations; these by their own deaths showed their art to be feigned and not real." By far the most important of such critics was Petrarch, whose great reputation and influence helped to create a strand of humanist rhetoric that was unfavorable to medicine. It has been shown that in the course of time Petrarch moved from an original response of fear and indignation at the judgement implied by the plague to an attitude of resigned and pious acceptance. Neither of these points of view reflects much confidence in the efforts of the medical profession. In the years immediately following the first great plague epidemic, Petrarch's attitude to medical men was one of active hostility that went far beyond pointing out their ineffectiveness in the face of major epidemics. This attitude is manifested in the *Invectiva contra medicum*, completed in 1353. The work grew out of an exchange of letters with a papal physician who had been incautious enough to object when, in 1351, Petrarch advised Pope Clement VI to avoid doctors during his illness. In the *Contra medicum* Petrarch deployed his unparalleled mastery of Latin rhetoric in a stream of vituperation. In particular, medicine is repeatedly attacked for its pretensions to rhetorical and philosophical learning, although it is allowed a modest place as a mechanical art. One sample of Petrarch's invective will suffice: to an apparent claim by the unfortunate physician that his palor was due to vigils spent in philosophical studies, Petrarch responded that it was the result of ill health produced by frequent examination of feces.

Influential though Petrarch's attitudes to the medical profession may have been, they were not necessarily characteristic of the Italian humanism of the fourteenth and fifteenth centuries taken as a whole. The development of certain north Italian cities as centers of academic medical learning from the thirteenth to the fifteenth centuries, is, after all, a well-known part of the general flowering of Italian urban culture and civic institutions in that age. Accordingly, it comes as no surprise to find either that the literate medical man's understanding of his own responsibilities continued to be shaped by the scholastic tradition, so successfully institutionalized in university faculties of medicine, or that a number of contemporaries outside the medical profession, literary humanists among them, pointed with pride to the achievements of Italian scholastic medicine. . . .

[A] physician has two distinct but intimately related functions, namely *understanding* and *healing*. To them may be added a third function, not spelled out by Avicenna, but implicit in his formulation and surely of great importance in the professional life of his Latin followers: that of providing a link between the other two by *explaining*.

These functions were not only diverse in themselves, but so also were the settings in which they were exercised in the Renaissance Italian cities. In the case of the university-trained physician, and still more in that of the professor of medicine, the achievement of *understanding* took place in the context of an academic community whose chief investigative and teaching tools were text analysis and structured debate, setting a high priority on the ability to demolish an opponent's arguments. By this means and in this atmosphere, the physician acquired knowledge of *theoria*, that is, of basic principles derived, and refined, from the study of authoritative medical texts. . . .

But university medical training further required the scholar to grasp principles and precepts of *practica*, a distinct academic discipline with its own professors and authoritative texts. Here, too, instruction was provided by means of formal scholastic exposition and debate, although not by those means alone, since attendance upon the practice of experienced physicians and, occasionally, at dissections of the human cadaver was also customary. It is by no means easy to determine the boundary between medical *theoria* and *practica* considered as academic disciplines, either from the standpoint of academic methodology or from that of subject matter. For example, discussion of the elements clearly belongs to *theoria* and lists of specific treatments for particular diseases to *practica*. But content relating (in our terms) to physiology and pathology might occur in either or both, and scholastic commentaries might be tools of teaching and study for *practica* as well as *theoria*. The medical scholar was supposed to be able to relate *theoria* to *practica*, but the fit did not necessarily have to be very close. In particular, it was generally recognized that the basis for many remedies was empirical rather than rational.

The contexts in which a medical man exercised his *explanatory* functions were a good deal more varied. A professor of medicine would, of course, be engaged in pedagogic explanation in the academic setting just described: lecturing to his students on assigned books, supervising their efforts at disputation, or engaging in various forms of physical demonstration if he conducted anatomies or allowed students to accompany him in his practice. Outside the universities, medical men of all kinds no doubt trained apprentices as their successors, and hence these practitioners too must have engaged in pedagogical explanation or demonstration to some extent. A university professor of medicine or, probably, any literate physician of some renown might also respond to requests for explanation or advice from lesser professional colleagues engaged exclusively in practice, who would in turn apply his recommendations to their patients. Many of the surviving *consilia* of well-known physicians appear to have been produced in this way. A few of them identify the addressee as a physician, or assume his access to medical books; almost all take for granted the recipient's Latinity and some background of medical knowledge.

And, of course, all medical practitioners engaged in some form of communication with their patients. While the nature of this communication is one of the most elusive aspects of the medical system under discussion, several considerations lead one to suppose that explanation played a major and esteemed part therein, at any rate to the extent that culturally, socially, or economically privileged patients were involved. One might note in this connection the general stress on regimen of the patient's entire mode of living. This ideal of medical supervision was no doubt fairly seldom realized in practice, except with a few wealthy and exceptionally cooperative patients, but it surely presupposes a flow of information and exhortation from doctor to patient. The same might be said for the importance attached to prognosis. The learned doctor's expression of sympathetic concern, his detailed instructions for the regulation of the patient's daily regime, his erudite explanations of the complexional origins of ill health, and his cautious prognosis of future developments constituted a significant part of what he had to offer.

Healing, or rather activities intended to promote healing, might also take place in a variety of contexts. Any medical man might treat his patients directly; but, depending on his and the patient's circumstances, he was also likely to instruct a variety of possible intermediaries, for example, his own assistants, the patient's family or servants, or a pharmacist, to prepare or administer remedies. In addition, as already noted, a learned physician might suggest in writing a course of treatment that would actually be carried out by a fellow physician. While it is possible to overstress the limitations of the therapy of the age (after all, minor surgery, laxatives, and opiates presumably worked well enough much of the time) it does seem likely that the prescribing physician often had relatively little scientific or administrative control over the substances finally ingested by or applied to the patient.

In the careers of individuals, the balance between understanding, explaining, and healing functions no doubt varied widely. Indeed, even within a single career the balance was probably often different at different times. Nor is there any need to suppose that fairly wide variations in balance would not be found generally acceptable and appropriate. Nonetheless, it is clear that the more highly trained [a] physician was, the more likely he was to spend time in the activities here grouped under the headings "understanding" and "explaining." It is also clear that while almost all physicians were active in healing, medical reputations were seldom made by healing alone.

One way of examining medical reputations is of course to turn to the written works of physicians themselves and note the pattern of citation of local and relatively recent predecessors. . . . Another avenue of approach is through works by nonmedical authors that are explicitly addressed to the subject of medicine. . . . For the present we shall focus . . . on a group of writings that include depictions of physicians with, in most cases, no discernible polemical purpose. . . . Suffice it to say that from the late fourteenth century, biographically organized collections that included modern individuals began to appear in some numbers. In some other cases, the developing interest in biography was fused with urban history, and led to the inclusion of accounts of outstanding citizens in works descriptive of single cities. . . .

Of much greater interest are the accounts of modern medical men provided by Filippo Villani in his *De origine civitatis Florentiae et eiusdem famosis civibus* (probably first written in 1381/82 and revised 1395/96.). Villani, who was a member of the circle of Salutati, came from a family of noted Florentine historians. No doubt he was fully familiar with his father Matteo's dramatic narrative of the plague in Florence. . . . As he informed his readers in one of his prefaces, in the biographical section of *De origine* he was interested mainly in the Florentine poets, but he decided also to include exemplary fellow citizens in other occupations. Four of these were physicians: Taddeo Alderotti (d. 1295), Dino del Garbo (d. 1327), Turisanus (Torrigiano de' Torrigiani, d. ca. 1319), and Tommaso del Garbo (Dino's son d. 1370). Villani's lives of physicians are of the first importance, because they developed patterns in describing medical accomplishment that seem to have become virtually standard *topoi* in the work of subsequent Latin humanists. Salient features are the assertion or assumption that medicine has made significant modern advances owing to the efforts of Italian physicians, the description of those advances as primarily involving improvements in the interpretation of ancient or Arabic texts, the inclusion of information about the written works of medical men and their activities as university professors, and a stress on the demand among the rich and powerful for the services of learned physicians.

The claim for modern revitalization of medical culture among the Italians of course parallels the similar and much better known contemporary claims for art and letters. One recalls Boccaccio's assertion that Giotto had revived "that art which had for so many centuries lain hidden" and his similar remark about Dante. Villani applied this idea to poetry and art and extended it to medicine and law. Thus, of Taddeo Alderotti he said that he was among the first of the moderns and that he opened up the profoundest secrets of the art which were lying hidden under the words of medical authorities. As a result, Taddeo's commentaries constituted a *glossa ordinaria* for medicine; he and the jurist Accursius were twin stars who made "easy and open" the two arts most useful for the preservation of human nature. We also learn from Villani that Taddeo's medical attentions were in demand throughout Italy, that he commanded enormous fees, and that his patients included a pope. Villani further underlined the novelty of Taddeo's enterprise by including vivid anecdotes showing him as a self-made man, intellectually, socially, and economically. . . .

Villani's work also seems to have been a source for the encomium of Italian scholastic physicians that Salutati included in his treatise on the relative merits of law and medicine, completed in 1398. Announcing that he did not begrudge "the glory of the discoverers of medicine," Salutati first listed various ancient and Arabic physicians and Maimonides and then passed abruptly to the moderns, introducing them as follows: "But that I may come to the Italians who have treated this learned medicine with marvelous subtlety. . . . " He included accounts of the same four physicians as Villani and, in very similar words, credited Taddeo with being the first to open up medical learning. But by adding discussions of Pietro d'Abano (d. ca. 1316) of Padua, Gentile da Foligno (d. 1348), who taught at Perugia and elsewhere, and Cristofano Degli Onesti (d. 1392) who taught at Bologna, Salutati made it clear that he regarded the modern revival of medicine as an achievement associated with the north and central Italian university centers in general and not just with Florence. Of course, in passing straight from the Arabs to the *italici* (by whom he meant Taddeo Alderotti and his successors), Salutati blandly and conveniently overlooked the contributions of both Salerno and Montpellier. One must admit that in so doing he displayed an attitude entirely consistent with the pattern of citation in the works of fourteenth- and fifteenth-century Italian medical authors themselves.

Salutati's praise of Italian academic physicians, and especially of Pietro d'Abano ("a universal man, more than a physician, truly a philosopher") certainly amounts to a rather handsome tribute to the regional tradition of scholastic medicine, especially considering that the context is a treatise in which law is judged superior to medicine on a variety of counts. According to Salutati, of the two disciplines law is nobler, more truly scientific, more useful to the community, and more spiritually uplifting. But Salutati's general polemical strategy throughout the treatise was to assimilate medical *theoria* wholly to *physica* or *philosophia*, while simultaneously pouring scorn on the degrading physicality, the non-rational basis, and the dubious or trivial results of the practical part of medicine. This disjunction was not, of course, at all characteristic of the higher reaches of the medical profession itself. And . . . such a disjunction was equally uncharacteristic of the treatment of medical men in the tradition of collective biography as it developed after Villani. Some of the collective biographies were, as one might expect, from erudite or literary writers, more inclined to emphasize the learning of their subjects than their activities as healers. Although they followed Salutati in assimilating theoretical medical studies to philosophy, none of these authors went so far as to denigrate medical practice. Moreover . . . several of them laid considerable stress on the importance, and indeed inseparability, of achievement in both the theoretical and the practical realms.

Furthermore, it is perhaps worth noting in passing that although Salutati's skepticism about neo-Galenic pharmacology and the inspection of urines may arouse our sympathy, he also objected on very similar grounds to one of the most significant innovations of fourteenth-century Italian university medical education, namely the dissection of the human cadaver for purposes of study. The latter opinion should perhaps serve as a warning against any too ready identification of Salutati's views of early Renaissance medicine with those of more recent critics of the system. . . .

. . . The topos of distinguished medical citizens was nowhere more carefully handled or more fully developed than by Michele Savonarola of Padua, in his work on the glories of that city, written in 1446. The author was both a former professor of medicine in the *studium* of Padua and also a man of pronounced humanistic and religious interests. In composing and arranging his accounts of notable medical men, he drew both upon the general tradition of humanist collective biography sketched above, and upon an insider's view (and knowledge) of the medical profession. A thoughtful prologue and asides explain his choice of occupational categories and their arrangement in a sequence of descending worth. With rather self-conscious detachment he rated law as nobler than medicine, remarking: "And [this is] although

I am surrounded by physicians, since I am one, thus in my view I have here, preferred truth to being in company." Within each category, Savonarola also ranked his subjects in order of merit, designating them as first, second, third, etc. That this is a preferential rather than a chronological order is indicated by the fact that two painters tie for first place in that category.

In assembling the subjects for his category of philosophers, Savonarola brought together two distinct approaches, both of which we have encountered before. Like Salutati, he believed that some physicians had really attained the status of natural philosophers; like Cino Rinuccini, he thought that some poets functioned as moral philosophers. Accordingly, four of his five philosophers are the scholastic physician Pietro d'Abano, in first place, and the humanist poets Petrarch, Mussato and Lovati. For Savonarola, philosophers came after theologians and before political and military leaders and jurists. After the jurists he placed doctors of arts and medicine who cannot be ranked as philosophers because of their *"illiberale et servile exercitium,"* but who nonetheless have "such worth in the excellence of their writings, the elegance of their works, and their ability to preserve health and restore it when lost . . . that mortals revere them as once they did the gods." The eight physicians in this category, of whom the earliest is Jacopo Dondi (d. 1359), were all professors of medicine and scholastic authors. In four cases, the primary emphasis is placed upon university teaching, commentaries, and *quaestiones*; in two others, although *theoria* and written works are alluded to, the chief points are skill in *practica* or a famous patient. In addition, Jacopo Dondi is praised as the author of a written work of such practical usefulness that it is indispensable for practicing physicians throughout Italy and Germany. The eighth account is of Giovanni Dondi, the clockmaker, "a great orator, a *medicus practicus*, an outstanding mathematician, and a man of extraordinary manual dexterity," but the focus is on his horological not his medical achievements.

Savonarola then turned to a separate category of *medici practici* whom, he declared, should by right follow the *medici theorici*. As one might expect, even in an author as careful about classification as Savonarola, the basis for assignment to one or the other category seems more a matter of emphasis than of any fundamental difference in approach. We have just seen that noteworthy ability in *practica* or even manual skill by no means disqualified candidates for inclusion in the category of *theorici*. Similarly, the *practici*, who seem mostly to be men of lesser reputation, include authors (identified as such) of scholastic commentaries on works on *practica*. Four of the eight *practici* appear in fact to have been professors, although their professorships may have been distinguished from those of their colleagues in *theoria*; the remainder were all university educated. . . .

Savonarola clearly displayed a wider knowledge of the recent history of medicine and perhaps a more informed appreciation of the way the relationship between medical *theoria* and *practica* actually worked within the university setting than the other authors considered; nonetheless, there is no doubt that his work belongs essentially to the same genre as theirs. What conclusions, then, can one reach about this body of material as a whole?

In the first place, there appears to be a fairly consistent tradition placing medicine among praiseworthy public activities. Law may be more prestigious, but this does not mean medicine is dismissed as unworthy. Furthermore, this tradition remained a living one; successive authors brought it up to date by the addition of more recent names. Secondly, in the hands of Villani and Salutati, medicine took its place among the disciplines restored to life by the efforts of modern Italians, and therefore as a source of pride. As with art and letters, there was certainly some historical basis for this attitude, although (also as with art and letters) it involved ahistorical notions of sudden disjunction and the overlooking of a significant and continuous earlier process of development. In the third place, the distinctive feature of this supposedly "new" medicine was its scholastic learning, in the setting of the north Italian universities. Accordingly, pride in that learning was a central feature in any praise accorded to medicine by Italian authors of the fourteenth and fifteenth centuries. At the same time, the medicine of illustrious physicians was almost always presented as including all three of the functions here characterized as understanding, explaining, and healing. The model physician . . . was a scholastic commentator and university professor who also attended patients. A reputation for scholastic learning was, moreover, clearly one of the factors that might draw patients to a particular physician. Nevertheless, although the two medical authors perhaps displayed slightly more enthusiasm for *practica* than the non-medical authors, none of the latter slighted or ignored it, and one, Bartolomeo Fazio, was fascinated by surgical skill.

The accounts of medical men discussed in this essay antedate important criticisms and demands for change that began to appear within the medical profession toward the end of the fifteenth century and to multiply in the early sixteenth. Those criticisms and demands were expressed in the call for a return to the original Greek texts of ancient medical works, in the growing dissatisfaction with the scholastic question method in science, and in the thrust toward greater precision in anatomy and botany and toward the systematization of clinical teaching. They did indeed in the end radically undercut Latin scholastic medicine, even though it long survived their first appearance. But the witness of the collective biographies suggests that, in the later fourteenth and the fifteenth centuries, not only within but also outside the medical profession, Latin medical learning and the healing activities of academically trained physicians were normally perceived as a harmoniously integrated and satisfactorily functioning system. Despite the proliferation of presumably equally effective (or equally ineffective) informally trained healers, despite the Plague, and despite the accusations of greed, philosophical inadequacy, or practical inefficacy launched at scholastic physicians by Petrarch and others, Italian university educated physicians were successful in retaining a large measure of social respect in this period. It is easy to see why this should be so. From the medical standpoint, learned explanation and sympathetic regimen, rather than cure (except in relatively minor or self-limiting illnesses), were and would long remain optimum therapeutic expectations. More generally, the learned commentaries and other writings of Italian medical authors were perceived, correctly, as a significant intellectual achievement in their own right. Hence the scholastic physician, carrying out his society's expectations concerning the definition and performance of his task, might expect in turn to enjoy the confidence of his patients, the respect of his colleagues and fellow citizens, and perhaps also to serve as a model to lesser medical men.

Sexuality and Medicine in the Middle Ages

DANIELLE JACQUART AND CLAUDE THOMASETT

Through Avicenna's influence, the consensus of doctors regarding the existence of female sperm was maintained; even in authors who granted it only a restricted role, the link between fecundity and a female emission was preserved. This enabled medical preoccupations to be displaced and created the possibility of making room for the beginnings of an erotic art: the quest for pleasure as such was to be one of the components of every discourse on the conditions for performing the sexual act, since in the background loomed the necessity of encouraging conception. Sterility and frigidity became synonymous. All of these factors led to the notion of sin being forgotten when this was necessary, and to the possibility of a freedom in thought and behaviour which might have struck us as irreversible, were it not for the opposing current transmitted by the Aristotelian vision of women and the failure of the centuries that followed the Middle Ages to follow up this vision of freedom. . . .

Avicenna . . . granted doctors freedom of expression with, in addition, a justification that could not be neglected in a society that made sexual intercourse serve the sole end of reproduction. Medieval writers backed Avicenna's assertion with an aphorism from another author writing in Arabic: "You must not be ashamed to ask the patient about everything." Doctors made use of this freedom of expression first of all in what seemed to be most within their field of competence, that is, in everything that had to do with the structure of the genitals and any incompatibilities that might arise between them—and so one comes across long lists of ointments, pessaries or fumigations designed to make the respective organs bigger or smaller, wider or narrower or stronger and so on. . . .

Doctors . . . accepted without hesitation all of Avicenna's prescriptions meant to make sexual intercourse easier or more pleasant; they even added a certain amount of advice drawn from other sources or from their own experience, but they did not always manage to do so without seeing them as a means of obtaining greater fecundity. With this type of prescription, we are still dealing with a sexuality in thrall to a purely medical approach. Another short paragraph from the *Canon* of Avicenna risked creating a greater difficulty, since its advice lay completely outside the framework of pharmacopoeia. Indeed, in the chapter devoted to curing sterility, the foreplay that should precede and accompany the sexual act is discussed. . . .

. . . By the end of the Middle Ages, medicine had placed itself staunchly on the side of the individual. Despite the many things that were not mentioned, Avicenna's lesson had been noted and Arab erotic lore was apparently becoming a component of the didactic message of certain doctors. Ovid was equally omnipresent. The question of female sperm provided an opportunity of affirming the benefits of shared pleasure, in a context that went beyond that of literature meant for doctors alone. . . .

. . . Although they avoided alluding to different positions, doctors found room in their works for a great deal of advice which diverged from anatomical or physiognomical description and bore a closer resemblance to an erotic science. In it could be discerned the manifestation of a medical reaction against the dangers that threatened civilization. Epidemics of the plague increased falls in the population, and the last centuries of the Middle Ages were characterized by the rise of an apocalyptic vision; fanatical preachers foretold the end of the world. Doctors were led to denounce the danger of such influences and to praise the joys of life rather than to act repressively. From the same point of view, Jacques Despars, in the fifteenth century, declared firmly that nobody should blush about their sexual life, and underlined the happiness that procreation could bring:

> [The man who suffers from a diminution of coitus] should become used to not blushing about the sexual act, or about listening to stories about it. Books discussing carnal love, the acts of Venus and their figures should be read in his presence, so that he will not blush either at talking about it openly, or at hearing it discussed, or at performing coitus when he so decides. He must frequently imagine the pleasures of love and he must bear in mind that to beget one's fellow-creatures constitutes for living beings an entirely natural task; he must remember that without coitus, the human species would be extinguished, and it is pleasant to have children who will produce others and keep the world going.

DOCUMENTS

The first selection—chronicles from Siena and from Padua—provides eyewitness accounts of the immediate effects of the Black Death on those two Italian cities in 1348. The accounts independently record enormous social disruption during the plague, which caused a widespread breakdown of social relations and morality. Writing some years later, the French physician Guy de Chauliac evokes his feelings of hopelessness in the face of the plague and shows the ineffectiveness of astrological medicine. The two forms of plague that he describes in the second document are bubonic—the most common, characterized by large swellings (buboes) of the lymph nodes—and pneumonic—caused by the bacillus entering the lungs. Pneumonic plague was nearly always fatal within hours or a few days; the bubonic variety claimed its victims after a week or so, but about one-third of those who contracted the disease—including Guy himself—survived it. Socino Benzi's enthusiastic biography of his father, Ugo, a great north Italian medical man of the early fifteenth century, documents in the third piece the prestige that medical professors enjoyed in court and university circles.

| The Plague Strikes Siena, 1348

The mortality began in Siena in May; it was a horrible and cruel matter, and I do not know where to begin to describe its cruelty and pitiless ways, which made almost all who saw it become stupefied with the pain. And it is not possible to de-

"The Plague Strikes Siena, 1348," from Antonio di Tura del Grasso, *Cronaca Senese*, eds. A. Lisini and F. Iacometti, Rerum italicarum scriptores, new ed. Vol. 15, part 6 (Bologna, Nicola Zanichelli, 1937), p. 555. Translated by Benjamin G. Kohl.

scribe the horrible thing; indeed one can be called blessed who did not see such horribleness. And those struck died almost at once; they would swell beneath their armpits and in their groin, and fall dead while talking. Father abandoned son, wife her husband, and one brother the other; each one fled and left the other, since this disease seemed to strike through breath and the eyes. And thus people died, and no one could be found to bury the dead for money or out of friendship, so members of each household buried their own dead in a ditch, without a priest, without services, without the tolling of the death bell. And in many places in Siena great pits were dug and filled with the multitude of the dead. And they died by the hundreds both day and night, and each was thrown in those pits and each layer covered with dirt. And as soon as these pits were filled, more pits were dug.

And I, Agnolo di Tura, called the Fat, buried five of my children with my own hands. But there were also bodies that were so poorly covered with earth that dogs dragged them out and ate many bodies, all through the city. And no one lamented the death of others, since each one awaited his own death. And so many people died, that everyone thought that the end of the world had come. And no medicine nor any other remedy worked, and the more remedies were administered, the sooner the victims died. And the governors [of Siena] appointed three citizens who received one thousand gold florins from the commune of Siena, which they were supposed to spend on the sick poor people and use to bury the poor who had died. And it was so horrible that I, the author, do not want to think about it, and, therefore, I will not talk about it any longer. And one finds that there died during this period in Siena 36,000 persons who were twenty years old or less. With the aged and others who died, this added up to a total of 52,000. In the suburbs of Siena died 28,000 persons, so that in all one finds that 80,000 persons died in the city and suburbs of Siena. And at this period there were left in Siena and its suburbs about 30,000 persons, of whom there remained in the city fewer than 10,000 persons. And those who survived were filled with despair and almost devoid of feeling. And many enclosures and other places were abandoned, and all the mines of silver, gold and copper, which existed in [the territory of] Siena, were abandoned as one can see, because in the countryside many more people died, and many areas and villages were abandoned since no person lived there. I will not describe the cruelty that happened in the countryside, how the wolves and other wild beasts devoured the badly buried bodies, and the other cruelties that would be too painful to read about.

| The Black Death Comes to Padua, 1348

Almighty God, who does not want the death of a sinner, but that he should convert and live, first warned, then struck the human race with this not untimely destruction. Wanting to afflict the human race with the greatest plague, unrivaled,

---

"The Black Death Comes to Padua, 1348," from G. Cortusio, *Cronica de novitatibus Padue et Lombardie*, ed. B. Pagnin, ibid., Vol. 10, part 5, p. 121. Translated by Benjamin G. Kohl.

He began it in the farthest reaches of the world and in the East unleashed the plague to work His horrible judgment. Indeed soon after it struck the Tartars, the Turks and all the other infidels, on the 25th of January 1348 at eleven in the evening, there was a terrible earthquake that lasted for half an hour to the terror of the Christians. After that, this unheard of plague crossed the seas into the regions of the Veneto, Lombardy, Tuscany, Germany, France and almost the whole world. Certain infected persons coming from the East carried this [disease]. These killed everyone by sight, touch or breath. This was an incurable infection that could not be avoided. This wife fled the embrace of her dear husband, father from son, brother from brother; on the contrary, people killed for the home, honors, and clothing of the sick. Quite often those burying, carrying, viewing or touching the dead expired almost at once. Thus, one infected sheep killed the whole flock. Thus, the occupants of a household where someone had died followed the others to the dogs. Even the bodies of nobles remained unburied. Many were buried at the high price by vile persons without [the benefit of] priests and candles. Indeed at Venice, where a hundred thousand perished, ships hired at a great expense carried the corpses to the islands. The city was almost deserted. One [sick] person came undetected to Padua, where he infected the whole city, so that one third of the population died. Cities, wanting to avoid this plague, prohibited the entry of all outsiders. Thus, merchants could not travel from city to city. Shut off, cities and castles became destitute. No voices were heard, except sighs, moans and laments. There ceased the voice of the bride and groom, the sound of the zither, the joyful song of the youth. Those plagues that raged in the time of the Pharaohs, of David, of Ezekiel and of Pope Gregory were now considered as nothing. For this plague encompassed the whole world.

This plague was worse for those infected as mentioned above, these vomited blood and died immediately. Others were sick with cancers or with worms. As death approached, almost all of these developed incurable boils around their genitals, under their armpits, and in other parts [of the body], attacked with poisonous fevers. These died on the first or second day; after the third day, there was rarely any hope for recovery; they lapsed into a coma, from which they never awoke, and died. Against this [plague] the physicians openly acknowledged that they were ignorant of any remedy; indeed the vast majority of them died from this very disease.

| A French Physician Survives the Plague, 1368

The mortality began with us in the month of January, and lasted for seven months. It was of two kinds. The first lasted for two months; it was characterized by a continuous fever and a spitting of blood, and men died of it within three days. The second lasted for the rest of the time; it too was characterized by continuous

"On Bubonic Plague" by Guy de Chauliac, trans. by M. McVaugh in *A Source Book in Medieval Science*, Edward Grant, ed., Harvard University Press, 1974, pp. 773–774. Reprinted by permission of the publisher.

fever, and by apostemes and carbuncles and tumors in the external parts, mainly the armpits and groin; and men died of it within five days. It was so contagious (especially that which involved spitting of blood) that one man caught it from another not just when living nearby but simply by looking at him; so much so that people died without servants and were buried without priests. Father would not visit son, nor son, father; charity was dead, and hope prostrate.

I call it great because it engaged all the world, or nearly. For it began in the East, and shooting out into the world, passed through our region toward the west. It was so extensive that it left scarcely the fourth part of the population alive. And it was unprecedented, since, although we read in the *Epidemics* of the mortality in the city of Thrace, and in Palestine, and of another which occurred in Hippocrates' time, and (in the *Euchymia*) of that which afflicted the Romans' subjects in Galen's time, and of that of the city of Rome in the days of Gregory [IX], none of these was as great as this one. For they affected only one area; this one, the whole world; they were curable in one fashion or another; this one, in none. Because of this physicians felt useless and ashamed, inasmuch as they did not dare visit the sick for fear of infection; and when they did visit them they could do very little and accomplished nothing, for all the sick died except for a few towards the end, who escaped with matured buboes.

Many have speculated on the cause of this great mortality. In some places they believed that the Jews had poisoned the world, and so they killed them. In others, they believed that it was the mutilated poor, and so they drove them away. And in still others, that it was the nobles, so that they feared to travel in the world. Finally it came to the point that a watch was kept in cities and towns, forbidding entry to anyone who was not well known. And if they found anyone with powders or ointments, they made him swallow them, fearing that they might be poisons.

But whatever the people said, the truth is that the cause of this mortality was twofold: one active and universal, one passive and particular. The active, universal cause was the disposition of a certain important conjunction of three heavenly bodies, Saturn, Jupiter, and Mars, which had taken place in 1345, the 24th day of March, in the fourteenth degree of Aquarius. For (as I have said in my book on astrology) the more important conjunctions presage marvelous, mighty, and terrible events, such as changes of rulers, the advent of prophets, and great mortalities; and they depend on the [zodiacal] sign and the aspects of the bodies in conjunction. It should not amaze you, therefore, that such an important conjunction signified a marvelous, awful mortality, for it was not just one of the greater ones but one of the greatest. Because the [zodiacal] sign was a human one, it foretold grief for humanity; and because it was a fixed sign, it signified long duration. For [the mortality] began in the East, a little after the conjunction, and was still abroad in the West in [13]50. It so informed the air and the other elements that, as the magnet moves iron, it moved the thick, heated, poisonous humors; and bringing them together within the body, created apostemes there. From this derived the continuous fevers and spitting of blood at the outset, when this corrupt matter was strong and disturbed the natural state. Then, as this lost its strength, the natural state was not so troubled, and expelled what it could, mainly in the armpits and groin, and so caused buboes and other apostemes, so that these external apostemes were the effects of internal ones. The particular, passive case was the disposition of each body, such as cachochymia, debility, or obstruction, whence it was that the working men and those living poorly died.

Men looked for a preventative treatment before the attack and for a curative one thereafter. For prevention nothing was better than to flee the area before becoming infected; and to purge oneself with pills, to diminish the blood by phlebotomy, to purify the air with fire, and to strengthen the heart with tyriac, fruits, and good-smelling things; to fortify the humors with Armenian *bolus*, and to resist decay with sharp [-tasting] things. For a cure men tried bleedings and evacuations, electuaries and cordial syrups. The external apostemes were brought to a head with figs and cooked onions mixed with yeast and butter; then they were opened and treated as ulcers. The tumors were cupped, scarified, and cauterised.

I myself did not dare to leave lest I lose my good name, but in continuous dread kept myself healthy as well as I could, using the remedies above. Nevertheless, towards the end of the mortality I fell into a continuous fever, with an aposteme in the groin; I was ill for six weeks, in such great danger that all my friends believed I would die; but the aposteme ripened, and was treated as I have described, and by God's will I survived.

Socino Benzi Honors
a Renowned Physician—His Father, 1440

He [Ugo Benzi] was of moderate height, of a countenance kindly and modest and ever inclined to dignified merriment. In his boyhood he was of such a rubicund complexion that to many he was known by the name of "Rosy." His hair was blond and thick, but in old age he acquired an honorable baldness. His beard was becoming and manly. He was no weakling and would have retained his natural strength unimpaired, had not study undermined his health; his unceasing toil—for he spared himself neither by day nor by night—brought on an infirmity of the stomach. He suffered also from kidney-stone, and finally from dysuria, not induced, as is usually the case, by intemperance, but by his excessive labors at the time when the thirst for knowledge urged him from one to another of the universities of Italy.

While still a child, even before he entered grammar school, he displayed such remarkable ability that it was a foregone conclusion he would make a great name for himself, however arduous a career in life he might adopt, for in all his elementary lessons he showed a lively intelligence and a tenacious memory. . . .

It was not long before Ugo's fame had spread to all the universities, for he toiled unceasingly at his studies. He even went so far as to shut himself up for several months in his lodgings, eating but one meal a day, and that a meager one; never lying on a bed, but sleeping on the ground; and devoting all his time to reading, writing, and memorizing. Hence it was that no one could grasp the tenets and arguments of philosophy or any other discipline more keenly, nor remember them more tenaciously, nor express them more glibly, than he. In short, his extraordinary quick-

"Life of Ugo Benzi, Eminent Physician" by Socino Benzi from *Ugo Benzi, Medieval Philosopher and Physician, 1376–1439* by Dean Lockwood, pp. 22, 24, 30–31. Copyright 1951 University of Chicago Press. Reprinted by permission of the publisher.

wittedness—which the peripatetics define as "the faculty of hitting upon the middle term instantaneously"—was admitted even by his detractors. Finally he made such progress that during his nineteenth year he declaimed in public on logic, philosophy, medicine, astronomy, arithmetic, geometry, music, grammar, and rhetoric—winning great glory for himself thereby.

For he was immediately invited to Pavia to teach logic in the University. His invitation to that famous Insubrian city, cradle of the arts and sciences, came from the bishop [Guglielmo Centuaria], famous for the sanctity of his morals as well as for the profundity of his learning. Ugo displayed such skill that all the students of dialectic left their former masters and flocked to him, for even against their will he was able to lure them to his classroom through his extraordinary learning and through his eloquence in lecturing, wherein he far excelled all other teachers of his generation. But in addition to these qualities he also displayed a remarkable degree of innate human kindness and an incredible affection for those whom he found eager to learn, so that he not only loved them, but even gave them material aid, so far as his means would allow. In this place he also published his very subtle *Treatise on the Art of Logic.* . . .

After remaining at Parma for four years he was called for a second time to Siena. So eager was he to revisit his birthplace and so weary of exile, that he gladly accepted the call, though some of his friends, who disagreed with him, advised against it. He had not been long in Siena before he found that his friends had advised him correctly, and that his patriotism, which he had always maintained to be man's greatest virtue, had done him great harm. For there are many of his fellow-countrymen who can bear witness that more than once he was falsely and secretly accused of capital offenses, and that his case was tried in his absence, at which time his friends, of whom he had many, appeared in his defense. Consequently, finding himself subject to malicious attacks by a small group of men, who were habitually inclined to the overthrow of the state, he decided to leave Siena; but only by the greatest effort and with the utmost difficulty did he succeed in obtaining leave. He accordingly went to Florence to teach medicine [in the university]. After he had lived there for a while, war and plague drove him to Bologna.

Here he was held in great honor by Gabriel Condulmer, the Venetian, who was at that time ruler of the city, but later became supreme pontiff [Eugene IV]. Ugo was now judged the foremost philosopher and physician of his time—and rightly! For who could adequately praise his diligence in attending the sick? Not only did he care for princes and potentates—many of whom by his skill he snatched from the jaws of death—but also for the poor and needy. So tirelessly did he devote himself to his art that they adored him as a god. And he aided them not only by his professional advice, but also in a more practical way, for he was most generous in giving financial help to those whom he found burdened with poverty and ill health. Who, moreover, could fail to admire his perspicacity in predicting the recovery or foretelling the death of his patients? He was so famous for his prognostications, that in wishing one's friends avoidance of misfortune, the phrase, "look out for a bad prognosis from Ugo," became proverbial. Thus it came to pass that patients not only from Italy, but also from Germany, Spain, distant Britain, and other foreign lands flocked to visit him, as if to consult an Apollo; and in Italy men of the highest rank and wealth, when stricken with disease, summoned him as their last resource. At this same time, by universal consent, he was granted Bolognese citizenship as a reward for his many splendid achievements; and the like honor was paid him in all the other Italian cities in which he lived. . . .

Finally, on the invitation of the Venetians, he went to Padua. It had been the greatest ambition of his life to teach in that university, for in the course of his career he had occupied a chair in every university of Italy save that alone. He was given a magnificent welcome. In response to popular demand, the civic authorities and all the members of the University who were engaged in the study of the arts met him outside the walls and escorted him into the city with great applause. Here for several years he taught medicine and at the same time engaged in frequent disputations on the most profound problems with such brilliant success that his fame spread to all the nations of the world.

Summoned, therefore, by Niccolo, Marquis of Ferrara, he entered the service of that illustrious prince, at whose court he remained for the rest of his days. How greatly the Prince honored Ugo is shown by the magnificent estates he bestowed on him at Rovigo, by the grief he expressed at his death, and finally by the honors he has since granted and the genereous benefits he has conferred on Ugo's sons.

FURTHER READING

William M. Bowsky, "The Impact of the Black Death upon Sienese Government and Society," *Speculum* 39 (1964), 1–34

_____, ed., *The Black Death: A Turning Point in History?*, 2d ed. (1978)

Anna M. Campbell, *The Black Death and Men of Learning* (1931)

Piero Camporesi, *The Incorruptible Flesh, Bodily Mutation and Mortification in Religion and Folklore* (1988)

Ann G. Carmichael, *Plague and the Poor in Early Renaissance Florence* (1986)

Carlo M. Cipolla, *Public Health and the Medical Profession in the Renaissance* (1976)

Samuel Kline Cohn, *The Cult of Remembrance and the Black Death: Six Renaissance Cities in Central Italy* (1992)

Robert Steven Gottfried, *The Black Death: Natural Human Disaster in Medieval Europe* (1983)

Dean Lockwood, *Ugo Benzi, Medieval Philosopher and Physician, 1376–1439* (1951)

Katherine Park, *Doctors and Medicine in Early Renaissance Florence* (1985)

John M. Riddle, *Contraception and Abortion from the Ancient World to the Renaissance* (1992)

Nancy G. Siraisi, *Avicenna in Renaissance Italy: The Canon and Medical Teaching in Italian Universities After 1500* (1987)

_____, *Medieval and Early Renaissance Medicine* (1990)

Sharon T. Strocchia, *Death and Ritual in Renaissance Florence* (1992)

Marcel Tetel, Ronald G. Witt, and Rona Goffen, eds., *Life and Death in Fifteenth Century Florence* (1989)

Lynn Thorndike, *A History of Magic and Experimental Science*, vols. 1–3 (1923–1934)

Graham Twigg, *The Black Death: A Biological Reappraisal* (1984)

Philip Ziegler, *The Black Death*, 2d ed. (1971)

CHAPTER **3**

The Economy of City
and Countryside

B y the later Middle Ages, central and northern Italy had become
one of the most heavily urbanized areas in Europe, with perhaps
one-third of the population residing in cities and towns of more
than two thousand inhabitants. Town and country enjoyed a symbiotic
relation. City elites, merchants, professionals, and tradesmen usually
owned rural property and enjoyed the products of vineyard, field, and
farmyard on their tables. Late-medieval Italian landowners were thus
among the first to collect money rents and initiate sharecropping
contracts, rather than extracting payment in labor, as they intensified
agricultural production for the marketplace. But banking and
manufacturing drove the Italian economy's rapid expansion.
Sophisticated bookkeeping techniques, developed during the
commercial revolution of the Middle Ages, permitted businessmen to
build large companies that combined textile manufacturing with the
high risks and high profits of international trade and banking.
Historians disagree, however, on how to measure the economy's overall
performance and thus in their assessment of the huge expenditure by
urban Italians on conspicuous consumption (spending to enhance social
standing).

ESSAYS

In the first essay, Giuliano Pinto of the University of Florence offers an explanation of
Siena's arrested economic development after its early leadership in international commerce and banking in the thirteenth century. He suggests that a combination of factors
led the rich Sienese merchant families to abandon their risk-taking mercantile ventures
and to invest heavily in agricultural properties instead. Pinto uses the example of Siena
to argue that the world of traditional, land-based aristocratic values endured in some
regions in clear opposition to the innovative, energetic urban merchants who propelled
Renaissance Italy to the forefront of economic and social change. Richard A. Goldthwaite, of The John Hopkins University, then broadly surveys the Renaissance economy—reasons for the concentration of wealth in Italian cities, the structure of wealth,
the performance of the economy—to explain the extraordinary levels of conspicuous
consumption for which Renaissance Italy is perhaps most famous. Judith C. Brown of

Stanford University follows with an analysis of women's increasing participation in the Florentine labor force that reveals a great deal about changes in the structure of labor in manufacturing and agriculture as capitalism spread.

Landed Property and Trade in Medieval Siena

GIULIANO PINTO

Siena has been described by Philip Jones as "the southernmost capital" of the commercial revolution of the Middle Ages: almost no other city of medieval Italy shows such a clear and wide contrast in its social and economic fabric between its period of greatest prosperity and the early modern period. In the second half of the thirteenth century, Siena was a star of the first order in the European economic sky. Sienese merchant and banking companies operated on a large scale in many parts of western Europe. They were prominent in the exchanges leading to the fairs of Champagne; and they had a strong presence in England, Germany and southern France (though less so in Flanders, Spain and the Levant). In Italy Sienese merchants had warehouses and sizable business at Pisa, Genoa, Venice and Naples (though their numbers were fewer in Sicily, which is indicative of their lesser interests in and contacts with the Mediterranean area).

For almost the entire thirteenth century, the Sienese families of the Piccolomini, Tolomei, Salimbeni, Bonsignori and Gallerani constituted, with only a few other Italian companies, the mercantile and banking aristocracy of Europe. Their good relations with the papal court—they served for a long time as papal bankers—brought them profitable financial operations and increased their prestige. The great Sienese companies were well-organized internally, were endowed with ample funds, were able to draw on the combined capital of their partners and enjoyed the confidence of their depositors and of the rulers, churchmen and businessmen with whom they had dealings. Siena's trading peak largely coincided with its period of greatest political power, which culminated in the victory over Florence at the battle of Montaperti in 1260. The same years saw the beginning or the completion of major building projects in Siena which had a lasting effect on the face of the city.

Two centuries later the picture had altered drastically. Siena's population had fallen to around 15,000, one third (more or less) of its level in the early thirteenth century. The city seemed a sleepy provincial town, despite the fact that it governed a vast (if little populated) territory of 7,000 sq. km. and 80,000 inhabitants in central-southern Tuscany. One of the few sparks of life in the city, and the only one that gave it a cosmopolitan air, was provided by the university and its crowd of foreign students. The documentary and literary sources are agreed on the character of

"Honor and Profit: Landed Property and Trade in Medieval Siena" by Giuliano Pinto from *City and Countryside in Late Medieval Renaissance Italy: Essays Presented to Philip Jones*, ed. by T. Dean and C. Wickham, Hambledon Press, 1990, pp. 81–91. Reprinted by permission of the author.

Siena's economy and society in the fifteenth and sixteenth centuries. The more well-to-do citizens, who also participated actively in political life, based their wealth almost exclusively on landed property and on livestock. Their tax-returns consist of lists of farms and houses, rarely of warehouses. Only a small group of families—a few dozen—were engaged in banking or in trade (in wool, silk, linen, leather), but their investments were modest (rarely exceeding 1,000 florins) and were accompanied by large investments in land. According to the records of a fiscal levy (lira) in 1453, the trading and manufacturing investments of the wealthier families amounted to less than a quarter of their total wealth. Government bonds formed another 10 percent; and the rest, around two-thirds, was derived from land. Even neighbouring cities such as Pisa and Arezzo (to say nothing of Florence) had much more pronounced trading and manufacturing contours; and they were subject cities, not capitals of vast territories, and were also still recovering from the crisis of Florentine conquest. As a region, the Sienese state was a producer mainly of raw materials (grain, livestock, metals) for the major markets of the Florentine state, and Florentine businessmen were active in Sienese markets, often supplanting local merchants.

Although this picture has many obscurities which still need to be clarified, it gives greater credibility and force to the numerous comments of observers, from both inside and outside Siena, who underlined the fact that high-ranking Senesi generally lived off landed rents and the salaries of office and showed detachment, if not distaste, for the world of business. The memory of the great thirteenth-century mercantile era hardly seemed to survive.

In attempting to explain this general picture, historians have used a variety of interpretations and evidence: the limits and inherent weaknesses of Sienese economic expansion; structural conditions and constraints; or the emerging difficulties of international trade. These, though unexceptionable in themselves, have, when put together, appeared insufficient or incomplete. . . . It would therefore seem more profitable to call attention to some internal peculiarities of Sienese society and economy in the thirteenth and fourteenth centuries. Recent historiography has not overlooked the deep bond between Sienese ruling groups and landed property. Around 1320, 2 per cent of citizen families owned one third (by value) of all urban and rural property. Four great families (the Gallerani, Salimbeni, Tolomei and Malavolti) held almost 20 percent of all landed wealth. This situation had arisen from an interest in land already at least a century old. In the course of the thirteenth century, the major families directed their economic energies in two quarters: to international expansion, especially in the banking sector, and to the massive acquisition of lands and castles, with corresponding seigneurial rights. They became at one and the same time great merchant bankers and great landowners and lords of castles, more so than the major families of other Tuscan cities, which had smaller territories and stronger rural aristocracies.

This planting of roots in the Sienese contado [countryside] took place only shortly after the period of great international successes; it suffices to recall only the main phases of the process. The Piccolomini, who in the early thirteenth century had banks in many European cities and were linked both to ecclesiastical and to lay potentates, in the same period obtained local fiefs from Frederick II in exchange for services to the Empire. The Salimbeni in the course of the thirteenth century took advantage of Siena's expansion to create a large power base in various parts of the *contado*; in 1275 they acquired, from the commune of Siena itself, in repayment of a debt, castles with attached seigneurial rights in the Val d'Orcia, the upper Val d'Elsa and the Val d'Ombrone. The Malavolti, in the decades around 1200, built up a strong core of properties around Monteriggioni, owing in part to their connections of alliance, and perhaps of marriage, with the major aristocratic family of the area (the Soarzi, lords of Staggia). The Bonsignori concentrated on an area further south, in the territory of the Ardenghesca, where they obtained rights over various castles. This agglomeration of great landed estates seems to involve motives and purposes beyond mere economic calculation. Investments in landed property in the country-side (rarely in the city) were not intended to diversify sources of wealth, nor to create a balance among different economic activities, but were a means of legitimising rapid social advance and of consolidating the power of individual clans (*consorterie*) through the possession of solid bases in the countryside and of huge agricultural sur-pluses, so as to provide armed men and faithful clients for use at opportune moments.

All this assumes special importance in the light of Paolo Cammarosano's recent, fundamental studies on Sienese society in the twelfth and thirteenth centuries. We now know that the great merchant families did not descend from the ranks of the rural aristocracy, even less from the comital houses. They arose within the city walls: "It was not the aristocracy which made the communal city, but the communal city which created an aristocratic class." If some families (for example, the Malavolti) appeared on the political stage in the period of the consular commune, most of them emerged later, at the end of the twelfth century, if not in the early thirteenth. Their strong roots in the *contado* were not therefore inherited from previous generations, but the outcome of a deliberate choice; and the cultural models of the traditional aristocracy would have conditioned that choice. This is shown by the marriage rela-tionships which soon bound these prominent urban families to the old nobility of the *contado*, and by the fact that the urban families not infrequently succeeded to the nobles' estates and seigneurial rights, or acted as intermediaries between the great dynasties of the territory and the commune of Siena.

Mercantile and aristocratic culture coexisted in Sienese society in the thir-teenth and early fourteenth centuries, as in most cities of north and central Italy. At Siena, however, the noble model acquired a particular attraction with the growth in importance of military and aristocratic forces during the city's constant warfare with its powerful neighbours. The noble model, at first perhaps only outwardly imitated, was later fully absorbed into urban life and enthroned among the aspirations and aims of the major families. The latter increasingly detached themselves from the popular traditions within which they had arisen, and created a *de facto* aristocratic class that was distinguished as much by its wealth (in trade and property) as by its attitudes and behaviour. At the same time mercantile culture failed to establish deep roots, or to become the common property of the higher social strata, or to be trans-mitted from generation to generation. It is symptomatic that a second generation of great merchant bankers did not come forward to fill the places of the great compa-nies that had failed or disappeared in the years around 1300. The failure of interna-tional companies was of course not altogether extraordinary in the later Middle Ages: companies' lives were always short, and their fall sometimes noisy; but other trading companies would take their place, as new businessmen (*gente nuova*) emerged into the international limelight. This happened in many cities of communal Italy; but not in Siena, where the opening of the fourteenth century closed an era. . . .

Faced with their first great difficulties—both structural and conjunctural—the Sienese commercial aristocracy showed no resistance, nor any will to respond. A return to the land, in terms of vast landed estates and seigneurial rights, seems to have been totally congenial to their mental patterns and ideals. Did they perhaps see in it an assertion of identity against the ruling classes of neighbouring cities? A more or less conscious desire to stand out and to create an identity would indeed seem to explain "archaic" behaviour among the Sienese aristocracy: the large expenditure on clothes and banquets, the taste for ceremony and festival, the cult of courtesy, the fine façades (and they were only façades) of the patrician palaces, the grandiose and unrealistic architectural projects, and the strong spirit of faction (manifested in the peculiar local subdivision into *Monti*).

In the management of the large estates, the more practical methods of the thirteenth century were slowly replaced by the detachment typical of rentiers. This was responsible, at least in part, for the economic decline in the fifteenth century of some families from the old urban aristocracy whose wealth had by then long been identified with the land.

The mercantile mentality and the world of business (*negotia*) seemed, from at least 1400, largely alien to the prevalent culture among the upper strata of Sienese society. Such activities became dishonourable for gentlemen, for whom living off the profits of the land or of public office was more appropriate. Indeed among the great families the concept of honour was often connected to the management of property. We should not be deceived by references in the fourteenth and fifteenth centuries to a lively trading sector in the city: Siena, after all, remained an important city (the second in Tuscany), with a large territory, and it continued to offer notable opportunities to small and middling traders operating at a local or regional level. But they remained small and middling merchants. Evidence pointing in the opposite direction is much more frequent in the sources. The contrast with Florence is striking: there trade continued to be praised as "that which alone can make cities rich from its many profits." . . .

Late medieval Siena represents a rare example of the accelerated development of processes and phenomena which in the rest of Italy had a slower pace and achieved their outcome only in the early modern period. Siena saw both a rapid and dazzling expansion and similarly rapid turning in on itself. The mercantile upswing and ideology were suddenly interrupted, before they could fully develop; they gave way to a brisk aristocratisation of society and to a recovery of traditional values. In the triumph of these values the close and "stifling" relationship with the land played a decisive part. The case of Siena thus provides material to reconsider two contradictory interpretations of late medieval Italy: one which exalts the role of the emergent bourgeoisie and one which speaks of the "myth of the bourgeoisie." Italian society between the twelfth and sixteenth centuries revolved around two opposite poles. On the one hand were the innovative elements, new economic activities (trade, banking, manufacture), and a different concept of society, of institutions and of relations between men and between groups. These elements, naturally gathered within cities, were promoted or adopted by largely new classes and represented a break with established values. On the other hand were the elements of tradition: the seigneurial world, the role of land as a sign of power, a more clearly hierarchical concept of society, all of which were expressed in particular styles of behaviour. From the dialogue between these two poles—but sometimes from the combination of individual elements—proceeded the diversity of social, political and institutional conditions in the Italian city communes. Siena, though showing a highly individual development, did not fall outside this general pattern.

The Preconditions for Luxury Consumption

RICHARD A. GOLDTHWAITE

The Renaissance has not been a very useful concept for organizing the materials of the economic history of Italy. Given the current state of the scholarly literature, we can talk about a "Renaissance economy" only in the obvious sense that economic activity was going on at the time. No one has shown how the term helps clarify structural, technological or any other kind of change the economy may have undergone, or indeed whether any such changes even took place to a significant degree during the period. For all the scholarship that has been expended on particular problems, economic historians have not generally been interested in looking at the period as a whole: medievalists find the crisis of the mid-fourteenth-century demographic catastrophes a convenient place for concluding their account of the commercial revolution and urban economic growth, and modernists pick up the story with their concern about why Italy got left behind in the rapid expansion of the European economy from the sixteenth century onwards. What happened in between is not very clear, and there certainly is no agreement on the overall performance of the economy.

Yet, in at least one way it is possible to talk about a Renaissance economy. If any distinctive economic activity marks the period, it is conspicuous consumption. The increased production of art, and luxury goods in general, is one of the most characteristic features of the Renaissance; and indeed it is at this time that art created consciously as such emerges as a distinct category of goods. The kinds of objects we today call art proliferated boundlessly, showing up in all walks of life, secular as well as religious, and they added up to a major change in the history of style. Even if there had been no stylistic innovation, however, all this consumption would be a notable

Richard A. Goldthwaite, "The Renaissance Economy: The Preconditions for Luxury Consumption," in *Aspetti della vita economica medievale,* Atti del Convegno di Studi. . .Melis (Florence, 1985), pp. 659–675. Reprinted by permission of Professor Richard Goldthwaite. A much expanded version of this essay constitutes the first part of *Wealth and the Demand for Art in Italy, 1300–1600* by R. Goldthwaite (Baltimore: The Johns Hopkins University Press, 1993).

phenomenon simply as economic activity: had palaces and churches, villas and gardens, sculpture and painting, domestic and liturgical furnishings all been produced in the traditional medieval style, we would still be confronted with an extraordinary abundance and variety of goods. Although the world has become infinitely more cluttered since the Renaissance, an argument can be made that modern consumer society, with its insatiable consumption setting the pace for the production of more objects and changes in style, had its first stirrings, if not its birth, in the habits of spending that possessed the Italians in the Renaissance. This increase in consumption is all the more surprising in an economy that had undergone a drastic reduction of population and at the same time seen a marked rise in the cost of labor. In short, as much as anything else, this demand signals much of what is new about the Renaissance and what sets Italy off, economically as well as culturally, from the rest of Europe at the time.

. . . Italy enjoyed extraordinarily favorable conditions for the development of a luxury market, and . . . these conditions go a long way toward an economic "explanation" of the Renaissance not as a new period in the history of taste but simply as a consumption phenomenon. Certain structural features of the Italian economy, in other words, help explain why demand was so vigorous and why therefore cultural production flourished. In any case, a survey of these conditions on the demand side of the luxury market touches on many features of the Italian economy that have been obscured, if not altogether ignored, in the endless and largely fruitless debate about how "hard" the times were, or were not. On this ground alone it seems worthwhile to shift attention from the performance of the economy to its structure.

That behind the extraordinary consumption that marks the Renaissance there was the immense wealth of Europe's most developed economy goes without saying. What gets lost in the old debate over the problem of whether at the time the Italian economy was prospering or contracting, however, is that the logic of the economic system argues for the continual accumulation of wealth throughout the later middle ages regardless of the level of performance. This system was oriented toward the export of goods and services and had built into it a favorable balance of payments. "Let us face it," argued a Florentine in the eighteenth century, looking back on better times, "our economy rested on a monopoly. We waxed rich thanks to the barbarous ignorance and indolence of others."

The strength of this economic system is well understood. In the commercial sector Italians monopolized the trade of those luxury items imported from the Near East and distributed throughout all of northern Europe; and they controlled both the maritime transport of these goods and the distribution network. With the possibility of transferring credit throughout this vast commercial network, extending across the Mediterranean and into all of western Europe, the Italians also became Europe's preeminent international bankers, and they used the resources of this sector for the further extension of their activity into government finance. Finally, Italy had a strong industrial sector oriented toward the production of luxury goods, above all textiles, for export to northern Europe and eventually, by the end of the fifteenth century with the establishment of the Ottoman Empire, also to the eastern Mediterranean.

This situation can be put into relief by looking at the debit side of the balance. The history of the development of textile production—both wool and silk—shows how the industry improved its competitive advantage in local markets against imports from abroad, how it expanded its own markets abroad, and finally how it reduced its dependence on raw materials imported from abroad. By the end of the fifteenth century, the wool industry was producing for important new markets opened with the establishment of the Ottoman Empire and was taking less wool from far-away England and more from central and southern Italy. The reversal in the silk market was even more complete. Whereas earlier Lucca was the only major center of production and raw and finished silk came into Italy from the east, in the fifteenth century Florence grew rapidly as a major producer; and by the sixteenth century silk cloth was being manufactured in numerous Italian towns for markets abroad all across Europe and in the Near East and silkworm culture was being vigorously promoted throughout Italy, in both the north and the south.

Looking over the international scene of Italian trade at the end of the fifteenth century it is not easy to find products of value that were imported in notable quantity. . . . Demand, directed by the desire for many new kinds of objects and increasingly conditioned by a highly self-conscious taste, generated productive forces within Italy itself; and by the sixteenth century, except for a few items, like tapestries from the north and carpets from the east, there were hardly any luxury goods manufactured abroad that Italians wanted. The rise in luxury consumption, in other words, did not mean a loss of wealth from the economic system; rather, it was a stimulus to further development within.

Trade was not the only activity that brought wealth into Italy. So did war. Throughout the middle ages Italy was a focus for the political ambitions of northern rulers, who drained off resources from their homeland to pay for their ventures. For some of the Holy Roman Emperors, from the Ottonians through the Hohenstaufens, Germany served as little more than a tax-base to finance their ambitions in Italy. The Angevins used their considerable wealth in France to finance their move into the Kingdom of Naples in 1268; and once there, their marriage into the Hungarian royal family enabled them to tap the most important source for gold in Europe to pay for their further military exploits in the south. When, in turn, the Aragonese came, first into Sicily in 1282 and then to the mainland in 1435, they had behind them the resources of their Iberian kingdoms, which included Barcelona, the only major European emporium of trade and banking in the Mediterranean outside of Italy; and wealth flowed into Naples once it became the capital of their new trans-Tyrrhenean empire. Moreover, all these foreign ventures in southern Italy in one way or another involved the Papacy, whose vital interests were at stake; and entering the fray, the Pope did not hesitate to tap the vast resources of the church all over Europe by declaring a new kind of crusade, now not in the Near East against infidels but in Italy itself against Christian enemies in the pope's backyard. These financial efforts were a major cause for the tightening-up of the church's revenue-collecting mechanism. The Avignon papacy made continuing use of its bureaucratic grip on the church throughout Europe in order to amass the resources for its primary objective during those years—the return to Italy; and the cost of the long, drawn-out campaign to carve out an independent papal state in central Italy was paid, in part at least, with church revenues from outside Italy. When, after 1494, Italy became the battleground for the major European kingdoms, more resources were poured into the country. It is very likely, too, that Italy actually profited from the eventual Spanish domination of much of the peninsula. The Genoese raked off considerable profits from their financial services to the monarchy in handling the transfer of American bullion to the north; and however oppressive the Spanish regime was in Lombardy, it is clear that not enough money was collected locally to pay the expenses of government, with the balance having to be imported. In short, for over 400 years, from the twelfth century (and probably earlier) to the sixteenth century, foreigners' involvement in Italy, however unfortunate the political and military consequences, must have resulted in flows of some wealth into Italy.

Although trade and military activity have a long history that made the accumulation of wealth a continuing phenomenon, that process must have accelerated at the end of the middle ages. It was at this time, at any rate, when the major political events noted above occurred and when shifts in commerce and growth of local industries strengthened the balance of payments. Moreover, the fourteenth-century plagues, for all their devastating effects, left in their wake many fewer people to enjoy the ever-greater wealth. If all these factors could somehow be measured we might be able to show how the per-capita wealth in Italy increased in a relatively short period of time—precisely the time when it began to manifest itself in spectacular luxury spending. In short, to explain where men got the money to finance their new spending habits we do not have to posit a withdrawal of wealth from investment nor in fact do we have to take sides at all in the debate over the performance of various sectors of the Italian economy that has distracted attention from the structural problems raised here.

Greater wealth is only part of the explanation for the greater consumption of luxury goods. The vigor of demand was also dependent on the structure of wealth. That structure consisted in, first, its distribution, both geographic and social, and, secondly, a certain weakness or instability in its ownership that resulted in its fluidity of redistribution. A structural analysis of wealth in Renaissance Italy along these lines reveals: 1) that wealth was distributed among a large number of consumers for the most part concentrated in many urban markets; 2) that the ranks of these consumers were constantly changing so that demand was sustained at a high level; and 3) that the rich tended to become richer, which meant a rise in the level of individual spending. These conditions taken all together go a long way in explaining why Italy probably enjoyed the most favorable condition in Europe for the development of a vigorous luxury market.

The distribution of wealth in Italy was largely determined by the political fragmentation of the peninsula into areas of widely varying economic development. Hence, no one capital city dominated as a governmental center that, like London and Paris, also tended to be the central market for the economic life of the country. Nor did any one city dominate the economic system. Between them Venice and Genoa enjoyed pre-eminence as ports, but neither had much importance as industrial and international banking centers, at least not before the sixteenth century; and the leading industrial and banking center, Florence, had by no means a monopoly in these sectors. Other towns, like Lucca, Milan and Bologna, had their particular economic activities of varying importance to the system as a whole. Rome had a unique economic position as the capital of an international ecclesiastical organization. Yet other provincial towns derived their economic vitality from the professionalization of war, as seats of independent condottieri who drained off the kind of wealth from the larger states that in the northern kingdoms remained confined to the political-military establishment therein. War, in other words, was an economic activity in Italy that redistributed wealth in a way that did not happen elsewhere in Europe; and its profits paid for much of the patronage in Ferrara, Mantua, Urbino and a host of smaller places. In short, the Italian economy for all its international orientation consisted of a complementary system of varied local economies.

. . . Wealth in Italy was urban not just in the sense that it derived from those industrial, commercial and financial activities characteristic of the economic development of towns but in the sense that rural wealth, too, was largely in the hands of men who lived in towns. In the Florentine state, for instance, almost two-thirds of the total wealth (as reflected in the 1427 Catasto) was owned by Florentines, who constituted only about one-sixth the population. This urban concentration of rural wealth followed from, on the one hand, the move by landowners into the towns during the early period of the commune and, on the other, the acquisition of land by the rising class of urban entrepreneurs as they reinvested their earnings. The former process alone, in fact, accounts for the economic vitality of many provincial towns, whereas the latter process—the purchase of land by townsmen—rarely led to the abandonment of the town for the country. It was otherwise in northern Europe, where land remained for the most part in the hands of men who lived in the country, whether older landlords who long resisted the move into the city or newer ones who abandoned the city for the country. Even in a highly urbanized region like Germany the wealth of the towns did not include much of the surrounding land. What made Italy distinctively different from the rest of Europe, in short, was not just the growth of towns, with all the economic developments associated therewith, but the much greater concentration in towns of the wealth of the whole economy, rural as well as urban—and even in Italy, for all its economic development, agriculture remained the largest sector of the economy. This fact has been somewhat obscured in the current debate over the relative importance of capitalist and landed classes in the economic and social system of Renaissance Italy. And yet, if demand itself is ever to be understood—apart from the economic structure it operates through, which is the subject of this essay—the analysis of the consumption habits of Italians will have to consider the difference in lifestyle not between a "bourgeoisie" and an "aristocracy" but between an elite that is entirely urban, whatever the nature of its wealth, and one that is entirely rural, like that in northern Europe. Travellers from both the north and the south clearly observed this difference at the time.

If the higher degree of the urbanization of wealth in Italy helps account for the earlier development there of a luxury market, it is in part because certain structural features within urban society also impinged on demand. First of all, in many of the major city-states the upper-class was not organized around a prince whose government skimmed off an inordinate share of the wealth to maintain a court, thereby heavily concentrating demand in a single agent and at the same time focusing on itself much of the consumption behavior of the upper-class. Some of the largest and wealthiest cities, like Genoa, Venice and Florence, were, of course, oligarchies with no formal court at all. When Venice extended its possessions on the terraferma, it left local urban oligarchies intact in cities like Verona, Padua, and Brescia rather than force a concentration of their wealth in the capital; and when the Medici consolidated their control over Florence as dukes, their court remained largely a private affair, with much of the older upper-class not socially involved in it at all.

Whatever the concentration at the top rung of society, wealth was widely enough distributed in Florence that the middling class of artisans—perhaps for the first time in the history of the west—began to show up in the luxury market. The considerable increase in real wages after 1348 put a larger share of wealth into their hands; and the number of highly skilled artisans increased with the growth of the luxury-crafts sector of the economy. Neri di Bicci's record book consists largely of his dealings with people more-or-less of his own class, and a century later Vassari tells us that some clients of the major artists of his day were men of this kind. It was, after all, a modest broker in the banker's guild who commissioned Botticelli's Adoration of the Magi in the Uffizi. The evidence of inventories across the fifteenth and sixteenth centuries confirms the growing quantity of furnishings, including art works, in the homes of Florentines well below the level of the patriciate.

Whatever the diffusion of wealth throughout Italian society, mobility within the structure of that society assured its frequent redistribution. Some of this flow was generated by the inherent instability of the political system arising from what Burckhardt called the illegitimacy of power. New men were forever showing up on the political scene; and the emergence of the five major states and the establishment of the precarious balance of power in the mid-fifteenth century did not mean the immediate elimination of many lesser despots. The kaleidoscopic changes especially in the Marches, the Romagna and Emilia reflected the fluidity of power and therefore of wealth among these men, many of whom enjoyed their moment of glory in the annals of patronage. Mobility was also built into the structure of the church hierarchy, obviously a major group within the Italian elite. Since the pope and the 25 to 30 cardinals in Rome could not assert familial claims to their office, the immense wealth of the church was constantly plundered to benefit their families. The rapid turnover in the holders of these offices and the lack of any dynastic continuity—there were 18 popes in the sixteenth century in contrast to 7 monarchs in France, 5 in England and Germany, and 4 in Spain—assured the rapid renewal of demand that is a major explanation for the extravagant patronage in the Holy City.

Finally, the mobility of wealth was inherent in an economic system largely based on commerce, finance and industry. In the business world fortunes came and went, new men were always showing up on the scene, and establishment figures were forever exiting. Something of this fluidity is reflected in the history of the most notable palaces in Florence, which were built by new fortunes or did not get finished for lack of funds or passed into new hands with a change in fortune. Some of the most familiar names in the annals of business history—Andrea Barbarigo, Francesco di Marco Datini, Giovanni di Bicci de' Medici, Filippo Strozzi the Elder—represented new wealth if not new families. So long as men kept their wealth in business they could not assure the financial stability of their families, many of whose histories reveal how elusive permanent wealth could be in the early Renaissance; and in any case veritable business dynasties are not easy to find. Moreover, whenever businessmen shifted their investments to land, as they increasingly did in the sixteenth century, whether because (as tradition has it) they were losing their nerve and wanted to secure their patrimonies, or whether simply because (as recent scholarship is revealing) agriculture offered better prospects for profits, their "move to the land" left room for new men to take their places in the business world and try their hands at making another fortune.

In short, Italian society was subject to a dynamic of change unlike that of any other in Europe. Elsewhere, wealth was predominantly in land and therefore less subject to instability, it was largely in the hands of a closed caste that experienced less mobility, and it moved from one generation to another over well-charted and confined genealogical routes.

Nevertheless, the growth of this sector had far-ranging effects on the Italian economy and society. It may seem obvious that all the money spent not only for architecture but for the furnishing of palaces and churches with everything from furniture and ceramics to painting and sculpture added up to a considerable investment in human capital: there were more skilled laborers and a larger variety of skills as a result. Already by the end of the fifteenth century artisan society in a place like Florence was larger and more complex than it had been earlier, say at the time of Dante. But there is more to this development than a mere quantitative change. Many of these new skills required highly individual talents, so that artisans had greater opportunity for creativity, some declaring for themselves an altogether new kind of creative freedom as artists. Moreover, the high degree of competition in the numerous markets of Italy stimulated these producers to be innovative and original, so that they themselves could actually mold new taste.

Why demand for art and the other luxury items we associate with the Renaissance arose in the first place, and how this demand shaped the growth of the luxury sector of the economy, are questions that lie beyond the scope of this discussion. Whatever its origins, however, demand was dependent on the level of wealth and operated in the economy by working its way through the structures of wealth; and the contention here has been that these conditions favored the development of a vigorous luxury market in Renaissance Italy. First, the general level of wealth was extraordinarily high due to the long cumulative advantage of a favorable balance of payments at the end of the middle ages; secondly, this wealth was widely distributed both geographically and socially and yet heavily concentrated in a large number of urban markets; thirdly, the political, economic and ecclesiastic elites were fluid, and the consequent social redistribution of wealth assured a constant renewal of demand; finally, the wealthy became much wealthier in the course of the Renaissance, especially in the sixteenth century. The timing of the Renaissance as a consumer phenomenon was very much a matter of the political situation—the emergence of strong oligarchical and despotic governments in the towns; the general, if precarious, stabilization of the political scene in the mid-fifteenth century; the success of the popes in establishing an independent state; and the overwhelming presence of Spain in the sixteenth century, which had its effect in freezing the political situation and thereby assuring stability, in radically transforming Naples into a significant new market, and in giving yet another infusion of wealth through use of the bankers of Genoa for the international transfer of bullion. Given these political developments, the analysis of the nature of wealth sketched out here goes a long way toward explaining the vigor of the luxury market, the geography of patronage (or the shifting of markets), and the duration of luxury spending, with its ever-greater extravagance from the Renaissance to the Baroque.

Women's Work in Renaissance Tuscany

JUDITH C. BROWN

In her pioneering essay, "Did Women Have a Renaissance?" the late Joan Kelly suggested that the very developments that opened up new possibilities for Renaissance men, namely the consolidation of the state and the emergence of capitalism, affected women so adversely that for them there was no renaissance.

In this essay, I hope to analyze the issue of women's economic status from a different perspective. I will use a variety of sources—guild records, population surveys, and literary evidence—to explore the lives of working women in Renaissance Florence and their relation to paid employment.

. . . Access to paid employment is not the only, or even the most important, determinant of economic power. As scholars continue to work on this subject, they will undoubtedly consider class, property rights, marriage relationships, and many other social and economic factors before they can arrive at any broad interpretations of the economic and social status of Renaissance women. Nonetheless, if we are to determine whether or not there was a renaissance for women in the economic realm, and by that, like Kelly, I mean an expansion of options available to them, then access to paid employment, the kinds of work women did, how and how much they were paid in comparison with men, all have to be given prominent consideration. Such an examination for Renaissance Florence may well reveal a different pattern from the one suggested by Kelly.

. . . To begin with, as in all other premodern cities, women often worked as helpers to their husbands, fathers, and brothers in workshops located in their homes. Although their work was economically significant both to their households and to the economy as a whole, its value was reflected only indirectly in the income earned by the males they helped. Their contribution to the productivity of their households is impossible to measure because it left few traces in the historical record, but this is not to say that it had no value. As Natalie Davis has shown, in their wills and other bequests, husbands and fathers frequently alluded to the approximate cash value they placed on the unpaid work performed by the women of their households.

In contrast to the large numbers of working women mentioned in documents of the late thirteenth and the first half of the fourteenth centuries, the records of the next two centuries reveal very few. The principal Florentine industry, woolen cloth manufacturing, which until the last quarter of the fourteenth century relied primarily on female weavers, turned to males, many of them foreigners, in the subsequent period. The nascent silk industry also relied primarily on male workers. While women continued to exercise certain traditionally female occupations such as midwifery, wet nursing, and domestic service, the guild records, wills, property transfers, and other legal documents no longer mention the large variety of female occupations evident in the notarial records and literary sources of the pre-plague period. The absence of working women from the historical records of the early Renaissance may simply be an anomaly, but that is not very likely in view of the large numbers of documents for this period. An explanation for this shift in employment patterns is readily available in regard to the wool industry: female weavers were replaced by male weavers from Germany. The reasons for the absence of women in other occupations are more difficult to discern. One plausible argument, advanced by David Herlihy and Christiane Klapisch, is that lower demographic pressures after 1348 enabled women to avoid the labor market and to enter the marriage market instead.

The long absence of women from the ranks of wage labor ended in the late sixteenth century, when once again women began to appear as part of the urban labor force. The account books of silk and wool manufacturers indicate that they made up a rising percentage of workers in the textile sector, which from mid-sixteenth century to mid-seventeenth century still employed between one-half and one-third of the labor force. By 1604, 62 percent of the weavers and approximately 40 percent of all wool workers were women, not counting the spinners who resided mostly in the outskirts of the city and who had always been female. . . .

The growth of paid employment for city women in late Renaissance Florence is related to structural changes that took place in the urban economy. In the last half of the sixteenth century the artisan sector flourished, as many of the old crafts expanded and a new set of luxury crafts developed in response to the growing demand by the European public for luxury products. Florentine workers eagerly set to accommodating the taste for ceramics, books, jewelry, furniture, coaches, and other objects with which the bourgeoisie and nobilities of Europe sought to enhance their prestige and their standards of material life. The emergence of a more diversified world of goods in the late sixteenth century created new employment opportunities for the Florentine population. Although few women found openings in the artisan sector, as men shifted from the production of textiles to that of luxury crafts, the women began to perform many of the previously male tasks in the wool and silk industries. This, more than anything else, probably explains the larger participation of women in the labor force.

Another reason may be the altered status of the guilds in the political economy of late Renaissance Florence. There is a small but growing body of evidence to indicate that throughout Europe there was an inverse relation between the ability of guilds to regulate economic activity and the extent of female participation in the labor force. Merry Weisner's work on women's occupations in Nuremberg suggests that as guilds consolidated their power in the sixteenth and seventeenth centuries, they passed regulations excluding women from traditional occupations and relegated them to the margins of the world of work. Similarly, evidence cited by Alice Clark for a variety of English towns suggests that starting in the sixteenth century guilds passed prohibitions against women weavers. In Florence, however, the guilds received a major setback as regulators of economic and political activity with the creation of the Medici principate in 1532.

During the first twenty years of their rule, the Medici abolished the most vital political functions of the guilds and reorganized them as eleven universities whose officers and economic policies were controlled by government officials. Since the early Medici dukes were particularly interested in promoting economic activity, they aimed in various ways to make the guilds less exclusive and more open to competition, whether from neighboring cities in the state or from within the ranks of Florentine labor. It is not surprising therefore to see women enter certain sectors of the labor force at a time when the guilds were at their weakest. This is not to argue that the Medici were champions of the economic emancipation of women or that women after the mid-sixteenth century had equal status in the guilds. Even in mid-seventeenth century, when there were many women masters in the wool and silk industries, very few appear in guild matriculation records and none became guild consuls. Still, the greater tolerance toward female workers in some types of work is revealed in the different ways that two guilds, one in the fourteenth century and the other in the sixteenth, reacted to the presence of women competitors. In the late fourteenth century, the guild of used clothing dealers (rigattieri) for a time barred women as itinerant hawkers, claiming that they infiltrated people's houses and "persuaded the women to buy to the detriment of their men [that is, of the men of their household]." Two centuries later, the linen guild, which now included the rigattieri, faced with large numbers of female tailors, did not seek to prohibit them from practicing their trade but argued instead that if they were going to work as tailors and maintain shops, they should pay the modest fee to matriculate in the guild.

While such structural factors may account for the increased participation of women in the labor force of late Renaissance Florence, they do not explain why Florentine males worked in luxury crafts while women were employed in the textile industries and a smaller number of other occupations. What determined the sexual segregation of labor in Florentine society? For an understanding of such problems, economists have relied in part on the very useful theory of human capital. According to this theory, investment in human capital, that is, in the acquisition of skills either through education, on-the-job training, or general training, has generally paid individuals a substantial rate of return because it has enabled them to learn difficult skills or to engage in a wide variety of well-paid occupations. Women are generally found in poorly paid, low-skilled occupations because they accumulate less human capital through their work experience. Women's function in the household economy as childbearers, providers of childcare, and domestic labor results in their more limited and discontinuous presence in the job market, making it harder for them to acquire the training necessary for highly skilled work. Barriers to skill acquisition, moreover, could be higher in premodern economies in which training often took place in the home. There was little incentive for parents to teach their daughters complex and hard to learn skills that they would hardly put to use before they married and left the paternal house. In Italy, where urban women married when they were still in their teens, this would have been a particularly important consideration. While some parents may have counted this training as part of their daughters' dowry, as was the case in some parts of Northern Europe, such an indirect return on their investment was far from certain as it might be difficult to find a husband whose trade could make use of the specialized skills previously acquired by his bride. Evidence from sixteenth-century Lyon and Venice suggests that very few women married men in the same occupations as their fathers. If the same were true in Florence, and preliminary analysis of the 1631 census and of guild records suggests that it was, then it would be

better for young girls to work on less skilled tasks where there were immediate returns and where the minimal skills acquired could be easily transferred to their new
households. Once there, the young wives of Florentine artisans would be in no position to acquire sophisticated new training. The cares of childbearing and domestic
work would ensure that they would simply maintain their previous skills or acquire
only those new ones that were easily learned.

The distribution of labor in late Renaissance Florence in large measure accords
with the pattern predicted by the human capital approach. Highly skilled artisans
were men, and women were relegated to textile work where there were fewer skill
requirements. In this regard, it is revealing that in the early Renaissance, when Florence produced a small quantity of simple woolen cloths alongside the more elaborate
woolens and silks for which the city became famous, a small number of women appear in the account books of Florentine wool manufacturers as weavers of the plainer
and coarser wools. None worked as weavers in the silk industry, which was entirely
devoted to the production of luxury cloths requiring a high degree of skill. In the late
Renaissance, however, when both wool and silk production shifted to cheaper,
coarser, and simpler cloths, women formed the majority of weavers in the two industries. But, significantly, the silk manufacturers who continued to produce elaborate
patterned silks generally turned to male weavers for those cloths while retaining
women to work on the rest.

But how are we to explain the high concentration of women in certain relatively low-skill jobs and their absence in others? Why are most women wool workers
engaged in weaving, warping, and spinning, but not in cleaning, combing, or carding
wool? Consistent with the human capital approach is the notion that women have
had first and foremost a reproductive responsibility in the home. This would limit
employment outside. Textile manufacturing was organized according to a putting-
out system in which the merchant consigned the raw silk or wool to workers who did
much of the processing of the raw material into cloth in their own homes. Occupations such as weaving, which were carried out in the home, could fit around
childrearing and household tasks. The compatibility of these different types of work
is illustrated by the fact that in the early seventeenth century, roughly 800 of the
1,025 female weavers surveyed by the Florentine wool guild had children. Other
occupations in the textile sector, such as cleaning or carding, were done in central
workshops and would have required women to give up their productive roles within
the household. It is not surprising then to find that there were no women engaged in
those types of jobs. . . .

These attitudes had far-reaching implications for women's lives and women's
employment in particular. In effect, they worked to keep women out of occupations
that required mobility and public exposure. This may explain the reasons given by
the second-hand clothing dealers in prohibiting female street hawkers. They attributed women's sales abilities to their "seduction" of weak-willed female customers
who succumbed to their sales pitch. Surely, the guild took a different view of the
male members of the trade who displayed similar skills.

Since women were considered flighty and incapable of complex reasoning, it
also followed that they were meant to obey orders, not give them. Most Renaissance
commentators subscribed to the Aristotelian notion that women are subject to the

authority of males. "They are madmen," says Giannozzo Alberti, "if they think true prudence or good counsel lies in the female brain." He adds, "all wives are thus obedient, if their husbands know how to be husbands." A century later, Orazio Lombardelli had this kind of admonition in mind when he instructed his new bride to be happy that God had granted her a husband such as he who would govern her in place of all others. Just as "the head adorns the body, the prince the city, the gem the ring, so the husband adorns the wife, and she should obey not only when he commands but when he doesn't."

Because the subjection of women to men was seen as part of the natural order, men probably resented employment situations that placed women in superior positions. This worked to keep women out of occupations in which there were distinct workshop hierarchies. Undoubtedly, masters' wives and female domestics helped out by cleaning the workshops, feeding the workers, stoking furnaces, and engaging in other secondary operations. They probably engaged in these tasks in greater numbers than appears from the written records. But although such work facilitated the functioning of their husband's or father's establishments, it also kept them apart from the ladder of advancement occupied by apprentices, journeymen, and masters in many of the crafts. Women's industrial and service occupations generally did not require them to have the extensive numbers of helpers required by workers in leather, stone, or metal crafts, among others. Theirs tended to be solitary jobs, and if help could be used, as was the case with silk throwsters, it was usually provided by other women. . . .

The restrictions on work faced by urban women were perforce different from those faced by women living in the country. For one, in rural Tuscany the agricultural family was to a large extent both the unit of production and of consumption. Wage labor was not very common. Secondly, because household tasks and the tasks of the farm could not be so easily separated, women naturally had provided a considerable portion of the labor force from time immemorial.

Yet, although female labor had always been important, we should nonetheless keep in mind that the extent of rural women's productive labor was closely related to the requirements of specific agricultural systems. In Tuscany, as elsewhere in Europe, these varied tremendously over short distances, as mountains, plains, rivers, and other geographic features helped determine the agricultural output. Some parts of Tuscany were almost entirely devoted to sheep raising, some to cereal cultivation or to mixed cropping that included viticulture and olive trees, and others added different crops ranging from flax to saffron. Institutional arrangements also differed widely. Some areas relied primarily on sharecropping, others on fixed rent tenancies, and still others on the family owned and operated farm. All of these factors had a bearing on how women were integrated into the agricultural work force, so that a valid generalization covering all these situations cannot be made.

Given these limitations, to what extent can one find in the countryside a parallel to the growing economic function of urban women in the late Renaissance? Despite obvious geographic differences among agricultural landscapes, we can observe similarities in agricultural developments that helped engender a new role for women. In some areas of the Florentine state, there was a growth of *agricultural promiscua*, multicrop farming that aimed, among other things, to give landlords a larger share of commercial crops and to make a more profitable use of available land and labor.

Gradually less land was devoted to cereals and a larger share was planted with vines, olives, and mulberry trees for sericulture. The spread of these crops was related to a growth in demand for Tuscan wines, a change in tastes, as consumers switched from eating animal fats to olive oil, and to the growth of the Florentine silk industry in the sixteenth and seventeenth centuries.

These new forms of land use, and especially those related to sericulture, had a profound impact on the role of women in the agricultural economy. Tuscan agriculture had always made use of labor-intensive techniques. But not all hands could be used for many of the time-consuming and important tasks. Most peasants, for example, did not own ploughs, so the cultivation of cereals depended on the use of the hoe (*vanga*)—a back-breaking, slow, and labor intensive method that was done most effectively by strong men. It has been estimated that a 25-acre farm devoted primarily to cereal cultivation, as was the case in much of Tuscany in the early Renaissance, required at least four to five men capable of using a *vanga*. For each of them, however, the rural population contained approximately five women, children, and elderly men, most of whom were idle or underemployed during much of the agricultural cycle. Because such a large proportion of the land was devoted to cereals, both the amount of land that could be farmed and the total agricultural output of the early Renaissance were very limited.

The extension of viticulture and olive trees created new opportunities for the previously underemployed workers in the farm. Women could tie the vines and harvest the grapes as easily as men. In some tasks, however, such as pruning olive trees and terracing hillsides, men still had a comparative advantage. The major breakthrough in establishing a more productive system of agricultural labor finally came with the introduction of mulberry trees and sericulture. Mulberry trees were raised first in the Valdi Nievole and the territory of Pisa and Pistoia after the mid-fifteenth century and, in response to market demands and government efforts, spread rapidly to other parts of the state, including the Valdelsa and the Arno valley. Tuscan sericulture increased by three-quarters from 1440 to 1576, more than doubled in the following twenty-five years, and increased by two and one-half times between 1610 and the mid-seventeenth century. In the last half of the 1600s, sericulture was a major agricultural activity in the Val di Nievole, Valle del Bisenzio, the Tuscan Romagna, the Val di Chiana, the Pratomagno, and parts of the Val d'Arno, with production reaching an average of 110,000 *libbre* of silk annually.

If cereal cultivation was male-labor intensive, sericulture was female and child intensive. Women and children gathered the leaves from the mulberry trees, which in many areas were kept suitably pruned to a small size. Women also raised the silk cocoons, as the English traveler Robert Dallington remarked during his Tuscan travels, when he saw peasant women hatching the silkworm eggs in their bosoms to supplement with their own bodies the insufficient warmth provided by the sun. Raising silk worms was a very labor intensive process, but it took only a few weeks and, in contrast to the labor inputs for other agricultural tasks, it required no special physical attributes, only constant vigilance. Practically all members of a household could be utilized. Women and children therefore performed these tasks while the men engaged in other forms of labor on the farm. The next stage of silk preparation, processing cocoons into raw silk by reeling and spinning, was also in the hands of women, assisted by children or otherwise unoccupied members of the household. Probably planting and pruning mulberry trees and cutting wood for the fires required in reeling were the only tasks performed by able-bodied men.

Sericulture thus constituted an important source of additional employment for Tuscan women and helped to link the household economy to the market place. The introduction of this activity into the rural economy of the late Renaissance resulted in a more intensive use of society's labor resources.

. . . When we consider the low level of output of premodern agricultural systems, when one out of every three or four years could bring famine, we can appreciate the importance of the integration of female labor into the agricultural world. Every person who could work to enlarge the agricultural surplus, every person who was not dependent on the meager output of others, helped to keep rural society from the brink of catastrophe. By contributing to the rising agricultural output of the early modern period, the work of women helped to improve people's material life and their chances for survival.

Documents

First, Paduan agricultural contracts from the early thirteenth century document the relations between urban proprietor and rural peasant in north Italy in the century before the Black Death. Note the differences between the short-term sharecropping lease requiring heavy payment in crops and the long-term lease for nominal money rents. What classes of persons are involved in each of the contracts? What were the economic or social purposes behind the *soceda* contract and the fief? Do these contracts always show the owner as the privileged party? How do the sharecropping contracts from Siena (near Florence), outlined in the second document, differ from those of Padua (near Venice), and where do the peasants seem more oppressed? In the third document Raymond de Roover, a business historian, devised a chart to describe the internal organization of a typical bank, this one owned and run by the Medici family. Aside from the international scope of their activities, notice how each step of the textile manufacturing process in Florence was handled by separate, independent workshops, not by the large, centralized factory that we associate with manufacturing today. Finally, the memoirs of Gregorio Dati, a Florentine merchant who lived around the turn of the fifteenth century, reveal how business partnerships were formed (sometimes with an infusion of capital from a wife's dowry) and then easily dissolved when no longer needed. This flexibility allowed businessmen to respond quickly to changing economic opportunities.

Paduan Agricultural Contracts, 1223[1]

SHARECROPPING LEASE [*LOCATIO*] FOR TEN YEARS

Symeon, notary, invests Albertino of Abate di Camponogara according to the law of rent for ten years with a piece of land lying in that place. It is bounded, etc. The aforesaid Albertino pledges to guarantee and defend the same land up to the aforesaid period to ten years that the aforesaid Albertino and his heirs have and hold the aforesaid land according to the law of rent up to the period of the ten years. Hence the aforesaid Albertino promises and agrees with the abovementioned Symeon, notary, in good faith and without fraud to work and plant, to drain and ditch the land and to plant willows, and to give to him [Symeon] a third part of the crop delivered to his house in Padua at Albertino's expense. Every year for ten years also [he will give] a shoulder and cake at the feast of St. Stephen [December 26]; and at Shrove Tuesday, two capons; at Easter twelve eggs; and at the feast of All Saints [November 1] a duck or a goose; and at the feast of St. Justina [October 7], twenty *soldi*. He is held to make these payments with the obligation of all of the goods present and future which he might own to pay all his dues and if there are damages to his part of the crop, he must still meet the aforementioned requirements and make good the damage with oath and other means of approval.

LEASE [*LIBELLUS*] FOR TWENTY-NINE YEARS

John, by the grace of God prior of the monastery of S. Ciprian, with the consent and will of his brothers here present, namely Valentino and Peter and others, for 100 Venetian *lire de piccoli* which he has confessed to have accepted numbered and accounted by himself in the name of the monastery and for the monastery from Albertino of Luciano, he [John] renounced all exceptions and agrees himself paid for the time of the contract, and together with his aforementioned brothers accepted this money for the use of the monastery. Now he [John] invests the same Albertino according to the law of the perpetual lease [*libelli perpetualis*] with a piece of land of building property [*terra casaliva*] with a house built upon it and with a court and garden belonging to it, lying in the city of Padua in the district of S. Lucia. It is bound on one side by a public road, on the other by [the land of] Egidiolo Filora, on one end by Symeon, notary, and on the other by Peter. Thus that the lease [*libellus*] or the investiture of a lease ought to be renewed every 29 years. At each renewal, Albertino and his heirs will have to give John or his successors, ten Venetian *soldi di piccoli* and, in turn, Albertino and his heirs ought to have, hold and possess the aforementioned piece of land with court and garden and with the house built on it with all his will and according to the law of perpetual lease renewable every 29 years. As is said,

---

1. Note on measures: One Paduan *campo* equals .386 hectare or about .954 English acre, and the Paduan *staio* equals about 3 liters, or .81 bushel.—Eds.

"Paduan Agricultural Contracts, 1223," ed. M. Roberti, "Un formulario inedito di notaio padovano del 1223," *Memorie del R. Istituto veneto* 27, no. 6 (1906), pp. 69–71. Translated by Benjamin G. Kohl.

without contradiction from or petition to John and his successors, [Albertino and his heirs ought to have] right of accession, entrance, entering and leaving, with the road and ditches and aqueducts, with above and below the ground and with all things that belong to these property, and with all rights, actions, and law, real and personal of the same land and buildings which belong to the aforementioned John in the name of the same monastery. Except according to the law and condition asserting and saying that the same land with building cannot be given, alienated or in any way obligated to any other except to the aforesaid Albertino, and it is free of all service. And if more than the said price will be demanded, it will be given and conceded to him purely and irrevocably, as is contained above in the contract of the lease.

FIEF [FEUDUM] OF A PIECE OF LAND

Lord Forzatè, *visdomino*, invested according to the law of fief Nicolò da Rutena with a piece of land of eight *campi* in the village of Corte. It is bordered as they have said, etc. And in this fief Nicolò's male offspring will succeed, and, lacking them, his female offspring succeed. And to the same Nicolò, Lord Forzatè gives this piece of land in fee, as is said, with accession, right of entrance, entering and leaving, with road and services and with ditches and with rights both above and below the ground and with all those things which belong to the fief, and with all rights and actions real and personal which belong to the same piece of land and for that land, he [Forzatè] appoints him [Nicolò] his procurator in legal actions. Also the said lord Forzatè promises the aforementioned Nicolò to guarantee and defend the aforementioned land for himself and his heirs from all men by legal action [*cum racione*]. And if he [Forzatè] will not be able to defend him, he promises and agrees to give him in the abovementioned place judgment of one good man instead. Thence, the aforesaid Nicolò swears his fealty [*fidelitatem*] to the same lord Forzatè against all persons except the fealty [owed to] his earlier lords [*anteriorum dominorum*].

DOWRY OF LAND AND MONEY

Marcourdo, notary, son of deceased Folberto of Noventa, confesses to have accepted a dowry from Patavina, his wife, two hundred *lire* in cash and in other evaluated goods, and a piece of land unevaluated lying the confines of Noventa, which is bordered in such a way, or the produce of one farmstead lying in the confines or village of Noventa worked by Spinello, a *precos* [a low-grade civil servant of the commune]. It is bordered by the confines of the farmstead and unevaluated. Hence, concerning this, the aforesaid Marcourdo, notary, agrees that he has received these in dowry at the time of the contract, and that he will defend them by his own law. He makes a donation because of the wedding of the said Patavina, his wife, of his own goods up to the sum of two hundred pounds plus however much the aforesaid piece of land will be worth or will be evaluated according to judgment of one good man or however much the crop of the aforesaid farmstead will be worth. By a pact concluded between them, it is stipulated that if the aforesaid Patavina, wife of the same Marcourdo, will die during the marriage between them without common offspring, then, Marcourdo will keep 25 *lire* of the aforesaid dowry, while the rest will be returned to the heirs of Patavina. If it happens, on the other hand, that the said Marcourdo will predecease his wife without common heirs, then the same Patavina ought to have her entire dowry plus 25 *lire* of the donation, as is contained in the above contract.

SOCEDA CONTRACT TO RENT A COW AND CALF

Zambenetto Fellinia confesses to have accepted in *soceda* from Matteo a cow and a calf, whence concerning this, Zambenetto renounces any exceptions and for the time of the contract agrees to defend the cow and calf himself for everyone by his own law. And according to the stipulation of the same Matteo, he [Zambenetto] promises and agrees to preserve the aforementioned *soceda* [partnership] in good faith for five years and to give him [Matteo] half of the aforesaid cow and calf and any new-born coming from them. Matteo retains in himself domain and property and almost possession of the same cow and calf, while the same Zambenetto keeps them in his possession for Matteo as long as the partnership will last. Beside, said Zambenetto promises (for himself and his heirs) according to the stipulation of the aforesaid Matteo to give annually as long as the partnership will last, to Matteo and his heirs every year at the feast of Santa Margherita [July 20] 4 *staii* Paduan of good wheat and four *staii* Paduan of good millet at the feast of Saint Justina [October 7].

Two Mezzadria Contracts from Siena, 1342–1343

SHARECROPPING CONTRACT MADE AT SIENA BETWEEN A CITIZEN AND PEASANT

Meo, son of the late Dona da Stigliano, of the Sienese contado, makes a contract with Jacopo, son of the late Niccolò di Mino Castaldi, of the quarter of San Salvatore of Siena, receiving for himself and for Agnese and Niccolò, his sister and brother, a farm with house, vineyard and land, located in the district of Stigliano, in the village called Poderino, with certain borders, to have beginning with the next feast of Saint Mary of August [August 15, 1342] for the next five years, to till on shares. And he [Meo] promises to contribute all seed, animals and tools. And he promises to work and till [the land] and transport to his [Jacopo's] home in Siena half of all the crops, namely, grain ground as flour, and whatever other crops there will be, at his own expense as ordered by said Jacopo. And he promises to give every year 110 pounds of pork at the feast of Christmas. And he promises also to keep sixteen sheep and one sow for three years, and give over one third of them with one half of their offspring [delivered] to Siena, plus one pair of good capons and one hundred eggs each year; and to spread all manure that there is on the said farm. And he promises to give five bushels of mixed grain at the end of the contract.

"Two Mezzadria Contracts from Siena," trans. B. G. Kohl from *Il contratto di Mezzadria nella Toscana medievale, I. Contado di siena, sec. XIII-1348*, ed. G. Pinto and P. Pirillo (Florence, Leo S. Olschki Editore, 1987), pp. 69–70, 183–184. Reprinted by permission of the publisher

Sharecropping Contract Made at Siena Between the Augustinian Hermits at Sant'Agostino and a Peasant

I Cennino, son of the late Martino da Orgia, the Sienese contado, confess to have received by the sharecropping contract from you, Friar Simone Orlandi, of the order of brothers of Sant'Agostino of Siena, official and representative of the said brothers, chapter and convent of Sant'Agostino, renting and conveying on behalf of the said brothers, chapter and convent, according to the contract drawn up in a public instrument in the hand of Ser Niccolò di Ser Mino notary, to rent and till on shares the lands and possessions located in the neighborhood of Orgia and other places listed below, for the next nine years. These properties are:

First, a parcel of land and vineyard located in the place called Fonte a Caprazoppa, which is bounded by the commune of Orgia, the property of Davino Memmi, and a public road.

Item, a parcel of tillable land located in the place called Goratello; which is bounded on one side by the heirs of Nero Pietro Daglioposi, on another by Andrea Scolaino, and another by Ciampoli Gani.

Item, another parcel of tillable land in the place called Citina, which is bounded on one side by the Church of San Bartolommeo of Orgia, and on another by the said Andrea Scolaino, and perhaps there are [other] borders.

And I promise to you, said Brother Simone, aforesaid representative, receiving for the said brothers, chapter and convent, diligently and well to work and till the said lands and vineyard, and to ditch and hoe, stake, water and prune the vines and to manure well the fields and to sow [them] with my own seed, all at my own expense, according to the practice of a good farmer without any neglect at any time. Likewise, I promise and agree to give and assign to you, Brother Simone, receiving all in the name of the said brothers, chapter and convent, every year one half of the crops and wine, which will be produced from the said possessions, and to transport and convey to the convent of the brothers of the aforesaid Sant' Agostino in Siena, all at his own expense, every year of produce and wine of the harvest, except that you said Cennino ought to have and receive from the said brothers, chapter and convent, for every year of this contract, 12 soldi for the cost of shipping the wine that you, the said Cennino, will transport to Siena at the time of the harvest or another time. Likewise, I promise and agree to you Brother Simone, the aforesaid representative, that I will not rent nor in any way alienate these possessions or any part of them to another person without the special permission and agreement of the said brothers, chapter and convent, for the term of the said contract. [There follows a fine of 25 lire for breaking the contract, formulas of guarantees, and the name and signature of the notary.]

ORGANIZATIONAL CHART OF THE MEDICI BANK, 1455

- **Head of the Firm** — Cosimo de' Medici
  - **General Manager and Partner** — Giovanni d'Amerigo Benci
    - **Silk Manufacturing** (One partnership) — Managers: Berlinghieri Berlinghieri, Jacopo Tanaglia
      - Production
        - Purchases Raw Silk
        - Throwing
          - In Throwing Mill
        - Boiling
          - Boilers
        - Weaving
          - Warpers
          - Weavers
        - Dyeing
          - Dyers
      - Sales, Exporters and Foreign Branches
    - **Local Banking**
      - Manager of Tavola in Florence: Giovanni di Baldino Inghirami
    - **Cloth Manufacturing** (Two partnerships) — Managers: 1. Antonio di Taddeo 2. Andrea Giuntini
      - Purchases — Wool from Local Importers and from Bruges and London Branches
        - Preparing the Wool
          - Woolwashers
          - Capodieci
          - Cleansers and Beaters
        - Spinning
          - Lanino
          - Stamaiuoli
          - Spinners
          - Spinners
      - Production
        - Weaving
          - Warpers
          - Weavers
          - Fattore di Pettine
          - Fattore di Cardo
          - Combers
          - Carders
      - Finishing
        - Menders
        - Stretchers
        - Burlers
        - Scourers
        - Fullers
        - Nappers
        - Shearers
      - Dyeing
        - In the Wool
        - In the Cloth
      - Sales — Retailers, Exporters, and Branches Abroad
    - **International Banking and Foreign Trade**
      - Branches beyond the Alps
        - Geneva — Manager Francesco Sassetti; Six Factors in 1469
        - Bruges — Manager Agnolo Tani, Tommaso Portinari; Seven Factors in 1469
          - Assistant Manager Antonio di Bernardo de' Medici
          - Wool trade Cristofano Spini
          - Banking Tommaso Guidetti
          - Bookkeeping Adoardo Canigiani
        - London — Manager Simone Nori; Three Factors
        - Avignon — Manager Giovanni Zampini; Two or Three Factors
      - Branches in Italy
        - Milan — Manager Pigello Portinari; Banking; Silk Trade Carlo Cavalcanti
        - Rome — Manager Roberto Martelli; Fiscal Agent of the Papacy
        - Pisa — Manager Ugolino Martelli; Trade
        - Venice — Manager Alessandro Martelli; Correspondence Antonio Tornabuoni; Errands Folco Portinari

Chart, "The Organization of the Medici Bank" in "The Medici Bank" by Raymond de Roover from *The Medici Bank, Its Organization, Management, Operations and Decline* by Raymond de Roover, New York University Press, 1948, p. 12.

A Businessman Records
His Financial Affairs, 1385–1403

In the name of God, the Virgin Mary and all the Saints—may they grant me health in soul and body and prosperity in business—I shall record here all my dealings with our company.

On 1 January 1385, Giovanni di Giano and his partners made me a partner in their silk business for as long as it may please God. I am to invest 300 gold florins which I have not got, being actually in debt to the business. However, with God's help, I hope to have the money shortly and am to receive two out of every twenty-four shares, in other words, a twelfth of the total profit. We settled our accounts on 8 June 1387, on Giovanni di Giano's death. May he rest in peace. My share of the profits for the two years and five months I had been a partner came to 468 gold florins, 7 *soldi a fiorino*.[1] Thanks be to God. We formed a new partnership on the following terms: Buonaccorso Berardi is to invest 8,000 florins and have eleven shares; Michele di Ser Parente is to invest 3,500 florins and have eight shares; Goro, son of Stagio Dati, is to invest 500 florins and have three shares; Nardo di Lippo is to invest 500 and have two shares. Thus the capital of the company shall amount to 12,500 gold florins. And if any partner invests additional money in the company, that investment will earn one-half of the percentage of the profits earned by the regular shares.

In God's name I shall continue my review of the accounts written above on page two of our company's agreements, and of my shares, balance sheets and profits and shall record what followed and is yet to follow. As appears in these accounts, we renewed our partnership on 1 January 1393 when I undertook to invest 1,000 florins. I did not actually have the money but was about to get married—which I then did— and to receive the dowry which procured me a larger share and more consideration in our company. Yet we achieved little that year.

I set out for Valencia in September 1393 in order to wind up matters there but did not get beyond Genoa. When I reached the Riviera, I was set upon and robbed by a galley from Briganzone and returned to Florence on 14 December, having lost 250 florins' worth of pearls, merchandise and clothes belonging to myself, and 300 gold florins' worth of the company's property.

When the partnership with Michele di Ser Parente expired, I set up shop on my own under the name of Goro Stagio and company. My partners are Piero and Jacopo di Tommaso Lana who contribute 3,000 [florins] while I contribute 2,000, and Nardo di Lippo who contributes his services. The partnership is to start on 1 January 1403 and to last three years. The clauses and articles of agreement and the amounts invested by each partner will be entered in a secret ledger covered with white leather belonging to our partnership.

"Merchant Memoirs" reprinted by permission of Waveland Press, Inc. from Gene Brucker, Editor, *Two Memoirs of Renaissance Florence: The Diaries of Buonaccorso Pitti and Gregorio Dati*, translated by Julia Martines, pp. 108–109, 110, 120–121. Copyright © 1967, reissued 1991 by Wavelend Press, Prospect Heights, Illinois.

1. The phrase *soldi a fiorino* refers to a money of account commonly used in Florentine monetary calculations. Twenty-nine soldi a fiorino were equivalent to one gold florin.

On my own account and with my own money, I paid 75 florins to the heirs of Simone Vespucci and their representative, Lapo Vespucci, for the goodwill and licence to exercise my profession in one of the shops of Por Santa Maria. The brokers were Andrea di Bonaventura and Niccolaio Niccoli. On 6 March 1403, Isau d'Agnolo and Antonio Manni, a silk merchant who was in the shop, received 25 florins from me. The broker was Meo d'Andrea del Benino. The fixtures and repairs cost me about 100 florins, so altogether, between the goodwill and the fixtures I paid 200 florins out of my own pocket, in God's name, for myself and my heirs. The site of the shop belongs to the Carthusian monks, from whom I am to rent it on the usual terms for 35 gold florins a year. Ser Ludovico of the guild drew up the lease, which is to run for five years from the beginning of February 1403.

As already stated, I have undertaken to put up 2,000 florins. This is how I propose to raise them: 1,370 florins and 25 *soldi a fiorino* are still due to me from my old partnership with Michele di Ser Parente, as appears on page 118 of my ledger for stock and cash on hand. The rest I expect to obtain if I marry again this year, when I hope to find a woman with a dowry as large as God may be pleased to grant me. If I do not marry, I will find the money some other way.

FURTHER READING

Trevor Dean and Chris Wickham, eds. *City and Countryside in Late Medieval and Renaissance Italy: Essays Presented to Philip Jones* (1990)
Raymond de Roover, *The Medici Bank* (1948)
_____, *The Rise and Decline of the Medici Bank* (1963)
Richard A. Goldthwaite, *The Building of Renaissance Florence* (1980)
_____, *Wealth and the Demand for Art in Italy, 1300–1600* (1993)
Barbara A. Hanawalt, ed., *Women and Work in Preindustrial Europe* (1986)
David Herlihy, *Pisa in the Early Renaissance* (1958)
_____, *Medieval and Renaissance Pistoia* (1967)
P. J. Jones, "From Manor to Mezzadria: A Tuscan Case-Study in the Medieval Origins of Modern Agrarian Society," in *Florentine Studies*, ed. N. Rubinstein (1968), 193–241
_____, "Italy," in *Cambridge Economic History of Europe, vol. 1: The Agrarian Life of the Middle Ages*, 2d ed. (1966)
Frederic C. Lane, *Andrea Barbarigo, Merchant of Venice* (1944)
_____, *Venetian Ships and Shipbuilders of the Renaissance* (1934)
Frederic C. Lane and Reinhold C. Mueller, *Money and Banking in Medieval and Renaissance Venice*, vol. 1 (1985)
Robert S. Lopez and Harry A. Miskimin, "The Economic Depression of the Renaissance," *Economic History Review*, 2d ser., 14 (1962), 408–426
Robert S. Lopez and Irving Raymond, *Medieval Trade in the Mediterranean World* (1955)
Gino Luzzatto, *An Economic History of Italy*, trans. P. J. Jones (1961)
Harry A. Miskimin, *The Economy of Early Renaissance Europe, 1300–1460* (1975)
Benjamin Nelson, *The Idea of Usury from Tribal Brotherhood to Universal Otherhood*, 2d ed. (1969)
Iris Origo, *The Merchant of Prato, Francesco di Marco Datini, 1335–1410* (1957)
J. C. Russell, *Medieval Regions and Their Cities* (1972)

CHAPTER 4

Urban Needs and Opportunities

The nature of urban life in Italian Renaissance cities has attracted much scholarly attention. Florence has been the focus of much of this attention, in part because two extraordinarily useful kinds of documents for urban history are most abundant in its archives: the detailed census records, known as the Catasto, and merchant diaries. Italian city dwellers were among the first Europeans to tax themselves, and they employed sophisticated techniques of record keeping to assess the tax-paying population as fairly as possible. Moreover, merchants not only kept detailed account books but also recorded important events of their personal and business lives in diaries, or *ricordanze*. The picture that emerges from these census records and private memoirs is of a world of dramatically fluctuating personal fortunes. Success in business and politics required constant vigilance, as well as the maintenance of a complex network of neighbors, kin, and associates for support and protection against the vagaries of fortune.

ESSAYS

In the first essay, Marvin Becker of the University of Michigan argues that warfare and the resultant public debt of the Italian city-states transformed urban experience in the fourteenth and fifteenth centuries. In order to meet the extraordinary costs of war, communes borrowed from their most wealthy members, eventually consolidating this temporary indebtedness into a funded debt, called the Monte. Because the citizens of each city-state shared the experience of making forced loans to their governments, they tended to identify with the interests of the ruling class in support of those governments. In the second essay, David Herlihy of Brown University uses the massive computer-assisted research that he and Christiane Klapisch-Zuber of the École des Hautes Études en Sciences Sociales in Paris conducted on the Florentine Catasto to examine issues of social mobility. Finding that the replacement rate (the ratio of young adults to their parents' generation) was high among wealthy Florentines and low among rural Tuscans, Herlihy posits great competition among the wealthier classes for the best jobs and the attraction of rural Tuscans to opportunities in the cities. Thus, the competitive individualism of Burckhardt's vision receives unexpected reinforcement from newly exploited statistical sources. Christiane Klapisch-Zuber, who has pioneered the study of Florentine *ricordanze*, examines the social relationships of a typical fifteenth-century merchant and his family in the third essay. She concludes that kinship ties and neighborhood alliances were of fundamental importance—and closely intertwined—in a family's commercial, political, and social success.

The Italian Urban Experience

MARVIN B. BECKER

Leonardo Bruni Aretino and Niccolò Machiavelli were quite correct in their assessment of the significance of the shift from citizen military service to an army of mercenaries. Although their judgments must be modified to indicate that hired troops were in evidence long before the period they deemed crucial, still their stress on this point was not misplaced. This thesis can be readily extended to include the effects of warfare in general upon the rise of late medieval and Renaissance territorial states as well as the decline of the commune in north and central Italy. . . .

Perhaps there is something of a liberal bias in the fact that modern scholars have discounted the obvious and primary activity of both late medieval and Renaissance city states—warfare—in order to concentrate upon questions of ideology and problems of class conflict. Similarly, scholarly concern with the rise and decline of private economies has led to a substantial neglect of public financing for war. Surely, an interest in ideology, class conflict, or business activity needs no justification, but those involved in causal investigations may have to inquire into martial affairs. A hypothesis of the present study can be stated thus: It was warfare and the attendant accumulation of indebtedness that undermined older political structures and styles of rule, while at the same time prompting the development of new political institutions and forms. Therefore, I shall concentrate upon the emergence of a new political matrix—a superstructure, if you will—that housed a variety of city-state societies, each with rather distinctive qualities. Yet another way of indicating my purpose is to suggest that the superstructure in Venice evolved as a resultant of forces comparable to those acting to generate similar structures in Florence or Genoa or Pisa or Milan. The possible advantage of this approach is twofold: first, hypotheses can be offered as to the nature of the causes at work undermining the older commune; secondly, certain of the characteristics of these emerging superstructures may be shared by several of the cities. Possibly we shall find that Renaissance political problems, whether Florentine, Venetian, or Genoese, were not so disparate. If this be so, then the possibility of formulating pragmatic definitions articulating features of these medieval and Renaissance political structures shall be enhanced. In any case, we can always plead in the name of methodological modesty, like the novelist Henry James, that all we are doing is seeking to put together what goes together.

The medieval commune that developed in north and central Italy was a config-

"Some Common Features of Italian Urban Experience" by Marvin B. Becker from *Medievalia et Humanistica* 1 (1970), 15 pages of text abridged from pp. 175–196. Reprinted with permission from the Medieval and Renaissance Society.

uration of economic, social, religious, and political organisms coexisting in a pluralistic, civic environment. The commune itself was at first only a sworn association of men devoted to keeping the urban peace, and this clearly implied making war. There were sworn associations of knights (*commune militum*) and sworn associations of foot soldiers (*commune peditum*). On the façades of cathedrals we would find the foot soldiers on the left hand of the Redeemer and the knights appropriately on His right. Guilds, religious confraternities, philopapal and philoimperial organizations were an essential part of this manifold political universe. Indeed, the medieval city-state can be likened to a body possessed of no political center of gravity. Fundamental to an appreciation of the political texture of this type of community is a comprehension of the abundant number of immunities, privileges, and ecclesiastical liberties. The city in medieval Italy was primarily an aristocratic foundation; likewise, the commune of the eleventh and twelfth centuries was chiefly a patrician construct. Moreover, where political development was most precocious, such as in Milan, the archbishops and other prelates played a decisive role in encouraging the formation of political associations. Two factors worth a brief glance are the persistence of urban forms of association throughout the early history of medieval Italy and the intense involvement of large segments of the population in the work of religious reform in cities such as Milan and Florence in the eleventh and twelfth centuries. The conglomerate character of the *civitas* can be observed if we realize that great feudatories and prelates, and even guilds, retained control of areas of life that today would be considered public. A guild might collect the wine tax or oversee the use of weights and measures; a great feudatory might hold the customs toll as a fief or exercise his jurisdiction over the market. The prelate held ecclesiastical court, claimed exemption from communal imposts, and denied the right of secular jurisdiction over his clergy.

By the twelfth century we note a peculiar mix of social classes and quasi-political bodies. While popular participation in the polis increased as a result of the revolutionary movement accompanying the Gregorian reforms in the latter half of the eleventh century, and was accelerated by struggles against the Holy Roman Emperors, still most urban regimes remained firmly in the hands of consular aristocracies. Indeed, these great families, often feudal in origin, had achieved a remarkable preeminence as a consequence of substantial victories over imperial armies. Their leadership over town militia and cavalry also proved essential for securing trade routes and commercial advantage. In Milan the *capitanei* [captains] and *valvassori* [vassals] dominated the military and juridical life of the community, replacing the ancient authority of the archbishop. In Pisa and Genoa their aristocratic counterparts were likewise preeminent, leading the grand naval expeditions that rolled back Mohammedan occupation of Mediterranean islands, giving their townsmen rich possibilities for trade and investment.

The late twelfth and early thirteenth centuries can be seen as the golden age of the upper and middling north Italian nobility. Already, half a century before, the German chronicler Otto of Freising had complained that few nobles placed fidelity to the Empire over loyalty to their natal *patria*. By an ancient Milanese custom the vassal of a lord did not forfeit his fief if he failed to join his *dominus* [lord] in war against the city. Again, Otto noted that the consulate of Milan was staffed by men from the high and middling nobility. When imperial authority receded and civil strife became intolerable, efforts were made to install more impartial magistrates. The institution of the podestà—a complex phenomenon at the least—was at first the exclusive preserve of urban nobility. While the paucity of evidence does not allow us to reconstruct in depth the effects of extensive participation by these nobles in the bureaucratic and juridical life of the polis, still, service in high magistracies worked to discourage old loyalties and habits. It is clear from the histories of Pisa, Pistoia, and Genoa that important sectors of the nobility were themselves sponsors of basic reforms, and even leaders of popular regimes. Certainly, a part of this can be attributed to demagoguery, but much more is explicable in terms of the high degree of military and juridical involvement in government of these aristocrats. Yet another more obvious force stemmed from extensive participation by Venetian patricians, Pisan feudatories, and Genoese consular nobility in the thriving commercial activities of the Dugento. That portion of the well-born most readily assimilated into business and government were as anxious to promote urban peace through law as were many of the haute bourgeoisie. . . .

Even at the moment of its greatest success citizen military service was proving inadequate to the demands of war and peace. Already, during the 1160's in Milan, the 1170's in Venice and Genoa, and the final decades in Siena and Pisa, it was clear that revision of military finances was vital. In Milan, during its struggle against imperial power over the second half of the twelfth century, the hire of substantial contingents of cavalry at high wages was required to supplement the citizen militia. This practice, endemic throughout north and central Italy, paralleled the discontinuance of gratuitous or meagerly paid citizen military service. By 1228 the Milanese citizen cavalry was being indemnified, and hired troops were bearing the brunt of warfare in the Piedmont. Economic interests in each of the major cities encouraged policies of conquest and firm control of territories so that trade might be secure and free from obstruction. . . .

Genoa offers a telling example of the new problems and pressures; her great naval expeditions in the eleventh and twelfth centuries had been mainly privately financed. Communal government tended to be lackluster in this pluralistic world of medieval politics. Influential nobility captained the forces, advanced monies, and shared the booty; later, the families of the consular aristocrats even held the conquered territories of the commune as fiefs. In the thirteenth century much of this underwent deep alteration: the navy was now financed by the communal treasury, and war became a public prerogative.

Communal administrative machinery was profoundly influenced by the experiences of the hundred years after 1150. Persistent experimentation led to the erection of bureaucratic and juridical systems that would prove effective in making warfare a public prerogative. Two vexing issues were to be confronted: first, how this shift might be adequately financed; and second, how to release the commune from military dependence on the consular aristocracy. Each of course was closely connected with the other. Perhaps, so that we may better see the connection, the word violence may be employed for the moment in place of the word war. Again, to illustrate from Genoese history, we find that the family of Folco di Castello, commanders of the Genoese contingent on the Third Crusade, attacked the communal magistrates in an attempt to seize power. In Pisa, Ubaldo Visconti tried to dominate the city, just as he controlled the island of Sardinia, that prize of the republic's wars. Against him stood the clan of Gherardesca. We could easily duplicate the circumstances for virtually each Italian town. The exercise of violence by the *millites* [knights] of the city was surely inflamed by chivalric codes placing primacy on the vendetta and blood feud. The contemporary word used to describe violence among noble *consorterie* [clans] was *guerra* [war]. To repress this *guerra* [war] the right to bear arms would have to be limited and the *potentes* [magnates] be compelled to use force only in ways commensurate with public order. The phrase appearing with monotonous regularity in documents of the period, "the peaceful and tranquil state of the city," expressed that ethos aiming to make the *buono stato* [good state] prevail. . . .

The epitomization of programs was realized, at least in theory, when Da Vialta and his subordinates attempted to draw up a general estimate of the value of all citizen property for the purpose of achieving greater equality in taxation. Special attention was focused on the troublesome question of greater parity between urban and rural imposts. The commune asserted the right to impose customs and hearth taxes; the former had frequently been retained by the nobility as a fief, while the latter were recognized as a regalian right, i.e., belonging to the Emperor. Finally, the effort to achieve equity was continued in levies upon noble and commoner, and even in those falling on the various grades of nobility. The difficulties confronting such a formidable enterprise were attested to by the halting, long-term endeavors to complete this type of estimate of wealth. The advantages to a militarily beleaguered community were obvious: taxes and loans could be assessed in proportion to citizen wealth. If the total were known, then the commune could assess that percent which would yield it the requisite sum.

Still, the press for further fiscal reorganization persisted; tensions between custom and innovation were strong and practical difficulties always baffling. Minor accomplishments of successive podestàs, who displaced ancient feudatories (the Visconti) from their role as collectors of taxes on tradesmen, contributed toward the gradual formation of a more unitary political structure. But the monies realized for the commune proved insignificant in meeting the escalating costs of warfare. In 1233 control of communal finances was centralized, and again the bureaucratic structure was renovated. This at precisely the moment when we observe the beginnings of the existence of a permanent mercenary army. The terrible years of hostilities with the Emperor demanded extreme citizen sacrifice. *Il popolo* [The people] claimed that they were assuming "the whole weight" (*totum pondus*) of military expenditures. In 1240 their leader, Pagano della Torre, . . . gained control of the communal government. With the support of other nobles (the Da Soresina, Crivelli, Pirovana) and the papal legate, he was able to put into effective operation the first extensive tax on fixed and movable properties. The difficult business of achieving an estimate of citizen holdings had been accomplished. . . . Until that decade nobles and clergy had effectively resisted its thorough implementation; the problem of medieval tax liability was always thorny. Should allodial tenures be liable for imposts or only benefices? What about land that had been exempted by imperial diploma? What of the clergy? (At this time they did not resist the levy because Milan was warring against the arch-heretic Frederick II.) What of the confraternities? (The question of status was particularly vexing, and again the Milanese clergy acknowledged communal rights only because of the exigencies of war.) The need for revenue again assumed primacy: war and the carrying charges on the public debt had prompted reforms that strengthened the fiscal authority of the commune.

Popular forces routed from the guilds were not strong enough to promote reorganization of the state and its finances. The path of the despot was presaged by the roles of such strong men as Gregorio da Montelongo and Beno de' Gozzandi, who responded to military needs by sponsoring administrative and fiscal reorganization of the commune during the middle years of the thirteenth century. These men were both foreigners and were expected to stand above factional interests, while Milanese families, with their followings, would soon enter a deadly contest for political control. While there were to be significant differences in political styles among the Della Torre, Visconti, and Sforza, still the march toward centralization and bureaucratization proceeded quite steadily. No matter who the ruling elite might be, deficit financing and warfare remained the essential problems. Without minimizing the differences between republics and despotisms, both were generating political superstructures with comparable features. The daily intrusion of political power into citizen life and the high degree of economic supervision by a centralized government were encouraged by identical sets of factors—budgetary and military considerations. Integration of territories and bureaucratic development maximized opportunities for citizen participation in diplomacy and civil service. While there was a substantial difference between the active citizen of a republic and his more docile Milanese counterpart, yet both political orders were staffed by numerous functionaries whose dedication to administrative problems was uncritical and lifelong. Such a reorganization was prompted largely by old familiar considerations. There was, however, an added incentive for the despot. He felt more secure with a standing army at his side. So, the citizen army was to undergo further eclipse.

Throughout north and central Italy we observe the creation of a creditor class as a consequence of expansion through diplomacy and warfare. Venice borrowed from a consortium to raise a subvention for the league organized against Frederick I. . . . Indeed, if there is a corollary to our single enduring socioeconomic fact that warfare and deficit financing were decisive for late medieval Italian urban experience, it might run thus: in Genoa and Venice in the thirteenth century, and Florence in the fourteenth, entry into the communal creditor class was the surest passport to political influence. By mid-fourteenth century those Florentine nobles who were no longer large-scale communal creditors lost much of their political standing, while "new citizens" who advanced capital to the government were playing crucial roles in public life.

For one hundred years the government set aside large sums during times of peace and prosperity for amortization of the principal. In 1363 a new technique was introduced when the government decided to employ public revenues to purchase shares of the debt; in this way the market price of these public stocks was to be shored up. It is not with the success of these policies or the fluctuations in the value of these shares that we are concerned; even the fact that the patrician ruling families were its principal shareholders is not central to the argument. That the parvenus benefited from certain aspects of tributary policies and were able to acquire sizable blocks of shares adds dimension to the observation that these centuries witnessed a tightening of the nexus between citizen and polis. What stands as most germane, however, is the astronomical leap in the total debt: in 1255 it was at the trifling figure of 15,000 *lire a grossi*; in 1279 it was 400,000; and by 1313 it totaled almost 2,800,000. There was a substantial reduction in the 1330's and 40's, but again the climb proved irrepressible; in 1353 it stood at 3,100,000, only to reach 12,300,000 at the conclusion of the War of Chioggia in 1381.

The costs of equipping war galleys, staffing them with mariners and troops, and maintaining the great Venetian arsenal served to prompt stricter enforcement of statal norms. To meet the carrying charges on this aggregate of indebtedness required the application of highly rationalized fiscal techniques. Chronic warfare allowed no surcease, and in time of stress the Venetian naval forces could boast of 36,000 sailors. Words attributed to doge Andrea Contarini, in 1381, make explicit that awareness which made the "buon stato" preeminent: "It is a manifest thing that the Republic can easily tolerate the adversity of private citizens, but that they are not sufficient unto themselves to sustain the adversity of all the realm." The state commenced to elevate itself above society with its central organs, the Senate and Council of Ten, exercising influence over the farthest reaches of civic life. The powerful bureaucracy, like capillaries, extended throughout the body politic. Soon Venetian humanists of the early fifteenth century celebrated the *Principatus Venetus*, as did Lorenzo Monacis in his *Chronicon de rebus Venetis*, as being that city where law prevailed and the doge ruled like a king. Gladly would the citizen sacrifice his life for this *Principatus*. Chroniclers maintained that any who opposed the Republic were in blasphemous contest, "contra divinam potentiam," for "divina providentia" herself ruled and ordered the city. Bernardo Guistinian, in his eulogy of the doge Francesco Foscari, set forth the sacrifices of the ancient Athenians, who won a maritime empire, as well as those of the Romans, who brought Carthage to heel and gained the expanses of the Mediterranean for the Eternal City.

During the early tenure of the podestà, at the close of the thirteenth century, the maritime and military aristocrats from the Visconti and Gherardesca families regularly occupied or dominated this magistracy. Yet the anatomy of the administration and bureaucracy was ever more discernible, and increasing participation by judges and notaries had become a fact of civic life. Pisa appears to have been the first of the Italian towns to apply the norms of Roman law to everyday political life. Written law vied with custom with the appearance of the *Breve populi*, first noted in 1171. Duties of new officials were defined with greater precision, and they were required to take an oath to observe the new rudimentary legal codes. In 1162 one of the consuls was himself a legal specialist, and soon this type of appointment became a commonplace with the creation of the *consul justiciae*. By the end of the century there were several of these magistrates, and their courts were exceedingly active. Gradually, then, there was a displacement of much judicial business from ecclesiastical and feudal courts into the tribunals of the commune.

Even under this canopy of law and increasing legal sensibility the familiar pluralism of communal life prospered, with guild courts . . . collecting customs receipts and the military nobility retaining their own organization with *capitanei militum* [captains of the knights]. But again warfare, deficit financing, and population increase worked to tip the balance toward more impartial and unitary regimes. Participation by the new citizens, first in the urban militia, then in the *societates armorum* [companies of foot], and finally as administrators and government creditors, was a relevant aspect of this transformation. Military service and then financial contribution brought greater equality to the ruling and bureaucratic cadres of the society. As in Arezzo, Ravenna, and Treviso, the formation of *il popolo* at Pisa was not exclusive nor were its leaders unmindful of the traditional claims of the nobility for status. Great nobles such as the Donoratico, who had rendered valuable service to the commune, took the sacred oath to the Pisan people. . . .

The need for revenue proved difficult to resist; there was a general administrative reform of fiscal and institutional procedures: between 1230 and 1288 communal income increased from 2,400 lire to 40,000 lire. Even taking into account coin devaluation and inflation, this was a sizable accomplishment. Still, it was not possible for the city to meet its military commitments. Efforts at the beginning of the century by foreign podestàs to install a revenue system based upon the imposition of direct taxes proved no more successful at Pisa than at many another Italian town. Chronic war with Genoa, culminating with the crushing defeat of Meloria in August of 1284, did not dissuade the Pisans from continuing an overly ambitious foreign policy. Contemporary chroniclers may have exaggerated the sums that the ill-fated expedition of Henry VII ("exercitus felicissimus Domini Imperatoris") cost his Pisan ally, but the bankruptcy of the public treasury attested to the barren fiscal facts. Failure to collect sufficient monies from direct taxes and the preference for interest-bearing loans caused an escalating debt. These risky imperialistic policies were underwritten by new and old citizens who advanced capital to the communal treasury. In a single register for the year 1304 (few survive for this period), we find that measures taken by the government concern almost exclusively militia activity, armaments, higher taxes, and the imposition of interest-bearing loans. Increasingly, members of the executive branch of the communal government (the *anziani* [elders]) were to be the principal creditors. These citizens formed companies (*societas*) to advance capital to the government. Less than two generations later their creditor organizations would be well represented in the regime, and management of the public debt would become a central concern of all Pisan regimes.

In Florence, conquest and expansion characterized the city's history from the eleventh through the fourteenth centuries. Indeed . . . the conquest of neighboring Fiesole in 1125 marked the beginnings of a new historical consciousness among Florentine chroniclers. The memory of this victory was ritualized when on St. John's Day former tenants of the bishop of Fiesole proceeded to the Florentine cathedral and rendered homage to their new lord. Later, Florence's subject cities were to bring wax candles of enormous size to the cathedral to be lit in homage to the city's patron saint on his name day. War against the counts Alberti, Adimari, Buondelmonti, and Foraboschi secured communications throughout Tuscany, and later, after innumerable additional campaigns. Florentine banking and business interests were also firmly ensconced. At first, the work of conquest was achieved by a communal army with a sprinkling of mercenaries who joined the forces of the bishop and his vassals. The great nobles (*cives maiores*), the counts Guidi, Alberti, Firidolfi, Pazzi, and Ricasoli, served personally in the armies of the commune and therefore were exempt from many imposts. By the end of the eleventh century levies for defense were being imposed regularly on the countryside, and by the start of the thirteenth century the lands of the nobility were declared liable for imposition of taxes. Meanwhile, over the twelfth century, the commune appropriated authority to impose the hearth tax; this was a prerogative belonging to the Empire. As a consequence of the war for Semifonte in 1201, the first direct taxes were placed upon citizen property at a rate fixed on a percentage basis in terms of the total evaluation.

Even before the establishment of *il primo popolo* in 1250, the guilds, stronger in Florence than in most Italian cities, had organized their own effective militia. These troops were able to replace the *societas militum* after 1282. Required cavalry were no longer furnished through personal service, but principally by means of a tax charge on landowners. The guilds attempted to concentrate effective military police power in the hands of their own armed companies. By the late thirteenth century the might of the greater guilds was such that the bankers and industrialists could successfully finance great military expeditions. Even as far back as 1265–66, Florentine cameral merchants had accepted the risks and reaped the benefits by underwriting the campaigns of Charles of Anjou. In fact, the bankers who had been banished from their *patria* by their Ghibelline adversaries in 1260 were little short of a government in exile. With the victories of Charles of Anjou over the imperial armies, the bankers were restored to their city and granted vital commercial privileges in the Italian holdings of the Angevin line. Further loans, perhaps more than a hundred thousand florins, gained Florence control over Poggibonsi and other Tuscan centers, as well as trading concessions in the kingdom of Sicily. It is well to remember that since Florence was required to import at least two-thirds of her wheat from abroad, favorable connections with Sicily and south Italy were essential. The wealth of the pro-papal Guelf party from confiscated Ghibelline properties was so substantial that she held current accounts with ten of the leading banking and commercial companies in the city. These same financial institutions were now assuming the bulk of banking activity for the papacy. Increasingly, the leaders of the greater guilds (members of the *calimala* [luxury cloth], *cambio* [banking], and *lana* [wool]) placed their capital at the disposal of the commune for the purpose of carrying out a very successful foreign policy. So triumphant was this program that by the decade of the 1280's Florence through her armies, diplomacy, coinage, and exchange came to exercise dominion over Tuscany.

The difference between the Florentine constitutional system and that of so many of her neighbors stemmed in part from the city's diversified banking, commercial, and industrial economy—exceptional for Tuscany. So well endowed and resolute were the greater guilds that a regime could be founded upon the effective rule of leading members of *arti*. What emerged at the early fourteenth century was a system of guild rule characterized by extensive immunities and privileges for the membership. This system of exemptions coexisted with a tendency toward relaxed rule of the countryside and an easy entente with the nobility. After 1315, direct taxation was abandoned; except in moments of emergency or under military despotism, it was not resorted to. While Florence's military objectives were at least as ambitious as those of other towns, she did not yet run the sizable budgetary deficits of her neighbors and rivals. In 1315, communal obligations totaled a trifling figure—somewhat less than 50,000 florins. Loans from bankers, the Guelf party, and wealthy guilds were of incomparable assistance to the treasury. But this casual regimen was soon to be undone: escalating wars and exaggerated imperial ambition promoted even larger deficits. Within a period of thirty years communal indebtedness increased more than tenfold.

It was to be the great work of the regimes after 1343, culminating in the formation of the territorial state of the late Trecento, that repressed recalcitrant patricians, obdurate magnates, and overly expansive corporate bodies. In the course of this process traditional forms of government intimately associated with the era of the medieval commune dissolved, while successive regimes replaced private immunities with public law.

Out of this experience emerged a cohesive aristocracy quite different from the patriciate of the communal age. They were concerned with the procedures of communal finance, the techniques of diplomatic maneuver, and the conduct of the interminable wars of the early Quattrocento. Sedition and violence were more sporadic than formerly, and the disputes between *optimates* [magnates] centered around the management of the funded communal debt or the extent to which the signory should sponsor mercantilistic programs. The ties of *consorteria* [clan] and even of guild slackened, and an intimate nexus developed among the great oligarchs, who were now virtually stockholders in a giant corporation called the state. They were joined in this partnership by the most affluent of the *novi cives* [new citizens]. Less and less was the signory forced to play its great medieval role of peacemaker. The canopy of law, bureaucracy, and public power spread increasingly over private lives. Swarms of treasury officers and judicial officials entered state service during the mid-Trecento, so that within a generation Florentine bureaucracy had increased threefold, with a corresponding increase in power. Further, the same men tended to continue in office throughout their adult lives. Regularization of political procedure contributed to the efficiency of law enforcement. Judicial dispensation and annulment of sentences eventually became rarities in the less permissive world of the new polis.

Under this stricter regimen the polis exercised tight controls over the countryside during the late Trecento so that additional revenues might be extracted. In the early 1380's "extraordinary" imposts were levied on rural property which very soon became a regular feature of the Florentine tributary system. Tax rates that in the early Trecento averaged only ten soldi per lira now doubled and tripled, while the communal intake even quadrupled. What had been a light burden was well on the way to becoming a rugged, persistent program. Originally, such imposts had accounted for only about 10 percent of the communal intake, but by the early fifteenth century the figure veered between 40 and 50 per cent of total tax revenue. Comparable patterns of rigor can be discerned in the rule of subject cities and allied territories, where communal policy was dictated increasingly by budgetary deficits and the pressing need to underwrite the inflated credit structure; within only a few years taxes in these areas doubled.

Persistent and expanding costs of warfare, as well as the inordinate pressure of trying to meet escalating carrying charges on a burgeoning public debt, had a relentless effect upon the style of politics and the tone of public life. As we have seen, in the first decade and a half of the fourteenth century, when the income of the republic was about 300,000 florins, the public debt (*Monte*) was between 47,500 and

50,000 florins. Carrying charges were a few thousand florins. By the late fourteenth century the public debt stood at 3,000,000 florins, and carrying charges approached 200,000 florins; the treasury was in arrears some 300,000 florins a year. Thus, in addition to warfare, the maintenance of citizen confidence in the fiscal reliability of the polis was a monumental problem for Florentine rulers. Moreover, during these years the increase in forced citizen loans . . . was staggering. The annual figure sometimes exceeded 1,000,000 florins. Such an assumption of fiscal liability on the part of the government was revolutionary and awesome.

The problem of finding fiscal support for this inflated credit structure compelled those in power not to overlook any potential source of revenue. That their quest met with some degree of success is attested to by the fact that the value of shares in the public debt did not decline appreciably between the 1380's and the 1430's. This search for revenue led to the integration of Florentine territory, the rise of empire, and a strenuous program of mercantilism. Indeed, growth of the public debt and large-scale warfare did much to destroy the communal regime.

After the first part of the fifteenth century fiscal innovation tended to be exceptional. Ties between the public and private economies did not slacken in Venice, Florence, Milan, or Genoa. When confidence in the public debt floundered late in the fifteenth century, leading Venetian bankers were compelled to close their doors—so tight was their dependency on the state. In Florence, during the first part of the fifteenth century, the *Monte delle doti* was established, allowing families to purchase state credits that later could be collected in the form of a marriage dowry when their daughters came of age. Again, in the late fifteenth century, when the strain on the public fisc was particularly intense, there was a serious decline in the number of marriages, so close were the bonds between families and state finances. Milan has been described as the first modern state, and judging from its expanded bureaucracy, extensive control over morals and commerce, as well as its sponsorship of mercantilistic policies, this characterization appears most apt. Here again, citizen dependence upon the public world of bureaucracy and finance was deepened. Genoa's reliance on the management of the public debt was so marked that by the fifteenth century the history of the commune became the record of the activities of the directors of the Casa di S. Giorgio.

Renaissance political structures were characterized by the emergence of a public economy generated largely from war, population growth, and deficit financing. Opportunities for the citizen bureaucrat and capitalist increased as the public sector assumed a more unitary form. Despite differences in the social structures and conditions of political participation in the several Italian Renaissance states, a tighter nexus was forged between public and private worlds. Opportunities for civic participation at the bureaucratic and administrative levels multiplied despite differences in constitutional systems. Neither despots nor republican governments could afford the luxury of ineffectual management of resources and state finances at a time when pressures from the public debt were relentless.

In patrician Venice, public office, with the exception of the chancellory, was the preserve of the bourgeoisie. At Milan the despots regularly balanced the claims of the various orders to public preferment and honor; commoners could readily purchase high office and even patents of nobility. Again, at Venice, during the time of the League of Cambrai and another time in 1510, venality was practiced on a large scale. The bourgeoisie made payments to the state; the monies were employed to hire troops, and the offices were declared hereditary. Interestingly enough, these were fiscal posts and not magistracies as they were in contemporary France. Florence was the most open of the political societies; the problem in the late fourteenth and early fifteenth century was one of staffing a burgeoning administration. Provincials were particularly valuable to the polis, and they had profitable and honorable careers in the bureaucracy. It was not by happenstance that so many of the civic humanists, who extolled the authority of the state and found justification for private wealth largely in terms of public power, came from the provinces. It was members of the Florentine administrative cadre who came to view warfare as natural to the human condition and who sought to provide theoretical justification for the republic's claims to empire. Bruni's celebrated *History* championed not only Florentine *libertas* but also conquest of a Tuscan empire. Some like Machiavelli, who argued that states must either expand or die, did not have to turn to antiquity for examples. Warfare and arms were central to civic humanism, and three generations of Renaissance historians rightly stressed the shift from citizen militia to mercenary army as the hallmark of the grandeur and decay of their times.

It remains only to suggest a preliminary context in which this evidence on the fiscal experience of Italian cities may be placed. In the case of Florence, Venice, and Genoa, military and naval expenditures consistently outstripped state income.

It would appear, then, that Italian public finance and the conduct of war were among the primary socioeconomic factors that promoted many of the startling political changes we associate with Renaissance statal structures. The system of immunities, privileges, and liberties in medieval Italian communes could not endure this protracted budgetary pressure. Moreover, the pluralistic communal world was an economic luxury that state treasuries could not abide. What emerged finally was a more unitary state economy, with wealth flowing from the private into the public sector.

Perhaps it would not be overzealous to make a few suggestions as to the possible general import of some of the economic data presented in this study. The exceptional ease with which Italian city-states could borrow large quantities of capital from their economically precocious citizenry permitted the region of north Italy to play a forceful political role on the European scene over the fourteenth and fifteenth centuries. With arms, mercenaries, money, and diplomacy they were able to endure, survive, overcome, and buy off invaders such as Henry VII, Lewis the Bavarian, Charles of Bohemia, and the many companies of freebooters. The contest continued, and it was no bloodless charade, as Jacob Burckhardt would lead his readers to believe. Contrary to the mythic vision of Machiavelli, the Italian professionals waged harsh war. The victory of Visconti cavalry led by Facino Cane and other *condottieri* [mercenary captains] over German forces near Brescia in 1401, the victory of Carmagnola over Swiss troops at the battle of Arbedo were but early examples of the capacity of Italians to succeed against foreign adversaries. The *condottieri* rendered value to their employers, the city-states. Machiavelli's overly celebrated description of the battle of Anghiari, where he tells us that one man was killed because he was trampled after tumbling from his horse, is a travesty in the best comic mode. Casualties in Italian battles of the period were comparable to those suffered in other European theaters.

Expansion of public credit permitted these states to achieve extraordinary eminence in the fourteenth and fifteenth centuries. Any judgment concerning the inability of north Italy to retain this prominence in the sixteenth century must reckon with the peculiar economic circumstances that promoted the earlier flourishing of public credit. The ability of Spain and France to command greater resources to make warfare a statal activity and to provision large standing armies was manifested at a time when the credit structure of north Italy could least sustain a comparable effort. For two centuries the Italian cities had incurred budgetary deficits truly exceptional in pre-modern history. Their military role as powers in Europe had been aggrandized, but except for Venice, whose resources were substantial, none possessed revenues ample enough to underwrite continued large-scale military operations.

If I suggest that the credit system in the fourteenth and fifteenth centuries did not favor impulses toward unification, then the thread of my generalizations may be stretched to the limit. Yet, without a secular ruler of inordinate prestige the likely road to unification in north Italy would be dominance by a single state. Milan was, of course, the logical contender for the role. Commanding more resources than her neighbors, she was to be checked by the ability of a smaller state (Florence) to expand its credit and thereby to wage war on equal terms. Indeed, governmental borrowing is exceedingly relevant when attempting to explain the parity of military capacity obtaining among the several states. In the fifteenth century, this encouraged an equilibrium that forestalled the dominance of one over the others. Ironically, this was the era most favorable to unification, since with massive intervention by foreign powers after 1494 it was less likely. Once military and tax reforms were installed in France and a standing army established, the propitious days had passed. The unification of Spain also darkened the hour for sixteenth-century Italy.

Lastly, it remains to repeat a disclaimer: My search was for factors common to the experience of several Italian city-states. Had my interest been in making distinctions as to differences in social and institutional forms, I would have stressed such features as the incidence of social mobility, transformations in clan structures, alterations in private modes of economic organization, and so on. Instead, an attempt has been made to construct pragmatic definitions applicable to the experience of several Italian states and to place them within a general matrix.

Social Mobility in Florence

DAVID HERLIHY

The economic expansion from approximately the year 1000 brought to Europe a rebirth of urban life, particularly notable in such regions as northern Italy or Flanders. The economic crisis of the closing Middle Ages (fourteenth and fifteenth

"Three Patterns of Social Mobility in Medieval Society" by David Herlihy from *The Journal of Interdisciplinary History*, III (1974), pp. 641–647, with the permission of the editors of *The Journal of Interdisciplinary History* and the MIT Press, Cambridge, Massachusetts. © 1973 by The Massachusetts Institute of Technology and the editors of *The Journal of Interdisciplinary History*.

centuries) does not seem to have influenced the proportion of the population living in towns. In Tuscany, for example, about a quarter of the population continued to live in cities during the last two hundred years of the Middle-Ages.

How did the presence of a large urban sector affect patterns of replacement and mobility in medieval society? The rich data from the Florentine Catasto of 1427 can give us partial but suggestive answers. Table 1 shows the distribution of minors, young adults, and older adults according to residence in the city of Florence, in the small cities (Pisa, Pistoia, Arezzo, Prato, and Volterra), and the surrounding rural areas.

The most remarkable result which emerges from Table 1 is the success with which the population of the city of Florence was maintaining its members. There is apparent no replacement deficit, in the sense of a smaller portion of minor children in comparison with that of adults, in the Florentine urban population, and only a minuscule deficit can be observed in the small cities. To be sure, the countryside included many stricken areas, such as the high mountains, and the global replacement ratios cannot be considered representative of the prosperous rural areas. Still, cities have a long-standing reputation for being, in comparison with rural areas, poor producers of children; this is not apparent in the Florentine domains in 1427.

However, to gain a better grasp of the patterns of replacement present in Tuscan society, we must take a closer look at our data. Did welfare, for example, have a different impact upon replacement in the cities than in the rural areas? Table 2 illustrates the distribution of minors, young adults, and older adults, according to four wealth categories, exclusively for the households of the city of Florence.

If the results of Table 2, for the city of Florence, are compared with those for the entire population of the Florentine dominions, then it becomes evident that the

TABLE 1   Residence and Age Distributions in Tuscany, 1427

	Residence			
	Florence	Small Cities	Countryside	Total
Ages:				
0–17				
Persons	15671	9930	81692	107293
Percent	14.6	9.3	76.1	100.0
18–47				
Persons	13230	8793	69547	91570
Percent	14.5	9.6	75.9	100.0
48–99				
Persons	7083	6543	47013	60639
Percent	11.7	10.8	77.5	100.0
Totals	35984	25266	198252	259502
Percent	13.9	9.7	76.4	100.0
Ratio: Minor/young adult	1.18	1.13	1.17	1.17

Note: Only persons with stated age are included.

TABLE 2   Welfare and Age Distributions at Florence, 1427

	Assessment (Florins)				
	0	**1–100**	**101–400**	**Over 400**	**Total**
Ages:					
0–17					
Persons	1713	2564	2969	8425	15671
Percent	10.9	16.4	19.0	53.7	100.0
18–47					
Persons	1635	2566	2770	6259	13230
Percent	12.3	19.4	20.9	47.3	99.9
48–99					
Persons	1095	1581	1788	2619	7083
Percent	15.5	22.3	25.3	36.8	99.9
Total	4443	6711	7527	17303	35984
Ratio: Minor/young adult	1.05	1.00	1.07	1.34	1.18

Note: Only persons with stated age are included.

poorer households of the urban population were conspicuously less successful than poorer families generally in rearing children. With "minor–young adult" ratios of 1.07 and less for the three lowest categories of assessed wealth (Table 2), those segments of the urban population were clearly not maintaining their numbers through natural increase. The apparent success of the city in rearing children was exclusively the success of its richer families, those with more than 400 florins of assessed wealth.

The influence of residence upon replacement seems, therefore, to have been strongest among, and indeed limited to, the poor and the lower middle classes. Table 3 cross-tabulates residence and age distributions for Florence, the small cities, and the countryside, but only for those persons found in households assessed at 400 or fewer florins.

Table 3, which incidentally surveys about 87 per cent of the inhabitants of the Florentine dominions, confirms that urban residence interfered with reproduction and replacement, but only at the lower levels of the social scale. (The assessment level between 300 and 400 florins would, however, include many artisans and shop-keepers in the city, who would have to be described as "middle class" in their social position.) The patrician families, in spite of their urban residence, continued to support large numbers of children in their households. (The median age of the population resident in households with more than 400 florins of assessment was 18, and for those with 400 or fewer florins it was 26. The rich households, in other words, were prolific in the numbers of children they were supporting. As servants were not registered in the Catasto, the children were all the products of the natural reproduction of the rich families.) On the assumption that the size of the population and its residential distribution were constant over time, then about 10 percent of the middle and lower classes of the urban population would have to be recruited by means other than natural reproduction and replacement. The replacement deficit of these groups

TABLE 3   Residence and Age Distributions in Tuscany, 1427
(Households Assessed at 400 or Fewer Florins)

	Residence			
	Florence	Small Cities	Countryside	Total
Ages:				
0–17				
Persons	7246	7416	77492	92154
Percent	7.9	8.0	84.1	100.0
18–47				
Persons	6971	6785	66412	80168
Percent	8.7	8.5	82.8	100.0
48–99				
Persons	4474	5469	45156	55099
Percent	8.1	9.9	82.0	100.0
Total	18691	19670	189060	227421
Percent	8.2	8.7	83.1	100.0
Ratio: Minor/young adult	1.04	1.09	1.17	1.14

Note: Only persons with stated age are included.

could be overcome either by encouraging immigration from the more prolific countryside, or by absorbing persons from the higher and more prolific urban social strata.
The patrician families were, however, likely to resist this second alternative.

Two principal conclusions flow from our data. The threat of losing status, which
particularly pressed the lower but still propertied classes in the countryside, reached
into much higher social levels in the city. The urban patriciate had to find careers for
its plentiful children, or watch them sink to lower social positions. Many, but clearly
not all, of the patrician sons and daughters could enter upon ecclesiastical careers or
join religious orders. Many more had to make their way in a highly competitive
world. Contemporaries were quite aware of the pressures working upon the patrician
families. A historian of Florence, Goro Dati, who appears in the Catasto, offered
this striking account of the behavior of the Florentines in the face of demographic
pressures:

> . . . the city of Florence is placed by nature in a rugged and sterile location
> which cannot give a livelihood to the inhabitants, in spite of all their efforts.
> However, they have multiplied greatly because of the temperate air, which is
> very generative in that locale. For that reason, for some time back it has been
> necessary for the Florentines, because they have multiplied in number, to seek
> their livelihood through enterprises. Therefore, they have departed from their
> territory to search through other lands, provinces and countries, where one or
> another has seen an opportunity to profit for a time, to make a fortune, and to
> return to Florence. . . . For some time now it has seemed that they were born for
> this, so large is the number (in accordance with what the generative air pro-
> duces) of those who go through the world in their youth and make profit and

acquire experience, daring (*virtu*), good manners and treasure. All of them to-gether constitute a community of so large a number of valiant and wealthy men which has no equal in the world.

Goro Dati was clearly not describing the humbler inhabitants of Florence, few of whom wandered great distances through the world, few of whom made fortunes. He described the life style of the patricians. Still, in his estimation that demographic pressures demanded that the sons even of the privileged assume and maintain an entrepreneurial stance, he now confirms what data from the Catasto also reveal.

The second conclusion from our data is that the replacement deficit from the middle and low classes of urban society engendered a recruitment of new men, par-tially from other cities, but pre-eminently from the villages and small towns of the countryside. Numerous men of talent responded to the call, and they especially filled the ranks of artisans, notaries, and government servants—careers where skill counted more than capital. Many great literary figures of Renaissance Florence came from rural or small-town origins—Boccaccio, Coluccio Salutati, Leonardo Bruni, Poggio Bracciolini, Marsilio Ficino, Angelo Poliziano, and others. Many artists were of similar derivation—Giotto, Masaccio, Leonardo da Vinci, Desiderio da Set-tignano, and more. Few of these gifted immigrants penetrated in the fourteenth and fifteenth centuries into the ranks of the patriciate. One ominous result of this mass recruitment of talented men was that it introduced them into society at levels—the middle urban classes—where their own reproduction was hampered. Ultimately, massive immigration may have been destructive of talented lines and wasteful of human capital. But in the short run, these gifted newcomers were given an opportu-nity to display their skills, and Florentine culture was immeasurably richer for it.

These, then, are the principal conclusions which our considerations of social mobility in the Middle Ages suggest. Because of differences in rates of replacement across the social spectrum, families in favored positions produced more heirs and successors than those on the less advantaged levels of society. The dominant trend of social mobility in this traditional society was therefore consistently downward. Still, markedly different results could follow, which pre-eminently reflected the eco-nomic conditions of the period. In the stagnant epoch of the early Middle Ages, the privileged tended to lose position, while some few lucky or talented persons gained it. The overall result was a shuffling of status; in consequence, juridical differences, notably between slave and free, were progressively obliterated. The economic take-off from the year 1000 enabled those facing a threat of losing status to assume the function of entrepreneurs. They had powerful incentives, and enough property, to be both willing and able to gamble upon their talents. Conditions of urban life height-ened pressures on the privileged, requiring them under penalty of loss of status to keep their sons in an entrepreneurial stance. Also, in increasing the difficulties of reproduction for the city poor, urban conditions forced a continuous recruitment of new men from the countryside, to which the talented and the motivated were espe-cially prone to respond. The pressures upon the rich, the opportunities offered to the talented poor, combined to lend to the late medieval and Renaissance town its cre-ative vitality. In sum, medieval society, rural and urban, presents dynamic patterns of social movement, which historians are only today coming to appreciate and study.

The Urban Territory
of a Florentine Merchant, 1400

CHRISTIANE KLAPISCH-ZUBER

Parenti, amici, vicini [kinsmen, friends, neighbors]: these three words are constantly found closely associated in the thoughts of Tuscans of the fourteenth and fifteenth centuries. Around 1400 a man like Giovanni Morelli will often use them to express the many relatives and associates on which an individual could rely; to be betrayed or abandoned by them signified to him ruin and poverty. With Morelli as with his contemporaries, kinship, friendship, and neighborliness are thus almost always evaluated in terms of their social utility. The same viewpoint will serve here to analyze the composition, the range, and the role of this "personal group" centered on a given individual; in particular, I shall try to determine whether the blood relationship is the dominant constituent of these ties. If we can define the criteria for the recruitment or exclusion of these persons—persons who permitted the individual to play his social role to the full—it should clarify the functions ideally assigned to kinship and to alliance, as well as the functions that these two sorts of ties (or their substitutes) really fulfilled. Some aspects of this problem may be clarified by examining one particular case.

A Florentine merchant, Lapo di Giovanni Niccolini dei Sirigatti, kept a *Libro degli affari proprii di casa* [Book of Domestic Affairs] from 1379 to 1421. Like other Florentine *ricordanze* [diaries], it evokes the pell-mell of daily life, notes the people Lapo encountered, and describes their dealings. In its conception and organization this book is by no means especially original; to the contrary, it is marked by the dryness of its observations and information. Lapo states his intention to record the "events of the house . . . all notations and memoranda and every thing that pertains to me"—all that regards him, then, and those close to him, members of his "chasa" [house]. (Lapo's spelling) As with so many other examples of this private literature, Lapo's book recounts day by day the events that affected the number or the status of the members of the household and the acquisitions, transfers, or exchanges of goods that influenced its wealth. In this way he records a great number of relatives, both consanguineal and affinal, and others connected with him in all sorts of ways. A further interest of his book is that the author, like many of his contemporaries, indulges late in life in the preparation of an annotated genealogical introduction designed to prove the antiquity and reinforce the social status of his lineage.

The Niccolini were a family relatively new to Florence, distinguishing themselves, toward the beginning of the fourteenth century, from the older lineage of the Sirigatti from Passignano, certain members of which had already arrived in the city by that time. Lapo's immediate ancestors were soon honored with municipal offices.

His grandfather, also named Lapo, was a prominent silk merchant . . . and became a
. . . [prior] in 1334 and *gonfaloniere di justizia* [standard bearer of justice] in 1341—the
highest civic magistracy in Florence. The father of our Lapo, Giovanni, was also
active in city government, although he never became *gonfaloniere*. When Lapo
wrote his genealogical introduction (between 1417 and 1421), he had already held
that position himself at least three times and had played an important role in Florentine politics. Why, in these circumstances, should he still feel the need to consolidate the political and social position of the family by evoking the Guelf loyalties of
his ancestors and their admission into the circle of "good citizens"? Honors had been
concentrated in one branch of the Niccolini family, and the lineage as a whole seems
still relatively humble around 1400, whether we consider the number of its members
and the influence of the entire group or the few individuals among them, notably our
Lapo, who monopolized political command and material success. The interchangeable responsibilities and roles that assured the strength of the great Florentine families were less secure among the Niccolini. A man like Lapo, who had achieved personal success, sought to deflect onto all those he considered his kin the prestige that
his grandfather, his father, his older brother, and he himself had acquired. Naturally,
he expected personal benefits in exchange, but his first concern seems to have been
dynastic. *Parenti, amici,* and *vicini* were to play an important role in this attempt at
consolidation. When he conforms to the traditional strategies of his circle—and
when he occasionally abandons these strategies in order to hasten their effects—
Lapo ingenuously reveals the accepted functions of those contacts. . . .

The family was first and foremost those who shared a house, the domestic group
that lived in common. It is significant that in his introduction Lapo emphasizes the
geographical roots of his line. Two houses in Via del Palagio del Podestà in the
quartiere [quarter] of Santa Croce, extending east along the Arno, gave tangible expression to the "Florentinity" of the Niccolini from the time they came to the city.
Those who were admitted to or excluded from these houses provide some measure of
who Lapo considered his intimates. But the "family," for a Florentine of the merchant aristocracy, also included the members of that spiritual *casa* [house] that was
the lineage—deceased family members whose last resting place the descendants provided and whose memory was kept alive by masses celebrated in the family chapel—
and living members scattered in different households, who by misfortune and awareness of their lineage were sometimes forced to unite under one roof. Lapo's book
permits us to survey a great number of these persons, and even his reticences are in
themselves significant.

First of all, the book offers a series of images, spread over forty years or so, that
serve as points of reference to show how the composition and the size of the domestic
group varied with the age of the head of household and with the tribulations undergone by the population as a whole.

. . . [F]raternal solidarity did not last long under a common roof. In September of
1385, less than one year after their marriages, the two couples moved apart and divided the goods that the 1382 agreement had left undivided. Since he was older,
Lapo quite naturally became head of *casa* Niccolini and acquired the principal house
on Via del Palagio del Podestà, in which he was to live until his death in 1430.

From this moment onward, births were to swell the household that occupied this dwelling. Lapo was prolific: he had seven children by his first wife, Ermellina da Mezzola, in less than sixteen years of marriage; and six by the second, Caterina Melanesi, in the first twelve years of their union. Around 1402 his roof sheltered ten persons, not counting the domestics, and around 1410, fifteen. He was at the time over 50. At the peak of his responsibilities as head of household, ten unmarried children lived at home, along with his old mother, who was at least 80, and his sister Monna, widowed for the second time and whom he had taken in with her daughter Nanna. The plague of 1417 carried away his eldest son and his youngest daughter, but these losses were made up for by taking in his three granddaughters—the daughters of his daughter Lena and his son-in-law Ugo Altoviti, orphaned when both parents also died of the plague—and he was again responsible for at least twelve persons. According to his *catasto* declaration of 1427, the household was at that time reduced to eight persons and one slave woman; Giovanni, now the eldest son, had married and left the house. At this point Lapo was living only with his wife, five children, and a grandnephew.

This reduction of his household late in life is also a characteristic that can be observed statistically in the households of city dwellers of his circle. Lapo's father had been able to continue to keep his married eldest son with him, with his wife and children, because his household did not have too many mouths to feed; but Lapo, at the same age, had a *famiglia grandissima* [very large family]. On several occasions he made an effort to make more room by getting his grown sons established elsewhere. His efforts were in vain: Niccolaio, the eldest, "too big a spender of his own money and others," preferred to shelter "his appetites and desires" within the familial cocoon. The plague of 1417 swept him away, eliminating the problem of a congested house in radical fashion. Giovanni, the next son, seems to have been in no greater hurry to submit to the holy laws of matrimony, even when Lapo paved the way with gold in 1418. While still seeking out a wife for him, Lapo offered him more than his share of his inheritance if he would leave the house. His efforts were crowned with success before the *catasto* of 1427, since Giovanni is listed on its books on his own, with a wife at last.

In the final analysis, Lapo owed the fairly simple structure of his household toward the end of his life to the fertility of his wives and to the fact that ten of his thirteen children survived to adulthood. People of his rank in Florence were happy to marry one or two of their sons without having them leave the flock, as his own father had done. But the variations in the composition of Lapo's household reveal the flexibility of rules of residence in Florence, which bent to the practical conditions of cohabitation. If Lapo's progeny had suffered a higher mortality rate, he very probably would have been encouraged to keep his married son at home.

We can also see that his house was on several occasions saturated by an influx of close relatives who were widowed or in need owing to the plague. As head of *casa* Niccolini, Lapo opened his doors wide to these relatives in difficulty, as familial ethics required. The solidarity of these *congiunti stretti*—blood relatives—is never better expressed than in the momentary reunions brought about by a death or a low blow of fortune. To belong to the same *casa* also meant to be able to take refuge or to gather under the same roof when danger threatened.

We would have to exclude wives from among these intimates—the *prossimani* that Lapo finds himself taking in—as they are never completely considered full-fledged members of the lineage into which they entered by marriage. Nothing could better reflect their floating status than a comment of Lapo's at the time of his mother's death in 1416. He remarks that she "came to [her] husband in the year of our Lord 1349, the first day of October 1349, so that she remained in our house 67 years, 2 months, and 26 days." The meticulousness of the reckoning reveals rather than masks the son's real feelings: this woman, who came of the Bagnesi family, remained all of her long life a transitory visitor in the Niccolini house.

Aside from those to whom blood and the family name gave full rights of residence, the material house might shelter more distant blood relatives, forced by an extraordinary or temporary situation to turn to the head of family. Consciousness of the spiritual *casa* (what Lapo calls the "familglia") reaches beyond those living in the same dwelling, however, even considering temporary additions to the household. Of blood relatives of all degrees mentioned in his *Libro*—those with whom he has dealings or whom he notes as among his contemporaries—only one-half (twenty-three persons) at one time or another share Lapo's roof. The rest break down into two groups of quite unequal size.

The first of these groups, and the largest, is made up of the families descended from his elder brother, Niccolaio, who were hard hit by the plague of 1417, and those of his sister Fia, whose four children remain within the two lineages to which she was successively allied. The second group is made up of more distant cousins. Lapo calls them *nostri consorti* (our consorts) and here they bear the name of Sirigatti alone. If we go back to their common ancestor, Arrigo, surnamed Sirigatto, who lived during the first half of the thirteenth century, these cousins are no less than five canonical degrees removed from Lapo. Aside from them, Lapo notes in his brief preliminary genealogy that his great-uncle Biagio Niccolini must have had at least six children, over whom, however, he casts a modest veil: "[they] were all wicked men—one more than the other—and [they] destroyed what their father had earned." This "wretched family" had only one descendant "about in the world" around 1420. The genealogy published by Passerini shows, furthermore, that Lapo passes over certain branches of the family in total silence, as well as certain individuals who bore the Niccolini name and lived not only during his lifetime but even in his neighborhood. Thus our author does not even mention a paternal great-uncle, Giovanni, and all his descendants, long settled in the *contado*. Men of war, businessmen who were unlucky or ran through their fortunes, men who tilled the earth—Lapo considers them marginal to society and better ignored.

When he cuts his ties with his cousins' descendants in this manner, Lapo greatly reduces the number of his useful blood relatives. His contemporaries—Giovanni Morelli, for example, and later Leon Battista Alberti—saw in immediate kin the persons whom it is natural, and thus logical, to trust in family or commercial affairs. Lapo thus has only a few "natural" contacts—collaterals or adult cousins who could come to his aid. In the family agreements noted in his *Libro*, few of the arbiters are recruited from among the Niccolini. In contrast, ser Niccolò Sirigatti, a notary and the oldest of the three *consorti*, is called on to play this role on two occasions: in 1380 to settle a matter between Lapo and his sister Monna, and in 1403 to draw up the accounts for the guardianship of Lapo's nephews. This "savio huomo" (wise man), as

Lapo calls him, enjoyed enormous prestige among the Niccolini and was certainly well informed of their affairs, since he acted as notary for Lapo's father from the mid-fourteenth century onward. A respected man (and of respectable age around 1400), he held important communal offices. His talents and his experience thus made him particularly well qualified to decide the affaires of his *consorti*. On the other hand, his nephew, also a notary, and his son seem never to have been called on to fulfill similar functions.

Lapo's book shows us what questions generally obstructed the solidarity and confidence normal among close kin. Paradoxically, the very means that their mutual confidence prompted relatives to employ in dealing with one another ended up working against them. Oral agreements that spared them the use of legal formulas and notarization were easily broken or reinterpreted, thus arousing the rancor of the other party. Lapo saves his bad humor and his scorn for those closest to him, in proportion to what he considers their betrayal: for his brother, who "per poco suo senno" (through his lack of good sense) failed to be grateful to Lapo for services rendered; for a female cousin who acts as if he, Lapo, were not going to keep his word; for his niece's husband, who was sticking his nose into his mother-in-law's affairs. . . .

All his life, Lapo fought a centrifugal tendency for dwellings constructed by his ancestors to be removed from the control of the head of the "house" of Niccolini. The changing fortunes of the second of the houses situated on the Via del Palagio are a good illustration of the need for geographical stability in order to maintain familial group identity. This house had fallen to the elder of the brothers, Niccolaio, in 1382. One of his sons, Giovanni, went bankrupt in 1409. To release him from prison, Lapo guaranteed a loan of 500 *fiorini* to satisfy his creditors, putting up the house as security. But when Giovanni died in 1417 without having been able to pay back his debts, Lapo found himself obligated, much against his will, to put the dowry of the deceased's widow before his own interests, and had to buy back for 350 *fiorini* a house that he already considered his own. Several years later, in writing the genealogical introduction to his book, he declares himself glad: "although in this way [the houses] were left to many institutions and to many persons and given by some people as a dowry, they have finally returned to us, and may it please God that it be so for long years to come. These words speak to a desire for geographical roots, expressed by the urban family as forcefully as by the rural family. . . .

Because the material and political bases of his family were as yet not solid, Lapo could afford even less than some others to ignore the need for support from a powerful circle of relatives. His *Libro* shows how, in the span of thirty years, the Niccolini acquired them.

For a Florentine of 1400, a *parente* [kinsman] designated above all a *congiunto di parentado*, an affine. The term included maternal kin as well, however, and sometimes also close blood relatives. We have a sample of what the term represented for Lapo in the arbiters he chose in 1416 to supervise the liquidation of a debt. The five names he put forth "come miei tutti parenti e amici fidati" (all as my relatives and trusted friends) were those of his son-in-law, the husband of his niece (his sister's daughter), an ally through his daughter, a first cousin (son of a maternal uncle), and one other person whose possible kinship with the Niccolini I have been unable to establish.

The matrimonial strategy that Giovanni Morelli recommended to his descendants when the possibility loomed that they might remain orphans and have to administer their own affairs is well known. In substance, Morelli advises them to acquire a substitute father, through friendship as long as they were too young to marry, or by alliance when that moment came. The geographical area in which friends and particularly affines should be recruited is the *gonfalone*, a subdivision of the *quartiere*, and, failing that, the *quartiere*. To look beyond the immediate neighborhood, a truly exceptional opportunity would have to present itself in the shape of "an excellent relative, able to give satisfaction in every way." Lapo's book enables us to verify whether the Niccolini observed this neighborhood endogamy and whether, when they did not, they acted from conscious matrimonial policy. . . .

The Niccolini's matrimonial strategy evidently depended on Lapo's personal achievement as the "strong man" of the lineage. Evidence of this can be seen by a comparison of the average sums given and received in dowry in the first period (until 1385) and in the second (1395–1410). While the dowries given by the Niccolini remain at the same level from the first to the second period (respectively 890 and 870 *fiorini* on the average), those they received increased notably, passing from 750 to 900 *fiorini* on the average. This rise probably reflects the rise in Lapo's own fortunes, for he now received more than he gave in matrimonial exchanges.

The strategy pursued by Lapo and those close to him becomes clearest if we look at its geographical dimensions. The alliances concluded plainly go beyond the borders of the *quartiere*; thus, if we remember Morelli's advice, they imply an abundance of exceptional opportunities offered to Lapo. Only one sister and the daughter of a sister were given in marriage (in 1385 and in 1410) to families in Santa Croce. But no Niccolini man took a wife within the *quartiere* during this period. On the other hand, there were many more exchanges with the families of Santa Maria Novella, in the west part of the city, since three Niccolini chose wives from that area and the family also gave three wives to it. The *quartiere* of Santo Spirito—across the Arno on the road to the family landholdings—and the *quartiere* of San Giovanni to the north gave two wives and took one each. The exchanges seem to be numerically equal with Santa Maria Novella, to show a profit with San Giovanni and Santo Spirito, and to show a debit with the home *quartiere* of Santa Croce. This balance suggests that the Niccolini were truly seeking out good matches outside their neighborhood and that they succeeded in making some major coups beyond its boundaries, to the detriment of local alliances. Alliance certainly appears to have contributed to their rise as it brought them closer, between 1400 and 1410, to the great commercial and banking families of the Ardinghelli, the Bischeri, Altoviti, the Rucellai, and the Albizzi. . . .

Blood relatives, as we have seen, are seldom seen as judges in the arbitration to which they are party. Affinal relatives, on the other hand, form the reserve troops from which Lapo calls up familial peacemakers: brothers-in-law first (his sisters' husbands or his wife's brother), then sons-in-law or his nieces' husbands, then relatives on the maternal side, and finally somewhat more distant affines. The frequent participation of his *parenti* [kin] shows that Lapo and his immediate family judged them knowledgeable enough concerning their family affairs to be able to take part, with the necessary discretion, in the resolution of thorny problems—as long as they were not directly involved. There are few of these family affairs, settled out of court—the appraisal of dowries, the division of estates, the settling of quarrels between a father and an independently established son, the repayment of non-interest loans conceded to friends, etc.—in which we do not see at least one of the arbiters drawn from this circle of in-laws. Their appearance was all the more welcome since a man of Lapo's age could not count on many of his close blood relatives. His paternal uncles were likely to be dead, like his father, whose contemporaries they were, while the maternal uncles, whose sister married young, were less distant from their nephew both in age and by their activity. In a society in which city men of this class married girls considerably younger than they, it is difficult to find a simple definition of the "generations" where affinal relatives are concerned. Thus, the husbands of sisters are contemporaries of the brother and can soon back him up in his affairs, while the wives' brothers, younger than the husband, will enter the picture later, and perhaps in a somewhat subordinate situation. A man of fifty, contemplating his approaching death, would do well to provide for paternal substitutes with sufficient life expectancy, choosing his wife's brothers rather than his own brothers or his sisters' husbands, who would be even older than he. Thus age gaps—one could almost say a generational gap—between spouses reinforced ties with the allied lineage from which the wife came, and also contributed to an early indifference toward the families into which the sisters had married.

The least we can say is that these situations of unequal age wove a subtle network of relations spaced out in time, in which one man benefited from the experience and authority of his maternal relations and of persons allied to him through his sisters before he could offer his protection to his own affines—his wife's brothers and his brothers' affines—and obtain their services and their advice. This spacing of ages helps us to understand how affines changed place so rapidly in family councils and why their participation in Niccolini affairs remained for the most part episodic. But the number and the diversity of these instances undeniably reveal Lapo's need to rely on a circle of relations much broader than the nucleus of blood relatives. . . .

In choosing his affines in other *quartiere*, Lapo created a sort of void between his blood relatives, crowded into their grouped houses, and *parenti* established farther away. This void was filled by the "allies of choice," the *amici* [friends] whose presence had the task of insuring the harmonious proximity of neighboring lineages.

In Florence, friendship or, as the Florentines of the fifteenth century said, *amore* [friendship] is not to be confused with kinship. *Parenti* are often closely connected with *amici*, however. . . . The arbiters Lapo retained on the occasion described in the text included one man who seemed to be neither a close relative nor an ally of Lapo, although his father, a banker, had been active a quarter-century earlier in the affairs of the Niccolini family. Still, this person does not permit us to say that Lapo established the same confusion between kin and "friends" that can be easily found in France of the same epoch. Who, then, were Lapo's friends?

Lapo presents an extremely small number of people as friends. Whereas he could rely on forty or so blood relatives and at least fifty affines, the number of his "friends" can be counted on the fingers on one hand. Excluding the five arbiters in 1416 who have been mentioned, those he declares as friends include, above all, a neighborhood notary, ser Antonio di ser Niccolaio di ser Pierozzo dall'Ancisa, and his entire family; Antonio di Bertone Mannelli, the beneficiary of a non-interest loan in 1383;

and an intermediary at the time of the sale of a parcel of land. Lapo's son Niccolaio had a bond of friendship with a certain Geppo di Bartolomeo. Ser Antonio dall'Ancisa, the notary Lapo turned to from 1407 on, also appears as his representative in delicate affairs, which is probably what earned him the title of "intimo amico." Lapo and he were tied by the godparental relationship, as were his son Niccolaio and his friend Geppo. The *amore* that Lapo claims to bear this ser Antonio and his family is expressed in the desire to render him services, and the occasions for doing so reveal something of the nature of friendship in the fifteenth century.

In 1416, soon after ser Antonio had helped Lapo to untangle a complicated affair, the notary, his brother, and his mother attempted to buy back their paternal house, which had been sold. Lapo guaranteed the 400 *fiorini* loan needed for this reacquisition, and he did so—"with no profit to myself, but for the love I bear that family." Thus *amore* permitted him to understand a friend's pressing need to regain possession of an ancestral house and made him rise above his appropriate and natural love of gain and the custom that dictated that a *servigio*, a courtesy, must always be repaid. The exchange of free favors seems to characterize relations between "friends," and—in a society in which every penny was counted—*amore* introduced a certain freedom of action. Behind this exchange, when it was disinterested, we can divine a certain desire to leave accounts perpetually open between friends, not to hold friends to an exact accounting in the repayment of loans.

For Lapo, however, friendship usually involved important social functions. Friends were a ready source of obliging intermediaries, lenders or guarantors of non-interest loans, sometimes arbiters in amicable settlements, and godfathers to the children. These varied functions enable us to enlarge somewhat the circle of Lapo's "friends" to include persons who are not specifically designated as such.

It is, first of all, in the give and take of daily business that these privileged relations of *amore* and confidence, which contemporaries naturally associated with kinship but which also characterized friendship, seem to be initiated. . . .

Friendship among the Niccolini tended toward kinship without ever—or hardly ever—reaching that point, except perhaps on the spiritual level. It appears as a geographically limited complement to marriage alliance, filling in gaps and for the most part exercising its role in situations where kinship did not operate. Friendship generally engaged individuals only. The godparent relationship, one of its best expressions, offered a tested means to reinforce the bonds between persons of the same geographical or business community without going so far as to ally their families. Thus "friends" were first of all privileged neighbors, encountered in the crush of the *bottega* or of the parish church, at the notary's down the street, or in the *loggia* of a neighboring house. These close encounters introduced a greater freedom in social relations. While blood relatives customarily ate together under the same roof and made this sharing into a right, and while affinally related families participated in the ritual feasting that sanctioned events important to their lineages, neighbors were invited to drop in for a glass of cool wine on a hot day or to stop for a snack outside the doorstep in simple gatherings that sealed neighborhood good feelings. When he drinks wine with the baker, Cisti, messer Geri Spina becomes his "friend." Thus Lapo must have drunk with the simple people among whom he chose certain of his *compari*. The goodwill of friends thus acquired or, more cynically, *comperati* (bought) (the expression is once again Morelli's) satisfied a sociability that could not find complete expression in the constraining setting of the family and the lineage, or in the more formal relations of affinity, while at the same time it provided a complementary and locally-based support network.

It is difficult to say whether Lapo is representative of people of his class in his systematic search for exogamous relationships and his utilization of *comparaggio* (the godparent relationship) on the very local level. An analysis of his book leads us to think that the small number of blood relatives available to be called on and the personal prestige he enjoyed early in life placed him in the somewhat exceptional position of needing to strengthen his prestige by allying himself out of the neighborhood and to compensate this exogamy by spiritual alliance in a more restricted area. His recourse to different forms of kinship shows that, at least around 1400, a successful man's opportunities for action were still largely founded on kinship—but there were also occasions on which matrimonial strategy and choice of *compari* might violate his contemporaries' principles of action.

DOCUMENTS

The Florentine Catasto of 1427, which for the first time assessed taxes based on income, Monte shares and credit (loans to the government), as well as real estate, personal property, and liquid wealth. This proved a major innovation in financing public budgets in the early Renaissance. Since deductions were allowed for members of each household— and every Florentine resident, both rich and poor, was required to submit a tax return— the Catasto also provides extensive demographic information. The first document provides several examples of Catasto *portate*, or returns, ranging from the very wealthy, down through the famous sculptor Lorenzo Ghiberti, to the ranks of a skilled laborer. The excerpts in the second document are comments on marriage, children, kinship, and other private family matters by the merchant Gregorio Dati in his *ricordanze*.

Tax Returns in Florence, 1427

TOMMASO DI FRANCESCO DAVIZZI AND HIS MOTHER

Tommaso di Francesco Davizzi and Monna Catelana his mother in the quarter of Santa Croce, *gonfalone* [district] of Leon Nero; they have a *prestanzone* [loan] rate of *f* 7.

To you, revered citizens, elected officials to do the Catasto of the property of every citizen of the city of Florence. I Tommaso di Francesco Davizzi report to you all moveable and immoveable goods, debtors and creditors of mine and of Monna Catelana my mother here in every detail and, following, all our obligations. First:

A half house, indivisible, where we presently live, situated in the *gonfalone* of Leon Nero in the parish of Sant'Iacopo tralle Fosse in Borgo Santa Croce. [Bounded]

"Florence's Catasto of 1427," trans. by Susannah Foster Baxendale, from *Readings in Medieval History*, ed. Patrick J. Geary, Broadview Press, 1989, pp. 805–811. Reprinted by permission of the publisher.

first, the said street; second, the heirs of Adovardo degli Alberti; third, Tommaso Davizzi and Nerozzo degli Alberti; fourth, Francesco d'Altobianco degli Alberti. Further, household furnishings for our use in the said house and in the summer house.

5 or 6 parts, indivisible, of a house situated in the said parish in the street called "of the Alberti's house." Bounded first, the street; second, the heirs of Adovardo degli Alberti; third, the abovenamed house of Monna Catelana and Monna Antonia d'Alberto degli Alberti; fourth, Francesco d'Altobianco degli Alberti. This [house] is rented by Tommaso Busini; he gives me ƒ20 yearly; I get, for my part, ƒ16 s13 d10 a year.

[He goes on to list 5/6 of a farm; 5/6 of a farm with one parcel of land; and a half farm]

I find myself in the partnership which I have with Tommaso and Simone Corsi, a base capital of   ƒ1500

We have not yet settled the accounts; we are overextended rather than settled; I will have to report to you what I have in the shop.

I find myself, next, bankrupt in the new company, current account   ƒ270

[He lists some small Monte credits]

Here next I will write all the debtors I find, those whom I reckon to be good for payment ultimately.

The heirs of Cipriano and Ser Luigi di Simone Guiduccini	ƒ60
Nastagio di Simone Guiduccini	ƒ35
Niccolò di Sanminiato de'Ricci	ƒ55
Antonio, priest, of Sant'Angelo	ƒ65
The Commune of Assissi for 10 *accatti*	ƒ28
Benedetto da Panzano	ƒ8s15
Pagolo Quaratesi	ƒ9s17
Rosso di Strozza	ƒ6s11
	ƒ267s20

Here next I will write all the credits to be recovered:

Cosimo and Lorenzo de'Medici and heirs	ƒ430
Monna Vaggia di Bindo Guasconi	ƒ150
Giovanni di Bartolo Morelli	ƒ500
Ilarione di Lipanno de'Bardi	ƒ42
Antonio di Salvestro and partners	ƒ20
Monna Antonia, wife of Piero Dini	ƒ50 +
The old company of Tommaso and Simone Corsi and with the remainder, I should have	ƒ450
	ƒ1542

Here below I will record the many debtors I find which are no-account, from whom I have not been able, in times past, to collect, nor do I expect to [ever]. These debtors are, that is:

Tommaso di Filippo di Michele   *f*4–1/2

Lorenzo and Giovanni di Scholai degli Pini; I paid for them to their syndic   *f*555

Santi Pisiro   *f*1

The heirs and estate of Bernardo degli Alberti, for the remainder of a finding I got
against them; and for money I paid to the *gonfalone* for them. They don't have
their property, so one must let it [the debt] ride.   *f* 765

Bartolo di Maschio   *f* 765

Giovanni Manini   *f*10

Monna Catelana is aged   44

Tommaso aged   26

Checca is a girl who Monna Catelana vowed to raise for the love of God since
she has neither daddy nor mama to raise her aged   4 or 6

[He is not given credit for Checca]

property   *f* 3361*s*4 *d*8
obligations   *f* 2042
remainder   *f*1319*s*4 *d*8

ALBERTO DI GIOVANNI DEGLI ALBERTI

Jesus

Before you, the wise and prudent officials of the Catasto, reported for me, Messer
Iberto di Giovanni degli Alberti, quarter of Santa Croce, *gonfalone* [left blank], parish of
San Iacopo tralle Fosse, who has a *prestanzione* rate of [left blank] that in this [my *portata*]
will mention to you of my little houses, my furniture and obligations. And first:

A farm situated in the Valdarno di Sopra . . . the farm is worked by Bartolomeo
di Iariotto and his brothers and they have rented it a long time. It yields 100 *staia* of
grain [a] year, sequestered by the official; and it isn't run with oxen nor [has it] *prestanza*.

Another farm without a house . . . For many years rented by Ghezo di Giunta da
Iarrano. It yields 100 *staia* of grain a year.

With [the following] obligations, first:

I Messer Alberto, aged   48

Mariotto di Duccio my blood cousin, aged   30

Luigi and Antonio di Niccolo di Luigi,
my second cousins, aged   45 and 35

[I am] omitting the other household members whom I know you won't accept.

I owe the Commune [blank], all that is posted in this last venture and even
perhaps some old *prestanze*.

The present document done in the name of Messer Alberto was written by the
hand of me, Valorino di Barna, at his behest and according to how he directed that
I set it out and record it by me myself. I know that the abovesaid matters are true, and
because I am still weak from a long illness, I can't come to depose [the *portata*], but
my son Lapozzo will come or Piero Cambini.

TOMMASA, WIFE OF BIVIGLIANO DEGLI ALBERTI

The property of Monna Tommasa, wife of Bivigliano degli Alberti, who [the
Alberti] were consigned [to exile] and daughter of Noffo Ridolfi. And taxed *iprestanze* in the quarter of Santa Croce in the *gonfalone* of Leon Nero.   *f*1*s*12*d*5

A "noble house" with a kitchen garden in the place called "in the woods" in the parish of San Piero a Ema.

Below I will write her debtors:

Piero di Nofri dell'Antella   ƒ33

Giovanni di [blank] who tends the vines [in the garden mentioned] holds a little farm which he rents from the commune. And because he works the farm and the said vineyard, I lent him ƒ40   [blank]

Below I will write her creditors:

Schiatta Ridolfi and Giovanni Giugni   ƒ20

I am here in his house [Schiatta's?] and I am about to take a rental [place]. Thus, use your discretion [as to how to tax me].

[In the official version, this portion is written: I am in the house of others and am about to take a house. Therefore take into account what is my [tax] responsibility.]

Monna Tommasa, aged	60
Bivigliano, her husband, aged	69
Francesco, her son, aged	42
Bertoldo, her son, aged	26
Monna Isabella, wife of Francesco her son, aged	24
Marco, son of the said Francesco, aged	6
Diamante, son of the said Francesco, aged	2-1/2
Bartolomea, daughter of the said Francesco, aged	3
Nera, daughter of the said Francesco, aged in months	18
Altobiancho, son of the said Francesco, aged in months	3
submitted 12 July 1427	

[She is given only her "mouth"]

property	ƒ 841
obligations	ƒ 220
remainder	ƒ 621

LORENZO GHIBERTI, SCULPTOR

A house located in the parish of S. Ambrogio
in Florence in the Via Borgo Allegri . . . with household furnishings for the use of myself and my
family. . . .   0
     A piece of land in the parish of S. Donato in Franzano. . . .   ƒ100–0–0
     In my shop are two pieces of bronze sculpture which
I have made for a baptismal font in Siena. . . . I estimate that they are worth 400 florins or thereabouts, of
which sum I have received 290 florins; so the balance is
110 florins.   ƒ110–0–0
     Also in my shop is a bronze casket which I made for

Cosimo de' Medici; I value it at approximately 200 florins, of which I have received 135 florins. The balance owed to me is 65 florins.

I have investments in the *Monte* of 714 florins.

ƒ65–0–0
ƒ714–0–0

I am still owed 10 florins by the Friars of S. Maria Novella for a the tomb of the General [of the Dominican Order, Lionardo Dati].

Obligations

Personal exemptions:

Lorenzo di Bartolo, aged 46	ƒ200–0–0
Marsilia, my wife, aged 26	ƒ200–0–0
Tommaso, my son, aged 10 or thereabouts	ƒ200–0–0
Vettorio, my son, aged 7 or thereabouts	ƒ200–0–0

I owe money to the following persons:

Antonio di Piero del Vaglente and company, goldsmiths	ƒ33–0–0
Nicola di Vieri de' Medici	ƒ10–0–0
Domenico di Tano, cutler	ƒ9–0–0
Niccolò Carducci and company, retail cloth merchants	ƒ7–0–0
Papi d'Andrea, cabinet-maker	ƒ16–0–0
Mariano da Gambassi, mason	ƒ7–0–0
Papero di Meo of Settignano (my apprentices Simone di Nanni of Fiesole in Cipriano di Bartolo of Pistoia the shop)	ƒ48–0–0
Antonio, called El Maestro, tailor	ƒ15–0–0
Domenico di Lippi, cutler	ƒ2–0–0
Alessandro Allesandri and company	ƒ4–0–0
Duccio Adimari and company, retail cloth merchants	ƒ8–0–0
Antonio di Giovanni, stationer	ƒ3–0–0
Isau d'Agnolo and company, bankers	ƒ50–0–0
Commissioners in charge of maintenance and rebuilding of the church of S. Croce	ƒ6–0–0
Lorenzo di Bruciane, kiln operator	ƒ3–0–0
Meo of S. Apollinare	ƒ45–0–0
Pippo, stocking maker	ƒ8–0–0
[Total of Lorenzo's taxable assets]	ƒ999–0–0
[Total obligations and exemptions]	ƒ1074–0–0

AGNOLO DI JACOPO, WEAVER

He and his mother own a house, in which they live, in the Via Chiara. . . .

	ƒ0
A loom which we operate, valued at	ƒ40–0–0
Giano di Masotto owes me	ƒ3–s5–0
Antonio di Fastello, parish of S. Stefano, owes me	ƒ25–0–0

Michele di Piero Serragli owes me	f21–0–0
Niccolò di Andrea del Benino owes me	f15–s8–0

Obligations

Personal exemptions:

Agnolo di Jacopo, aged 30	f200–0–0
Mea, his wife, aged 28	f200–0–0
Taddea, his mother, aged 72	f200–0–0
I owe Giano di Manetto	f3–s5–0
[Agnolo's taxable assets]	f104–s13–0
His obligations and exemptions]	f603–s5–0

A Merchant Comments
on Family Matters, 1420

On 31 March 1393, I was betrothed to her and on Easter Monday, 7 April, I gave her the ring. On 22 June, a Sunday, I became her husband in the name of God and good fortune. Her first cousins, Giovanni and Lionardo di Domenico Arrighi, promised that she should have a dowry of 900 gold florins and that, apart from the dowry, she should have the income on a farm in S. Fiore a Elsa, which had been left her as a legacy by her mother, Monna Veronica. It was not stated at the time how much this amounted to, but it was understood that she would receive the accounts. We arranged our match very simply indeed and with scarcely any discussion. God grant that nothing but good may come of it. On the 26th of that same June, I received a payment of 800 gold florins from the bank of Giacomino and Company. This was the dowry. I invested it in the shop of Buonaccorso Berardi and his partners, and it is recorded here, on page 2 among the profits. At the same time I received the trousseau which my wife's cousins valued at 106 florins, in the light of which they deducted six florins from another account, leaving me the equivalent of 100 gold florins. But from what I heard from her and what I saw myself, they had overestimated it by 30 florins or more. However, from politeness, I said nothing about this.

I have not declared this dowry nor insured it on account of their negligence and in order to put off paying the tax. They dare not urge me to do so since they are obligated towards me. Yet I must do so, and if by God's will something were to happen before I do, I want her to be as assured as can be of having her dowry, just as though it had been declared and insured. For the fault is not hers. It turns out that the income she is to receive comes from a farm in S. Fiore on the Elsa on the way to Pisa. It is a nice piece of property which apparently belonged to Pagolo Guglielmi.

"Merchant Memoirs" reprinted by permission of Waveland Press, Inc. from Gene Brucker, Editor, *Two Memoirs of Renaissance Florence: The Diaries of Buonaccorso Pitti and Gregorio Dati*, translated by Julia Martines, pp. 114–115, 126–128, 132. Copyright © 1967, reissued 1991 by Waveland Press, Prospect Heights, Illinois.

Giovanni and Lionardo bought it from Betta's mother, Monña Veronica, or rather bought a half-share in it for 500 gold florins and paid a tax on this sale. Later they sold back their share to Monna Veronica, paying another tax, for 575 florins. These transactions are recorded in the register of taxes on contracts in register 500, 40; 500, 41 and 500, 42. When Monna Veronica died in April 1391, she left the income from this farm to Betta and to her children after her.

On 26 September 1402, as Simone was in Florence for a while before leaving for Catalonia, and as the penalties for evading the tax on contracts were remitted by law for those who paid that day, I and Simone declared the dowry of 900 gold florins received from Leonardo and Domenico. The notary was Ser Giunta Franceschi and on the 30th of the same September, I paid 30 gold florins, being 3 1/3 per cent, to the account of the taxes on contracts.

Our Lord God was pleased to call to himself the blessed soul of Isabetta, known as Betta, on Monday, 2 October, between four and five o'clock in the afternoon. The next day, Tuesday, at three in the afternoon, she was buried in our grave at S. Spirito. May God receive her soul in His glory. Amen.

Glory, honor and praise be to Almighty God. Continuing from folio 5, I shall list the children which He shall in His grace bestow on me and my wife, Ginevra.

On Sunday morning at terce, 27 April of the same year, Ginevra gave birth to our first-born son. He was baptized at the hour of vespers on Monday the 28th in the church of S. Giovanni. We named him Manetto Domenico. His sponsors in God's love were Bartolo di Giovanni di Niccola, Giovanni di Michelozzo, a belt-maker, and Domenico di Deo, a goldsmith. God make him good.

At the third hour of Thursday, 19 March 1405, Ginevra gave birth to a female child of less than seven months. She had not realized she was pregnant, since for four months she had been ailing as though she were not, and in the end was unable to hold it. We baptized it at once in the church of S. Giovanni. The sponsors were Bartolo, Monna Buona, another lady, and the blind woman. Having thought at first that it was a boy, we named it Agnolo Giovanni. It died at dawn on Sunday morning, 22 March, and was buried before the sermon.

At terce on Tuesday morning, 8 June 1406, Ginevra had her third child, a fine full-term baby girl whom we had baptized on Friday morning, 9 June. We christened her Elisabetta Caterina and she will be called Lisabetta in memory of my dead wife, Betta. The sponsors were Fra Lorenzo, Bartolo, and the blind woman.

On 4 June 1407, a Saturday, Ginevra gave birth after a nine-month pregnancy to a little girl whom we had baptized on the evening of Tuesday the 7th. We named her Antonia Margherita and we shall call her Antonia. Her godfather was Nello di Ser Piero Nelli, a neighbor. God grant her good fortune.

At terce, Sunday, 31 July 1411, Ginevra gave birth to a very attractive baby boy whom we had baptized on 4 August. The sponsors were my colleagues among the standard-bearers of the Militia Companies with the exception of two: Giorgio and Bartolomeo Fioravanti. We called the child Niccolò. God bless him. God was pleased to call the child very shortly to himself. He died of dysentery on 22 October at terce. May he intercede with God for us.

At terce on Sunday, 1 October 1412, Ginevra had a son whom, from devotion to St. Jerome—since it was yesterday that her pains began—I called Girolamo

Domenico. The sponsors were Master Bartolomeo del Carmine, Cristofano di Francesco di Ser Giovanni, and Lappuccio di Villa, and his son Bettino. God grant him and us health and make him a good man.

God willed that the blessed soul of our daughter Betta should return to Him after a long illness. She passed away during the night between Tuesday and the first Wednesday of Lent at four in the morning, 21 February 1414. She was seven years and seven months, and I was sorely grieved at her death. God grant she pray for us.

On 1 May 1415, at the hour of terce on a Wednesday, God granted us a fine little boy, and I had him baptized at four on Saturday morning. Jacopo di Francesco di Tura and Aringhieri di Jacopo, the wool merchant, were his godfathers. May God grant that he be healthy, wise, and good. We named him after the two holy apostles, Jacopo and Filippo, on whose feast day he was born and we shall call him Filippo.

At eleven o'clock on Friday, 24 April 1416, Ginevra gave birth to a baby girl after a painful and almost fatal labor. The child was baptized immediately on S. Marco's Day, the 25th. We called her Ghita in memory of our mother. Monna Mea di Franchino was her godmother.

Manetto died in Pisa in January 1418. He had been very sick and was buried in S. Martino. Pippo died on 2 August 1419 in Val di Pesa in a place called Polonia. This is recorded in notebook B.

At two o'clock on the night following Monday 17 July, Lisa was born. She was baptized by Master Pagolo from Montepulciano, a preaching friar, on Wednesday at seven o'clock. God console us, amen. She later died.

Altogether Ginevra and I had eleven children: four boys and seven girls.

After that it was God's will to recall to himself the blessed soul of my wife Ginevra. She died in childbirth after lengthy suffering, which she bore with remarkable strength and patience. She was perfectly lucid at the time of her death when she received all the sacraments: confession, communion, extreme unction, and a papal indulgence granting absolution for all her sins, which she received from Master Lionardo, who had been granted it by the Pope. It comforted her greatly, and she returned her soul to her Creator on 7 September, the Eve of the Feast of Our Lady, at nones: the hour when Our Blessed Lord Jesus Christ expired on the cross and yielded up his spirit to our Heavenly Father. On Friday the 8th she was honorably buried and on the 9th, masses were said for her soul. Her body lies in our plot at S. Spirito and her soul has gone to eternal life. God bless her and grant us fortitude. Her loss has sorely tried me. May He help me to bring up the unruly family which is left to me in the best way for their souls and bodies.

God who shows his wisdom in all things permitted the plague to strike our house. The first to succumb was our manservant Paccino at the end of June 1420. Three days later it was the turn of our slave-girl Marta, after her on 1 July my daughter Sandra and on 5 July my daughter Antonia. We left that house after that and went to live opposite, but a few days later Veronica died. Again we moved, this time to Via Chiara where Bandecca and Pippa fell ill and departed this life on 1 August.

All of them bore the marks of the plague. It passed off after that and we returned to our own house. May God bless them all. Bandecca's will and her accounts appear on page . . . of my ledger A.

FURTHER READING

W. M. Bowsky, *The Finance of the Commune of Siena, 1287–1355* (1970)

Samuel K. Cohn, *The Laboring Classes in Renaissance Florence* (1980)

David Herlihy and Christiane Klapisch-Zuber, *Tuscans and Their Families: A Study of the Florentine Catasto of 1427* (1985)

Dale and F. W. Kent, *Neighbours and Neighbourhood in Renaissance Florence* (1982)

Richard Mackenney, *Tradesmen and Traders: The World of the Guilds in Venice and Europe* (1987)

A. Molho, *Florentine Public Finances in the Early Renaissance, 1400–1433* (1971)

Donald Queller, *The Venetian Patriciate: Myth vs Reality* (1986)

Dennis Romano, *Patricians and Popolani: The Social Foundations of the Venetian Renaissance State* (1987)

Ronald Weissman, *Ritual Brotherhood in Renaissance Florence* (1982)

PART III

Political Forms

Botticelli, *Portrait of a Young Man Holding a Medallion of Cosimo de'Medici.* (c. 1473) Portrait-painting was a new, secular art form developed in fifteenth-century Italy.

CHAPTER **5**

Renaissance Venice and Florence Emerge

The two most singular cities of the Italian Renaissance, Venice and Florence, received the essential elements of their constitutions in the later years of the thirteenth century. Economic power and class dominance helped to define those who could enjoy political rights, as merchants and traders seized the opportunity to make themselves the leaders of their states.

In the struggle for political rights in Florence, the new guild-dominated regimes composed of prosperous non-nobles challenged the older aristocratic commune for greater access to power. The prosperous non-nobles of the guilds passed a series of harsh laws directed against the sub-group of the Florentine aristocracy known as magnates. Usually enjoying knightly status and notorious for their violent feuding, the magnates were excluded from political power in Florence by the end of the thirteenth century. The magnates were supplanted by members of the greater guilds who were elected to serve in the priorate and higher councils of the government. Thus membership in the basic economic units of the city, the merchant and industrial guilds, became the basis for all future political participation in Florence.

In Venice membership in the sovereign assembly of the citizens, the Great Council, became ever better defined in the late thirteenth and early fourteenth centuries. Venetian merchants returning from trading posts and colonies in the Eastern Mediterranean (then called the Levant) were awarded the right to sit in the Council, as were some worthy commoners, after elaborate investigations proved their political reliability and citizen status. This movement back to Venice culminated in 1297 with the enlargement of the Great Council, the repository of sovereignty that was responsible for the election of officials, including the Doge himself. In the first half of the Trecento, membership in the Great Council became hereditary, identified with the nobility of Venice whose names and families were inscribed in the Golden Book. Thus the rulers of Venice were hardening themselves into a caste, which enjoyed its right to rule because of concern for the public interest and a political culture that preached and sometimes even practiced noble self-sacrifice for the greater good of the state.

ESSAYS

In the first essay John Najemy of Cornell University finds in Florence the gradual adoption of guild membership as the main criterion for holding political office. For him "corporatism" became the main criterion for political rights as a guild-dominated regime came to rule Florence in the early Renaissance. The second essay is drawn from a chapter on the "Growing Structure of the Commune" in Frederic Chapin Lane's magisterial survey of Venetian history. Lane (1900–1984), who spent his career at The Johns Hopkins University, where he became the dean of Venetian historical studies in the United States, draws on earlier archival and manuscript research to argue that the so-called closing of the Great Council was actually an enlargement of its membership. As Venetian merchants fled back to Venice with the fall of the Crusading States in the Levant, influential members of the patriciate jockeyed to gain a place in the city's assembly and offices. The result was the locking in of important men of the city to run the government.

Guild Republicanism in Trecento Florence

JOHN M. NAJEMY

The familiar image of republican Florence as a political community has been dominated by ideas and assumptions largely inherited from the civic humanists of the fifteenth century, and in particular from Leonardo Bruni. This view of Florentine politics rests on two central notions: first, on the idea of the sovereign, centralizing state, the embodiment of the *res publica* and the locus of all political life; and, second, on the conviction that the operative components of this civil community were individual citizens to whom an equal degree of liberty was guaranteed by the state and from whom the exercise of active responsibility was expected within the state. For Bruni's contemporaries, these notions clarified and simplified the moral dimension of political life by focusing loyalty and responsibility in the abstract idea of a state that existed above parties and factions and that derived its legitimacy from the express or implied consensus of its politically active citizens.

For modern historians—both the believers in and the debunkers of the ennobling myths of Florentine republicanism—the assumptions of the civic humanists have proved to be congenial territory. To the believers, they provide the comforting confirmation of the unity of theory and practice. To the skeptics, they furnish the foil against which the cynical realities of patronage and elitist politics clearly emerge. Both camps have assumed that the alternative frames of reference for understanding Florentine politics consist in either the success or the failure of Bruni's twin notions. According to this view, the significance of the Florentine political experience in the two and a half centuries of the republic lies either in the successful realization of the goals of centralized state sovereignty and the consensus politics of participatory individualism or in their failure and the consequent affirmation of private and factional

"Guild Republicanism in Trecento Florence" by John Najemy from *American Historical Review* 84 (1979), pp. 53–71. Reprinted by permission of the American Historical Association.

politics. Within the scope of these alternatives, historians of Florence have set out to measure the strength of the republic by gauging the extent to which the sovereign power of the state was or was not impaired by competing loyalties and allegiances and by assessing the size of the political class through a counting of officeholders or eligibles. Both investigations have yielded useful and important results, but their application to this conceptual framework assumes only one kind of republicanism and one kind of participatory politics. Yet for a century and a half before Bruni's generation another kind of republicanism, based on the corporate politics of the guild system, was both a real and a controversial alternative in the world of Florentine politics.

In Italy as in much of Europe, corporate and associative forms of organization proliferated during the thirteenth century: communes, guilds, parties, *consorterie* [clans], confraternities, companies, and universities—all of them classifiable under the generic term of *universitates* [associations]. The phenomenon was spontaneous, complex, and infinitely varied, yet it generally tended toward the realization of the basic features of medieval corporation law within the framework of what Walter Ullmann has called the "ascending theory" of government. Each corporation was in essence the product of collective self-government by a body of equals. Many were based on some social, professional, or voluntary principle of selective inclusion. The legal principles used by the canon lawyers to explain the nature of ecclesiastical corporations in the thirteenth century were also applicable to the experience of the many secular corporations of late medieval Italy. A corporation was inherently the free creation of its members, acting voluntarily and in concert. The powers exercised in the name of the corporation were held to reside in the community of the members. The membership of the corporation, or a council representing the same, delegated those powers to elected heads, who served for limited terms and with the specific mandate to preside over the corporation, or to represent it, within the limits of its written constitution, according to the will of the majority, and for the common good of the community. The corporations acquired a legal personality and began to perform functions of a semi-public nature. Many of them, especially the communes and some organizations of merchants, also gained the power to make and enforce their own laws. Self-regulation and limited but increasing legislative power and jurisdiction were the first steps toward the assumption by medieval corporations of an autonomous political existence. To this point the development was principally internal and common to a variety of different corporations and organized *societates* [guilds].

The guilds of the Italian communes shared in this general process of corporate growth. In most cities there was a large increase in the number of guilds and a rapid extension of their political functions. With the upsurge in population and vigorous social mobility during the second half of the thirteenth century, wave after wave of new social and professional groups began to organize themselves in societies, confraternities, and guilds. The political and institutional dimension of this social revolution, often referred to as the rise of the *popolo* [people], was firmly grounded in the principles of corporatism. Logically enough, the strongest and best organized of these societies discovered that their greatest potential for political advancement lay in the direction of corporate federation. Through the political and sometimes military union of a large number of guilds under a common banner, the corporate model of political organization was, in effect, extended from the level of the single corporation, consisting of individual members, to the corporate federation, consisting of individual guilds. The same notions of corporation theory that had been applied to the experience of individual guilds were now applied to what was in essence a giant corporation of many guilds. The federation was the voluntary creation of its constituent parts; power and legitimacy derived from the community of corporations and from the express consent of the elected representatives of each participating corporation. Notions of delegation, representation, and consent regulated the life of the federation as they did that of individual corporations. Each guild within the federation was considered an equal and free member of the corporate community, just as the status of each individual member of a corporation or guild was held to be one of equality and autonomy vis-à-vis the other members. . . . The creation of federations or unions of guilds, representing coalitions of new or newly prominent social classes, was achieved at different times during the course of the thirteenth century in a number of places including Padua, Bologna, Rome, Milan, and Florence. . . .

In Florence, the guilds did not content themselves with achieving the condition of an "estate" or "order" within the commune. They proceeded instead to a third stage in which the very sovereignty of the commune was absorbed by the corporate federation itself. The aim of the guild movement in Florence was to achieve the greatest possible degree of association between the commune and the corporate federation. To the extent that this was achieved, it became possible and, indeed, necessary to apply to the organization of Florentine communal government those same basic principles of corporation law that had been nourished on the level of single corporations and that had subsequently been elaborated within the framework of the guild federation. The affirmation of these corporate principles of political organization at the level of communal government produced what can be called "guild republicanism."

Guild republicanism first became a reality in Florence during the 1290s. The creation in 1282 of a new chief magistracy of communal government called the "Priors of the Guilds" was a preliminary step (the very name of the new office suggests the merging of the legal identities of the commune and the guild federation), but not until 1292 did the adherents of the guild movement succeed in implementing a specifically corporate approach to the election of the priorate. In the electoral debate of November 1292, which marks the real beginning of the popular government based on corporate principles, it was decided that the new Priors would be elected according to a system that called for independent nominations from each of twelve guilds and that allowed no more than one Prior from any guild in each term of office. Inherent in this apparently simple innovation in electoral procedure were two ideas of potentially revolutionary significance: first, that each of the guilds would participate, through its Consuls, autonomously and on an equal basis with the other guilds, in the electoral process; and, second, that, as far as possible, the guilds were to be evenly represented in the priorate. . . . The Ordinances of Justice of January 1293 gave formal constitutional expression to the vision, implied in the outcome of the November debate, of the Florentine commune as a sovereign federation of equal and autonomous guilds, and it did so in unmistakably corporate language. The opening lines of the first rubric, which established the legal framework for the union of the twenty-one guilds in their "good, pure and faithful society and company," echo the famous dictum of Roman law, *quod omnes tangit*, which was the basis of many attempts during the late Middle Ages to understand the nature of representative and corporate systems of government: "That is judged to be most perfect which consists of all its parts and which is approved by the consent of them all. . . ." The "parts" were, of course, the guilds themselves, and this opening clause forcefully asserted that the legitimacy of the corporate federation (which, according to these same Ordinances, was now entrusted with both the election and the defense of the central magistracy of communal government) had henceforth to derive from the consent of the equal partners of the corporate union. The decentralized sovereignty of the guild federations and the interposition of the corporations between citizens and commune effectively made the guilds the vehicles for the expression and interpretation of the popular will.

To appreciate fully the implications of this constitutional arrangement, it is useful to have some idea of the size of the guild community that was called upon to participate in the federation. Working from some precise matriculation figures and a few hopeful guesses, a reasonable estimate for the period around 1300 would be in the range of seven to eight thousand matriculated members of the twenty-one guilds, with perhaps fifty-five hundred to six thousand in the top twelve guilds. In a population of about one hundred thousand, the guild community thus included more than a third of the adult males of the city. What made the new arrangement revolutionary in terms of the social bases of politics was that these guilds represented the interests of specific professional and occupational groups. The corporate formula for attaining the consent upon which the legitimate exercise of the government's power was now based guaranteed an equal voice to each of the participating guilds and thereby institutionalized the representation of a wide range of social groups with varying economic and class interests.

This complex of ideas about the nature of politics in a commune ruled by a corporate federation did not die in Florence with the failure of that first guild government. It survived—fitfully, unevenly, and in an increasingly radical form—through most of the fourteenth century. The guilds, of course, remained, and so, in theory at least, did the corporate union of the twenty-one guilds. But, as a matter of policy, the oligarchic governments did not stress the close constitutional association of the commune and the corporate federation. These governments sought to disengage the electoral process from the corporate principles of the guild system and to base the legitimacy of government and the consent of the community on grounds other than those of the decentralized sovereignty of the guilds. Although these aims were definitively achieved by the end of the fourteenth century, guild republicanism did not die easily. On a number of occasions during the century, this alternative conception of the Florentine body politic reappeared in the political arena as the constitutional claims of the corporate system were reasserted. Two of these occasions are worth looking at in some detail.

One of the most striking instances of the revival of Florentine corporatism occurred in the crisis of the 1340s. The circumstances are well known: oligarchic government was severely compromised by military failures in 1341, by the disastrous appeal to a foreign tyrant in 1342–43, and by the impending collapse of several of the largest banking companies. In the fall of 1343, the proponents of guild government resurrected the ideas of 1293 with a new and more radical formula: "the Florentine Republic," it was asserted in at least two official documents of these years, "is ruled and governed by the guilds and guildsmen of the same city, and especially by the Consuls of those guilds. . . ." In this formula the verbs *regitur* [rule] and *gubernatur* [govern] themselves connote sovereignty, and the *res publica,* so dear to the civic humanists of the fifteenth century, is here made to coexist with and, indeed, is "ruled and governed" by those most unclassical institutions, the guilds. There is, moreover, a remarkable parallel between this self-definition by the new popular regime and the description of it by Giovanni Villani, who excoriated this government for its dependence on "guildsmen, manual laborers and illiterates, since most of *the Consuls of the twenty-one guilds, by whom the commune was then being ruled, were lowly guildsmen. . . .*" Villani's echo of the formula for corporate sovereignty, coming as it does from a harsh critic of the regime, is a compelling confirmation of the popular government's own conception of its constitutional order.

How accurate were these claims? Perhaps the most dramatic example of the expansion of guild power and the impact of corporate politics in these years can be seen in the role that the guilds played in the settlement of major bankruptcies. One of the prime objectives of the guild regime that came to power in the fall of 1343 was to establish firm control over the institutions which would be called upon to deal with these complex litigations and especially to resolve the conflicting claims of foreign creditors and appeals for delay from hard-pressed bankers and merchants who hoped to shift the burden of the claims against them onto their own debtors. Chief among these institutions was the Mercanzia, which had been founded in the first decade of the fourteenth century to deal with a similar banking and credit crisis. The Mercanzia was an oligarchic institution dominated from its inception by the international bankers and merchants of the five major commercial guilds (Calimala, Cambio, Lana, Por Santa Maria, and Medici e Speziali). The Mercanzia's five governing councillors (one from each of the five guilds) had traditionally used their power to protect this commercial oligarchy and its vital economic interests. It was to the Mercanzia that the petitions of creditors came and from which the threatened bankers expected a sympathetic hearing. But the government of the guilds had other plans for the Mercanzia: in July 1344 an *ad hoc* Committee of Twelve was created and joined to the five councillors. Special legislation authorized the Twelve and the Five, sitting together as a single body, to administer the settlement of creditors' claims through the seizure, distribution, and sale of the goods and assets, including land, of the bankrupt merchants.

The popular government, in short, steered the banking crisis toward a solution that meant disaster for the great companies by allowing the claims of creditors to be satisfied directly through the liquidation of the enormous landholdings that served as the indispensable security in the high-risk deposit banking business. The joint committee of the Five and the Twelve became the ultimate arbiter in this process at a time when the greatest banking companies of Florence were collapsing. It was thus a matter of enormous importance that the all-powerful Twelve (who could, of course, out-vote the Five and were essentially in control of the situation) were elected by the

Consuls, not of the five guilds of the Mercanzia, but of all twenty-one guilds of the corporate federation.

Nor was this the only application of the principles of Florentine corporatism in the bankruptcy crisis. Early in 1346, as the fate of the powerful Bardi company was about to be decided, the Consuls of the bankers' guild held a council meeting to discuss what advice the guild should give to the government "concerning the assets of bankrupt merchants." The government very likely requested such advice from the bankers' guild and perhaps from other guilds as well. In any case, the result of this open debate in the guild's "representative assembly" was a recommendation that officials of the commune be empowered to seize the landholdings of bankrupt merchants and to prevent them from being used or inhabited until the claims of creditors had been satisfied according to stipulated agreements. The details and the outcome of this policy of the guild government must await further study, but the important point here is that the popular government, facing the greatest economic crisis in the history of the Florentine merchant oligarchy, calmly formulated a policy based on the direct consultation of at least some sectors of the guild community and carried out that policy through a committee that was elected and directed by the Consuls of all twenty-one guilds. It hardly needs to be added that the Bardi were indeed ruined.

From this specific instance of guild government, it becomes easy to understand why, in the minds of many prominent Florentines like Giovanni Villani, who agonized over the destruction of the Bardi, the whole idea of government by or through the guilds began to be very distasteful. Villani had no quarrel with the Ordinances of Justice as the foundation of a convenient and patriotic historical myth. But the actual implementation of that document's constitutional principles in the delicate circumstances of the 1340s was another matter altogether. It was madness, he believed, to expect that lowly guildsmen, from each and every one of the twenty-one guilds, could properly care for the affairs of the republic. The guild idea had been revived at a time when the economic survival of the Florentine oligarchy was in doubt, and what Villani accurately perceived was that the implementation of corporate principles at such a time was bringing Florence dangerously close to a condition of class conflict in which his own class was at a distinct constitutional disadvantage. For, in any arrangement in which the twenty-one guilds spoke with twenty-one equal voices on public issues, the oligarchy was bound to be hopelessly outnumbered. The dangers for the oligarchy inherent in the principles of 1293 began to be understood, and one of the first acts of the restored oligarchic regime of 1348 was to reduce the number of minor guilds from fourteen to seven through the consolidation of several corporations. This attempt to deprive the nonoligarchic guilds of their numerical advantage in the corporate federation lasted only two years. But the fears engendered by the revival of corporate principles of government in the 1340s were never allayed in the minds of Florentine merchants and bankers. The alienation of the Florentine upper classes from the ideals of their own corporate past was crucial to the ultimate failure of guild republicanism.

The increasing radicalization of the guild movement in that same decade of crisis also contributed to the alienation of the upper classes from the assumptions of corporate politics. As a result of the bankruptcy settlements and the early legislation on the funded public debt, government by the guilds was now associated with an openly anti-oligarchic stance on economic issues. But the movement was radicalized in another and perhaps more profound sense in these years. The notion of the guild community as a voluntary federation of equal and autonomous members tended, in the nature of things, to be an expansive ideal. Popular governments often needed support for their constitutional and political programs and were most likely to find it lower down in the social and professional hierarchy among those groups willing to trade such support for recognition of their own corporate and political aspirations. Although the oligarchy was beginning to recoil from the idea, the constituencies of the established guilds had, in fact, set an important example by embracing the idea of corporate organization as the most effective means for safeguarding their class interests.

This example was not lost on those artisan and working elements of Florentine society that did not have their own legally recognized guilds. . . . As early as the fall of 1342, the dyers of the textile industries petitioned Walter of Brienne for a guild of their own to be equal in standing to the established guilds. In 1345 the government dealt harshly with Ciuto Brandini, the leader of a workers' movement that aimed at the creation of a corporation—a union, we would say—in defense of their interests. He was executed by a government that wrapped itself in the principles of corporatism, for the crime of having attempted to establish a corporation for workers. For the upper ranks of the guild community, which felt threatened by such attempts, class interests and constitutional principles began to veer apart. The growing hostility of the established guilds toward the corporate aspirations of those without guilds seriously weakened the long-term prospects of guild republicanism. The guild movement began to discover that it was alienating both the upper and the lower ranks of Florentine society. Caught in an unstable position between the oligarchy, which despised the corporate system of government, and the lower classes, which desired nothing more than to become a part of it, the guild movement was increasingly isolated and on the defensive.

Amid these internal tensions and unresolved contradictions the theories of guild government were revived in the long social crisis of the 1370s and early 1380s. The reaffirmation of corporate principles began as early as 1370 in the wool guild. In opening the election of the guild notary in that year to the full membership of the guild's council, the proponents of reform resurrected a classic formula: "it is just and consonant with law," they asserted, "that this election be held by the guild and its members, since *that which touches all must be approved by all*." These reforms culminated in January 1374 with a provision that made it obligatory for the Consuls to hold regular meetings of the guild council at least twice in each consular term of four months. But it is the prologue of this provision that sums up in the most optimistic terms the basic assumptions of corporate politics underlying this renewal of the ideals of consent and representation in the guild:

> Whenever it happens, as a result of some compelling necessity, that the Consuls of this guild convoke and assemble good and expert members of the guild in the guildhall, and seek counsel and confer with them on matters of utility and benefit to the guild, with the assembled members of the guild continuously consulting and talking with each other in these assemblies and meetings, the result is that many issues are raised and brought to the attention of the Consuls of the

guild, which redound to the honor, utility, and convenience of the guild and its members.

Regular meetings and spontaneous consultation among the members, faith in the collective wisdom of the members to discern the common good, initiatives emerging from such exchanges to mold the policies of the leadership—such were the basic ideals of guild republicanism and of the ascending quality of corporate government. The implementation of these ideals within the community of the Florentine guilds during the decade of the 1370s enabled the guilds to become the focal points of initiative, opposition, and ultimately revolution in 1378.

The revival of corporate principles within individual guilds was paralleled in these years by their reaffirmation at the level of the corporate federation. Sometime in the summer or fall of 1378, an advisory committee of twelve citizens submitted to the Signoria a long list of recommendations, or "ricordi," dealing with the most difficult and sensitive issues facing the government. At the end, the authors reminded the Signoria that in turning these proposals into legislation they must not forget to consult with the *Capitudini*, or Consuls, of the guilds:

> Finally, it seems to us that, if it seems fitting to you, all of the aforementioned matters should be brought up and discussed with the Consuls of the guilds, and *their advice on these questions should be requested*; so that, if all or part of these proposals become law, it will have been done with the agreement and consent of the guild Consuls; *and then it can truly be said that it has been done with the consent of the whole city*.

Here again, in a most revealing formulation, is the fundamental assumption that the exercise of communal sovereignty was ultimately dependent upon the consent that could only be obtained from a consultation of the guild community. Such consent was, moreover, equivalent to the consent "of the whole city." The implication is clear that, without the approval of the Consuls of the individual guilds of the corporate federation, the enactment of the committee's proposals would be vulnerable to the charge that they did not enjoy the legitimizing support of the popular will.

In the circumstances of 1378, of course, the consent of the guild community came closer to the consent of the "whole city" than it did in more normal times. The revolution of that summer resulted in the expansion of the corporate federation to include three new guilds, two for the skilled artisans of the textile industries and one for the unskilled Ciompi. The reassertion of corporate principles of government both within the guilds and within the federation was accompanied by an extension of those principles to a wider range of social groups. From this perspective, the events of 1378 may reasonably be viewed as a "guild revolution" and as the last serious attempt by Florentines to construct a polity on corporate principles.

The government that emerged from this revolution prevailed for another three and a half years. How it viewed itself can be seen in a *missiva* [letter] of 1380, written by the chancellor, Coluccio Salutati, concerning the conspiracy of a band of exiled Guelfs against the regime. Among the crimes planned by these exiles, he wrote, were murder, torture, arson, and the destruction of "the most honorable corporations of the guilds of our city, *through which, by the grace of God, we are what we are*, and without which, should they ever be suppressed, the very name of the Florentines would without doubt be erased from the face of the earth." *Per quas sumus quod sumus:* through which we are what we are—half a generation later this would certainly have seemed an extravagant and almost incomprehensible claim, especially from a chancellor of the republic. But for the Salutati of 1380, working for a government that based its legitimacy on the corporate principles of guild republicanism, it was perhaps only natural to proclaim that the very identity of the Florentines and the reputation of the city were bound up with the survival and prosperity of their guilds. That a humanist chancellor of the republic could have uttered such sentiments may serve as testimony to the extraordinary power of the guild idea as public policy in those years.

Why, then, did the idea fail? Aspects of the answer have already been suggested. The guild republicanism of the Florentine corporate community was, to be sure, an expansive but never a universal ideal. Although the guild constitution had been built on the fundamental right of corporate association, the established guilds denied this same right to the lower orders of Florentine society. Guild republicanism might have succeeded as a socioconstitutional system if its basic principles had been allowed to extend far enough. Paradoxically, the success of the guild idea in 1378 assured its ultimate failure. The Florentine upper classes were profoundly frightened by the social radicalism of the guild revolution of 1378–82, and the impact of the experience cast a long shadow over the next generation. Bankers, manufacturers, and international merchants, realizing that the principles of the corporate state were an ever-recurring danger to their own security and hegemony, began to see the guilds in a different light; no longer were the guilds considered central to the Florentine political system or to its historical traditions. . . .

The first chronicler to articulate an open hostility, not merely toward individual actions of the guilds and their Consuls, but to the very assumptions and foundations of corporate politics, was Marchionne di Coppo Stefani, who wrote in the aftermath of 1378. The spectacle of the independent guild of dyers making life miserable for the woolen cloth manufacturers of the Arte della Lana was more than Stefani could tolerate, and he began to associate the whole idea of guild government, not altogether wrongly, with social and class revolution. This negative posture toward the aims of corporatism in his own day led Stefani, like Villani, to play down the significance of the guilds in the political history of Florence. They appear in his account of the distant 1260s, but not in that of the 1290s, and only sporadically in that of the 1340s. Stefani not only neglected guild history; he specifically rejected the underlying principles of any corporate polity. The "popolazzo" and the "mezzani" of Florence, he asserted, exist "con niun ordine"—that is, in the absence of any established institutional framework. Here, in view of the experience of 1378, the wish was certainly father to the thought, but Stefani's explanation for the presumed inability of the Florentine middle and lower classes to organize themselves politically is nonetheless revealing: "they are too numerous to be gathered together or to come to any firm decisions." By rejecting the possibility of meaningful consent obtained through the collective participation or representation of communities of equal members, Stefani, in effect, denied the validity of the corporate state. . . .

But in rejecting the ideals and assumptions of corporatism, Stefani began to put something in their place. He praised the patrician families of Florence, "the *grandi* of wisdom, gentility, and order," for the manner in which they made decisions among themselves: by honoring and "revering the wisest person of their line or, at the most, the wisest few." Because there are "fewer of them to be convened and consulted," it is easier for them to discuss their affairs and to bring into harmony *"la volontà degli appetiti."* Here was an alternative vision of the political process based on the related notions of decision-making authority concentrated in the hands of the experienced few and willing consensus of a wider community that "reveres" their wisdom and judgment. In essence, Stefani substituted the patrilineal family—with its built-in hierarchy and notions of descending, but benevolent, authority—for the fraternal corporation of equal members—in which authority ascended from the membership to its delegated leaders—as the preferred model for understanding and ordering the political world of the commune. The use of the family as a model for conceptualizing political relationships in a community dominated by aristocratic power and hierarchical values (which nonetheless felt the need to justify the existence of the ruling "one or few" with the notion that their authority served the common good and thereby rested on the implicit consent of its beneficiaries) was destined for a long and successful career in the second century of the Florentine republic. Again, it was Bruni in the *Life of Dante* who popularized the idea with Aristotelian notions of the family as the "original" and fundamental political unit, "from the multiplication of which is born the city." In this transformed world of political assumptions, it was no accident that the most powerful and revered Florentine of them all, Cosimo de' Medici, was dubbed *pater patriae* [father of his country]. . . .

The rejection of corporatism and the tentative formulation of a contrasting model of consensus politics, pioneered by Stefani in the 1380s, were assimilated and elaborated into a new vision of Florentine republicanism in the early fifteenth century by Leonardo Bruni. In his hands, the guilds were written out of Florentine history, expunged from the tradition they had helped to shape.

In the *Histories of the Florentine People,* he mentioned them only in the context of the 1378 revolution, as if to emphasize their subversive and socially disruptive tendencies. That the guilds had a significant or lasting impact on Florentine politics or society would be impossible to tell from the pages of Bruni's *Histories.* So Bruni grounded his new republicanism in the centralized sovereignty of the state and in the consensus of a broad, unified, and undifferentiated political class. And, in fact, the number of Florentines considered and accepted for high office was enormously expanded in these years: nominations for the *Signoria* in the much smaller urban population of 1433 were nearly twice what they had been in the mid-fourteenth century; the number of approved candidates, over two thousand in the scrutiny of 1433, was three times greater than in 1391. This explosion of the office-holding class provided the wide base for the consensus politics of the Albizzi years. Of course, only a fraction of this class enjoyed the authority of the decision-making inner circle, and the difference between a Buonaccorso Pitti, on the one hand, and a Goro Dati or a Giovanni di Paolo Morelli, on the other, is a measure of that distinction, even within the limits of the upper class.

Ultimately, consensus politics turned on a separation between participation and power. The legitimacy and stability of this system depended upon the consensus represented by the thousands whose names were introduced into the electoral process and who thereby gained, as Bruni so accurately observed in the funeral oration on Nanni Strozzi, the "hope" of ascending to the honors of high office. The political class of the guilds was co-opted to the purposes of the ruling group and wooed away from its traditional, but essentially always ambivalent, attachment to corporate politics. In the process the guilds were reduced to offices of the state, subordinated legally and constitutionally to a sovereignty in which they no longer had any part. If the corporate ideal can be said to have survived beyond the 1380s or the 1390s, it was largely in the form of legislative obstructionism on the part of disgruntled artisans or futile conspiracies hatched by still unresigned workers. In the eyes of the upper classes, however, it survived only as conspiracy and sedition perpetrated by malcontents, not as a political and constitutional program grounded in the respectability of law and custom. Cut off from their political function, the guilds no longer served as vehicles through which the aspirations and grievances of social groups could find adequate, rational, and effective expression. . . .

The Venetian Aristocracy Takes Control

FREDERIC C. LANE

Unity within the [Venetian] aristocracy was equally important in maintaining peace within the city. In communes that were shaken by uprisings of the middle or lower classes, fights between members of the ruling class gave the rioters their chance. Venice could restrain family rivalries more easily because it inherited from the Byzantine Empire a tradition of unified allegiance to a sovereign state. This unity was reinforced by many institutional arrangements . . . : the large number of offices and councils, the brief terms of office holders, and their ineligibility to succeed themselves. These practices made it possible to disperse powers and honors widely. No family was allowed more than one member on the Ducal Council, on any important nominating committee, or on any important administrative board. Whenever a nominee for office was being voted on, his relatives were required to withdraw.

Rivalries were reduced also by outlawing campaigns for office. Theoretically, the office sought the man, and anyone elected to office was required to serve. If he refused, he was subject to a heavy fine and made ineligible for other offices, unless excused by the Ducal Council, as he would be if he was legitimately absent from the city or about to leave on a trading voyage for which he had made contracts. Some offices were profitable and were desired on that account, so there were restrictions on the extent to which members of the nominating committees could name each other for such posts. Others, such as some of the ambassadorial missions, entailed heavy expense, and even rich men would have avoided them if possible—unless they had political ambition to match their wealth and desired the honor. But a man was not supposed to choose offices he wished to stand for; he was obligated to accept the posts for which he was picked. The requirement that a man must serve when selected

"The Venetian Aristocracy Takes Control" from Venice, A Maritime Republic by Frederic C. Lane, pp. 106–117. The Johns Hopkins University Press, Baltimore/London, 1973. Reprinted by permission of the publisher.

expressed the Commune's claim to unqualified allegiance and accustomed members of the ruling class to subordinating their individual interests to those of the state.

We regard political parties as an essential part of any government reflecting the will of the community, but George Washington and other founders of our nation shared the view which was that of the Venetians and indeed all earlier republicans, namely, that party rivalry was vicious, the destroyer of freedom. Like the Venetians, our Founding Fathers tried to avoid it by various devices, such as the Electoral College—unsuccessfully, as events proved.

Among the devices which they did not adopt but which the Venetians applied quite effectively, in addition to obligatory office-holding, was nomination by lot. It was quite common in the Italian city-states of the Later Middle Ages to place the names of qualified citizens in a bag or urn and to draw them out blindly. Such practices, used in various ways, introduced an element of chance and of rotation into the selection of officeholders. Drawing lots prevented a few men, those best known on account of achievements or family, from being the only ones to obtain the honor and power that went with office-holding. It also prevented election campaigns which would intensify rivalries, hatreds, and the organization of factions. Its disadvantage of course was that it gave out offices without distinguishing between men of more and less zeal and capacity.

The Venetians found a compromise which lessened the disadvantages while keeping the one main advantage, the moderation of factionalism. Selection of men for councils and magistracies at Venice consisted of two parts: nomination (which they called *electio*) and approval (which we would call election). At first the nominations seem to have all been made by the doge and his Council, but before the end of the thirteenth century, important nominations were made by committees whose members were chosen by lot. It was provided after 1272 that at least two nominating committees, each chosen by lot, be required to meet immediately and report a candidate or a slate of candidates to be voted on immediately, the same day if possible. The selection of the nominating committee by lot and the immediacy of the nominating and the voting were expressly designed to prevent candidates from campaigning for office by appeals that would inflame factions. On the other hand, the need of obtaining the approval of the Great Council was a protection against the choice of incompetents.

In spite of the laws, men did seek particular offices, sometimes for personal advantage, as is illustrated by one of the very few tales of practical personal politics in late thirteenth-century Venice. Nicolò Querini, a member of one of the richest and most powerful families, sought to be chosen governor of Negroponte, hoping to use the post to advance an inherited personal claim to a nearby Aegean island. After he had failed in spite of great efforts ("gran practica," a contemporary called it), his son Matteo Querini was named as one of the two nominees for that post chosen by the nominating committees. When this was reported to the doge at noon as he was dining, he exclaimed: "Then the son will be where the father could not get to be!" But the Great Council approved the other nominee instead of Matteo Querini.

The most sought-after office, that on which party rivalries were sure to focus if there were parties, was the dogeship. The closely contested election of 1229, when Giacomo Tiepolo and Marino Dandolo received equal votes in the nominating committee and Tiepolo obtained the honor by lot, showed the danger. While the dogeship gave many advantages in providing a strong executive, it had the disadvantage of focusing family ambitions and rivalries. To obfuscate these rivalries as much as possible and to remove their poison, the Venetians elaborated a series of nominations of nominating committees by nominating committees and by lot. In its completed form in 1268, the process was as follows:

> From the Great Council there was chosen by lot 30;
> the 30 were reduced by lot to 9;
> the 9 named 40;
> the 40 were reduced by lot to 12;
> the 12 named 25;
> the 25 were reduced by lot to 9;
> the 9 named 45;
> the 45 were reduced by lot to 11;
> the 11 named 41;
> **the 41 nominated the doge,
> for approval by the Assembly**

This seems like the *reductio ad absurdum* in indirect election of a chief executive, but it worked. The result was not absurd, its aim was achieved; the interjections of selection by lot blurred factional alignments.

In spite of all the efforts to moderate their influence, factions persisted. The denunciations and safeguards are in themselves evidence of the concern with family rivalries. In overcoming them the crowning measure was a reform in the composition of the Great Council.

Although the Great Council elected all magistrates and had the final word in settling issues, the methods of selecting its own members were rather casual, easily changed, and somewhat haphazard until nearly the end of the thirteenth century. A majority of its members were in the Great Council because of some office they held or had held, such as a judgeship or a post in the Forty or Senate. Each year a nominating committee chosen partially by lot or by a system of rotation, and frequently as small as four, named one hundred additional members for the following year, members who would not be distracted from attendance by having other functions. Since only one slate of nominees was prepared, nomination was practically equivalent to election. To give to just four men chosen almost at random the power to name each year members of the supreme legislative body would have been extremely unsettling if the committee had not been bound, as were the censors in ancient Rome in their naming of the Senate, by some well-established customs about who should be chosen. Indeed membership lists show that all sections of the city and a few score families were always represented.

But there was a margin of uncertainty which widened in the latter part of the century. The majority were nobles, but some commoners also were members of the Great Council. And among the nobles there might be some question as to who was really Venetian, a question which could arise especially in regard to men whose families had been living for some time in the East, and in regard to some of the Dalmatian counts. Two dangers created a desire for change. On the one hand, a member of the nominating committee might name someone he personally admired or to whom he was personally beholden but who did not belong to a family traditionally represented in the Great Council, being instead from a family of recent immigrants and recent wealth and without any distinguished record of public service. On the other hand, as the population multiplied, which it did markedly during the thirteenth century, the nominating committee might not find room among its hundred nominees for all those who had been members and felt that their family and their public services gave them a right to continue to belong.

Proposals were made in 1286 and 1296 for changing the procedures in the yearly selection of members for the Great Council and were voted down. They were designed to deal with the first of the above mentioned difficulties, the selection of undesirables. All of them would have made the men named by the nominating committees subject one by one to a vote of approval in whole or in part, by the Ducal Council, the Forty, or the Great Council, or some combination of these councils. The resolution of 1286, that about which there is the fullest record, would have excepted from such a vote those whose paternal ancestors had been a member of one of the governing Venetian councils. It was opposed by the doge then in office, Giovanni Dandolo, who favored continuing the existing system. He was a member of one of the most solidly entrenched old families, and the majority which voted down that proposal and two others consisted overwhelmingly of nobles from relatively old families. Probably they had less objection to the emphasis on ancestors than to the provisions which would in effect have reduced the importance of the electors chosen by lot and would have given any faction which gained control of the approving bodies a chance to eliminate opposing factions from the Great Council and thus from all participation in Venetian public life.

This objection did not apply to the reform which was adopted in 1297. It contained provisions dealing simultaneously with both dangers—the danger of undesirable additions and that of excluding men who were accustomed to being included. It took care of the second of these difficulties by removing all limitations on the size of the Council and providing that all those who were already members of the Great Council or had been members during the last four years were to be members thereafter if approved by as many as twelve votes in the Council of Forty. No wonder that this proposal, giving practical assurance that those already in would continue to be members, gained a sufficient number of the members' votes! At the same time, the new law provided that other persons might be proposed for membership by a nominating committee of three when this was proposed by the doge and by his Council. These other nominees were subject to approval also in the Council of Forty, where at first they also needed a mere twelve votes out of forty to be approved. Under this procedure and the doge's sponsorship, a number of commoners of old Venetian families were made permanent members of the Council. Also a dozen or so families from Beyond-the-Sea, refugees after the fall of Acre in 1291, were admitted to the Great Council. Its membership more than doubled, rising to over 1100.

This enlargement of the Great Council was put through by a relatively young man, Pietro Gradenigo, who succeeded Giovanni Dandolo as doge. The change he directed in the composition of the Great Council was probably designed deliberately to increase its authority and enable it to eclipse the General Assembly. At the death of Giovanni Dandolo, the populace was clamoring for the election of Giacomo Tiepolo, son of the former doge Lorenzo and himself also a victorious admiral. Since Giacomo's father and grandfather had both been doges, his election might seem to recognize an hereditary right and be a return to the dynastic politics of which Vitale II Michiel had been the last, ill-fated practitioner. The popular demand for Giacomo Tiepolo made the other nobles all the less willing to name him. They did not wish to return to the selection by unruly popular assemblies such as were vaguely recalled to have functioned before 1172; they meant to keep the choice of the doge in the hands of their elaborately selected nominating committee. In view of the Dandolo-Tiepolo rivalry, there might have been civil war in Venice in 1289 if Giacomo Tiepolo had tried to use his popularity to gain the dogeship. On the contrary, he withdrew from the city in order to avoid a conflict, yet another man who made a major contribution to the solidity of Venetian institutions by his readiness to step aside. After the usual interlude of twenty days and after going through the sequence of selection procedures established in 1268, the nominating committee of forty-one named Pietro Gradenigo, a member of one of the oldest established families who, at thirty-eight, had already held many offices and was serving as the Podestà of Capodistria. The choice was not popular, and Doge Gradenigo is said to have cherished a resentment against the common people who had shouted for the selection of Tiepolo. This is one explanation of his leadership in reforming the Great Council. Certainly one effect of the reforms was that the General Assembly became less important than ever.

Other effects were that the line between nobles and commoners was redrawn and the admission of new families into the governing class was made more difficult in the future. True, Gradenigo's reform had involved the acceptance, in about 1300, of many new families as noble. It is a mistake to consider it a move directed against commoners as a class and resented by them for that reason. To be sure, some commoners who thought they ought to have been made members of the Great Council and who were not among those admitted hated Gradenigo and conspired to kill him. For such a plot, a certain Marino Boccono was hanged between the two columns in 1300. On the other hand, there was no general movement of rebellion among commoners. The reform was put through in the middle of the Second Genoese War; it became effective just after the most costly of Venetian defeats, that in 1298 at Curzola, where the fleet was under the command of a Dandolo, a son of the former doge Giovanni. In contrast, the naval hero of the war, who even after the defeat made a daring raid into Genoa's own harbor, had the suggestively humble name of Domenico Schiavo. The giving of high naval commands to commoners in the last years of that war argues against any general antagonism between nobles and commoners. While some commoners had reasons to feel aggrieved, others had reasons to be pleased with the way the doge had widened the ruling class.

Liberality in accepting new men was short-lived. Within a few years, curbs were imposed on their admission to the Great Council. First they were required to have not merely twelve approving votes in the Council of Forty but a majority, then 25 approving votes, then 30. Additional restrictions were climaxed by a clear declaration in 1323 that, in order to be a member of the Great Council, a man must show that he had an ancestor who had held high posts in the Commune. By that date, membership in the Great Council had become permanent and hereditary and a prerequisite for election to any other council or magistracy.

Thereafter, the old line between nobles and commoners disappeared. Membership in the Great Council became the basis for that distinction. All members of the

Great Council were considered nobles, and nobility was viewed not as a matter of personal life style, but as hereditary.

In thus enlarging and giving hereditary status to Venice's ruling class, Gradenigo cushioned the impacts of factional rivalries. In cities such as Florence, in which such rivalries led to abrupt shifts of power from one faction to another, the usual instrument for effecting the shift was a general assembly of the populace, for that could be relatively easily packed or swung one way or the other by changes in mood or by intimidation. Venice's Great Council, which completely replaced the General Assembly as the supreme body, could not be so manipulated. Hereditary life membership in that Council gave assurance to all members of the ruling class that they would not suddenly find themselves excluded. They were "locked" into an assured place in Venice's political life; for this reason, the reform of 1297 may with good reason be called the "*Serrata*," as is customary. But the main moderating effect of the reform came simply from having so many different families, nearly two hundred, sharing power. The bitter animosity between some of them was submerged by the concern of other families with other issues. It became less difficult to find nobles who would act with impartiality.

In short, Gradenigo strengthened the hold of the aristocracy by enlarging its membership. A nearly contemporary lawyer and political thinker, Bartolus, who praised Venice as a successful aristocracy, regarded this as the essential. Venice, he said, was the kind of government classified as a Rule by the Few, but, he went on, "although they are few compared to the whole population of the city, they are many compared to those ruling in other cities, and because they are many, the people are not resentful of being governed by them. Also because they are many, they are not easily divided among themselves; moreover, many of them are men of moderate wealth, who are always a stabilizing force in a city."

In spite of all the measures devised to restrain factionalism, it led to one violent explosion under Doge Pietro Gradenigo. Like the crises which in most cities destroyed republican government and established tyranny, this crisis at Venice also came after a failure in foreign policy. It exploded in 1310, during the war with the pope over Ferrara. . . . [as part of] Venice's assertion of her lordship of the gulf. Doge Gradenigo was the leader in the aggressive policy; he sought to take advantage of the situation within Ferrara to bring it definitely under Venetian rule, in spite of the opposition of the city's overlord, the pope. Even when smitten by the papal excommunication and interdict, by the defeat of the Venetian army in Ferrara, and by the heavy material losses suffered abroad by Venetian merchants whose wares and persons were subject to seizure under the terms of the pope's interdict, the doge refused to yield.

Gradenigo's readiness to defy the pope had been opposed all along by some rival leaders, notably by a branch of the Querini family. Personal quarrels embittered the relations between them and the doge's leading supporters, the Giustiniani and the Morosini. A member of the Morosini family who was serving as a Lord of the Nightwatch tried at the Rialto to search a Querini to see if he was violating the law against concealed weapons. The zealous official was tripped up and humiliated, and the offending Querini fined, so both were resentful. Other Querini of the branch called the Querini of the Big House (de cà Mazor) wished revenge on a Dandolo who, when serving as State's Attorney, had been zealous in prosecuting them for an outrage committed against a Jew in Negroponte. Bitterest of all was Marco Querini, son of the Nicolò mentioned earlier, because he felt he had been inadequately supported when in command at Ferrara and unjustly blamed for the defeat. A conspiracy to kill the doge and seize power was initiated by Marco Querini who brought in his son-in-law, Bajamonte Tiepolo, to lead the revolt. Bajamonte was a son of the Giacomo Tiepolo who had stepped aside at the time of Gradenigo's election. In contrast to his father, Bajamonte was the kind of a man who justified the aristocracy's fear of giving too much prestige to any one family. When castellan at Modon, he had entertained in princely fashion and boasted of it, claiming it justified his appropriation of funds while in that office, an offense for which he was condemned to a heavy fine. Feeling that his honor was affronted, he withdrew from the city until called by Marco Querini to lead a revolt, which, if it had succeeded, might have made him the city's Signore. In other Italian cities, partisans of the pope in quarrels with the emperor were called Guelfs, and the Tiepolo-Querini faction were regarded as Venetian Guelfs since they were plotting against a government at war with the pope. But the conspiracy was motivated less by attachment to the pope and respect for his claims than by personal ambitions and hatreds.

The palaces of the Querini and Tiepolo were located across the bridge and behind the markets and shops of the Rialto. Their plan was to assemble their supporters there at night and next morning to cross the Grand Canal and proceed in two streams to the Piazza San Marco, one down the Mercerie to the eastern end of the Piazza, the other through the Calle dei Fabbri to its western end. Then they would unite in storming the ducal place and be joined therein by a contingent which was to be brought across the lagoons by Badoero Badoer, a noble who was related to the Guelfs of Padua and who had large possessions on the mainland. But the doge received a warning, for in seeking supporters the conspirators approached at least one commoner who had second thoughts and turned informer. Gradenigo then acted with the decisiveness which characterized all his career. That same night he called to the Ducal Palace his Councillors and the chiefs of the great families on whose support he could count, and who brought supporters; he alerted the Arsenal; and he instructed the Podestà of Chioggia to intercept Badoer's band. The conspirators failed to synchronize their attacks. Tiepolo's column was delayed while his supporters plundered the public treasury at the Rialto, and Badoer did not get started on time because of a violent thunderstorm. Querini's column arrived first at the Piazza San Marco. It was at once engaged, and Querini was killed in the fighting. Tiepolo's column found itself under attack in the narrow confines of the Mercerie before it ever arrived at the Piazza. At the peak of the tumult, a woman looking out from an upstairs window let fall a heavy pot or mortar which struck Tiepolo's standard bearer so that the flag fell to the ground. Lacking a rallying point, his men retreated. The doge was thus victorious: Marco Querini was dead; Badoero Badoer was captured in armed rebellion and immediately executed; Bajamonte Tiepolo and the other nobles who had retreated safely to their palaces accepted terms which required them to go into exile.

Because the Tiepolo family enjoyed such a large popularity through many generations, some historians of later centuries pictured Bajamonte Tiepolo as a champion of the common people against a jealous oligarchy and the revolt of 1310 as an expression of popular discontent with the way in which Doge Gradenigo had re-formed the Great Council. That is part of the Jacobin myth about Venice. Jacobins proposed to erect a monument to Bajamonte Tiepolo as a champion of democracy! In fact, he seems to have been simply a disgruntled noble who would have put his clique of nobles in power and might have proceeded to become the Signore of Ven-ice, creating the kind of one-man rule that was at about that time being created in Milan by the Visconti, in Padua by the Carrara, in Verona by the Scaligers, and so on. Certainly, he had considerable support among the common people, attracted by his family name, unsympathetic towards Gradenigo, and resentful of the suffering imposed by the war. Also, many of the parish priests participated in his conspiracy. But there was no general uprising; the "little people" were divided. Nor is there any sign of a link between the Querini-Tiepolo conspirators and the guilds; the only guild mentioned in connection with the revolt was that of the painters who com-pleted the rout of Querini's column by valiant fighting around their headquarters at San Luca. They were rewarded by the right to hoist their banner on a flag pole set up in the square where they had fought. The woman whose falling mortar had struck down Tiepolo's standard bearer received the reward she requested: permission to fly the banner of San Marco from her window on holidays, and assurance that the rent on her apartment would never be raised by the Procurators of San Marco, her land-lords. (The Procurators did raise it in 1436, when her great grandson was serving in the fleet, but he successfully petitioned in 1468 for restoration of the old rate.) The palaces of the Querini and Tiepolo were destroyed, and a marker set up instead, to assure that Bajamonte would go down in history as the vilest of traitors ("il pessissimo traditore").

The difficult problem faced by the government immediately was the punish-ment of those implicated, and especially of those who had been permitted to go into exile. In other Italian cities, factional fights led to the formation of large bands of exiles (*fuorusciti*) who continued sometimes for generations to plot a revolution which would permit their return. The Genoese Ghibellines were able just about this time to create a government-in-exile which waged war on its own account and con-trolled several of the Genoese colonies. The many exiled Florentines who hoped for an overthrow permitting them to return to their native city are well known, because one of them was Dante. It seemed in 1310 that Venice's rulers might similarly be threatened by fuorusciti plotting their return. The terms under which Bajamonte Tiepolo and his band were permitted to leave Venice limited the places where they might go, but the leaders at once violated these limits and began seeking support among the Guelfs in nearby Padua and Treviso and among friends and relatives in Dalmatia and the Balkans. To counter such moves and to suppress any new plots, a special commission of ten men was created in 1310. It proved so useful that this Council of Ten became a permanent and prominent part of the Venetian system of interlocking Councils.

The Ten had chairmen of their own, three *Capi* [Heads], each of whom held his post for just one month before it passed to a colleague. Membership in the council was for only one year, and no two members could be of the same family. At first, its business consisted in overseeing the sentences against the exiles. It alleviated the penalties for those who showed themselves submissive, but tracked the others from place to place and set a price on their heads. Ten to twenty years later, it was making payments to successful killers. Partly by leniency but mainly by efficiency they eliminated Venetian fuorusciti.

After the danger from Bajamonte Tiepolo and his followers was eliminated, the Council of Ten almost lapsed, but gradually it built a permanent place for itself in a dual role. Firstly, it was small enough so that the doge and his Council could take to it for action matters whose urgency and secrecy made seem undesirable consultation with any larger council. Secondly, it took the initiative in internal police. It was on the look-out to suppress not only any possibility of armed insurrection, but also any noble acting as if above the law, and any attempt to organize a faction or party even if merely by soliciting and swapping votes. They permitted no organized opposition. Indeed, any beginning of organized parties, even if initiated by those in power, would have been judged a corruption of public spirit.

The enlargement of the Great Council and the addition of the Council of Ten rounded out the aristocratic structure of governing bodies. They provided steadiness, fast action in emergencies, and involvement of the whole aristocracy in the deliberations leading to important decisions. Compared to the conditions in most cities, there was a general feeling of solidarity and loyalty among the Venetian nobility, and even in the relations between the ruling class and the rest of the people. But this cohesion was only relative and it was severely tested later in the fourteenth century.

DOCUMENTS

A series of reforms in Florence of the late thirteenth century culminated in enactments known as the Ordinances of Justice of 1295, whereby political participation was restricted to those enjoying guild membership. Through these ordinances, excerpted here first, the turbulent magnates were, nominally at least, excluded from any political rights and compelled to post large bonds to ensure their good behavior. Though written in 1523, Gasparo Contarini's famous analysis of the Venetian constitution—the second document—reflected the customs and outlook of an earlier age, before Venice acquired its mainland empire and developed a large bureaucracy to govern it. Thus, the account of the intricate alternation of election by lot and vote documents the reforms of the late thirteenth century that aimed at eliminating faction within the ruling patriciate of Venice. In the late Elizabethan version presented here, spelling and diction have been modernized.

| The Ordinances of Justice of Florence, 1295

CHAPTER 1. ON THE UNION, OATH, AND AGREEMENT OF THE GUILDS EXPRESSED IN THIS ORDINANCE

Since this most perfect ordinance is approved so that it consists of all its members and its jurisdiction is approved by all. Thus, it is ordained and provided that the Twelve Major Guilds are approved by the authority and power of the Podestà, the Defender and the Captain, the Priors of the Guilds and the *savi*, namely:

Judges and Notaries
Calimala Merchants
Bankers
Wool manufacturing
Merchants of Por Santa Maria
Physicians and Apothecaries
Furriers
Butchers
Shoemakers
Masons and carpenters
Blacksmiths
Retail Cloths Dealers (*Rigattieri*)

And also the other [nine] guilds of the City of Florence, which are the following:

Wine Retailers
Innkeepers
Retailers of Salt, Oil and Cheese
Tanners
Armorers and Swordmakers
Locksmiths and Iron Workers
Harness Makers and Shield Makers
Woodworkers
Bakers

These guilds, which have and are wont to have banners from the Commune of Florence for five years hence, and the masters of the same guilds, whose certain protector is the City and Commune of Florence, ought and are held to have appointed suitable and sufficient Sindici legitimately by the Rectors and Consuls of each of these same guilds. . . . And these same Sindici are required to appear with full and sufficient authority before the Lord Captain and Defender of the City of Florence. And the Sindici should swear, touching the Bible, just as the said Lord Captain

"The Ordinances of Justice of Florence, July 1295," from G. Salvemini, *Magnati e popolani a Firenze, 1280–1295* (Florence, 1899), Appendix, pp. 385–386, 389–390, 394–395. Translated by Benjamin G. Kohl.

would have the same Sindici make their oath. And also the said Sindici should promise, one and all, to ensure and oversee that the Guilds, of which they are and will be Sindici, and the members of the same Guilds and require and observe that all the Guilds shall form a good and pure and faithful Union and Company. And that one and all are of one mind and in agreement concerning the honor and defense and exaltation of peaceful and tranquil state of the Lord Podestà, the Lord Captain of the People and the Priors and the Standardbearer of Justice, and of the Guilds and Guildsmen of the City and District of Florence and of all the Florentine People. The said Sindici also swear and promise, one and all, to ensure and oversee that the Guilds, of which they are Sindici, and the members of these same Guilds, will obey the Podestà, the Captain, the Priors and the Standardbearer of Justice, in all and every matter which pertain and look to the honor of the aforesaid Lords and the exaltation, defense and good and peaceful state of the Commune, People and Guilds and Guildsmen of the said City of Florence. And also that the said Guilds and their standardbearers and members shall furnish and provide counsel, aid, assistance and favor to the Podestà, the Captain, the Priors and the Standard-bearer of Justice, whenever and as often as these officials may require and order and shall be ready to come, armed or unarmed, obeying and executing, freely, man-fully and suitably, the commands and orders of these officers, thus obeying com-pletely and fulfilling effectively all that is contained in the Ordinance of Justice here written. . . .

Chapter 3. On the Election and Office of the Lord Priors of the Guilds

Likewise wanting to provide usefully concerning the election and office of the Lord Priors of the Guilds on behalf of the masters of the Guilds and the People [of Flor-ence] and also for the republic, and considering the content of chapters established by the Lord Captain discussing the election of the priors, it is provided and ordained that the election of future priors of the Guilds shall be carried out in the following manner. Henceforth, the Lord Defender and Captain of the city of Florence, with the agreement and permission of the Priors of the Guilds in a place agreed to by the priors, one day before the expiration of the term of the current priors, or earlier if the Priors so desire, will call together the Heads of the twelve major guilds and the ap-pointed "good men" from the masters, and these shall elect the new Priors of the Guilds. In the presence of the current Priors the Captain shall propose to the same Heads and "good men" how and in what form should take place the election of the new priors of the guilds—who ought to be six in number, namely one from each *sestiere* [sixth of the city] and serve for a term of two months. . . . Thus, those six, who are elected according to the form and method provided, are and ought to be for the next two months the Priors of the guilds and masters of the Commune of Florence, with their term to begin within fifteenth day of that month. Thus, every year every two months at the aforesaid time the election of the Priors is to proceed in this way and form, which henceforth is to be observed. First, in the election of any future Prior, before anyone could be proposed or elected, it must be determined by lot in which *sestiere* the election should take place first, in which second, and so forth. And thereafter, the Heads and the "good men" must swear, touching Scripture, that they are conducting the election according to the legal and proper rules determined for the election of the Priors, as established by the masters of the Guilds and the people and Commune of Florence. And according to these rules they will permit to be nominated and elected to the office of Priors only those persons, whom they judge and consider most suitable and proper to exercise the office of the Priorate. And they will not nominate or elect or give assent to anyone who will offer or have offered on his behalf bribes, so that he would be elected to the Priorate. . . . Moreover, since they name and place in writing the names of those whom they want to be elected Priors, they must be certain that they place in nomination only the most prudent, suitable, and legal of the guild masters of the city of Florence, who have been continually plying their trade, or who have been inscribed in the matriculation book of one of the guilds of the city of Florence, provided that they are not knights. And the Heads and "good men" ought to declare and make public who is eligible for election in each Guild and which members of each Guild are actually plying their trade, or are inscribed in the Guild's matriculation book, for only these, as has been stated, can be nominated. And if it happens that the said electors nominate one or several persons who would represent two or more Guilds, the council must determine which guild the nominee is to represent and which Guilds are still in need of representation.

And so that the elections of the future Priors will observe due harmony and proper equity, the following rules should be observed. No one can in any way and manner be elected to the Priorate: from the Heads of the twelve Guilds or from the "good men" making the nominations; who has a member of his family or clan in the Priorate at the time of the election; who has been a member of the Priorate at any time during the last two years; or who does not continually ply his trade or who is not inscribed in the matriculation book of one of the Guilds of the city of Florence; or who is a knight. Nor can there ever be elected two or more Priors from one and the same Guild. And if there is an election of any Prior which contravenes these rules, it is null and void.

CHAPTER 6. ON THE PENALTIES TO BE IMPOSED AGAINST MAGNATES HARMING COMMONERS

It is provided and ordained that if any magnates whosoever of the City and District of Florence should, with malice aforethought, kill or have killed or wound or have wounded any commoner (*popolano*) of the City and District so that from such a wound death should ensue, then the Lord Podestà should condemn the magnate, who did or caused to have done such a crime, to death by beheading, if he should come into the custody of the Commune of Florence. And moreover the Podestà is held and ought to confiscate and have confiscated all the property of such criminals, and such property ought to come into the possession of the Commune of Florence and be sold by the Commune of Florence. If indeed such criminals are not in the custody of the Commune of Florence, still they should be condemned to the death penalty, so that if they come into the custody of the Commune of Florence in the future, they are beheaded so that they die. And nonetheless the sureties of such magnates and criminals, who stand surety for these same criminals with the Commune of Florence, should and ought to be compelled by the Lord Podestà of Florence to pay that amount of money which they guaranteed for the magnates and criminals. And so that the surety may be recompensed for the same amount of money that he has paid, the surety should have access to the property of the criminal himself and should make a diligent accounting of that property. Any property exceeding the amount compensated to the surety should come to the Commune of Florence. If indeed any Magnate should wound or make to wound, with malice aforethought, with any kind of weapon or sword any commoner of the City or District of Florence in the face so that blood spurts from the wound and the wound is disfiguring, or should wound or cause him to be wounded, with malice aforethought, in any member so that the member should be permanently disabled, if such a criminal should come into the custody of the Commune of Florence, the Podestà should condemn him to a fine of 2,000 lire. If the criminal does not pay the fine, within ten days from the day of the sentence, his right hand should be amputated so that it is severed from his arm. If indeed the criminal has not come into the custody of the Commune, the Podestà should still condemn him to a fine of 2,000 lire. And if at some future time, the criminal shall come into the custody of the Commune of Florence, and if he does not pay the fine within ten days, let his hand be amputated so that it is completely severed from the arm.

| Venice Elects a New Doge, 1523

To elect a new Doge, all the citizens who are above thirty years old assemble in the Great Council Hall, for no one under the age is, by ancient custom, admitted to the Great Council or its sessions. Then all the citizens are counted and for each present a ball is placed in an urn; thirty of the balls are gold, the rest silver. And the urn is placed before the tribunal of the session, where the Ducal Councillors stand, and from the urn a young boy draws out each ball. Each citizen is called and approaches the urn according to his order and rank in the assembly. But no one is allowed to put his hand into the urn (as happens in other elections); only the young boy is permitted to draw out a ball for each of them. Those who receive a silver ball immediately leave the room. But anyone lucky enough to get one of the gold balls has his name announced in a loud voice by the secretary and at once enters an inner waiting room, while his kin and relatives arise from his seats and gather in one part of the hall. The kindred are counted and each receives a silver ball drawn from the urn, and they all immediately leave the hall. When all thirty gold balls have been given out, these become the first committee of electors, and the rest of the Great Council is dismissed. Then the thirty again conduct another lottery before the Ducal Councillors and are reduced by lot to nine. These nine are made the new electors and retire, locked in a small room, so no servant and other person is allowed to speak

"Venice Elects A New Doge, 1523," from G. Contarini, *The Commonwealth and Government of Venice*, trans. L. Lewkenor (London, 1599: repr. New York: Da Capo, 1969), pp. 53–66, spelling and diction modernized.

with them until they have chosen forty new men to be electors. Each of these new electors must be chosen by six of the nine. Thus, if there are four votes against one of those proposed, he cannot be elected.

As soon as the nine have chosen forty men, they send word by their porter to the Ducal Councillors. Unless it is very late in the day, the Councillors call and assemble the Great Council. The names of the forty new electors are written down. Then the chief secretary ascends the tribunal and announces in a loud voice the name of each of the forty who has been elected. When a citizen hears his name announced, he leaves his seat and goes to the tribunal, and thence into the small inner room. If any of the forty chosen is not in the chamber, the Ducal Councillors and three heads of the Forty inquire of him and have him searched for throughout the city of Venice. As soon as he is found, he is immediately brought to the Ducal Place and into the chamber, and thence into the committee with his fellow members, without allowing him to speak with anyone on the way. By this means the forty come together unaware of who are the other members of the committee. When they are assembled in their small room, the Great Council is again dismissed. Then these forty enter the Great Council and are reduced by lot to twelve. The twenty-eight who are not chosen by lot are then dismissed. Then the twelve meet and chose twenty-five others, each by a majority of at least eight votes. When this is done, they send word by messenger to the Ducal Councillors. If there is still daylight left, the Councillors again assemble the Great Council. In the same way, each of the twenty-five is called unaware of his election until that moment. When the committee is complete, the Great Council is again dismissed. Then this new committee of twenty-five is reduced by lot to nine. Those chosen remain while the rest go away. Then the nine elect a new committee of forty-five, with each member being chosen by at least six votes. When the forty-five are chosen, the Great Council is again assembled and the Secretary announces the name of each member. These are in the usual manner reduced by lot to eleven, and the eleven choose forty-one of the best citizens in Venice. The forty-one then promptly withdraw to an inner room, and this committee has the authority to elect a new Doge. As is the ancient Venetian custom, no more than one member of any family can sit on the electoral committee.

Our ancestors, who were very wise and virtuous men, devised these strange and intricate procedures so that the entire patriciate have seem to have a hand in the selection of a new Doge. . . . By alternating election with choice by lot, the determination of whole was made with all personal pretensions and ambitions eliminated. . . . Moreover, the forty-one electors always go immediately into the Senate's Chamber, where they hear a divine service. And with their hands touching the altar, they swear to God and to the Republic that they will choose as Doge only someone they consider best qualified for the office, someone who will love his country and lead Venice with piety, prudence, and great care.

FURTHER READING

Marvin B. Becker, *Florence in Transition*, 2 vols. (1967–68)
Daniel Bornstein, trans., *Dino Compagni's Chronicle of Florence* (1986)

William Bowsky, *A Medieval Italian Commune, Siena Under the Nine, 1287–1355* (1981)

Gene Brucker, *Florentine Politics and Society, 1343–1378* (1962)

_____, *The Civic World of Early Renaissance Florence* (1977)

David Chambers, *The Imperial Age of Venice, 1380–1580* (1970)

George Dameron, "Revisiting the Italian Magnates: Church Property, Social Conflict, and Political Legitimization," *Viator* 23 (1992), 167–187

Robert Finlay, *Politics in Renaissance Venice* (1980)

J. R. Hale, ed., *Renaissance Venice* (1973)

George Holmes, *Florence, Rome and the Origins of the Renaissance* (1986)

J. K. Hyde, *Padua in the Age of Dante* (1966)

_____, *Society and Politics in Medieval Italy: The Evolution of the Civil Life* (1973)

Frederic C. Lane, "The Enlargement of the Great Council of Venice," in *Florilegium Historiale, Essays presented to Wallace K. Ferguson*, eds. J. G. Rowe et al. (1971), 236–274

_____, *Venice, A Maritime Republic* (1973)

Carol Lansing, *The Florentine Magnates: Lineage and Factions in a Medieval Commune* (1991)

John Larner, *Italy in the Age of Dante and Petrarch, 1216–1380* (1980)

John Najemy, *Corporatism and Consensus in Florentine Electoral Politics, 1280–1400* (1982)

Guido Ruggiero, "Modernization and the Mythic State in Early Renaissance Venice: The Serrata Revisited," *Viator* 10 (1979), 245–256

_____, *Violence in Early Renaissance Venice* (1980)

Ferdinand Schevill, *A History of Florence* (1936)

Daniel Waley, *The Italian City-Republics*, 3d ed. (1990)

Forms of Government in Renaissance Italy

I n the century following publication of Burckhardt's "State as a Work of Art," historians typically divided the governments of Renaissance Italy into communes and despots: the "good" republics of Florence and Venice as opposed to the "bad" signorial dynasties of the Visconti in Milan, the Carrara in Padua, the Este in Ferrara, and the Malatesta of Rimini. Recent research on the signorial regimes (the rule of single families over the cities of central and northern Italy) has shown that this dichotomy is far too simple. Within both republican and despotic regimes, there always lurked a small and controlling oligarchy.

By the middle of the fourteenth century, virtually every city north of the Appenines, except Venice, had come under the rule of a local dynasty. Some, such as the Della Scala in Verona and the Carrara in Padua, were exterminated in the course of the creation of the great territorial states of the fifteenth century; Milan under the Visconti and later the Sforza princes came to dominate nearly all of Lombardy, and Venice conquered northeast Italy. Thus larger territorial states, ruled by both lords and republics, came to characterize the political divisions of Italy in the High Renaissance.

The major change in Tuscany during this period was the emergence of the veiled despotism of the Medici dynasty in Florence, which came to power in a bloodless coup led by Cosimo de' Medici in 1434. In fact, the art of Medici government was retaining a semblance of republican institutions while concentrating power in the hands of a small clique of supporters bound to the ruling family by ties of kinship, friendship, clientage, and political interests (see Klapisch-Zuber essay, Chapter 4).

Essays

In the first essay, Philip Jones of Brasenose College, Oxford University, questions the traditional division of Renaissance governments into communes and despots. He shows that despotic regimes were not as efficient and powerful as they are often portrayed to be, nor were the republics so democratic and innocent of power politics. In both cases, rule by oligarchies blurred distinctions between the two forms of government. In the second selection, Dale Kent, an Australian historian trained at the University of London and now teaching at the University of California, Riverside Campus, offers an anatomy of the nascent Medici regime that reveals the complexity and fragility of the social and political networks on which government by oligarchy in Florence was based.

Communes and Despots in Late-Medieval Italy

P. J. JONES

It is a commonplace of political history that in the later Middle Ages the city states of north and central Italy were the scene of a conflict in the theory and practice of government between two contrasted systems: republican and despotic (or in contemporary terminology, government "à commune," "in libertà" etc., and government "a tiranno," *signoria* or *principato*). The conflict began about the mid-thirteenth century, and in most places, sooner or later, was settled in favour of despotism.

At the close of the Middle Ages there were few towns which were both independent and freely self-governing; fewer still which could look back on a history of unbroken liberty. Even by those most concerned to preserve it, the day of the small, independent, commune was admitted to be over. And certainly, in retrospect, for most communes the period of effective autonomy, between feudal and despotic rule, must have seemed brief enough: a few generations of turbulent self-rule or partial self-rule in the shadow of local feudatory or magnate. In an age when, even in Italy, most government was seigneurial or royal, what is remarkable is not the return to monarchy, but rather its interruption.

For Italian political theorists monarchy remained the common ideal of government, not only for civilian and canon lawyers or academic philosophers, but also for humanist writers, of whom a number in the fifteenth century composed conventional tracts on the rule of princes. Princely rule, however, was not the exclusive ideal. On the contrary, it was precisely in the later Middle Ages, when monarchy was everywhere gaining ground and political indifference increasing, that Italy was swept, in the words of one writer, by "a current of republicanism" in sentiment and doctrine. The inspiration of both ideals was no doubt often literary, and their expression rhetorical and abstract: in differing degrees monarchists and republicans alike fed upon classical tradition, as interpreted in the legal and philosophical learning of the Middle Ages or rediscovered by humanistic study; and both were concerned with ideas more than programmes of political action. But, for all the divorce existing between the active and contemplative life, the time and place of these writings, and the themes commonly developed, betray quite clearly also the influence of events. Such influence is evident in the new emphasis laid by Marsilius of Padua and others on the principle of popular sovereignty; it is evident even more in the theory, conse-

"Communes and Despots in Late-Medieval History" by P. J. Jones from *Transactions of the Royal Historical Society*, 5th ser., 15, 1965, pp. 71–95. Reprinted with permission of The Royal Historical Society.

crated by Bartolus, of the sovereign city state and of tyranny as a usurpation of sovereign civic authority; but most of all it is evident in a new preoccupation with the rival merits of despotic and communal government. Hints of this appear quite early in chronicle-writing and satire. Then, from the later-fourteenth century, as republican Florence and Venice became involved in growing conflict with the despotism of Milan, professional *literati* began increasingly to take sides: principles of "civic humanism" emerged, and the power of the pen began to be compared with the power of the sword. Florence, in particular, became a centre of republican diplomacy and propaganda, and, nurtured largely by war, a specifically Florentine folk-lore of republicanism developed, a belief, partly conventional, partly sincere, in the sturdy democratic virtues of the Florentine business class. The Venetians were less demonstrative, but their constitution, misinterpreted, became the republican ideal. Less vociferous also were the partisans of despotism, but they engaged in the literary war; and so, in scattered writings, polemical and academic, the elements were slowly prepared of a debate about government, which, purged of rhetoric and redefined in realistic terms, was brought to a conclusion by Machiavelli, Guicciardini and others in the sixteenth century. The arguments on both sides were predictable and simple. The republicans' theme was liberty, liberty in the double sense of elective government and independence of foreign domination. The monarchists' theme was order, peace and unity. Both claimed to represent the rule of law (not least in defence against the other), and both expressed devotion to cultural values.

. . . What remains indeterminate is the effect, within states, of differences of regime and the true measure of contrast between communes and *signorie*.

In no sense, it need hardly be said, was it a contrast of democracy and dictatorship. Despotic government was not totalitarian; communal government, though sometimes called *democratia*, knew nothing of manhood suffrage. By the statutes of most Italian towns, qualification for citizenship, and even more for office, was restricted almost exclusively to property-owning burgesses of local origin and prolonged residence. Rustics, the largest class, though combined in rural communes, were defined by law as natural inferiors and were almost nowhere granted political rights; nor were the humbler townsmen, the wage-workers and "plebei" (Giannotti); nor finally were the citizens of independent towns, incorporated by conquest in expanding territorial states. Though allowed some powers of self-government, they were not admitted to political representation. Representative parliaments, in Italy as elsewhere, were the creation not of urban but of feudal regimes. Under the rule of the richer republics, Venice and still more Florence, subordinate communities were degraded to a position of colonial dependence and ruthlessly exploited in the economic interest of the dominating town. "Florentina libertas" was for Florentines alone.

But if political rights, on republican principles, were narrowly distributed, narrower still, in republican practice, was the normal distribution of power. Despite all constitutional checks and balances, power in the Italian communes clung obstinately to wealth and migrated with movements of wealth, and through all revolutions of political and economic regime, oligarchy, in fact or law, was the predominant form of government. In the first century of the commune this represented, in contemporary language, government of those called *minores* or *pedites*, who constituted the *populus*, by the class of *maiores* or *milites*, a composite group of feudal gentry and merchants, who in Florence, for example, may have numbered some 100 families. In a few towns, notably Venice, this patrician regime survived unchallenged for as long as the commune lasted; but in most places, from about 1200, it began to break up. On the one hand the governing class fell apart into rival factions; on the other the *populus* or *popolo*, enriched by trade and enlarged by urban immigration, began to rebel against magnate domination, and in the course of the thirteenth century secured a share, and in places control, of the communal government. These fratricidal divisions, partly of social origin, more often political or personal, are the familiar theme of medieval Italian history. More difficult to establish is their effect on the tenure of power. A common result of party warfare was mass emigration and persecution; hundreds of citizens were excluded from political life. Against this, the emancipation of the *popolo* certainly admitted large numbers to nominal rights of government, though in places it also resulted in partial or total disfranchisement of the *grandi* (at Florence in 1295 about 150 families). But at no time did the *popolo* include the whole people, or even the whole commune. Rather was it a "party," the *pars populi*, for which the property qualification might be higher than that for the commune. The groups most powerfully represented were the richer trade guilds, especially the guilds of bankers, business men and industrialists—the *popolani grassi*. At Florence in the 1330's over 70 per cent of all major offices were held by members of the three wealthiest guilds: *Lana, Cambio,* and *Calimala.* Then, in 1343, by a popular revolution, the full corporation of 21 guilds gained access to governing power. The effect of this, it has been calculated, was to render eligible for high office some 3,500 men, from a total urban population of 75,000–80,000 souls. In the sequel the number increased slightly, but at no stage was more than one-tenth of the eligible class effectively qualified for office, about 750 persons at most, and of these an excessive proportion were still drawn from the upper guilds or from client lower guildsmen. Such was the type of government described by contemporaries as *democratia* and represented by Florentines as an egalitarian, broadly-based polity; and indeed, as long as it lasted, the Florentine constitution of the mid-Trecento, un-Athenian though it was, was probably as democratic as any regime, in the larger medieval communes. But it did not last, and few regimes were ever like it. . . .

The political creed of this urban patriciate is clearly stated, at the end of the period, by the aristocratic Guicciardini and other Florentine writers. According to them, government belonged properly to the wealthy and the wise. Democracy was a dangerous delusion, which identified liberty with licence. But if government by the many threatened government by the few, then it was better to have government by one. Not surprisingly similar views were entertained by despots. "It seems to me," wrote the duke of Milan, Filippo Maria Visconti, "that it's better to obey a prince or king, whatever his disposition, than submit to being governed by a rabble of artisans or by rulers of whom we cannot even tell who their fathers were." Such precise opinions are not often recorded; but, that they represent the traditional prejudices of the Italian upper class, there can be little doubt. And it is in these class prejudices, aggravated by the rise of *gente nuova* and enflamed by anti-magnate laws, that the source of Italian despotism must be principally sought. Not only did most despots derive from the upper class, as feudatories like the Visconti, or plutocrats like the Medici. From Ferrara in the early-thirteenth century, where the first stable *signoria* was formed, to Florence in the early-sixteenth century, where the last was successfully established, the interests which promoted or most readily accepted despotism are to be identified primarily among members of this class. If they could not be natural rulers, they would be natural counsellors. No doubt a single formula cannot cover all cases. There were some ephemeral *signorie* which were founded by noble demagogues, "class traitors" as they have been called; while others, more enduring, arose through popular magistracies or by acclamation in popular assemblies. But popular acclamation is no proof of popular initiative; rather were mass assemblies repudiated as a tyrannical device in towns where republican institutions were temporarily reinstalled. And this is only one sign that the most strenuous resistance to incipient *signorie* came from the middle-class *popolo*. However popular in form, in Italy unlike the ancient world, the origins of despotism lay in oligarchy rather than democracy. . . .

Beginning with the rudest elements they [the Italian towns] had managed to construct, between the eleventh and thirteenth centuries, an elaborate constitution, a strong administration, and the nucleus of a permanent bureaucracy. At the same time they had striven to restore the ancient unity of town and *territorium* [territory], and assert, in fact if not in doctrine, the principle of legal sovereignty within the boundaries of the *civitas*. Externally, they had freed themselves, in Tuscany and the North, from all but the titular supremacy of the Empire, and in the States of the Church, from all but the minimum claims of papal suzerainty. Internally, they had waged war on private jurisdiction, challenged feudal immunities and ties of fealty, and, by the class legislation of the *popolo*, reduced the legal and fiscal privileges of the nobility. They had also gone further than most medieval states in contesting the privileges of the Church, taxing the clergy, disputing and even suppressing the payment of tithe, and passing drastic mortmain laws to limit church property. In law, particularly, they had evolved, by 1300, from a confusion of Germanic custom, case-law, and Roman jurisprudence, an impressive body of statutes; and beside the justice of statute they had started to develop an equitable jurisdiction which disregarded *ius scriptum* in the name of *humanitas*. In the process of legislation they had gone far to substitute territorial for personal law, supersede private initiative in the execution of justice, and revive the notion of crime as an offence against the state. Progress was equally marked in the sphere of public finance. In indirect taxation, the communes exhibited great ingenuity in devising gabelles and customs duties; in direct taxation they replaced the primitive hearth-tax *(focaticum)* by a new form of property-tax *(libra)*, which was graduated according to wealth on the basis of cadastral surveys *(estimi, catasti)*; and in the management of revenue they began to adopt from business practice advanced techniques of accountancy. The uniformity of development, in all branches of government, was not the product of chance. Despite political disunity, there was a lively exchange of statutes and institutions, which prepared the way from an early date for regional systems of law and administration. Similarly in economic policy, protectionist though it was, towns worked to establish some regional uniformity, by standardizing measures and negotiating treaties for the equalization of coinage.

In discussing communes and *signorie*, however, and the transition from one to the other, it is customary to emphasize, in common with contemporary critics, not the creative achievement, but the practical deficiencies of the Italian city state. Too often, it is pointed out, the elaborate constitution, which the statutes describe, concealed a confusion of offices, courts, and councils, created but never co-ordinated by successive revolutions. Similarly the administration, however intricate, was still too much dependent on private service and hand-to-mouth expedients. For military defence, as late as the fifteenth century, there was no regular army, nor, except in Venice, any permanent fleet. For the routine conduct of government the judiciary and bureaucracy were often insufficient and persistently underpaid. Accordingly, under all regimes, justice was denounced as ineffective and corrupt, open to manipulation by the *optimates*. The influence of wealth was encouraged by the widespread survival in municipal law of the Germanic system of money penalties for crime and fixed tariffs of fines; the death penalty, even when imposed, was commonly commuted for the rich. In other ways also statutes countenanced inequality before the law. In many towns peasants were punished more severely than burgesses; under the class laws of the *popolo*, nobles paid more heavily than commoners; and by a large number of statutes landowners were granted generous powers of imprisonment and distraint over their tenants, and employers over their workmen. The fiscal system, as it finally evolved, was hardly less inequitable. In all communes the country was taxed more harshly than the town; in most, movable wealth escaped direct taxation; while at Florence and certain other large cities direct taxes were neglected, or for burgesses even suppressed, in favour of a system of redeemable government loans, secured against items of income. The effect of this, at the best, was to pervert state finance in the interest of the rich, who could lend, for themselves and others, on profitable terms; at the worst it involved nothing less than the practical transfer of public revenue to a narrow financial oligarchy. Such was the result, by the fifteenth century, at Florence, Bologna, and, most conspicuously, Genoa, where in 1405 the shareholders of the public debt took over the control of revenue, and eventually some political powers as well. Hence P. C. Decembrio's gibe that the Genoese could not distinguish public from private rights, and Machiavelli's description of Genoa as two states not one.

By later writers, familiar with the modern state, the Machiavellian analysis has been extended to the Italian cities generally: they were not sovereign communities, and their authority was not single but divided. However independent in practice, they continued to acknowledge in theory, and reluctantly in fact, the supremacy of imperial or, still more, papal overlordship; however much anti-clerical, they were forced to recognize the privileges of the clergy; and however much anti-feudal, they all tolerated in varying degrees the persistence of feudal franchise. As the greater communes expanded, their jurisdiction was regulated by individual compact with dependent towns and lords, who were often more nearly confederates (*accomandati*) than subjects. Territorially, therefore, the city state was never unified, but remained throughout an association of communities and powers. No doubt the same was true of other medieval regimes. Peculiar, rather, to the Italian towns, was the composite structure of the communal polity itself. It evolved as a combination of semiautonomous groups and institutions; and among these the majority of citizens only too readily divided their allegiance.

First and most fundamental was the family-group or clan. Though never, like the early *polis*, a coalition of clans, the Italian commune, in all its history, knew no more powerful influence than that defined by Leon Battista Alberti as "the strongest of all bonds, the bond of blood." In Italy, as elsewhere, loyalties and functions which, in the early Middle Ages, had been claimed by the family, were surrendered only reluctantly to the re-emergent state. The large family unit, especially among the nobility, was defended by rules of law, administration, and inheritance. Its members lived together, under a close common discipline, and their home was often literally a castle: a fortified keep or tower within the city walls, with drawbridges and all the apparatus of war, in later times including private artillery. The clan was expected to co-operate in all activities, but in none so much as defence. Accordingly one inveterate custom of communal society was the practice of vendetta. The vendetta rested as a duty of honour on all members of the family, and recourse to public justice was considered an indignity: in the Florence of the great merchant dynasties, Bardi and Frescobaldi, "justice," it is said, was regarded still "as a private prerogative rather than a public responsibility." Feuds were often bitterly ferocious, and by encouraging habits of personal violence, especially among *magnati*, they aggravated social conflict; yet law and public opinion were slow to condemn the feud, and most Italian statutes tried only to restrain it. Nor was it only by the right of vendetta that the family restricted the action of the state. Consolidated in large groups, with up to 100 men-at-arms, many clans increased their strength still further by artificial unions, *consorterie* or *alberghi*, and in the thirteenth century these family federations often came to form nothing less than communes on their own. They had elected officials, councils or parliaments, jurisdiction and police powers, and codes of private statute. Some of these codes survive, and perhaps no records come closer to the facts behind the theory of the city state. Most explicit are certain clan-statutes from thirteenth-century Lucca, which provide that in the event of political disturbance the members should meet and decide: "whether to serve the commune or to serve each one his friends." The issue is succinctly put: for the state, or against it. The dilemma, however, should not be pressed too far. In the Italian towns, service for the commune was often indistinguishable from service for friends. From the thirteenth to the sixteenth century no complaint recurs more insistently in Italian political writing, and no fact is more frankly confessed, than that men practised politics for office and sought office for family advantage—to gain access, as one Florentine put it, to the public "manger," the *mangiatoia* of lucrative appointments, government contracts and leases, tax-farms and the rest.

It was largely against the excesses of family power and influence that the popular movements in the commune were directed; and during periods of more democratic rule, there are certainly signs that law and government tended to become more impersonal and controls more strict on violence and vendetta. But it was not only with ties of kindred that the commune had to contend. Beyond the family were other associations—the trade-guild, the social class, and most of all, the party; and it is characteristic that, like the *consorterie*, the guilds, the parties, and even the social classes, all came to assume a corporate organization, modelled on that of the commune. They exacted oaths of fealty, they had laws and jurisdiction, assemblies and officials, and in certain cases they established military or para-military formations. Nominally these groups were all subject to the commune; practically they were rival corporations, which strove to absorb the commune and identify the state with a class or party. By the later-thirteenth century they had generally achieved their aim. In many towns the organization of the *popolo* had in effect replaced the commune, in most the commune had become officially Guelf or Ghibelline, and, however democratic the form of government, membership of a particular class, party, or guild, had almost everywhere become a qualification for citizenship or office.

In the great majority of city states the triumph of corporate interest, whether popular or partisan, marked the final phase of republican independence. In a few towns like Florence the commune survived, but only to continue the conflict with sectional loyalties, in which eventually party once again prevailed over the state. And from the partisan state emerged the despotic state. However different in detail the constitutional process of their rise, nearly all Italian despots were alike in one thing: they came to power first as leaders of faction.

By origin, therefore, Italian despotism was the product of restrictive tendencies, oligarchical and factious, in states imperfectly sovereign and unified. This focusses attention on the question, how far, by 1500, the despots managed to repudiate their origins and remove the imperfections of the city state?

Formally, it is well known, the city state long remained unmodified, in its laws and institutions, by the revolution of political system; and what changes occurred were often prepared or accompanied by similar developments under republican regimes. Not only did the name and corporate notion of the commune survive; the communal constitution also persisted, with its magistrates and councils, through which, with varying degrees of freedom, the subordinate community continued to elect officials, enact laws, and raise and administer taxes. One particular sign of this formal partnership between commune and despot was the indifference with which, in many towns, lords as powerful as the Visconti continued until quite late to draw fixed salaries like common magistrates. No less evident was the conservatism in law and administration. In law, the municipal statutes, supplemented by *ius commune*, remained the basis of justice; and although commonly revised and reinforced by seigneurial decree, they suffered little change of substance. There is evidence of an increasing claim by the state to responsibility for the punishment of crime, and a growing severity in penalties for offences; but this was common to all regimes, and in spite of it, under lords and communes alike, the habit of feud continued, and in places also the ancient right of kindred to a share of money fines. Similarly, in state finance and accountancy, contrary to some opinions, the despots were responsible for no great technical advance. The prevailing forms of taxation remained unchanged, and so did the trend of development in military and all other charges on the population. Indirect taxes were the richest source of revenue; of other burdens, armed service and *corvées* were levied only from the rural areas; townsmen, when not wholly exempt, commuted such services to money. For waging war, therefore, despots, like republics, relied mostly on mercenary companies, reinforced by rural levies, though from the later Trecento some *signori* were starting to retain a small corps of permanent, stipendiary troops (*provvisionati*, etc.).

With the notable exception of military organization, which they mistook for a political issue, contemporary publicists paid little attention to administrative detail. For republican writers the survival, in despotic states, of communal institutions was a mere "pasci-popolo," a sop to popular sentiment, which could not conceal the realities of power. Whatever the constitutional forms, under despotism all political matters, from rights of citizenship upwards, were controlled if not decided by the lord. If communal councils met, their work, numbers, and attendance, were all determined from above. The general councils especially retained little power, and in places their membership was drastically reduced; while the smaller councils, though still conceived as representing the commune, were in practice transformed into administrative organs of the despot. Similarly, all officials of importance were appointed by the *signori*, and often prolonged in office beyond the statutory term. Statutes, like government, now rested on the sanction of the despot: his decrees took precedence of the codes and common law, and in the administration of justice he claimed and freely exercised an exclusive right of dispensation. The same power was exercised in respect of taxation. Financial rights were commonly among the last to be surrendered by the commune; but whatever the conventions in use, final control of revenue belonged in practice to the lord, and it was only a matter of time before the imposition, collection, and administration of taxes passed in form as well as fact to the lord and his officials.

In most cases this redistribution of authority between commune and lord was a natural development from the plenitude of power . . . with which the great majority of despots had been invested at an early stage of their rise. To begin with, such power derived almost everywhere from an act of popular election, repeated with each new ruler; but, as time went on, an increasing number of *signori* contrived to reduce the ceremony of election to a mere matter of form. This they did, in part, by securing hereditary tenure of power by direct grant or by associating heirs with the government; but a no less favoured device was to seek from the nominal overlord, emperor or pope, the title of temporal vicar, or later of margrave or duke, which without any actual surrender of power conferred an independent warrant for the exercise of authority. As far as possible also, the *signori* tried to dissociate themselves from the partisan allegiance with which they began: after a suitable interval, exiled factions were restored; persons of all denominations were drawn into service; and the very names of parties were proscribed. And so both the partisan and electoral basis of despotic rule were slowly superseded: to the figure of the factious leader, with delegated power from the commune, succeeded the figure of the Prince, who delegated power to the commune, and was expected to exert an equal authority over all sectional interests.

For this ideal of princely rule evidence has been found, not only in the theory, but also in the practice of despotism. Thus, intermittently, it can be shown, *signori* sought to enforce greater equity in the administration of justice and the distribution of taxes between different classes and different parts of their dominions; even in the smaller *signorie* the tendency appears to release rural districts from dependence on the towns, and smaller towns from subjection to the larger. In defiance of local discontent despots drew their servants from all over their territory and all over Italy. The Visconti and the Sforza even made use of clerks, excluded from secular office under the commune. They also allowed the clergy access to urban statute, from which they had formerly been debarred as forenses [non-citizens]. Such levelling of status was simply part of a wider policy to assert untrammelled authority over all forms of privilege, corporate or territorial. Wherever they could, the despots acted, like Bernabò Visconti, as "pope, emperor and lord" in their domains. So independent lordships were forced into submission, and feudal grants from outside subjected to authorization. Unlicensed clan-associations were also forbidden, at least in the state of Milan; and everywhere the trade-guilds were reduced to subordination and deprived of political power. The privileges of the Church were more recalcitrant, and in the smaller despotisms, of the Papal States especially, remained virtually free from interference; but in the Milanese dominions they continued to be closely restricted: benefit of clergy was generally allowed, but clerical appointments were controlled by seigneurial licence, clerical wealth was regularly taxed, without papal or local consent, and clerical property was limited by statute. It was in the larger states, finally, and most conspicuously Milan, that the common subjection of different groups and territories to one overriding authority began to assume expression, from the mid-fourteenth century, in a certain community of law and administration. General decrees were published, statutes were extended from one town to another, and local courts were opened to citizens of other communes. In the Milanese dominion, under Giangaleazzo Visconti, regional courts were created for the eastern and western territories; and in a number of states, central appeal courts were introduced, the administration of finance slowly centralized, and in all branches of government the impersonal power of a specialized bureaucracy increasingly interposed below the personal power of the lord.

It is in tentative developments like these that the first beginnings have been seen in Italy of a new kind of state, the "Renaissance" state, unitary, absolute, and secular, built on new foundations and a new class structure, and serving as a model to the rest of western Europe. Yet, measured beside the achievements of western monarchy, they are perhaps not remarkable; and even in Italy itself, it is hard to draw sharp differences between work done by despots and that begun by communes and continued independently by contemporary republics. In much of their policy, indeed, republican Venice and Florence would seem to have been less tolerant than despots of autonomous authority, clerical, feudal, or urban. What rather calls for emphasis, in the constitutions of despotic states, is the obstinate survival of diversity and privilege. In the domain of law, local statutes continued to vary widely, even in the most ruthlessly centralized states, and in a number of critical cases, so powerful a lord as Giangaleazzo Visconti was unable to impose uniformity of law or reciprocity of rights between towns. Laws, courts, and jurisdictions were confused and contradictory, and in the costly muddle resulting, the poorer litigants particularly suffered. Uncontrolled custom persisted, and even the corpus of seigneurial decrees remained uncodified. The unification of despotic states was never more than rudimentary. It is sufficient to note the frequency with which lords shared their dominions on inheritance or divided them by appanage. Rarely did their native towns assume the status of capital cities; and where, as at Milan, a capital did develop, one effect was to give the citizens a privileged place in preferment which offended local feeling. In all the subject communes local feeling and privileges remained indomitably strong, and so, very often, did the old party loyalties and divisions. In a number of towns, indeed, as late as the fifteenth century, the authority of *signori* was still indissolubly tied to partisan support. And so it is not surprising that, at moments of political crisis, the most imposing of despotic states fell apart in the space of weeks or days, as happened twice in the duchy of Milan, in 1402 and 1447.

To the end of the Middle Ages, therefore, the unity of despotic states remained more personal than territorial, based rather on centralization of authority than equalization of rule. And this appears even more clearly in the policy of *signori* towards classes and corporations. They were more concerned to authorize than eradicate privilege. Thus the trade-guilds, though reduced to subordination, retained their courts and jurisdiction, and in Milan and certain other towns, the powers of the courts merchant were actually increased. Similarly the clergy, where subject, as in the duchy of Milan, to the claims of secular government, were in practice granted increasing fiscal immunities, obtaining by charter of privilege what, in canon law, was their right. Most *signori*, in fact, though ready enough to occupy ecclesiastical property by lease or feudal tenure, were lavish of gifts and favours to the Church. But the beneficiaries were mostly the greater monasteries and prelates, not the clerical order at large. The same distinction occurs in the secular policy of despots. Though commonly said to have shown favour to the peasantry, in reality they did little to moderate rural burdens, and nothing at all to reduce the judicial privileges of citizens and landlords. Nor were such measures to be expected. Themselves great landowners, it was from the class of . . . [nobles] that most despots came; it was by this class that they largely rose to power; and it was through this class, finally, that they principally governed and were recommended to govern. With the accession of *signori, the popolo*, with its class laws and organization, was almost everywhere suppressed. Nobles and patricians held the leading posts (or emoluments) of church and state, and they also dominated the municipal assemblies, which progressive reduction of membership made increasingly aristocratic in composition. As Machiavelli was among the first to observe, aristocracy and monarchy went together. Identifying republics with social equality and lordships with inequality, he remarked that a prince, without a nobility, could not administer government, and that where no nobility existed, it would have to be created. That the Italian despots, however, as is sometimes affirmed, created a new nobility and built their power on upstarts, is far from evident. New men, of course, there were. There always are. But this is a fact of biology as much as history. What history rather shows is the tenacious survival in Italy of old-established families, both feudal and patrician, within a narrow class of *optimates* (250 or so at Milan, a mere 30 to 40 at Camerino), which, through all political changes, seems not to have varied much in size nor greatly in composition. Of the *signori* it is truer to say that, from a combination of families, old as much as new, they established their own *clientela* of magnates and vassals, using the well-tried devices of intermarriage, privilege, and feudal benefaction. With the resurrection of monarchy, feudalism also revived. Beside the older feudal lordships, which although reduced to dependence were rarely reduced in power, a growing number of new fiefs were granted, often endowed with ampler rights than the old; and if this increased the number of places independent of the towns, it also reversed the unifying process by which the towns had once subdued them. No less common than feudal grants were grants of tax-immunity, the effect of which was to shift a growing burden to the lower classes. It is not in the despotic states, but in the republican state of Florence, that the most radical experiment is found in equitable taxation. Under the despots tax inequality flourished, to the profit of rich and noble, and so too did the privileges of magnates before the law. . . .

"In all ages," it has been said, "whatever the form and name of government, be it monarchy, republic, or democracy, an oligarchy lurks behind the facade." This observation, inspired by Roman Italy, may be extended also to medieval Italy. Between republics and despotisms the resemblances seem at least as great as the differences. In political organization both prolonged the past without radical alteration; and not the least striking resemblance between them is their unqualified failure, in common with other forms of European government, to support the fashionable concept of "Renaissance state" or "Renaissance monarchy." Rather do they confirm the view which sees, all over Europe, from the close of the early Middle Ages, a continuous development in the theory, practice and "reason" of the state, itself part of a larger movement, economic as well as political, which transgresses the traditional frontiers of "medieval," "Renaissance" and "modern" history. In Italy at any rate the "Renaissance state" is a fiction to be banished from the books. Here, down to the eighteenth century, government remained, in the words of one observer, "an invincible confusion" . . . and not till the eighteenth century, when despotism became "enlightened," was any attempt made to impose an egalitarian state. In this period, in all states, the same interests prevailed, power and office were effectively restricted to the same privileged order, and from the mass of people, under republics and despots alike, the same complaints monotonously arise: against unjust taxation, against corrupt and costly justice, against local and personal privilege. In the language of Tudor England, government for them was "nothing but a certain conspiracy of riche men procuring their own commodities under the name and title of the Common Wealth." Nor did political writers take a very different view: to Bartolus, to Machiavelli, to Francesco Vettori, all Italian governments were "tyrannies"—of party, of class, of despots. In a more sombre spirit, they shared the opinion later expressed by Dr. Samuel Johnson, when invited to comment on the theme of political liberty: "Sir, that is all visionary. I would not give half a guinea to live under one form of government rather than another."

The Rise of the Medici

DALE KENT

The Florentine constitution, the essential elements of which were established in 1282 and survived until the fall of the republic in 1533, seems designed to prevent the operation of private interest in government at the expense of the common good by the incorporation of two major features—a high degree of citizen participation on one hand, and an almost total lack of general representation on the other. Of course Florentine government was elitist, or oligarchic; in the fifteenth century, for example, participation was restricted to a group of some 2,000 to 3,000 upper-class men who, along with their wives and children, could not have represented more

"Introduction" from *The Rise of the Medici: Faction in Florence, 1426–1434* by Dale Kent, pp. 12–30, passim. Copyright © Oxford University Press 1978. Reprinted by permission of the publisher.

than a fifth of the total population of about 40,000 in this period. Within this group, however, the governing offices were widely distributed, and most of its members would have had in their lifetimes considerable experience of participation in active political life.

The constitution made elaborate provision for the constant circulation of offices, of which over 3,000 fell vacant in any given year. The system of government incorporated three main groups. At its head was an executive consisting of the *Signoria* and its two auxiliary colleges; they initiated legislation which was enacted by a complex of councils and administered by a multitude of special commissions. Membership of most of the more important of these bodies was determined by lot. A scrutiny of guild members occurred at regular intervals, and tickets bearing the names of all those eligible to hold offices were placed in bags from which the appropriate number was drawn when positions fell vacant. Terms of tenure were generally comparatively brief, especially in some of the more powerful magistracies, like the *Signoria*, whose members held office for only two months. The essential intention of this system was to make the elevation of individual citizens to positions of power brief and unpredictable, and thus to minimize the possibility of their using such positions to build up a base for the extension of personal power or the advancement of their private interest.

At the same time the constitution also provided against the expression of such private and particular interests as are represented through parties in a modern parliamentary democracy. Political scientists stress the peculiar position occupied by political parties even in modern democracies, pointing out that they are essentially "private associations to which the law does not give more rights and duties than to other private organizations, but they are usually seen to fulfil an essential representative function without which such governments could not function." In the Florentine system this representative element was almost entirely absent. Citizens were to act *ex officio* and when voting in the councils, solely "according to conscience." Soliciting of votes, or even prior agreement by interested persons on specific issues, was strictly forbidden. Thus parties in the modern sense, as channels for expression and representation of particular interests in government, had no legitimate place in the Florentine system; the only expression of private interest of which the law took account was the aggregate of individual opinions measured in the totals of "yes" and "no" votes on proposals put before the councils, and the numerous private petitions which testify to the need for such expression, and which opened a doorway to the soliciting of support.

For ultimately these provisions of a "jealous constitution" played an essential role in fostering the very factionalism which they were designed to prevent. A system of government in which such large numbers of private citizens participated could not function in practice without some channels for the representation and expression of the interests of some private individuals and groups, and the lack of continuity in government due to the rapid rotation of key magistracies merely accentuated the weakness of a state still very much in the process of consolidation. As in most societies in which the state is unwilling or unable adequately to defend the interests of the individual, extra-constitutional and unofficial bodies of a sublegal status tended to assume this function. By the beginning of the fifteenth century elements of the centralized state were gaining ground, and the influence and power of some independent corporate entities, like the *Parte Guelfa* and the guilds, had greatly declined. However, as Gene Brucker has observed, early Renaissance Florence was still very far from being an expression of Burckhardtian individualism; in this highly personalized and face-to-face environment a multitude of concrete loyalties competed with the abstraction of the commune in their claims on every citizen. Florentine society was a complex of interest groups from which very few men in the normal pursuit of their personal and civic concerns could stand entirely apart, and indeed most were entwined from birth to death in a network of associations and relationships from which their individual interests and concerns could not easily be disentangled.

At the logical centre of this network was the kin group, extended further by marriage and by relationships with neighbours, business partners, and other natural associates collectively subsumed under the designation *amici*. Friends, relatives, and neighbours constitute the great trinity of Florentine social bonds, which is constantly invoked throughout the period of the republic. Some rare souls, like Ser Lapo Mazzei in the second half of the fourteenth century, might succeed in avoiding such entanglements, but notably even he was moved to comment on the unusualness of his own situation: "There can be no one freer than I; I am bound neither to relatives nor to factions, nor is there anyone with whom I would wish to have such ties." Most would have concurred with Giovanni Rucellai, writing half a century later, when he advised his sons of the great happiness and benefit to be derived "from enjoying the favour and goodwill of kinsmen and relatives and neighbours and all the rest of the men of your district." The value of these associations lay in the support which these groups lent to the individual in all his activities. Giovanni Morelli's *Ricordi* of the early fifteenth century, also designed for the instruction of his heirs, advised them never to take any important step without such assistance, but "with the suitable and sound advice of your good relatives and friends make up your mind about everything that concerns you"; he stressed the folly of those who acted entirely without consulting "anyone else, either relative or friend." These imperatives involved citizens in practice in networks of patronage whose role in Florentine society was fundamental, but whose operation and effect on political life have hitherto been insufficiently acknowledged and explored.

The extent to which they potentially conflicted with the interests of the state and the good of the commune is implicit in recommendations such as that of Gino Capponi to his sons in 1420: "Above all else stick together with your neighbours and kinsmen; assist your friends both within and without the city." The private letters in which individuals often solicited the aid of their *amici* suggest that the range of problems with which they were expected to assist was as broad as the range of the Florentine patrician's interests and concerns, from the contracting of a marriage or the purchase of a house to the carrying-through of a business deal or the obtaining of a tax concession. However, as most upper-class citizens were closely involved with government, a great many letters contain requests for *amici* to circumvent the restrictive constitutional procedures and to arrange unofficially for the appointment of the writer or one of his friends to a particular public office. There was, moreover, a further sense in which most other concerns were ultimately related to politics. Studies of many aspects of Florentine society have tended to confirm the extent to which the Florentine patrician was a political animal, who regarded political pre-eminence as the crowning reward of economic success and social distinction; at the same time, these attributes could seldom successfully be preserved if they were not protected through political influence. No doubt Lorenzo the Magnificent was not in fact the first to observe that "in Florence a man cannot prosper if he has no share in government."

Where individual concerns were so powerfully affected by the possession of political influence and the exercise of political office, and the public sphere so intimately related to the private, the interest groups based on non-political associations whose members turned traditionally to each other for support might swiftly be transformed into political action groups or parties in times of crisis. The way in which such groups coalesced along the lines of traditional association is nicely illustrated in . . . the Black-White feuds in Florence at the beginning of the fourteenth century. . . . When the barricades went up *amici* [friends], *parenti* [kin], and *vicini* [neighbors] did not inevitably find themselves on the same side; sometimes the intimate pressures of these relationships led in practice to division instead of unity. There are a number of colourful examples in the history of Florence of feuding neighbours, families riven by internal conflict, companies ruined by dissension. However, regardless of the actual directions in which they were driven, Florentines responded to such situations not simply as individuals, but as members of a group or groups bound together by ties of kinship, marriage, neighbourhood, friendship, and custom.

It is clear that the basic principles of political life, and the social conditions which moulded and modified them, had not essentially changed by the beginning of the fifteenth century when the Medici family began its rise to power, except that, as Giovanni Morelli observed in recalling the epic feuds of the Florentine past, "then they used to persecute one another with sword in hand rather than with their votes as they do today." Long before the triumph of the Medici in 1434, once seen as the event which put an end to the actuality of republican government, the realities of power had ceased to correspond to the constitutional prescriptions for its distribution, and indeed the question of where ultimate political influence resided at any given time continues to tantalize students of Florentine politics and society. Certainly according to Cavalcanti, the commune in his time "was governed more from the dinner-table and the study than from the Palace," and he coined the aphorism that "many were elected to offices but few to government." In this sense, then, the story of parties in our period is the story of conflict, not only, or even most profoundly, between opposing factions, but also between unofficial government in the private interest and constitutional government in the public interest; these are the terms in which the problem was perceived in the mid-twenties when a new drive to extirpate factionalism was instituted in the name of the common good.

Both personal and official documents of this period reflect the impression that factionalism, endemic in Florence for reasons which we have discussed, intensified in a wave of unrest from the early twenties onwards. About this time the prominent patrician Buonaccorso Pitti bemoaned in his diary the growth of parties and divisions between the leading citizens, maintaining that on account of these "the welfare and honour of our Commune would be neglected." Bouts of legislation in 1421,

1426, and particularly 1429 suggest that his concern was shared by the ruling group in general; Cavalcanti claimed that Cosimo himself "always sought to put the interest of the Commune above everything else and used to say: Nature teaches us that for the sake of preserving the whole, the part must consider itself of no importance."

The extent to which the issue appeared as a conflict between private and public interest is most clearly seen in the focus of attention on the role of the *Signoria*, the eight Priors led by the Gonfalonier of Justice who constituted the chief magistracy of the state and were virtually its visible embodiment. On appointment to this office, citizens were ideally considered to have shed their private concerns and transcended their personal limitations. Immured in the palace of the Priors for the duration of their two-month term, detached quite literally from their customary environment and interests, they stood for the commune, and were "the principal source of authority and direction for the whole city." In accordance with the view that good government was necessary to the spiritual as well as the secular health of citizens, its maintenance was a sacred trust; notably amidst the multitude of sacred places, objects, and times upon which public religious ritual rested, the only sacred element in the secular sphere was the communal power. In his study of this subject, Richard Trexler has compared the Priors of Florence to "sacred but lay monks whose holiness was in their activity," and who "had acceded to their office . . . through ceremonies resembling rites of passage."

Certainly in their official capacity they were regarded with a reverence akin to piety. Averardo de' Medici bowed to the authority temporarily vested in his partisan enemies as members of the *Signoria*, while taking the opportunity to make a nice distinction between person and office, when he accepted their sentence of exile with the declaration that he never had and never would deny the authority of that "honorable, almost divine magistracy, supreme even to the Lord Priors and rulers of the Republic themselves." The disregard of this deeply held principle in their defiance of the *Signoria* may well have been a significant factor in the downfall of his enemies. Open defiance, however, was not the only, or at all the most characteristic, threat to the supremacy of the *Signoria* as the guardians of government in the interests of the whole, rather than a part of the ruling group. One of the greatest statesmen of his age, Gino di Neri Capponi, put his finger precisely on the problem confronting Florentines in 1420 when he laid down as his first maxim concerning the conduct of the patrician that "the Commune of Florence will preserve its authority in so far as . . . it does not allow any particular citizen or family or group of conspirators within it to become more powerful than the *Signoria*." In a series of meetings of the advisory council to the *Signoria*, convened throughout 1429 and in the early months of 1430 to discuss the means of achieving a unified citizenry, the insistence that no one should seek "to be equal to, or wish to be greater than, the *Signoria*," is a recurring theme. Notably it was on the grounds of their "wishing to violate the ordinances of the Priorate and Gonfalonier of Justice of the Florentine people" that the Medici were condemned.

Early in the course of these discussions an oath was drawn up to be sworn on the Bible by as many citizens from the *reggimento* as possible. They were required to promise simply "to divest themselves completely of all partisan and factional loyalties," and "to consider only the welfare and honour and greatness of the Republic, and of the *Parte Guelfa*, and of the *Signoria*." Later the tone of discussions in the *Consulte e Pratiche* was to become more intense, and there was a growing emphasis on spiritual sanctions against partisanship and factionalism which divided citizens. In the *Pratica* of 25 January 1429 the opening speaker, Lorenzo Ridolfi, pronounced that: "Just as we should adore one God, so you, Lord Priors, are to be venerated above all citizens, and those who look to others are setting up idols, and are to be condemned." Shortly after, Palla Strozzi signified his full agreement with this proposition, and the same theme was later taken up again by Giovanni Morelli who urged the *Signoria* to action with the reminder that "Our Lord stood in the midst of his disciples, and said, peace be unto you! In the same way you, Lord Priors, etc. . . . He who creates a party, sells his liberty . . .".

The extent to which moral aims and ideals, generated in both the secular and the spiritual worlds of the Florentine citizen, were fused in his view of the sacred role of the *Signoria* in suppressing private factions in the interests of the public welfare, finds perfect expression in these passages, which vividly evoke the atmosphere in which the struggle for power between the Medici and their opponents took place. They may help us perhaps to understand why citizens steadfastly continued to defend the letter of the constitution against the expression of separatist interests which had patently undermined it, and to explain the secrecy and stealth with which the manoeuvres of the latter were executed, and which make the task of the historian in identifying and describing these groups and their activities so particularly difficult.

As a consequence of the debates on faction, the office of *Conservatori delle Leggi* was set up early in 1429 with the task of examining evidence of citizens in official positions violating the laws of the commune, and putting private interest above public duty. An anonymous denunciation to this body in October 1429 describes an illegal association purposely created to perform particularly those services and functions generally expected of friends, neighbours, and relatives; indeed members were invited to regard one another in familial terms. They were encouraged to join the group with the inducement that they would henceforth be assured of guidance and protection: "You will be told what you have to do day by day . . . for we must do what our superiors, like fathers, . . . command. You yourself need never worry about anything: in every matter you will have many to defend and honour you." With the observation that "the Commune must maintain its citizens subject to the laws rather than the laws to the citizens," the informant expressed the hope that God would aid the magistracy in its investigations, so that through the formation of such private associations for mutual aid and protection "the Commune should not perish." Nevertheless, an organization such as this represented in fact only a short step further in evolution from the customary associations of friends, neighbours, and relatives whose role and relationships it sought to duplicate in a more formalized way. For as a friend observed, writing to Forese Sacchetti in 1427, "after all, you can do nothing unless, when the need arises, your friends and relatives are willing to exert themselves in your interest—especially in legitimate and honourable matters."

Despite these obvious similarities, the leaders of the *reggimento* in the twenties and thirties generally failed to acknowledge that some conflict between the two guiding principles of Florentine life—concern for the public welfare and loyalty to personal associates—was inevitable. No doubt this was partly because they and their friends were so involved in government that they tended to regard their share in the state . . . as almost a personal possession or attribute, and it was often difficult for them to distinguish effectively between public and private interest. So they continued, somewhat ingenuously, to declare that "they had never belonged to any faction," nor had any enemies other than those of the *Signoria* had "never taken part in discussions outside the Palace," but nevertheless had favoured "one man more than another according to rank and . . . [family]." However, they soon began to recognize that the best possible hope of eliminating the problem lay in ameliorating those injustices from which parties or groups of *amici* primarily sought to defend their members.

In 1422 and 1426 the main focus of contemporary concern over "parties" were various permanent but unofficial associations which could be used as a cover for the operation of political groups. Chief of these were the religious confraternities, which bore the main brunt of the early phases of the attack on factions. But by 1429, in discussions of the problem in the *Consulte e Pratiche*, there was less emphasis on wiping out potentially subversive associations, and more on the attempt to define the underlying causes and preconditions of the growth of parties. Like Cavalcanti and Buoninsegni, speakers in the council debates stressed the distribution of political offices and taxes as sources of dissension; most fundamentally, the struggle was seen as one between those seeking to increase their status and their share in government, and those at whose expense these gains would be made— the already powerful citizens whose best interests lay in preserving the *status quo*.

. . . The parties of the Medici and their opponents broadly corresponded in fact to these two sections of the *reggimento*, and . . . they were basically interest groups which, committed to the defence of their members in this as in other respects, became in the process political action groups, or, as the Florentines pejoratively called them, . . . [sects] within the ruling elite. Such parties, then, were not so much specifically political organizations, as in the modern sense, but rather natural outgrowths of permanent and fundamental elements in the structure of Florentine society. Thus the most natural approach to our original problems concerning the origins, nature, and membership of parties is through the identification and exploration of these networks of association and patronage.

This process is much easier in the case of the Medici than for their opponents. Given the nature of parties as we have described them, it is hardly surprising that there are no lists of partisans, and only a handful of leading Mediceans are mentioned by name in the few contemporary comments. Attempts to infer that those particularly prominent in government, or notably favoured by the Medici after 1434, were necessarily their partisans in the preceding years, are partly vitiated by the consideration that after 1434, support of the Medici and support of the state and the government was to a large extent one and indistinguishable, and while the Medici undoubtedly advanced their friends, they did not necessarily discriminate against the solid body of the patriotic supporters of the constitution and its representatives, whoever these might be. However, the Medici family obviously provide a focal point, and the magnificent collection of their letters relating to the years 1426 to 1434 are the primary means of exploring most of the problems which concern us. Unfortunately no comparable evidence survives to illuminate their opponents, but on the other hand, the list of those exiled by the Medici on their return to Florence in 1434 constitutes a solid if limited definition of the core of that group to serve as a starting-point for our investigation. The personal lives, interests, and associations of both groups are greatly illuminated by the evidence of marriage records, private diaries, letters, genealogical miscellanies, and, above all, tax returns, which are such a mine of information concerning the diverse affairs of every citizen of property after 1427.

Although the sum of our findings from this evidence enables us to confirm and illustrate the connection between these parties and traditional networks of association and interest, the precise relationship of parties to patronage groups remains a problem of some complexity. At the simplest level, it was natural for an individual to seek assistance with his concerns from kinsmen, and, by extension, from those related to him by marriage. Particularly if the power and influence of these most obvious patrons and supporters were limited, he might seek to extend the range of assistance on which he could call by cultivating other relationships with more powerful citizens; thus Morelli, an orphan from a family of comparatively modest status in the city, recommended his sons "to acquire at least one friend or more in your *gonfalone*" and to align themselves in business "with a suitable man, wealthy . . . and especially with political influence, or from a traditionally pre-eminent family." The latter in return would benefit through his honour and status being increased by the enjoyment of a following of citizens dependent on his influence, and with obligations to him which might be satisfied by the requirement of general and specific support and service.

Since most citizens were bound above and below by a veritable mass of such reciprocal obligations of aid and service, to social superiors, equals, and inferiors, in any particular case where assistance was needed the appropriate patron or patrons might be sought from a multitude of associates, related either horizontally or laterally on the social scale; hence it is impossible to say where a patronage network began and ended. It was essentially fluid rather than finite, and the links between men involved in the activation of a chain of patronage could either be of long standing, or forged specifically for the occasion, in which case they might either be subsequently neglected or solidify into permanent relationships.

However, such networks did tend to cluster and coalesce around prominent individuals or great families in a particularly favourable position to dispense patronage, and as Morelli's injunctions imply, citizens regularly sought patronage or service within the general bounds of a particular group, or complex of groups, focused on or led by the greater families. The families of the Medici and their most prominent opponents stood at the centre of such groups, and the evidence relating to the two parties suggests that when clients became partisans, the ties which held the group together were largely the reciprocal obligations of a patronage network. Nevertheless, the precise relationship of patronage network to party within each was rather different, and seems to have been the chief determinant of important differences between the structure and functions of the two parties.

The opposition to the Medici coalesced essentially in response to the threat which the Mediceans offered to the *status quo;* it was based on a fairly selective recruitment from a number of patronage networks only loosely connected with one another, and led by the several prominent families on whom those networks had

chiefly focused. While this process, and the party which it created, is essentially similar to that . . . [of] the early fourteenth century, the Medici letters, the actions of
their party, and the nature of its subsequent success all suggest that the growth of the
Medici party represented less the natural transformation of interest groups into action groups under the pressure of events, and more the planned and purposeful consolidation of existing social ties, and the creation of new reciprocal obligations, with
the express aim of more effective political action. Of course it is impossible to investigate the origin and nature of all the social bonds which cemented the Medici party,
and great Florentine families had traditionally cultivated personal followings. The
Medici family, however, began the fifteenth century at a peculiar political disadvantage which would, in the natural course of events, have debarred them from acquiring much influence within the ruling group. Thirty years later they exercised an effective ascendancy over it, with the aid of a particularly unified and closely knit
group of supporters. In this respect their party differed from those typical of preceding centuries, and of their opponents; it was, apparently, not so much a new style of
party, as a necessary modification of the old formula. Based, like its opposition, on a
network of patronage which began with kin and extended to incorporate others as
necessary and desirable, the Medici party seems to have relied more on friends than
family for some essential services because the social and political position of the latter was too weak to provide them. The fact that the Medici party was created mainly
by the extension of patronage, and the formation of ties with smaller or newer or
politically unpopular families, not solidly entrenched within the ruling group and
the social networks which dominated it, made the partisans particularly dependent
on their wealthy and socially distinguished patrons, and the latter the undisputed
leaders of a network of patronage and association which was particularly dense and
centralized.

  This would seem to have been an important factor in its success, and indeed the
Medici party achieved a success quite unique in Florentine history in promoting the
interests of its members; the Medici ascendancy represented almost the complete
triumph of unofficial government in the private interest over constitutional government in the public interest. Paradoxically, however, Medici government came near
in practice to resolving this eternal conflict simply because its dominance precluded
the creation of effective opposition parties, and achieved in time the incorporation
of virtually the entire ruling group into its own ranks; for the first time a single party
embraced the state and was able to define public interest in terms of its own private
needs.

  It is the party and its activities before 1434 which constitute the essential subject of this study. My intention is not ultimately to explain or to account entirely for
the victory of the Medici over those who opposed their aims, and indeed I am not in
a position to do so. There is evidence . . . to suggest that their enormous wealth, the
decisive economic influence which it enabled them to exert within the city, the
powerful foreign friendships which it brought in its train, made their triumph a diplomatic and financial necessity once their ambitions had been openly declared, and
challenged. An adequate consideration of these themes would require a study much
broader in scope than the present one, which is basically concerned with the means
by which the Medici family translated economic success into political predominance

in the traditional Florentine fashion, in a virtuoso exploitation of the vital weakness of the republican system—the disjunction between the official structure of government and its effective sources of political power in the social structure of its ruling class.

DOCUMENTS

The typical chief magistrate of the communes of early Renaissance Italy was the *podestà*, usually a foreigner serving with broad power for a short term of office. The statutes excerpted here on the duties of the *podestà* of Treviso underscore the need for him to stand above faction to ensure impartiality in government. In the signorial regimes, on the other hand, miniature courts were created whereby the lord oversaw the tasks of war and diplomacy aided by a small staff of advisers and intellectuals. In the second selection, Giovanni Conversini da Ravenna, an early humanist, records vividly the pettiness and humiliations of life at the Carrara court in Padua. However, when republican Venice conquered Padua two decades later, the Venetian government used despotic brutality to extinguish the Carrara dynasty. The Paduan chronicler, G. Gatari describes this process in the third document. Finally, in his famous collective biography the Florentine bookseller and observer, Vespasiano da Bisticci, characterized the mores and interests of the elder Cosimo de' Medici, who ruled Florence "behind the scenes" from 1434 until his death in 1464.

| A Podestà Swears to Do His Duty, 1313

I swear on God's holy gospels that in good faith and without fraud—unmoved by love and hate, [concern for] my own comfort and harm—that to the best of my ability and knowledge, I shall, through myself, my judges and knights, rule the commune of the city of Treviso, its suburbs and its whole district as peacefully and quietly as I can; and I shall preserve and increase in every way the same city, suburbs, district, its laws, jurisdictions, possessions, income, property and revenue, that it now has and will have in the future.

And I shall maintain the well-being of the citizens of Ceneda and especially those of Conegliano, who observe and shall wish to observe pacts and treaties, which they or their forebears made and had made with the commune of Treviso and with the Trevisans, to the laud, honor and glory of God, and to the perpetual peace, tranquility and community that the same city [of Treviso] and its district always desire.

And if there are any wars and discords now or in the future in the city of Treviso, in its suburbs and any part of its district, which God forbid, among any persons subject to the podestà's jurisdiction, that I shall bring them to peace and concord as I

"A Podestà Swears to Do His Duty, 1313," from *Gli Statuti del comune di Treviso (sec. XIII–XIV)*, ed. B. Betto (Rome, 1984), Vol. 1, pp. 28–32. Translated by Benjamin G. Kohl.

judge and think best, and I shall attend to this matter without fraud, lest discords should arise and grow in the future.

And I shall govern all citizens and contado-residents of the city-state of Treviso, all magnates and other persons, resident in the city and its suburbs as well as in the district, in honorable, peaceful and tranquil state according to the pacts, statutes and ordinances of the same city.

And I shall see to it that the oaths and pacts of the commune of Treviso are observed and fulfilled, and specially the pact made and signed in good faith with Conegliano; and I shall attend to the matter, namely, that the pacts and agreements with that city are preserved.

Neither have I made, nor shall I make or agree to make any pact or agreement with any person or persons living in the city of Treviso, or in its district or in foreign parts, during my term of office, which would be to the harm and prejudice of the commune of Treviso, or any particular persons.

And I shall preserve all pacts made and signed between the commune of Treviso and Guecellone and Gabriele da Camino [would-be lords of the city of Treviso] and between the same commune and Biachino, son of Gabriele da Camino, and all and any other pacts, and make sure that they are observed by all and every persons and by their heirs, who should observe these pacts now and in the future with the commune of Treviso. And I shall make certain that the podestà, who shall succeed me in this office, shall likewise swear to have these pacts preserved. And I shall give justice and render legal decisions impartially to all persons—widows as well as orphans, commoners as well as the powerful—whosoever is from the city of Treviso, its suburbs and its district, all according to legal procedure and according to the rules and laws, statutes and customs of the city of Treviso, just as I shall consider [these laws] ought to be carried out and observed. And at least once every month, I shall read myself or have read to me this oath so that I shall hear and clearly understand its entire tenor; and I shall carry out personally or have carried out what is contained in it, without asking for any dispensation from this [obligation].

A Humanist Records the Pettiness of Court Life in Padua, 1382

It was, as you know, some years ago that I came down from the Alpine regions to Padua, alone, poor, but free, unaccustomed to life in a city; there I spent a few days, troubled over my future— whether I should go to Bologna or to Florence; off toward Venice all was precluded by a raging war. Picture me than, a person wanting very little the situation he was in and hoping for even less (for who would entertain hope of being raised soon from a schoolroom to mingle among the highest of courtiers?), a person whom that illustrious leader now ordered summoned to Padua. Just as I was,

---

"A Humanist Records the Pettiness of Court Life in Padua, 1382," from Giovanni Conversini da Ravenna, "On His First Entrance into Court," from *Two Court Treatises*, eds. B. G. Kohl and J. Day (Munich: W. Fink Verlag, 1987), pp. 27–33.

in clothing that was rustic and well suited to the rain then falling, I get brought to court.

When I had arrived there a certain one of the attendants, Montorso, a man quite sharp and adept indeed at life in a court, launched himself at me as though at something just snatched from an African's hut: "Listen now," he says, "you are summoned before the prince. Comport yourself properly, showing him reverence, on bended knee, and with your head uncovered. Addressing rulers before being spoken to is bad form." Thus, with "all due respect" (that is a quality alien to the usage of courtiers), he was giving me advice, himself a stripling and of my own station in life. I stood in silent astonishment—either at the rashness of this man who would without knowing me try to lick me into shape to meet the prince, or else at the foolishness of the man, for although he had some account of me through talk or other report of my affairs—of whatever sort these were purported to be—yet now he did not trust this little old fellow, someone occupied with books, to know with what high respect kings must be approached. In any case, because he had prevailed upon his ruler concerning me, and because everyone wants what he offers up regarded as utterly excellent, he was seeing to it that naught lacked by whose presence we be found—himself as good as his word, and I meet and proper.

Yet, when summoned there, I had encouraged myself thus: "A great and powerful ruler is speaking, but he is human; he surpasses you in point of fortune, but you surpass him in point of talent; it is material goods you lack, but he lacks your education; you are able to improve yourself by your own wits, and to improve him by telling of splendid models and examples from the past and by reading him things he will find most useful." Well, what happened? I am brought before him. The great man receives me in kindly and polite manner—he is by nature a most pleasant person. Throwing aside on the spot the dice that had occupied him, he bends all his attention upon me. When he has, in asking many questions, sent the conversation off in every direction—as though I were a person versed in the greatest number of topics— he orders a Bible brought in; after further inquiries and answers about the Bible we parted—I to some reading, he to some rest.

Summoned back again during the first watch of the night, I find him dining, and during his dinner he kept me in motion in every direction with questions about any number and variety of things. In all this I felt astonished not so much at him as he interrogated me (indeed, to judge from his experience in affairs and his encirclement by scholars he could not but be an exceedingly well-taught questioner), as at myself yielding satisfaction all around during this inquisition. But God Almighty and my own good fortune—they put me in this spot—sufficed. And they sufficed better than I understood. In making me time and again the object of his attention that great and greatly wise man decreed that, on his express orders and forthwith, I was to be numbered among those he trusted most and saw most often. For in fact whether walking, thinking, eating, reclining, he would ask for the presence of—me.

It had been usual with him to honor nobody with any long or pronounced intimacy (except for a person kept by him after long passage of time and experience), nor again to lavish his generosity on anyone without the test of time. But in my case, and at the very outset (and that is accounted the signal honor in the eyes of the courtiers) he made me one of his inner circle and adorned me with his benefactions.

There were those who would say, in wonderment: "You have attained special favor with the prince, a beneficence on his part that is hasty and in anticipation of your scarcely demonstrated merits. For either his usual behavior is changed or else a fortune that is especially propitious has you in her gaze." Further, there was a time when I brought out into the open with several friends the strife that arose from that kind of admiration aimed at me. And I used to say that private citizens ought to be found irreproachable in their dealings with each other, and affable, and in just the way a servant becomes more adept with duties to perform and more dependable when trusted, so they should become day by day more productive; that in fact the people in whose hands lies the unchecked right of distributing rewards and punishments readily both bless with honor and heap with material rewards the ones they add to the household staff—because assuredly nothing discovers a man's spirit so exactly as riches and higher rank; hence that saying of Bias quoted by the moral philosopher, that "princehood reveals the man." Thus if rulers support and aid the attendants in their own courts with material rewards and honors, they esteem those attendants found faithful and then more faithful still as being precisely the ones they would want to have been beforehand in rewarding. Moreover, for the wicked to set about plundering although due rewards are given them—this, by heavens, is a deed of dishonor as great as is the deed of honor in conferring rewards when one recognizes the occasion for it. For these reasons I used to maintain that kings were acting judiciously when they had been quick to show themselves liberal toward their followers. To be sure, to inflict delays upon one who expects and needs his reward, to defer until he is on the threshold of despair—this would seem the course of the prudent ruler perhaps, but of the liberal one not at all. Soldiers' wages and even the prices demanded for purchases are to be paid out unfazed in face and ready in hand: how much more so the disbursements of generosity, and especially those from a prince's hand? It should be his goal to do good works spontaneously, and for the benefit of no end of people. For in this way from his surpassing means he attains their most illustrious use and their sweetest fruit, since princehood has nothing more noble or more divine about it than its good offices for the greatest number possible. Truly whoever strives for that pinnacle of power for another purpose beyond benefit to the many is to be deemed no prince, but the basest of tyrants, and just what sort of master of others he will prove to be, let those who suffer the experience testify.

An Account of the End
of the Carrara Dynasty, 1406

In these days, when the war [between Venice and Padua] was over, Messer Giacomo dal Verme, a great enemy of the Carrara clan, came to Venice, where he was honorably received by the government and invited to be present at the deliberations concerning what was to be done with the [captured] members of the Carrara

"An Account of the End of the Carrara Dynasty, 1406," from A., B., and G. Gatari, *Cronaca carrarese*, eds. A. Medin and G. Tolomei, Rerum Italicarum Scriptores, new ed., Vol. 17, part 1 (Bologna, 1909–1932), pp. 579–582. Translated by Benjamin G. Kohl.

house. Messer Giacomo used all his cunning with the Venetian government, arguing with great force that the Carrara lord had been very harmful to him and that considering the great intelligence of the Carrara lord, if he were left alive he would escape and would always seek to avenge himself. Moreover, [the Carrara lord] could always demand that new dominions should be given to him, and when these were not granted, hatred would be born. And thus the ancient proverb is still very true: dead men don't make wars. And so he recommended with all the force he could, that the Carrara should be executed. And this advice was at once adopted by the Council of Ten who decreed that the [Carrara] lord and his sons must die. And immediately the *Signoria* send for Fra Zuan Benedetto, an old servant of God, so that the Carrara lord could confess his sins, and the friar was ordered to go to the prison and announce his fate to the lord. And this he did, and when the Carrara lord heard he spoke these words: "Why do I have to die? Isn't it bad enough that you've taken my lordship and my lands and goods and thrown me unjustly into prison with my sons, and threaten my life? I am in your power and you can do with me as you wish. And still if you really want, you can stop this from happening." But Fra Zuan Benedetto simply comforted him and confessed his sins once more and had him devoutly receive the blessed body of Christ. With the lord shedding many tears, the friar left. When he had left, into the prison entered two men from the Council of Ten, two heads of the Forty, and two Ducal Councillors with many others, including Bernardo Priuli with about twenty cutthroats. And then the door of the Carrara lord's cell was opened, and in came Bernardo Priuli with his followers. And the lord put up a great defense against them. But with great effort, they beat him with clubs on his feet and arms, and pushed him around, and stripped off his clothes, and hit him in the face and on the head. And they threw him to the ground, hitting and punching him as he lay there. And they wound a double cord around his throat and strangled him with such force that his soul departed his body, and in that way [the Carrara lord] ended his life.

On the next day his body was carried to the church of Santo Stefano of the Eremitani [in Venice] to be buried on the 17th of January 1406 with about fifty candles and dressed in his suit of Alexandrian velvet. His face was quite bruised and battered, but his body was girded with a gold sword and he wore two golden spurs on his feet. Lord Francesco Novello da Carrara was not very large, but of normal stature, heavy with strong limbs more than other men. He was swarthy in complexion and rather proud in bearing, discerning in his speech, gracious and merciful to his people. Everyone thought him most wise and strong in body.

After the execution of the lord Francesco Novello, the *Signoria* ordered that his sons be treated likewise, and on its order, Fra Zuan Benedetto blessed them and gave them communion. And both of them wept with the saddest tears and most bitter cries as the friar gave each final kisses on their mouths and held them closely in his arms, so that all who were present wept in pity. Finally the two brothers were separated and Messer Francesco Terzo was led to the cell where his father had died. There Bernardo Priuli and some of his accomplices strangled Francesco Terzo and he died in that manner. Then they returned to the cell of Messer Giacomo da Carrara, who was very frightened. In a low and trembling voice he asked if his father were dead and when they said yes, he let out a deep sigh and raised his eyes to heaven, saying: "Lord God, have mercy on his soul and on mine." And then he asked permission to write a letter to his wife, Bellafiore da Varano, and this request was granted to him. Writing this letter with a shaky hand and eyes full of tears, he stated that when he finished the letter it would be his turn to die in the prison of the government of Venice and that he was quite prepared for his own death; therefore, he commended his soul to her and would say no more. Then he gave the letter to an official standing there, who sent it to the wife. Then lord Giacomo walked into the crowd with his hands raised, saying [in Latin] these words to the Lord Jesus Christ: "Into your hands, Lord, I commend my spirit." When he had finished speaking, Bernardo Priuli killed him in the same way he had the others, by strangulation with a double cord so that his blessed soul departed the cold earthly body and ascended to the Creator in heaven. And then the two dead bodies of the brothers were placed in a boat and carried with a few candles to the church of San Marco Boccalame in the lagoon. There both were buried in the middle of the night without the benefit of any divine office, on the 19th of January 1406. Messer Francesco Terzo was thirty-one years old, a large man, who because of his height inclined his head toward the ground. And he was large limbed, very strong, a valiant fighter, wise, disdainful, cruel and very vindictive. Messer Giacomo da Carrara was twenty-five years old, tall and well built, as fine a knight as in all of Lombardy. He was pale like his mother, sensitive, a lover of God, benign and merciful, gentle and mild in his speech, kindly, even angelic in bearing, tough and spirited, strong and adventurous, who in another life would have been a Scipio Africanus. In that way, the two brothers ended their lives.

Vespasiano da Bisticci's Portrait of Cosimo de' Medici

Cosimo di Giovanni de' Medici was of most honourable descent, a very prominent citizen and one of great weight in the republic. He was well versed in Latin letters, both sacred and secular, of capable judgment in all matters and able to argue thereupon. His teacher was Roberto dei Rossi, a good Greek and Latin scholar and of excellent carriage.

Returning to Cosimo, he had a knowledge of Latin which would scarcely have been looked for in one occupying the station of a leading citizen engrossed with affairs. He was grave in temperament, prone to associate with men of high station who disliked frivolity, and averse from all buffoons and actors and those who spent time unprofitably. He had a great liking for men of letters and sought their society, chiefly conversing with the Fra Ambrogio degli Agnoli, Messer Lionardo d' Arezzo, Nicolao Nicoli, Messer Carlo d' Arezzo and Messer Poggio. His natural bent was to discuss matters of importance; and, although at this time the city was full of men of distinction, his worth was recognised on account of his praiseworthy qualities, and he began to find employment in affairs of every kind. By his twenty-fifth year he had

"Portrait of Cosimo de' Medici" by Vespasiano da Bisticci from *The Vespasiano Memoirs*, Routledge Kegan Paul, 1926, pp. 213–219, 224–234. Reprinted by permission of the publisher.

gained great reputation in the city, and, as it was recognised that he was aiming at a high position, feeling ran strong against him, and the report of those who knew roused a fear that he would win success. The Council of Constance, gathered from all parts of the world, was then sitting; and Cosimo, who was well acquainted with foreign affairs as well as those of the city, went thither with two objects: one to allay the ill-feeling against him, and the other to see the Council which had in hand the reform of the Church, now greatly vexed by divisions. After staying some time at Constance, and witnessing the procedure of the Council, he visited almost all parts of Germany and France, spending some two years in travel. He hoped thus to let cool the ill-feeling against him which had greatly increased. He understood his own disposition which made him discontented with low estate, and made him seek to rise out of the crowd of men of small account. Many people remarked this tendency, and warned him that it might lead him into danger of death or exile. By way of lessening this resentment he began to absent himself from the palace, and to consort with men of low estate without either money or position, all by way of temporising; but his foes took this in bad part, affirming that what he did was a mere pretence to abate the suspicions of others. . . .

Now Cosimo being exiled his enemies in Florence used every means to ruin his credit both in Rome and in the city. But his wealth was so great that he was able to send to Rome enough money to re-establish his position. In fact, his credit increased vastly everywhere, and in Rome many who had withdrawn their money brought it back to his bank. In Venice Cosimo was held in the highest esteem, and those who had banished him—men of no reputation and with no idea of order in the state—did not realise that they would have to deal with such a powerful foe. They were new to the art of government, having had no practice in the same, and knew not how to rule. When trouble arose they soon changed their course, desiring to return to peaceful ways and let the city resume its tranquil and comfortable life in which no one citizen had more power than another, except those who had been placed by lot in posts of dignity. And though they had established a Balia and closed the ballot, they now ordered another scrutiny which deprived no citizen of his privileges, but gave them to all who had a right thereto. While Cosimo tarried at Venice, he was greatly esteemed by all the Venetians, who determined to despatch an ambassador to encourage the Signoria and those in power to recall him from exile. They began to favour him in diverse ways, secretly, and to arrange for his return; and as many in Florence were on his side, before a year had passed they made a plan to procure his recall by the help of the Priorato which was friendly to him. At the end of the year his adversaries took up arms, being suspicious as to what might be the results of his return, whereupon Pope Eugenius, like a good pastor, appeared as a mediator to arrange a peace between the two parties of citizens. Those of the government of 1433, who had taken up arms, laid them down and submitted themselves to the good faith of the Pope. But though they were under the Papal guarantee, they were exiled after Cosimo's return. In this matter Pope Eugenius was deceived, for he believed that good faith would be kept on both sides and the city pacified.

Cosimo having come back to Florence, to the great satisfaction of the citizens and of his own party, his friends procured the banishment of divers of those who had opposed his recall, and of those who were neutral; at the same time bringing forward new people. He rewarded those who had brought him back, lending to one a good sum of money, and making a gift to another to help marry his daughter or buy lands, while great numbers were banished as rebels. He and his party took every step to strengthen their own position, following the example of those of the government of 1433. In Florence there were many citizens who were men of weight in the state; and, as they were friendly to Cosimo and had helped to recall him, they retained their influence. Cosimo found that he must be careful to keep their support by temporising and making believe that he was fain they should enjoy power equal to his own. Meantime he kept concealed the source of his influence in the city as well as he could. I have no wish to set down here everything that I could tell, for what I write is only by way of memorandum. I leave the rest to anyone who may write his life. But I say that anyone who may be fain to bring new forms into the state, that those who wrought the changes in 1433, brought ruin to themselves and to the state also. Many leading citizens, men of weight, never wished for these changes, declaring they had no wish to dig their own graves.

Cosimo, after he had settled the government, called for a Balia which banished many citizens. At this time Duke Francesco was in command of the allied forces of Florence and Venice near Lucca; the two republics having agreed to share the cost of the soldiers' pay, but now the Venetians refused to contribute their part. Whereupon, after several letters had been sent in vain, Cosimo, as one highly esteemed in Venice, was sent to request the Venetians to hold to their promise and to pay the sum due to Duke Francesco.

On Cosimo's arrival all the citizens deemed that the Signory should take a new line and observe the promise they had made. Cosimo pressed his claims with the strongest arguments, but the Venetians kept obstinately to their view, for they were determined that the Florentines should not get Lucca without paying for it. When Cosimo perceived that they were set on this policy, and that they declined to recognise the benefits they had received, he grew to hate them on account of their bad faith; so he wrote to Florence asking leave to withdraw and return by way of Ferrara, where Pope Eugenius had gone with all his court. When he arrived, he waited upon the Pope according to his commission and made complaint of the ingratitude of the Venetians. But Eugenius made light of this, knowing their character, and the College of Cardinals was of the same mind. From the way in which the Venetians bore themselves towards the Pope, they greatly roused his anger, as it appeared from what happened later. Cosimo went on several embassies and brought back great honour to the city. . . .

. . . He had dealings with painters and sculptors and had in his house works of divers masters. He was especially inclined towards sculpture and showed great favour to all worthy craftsmen, being a good friend to Donatello and all sculptors and painters; and because in his time the sculptors found scanty employment, Cosimo, in order that Donatello's chisel might not be idle, commissioned him to make the pulpits of bronze in S. Lorenzo and the doors of the sacristy. He ordered the bank to pay every week enough money to Donatello for his work and for that of his four assistants. And because Donatello was wont to go clad in a fashion not to Cosimo's taste, Cosimo gave him a red mantle and a cowl, with a cloak to go under the mantle, all new, and one festal day in the morning he sent them in order that Donatello might wear them.

After a day or two of wear he put them aside, saying that he would not wear them again as they were too fine for him. Cosimo was thus liberal to all men of worth through his great liking for them. He had good knowledge of architecture, as may be seen from the buildings he left, none of which were built without consulting him; moreover, all those who were about to build would go to him for advice.

Of agriculture he had the most intimate knowledge, and he would discourse thereupon as if he had never followed any other calling. At S[t]. Marco the garden, which was a most beautiful one, was laid out after his instructions. Hitherto it had been a vacant field belonging to some friars who had held it before the reformation of the order by Pope Eugenius. In all his possessions there were few farming operations which were not directed by him. He did much fruit planting and grafting; and, wonderful as it may seem, he knew about every graft that was made on his estates; moreover, when the peasants came into Florence, he would ask them about the fruit trees and where they were planted. He loved to do grafting and lopping with his own hand. One day I had some talk with him when, being then a young man, he had gone from Florence—where there was sickness—to Careggi. It was then February, when they prune the vines, and I found him engaged in two most excellent tasks. One was to prune the vines every morning for two hours as soon as he rose (in this he imitated Pope Boniface IX, who would prune certain vines in the vineyard of the papal palace at Rome every year in due season. Moreover, at Naples they have preserved till this day his pruning-knife with two silver rings, in memory of Pope Boniface). Cosimo's other employment, when he had done with pruning, was to read the *Moralia* of S[t]. Gregory, an excellent work in thirty-five books, which task occupied him for six months. Both at his villa and in Florence he spent his time well; taking pleasure in no game, save chess, of which he would occasionally play a game or two after supper by way of pastime. He knew Magnolino, who was the best chess player of his age. . . .

Cosimo was always liberal, especially to men of merit. The majority of men who affect letters, without any other profitable employ, are poor in goods; men like Friar Ambrogio degli Agnoli, a man of religion, very holy and devoted to his order. Cosimo helped his monastery in all its needs, and a day seldom passed when he did not repair to the Agnoli, where he would find Nicolao Nicoli and Lorenzo his own brother, and would spend several hours with them. While Friar Ambrogio would translate S. John Chrysostom on the Epistles of S. Paul—as is told in his life—Nicolao wrote down what Fra Ambrogio translated, and, rapidly as Nicolao could write, he could not write fast enough for Fra Ambrogio's dictation and often was forced to beg him to go slower. This I heard from Cosimo who was present.

Nicolao had spent most of his substance in books and wanted for necessaries—as we may read in his Life. Cosimo, hearing of this, bade him not stint himself and told him that the bank had been ordered to advance him what he wanted, which the cashier would pay on receiving his bill. Nicolao duly took advantage of Cosimo's liberality; most praiseworthy because it served the needs of so illustrious a man as Nicolao. During his life he drew from the bank five hundred ducats, thus making a good show before the world, which he could hardly have done but for Cosimo, who, when he went to Verona to avoid the plague, took with him no buffoons or heralds but Nicolao Nicoli and Messer Carlo d' Arezzo with whom he could discuss literature. Cosimo made no demand on Nicolao for the five hundred ducats, having always treated this loan as a gift, and in this fashion he succoured all good and learned men in their need. They are indeed good men who practise liberality like Cosimo.

I must not forbear to tell of his great generosity to Maestro Tomaso da Serezana, afterwards Pope Nicholas, while he was Bishop of Bologna, without income, seeing that Bologna had rebelled against the Church. Pope Eugenius sent him, together with Messer Giovanni Carvagialle, on an embassy into France, but being short of funds he could give them but little for the journey. Messer Tomaso being in Florence, I, as a scribe, went to see him, whereupon he desired me to wait upon Cosimo on his behalf to beg for a loan of a hundred ducats, because Pope Eugenius had not given him money enough for so long a journey. When I had done this errand Cosimo, without much consideration, said, "Tell him I will send to him Roberto Martelli, and will let him have what money he wants." I had only just returned to him when Roberto appeared with a general letter of credit to all Cosimo's agents, instructing them to pay to Maestro Tomaso whatever sum he might want and without limit. When Maestro Tomaso read of this unheard-of liberality—for he was only known to Cosimo by his good name—he expressed to Roberto his unbounded gratitude, in that more had been done for him than he had asked for, whereupon Roberto said that it was but a trifle granted on account of Cosimo's goodwill.

On his travels he drew two hundred ducats on his letter of credit; and, on his return to Florence, found himself still in want of money to go on to Rome. There was a pardon at S. Giovanni and there Messer Tomaso met Cosimo coming out of church and thanked him for all he had done. He went on to tell him that he wanted another hundred ducats to take him to Rome, whereupon Cosimo said he would send Roberto with a commission for whatever he might want, and when he came Tomaso would accept no more than a hundred ducats. While he was at Viterbo a cardinal's hat was sent to him, and also one for his companion Giovanni Carvagialle, a Spaniard. Before the year was out he was made Pope, taking his title, Nicolas, from the Cardinal of S. Croce who had advanced him. After his election one of his first acts was to make Cosimo his banker in acknowledgment of the benefits he had received. In the year of Jubilee some hundred thousand ducats came to the Church, and Cosimo was well repaid for his generous accommodation. Cosimo had a beneficent eye, always friendly to men of merit, and knowing how to estimate their worth and to serve them. He was always ready to do what was asked of him, and besides he did much of his own accord. . . .

He also befriended Marsiglio, son of Ficino, a man of good talent and carriage and learned in Greek and Latin. His means were small, and to keep him from poverty Cosimo bought for him a house in Florence and a farm at Careggi, giving him thus income sufficient to allow him to live with one or two companions, and generally to serve his need. A servant of his had worked hard for many years at a wage agreed upon of so much a month; and when incapacitated he paid the man just the same, whereas many others would have just given him house-room, or handed him over to some guild to support. Cosimo was fain to support his servant out of his own purse, not out of that of others, so he gave him a house and farm out of which he might gain a living for himself and his wife as a recompense for his labour. . . .

. . . It happened that a certain of . . . [Cosimo's] kinsmen—who indeed was very rich—never met him without pouring out grievances, declaring that he was poverty-stricken, and every day he would tell the same tale. Cosimo made up his mind not to answer him so as to escape this worry, but one day, in the Piazza de' Signori, he met this kinsman who straightway began to repeat the same old tale. When he had come to an end Cosimo called him by name and said to him, "You are my kinsman, and nothing is more displeasing to me than your constant cry of poverty; because the man who proclaims himself a pauper always suffers hurt thereby. Otherwhere than in Florence everyone makes himself out to be richer than he really is, but in Florence the custom is the opposite: so that a man gains in one respect and loses in all the rest, which is a grave matter. Reverting to your own case, can a man be called poor who has sixty thousand florins with the Lombards: who is concerned with trade in Rome, in Florence and in divers other places: who holds possessions, like you, on all sides, which you have bought regardless of price, outbidding all the rest: who builds sumptuous town and country houses: who lives in the state you and your family maintain with your horses and fine attire, the handsomest in Florence?" Thus Cosimo laid the situation before him: he could make no reply as it was all true. This natural medicine cured him completely and he never grumbled again.

It happened that the surveyor of his building works cheated him of a large sum of money. Having investigated the business, Cosimo, like the wise man he was, did not fly into a rage, but simply withdrew the commission from the surveyor, and told him that he had no further need of his services, and that he had advanced to him as his agent a sum of money amounting to a hundred thousand florins. The story of this man and what he had done was soon spread all about the city; men talked of little else, and wherever he went he met with blame. One day he met Cosimo, whom he had robbed and in my presence thus addressed him: "Cosimo, all over Florence men are saying that I robbed you and that on this account you dismissed me from the surveyorship of your buildings." Cosimo in his reply did not repeat that this man had robbed him (as indeed he had), but said, "What would you have me do?" Said the other, "I would that should anyone ask you whether I had robbed you, you should answer, 'No.'" Then said Cosimo, "Get some one to ask me this question and I will tell the whole story." Some others, who were by, when they heard him began to laugh and said nothing about the matter, nor was anyone bold enough to comment on anything a man of worship like Cosimo might say. No other would have shown such great patience.

Cosimo used to say that in most gardens there grew a weed which should never be watered but left to dry up. Most men, however, watered it instead of letting it die of drought. This weed was that worst of all weeds, Envy, and that there were few except the truly wise who did not make shipwreck through it. In his latter days Cosimo fell into irresolute mood, and would often sit for hours without speaking, sunk in thought. In reply to his wife who remarked on his taciturnity he said, "When you propose to go into the country, you trouble yourself for fifteen days in settling what you will do when you get there. Now that the time has come for me to quit this world and pass into another, does it not occur to you that I ought to think about it?" For about a year before he died his humour was to have Aristotle's *Ethics* read to him by Messer Bartolomeo da Colle, the chancellor of the palace, and he brought Donato Acciaiuoli to arrange in order the writings on the *Ethics* which he had collected under Messer Giovanni [Argiropolo] and when these came to Cosimo, Messer

Bartolomeo read them to him, after emendation by Donato, and this emended text of the *Ethics* is the one now in use. Many other things might be told of Cosimo by one who purposed to write his Life, but I am not set on this task. I have only set down matters concerning him which I myself have seen or heard from trustworthy witnesses. I leave all the rest to anyone who may undertake the work of writing the Life of so worthy a citizen, the ornament of his age. What I have written is the actual truth according to what I have heard and seen, neither adding nor omitting anything. Whoever may put together this Life may be vastly more lengthy than I have been, and let things be more clearly portrayed.

FURTHER READING

Francis Ames-Lewis, ed., *Cosimo "il Vecchio" de' Medici, 1389–1464* (1992)
Alison Brown, *The Medici in Florence* (1992)
Gene Brucker, "The Medici in the Fourteenth Century," *Speculum* 32 (1957), 1–26
_____, *Renaissance Florence* (1983)
Trevor Dean, *Land and Power in Late Medieval Ferrara: The Rule of the Este, 1350–1450* (1988)
Louis Green, *Castruccio Castracani, a Study of the Origins and Character of a Fourteenth-Century Despot* (1986)
James Grubb, *Firstborn of Venice: Vicenza in the Early Renaissance State* (1988)
Werner Gundersheimer, *Ferrara: The Style of a Renaissance Despotism* (1973)
Curt Gutkind, *Cosimo de' Medici, Pater Patriae* (1938)
J. R. Hale, *Florence and the Medici, the Pattern of Control* (1977)
P. J. Jones, *The Malatesta of Rimini and the Papal State* (1972)
Dale Kent, *The Rise of the Medici: Faction in Florence, 1426–1434* (1978)
B. G. Kohl, "Government and Society in Renaissance Padua," *Journal of Medieval and Renaissance Studies* 2 (1972), 201–222
John Larner, *The Lords of the Romagna* (1965)
John Law, "The Renaissance Prince," in E. Garin, ed., *Renaissance Characters* (1991), 1–21
Michael Mallett, *Mercenaries and Their Masters* (1972)
Anthony Molho, "Cosimo de' Medici, *Pater Patriae* or *Padrino*." *Stanford Italian Review* 1 (1979), 5–33
Peter Partner, *The Pope's Men: The Papal Civil Service in the Renaissance* (1990)
Mark Phillips, *The Memoir of Marco Parenti: A Life in Medici Florence* (1987)
Nicolai Rubinstein, *The Government of Florence Under the Medici (1434–94)* (1966)
_____, ed., *Florentine Studies, Politics and Society in Renaissance Florence* (1968)

Machiavelli's World

The Italian Renaissance's most famous thinker, Niccolò Machiavelli (1469–1527), came to maturity in an age of chaos and uncertainty. The French invaded Italy in 1494; the invasion was followed by the Italian Wars, which pitted the Habsburgs of Germany and Spain against the Valois dynasty of France for control of the peninsula. In the words of one historian, "The nub of Machiavelli's writing is in the plight of Italy."

Born into an old but not well-to-do Florentine family, Machiavelli spent the first fourteen years of his adult life in the service of the Florentine state. As a diplomat in the field, he observed firsthand the power of the German emperor and the French monarch and the ruthless policies of the pope's son, Cesare Borgia, in his attempts to pacify the Romagna in 1502. Distrustful of reliance on mercenary troops, Machiavelli oversaw the training of a Florentine militia as he became a major figure in the regime of Piero Soderini, who governed Florence as a republic following the expulsion of the Medici in 1494.

With the restoration of the Medicean rule upon the election of Giovanni de' Medici as Pope Leo X in 1512, Soderini's regime fell. Machiavelli was toppled with it and, after brief imprisonment and torture, was exiled to his family's small farm outside Florence. There Machiavelli resolved to apply the lessons of politics he had learned as a statesman and the lessons of history he had gleaned from his readings about the ancients, especially Livy's account of the history of the early Roman republic.

The result of his studies was one of the most influential books of advice to rulers ever written, *The Prince*. Machiavelli dedicated the treatise to members of the Medici dynasty, no doubt hoping to curry favors with the new rulers of Florence and win back his political office. But *The Prince* was far more than simply a ploy to gain political preferment; it radically altered the conventions of the manual of political advice. Machiavelli saw politics in the context of problem solving and created a handbook that would provide effective solutions to contemporary problems, for which the answers from the older moral traditions of medieval Christianity and Roman Stoicism had proved inadequate. At the same time, Machiavelli was deeply indebted to the teachings of ancient moralists, who preached an ethic very different from his own. *The Prince* has been seen at two ends of a spectrum: as a callous political satire—an essay on how not to be a successful prince—and as a useful, pragmatic, sometimes cynical guide to effective political rule. The truth probably lies somewhere in between.

The Prince was written by an experienced statesman, in the enforced leisure of political exile, who resolved to "tell it like it is." Machiavelli no doubt lamented the harshness of his prescriptions for princely success; the demands he placed on his prince were great—nothing less than the liberation of Italy by harnessing the vagaries of fortune. Indeed he clearly came to prefer the edifying classical past of the Roman republic—examined diligently and at length in his *Discourses on the First Decade of Livy,* which every student must take into account for a rounded picture of Machiavelli's thought. But Machiavelli's *Prince* demands attention as the most startling solution to the new imperatives facing Italian leadership in the early sixteenth century.

Essays

Trained at Harvard in the diplomatic and political history of early modern Europe, Garrett Mattingly taught for many years at Columbia University, where his lectures were as famous for their sparkling wit as his books were for their grace and style combined with painstaking research. His famous essay reprinted here as the first selection sees *The Prince* as a prime specimen of political satire. In biting irony, Mattingly describes Machiavelli as deeply cynical, using Cesare Borgia, an example of a conspicuous "loser," as a famous instance of how not to rule as prince.

By contrast, Quentin Skinner, professor of political science at Cambridge University and an incisive student of early modern political thought, views *The Prince* as a serious and revolutionary work in the genre of advice handbooks for princes. Writing in the turbulent age of the French invasion and subsequent Italian Wars, Machiavelli called the old rules of conduct and morality inadequate for the new, dangerous, and unstable situations.

It is perhaps too simple to explain these conflicting interpretations as methods and sensibilities of the historian as opposed to the theorist. Nevertheless, both reveal the difficulty of interpreting Cesare Borgia as a model for the "new prince" and the possibility that *The Prince* can be interpreted as either a work of ironic resignation or a handbook for a new savior of Italy.

The Prince: Political Science or Political Satire?

GARRETT MATTINGLY

The reputation of Niccolò Machiavelli rests on a curious paradox, a paradox so conspicuous and so familiar that we have almost entirely forgotten it. After the collapse of the Florentine republic, which he had served faithfully for fourteen years, Machiavelli relieved the tedium of exile and idleness by taking up his pen. He wrote poems—verse, at least—and tales and plays, including one comedy which is a classic. But mostly he wrote about politics. He was mad about politics. He says in one of his letters that he had to talk about it; he could talk of nothing else. So, in short discourses and political fables, in a history of Florence, in a treatise on the art of war and, notably, in a series of discourses, nominally on the first ten books of Livy, he strove to pass on to his fellow countrymen the fruits of his experience, his reading and his meditation. These are solid works, earnest and thoughtful, often original and provocative. Scholars who have read them usually speak of them with great respect. But not many people ever look at them, and most of those who do have had their curiosity aroused by the one little book which everyone knows: *The Prince*.

The Prince is scarcely more than a pamphlet, a very minor fraction of its author's work, but it overshadows all the rest. Probably no book about politics was ever read more widely. Certainly none has been better known to people who have never read it. Everyone knows that Machiavelli recommended hypocrisy and ingratitude, meanness, cruelty, and treachery as the traits proper to princes. Everyone recognizes "Machiavellian" as an adjective for political conduct that combines diabolical cunning with a ruthless disregard for moral standards. But *The Prince* obsesses historians and political philosophers who know a good deal more about it than that. Its burning prose still casts a lurid glow over the whole landscape of Renaissance Italy: historians who ought to know better call the whole period "the age of Machiavelli" and describe it as if it were chiefly characterized by the kind of behavior on which *The Prince* dwells; and philosophers, undertaking to describe Machiavelli's political thought, after carefully apprising their readers of the greater weight and complexity of the *Discorsi* and his other writings, end up by choosing half or more of their quotations from one slender volume. But *the Prince* is a short book, and most people remember short books better than long ones. Moreover, *The Prince* is easily Machiavelli's best prose. Its sentences are crisp and pointed, free from the parenthetical explanations and qualifying clauses that punctuate and clog his other political writings. Its prose combines verve and bite with a glittering, deadly polish, like the swordplay of a champion fencer. It uses apt, suggestive images, symbols packed with overtones. For instance: A prince should behave sometimes like a beast, and among beasts he should combine the traits of the lion and the fox. It is studded with epigrams like "A man will forget the death of his father sooner than the loss of his

"Machiavelli's Prince: Political Science or Political Satire?" by Garrett Mattingly, reprinted from *The American Scholar*, Volume 27, Number 4, Autumn 1958, pp. 482–491. Copyright © 1958 by the United Chapters of Phi Beta Kappa.

patrimony," epigrams which all seem to come out of some sort of philosophical Grand Guignol and, like the savage ironies of Swift's *Modest Proposal*, are rendered the more spine chilling by the matter-of-fact tone in which they are uttered. And this is where the paradox comes in. Although the method and most of the assumptions of *The Prince* are so much of a piece with Machiavelli's thought that the book could not have been written by anyone else, yet in certain important respects, including some of the most shocking of the epigrams, *The Prince* contradicts everything else Machiavelli ever wrote and everything we know about his life. . . .

The notion that *The Prince* is what it pretends to be, a scientific manual for tyrants, has to contend not only against Machiavelli's life but against his writings, as, of course, everyone who wants to use *The Prince* as a centerpiece in an exposition of Machiavelli's political thought has recognized. . . . The standard explanation has been that in the corrupt conditions of sixteenth-century Italy only a prince could create a strong state capable of expansion. The trouble with this is that it was chiefly because they widened their boundaries that Machiavelli preferred republics. In the *Discorsi* he wrote, "We know by experience that states have never signally increased either in territory or in riches except under a free government. The cause is not far to seek, since it is the well-being not of the individuals but of the community which makes the state great, and without question this universal well-being is nowhere secured save in a republic. . . . Popular rule is always better than the rule of princes." This is not just a casual remark. It is the main theme of the *Discorsi* and the basic assumption of all but one of Machiavelli's writings, as it was the basic assumption of his political career.

There is another way in which *The Prince* is a puzzling anomaly. In practically everything else Machiavelli wrote, he displayed the sensitivity and tact of the developed literary temperament. He was delicately aware of the tastes and probable reactions of his public. No one could have written that magnificent satiric soliloquy of Fra Timoteo in *Mandragola*, for instance, who had not an instinctive feeling for the response of an audience. But the effect of the publication of *The Prince* on the first several generations of its readers in Italy (outside of Florence) and in the rest of Europe was shock. It horrified, rebelled, [*sic*] and fascinated like a Medusa's head. A large part of the shock was caused, of course, by the cynical immorality of some of the proposals, but instead of appeasing revulsion and insinuating his new proposals as delicately as possible, Machiavelli seems to delight in intensifying the shock and deliberately employing devices to heighten it. Of these not the least effective is the way *The Prince* imitates, almost parodies, one of the best known and most respected literary forms of the three preceding centuries, the handbook of advice to princes. This literary type was enormously popular. Its exemplars ran into the hundreds of titles of which a few, like St. Thomas' *De Regno* and Erasmus' *Institutio principis christiani*, are not quite unknown today. In some ways, Machiavelli's little treatise was just like all the other "Mirrors of Princes"; in other ways it was a diabolical burlesque of all of them, like a political Black Mass.

The shock was intensified again because Machiavelli deliberately addressed himself primarily to princes who have newly acquired their principalities and do not owe them either to inheritance or to the free choice of their countrymen. The short and ugly word for this kind of prince is "tyrant." Machiavelli never quite uses the word except in illustrations from classical antiquity, but he seems to delight in dancing all around it until even the dullest of his readers could not mistake his meaning. Opinions about the relative merits of republics and monarchies varied during the Renaissance, depending mainly upon where one lived, but about tyrants there was only one opinion. Cristoforo Landino, Lorenzo the Magnificent's teacher and client, stated the usual view in his commentary on Dante, written when Niccolò Machiavelli was a child. When he came to comment on Brutus and Cassius in the lowest circle of hell, Landino wrote: "Surely it was extraordinary cruelty to inflict such severe punishment on those who faced death to deliver their country from slavery, a deed for which, if they had been Christians, they would have merited the most honored seats in the highest heaven. If we consult the laws of any well-constituted republic, we shall find them to decree no greater reward to anyone than to the man who kills the tyrant." So said the Italian Renaissance with almost unanimous voice. If Machiavelli's friends were meant to read the manuscript of The Prince and if they took it at face value—an objective study of how to be a successful tyrant offered as advice to a member of the species—they can hardly have failed to be deeply shocked. And if the manuscript was meant for the eye of young Giuliano de' Medici alone, he can hardly have been pleased to find it blandly assumed that he was one of a class of whom his father's tutor had written that the highest duty of a good citizen was to kill them.

The literary fame of The Prince is due, precisely, to its shocking quality, so if the book was seriously meant as a scientific manual, it owes its literary reputation to an artistic blunder. And if it was meant for a Medici prince, it has at its core an even more inexplicable piece of tactlessness. For to the Medici prince, "to a new prince established by fortune and the arms of others," Machiavelli offers Cesare Borgia as a model. There was just enough truth to the suggestion that Giuliano de' Medici owed his principate "to the arms of others"—after all, it was the Spanish troops who overthrew the republic as it was French troops who established Cesare in the Romagna— to be wounding. There was just enough cogency in the comparison between the duke of Valentinois, a pope's son, and the duke of Nemours, a pope's brother, to make it stick. These things merely heightened the affront. A Medici, of a family as old and as illustrious as any in Florence, a man whose great-grandfather, grandfather, and father had each in turn been acknowledged the first citizen of the republic and who now aspired to no more than to carry on their tradition (or so he said) was being advised to emulate a foreigner, a Spaniard, a bastard, convicted, in the court of public opinion anyway, of fratricide, incest, and a long role of abominable crimes, a man specially hated in Tuscany for treachery and extortion and for the gross misconduct of his troops on neutral Florentine soil, and a man, to boot, who as a prince had been a notorious and spectacular failure.

This almost forgotten fact lies at the heart of the mystery of The Prince. We remember what Machiavelli wrote about Cesare in his most famous work, and we forget what Cesare was. But in 1513 most Italians would not have forgotten the events of 1503, and unless we assume that Machiavelli himself had forgotten what he himself had reported ten or eleven years before, we can scarcely believe that his commendation of the Borgia was seriously meant. If we take The Prince as an objective, scientific description of political reality, we must face contradiction not only by what we know of Machiavelli's political career, of his usual opinions and of his literary skill, but also by the facts of history as reported by, among others, Machiavelli himself.

Let us take just a few instances, the crucial ones. Relying on assertions in Chapter Seven of *The Prince*, most historians in the past hundred years have written as if the Borgia had restored peace and order in the Romagna, unified its government and won the allegiance of its inhabitants. Part of the time this must have been going on, Machiavelli was an envoy in the duke's camp. Although he does warn the signory repeatedly that Valentino is a formidable ruffian, daring, unscrupulous, and of unlimited ambition, he never mentions these statesmanlike achievements—nor do any of the other reports from observers in the area, Spanish, French, Venetian, Sienese; nor do any other contemporary sources. All the indications are quite contrary. The most probing recent study of Valentino's career, Gabriele Pepe's *La Politica dei Borgia*, sums the matter up by saying that the duke did nothing to end factional strife and anarchy in the Romagna; he merely superimposed the brutal rule of his Spanish captains on top of it.

We can make a concrete check on a related instance. After saying in Chapter Thirteen that the duke had used first French troops, then mercenaries under *condottieri* captains and then his own men, Machiavelli comments, "He was never esteemed more highly than when everyone saw that he was complete master of his own forces." But in the *Legazione*, Machiavelli never once refers to the military capacity of the duke or praises the courage or discipline of his army. Instead, as late as December 14, 1502, he writes from Imola of the troops under Cesare's own command: "They have devoured everything here except the stones . . . here in the Romagna they are behaving just as they did in Tuscany last year [of their passage then, Landucci had noted in his diary that none of the foreign armies that had crossed Tuscany in the past seven years had behaved so abominably as these Italians under the papal banner] and they show no more discipline and no less confusion than they did then." There is no subsequent indication that Machiavelli ever changed his mind.

Nowhere is *The Prince* more at odds with the facts of history or with Machiavelli's own previous judgments than in the famous concluding passage of Chapter Seven on which any favorable opinion of Cesare's statecraft must be based. The passage in *The Prince* reads: "On the day Pope Julius II was elected, the Duke told me that he had thought of everything that might happen on the death of his father and provided for everything except that when his father died he himself would be at death's door . . . only the shortness of the life of Alexander and his own sickness frustrated his designs. Therefore he who wants to make sure of a new principality . . . cannot find a better model than the actions of this man." Could Machiavelli have believed this in 1513? He certainly did not believe it in 1503. He did not even record then that Cesare ever said anything of the sort; and though it would not be unlike some of the duke's whimperings, he could not have said it on the day of Julius II's election, when he was boasting to everyone that the new pope would obey him. In any case, Machiavelli would have believed what, in *The Prince*, he said the duke said, as little as he believed the bluster that, in 1503, he actually reported. By November of 1503, nobody could have believed it. In fact, even in August, when Alexander VI died, at the age of seventy-two after a papacy of eleven years (not such a short life and not such a short reign), most people in Rome, including all of the ambassadors whose reports survive and most of the cardinals with whom they had talked, felt sure Cesare was finished. He had always ridden on his father's shoulders, and he was hated, feared, and despised even by most of the faction who had stood by the old pope. No one trusted him, and there was no one he could trust. No pope would dare support him, and without papal support his principate was built on quicksand. He had never, in fact, faced this eventual predicament, and he did not face it when it arose. It is true that he was ill in August with a bout of malaria, but not too ill to stall the election and then maneuver the choice of the old and ailing Pius III, thus delaying an unavoidable doom. Julius II was not elected until November. In all those months and even after the election, Italy was treated through the eyes of its ambassadors to the spectacle of the terrible Borgia duke writhing in an agony of indecision, now about to go to Genoa to raise money, now ready to start for an interview with the king of France, now on the point of leading his troops back to the Romagna, but in fact hovering about the curia, plucking the sleeves of cardinals and bowing and smiling to envoys he used to bully, sometimes swaggering through the streets with the powerful armed guard he felt he needed to protect him from the vengeance of the Orsini, sometimes shaking beneath bedclothes with what might have been fever and might have been funk. We catch a glimpse of him at midnight in the chamber of Guidobaldo de Montefeltro, the duke of Urbino, who had been newly restored to his former estates by the loyalty of his subjects, and to his former rank of *gonfaloniere* [standard-bearer] of the church by the new pope. There Cesare kneels on the floor, sobbing in pure terror, begging the old friend whom he had betrayed and robbed, with incredible meanness, not just of his duchy, but of his books and his antique medals, not to kill him, please not to kill him, to leave him at least his life, until Guidobaldo, beyond any feeling about this curious monster, says he does not wish to kill him; he only wishes him to go away.

Shortly thereafter Cesare slinks off to Naples and imprisonment, followed by the scornful laughter of Italy. For nothing is more absurd than the great straw-stuffed giants of carnival, and when such a giant has for a season frightened all Italy, the laughter is that much the louder. Machiavelli was one of the ambassadors in Rome. He knew all this as well as anyone. One can read in dispatches his growing impatience with the duke, his growing contempt for Cesare's wild talk, aimless shifts of plan, alternate blustering and whining. "The duke, who never kept faith with anyone," he wrote, "is now obliged to rely on the faith of others." And later, "The duke, who never showed mercy, now finds mercy his only hope." Later in his historical poem, *Decennali*, Machiavelli made his distaste for the Borgia clear enough. Did he really mean to propose him in 1513 as a model prince? Was he writing as a friend of tyrants or as a dispassionate scientific observer when he said he did? . . .

To read *The Prince* as satire not only clears up puzzles and resolves contradictions; it gives a new dimension and meaning to passages unremarkable before. Take the place in the dedication that runs "just as those who paint landscapes must seat themselves below in the plains to see the mountains, and high in the mountains to see the plains, so to understand the nature of the people one must be a prince, and to understand the nature of a prince, one must be one of the people." In the usual view, this is a mere rhetorical flourish, but the irony, once sought, is easy to discover, for Machiavelli, in fact, takes both positions. The people can only see the prince as, by nature and necessity, false, cruel, mean, and hypocritical. The prince, from his lofty but precarious perch, dare not see the people as other than they are described in Chapter Seventeen: "ungrateful, fickle, treacherous, cowardly, and greedy. As long as you succeed they are yours entirely. They will offer you their blood, property, lives, and children when you do not need them. When you do need them, they will turn against you." Probably Machiavelli really believed that this, or something like it, happened to the human nature of a tyrant and his subjects. But the view, like its expression, is something less than objective and dispassionate, and the only lesson it has for princes would seem to be: "Run for your life!"

Considering the brevity of the book, the number of times its princely reader is reminded, as in the passage just quoted, that his people will overthrow him at last is quite remarkable. Cities ruled in the past by princes easily accustom themselves to a change of master, Machiavelli says in Chapter Five, but "in republics there is more vitality, greater hatred, and more desire for vengeance. They cannot forget their lost liberty, so that the safest way is to destroy them—or to live there." He does not say what makes that safe. And most notably, with savage irony, "the duke [Borgia] was so able and laid such firm foundations . . . that the Romagna [after Alexander VI's death] waited for him more than a month." This is as much as to put Leo X's brother on notice that without papal support he can expect short shrift. If the Romagna, accustomed to tyranny, waited only a month before it rose in revolt, how long will Florence wait? Tactlessness like this is unintelligible unless it is deliberate, unless these are not pedantic blunders but sarcastic ironies, taunts flung at the Medici, incitements to the Florentines.

Only in a satire can one understand the choice of Cesare Borgia as the model prince. The common people of Tuscany could not have had what they could expect of a prince's rule made clearer than by the example of this bloodstained buffoon whose vices, crimes, and follies had been the scandal of Italy, and the conduct of whose brutal, undisciplined troops had so infuriated the Tuscans that when another band of them crossed their frontier, the peasants fell upon them and tore them to pieces. The Florentine aristocrats on whom Giovanni and cousin Giulio were relying to bridge the transition to despotism would have shared the people's revulsion to Cesare, and they may have been rendered somewhat more thoughtful by the logic of the assumption that nobles were more dangerous to a tyrant than commoners and should be dealt with as Cesare had dealt with the petty lords of the Romagna. Moreover, they could scarcely have avoided noticing the advice to use some faithful servant to terrorize the rest, and then to sacrifice him to escape the obloquy of his conduct, as Cesare had sacrificed Captain Remirro. As for the gentle, mild-mannered, indolent Giuliano de Medici himself, he was the last man to be attracted by the notion of imitating the Borgia. He wanted no more than to occupy the same social position in Florence that his magnificent father had held, and not even that if it was too much trouble. Besides, in the days of the family's misfortunes, Giuliano had found shelter and hospitality at the court of Guidobaldo de Montefeltro. Giuliano lived at Urbino for many years (there is a rather charming picture of him there in Castiglione's Il Cortegiano), and all his life he cherished deep gratitude and a strong affection for Duke Guidobaldo. He must have felt, then, a special loathing for the foreign ruffian who had betrayed and plundered his patron, and Machiavelli must have known that he did. Only a wish to draw the most odious comparison possible, only a compulsion to wound and insult, could have led Machiavelli to select the Borgia as the prime exemplar in his "Mirror of Princes."

There is one last famous passage that reads differently if we accept *The Prince* as satire. On any other hypothesis, the final exhortation to free Italy from the barbarians sounds at best like empty rhetoric, at worst like calculating but stupid flattery. Who could really believe that the lazy, insipid Giuliano or his petty, vicious successor were the liberators Italy awaited? But if we have heard the mordant irony and sarcasm of the preceding chapters and detected the overtones of hatred and despair, then this last chapter will be charged with an irony turned inward, the bitter mockery of misdirected optimism. For before the Florentine republic had been gored to death by Spanish pikes, Machiavelli had believed, as he was to believe again, that a free Florentine republic could play the liberator's role. Perhaps, since he was all his life a passionate idealist, blind to reality when his desires were strong, Machiavelli may not have given up that wild hope even when he wrote *The Prince*. If he had not, then the verses at the end take on a new meaning, clearer perhaps to his contemporaries than they can be to us.

> Virtù contro a furore
> [Valor against wild rage]
> Prenderà l'arme, e fia il combatter corto;
> [Will take up arms, and the combat will be short;]
> Chè l'antico valore
> [Because ancestral courage]
> Nell'italici cor non è ancor morto.
> [In our Italian hearts is not yet dead.]

The antique valor Petrarch appealed to was, after all, that of republican Rome. Perhaps that first sharp combat was not to be against the barbarians.

However that may be, we must agree that if *The Prince* was meant as a satire, as a taunt and challenge to the Medici and a tocsin to the people of Florence, then it must have been recognized as such by the Florentine literati and by the Medici themselves. If so we have the solution to two minor puzzles connected with this puzzling book. A rasher ruling family than the Medici might have answered the challenge by another round of torture and imprisonment or by a quiet six inches of steel under the fifth rib. But brother Giovanni and brother Giovanni's familiar spirit, cousin Giulio, though in fact they were aiming at exactly the kind of despotism that Machiavelli predicted, hoped to achieve it with a minimum of trouble by preserving for the time being the forms of the republic. It would not do, by punishing the author, to admit the pertinence of his satire. So the Medici did nothing. But they were not a stupid family, and they cannot have been very pleased. This would explain some puzzling things: why, for example, the ardent republicans among Machiavelli's friends, like Zanobi Buondelmonti, were not alienated by *The Prince*, and why the former republicans in Medici service among his correspondents, like Vettori, for instance, refer to it so seldom and with such muffled embarrassment. It would also explain why, among all the manuscripts of *The Prince* dating from Machiavelli's lifetime (and it seems to have had a considerable circulation and to have been multiplied by professional copyists), we have never found the copy which should have had the best chance of preservation—I mean that copy, beautifully lettered on vellum and richly bound, presented with its dedication to the Medici prince. Not only is it absent from the Laurentian library now, there is no trace that it was ever there. There is no evidence that it ever existed. Probably Machiavelli figured that the joke was not worth the extra expense.

Machiavelli's Advice to Princes

QUENTIN SKINNER

Arms and the man: these are Machiavelli's two great themes in *The Prince*. The other lesson he accordingly wishes to bring home to the rulers of his age is that, in addition to having a sound army, a prince who aims to scale the heights of glory must cultivate the right qualities of princely leadership. The nature of these qualities had already been influentially analysed by the Roman moralists. They had argued in the first place that all great leaders need to some extent to be fortunate. For unless Fortune happens to smile, no amount of unaided human effort can hope to bring us to our highest goals. . . . They also maintained that a special range of characteristics—those of the *vir* [man]—tend to attract the favourable attentions of Fortune, and in this way almost guarantee us the attainment of honour, glory and fame. The assumptions underlying this belief are best summarised by Cicero in his *Tusculan Disputations*. He declares that, if we act from a thirst for *virtus* without any thought of winning glory as a result, this will give us the best chance of winning glory as well, provided that Fortune smiles; for glory is *virtus* rewarded.

This analysis was taken over without alteration by the humanists of Renaissance Italy. By the end of the fifteenth century, an extensive *genre* of humanist advice-books for princes had grown up, and had reached an unprecedentedly wide audience through the new medium of print. Such distinguished writers as Bartolomeo Sacchi, Giovanni Pontano and Francesco Patrizi all wrote treatises for the guidance of new rulers, all of which were founded on the same basic principle: that the possession of *virtus* is the key to princely success. As Pontano rather grandly proclaims in his tract on *The Prince*, any ruler who wishes to attain his noblest ends "must rouse himself to follow the dictates of *virtus*" in all his public acts. *Virtus* is "the most splendid thing in the world," more magnificent even than the sun, for "the blind cannot see the sun" whereas "even they can see *virtus* as plainly as possible."

Machiavelli reiterates precisely the same beliefs about the relations between *virtù*, Fortune and the achievement of princely goals. He first makes these humanist allegiances clear in chapter 6 of *The Prince*, where he argues that "in princedoms wholly new, where the prince is new, there is more or less difficulty in keeping them, according as the prince who acquires them is more or less *virtuoso*." This is later corroborated in chapter 24, the aim of which is to explain "Why the princes of Italy have lost their states." Machiavelli insists that they "should not blame Fortune" for their disgrace, because "she only shows her power" when men of *virtù* "do not prepare to resist her." Their losses are simply due to their failure to recognise that "those defences alone are good" which "depend on yourself and your own *virtù*." Finally, the role of *virtù* is again underlined in chapter 26, the impassioned "Exhortation" to lib-erate Italy that brings *The Prince* to an end. At this point Machiavelli reverts to the incomparable leaders mentioned in chapter 6 for their "amazing *virtù*"—Moses, Cyrus and Theseus. He implies that nothing less than a union of their astonishing abilities with the greatest good Fortune will enable Italy to be saved. And he adds—in an uncharacteristic moment of preposterous flattery—that the "glorious family" of the Medici luckily possess all the requisite qualities: they have tremendous *virtù*; they are immensely favoured by Fortune; and they are no less "favoured by God and by the Church."

It is often complained that Machiavelli fails to provide any definition of *virtù*, and even that (as [J.H.] Whitfield puts it) he is "innocent of any systematic use of the word." But it will now be evident that he uses the term with complete consistency. Following his classical and humanist authorities, he treats it as that quality which enables a prince to withstand the blows of Fortune, to attract the goddess's favour, and to rise in consequence to the heights of princely fame, winning honour and glory for himself and security for his government.

It still remains, however, to consider what particular characteristics are to be expected in a man of *virtuoso* capacities. The Roman moralists had bequeathed a complex analysis of the concept of *virtus*, generally picturing the true *vir* as the pos-sessor of three distinct yet affiliated sets of qualities. They took him to be endowed in the first place with the four "cardinal" virtues of wisdom, justice, courage and temperance—the virtues that Cicero (following Plato) begins by singling out in the opening sections of *Moral Obligation*. But they also credited him with an additional range of qualities that later came to be regarded as peculiarly "princely" in nature. The chief of these—the pivotal virtue of Cicero's *Moral Obligation*—was what Cic-ero called "honesty," meaning a willingness to keep faith and deal honourably with all men at all times. This was felt to need supplementing by two further attributes, both of which were described in *Moral Obligation*, but were more extensively an-alysed by Seneca, who devoted special treatises to each of them. One was princely magnanimity, the theme of Seneca's *On Mercy*; the other was liberality, one of the major topics discussed in Seneca's *On Benefits*. Finally, the true *vir* was said to be characterised by his steady recognition of the fact that, if we wish to reach the goals of honour and glory, we must always be sure to behave as virtuously as possible. This contention—that it is always rational to be moral—lies at the heart of Cicero's *Moral Obligation*. He observes in Book II that many men believe "that a thing may be morally right without being expedient, and expedient without being morally right." But this is an illusion, for it is only by moral methods that we can hope to attain the objects of our desires. Any appearances to the contrary are wholly deceptive, for "expediency can never conflict with moral rectitude." . . .

Machiavelli's criticism of classical and contemporary humanism is thus a simple but devastating one. He argues that, if a ruler wishes to reach his highest goals, he will *not* always find it rational to be moral; on the contrary, he will find that any consistent attempt to "practise all those things for which men are considered good" will prove a ruinously irrational policy. But what of the Christian objection that this is a foolish as well as a wicked position to adopt, since it forgets the day of judgement on which all injustices will finally be punished? About this Machiavelli says nothing at all. His silence is eloquent, indeed epoch-making; it echoed around Christian Europe, at first eliciting a stunned silence in return, and then a howl of execration that has never finally died away.

If princes ought not to conduct themselves according to the dictates of conventional morality, how ought they to conduct themselves? Machiavelli's response—the core of his positive advice to new rulers—is given at the beginning of chapter 15. A wise prince will be guided above all by the dictates of necessity: "in order to hold his position," he "must acquire the power to be not good, and understand when to use it and when not to use it" as circumstances direct. Three chapters later, this basic doctrine is repeated. A wise prince "holds to what is right when he can," but he "knows how to do wrong when this is necessitated." Moreover, he must reconcile himself to the fact that "he will often be necessitated" to act "contrary to truth, contrary to charity, contrary to humanity, contrary to religion" if he wishes "to maintain his government."

. . . The crucial importance of this insight was first put to Machiavelli at an early stage in his diplomatic career. It was after conversing with the cardinal of Volterra in 1503, and with Pandolfo Petrucci some two years later, that he originally felt impelled to record what was later to become his central political belief: that the clue to successful statecraft lies in recognising the force of circumstances, accepting what necessity dictates, and harmonising one's behaviour with the times. A year after Pandolfo gave him this recipe for princely success, we find Machiavelli putting forward a similar set of observations as his own ideas for the first time. While stationed at Perugia in September 1506, watching the astonishing progress of Julius II's campaign, he fell to musing in a letter to his friend Giovanni Soderini about the reasons for triumph and disaster in civil and military affairs. "Nature," he declares, "has given every man a particular talent and inspiration" which "controls each one of us." But "the times are varied" and "subject to frequent change," so that "those who fail to alter their ways of proceeding" are bound to encounter "good Fortune at one time and bad at another." The moral is obvious: if a man wishes "always to enjoy good Fortune," he must "be wise enough to accommodate himself to the times." Indeed, if everyone were "to command his nature" in this way, and "match his way of proceeding with his age," then "it would genuinely come true that the wise man would be the ruler of the stars and of the fates."

Writing *The Prince* seven years later, Machiavelli virtually copied out these "Caprices," as he deprecatingly called them, in his chapter on the role of Fortune in human affairs. Everyone, he says, likes to follow his own particular bent: one person acts "with caution, another impetuously; one by force, the other with skill." But in the meantime, "times and affairs change," so that a ruler who "does not change his way of proceeding" will be bound sooner or later to encounter ill-luck. However, if "he could change his nature with times and affairs, Fortune would not change." So the successful prince will always be the one "who adapts his way of proceeding to the nature of the times."

By now it will be evident that the revolution Machiavelli engineered in the *genre* of advice-books for princes was based in effect on redefining the pivotal concept of *virtù*. He endorses the conventional assumption that *virtù* is the name of that congeries of qualities which enables a prince to ally with Fortune and obtain honour, glory and fame. But he divorces the meaning of the term from any necessary connection with the cardinal and princely virtues. He argues instead that the defining characteristic of a truly *virtuoso* prince will be a willingness to do whatever is dictated by necessity—whether the action happens to be wicked or virtuous—in order to attain his highest ends. So *virtù* comes to denote precisely the requisite quality of moral flexibility in a prince: "he must have a mind ready to turn in any direction as Fortune's winds and the variability of affairs require."

Machiavelli takes some pains to point out that this conclusion opens up an unbridgeable gulf between himself and the whole tradition of humanist political thought, and does so in his most savagely ironic style. To the classical moralists and their innumerable followers, moral virtue had been the defining characteristic of the *vir*, the man of true manliness. Hence to abandon virtue was not merely to act irrationally; it was also to abandon one's status as a man and descend to the level of the beasts. As Cicero had put it in Book I of *Moral Obligation,* there are two ways in which wrong may be done, either by force or by fraud. Both, he declares, "are bestial" and "wholly unworthy of man"—force because it typifies the lion and fraud because it "seems to belong to the cunning fox."

To Machiavelli, by contrast, it seemed obvious that manliness is not enough. There are indeed two ways of acting, he says at the start of chapter 18, of which "the first is suited to man, the second to the animals." But "because the first is often not sufficient, a prince must resort to the second." One of the things a prince therefore needs to know is which animals to imitate. Machiavelli's celebrated advice is that he will come off best if he "chooses among the beasts the fox and the lion," supplementing the ideals of manly decency with the indispensable arts of force and fraud. This conception is underlined in the next chapter, in which Machiavelli discusses one of his favourite historical characters, the Roman emperor Septimius Severus. First he assures us that the emperor was "a man of very great *virtù*." And then, explaining the judgement, he adds that Septimius' great qualities were those of "a very savage lion and a very tricky fox," as a result of which he was "feared and respected by everybody."

Machiavelli rounds off his analysis by indicating the lines of conduct to be expected from a truly *virtuoso* prince. In chapter 19 he puts the point negatively, stressing that such a ruler will never do anything worthy of contempt, and will always take the greatest care "to avoid everything that makes him hated." In chapter 21 the positive implications are then spelled out. Such a prince will always act "without reservation" towards his allies and enemies, boldly standing forth "as a vigorous supporter of one side." At the same time, he will seek to present himself to his subjects as majestically as possible, doing "extraordinary things" and keeping them "always in suspense and wonder, watching for the outcome."

In the light of this account, it is easy to understand why Machiavelli felt such admiration for Cesare Borgia, and wished to hold him up—despite his obvious limitations—as a pattern of *virtù* for other new princes. For Borgia had demonstrated, on one terrifying occasion, that he understood perfectly the paramount importance of avoiding the hatred of the people while at the same time keeping them in awe. The occasion was when he realised that his government of the Romagna, in the capable but tyrannical hands of Remirro de Orco, was falling into the most serious danger of all, that of becoming an object of hatred to those living under it. . . . Machiavelli was an eye-witness of Borgia's cold-blooded solution to the dilemma: the summary murder of Remirro and the exhibition of his body in the public square as a sacrifice to the people's rage.

Machiavelli's belief in the imperative need to avoid popular hatred and contempt should perhaps be dated from this moment. But even if the duke's action merely served to corroborate his own sense of political realities, there is no doubt that the episode left him deeply impressed. When he came to discuss the issues of hatred and contempt in *The Prince*, this was precisely the incident he recalled in order to illustrate his point. He makes it clear that Borgia's action had struck him on reflection as being profoundly right. It was resolute; it took courage; and it brought about exactly the desired effect, since it left the people "gratified and awestruck" while at the same time removing their "cause for hatred." Summing up in his iciest tones, Machiavelli remarks that the duke's conduct seems to him, as usual, to be "worthy of notice and of being copied by others."

Machiavelli is fully aware that his new analysis of princely *virtù* raises some new difficulties. He states the main dilemma in the course of chapter 15: on the one hand, a prince must "acquire the power to be not good" and exercise it whenever this is dictated by necessity; but on the other hand, he must be careful not to acquire the reputation of being a wicked man, because this will tend to "take his position away from him" instead of securing it. The problem is thus to avoid appearing wicked even when you cannot avoid behaving wickedly.

Moreover, the dilemma is even sharper than this implies, for the true aim of the prince is not merely to secure his position, but is of course to win honour and glory as well. As Machiavelli indicates in recounting the story of Agathocles, the tyrant of Sicily, this greatly intensifies the predicament in which any new ruler finds himself. Agathocles, we are told, "lived a wicked life" at every stage of his career and was known as a man of "outrageous cruelty and inhumanity." These attributes brought him immense success, enabling him to rise from "low and abject Fortune" to become king of Syracuse and hold on to his principality "without any opposition from the citizens." But as Machiavelli warns us, in a deeply revealing phrase, such unashamed cruelties may bring us "sovereignty, but not glory." Although Agathocles was able to maintain his state by means of these qualities, "they cannot be called *virtù* and they do not permit him to be honoured among the noblest men."

Finally, Machiavelli refuses to admit that the dilemma can be resolved by setting stringent limits to princely wickedness, and in general behaving honourably towards one's subjects and allies. This is exactly what one cannot hope to do, because all men at all times "are ungrateful, changeable, simulators and dissimulators, runaways in danger, eager for gain," so that "a prince who bases himself entirely on their word, if he is lacking in other preparations, falls." The implication is that "a prince, and above all a prince who is new" will often—not just occasionally—find himself forced by necessity to act "contrary to humanity" if he wishes to keep his position and avoid being deceived.

These are acute difficulties, but they can certainly be overcome. The prince need only remember that, although it is not necessary to have all the qualities usually considered good, it is "very necessary to appear to have them." It is good to be considered liberal; it is sensible to seem merciful and not cruel; it is essential in general to be "thought to be of great merit." The solution is thus to become "a great simulator and dissimulator," learning "how to addle the brains of men with trickery" and make them believe in your pretence.

Machiavelli had received an early lesson in the value of addling men's brains. . . . He had been present when the struggle developed between Cesare Borgia and Julius II in the closing months of 1503, and it is evident that the impressions he carried away from that occasion were still uppermost in his mind when he came to write about the question of dissimulation in *The Prince*. He immediately refers back to the episode he had witnessed, using it as his main example of the need to remain constantly on one's guard against princely duplicity. Julius, he recalls, managed to conceal his hatred of Borgia so cleverly that he caused the duke to fall into the egregious error of believing that "men of high rank forget old injuries." He was then able to put his powers of dissimulation to decisive use. Having won the papal election with Borgia's full support, he suddenly revealed his true feelings, turned against the duke and "caused his final ruin." Borgia certainly blundered at this point, and Machiavelli feels that he deserved to be blamed severely for his mistake. He ought to have known that a talent for addling men's brains is part of the armoury of any successful prince.

Machiavelli cannot have been unaware, however, that in recommending the arts of deceit as the key to success he was in danger of sounding too glib. More orthodox moralists had always been prepared to consider the suggestion that hypocrisy might be used as a short cut to glory, but had always gone on to rule out any such possibility. Cicero, for example, had explicitly canvassed the idea in Book II of *Moral Obligation*, only to dismiss it as a manifest absurdity. Anyone, he declares, who "thinks that he can win lasting glory by pretence" is "very much mistaken." The reason is that "true glory strikes deep roots and spreads its branches wide," whereas "all pretences soon fall to the ground like fragile flowers."

Machiavelli responds, as before, by rejecting such earnest sentiments in his most ironic style. He insists in chapter 18 that the practice of hypocrisy is not merely indispensable to princely government, but is capable of being sustained without much difficulty for as long as may be required. Two distinct reasons are offered for this deliberately provocative conclusion. One is that most men are so simpleminded, and above all so prone to self-deception, that they usually take things at face value in a wholly uncritical way. The other is that, when it comes to assessing the behaviour of princes, even the shrewdest observers are largely condemned to judge by appearances. Isolated from the populace, protected by "the majesty of the government," the prince's position is such that "everybody sees what you appear to be" but "few perceive what you are." Thus there is no reason to suppose that your sins will find you out; on the contrary, "a prince who deceives always finds men who let themselves be deceived."

The final issue Machiavelli discusses is what attitude we should take towards the new rules he has sought to inculcate. At first sight he appears to adopt a relatively conventional moral stance. He agrees in chapter 15 that "it would be most praiseworthy" for new princes to exhibit those qualities which are normally considered good, and he equates the abandonment of the princely virtues with the process of learning "to be not good." The same scale of values recurs even in the notorious chapter on "How princes should keep their promises." Machiavelli begins by affirming that everybody realises how praiseworthy it is when a ruler "lives with sincerity and not with trickery," and goes on to insist that a prince ought not merely to seem conventionally virtuous, but ought "actually to be so" as far as possible, "holding to what is right when he can," and only turning away from the virtues when this is dictated by necessity.

However, two very different arguments are introduced in the course of chapter 15, each of which is subsequently developed. First of all, Machiavelli is somewhat quizzical about whether we can properly say that those qualities which are considered good, but are nevertheless ruinous, really deserve the name of virtues. Since they are prone to bring destruction, he prefers to say that they "look like virtues"; and since their opposites are more likely to bring "safety and well-being," he prefers to say that they "look like vices."

DOCUMENTS

The exchange of letters between Machiavelli, exiled after 1512 to his farm at San Casciano in Tuscany, and his friend in Rome, Francesco Vettori, provides the setting for the composition of *The Prince*. In the first selection, Vettori, a Florentine patrician and statesman, describes his rather luxurious life as Florence's envoy to the papal court in Rome, where he hobnobbed with Pope Leo X, cardinals, and other diplomats. In his famous reply of December 10, 1513, the second selection, Machiavelli stresses his poverty and misery, alleviated only by his "conversation with the ancients" in his evening study of classical history. Composed with ironic intent as the mirror image of Vettori's life in Rome, Machiavelli's depiction of his grim exile in the Tuscan countryside is no doubt exaggerated. These two letters nevertheless provide deeply personal and contrasting visions of life in the era of the Italian Wars.

In *The Prince*, Machiavelli used the lessons of ancient history and contemporary events to educate a "new prince" to succeed in a volatile, even dangerous, political context. The third selection comprises excerpts from several chapters in *The Prince*. Chapter 7 presents Machiavelli's view of Cesare Borgia. Chapters 15, 17, and 18 address the prince's need to use evil methods for his own preservation. Finally, Chapters 24 through 26 examine how Italian princes have lost their states. Machiavelli then posits that fortune is a woman, controlled better by a bold prince than a cautious one, and he concludes with an exhortation to a "new prince" to free Italy from the barbarians.

Francesco Vettori Describes His Life in Rome, 1513

Distinguished Niccolò of messer Bernardo Machiavelli.
In Florence.

My dear friend,

In this letter I thought I would write to you about my life in Rome. And it seems sensible to start by telling you about where I live, because I've moved, and I'm no longer as near the courtesans as I was this summer. My rooms are in S. Michele in Borgo, very close to the Vatican [Palace] and St. Peter's Square, although a little isolated, because it's on the other side of the hill called Janiculum by the ancients. The house is very nice, with many small rooms, and it faces the breeze from the north, so it's well ventilated. From the house one enters directly into the church, as I do often, being a religious person, as you well know. Actually, the church is a good place to take a walk, because no mass or other divine office is said there but once a year. From the church one enters a garden, which used to be well kept and pretty but now is largely overgrown, even though it's always being tended. From the garden one can climb the Janiculum hill and wander on winding paths among the vines for pleasure, without being seen by anyone; here, according to the ancients, were the gardens of Nero, the remains of which can still be seen. I live in this house with nine servants, Brancaccio, a chaplain, and a secretary, and seven horses, and I spend my entire salary liberally. When I first arrived, I started out wishing to live in magnificence and with refinement, inviting guests, offering three or four courses, eating from silver dishes and other finery; then I realized that I was spending too much and I wasn't living any better; so I decided to invite no one and to live an ordinary existence; I returned the silver to those who had lent it to me, so as not to have to keep it safe, and also because they often asked me to intercede with Our Lord [the pope] about a problem of theirs; I did this, but they weren't satisfied, so I decided to abandon the matter and give trouble or responsibility to no one, as long as none were given to me.

During this season, I rise in midmorning and, dressed, go straight to the Palace—not every day but one out of every two or three. When there, I sometimes speak twenty words to the pope, ten to Cardinal [Giulio] de' Medici [later Pope Clement VII], six to the magnificent Giuliano; and if I cannot speak with him, I speak with Piero Ardinghelli [the papal secretary], then to a few ambassadors who are in the papal apartments; and I come by some minor information of little importance. Having done this, I come home, except on the days when I dine with Cardinal de' Medici. At home, I eat with my household and occasionally one or two guests, such as Ser Sano or Ser Tommaso who was in Trent, Giovanni Rucellai, or Giovanni Girolami. After eating, I play [cards] if I have a companion, but when alone I stroll

From Machiavelli, *Lettere*, ed. Franco Gaeta (Milan:Feltrinelli, 1961), pp. 297–300. Translated by Alison A. Smith.

through the church and the garden. If the weather is nice, I ride a horse a short distance from Rome. At night I return home, where I have collected many histories, especially of the Romans, such as Livy, with Florus's epitome, Sallust, Plutarch, Appian of Alexandria, Cornelius Tacitus, Suetonius, Lampridius and Spartianus, and those others who write of emperors—Herodian, Ammianus Marcellinus, and Procopius. I pass the time with these, and reflect on how poor Rome, which used to make the whole world tremble, once supported such emperors, and think that it is not so strange after all that Rome has tolerated popes of the quality of the last two [Alexander VI and Julius II]. I write a letter once every four days, to the Ten of War [War Commission] in Florence, and tell what stale, uninteresting news I have, because, as you well understand, I have nothing else to write. Then I go to sleep, after having supped and chatted with Brancaccio and Giovanbattista Nasi, who is with me often. On feast days I hear mass, unlike you, who occasionally skip it. If you ask me if I have a courtesan, I tell you that when I first came here, I had several, as I wrote to you; then, afraid of the summer air, I restrained myself. Nonetheless, I have had one who comes of her own accord, is quite pretty, and who speaks pleasantly. And even in this isolated place I have a neighbor (a woman) you wouldn't mind; and even if she is related to nobility, she'll do a few favors.

My dear Niccolò, I invite you to partake of this life. If you come you will make my happy, and then we can go home together. Here you have nothing to do but go about observing and then return home to tell stories and laugh. Nor do I wish you to believe that I live like an ambassador, because I always want to be free. Sometimes I wear long robes, sometimes short; sometimes I ride alone, with servants on foot, sometimes they come on horseback. I never go to cardinals' houses, and the only one I would visit anyway is Medici and sometimes Bibbiena, when he is well. And let people say what they wish, but if they don't like what I'm doing, let them call me back to Florence. When I return to Florence at the end of my term (in about a year), I hope that I will break even, after selling my clothes and horses, and not have to spend any of my own money here. And I want you to believe the following, which I say without flattery: Even though I have suffered little here, still the crowds are so large that little can be accomplished without much effort, and I don't like the people very much, nor have I found anyone with better judgment than yours. "But we are dragged by the fates": That, when I talk at length with people or read their letters, I am amazed that they have achieved any distinction at all that isn't empty ceremony, lies and fantasy, and there are few who are anything out of the ordinary. Bernardo da Bibbiena, now a cardinal, in truth has a very good mind, and he is a witty, distinguished man who has worked very hard; nonetheless, he is sick now, and has been for three months, nor do I know if he will return to good health. So often we tire ourselves out hoping to find rest, and aren't able to; and still we're happy, come what may. Remember that I am at your service, and that I recommend myself to you, to Filippo and Giovanni Machiavelli, to Donato, to messer Ciaio. And no one else. May Christ be with you.

| Machiavelli on a Typical Day at His Farm, 1513

10 December 1513, Florence
To Francesco Vettori, his benefactor, in Rome

Magnificent Ambassador:

"Never late were favors divine." I say this because I seemed to have lost—no, rather mislaid—your good will; you had not written to me for a long time, and I was wondering what the reason could be. And of all those that came into my mind I took little account, except of one only, when I feared that you had stopped writing because somebody had written to you that I was not a good guardian of your letters, and I knew that, except Filippo [Casavecchia] and Pagolo [Vettori, brother of Francesco Vettori], nobody by my doing had seen them. I have found it again through your last one of the twenty-third of the past month, from which I learn with pleasure how regularly and quietly you carry on this public office, and I encourage you to continue so, because he who gives up his own convenience for the convenience of others, only loses his own and from them gets no gratitude. And since Fortune wants to do everything, she wishes us to let her do it, to be quiet, and not to give her trouble, and to wait for a time when she will allow something to be done by men; and then will be the time for you to work harder, to stir things up more, and for me to leave my farm and say: "Here I am." I cannot however, wishing to return equal favors, tell you in this letter anything else than what my life is; and if you judge it is to be swapped for yours, I shall be glad to change it.

I am living on my farm, and since I had my last bad luck, I have not spent twenty days, putting them all together, in Florence. I have until now been snaring thrushes with my own hands. I got up before day, prepared birdlime, went out with a bundle of cages on my back, so that I looked like Geta when he was returning from the harbor with Amphitryo's books. I caught at least two thrushes and at most six. And so I did all September. Later this pastime, pitiful and strange as it is, gave out, to my displeasure. And of what sort my life is, I shall tell you.

I get up in the morning with the sun and go into a grove I am having cut down, where I remain two hours to look over the work of the past day and kill some time with the cutters, who have always some bad-luck story ready, about either themselves or their neighbors. And as to this grove I could tell you a thousand fine things that have happened to me, in dealing with Frosino da Panzano and others who wanted some of this firewood. And Frosino especially sent for a number of cords without saying a thing to me, and on payment he wanted to keep back from me ten lire, which he says he should have had from me four years ago, when he beat me at *cricca* [a card game] at Antonio Guicciardini's. I raised the devil, and was going to prosecute as a thief the waggoner who came for the wood, but Giovanni Machiavelli came between us and got us to agree. Battista Guicciardini, Filippo Ginori,

---

"Machiavelli on a Typical Day at His Farm, 1513," from Allan Gilbert trans. *Machiavelli: The Chief Works and Others*, Vol. 2, 1965, pp. 927–930, Duke University Press. Reprinted by permission of the publisher.

Tommaso del Bene and some other citizens, when that north wind was blowing, each ordered a cord from me. I made promises to all and sent one to Tommaso, which at Florence changed to half a cord, because it was piled up again by himself, his wife, his servant, his children, so that he looked like Gabburra when on Thursday with all his servants he cudgels an ox. Hence, having seen for whom there was profit, I told the others I had no more wood, and all of them were angry about it, and especially Battista, who counts this along with his misfortunes at Prato.

Leaving the grove, I go to a spring, and thence to my aviary. I have a book in my pocket, either Dante or Petrarch, or one of the lesser poets, such as Tibullus, Ovid, and the like. I read of their tender passions and their loves, remember mine, enjoy myself a while in that sort of dreaming. Then I move along the road to the inn; I speak with those who pass, ask news of their villages, learn various things, and note the various tastes and different fancies of men. In the course of these things comes the hour for dinner, where with my family I eat such food as this poor farm of mine and my tiny property allow. Having eaten, I go back to the inn; there is the host, usually a butcher, a miller, two furnace tenders. With these I sink into vulgarity for the whole day, playing at *cricca* and at trich-trach, and then these games bring on a thousand disputes and countless insults with offensive words, and usually we are fighting over a penny, and nevertheless we are heard shouting as far as San Casciano. So, mixed up with these lice, I keep my brain from growing mouldy, and satisfy the malice of this fate of mine, being glad to have her drive me along this road, to see if she will be ashamed of it.

On the coming of evening, I return to my house and enter my study; and at the door I take off the day's clothing, covered with mud and dust, and put on garments regal and courtly; and reclothed appropriately, I enter the ancient courts of ancient men, where, received by them with affection, I feed on that food which only is mine and which I was born for, where I am not ashamed to speak with them and to ask them the reason for their actions; and they in their kindness answer me; and for four hours of time I do not feel boredom, I forget every trouble, I do not dread poverty, I am not frightened by death; entirely I give myself over to them.

And because Dante says it does not produce knowledge when we hear but do not remember, I have noted everything in their conversation which has profited me, and have composed a little work *On Princedoms*, where I go as deeply as I can into considerations on this subject, debating what a princedom is, of what kinds they are, how they are gained, how they are kept, why they are lost. If ever you can find any of my fantasies pleasing, this one should not displease you; and by a prince, and especially by a new prince, it ought to be welcomed. Hence I am dedicating it to His Magnificence Giuliano [de' Medici, later duke of Nemours, son of Lorenzo the Magnificent]. Filippo Casavecchia has seen it; he can give you some account in part of the thing in itself and of the discussions I have had with him, though I am still enlarging and revising it.

You wish, Magnificent Ambassador, that I leave this life and come to enjoy yours with you. I shall do it in any case, but what tempts me now are certain affairs that within six weeks I shall finish. What makes me doubtful is that the Soderini we know so well are in the city, whom I should be obliged, on coming there, to visit and talk with. I should fear that on my return I could not hope to dismount at my house but should dismount at the Bargello, because though this government has mighty foundations and great security, yet it is new and therefore suspicious, and there is no lack of wiseacres who, to make a figure, like Pagolo Bertini, would place others at the dinner table and leave the reckoning to me. I beg you to rid me of this fear, and then I shall come within the time mentioned to visit you in any case.

I have talked with Filippo about this little work of mine that I have spoken of, whether it is good to give it or not to give it; and if it is good to give it, whether it would be good to take it myself, or whether I should send it there. Not giving it would make me fear that at the least Giuliano will not read it and that this rascal Ardinghelli will get himself honor from this latest work of mine. The giving of it is forced on me by the necessity that drives me, because I am using up my money, and I cannot remain as I am a long time without becoming despised through poverty. In addition, there is my wish that our present Medici lords will make use of me, even if they begin by making me roll a stone; because then if I could not gain their favor, I should complain of myself; and through this thing, if it were read, they would see that for the fifteen years while I have been studying the art of the state, I have not slept or been playing; and well may anybody be glad to get the services of one who at the expense of others has become full of experience. Of my honesty there should be no doubt, because having always preserved my honesty, I shall hardly now learn to break it; he who has been honest and good for forty-three years, as I have, cannot change his nature; and as a witness to my honesty and goodness I have my poverty.

I should like, then, to have you also write me what you think best on this matter, and I give you my regards. Be happy.

Excerpts From *The Prince*

CHAPTER 7
NEW PRINCEDOMS GAINED WITH OTHER MEN'S FORCES AND THROUGH FORTUNE

Those who—though only citizens—become princes simply through Fortune, with little effort become so, but with much effort sustain themselves, for they have no difficulties along the road, because they fly over it, but all the difficulties appear when they are settled. Princes are of this sort when a state is granted to anybody either for money or as a favor from him who grants it, as happened to many in Greece in the cities of Ionia and the Hellespont, where they were made princes by Darius so they would hold those cities for his security and glory. So were set up also those emperors who, though mere citizens, through bribery of the soldiers attained the imperial throne. Such rulers depend solely on a king-maker's will and Fortune—two things most uncertain and unstable; they do not know how to and cannot hold the

Excerpts from *The Prince* from Allan Gilbert trans. *Machiavelli: The Chief Works and Others*, Vol. 1, 1965, pp. 17–18, 24–26, 27–34, 57–59, 61–67, 88–96, Duke University Press. Reprinted by permission of the publisher.

rank bestowed on them. They do not know how because, if a man is not of great intelligence and vigor, it is not reasonable, when he has always lived in a private station, that he should know how to command; they cannot, because they do not have forces that are sure to be friendly and faithful. Besides, these states that come of a sudden, like all things in nature that spring up and grow quickly, cannot have roots and other related parts. Hence the first unfavorable weather destroys them. Such men as I have spoken of, who so swiftly have become princes, can survive only if they are of such capacity that what Fortune has put into their laps they can straightway take measures for keeping, and those foundations that other princes laid before gaining their positions they can lay afterward. On both these ways that have been mentioned (that is, on becoming prince either through strength and wisdom or through Fortune) I intend to bring forward two instances within the days of our recollection: Francesco Sforza and Cesare Borgia.

Francesco, by the necessary methods and by means of his great ability, though born to a private station, became Duke of Milan; and what with a thousand exertions he gained, with little effort he kept.

On the other side, Cesare Borgia, called by the people Duke Valentino, gained his position through his father's Fortune and through her lost it, notwithstanding that he made use of every means and action possible to a prudent and vigorous man for putting down his roots in those states that another man's arms and Fortune bestowed on him. As I say above, he who does not lay his foundations beforehand can perhaps through great wisdom and energy lay them afterward, though he does so with trouble for the architect and danger to the building. So on examining all the steps taken by the Duke, we see that he himself laid mighty foundations for future power. To discuss these steps is not superfluous; indeed I for my part do not see what better precepts I can give a new prince than the example of Duke Valentino's actions. If his arrangements did not bring him success, the fault was not his, because his failure resulted from an unusual and utterly malicious stroke of Fortune.

Alexander VI [Roderigo Borgia, pope from 1492 to 1503], in his attempt to give high position to the Duke his son, had before him many difficulties, present and future. First, he saw no way in which he could make him lord of any state that was not a state of the Church, yet if the Pope tried to take such a state from the Church, he knew that the Duke of Milan and the Venetians would not allow it because both Faenza and Rimini were already under Venetian protection. He saw, besides, that the weapons of Italy, especially those of which he could make use, were in the hands of men who had reason to fear the Pope's greatness; therefore he could not rely on them, since they were all among the Orsini and the Colonnesi and their allies. He therefore was under the necessity of disturbing the situation and embroiling the states of Italy so that he could safely master part of them. This he found easy since, luckily for him, the Venetians, influenced by other reasons, had set out to get the French to come again into Italy. He not merely did not oppose their coming; he made it easier by dissolving the early marriage of King Louis. The King then marched into Italy with the Venetians' aid and Alexander's consent; and he was no sooner in Milan than the Pope got soldiers from him for an attempt on Romagna; these the King granted for the sake of his own reputation.

Having taken Romagna, then, and suppressed the Colonnesi, the Duke, in attempting to keep the province and to go further, was hindered by two things: one, his own forces, which he thought disloyal; the other, France's intention. That is, he feared that the Orsini forces which he had been using would fail him and not merely would hinder his gaining but would take from him what he had gained, and that the King would treat him in the same way. With the Orsini, he had experience of this when after the capture of Faenza he attacked Bologna, for he saw that they turned cold over that attack. And as to the King's purpose, the Duke learned it when, after taking the dukedom of Urbino, he invaded Tuscany—an expedition that the King made him abandon. As a result, he determined not to depend further on another man's armies and Fortune.

The Duke's first act to that end was to weaken the Orsini and Colonnesi parties in Rome by winning over to himself all their adherents who were men of rank, making them his own men of rank and giving them large subsidies; and he honored them, according to their stations, with military and civil offices, so that within a few months their hearts were emptied of all affection for the Roman parties, and it was wholly transferred to the Duke. After this, he waited for a good chance to wipe out the Orsini leaders, having scattered those of the Colonna family; such a chance came to him well and he used it better. When the Orsini found out, though late, that the Duke's and the Church's greatness was their ruin, they held a meeting at Magione, in Perugian territory. From that resulted the rebellion of Urbino, the insurrections in Romagna, and countless dangers for the Duke, all of which he overcame with the aid of the French. Thus having got back his reputation, but not trusting France or other outside forces, in order not to have to put them to a test, he turned to trickery. And he knew so well how to falsify his purpose that the Orsini themselves, by means of Lord Paulo, were reconciled with him (as to Paulo the Duke did not omit any sort of gracious act to assure him, giving him money, clothing and horses) so completely that their folly took them to Sinigaglia into his hands. Having wiped out these leaders, then, and changed their partisans into his friends, the Duke had laid very good foundations for his power, holding all the Romagna along with the dukedom of Urbino, especially since he believed he had made the Romagna his friend and gained the support of all those people, through their getting a taste of well-being.

Because this matter is worthy of notice and of being copied by others, I shall not omit it. After the Duke had seized the Romagna and found it controlled by weak lords who had plundered their subjects rather than governed them, and had given them reason for disunion, not for union, so that the whole province was full of thefts, brawls, and every sort of excess, he judged that if he intended to make it peaceful and obedient to the ruler's arm, he must of necessity give it good government. Hence he put in charge there Messer Remirro de Orco, a man cruel and ready, to whom he gave the most complete authority. This man in a short time rendered the province peaceful and united, gaining enormous prestige. Then the Duke decided there was no further need for such boundless power, because he feared it would become a cause for hatred; so he set up a civil court in the midst of the province, with a distinguished presiding judge, where every city had its lawyer. And because he knew that past severities had made some men hate him, he determined to purge such men's minds and win them over entirely by showing that any cruelty which had gone on did not originate with himself but with the harsh nature of his agent. So getting an opportunity for it, one morning at Cesena he had Messer Remirro laid in two pieces in the public square with a block of wood and a bloody sword near him. The ferocity of this spectacle left those people at the same time gratified and awe-struck.

But let us turn back to where we left off. When the Duke had become very powerful and in part secure against present perils, since he was armed as he wished and had in great part destroyed those forces that, as neighbors, could harm him, he still, if he intended to continue his course, had before him the problem of the King of France, because he knew that the King, who too late had become aware of his own mistake, would not tolerate further conquest. For this reason the Duke was looking for new alliances and wavering in his dealings with France, as when the French moved upon the Kingdom of Naples against the Spaniards who were besieging Gaeta. And his intention was to make himself secure against them; in this he would quickly have succeeded if Alexander had lived. So these were his ways of acting as to present things.

But as to future ones, he had to fear, first of all, that the next man in control of the Church would not be friendly to him but would try to take from him what Alexander had given. Against this he planned to secure himself by four methods: first, to wipe out all the families of those lords he had dispossessed, in order to take away from the Pope that opportunity; second, to win to his side all the men of rank in Rome, as I have said, so that by means of them he could keep the Pope in check; third, to render the College as much his own as he could; fourth, to conquer so large an empire, before the Pope died, that he could by himself resist a first attack. Of these four things, on Alexander's death he had completed three; the fourth was almost as good as complete: of the dispossessed rulers he had killed as many as he could reach, and very few escaped; the Roman men of rank he had won over; and in the College he had a very large party; and as to further conquest, he had planned to become ruler of Tuscany, he already possessed Perugia and Piombino, and Pisa he had taken under his protection. And as soon as he no longer needed to defer to the King of France (and he would not need to do so much longer, since already the French were deprived of the Kingdom by the Spaniards, in such a way that each of them would have to buy his friendship), he would jump into Pisa. After this, Lucca and Siena would yield at once, partly through envy of the Florentines, partly through fear. The Florentines would have no recourse. If he had carried out these plans (and he would have carried them out the very year when Alexander died), he would have gained such forces and such reputation that he could stand by his own strength and would no longer rely on other men's Fortune and forces, but on his own vigor and ability.

But Alexander died five years after the Duke first drew his sword. He left Cesare with the province of Romagna alone secure, with all the others in the air, between two very powerful hostile armies, and sick unto death. Yet there was in the Duke so much courage and so much ability, and so well he understood how men can be gained or lost, and so strong were the foundations which in so short a time he had laid that, though alone, if those armies had not been upon him or if he had been in health, he would have mastered every difficulty. And that his foundations were good, we see; for Romagna continued waiting for him more than a month; in Rome, though but half alive, he was secure; and though the Baglioni, Vitelli, and Orsini came into Rome, they did not proceed further against him; if he could not set up as pope the one he wanted, at least he could make sure it would not be someone he did not want. If on Alexander's death he had been in health, everything would have been easy for him. And he said to me himself, on Julius II's accession-day, that he had imagined what could happen when his father died, and for everything he had found a solution, except he had never imagined that at the time of that death he too would be close to dying.

Having observed, then, all the Duke's actions, I for my part cannot censure him. On the contrary, I think I am right in bringing him forward in this way as worthy of imitation by all those who through Fortune and by means of another's forces attain a ruler's position. Since his courage was great and his purpose high, he could not conduct himself otherwise; and his plans were opposed only by the shortness of Alexander's life and his own sickness. Anyone, therefore, who thinks it necessary in his princedom newly won to secure himself against his enemies, to win friends, to conquer by force or by fraud, to make himself loved and feared by the people, followed and respected by the soldiers, to destroy those who can or are likely to injure you, to replace ancient customs with new ways, to be severe and agreeable, magnanimous and liberal, to destroy disloyal armies, to raise new ones, to keep the friendship of kings and of princes in such a way that they are compelled either to aid you with a good grace or to harm you with reluctance, cannot find more recent instances than this man's actions.

The single thing for which we can blame him is the election of Julius as pope. In this he made a bad choice because, as I have said, if he could not set up a pope to suit himself, he could exclude from the papacy whomever he wished. He should never have let the papacy go to any cardinal whom he had injured or who, on becoming pope, would need to fear him, because men do injury through either fear or hate. Those whom Cesare had injured were, among others, San Piero ad Vincula, Colonna, San Giorgio, and Ascanio. Any of the others on becoming pope would need to fear him, except Rouen and the Spaniards; the latter were made secure by their alliance and indebtedness, the former by his power, since he was closely connected with the kingdom of France. Therefore the Duke should by all means have chosen a Spaniard as pope, and if he could not, should have agreed to Rouen not to San Piero ad Vincula. To believe that new benefits make men of high rank forget old injuries is to deceive oneself. In this choice, then, the Duke blundered, and it caused his final ruin.

CHAPTER 15
THOSE THINGS FOR WHICH MEN AND ESPECIALLY PRINCES ARE PRAISED OR CENSURED

Now it remains to examine the wise prince's methods and conduct in dealing with subjects or with allies. And because I know that many have written about this, I fear that, when I too write about it, I shall be thought conceited, since in discussing this material I depart very far from the methods of the others. But since my purpose is to write something useful to him who comprehends it, I have decided that I must concern myself with the truth of the matter as facts show it rather than with any fanciful notion. Yet many have fancied for themselves republics and principalities that have never been seen or known to exist in reality. For there is such a difference between how men live and how they ought to live that he who abandons what is done for what ought to be done learns his destruction rather than his preservation, because any man who under all conditions insists on making it his business to be good will surely be destroyed among so many who are not good. Hence a prince, in order to hold his position, must acquire the power to be not good, and understand when to use it and when not to use it, in accord with necessity.

Omitting, then, those things about a prince that are fancied, and discussing those that are true, I say that all men, when people speak of them, and especially princes, who are placed so high, are labeled with some of the following qualities that bring them either blame or praise. To wit, one is considered liberal, one stingy (I use a Tuscan word, for the *avaricious* man in our dialect is still one who tries to get property through violence; *stingy* we call him who holds back too much from using his own goods); one is considered a giver, one grasping; one cruel, one merciful; one a promise-breaker, the other truthful; one effeminate and cowardly, the other bold and spirited; one kindly, the other proud; one lascivious, the other chaste; one reliable, the other tricky; one hard, the other tolerant; one serious, the other light-minded; one religious, the other unbelieving; and the like.

I am aware that everyone will admit that it would be most praiseworthy for a prince to exhibit such of the above-mentioned qualities as are considered good. But because no ruler can possess or fully practice them, on account of human conditions that do not permit it, he needs to be so prudent that he escapes ill repute for such vices as might take his position away from him, and that he protects himself from such as will not take it away if he can; if he cannot with little concern he passes over the latter vices. He does not even worry about incurring reproach for those vices without which he can hardly maintain his position, because when we carefully examine the whole matter, we find some qualities that look like virtues, yet—if the prince practices them—they will be his destruction, and other qualities that look like vices, yet—if he practices them—they will bring him safety and well-being.

Chapter 17
Cruelty and Mercy: Is It Better to be Loved Than Feared, or the Reverse?

Passing on to the second of the above-mentioned qualities [cruelty and mercy], I say that every sensible prince wishes to be considered merciful and not cruel. Nevertheless, he takes care not to make a bad use of such mercy. Cesare Borgia was thought cruel; nevertheless that well-known cruelty of his re-organized the Romagna, united it, brought it to peace and loyalty. If we look at this closely, we see that he was much more merciful than the Florentine people, who, to escape being called cruel, allowed the ruin of Pistoia. A wise prince, then, is not troubled about a reproach for cruelty by which he keeps his subjects united and loyal because, giving a very few examples of cruelty, he is more merciful than those who, through too much mercy, let evils continue, from which result murders or plunder, because the latter commonly harm a whole group, but those executions that come from the prince harm individuals only. The new prince—above all other princes—cannot escape being called cruel, since new governments abound in dangers. As Virgil says by the mouth of Dido, "My hard condition and the newness of my sovereignty force me to do such things, and to set guards over my boundaries far and wide."

Nevertheless, he is judicious in believing and in acting, and does not concoct fear for himself, and proceeds in such a way, moderated by prudence and kindness, that too much trust does not make him reckless and too much distrust does not make him unbearable.

This leads to a debate: Is it better to be loved than feared, or the reverse? The answer is that it is desirable to be both, but because it is difficult to join them together, it is much safer for a prince to be feared than loved, if he is to fail in one of the two. Because we can say this about men in general: they are ungrateful, changeable, simulators and dissimulators, runaways in danger, eager for gain; while you do well by them they are all yours; they offer you their blood, their property, their lives, their children, . . . when need is far off; but when it comes near you, they turn about. A prince who bases himself entirely on their words, if he is lacking in other preparations, falls; because friendships gained with money, not with greatness and nobility of spirit, are purchased but not possessed, and at the right times cannot be turned to account. Men have less hesitation in injuring one who makes himself loved than one who makes himself feared, for love is held by a chain of duty which, since men are bad, they break at every chance for their own profit; but fear is held by a dread of punishment that never fails you.

Nevertheless, the wise prince makes himself feared in such a way that, if he does not gain love, he escapes hatred; because to be feared and not to be hated can well be combined; this he will always achieve if he refrains from the property of his citizens and his subjects and from their women. And if he does need to take anyone's life, he does so when there is proper justification and a clear case. But above all, he refrains from the property of others, because men forget more quickly the death of a father than the loss of a father's estate. Besides, reasons for seizing property never fail, for he who is living on plunder continually finds chances for appropriating other men's goods; but on the contrary, reasons for taking life are rarer and cease sooner.

But when the prince is with his armies and has in his charge a multitude of soldiers, then it is altogether essential not to worry about being called cruel, for without such a reputation he never keeps an army united or fit for any action. Among the most striking of Hannibal's achievements is reckoned this: though he had a very large army, a mixture of countless sorts of men, led to service in foreign lands, no discord ever appeared in it, either among themselves or with their chief, whether in bad or in good fortune. This could not have resulted from anything else than his well-known inhuman cruelty, which, together with his numberless abilities, made him always respected and terrible in the soldiers' eyes; without it, his other abilities would not have been enough to get him that result. Yet historians, in this matter not very discerning, on one side admire this achievement of his and on the other condemn its main cause.

And that it is true that Hannibal's other abilities would not have been enough, can be inferred from Scipio (a man unusual indeed not merely in his own days but in all the record of known events) against whom his armies in Spain rebelled—an action that resulted from nothing else than his too great mercy, which gave his soldiers more freedom than befits military discipline. For this, he was rebuked in the Senate by Fabius Maximus, who called him the destroyer of the Roman soldiery. The Locrians, who had been ruined by a legate of his, Scipio did not avenge nor did he punish the legate's arrogance—all a result of his tolerant nature. Hence, someone who tried to apologize for him in the Senate said there were many men who knew better how not to err than how to punish errors. This tolerant nature would in time have damaged Scipio's fame and glory, if, having it, he had kept on in supreme command; but since he lived under the Senate's control, this harmful trait of his not merely was concealed but brought him fame.

I conclude, then, reverting to being feared and loved, that since men love at their own choice and fear at the prince's choice, a wise prince takes care to base himself on what is his own, not on what is another's; he strives only to avoid hatred, as I have said.

CHAPTER 18
HOW PRINCES SHOULD KEEP THEIR PROMISES

How praiseworthy a prince is who keeps his promises and lives with sincerity and not with trickery, everybody realizes. Nevertheless, experience in our time shows that those princes have done great things who have valued their promises little, and who have understood how to addle the brains of men with trickery; and in the end they have vanquished those who have stood upon their honesty.

You need to know, then, that there are two ways of fighting: one according to the laws, the other with force. The first is suited to man, the second to the animals; but because the first is often not sufficient, a prince must resort to the second. Therefore he needs to know well how to put to use the traits of animal and of man. This conduct is taught to princes in allegory by ancient authors, who write that Achilles and many other well-known ancient princes were given for upbringing to Chiron the Centaur, who was to guard and educate them. This does not mean anything else (this having as teacher one who is half animal and half man) than that a prince needs to know how to adopt the nature of either animal or man, for one without the other does not secure him permanence.

Since, then, a prince is necessitated to play the animal well, he chooses among the beasts the fox and the lion, because the lion does not protect himself from traps; the fox does not protect himself from the wolves. The prince must be a fox, therefore, to recognize the traps and a lion to frighten the wolves. Those who rely on the lion alone are not perceptive. By no means can a prudent ruler keep his word—and he does not—when to keep it works against himself and when the reasons that made him promise are annulled. If all men were good, this maxim would not be good, but because they are bad and do not keep their promises to you, you likewise do not have to keep yours to them. Never has a shrewd prince lacked justifying reasons to make his promise-breaking appear honorable. Of this I can give countless modern examples, showing how many treaties of peace and how many promises have been made null and empty through the dishonesty of princes. The one who knows best how to play the fox comes out best, but he must understand well how to disguise the animal's nature and must be a great simulator and dissimulator. So simple-minded are men and so controlled by immediate necessities that a prince who deceives always finds men who let themselves be deceived.

I am not willing, among fresh instances, to keep silent about one of them. Alexander VI never did anything else and never dreamed of anything else than deceiving men, yet he always found a subject to work on. Never was there a man more effective in swearing and who with stronger oaths confirmed a promise, but yet honored it less. Nonetheless, his deceptions always prospered as he hoped, because he understood well this aspect of the world.

For a prince, then, it is not necessary actually to have all the above-mentioned qualities, but it is very necessary to appear to have them. Further, I shall be so bold as to say this: that if he has them and always practices them, they are harmful; and if he appears to have them, they are useful; for example, to appear merciful, trustworthy, humane, blameless, religious—and to be so—yet to be in such measure prepared in mind that if you need to be not so, you can and do change to the contrary. And it is essential to realize this: that a prince, and above all a prince who is new, cannot practice all those things for which men are considered good, being often forced, in order to keep his position, to act contrary to truth, contrary to charity, contrary to humanity, contrary to religion. Therefore he must have a mind ready to turn in any direction as Fortune's winds and the variability of affairs require, yet . . . he holds to what is right when he can but knows how to do wrong when he must.

A wise prince, then, is very careful never to let out of his mouth a single word not weighty with the . . . five qualities; he appears to those who see him and hear him talk, all mercy, all faith, all integrity, all humanity, all religion. No quality does a prince more need to possess—in appearance—than this last one, because in general men judge more with their eyes than with their hands, since everybody can see but few can perceive. Everybody sees what you appear to be; few perceive what you are, and those few dare not contradict the belief of the many, who have the majesty of the government to support them. As to the actions of all men and especially those of princes, against whom charges cannot be brought in court, everybody looks at their result. So if a prince succeeds in conquering and holding his state, his means are always judged honorable and everywhere praised, because the mob is always fascinated by appearances and by the outcome of an affair; and in the world the mob is everything; the few find no room there when the many crowd together. A certain prince of the present time, whom I refrain from naming, never preaches anything except peace and truth, and to both of them he is utterly opposed. Either one, if he had practiced it, would many times have taken from him either his reputation or his power.

CHAPTER 24
WHY THE PRINCES OF ITALY HAVE LOST THEIR STATES

The things written above [in the entire work preceding], carried out prudently, make a new prince seem an old one, and make him quickly safer and firmer in his position than if he were in it by right of descent. Because the actions of a new prince are more closely watched than are those of a hereditary prince; and when these reveal strength and wisdom, they lay hold on men and bind them to him more firmly than does ancient blood. Because men are more affected by present things than by past ones; and if in present conditions they prosper, they rejoice and ask nothing more; in fact, they will in every way defend a new prince, if in other things he does not fail himself. Thus he will gain double glory, for he will both begin a new princedom and will ennoble and strengthen it with good laws, good arms, and good examples. On the other hand a man born a prince who through imprudence loses his princedom will incur double shame.

And if we consider those rulers who in Italy have lost their positions in our times, as the King of Naples, the Duke of Milan, and others, we find on their part, first, a common failure in their armies, for the reasons that we have discussed above at length. Then we see that some of them either suffered hostility from the people or, if the people were friendly to them, did not know how to secure themselves against the rich. Without these defects, princes do not lose their states if they are strong enough to keep an army in the field. Philip of Macedon, not Alexander's father but the one who was conquered by Titus Quintius, did not have much power in comparison with the greatness of the Romans and of Greece, who attacked him. Nonetheless, being a soldierly man and one who knew how to get on with the people and to secure himself against the rich, for many years he kept up the war against the invaders, and if at the end he lost the control of some cities, nevertheless he still retained his kingdom.

Therefore these princes of ours, who have been many years in their princedoms, and then have lost them, should not blame Fortune, but their own laziness. Never in good weather having imagined there could be a change (it is a common defect in men not to reckon, during a calm, on a storm), when at last bad weather came, they thought only of running away and not of defending themselves; and they hoped that the people, sickened by the conquerors' arrogance, would call them back. This plan, when there are no others, is good; but all the same it is very bad to abandon other expedients for this one, because you should never be content to fall, trusting that someone will come along to pick you up. Either that does not happen, or, if it happens, it brings you no security, because such a resource is abject, and does not depend upon yourself. And those defenses alone are good, are certain, are durable, that depend on yourself and your own abilities.

CHAPTER 25
FORTUNE'S POWER IN HUMAN AFFAIRS
AND HOW SHE CAN BE FORESTALLED

As I am well aware, many have believed and now believe human affairs so controlled by Fortune and by God that men with their prudence cannot manage them—yes, more, that men have no recourse against the world's variations. Such believers therefore decide that they need not sweat much over man's activities but can let Chance govern them. This belief has been the more firmly held in our times by reason of the great variations in affairs that we have seen in the past and now see every day beyond all human prediction. Thinking on these variations, I myself now and then incline in some respects to their belief. Nonetheless, in order not to annul our free will, I judge it true that Fortune may be mistress of one half our actions but that even she leaves the other half, or almost, under our control.

I compare Fortune with one of our destructive rivers which, when it is angry, turns the plains into lakes, throws down the trees and the buildings, takes earth from one spot, puts it in another; everyone flees before the flood; everyone yields to its fury and nowhere can repel it. Yet though such it is, we need not therefore conclude that when the weather is quiet, men cannot take precautions with both embankments and dykes, so that when the waters rise, either they go off by a canal or their fury is neither so wild nor so damaging. The same things happen about Fortune. She shows her power where strength and wisdom do not prepare to resist her, and directs her fury where she knows that no dykes or embankments are ready to hold her. If you consider Italy—the scene of these variations and their first mover—you see that she is a plain without dykes and without any embankment; but if she were embanked with adequate strength and wisdom, like Germany, Spain, and France, this flood either would not make the great variations it does or would not come upon us. I think this is all I need to say in general on resisting Fortune.

Limiting myself more to particulars, I say that such princes as I have described live happily today and tomorrow fall without changing their natures or any of their traits. This I believe results, first, from the causes lengthily discussed in the preceding pages, namely, that any prince who relies exclusively on Fortune falls when she varies. I believe also that a prince succeeds who adapts his way of proceeding to the nature of the times, and conversely one does not succeed whose procedure is out of harmony with the times. In the things that lead them to the end they seek, that is, glory and riches, men act in different ways: one with caution, another impetuously; one by force, the other with skill; one by patience, the other with its contrary; and all of them with these differing methods attain their ends. We find also that of two cautious men, one carries out his purpose, the other does not. Likewise, we find two men with two differing temperaments equally successful, one being cautious and the other impetuous. This results from nothing else than the nature of the times, which is harmonious or not with their procedure. From that results what I have said: that two men, working differently, secure the same outcome; and of two working in the same way, one attains his end, and the other does not. On this depend variations in success: if, for one whose policy is caution and patience, times and affairs circle about in such a way that his policy is good, he continues to succeed; if times and affairs change, he falls, because he does not change his way of proceeding. Nor is any man living so prudent that he knows how to accommodate himself to this condition, both because he cannot deviate from that to which nature disposes him, and also because, always having prospered while walking in one road, he cannot be induced to leave it. Therefore the cautious man, when it is time to adopt impetuosity, does not know how. Hence he falls; yet if he could change his nature with times and affairs, Fortune would not change.

Pope Julius II proceeded impetuously in all his affairs; and he found the times and their circumstances so in harmony with his own way of proceeding that he was always successful. Consider the first expedition he attempted against Bologna, while Messer Giovanni Bentivoglio was still alive. The Venetians did not approve it, neither did the King of Spain; with France, Julius was negotiating about such an expe-dition; nonetheless, in his energy and impetuosity he started in person on that cam-paign. This move made Spain and the Venetians stand uncertain and motionless, the latter through fear, and the other through his wish to regain the whole Kingdom of Naples. And on the other side the Pope dragged after him the King of France, because that King, seeing that Julius had already moved, and wishing to make him a friend in order to humble the Venetians, judged himself unable to deny the Pope soldiers without harming him quite evidently. Julius, then, accomplished with his impetuous movement what no other pontiff, with the utmost human prudence, would ever have accomplished; if he had waited until he could leave Rome with his terms fixed and all things in order, as any other pontiff would have done, he would never have succeeded, because the King of France would have had a thousand ex-cuses and the Venetians would have roused in him a thousand fears. I shall omit his other actions, which were all of the same sort, and for him all came out well. And the shortness of his life did not allow him to get any taste of the opposite; because if times had come when he needed to proceed with caution, they would have brought about his downfall; for never would he have turned away from those methods to which his nature inclined him.

I conclude then (with Fortune varying and men remaining stubborn in their ways) that men are successful while they are in close harmony with Fortune, and when they are out of harmony, they are unsuccessful. As for me, I believe this: it is better to be impetuous than cautious, because Fortune is a woman and it is necessary, in order to keep her under, to cuff and maul her. She more often lets herself be overcome by men using such methods than by those who proceed coldly; therefore always, like a woman, she is the friend of young men, because they are less cautious, more spirited, and with more boldness master her.

CHAPTER 26
AN EXHORTATION TO GRASP ITALY
AND SET HER FREE FROM THE BARBARIANS

Having taken account, then, of everything discussed above, and meditating whether at present in Italy conditions so unite as to offer a new prince glory, and whether the matter to be found here assures to a prudent and able ruler a chance to introduce a form that will bring him glory and her people general happiness, I believe so many things now join together for the advantage of a new prince that I do not know what time could ever be more fit for such a prince to act. . . . to show Moses' ability the people of Israel needed to be enslaved in Egypt, and to reveal Cyrus' greatness of spirit the Persians had to be oppressed by the Medes, and to exhibit Theseus' excel-lence the Athenians had to be scattered, so to reveal an Italian spirit's ability Italy needed to be brought to her present condition, to be more slave than the Hebrews, more servant than the Persians, more scattered than the Athenians, without head, without order, beaten, despoiled, lacerated, devastated, subject to every sort of ruination.

And though up to now various gleams have appeared in some Italians from which we might judge them ordained by God for her redemption, nevertheless we have seen later that, in the highest course of their actions, they have been disapproved by Fortune. Hence, as though without life, she awaits whoever he may be who can heal her wounds and put an end to the devastation and plunder of Lombardy, to the robbery and ransom of the Kingdom and Tuscany, and cure her of those sores already long since festered. She is now praying God to send someone to redeem her from such barbarous cruelty and arrogance; she is now also ready and willing to follow a banner, if only there be one who will raise it.

There is not, at present, anyone in whom she can have more hope than in your glorious family [the Medici family], which through its fortune and its wisdom and strength, favored by God and by the Church—of which it is now head—can make itself the leader of this redemption. That will not be very hard if you bring before you the actions and the lives of those named above [Moses, Cyrus, Theseus]. And though these men were exceptional and marvelous, nevertheless they were men; and every one of them had a poorer chance than the present one, because their undertaking was not more just than this, nor easier, nor was God more friendly to them than to you. Here justice is great, "for a war is just for those to whom it is necessary, and arms are sacred when there is no hope except in arms." Now your opportunity is very great, and when there is great opportunity, there cannot be great difficulty, if only your family will use the methods of those whom I have set up as your aim. Besides this, now we see marvelous, unexampled signs that God is directing you: the sea is divided; a cloud shows you the road; the rock pours out water; manna rains down; everything unites for your greatness. The rest you must do yourself. God does not do everything, so as not to take from us free will and part of the glory that pertains to us.

It is not astonishing if none of the Italians mentioned above [Francesco Sforza, Cesare Borgia, and Pope Julius II] has been able to do what we hope your illustrious family will do, and if, in so many convulsions in this land and in so much warfare, Italy's military vigor always seems extinct. The cause is that her old institutions were not good, and no one has been wise enough to devise new ones; and nothing does so much honor to a man newly risen to power as do the new laws and new institutions he devises. These things, when they are well based and have greatness in them, win a new ruler reverence and awe. And in Italy there is no lack of matter on which to impose any form; there is great power in the limbs, if only it were not wanting in the heads. Observe in duels and in combats by small numbers how superior the Italians are in strength, in skill, in intelligence; but when they are in armies, they make no showing. And it all results from the weakness of the heads; because those who are wise are not obeyed—and each one thinks he is wise—since up to now no one has risen so high, in both ability and Fortune, that to him the others yield. This is the reason why for so long a time, in the many wars fought in the past twenty years, whenever there has been an army wholly Italian, it has always failed when tested. To this the chief witness is the Taro, then Alessandria, Capua, Genoa, Vailà, Bologna, Mestre.

If then, your glorious family resolves to follow the excellent men I have named who redeemed their countries, she must before all other things, as the true foundation of every undertaking, provide herself with her own armies, because there cannot be more faithful or truer or better soldiers. And though each one of them is good, they will become better if united, when they see themselves commanded by their own prince and by him honored and maintained. It is necessary, therefore, for her to prepare such armies in order with Italian might to defend herself against foreigners.

And though the Swiss and the Spanish infantry are considered formidable, nonetheless in both there is a defect, by reason of which a third type could not merely withstand them but could feel certain of defeating them, because the Spanish cannot repel cavalry, and the Swiss need to dread infantry when they meet in combat any as stubborn as themselves. Hence experience has shown and will show that the Spanish cannot repel French cavalry, and the Swiss are destroyed by Spanish infantry. And though of this last there has been no complete demonstration, yet one was suggested at the battle of Ravenna, where the Spanish infantry were face to face with the German battalions, which use the same battle array as the Swiss; there the Spanish, with the agility of their bodies and the help of their bucklers, got within the pikes, underneath them, and were safe in attacking the Germans, without the latter having any defense; had the Spaniards not been charged by the cavalry, they would have destroyed all the Germans. A prince who recognizes the defects of both these types of infantry, then, can organize a new one that will repel cavalry and not be afraid of infantry. This will be effected by the nature of their weapons and by change in their tactics. And these are among the things that, as new institutions, give reputation and greatness to a new prince.

By no means, then, should this opportunity be neglected, in order that Italy, after so long a time, may see her redeemer come. I cannot express with what love he will be received in all the provinces that have suffered from these alien floods, with what thirst for vengeance, with what firm loyalty, with what gratitude, with what tears! What gates will be shut against him? What peoples will refuse him obedience? What envy will oppose him? What Italian will refuse him homage? For everyone this barbarian tyranny stinks. Let your glorious family, then, undertake this charge with that spirit and that hope with which men undertake just labors, in order that beneath her ensign this native land of ours may be ennobled and, with her guidance, we may realize the truth of Petrarch's words:

> Valor against wild rage
> Will take up arms, and the combat will be short,
> Because ancestral courage
> In our Italian hearts is not yet dead.

FURTHER READING

C. M. Ady, *Lorenzo de' Medici and Renaissance Italy* (1955)

Hans Baron, "Machiavelli: The Republican Citizen and the Author of the Prince," *English Historical Review* 76 (1961), 217–253

———, "The *Principe* and the Puzzle of the Date of Chapter Twenty-six," *Journal of Medieval and Renaissance Studies* 21 (1991), 83–102

———, "The *Principe* and the Puzzle of the Date of the *Discorsi*," *Bibliotheque d'Humanisme et de Renaissance* 18 (1965), 405–428

Gisela Bock et al., eds., *Machiavelli and Republicanism* (1990)

H. C. Butters, *Governors and Government in Early Sixteenth-Century Florence* (1985)

Federico Chabod, *Machiavelli and the Renaissance*, trans. D. Moore (1958)

Sebastian de Grazia, *Machiavelli in Hell* (1989)

Felix Gilbert, *Machiavelli and Guicciardini: Politics and History in Sixteenth-Century Florence* (1965)

_____, *History: Choice and Commitment* (1977). Gathers important earlier essays on Machiavelli.

Myron P. Gilmore, ed., *Studies on Machiavelli* (1972)

J. R. Hale, *Machiavelli and Renaissance Italy* (1960)

J. H. Hexter, *The Vision of Politics on the Eve of the Reformation* (1973)

Mark Hulliung, *Citizen Machiavelli* (1983)

De Lamar Jensen, ed., *Machiavelli: Cynic, Patriot or Political Scientist?* (1960)

Machiavelli, The Chief Works and Others, trans. Allan Gilbert (3 vols. 1965). The best translation of letters and major works.

Michael Mallett, *The Borgias* (1969)

Garrett Mattingly, *Renaissance Diplomacy* (1955)

John M. Najemy, *Between Friends: Discourses of Power and Desire in the Machiavelli-Vettori Letters* (1993)

Hanna Fenichel Pitkin, *Fortune Is a Woman: Gender and Politics in the Thought of Niccolò Machiavelli* (1984)

J. G. A. Pocock, *The Machiavellian Moment* (1975)

The Portable Machiavelli, ed. and trans. Peter Bondanella and Mark Musa (1979). Excellent selection of Machiavelli's most important works.

Roberto Ridolfi, *The Life of Niccolò Machiavelli*, trans. C. Grayson (1963)

N. Rubinstein, "Politics and Constitution in Florence at the End of the Fifteenth Century," in *Italian Renaissance Studies*, ed. E. F. Jacob (1960), 143–183

Silvia Ruffo-Fiore, *Niccolò Machiavelli* (1982)

Christine Shaw, *Julius II, The Warrior Pope* (1992)

Quentin Skinner, *Machiavelli* (1981)

J. N. Stephens, *The Fall of the Florentine Republic, 1512–1530* (1983)

Nancy Struever, "Machiavelli: Narrative as Argument," in her *Theory as Practice: Ethical Inquiry in the Renaissance* (1992), 147–181

J. H. Whitfield, *Discourses on Machiavelli* (1969)

PART IV

Humanism

Botticelli, *St. Augustine in His Cell* (c. 1480). The
image of an intellectual, surrounded by
manuscripts as well as scientific instruments, his
bishop's miter at his elbow.

CHAPTER **8**

Petrarch's Revolution

Italian humanism arose in northern Italy—in the cities of Padua, Bologna, Milan and Verona—in the age of Dante (1265–1322). Its growth was fostered by members of the nascent professional classes, including lawyers, notaries, schoolmasters, and chancery officials. These Italian writers were primarily rhetoricians (skilled in the use of language) who looked to ancient pagan writers for inspiration and instruction. Combining study of Roman poetry, history, and rhetoric with works of Roman Stoicism, the early humanists revived the traditional view of the rhetorician as a moral philosopher and champion of virtue. In so doing, they first relied on the rules of speech and letter writing contained in the *ars dictaminis* (the medieval art of composition) but later emulated the genres and works of ancient Roman authors. Many of the early Italian humanists considered themselves direct successors to ancient writers—for example, Albertino Mussato wrote a Latin tragedy on the excesses of the contemporary tyrant Ezzelino da Romano, in close imitation of the tragedies of Seneca—and this enthusiasm for the ancients led them to gain a profound appreciation of the writings of Livy, Cicero, Virgil, and Seneca.

The key figure in the establishment of Renaissance humanism was Francesco Petrarca (1304–1374), often called the first modern man of letters. He found ancient culture relevant to his own moral problems and the solutions to them. Throughout his long life Petrarch wrote numerous letters, offering advice on many subjects to a variety of persons. He engaged as well in polemics on several subjects: against medical doctors, against critics of Italy, and against those who criticized him and his concept of humanistic learning. He was at the same time the foremost Italian love poet of his age, and his deep commitment to investigating questions of religious belief and human existence made him a new sort of moral philosopher. His intellectual evolution and the complexity of his thought, however, complicate our understanding of his intentions and the true meaning of his works.

Petrarch's great personal charm, capacity for trenchant social criticism, and reputation as a great love poet and student of human nature showed aspiring young scholars that a career in letters could bring fame and success. He became a culture hero admired and emulated by the best minds of the next generation. By the time of his death, Petrarch's revolution was on its way to becoming permanent. The humanist as social critic, moral thinker, and student of classical culture was becoming a distinctive feature of Renaissance culture.

ESSAYS

Trained at Harvard and a professor of Renaissance history at Duke University, Ronald G. Witt has specialized in early humanism, especially the career and thought of Coluccio Salutati (the Chancellor of Florence, 1375–1406; see introduction to Chapter 9). In the first essay, Witt investigates the antecedents of Renaissance humanism, taking as his definition Paul Oskar Kristeller's famous cycle of five disciplines of the *studia humanitatis*, thus, identifying humanism as the study of grammar, rhetoric, poetry, history, and moral philosophy (see Chapter 10). Witt finds that the medieval *ars dictaminis* of speech making and letter writing in Italy coexisted with the more grammatical and literary concerns of humanism. With Petrarch the personal style of humanism triumphed as a form of public discourse; humanist oratory came only in the fifteenth century, in the speeches of Pier Paolo Vergerio.

Perhaps the most influential student of Renaissance culture in our century has been Hans Baron (1900–1988). Born and educated in Berlin, Baron studied in Italy before fleeing Germany under threat of Nazi persecution. Settling in the United States on the staff of the Newberry Library and as lecturer in Renaissance studies at the University of Chicago he made intensive investigations of the evolution of Petrarch's thought. In the selection that follows, Baron attempts to discover what is modern in Petrarch's outlook and how his thought evolved, as youthful enthusiasm for classical antiquity gave way to deep concern for Christian salvation. Baron finds this conflict between Petrarch's yearning for fame and glory in this world and redemption from his own sinfulness in the next most clearly posed in the *Secretum*, Petrarch's imagined interior dialogue between Saint Augustine and himself (which is reprinted in part in the Documents section of this chapter).

The Beginnings of Humanism

RONALD G. WITT

[T]he approach to rhetoric of] Brunetto Latini, the most important Florentine thinker of the mid-thirteenth century, . . . is vital for an understanding of *ars dictaminis* [the art of letter-writing] because more than any other author, he endeavors to describe in detail the nature and function of the letter. Although he exaggerates somewhat the extent to which most *dictatores* [letter-writers] assimilated the oration to the letter, Latini makes explicit the basic assumption common to all schools of *ars dictaminis* that the teachings of ancient oratory serve as background for the composition of letters. In the process he reveals the tension between the more customary medieval rhetoric of harmony and the rhetoric of conflict espoused by the *stilus rhetoricus* [rhetorical style]. Furthermore, his writings show that the renewed interest in detailed study of ancient textbooks on oratory merely served to reinforce the *ars dictaminis* tradition generally.

"The Beginnings of Humanism" by Ronald G. Witt from "Medieval 'Ars Dictaminis' and the Beginnings of Humanism: A New Construction of the Problem," from *Renaissance Quarterly* 35 (1982) pp. 16–35. Reprinted by permission of the publisher.

Latini's discussion of rhetoric and *ars dictaminis* occurs principally in two works, both written in France in the early 1260s, the *Rettorica* and the *Tresor*. The first is a translation into Tuscan with commentary of a portion of Cicero's *De Inventione* while the second, written in French, is an encyclopedic work containing, in the third and last book, an extensive discussion of the nature of rhetoric and political science. He had no intention of being critical of current *dictamen* [letter-writing] practices but rather was concerned with defining the place of *dictamen* in the larger field of rhetoric as defined by Cicero. His basic premise in both works is that Cicero's instructions for composing orations also apply to letter writing. From Cicero he learned of the ancient debate on the scope of rhetoric. On the one hand, an ancient orator like Gorgias insisted that any subject could be treated rhetorically, while on the other, Aristotle, with whom Cicero agreed, maintained that there were only three kinds of orations: those dealing with demonstrative, deliberative, and judicial issues. Cicero further restricted the field of oratory by limiting it to controversies dealing with specific individuals and matters involving them. Latini endorses the position of Aristotle and Cicero without noting that traditionally *dictatores* had simply assumed that any subject could be treated in a letter. In Latini's view the *dictator* can speak and write rhetorically only about controversial questions "where there is someone to oppose his statements." By implication the *stilus rhetoricus* would seem to be the only style fitted to expressing one's position in the context of debate, but, as the analysis develops, it becomes clear that the author does not intend to favor any particular style. His concern is to give *ars dictaminis* a structure derived from ancient teachings.

To critics who maintain that there are many letters where no controversy is involved, Latini replies in the *Rettorica* that most letters contain one, if only implicitly, but if none can be found, then the subject of the letter is not suitable for rhetorical treatment. In this earlier work, however, Latini clearly has second thoughts. Acknowledging that letters of friendship often do not reflect even an implicit debate and being unwilling to exclude such an important form of letter from the scope of *dictamen*, he does a *volte face* [an about-face]. Insisting in the *Rettorica* that *dictamen* is a branch of rhetoric, he maintains at the same time, in contradiction to his initial position, that, unlike oratory, the letter is fitted to treat every subject and offers a definition of *dictamen* which would have been acceptable to any *dictator*: "Dictamen is a proper and ornate treatment of everything, appropriately applied to that thing." A letter he continues a bit below, still trying to cover himself with Cicero's sanction, "must be furnished with attractive and pleasing words and full of good meaning, and also ornateness is demanded in every part of rhetoric as said above in the text of Cicero." Apparently the rhetoric of conflict and that of harmony are no longer contradictory but are viewed as different aspects of the same art. While some letters deal with conflict, others do not. In any case, he assures his reader that with help of his commentary on the *De inventione* he will be able to understand the art of composing both orations and letters. Mired in hopeless contradictions he breaks off the treatise.

In the discussion of *ars dictaminis* in the *Tresor*, Latini exhibits no such ambivalence when stipulating that only letters dealing with a controversial topic deserve rhetorical treatment. He says nothing of any category of letter not fitting this description but leaves the impression that most correspondence meets the requirement of containing some controversial point, at least by implication. Obviously suppressing his doubts and guided by a deeply felt need to ground *dictamen* on ancient rhetorical teachings, Latini in the *Tresor* ruthlessly tries to make the letter conform to Cicero's criteria of controversy.

The impression left by both works is that like other *dictatores* Latini would not abandon the idea that the letter was analogous to the speech. What seemed at the start of writing the *Rettorica* an easy thing to illustrate became a mass of confusion. When unable to apply Cicero's requirement of controversy to letters of friendship, Latini simply abandoned that prescription, while claiming the rest of Cicero's rhetorical teachings for the *ars dictaminis*. Unwilling to make this concession in the *Tresor*, he discussed the letter and the speech as if there were no difference except that one was written and the other spoken. Whether devoted to the rhetoric of harmony or conflict, *dictatores*, Latini concluded, considered the letter formal in tone and tightly organized into clearly articulated segments like the oration. Beautifully adapted to public communication, such a conception thwarted expression of intimate thoughts and emotions.

Indeed, while the thirteenth century with the *stilus rhetoricus* might be considered the apogee in the development of the public letter, it represents a low point for the private letter. Nowhere is this more clearly illustrated than in the correspondence of Dante, the greatest proponent of the oratorical style in the generation after Latini. The Florentine poet's public letters, for instance, those directed to Florence, Henry VII, and the cardinals, are powerful, moving documents of his political passion. In contrast, those directed to personal acquaintances have none of those qualities of revealing intimacy which make such letters interesting and aesthetically attractive. In Dante's case, the weakness of these personal letters surely does not stem from shortcomings in his personality or talents but from the means of expression available to him.

Latini's efforts to interpret Cicero's rhetorical teachings in the interest of contemporary needs mark the beginning of a new intensity of concern for both Ciceronian manuals in the schools of rhetoric themselves. Given the present state of scholarship, there is as yet no basis for connecting the *De inventione* commentary of Latini in the 1260s and that of Jacques de Dinant on the *Ad Herennium* in the same period with the rash of commentaries—especially on the pseudo-Ciceronian work—beginning around 1300. Perhaps as early as 1292 Giovanni di Bonandrea began his commentary on the *Ad Herennium*. His disciple, Bartolino di Benincasa, composed his own more famous one sometime after 1321. As for *ars dictaminis*, if the number of new manuals decreased significantly after 1290, the reason lies more in the amazing success of Bonandrea's "best seller," the *Brevis introductio ad dictamen*, than in any "classicizing" prejudice against *dictamen*. Indeed, the closer study of Cicero's oratorical techniques and instruction to *colores rhetorici* [shades of rhetoric] characteristic of the commentaries only served to endorse the basic assumptions inherent in *dictamen*. . . .

The proto-humanist movement appears to have been intimately related to developments in subjects generally assigned in the medieval program of studies to grammar. Like his ancient counterpart, the grammarian of the Middle Ages dealt with the grammar of the language and analyzed great literary masterpieces. While in antiquity the primary focus of the grammarians was poetic literature and the rhetoricians studied mostly prose, the medieval grammarians monopolized the teaching of both. Textual analysis involved among other things discussing the biography of the author, the historical and mythological references found in the work and the various figures used, as well as subjecting the text's vocabulary to etymological study to bring out the hidden truths. Although there was ancient precedent for the medieval grammarian's emphasis on the ethical implications of the reading material, part of the motivation lay in his desire to justify devoting so much of the classroom time to reading pagan authors. . . .

The proto-humanists from Lovato [early fourteenth century] on reinvigorated grammatical studies, and the various areas in which they themselves did creative work demonstrate their orientation. Members of the movement produced hundreds of poems imitating ancient examples and at least one play, *The Ecerinis,* based on Seneca's tragedies. Although many of the poems took the form of epistles, there is— with one notable exception to be discussed—an absence of surviving prose letters and orations by these men. How is this to be explained? The obvious effort of the group in their historical works to imitate ancient Latin writers indicates their will- ingness to reform prose style. Nor can there by any doubt that they wrote speeches and prose letters. The most probable conclusion is that whereas they felt able to reform poetry and even historical writing, they could not challenge the domination of *ars dictaminis* in these other areas. Men with a new kind of taste, they wrote letters and composed orations in the traditional fashion, but, taking no pride in them, they left the survival of these works more or less to chance. While reform of oratory must await the third generation of Italian humanists, reform in writing letters, that is, personal correspondence, constitutes one of the major elements of Petrarchan humanism.

Close study of the surviving correspondence of writers like Seneca and Pliny doubtless made the proto-humanists aware of major differences between ancient epistolary style and their own. . . .

Among the proto-humanists, however, one scholar, like Giovanni [del Virgilio] also a *dictator,* apparently rebelled against the modern practice. Little is known of Geri d'Arezzo or of the influences affecting his work, but he clearly had the courage to choose between the ancient and modern approach to letters. Of his once volumi- nous correspondence, only six short personal letters survive. But these are sufficient to show that Geri is resolved to develop a new stylistic approach to writing such letters. He refuses to follow the prescribed five-part letter form strictly; the violations of the *cursus* are frequent enough to suggest that they are intentional; the tone de- sired, if not completely realized, is one of informality. His letters emulate conversa- tion, not speeches.

Geri obviously wished to substitute a new model for the old ones associated with *ars dictaminis.* Educated presumably in Arezzo in the last decades of the thirteenth century, he would have been a student in the commune's schools in the period of Arezzo's cultural brilliance. Geri studied the letters of Seneca and Pliny closely, ei- ther at Arezzo or later when a student at Bologna, and his style is marked by the contact. Geri's surviving correspondence betrays frequent plagiarisms from Pliny's epistolary collection. His letter on the death of the Duke of Calabria of 1329 reveals the author's desire to imitate an ancient letter in its details.

Geri's advance was hesitant. Hesitancy, however, was not Petrarch's problem after 1345 when Cicero revealed to him the potentialities for expression available in the personal letter. That encounter caused him to reread Cicero in an effort to ferret out the great writer's fragmentary references to epistolography. Not Cicero the teacher of rhetoric, but Cicero the letter writer gave Petrarch means by which he could utter his inmost thoughts and give form to the sinuosities of his personality for the benefit of the learned men of his generation.

Petrarch's letter of dedication of his *Familiares* addressed to Ludwig von Kempen provides an unsystematic discussion of Petrarch's stylistic approach to the private letter. In writing such letters, Petrarch insists he would not use "great power of speech" if he had it. Even Cicero, who doubtless possessed immense oratorical gifts, did not display them in such cases. Rather, in his letters and, where appropriate, in his books Cicero employed "an 'equable' style" and "'a temperate type of speech.'" In his own case, involved neither in politics nor lawsuits, he has no need for such eloquence and, at any rate, his ability is untried. "Therefore," Petrarch concludes, "you will enjoy, as you have my other writings, this plain, domestic and friendly style, forgetting that rhetorical power of speech which I neither lack nor abound in and which, if I did abound in, I would not know where to exercise. And as a faithful follower you will find words that we use in ordinary speech proper and suitable for expressing my ideas." . . .

Reaffirming that he intended to write in a friendly manner (*familiariter*) to his friends, Petrarch promises to offer in the pages that follow a series of letters dealing with all sorts of subjects but one which in a sense does "almost nothing more than to speak about my state of mind or any other matter of interest which I thought my friends would like to know." For Cicero the task of the private letter was the same: "to make the recipient more informed about those things he does not know." Thus, Ludwig will find few masterpieces in the collection but many written in a rather simple and unstudied manner about personal affairs. Like Cicero, he has, where appropriate, made ethical observations.

Petrarch's conception of the personal letter as a conversation was perhaps totally inspired by his discovery of the *Ad Atticum* in the library of the cathedral chapter in Verona in 1345. From his encounter with the lively, gossipy, revealing letters of the great Roman so very different in nature from the medieval tradition of letter writing, he emerged disappointed with the inconsistent character of his hero but resolved to create a collection of his own. His first effort, written immediately following the discovery, was a letter to Cicero in which he upbraided the dead man for his conduct. Significantly, Petrarch's new approach to the letter derived inspiration from Cicero's actual correspondence, and only after appreciating the style did he understand Cicero's remark in the *De officiis*, I, I.3, cited in the dedicatory letter.

Over the next fifteen years Petrarch not only fabricated a number of letters purporting to have been written earlier in his life, but he also reworked those of which he had retained a copy. Had the originals of these letters actually sent before 1345 survived, they presumably would have been more consonant with the medieval tradition than those actually in the present collection. As it was, the *Familiares*, shaped after 1345, demonstrated to the contemporary learned world a novel yet ancient conception of the private letter and inaugurated a new epoch in the history of epistolography in Western Europe.

Geri d'Arezzo had pioneered stylistic reform in his personal correspondence, but Petrarch far surpassed him. A major factor influencing the latter was that he was not a *dictator* by profession, but a private man. Even when he spoke on issues of public life, he spoke with a certain detachment from political partisanship, a freedom not enjoyed by the chancery official or the professional teacher. While Boccaccio's more precarious financial situation made him vulnerable to pressures of earning a living, his literary interests, like those of Petrarch, were overwhelmingly those of the private individual. . . .

The life largely free of financial concerns or political involvement was conducive to the kind of humanistic endeavor Petrarch pursued. His search for manuscripts, his concern for collating texts, establishing facts of literary history, and reforming language are marks of a humanism essentially grammatical and philological in character. His approach to history as teaching by example as well as his general focus on the relationship between ethics and learning were traditional in the schools of grammar. In his case, however, the ethical orientation of scholarship was clarified and enhanced by an intensive reading of Cicero. Furthermore, as a private man he attained a degree of integration of this early grammatical humanism with his style of life which was denied the proto-humanists, who had to lead public lives as professional rhetoricians.

Although he attempted to apply his familiar style to oratory, as noted above, he took no risk with official or business letters. Correspondence between princes and city-states, which offered a wide field for displaying one's eloquence, remained largely untouched by the new style. Petrarch himself occasionally demonstrated his ability to compose in the medieval style when called upon to write a public letter on behalf of a government. Among Petrarch's immediate followers Coluccio Salutati devoted much of his time to writing this official kind of letter. In fact, down to the late fifteenth century, after more than a hundred years of humanistic letter writing, public letters remained the preserve of a conception of letter writing that evolved in the centuries before Petrarch's birth.

As the fifteenth century progressed, official letters sent in the name of a ruling authority increasingly lost importance as a means of carrying on diplomatic relations and political propaganda. There were more embassies, while letters and tracts composed by humanists in their own name and written in humanistic Latin became the major vehicle for propaganda. However, despite decreasing practical importance, official Latin epistolography in the fifteenth century remained strongly tied to the teaching of the *dictatores* of the eleventh to the thirteenth centuries. Singling out the personal letter for special treatment as Petrarch had done was to be a long-standing practice among the humanists, who, like Petrarch, conceded the advantages of *ars dictaminis* in other areas of epistolography.

No one reading Petrarch's correspondence or his other writings could of course consider his letters uninformed by the teachings of classical rhetoric. The creation of the "domestic" style, a *stilus humilis,* surely demanded a deep knowledge of the art and a superb gift for sensing appropriateness of style. His writings reflect an expanded understanding of the functions and complex character of rhetoric. Nevertheless, in at least three respects he is anti-rhetorical. He rejected the practice of contemporary rhetoric of treating all letters oratorically. Moreover, a subjective element pervading his thought tended to undercut the rhetorician's aim of moving the audience toward a specific end. Finally, his breadth of interests and the depth to which he pursued them testify to his rejection of the narrow technical approach to rhetoric prevailing among the *dictatores*. He would readily agree with the Cicero of the *De oratore*, who criticized his juvenile *De inventione* by condemning the "exponents of the science of rhetoric" who "only write about the classification of cases and the elementary rules and the methods of stating the facts." Rather the orator's "eloquence is so potent a force that it embraces the origins and operation and developments of all things, all the virtues and duties, all the natural principles governing the morals and minds and life of mankind, and also determines their customs and laws and rights, and controls the government of the state, and expresses everything that concerns whatever topic in a graceful and flowing style."

While Petrarch considered himself an orator—not a rhetorician—according to his understanding of Cicero's definition, his desire for the private life and his central concerns were in fact more those of the poet and literary scholar. The same thing was true for Boccaccio. The movement they initiated grew directly out of a medieval grammatical tradition whose previous high point had been the twelfth-century French humanists. Short of applying one's learning and eloquence to the needs of the state as a citizen or, better still, through some official charge, Cicero's ideal of the orator was unattainable. As articulated by Cicero and before him by Greek writers going back to Isocrates, the full potential in the ideal could be realized only within a republican setting. Even Coluccio Salutati, for thirty-one years chancellor of the Florentine Republic, achieved only an uneasy reconciliation between the demands of grammatical-philological humanism and his commitment to Florence as a citizen-patriot.

With Vergerio's generation at the close of the fourteenth century humanism began to affect oratory stylistically and to overcome another stronghold of *ars dictaminis*. Once humanism dominated the schools of rhetoric and the chanceries of Italy, scholarly and literary concerns became welded to professional commitment, and the age of rhetorical humanism began. . . . While they by no means neglected the other *studia humanitatis*, most humanists earned their livelihood by their knowledge of classical rhetorical models and their skill in knowing when and how to use them.

I would, however, make one modification in defining the fifteenth-century humanists as rhetoricians. For the most part, the advent of humanism in the domain of rhetoric proper merely encouraged the replacement in schools and chanceries of one group of technicians, the *dictatores*, by another, the humanists, who, more skillful, were capable of using both humanistic and traditional styles as the need arose. The appropriation of oratory by humanism, nevertheless, facilitated a more significant and related development: that is, the realization of Cicero's ideal of the orator. It was not coincidental that Leonardo Bruni made his first statement of a consistent republican view of politics and history in the form of an oration in 1403/4.

Like other humanists, Bruni devoted himself to wide study of the *studia humanitatis*, but with exceptional single-mindedness he subordinated the grammatical and philological aspects of humanism to the tasks of the orator. Deriving the definition from the ancient tradition, Bruni presented the orator as devoting his life to serving and preserving a society of free men through his learning and eloquence. Whereas Petrarch established the personal voice to express a new cluster of ideas and emotions centered on subjective experience, two generations later Bruni discovered the voice of the citizen and through it communicated his interpretation of the historic struggle of freedom and liberty in human society and of the role of political participation in the development of the complete individual.

Petrarch and the Discovery of Human Nature

HANS BARON

Writers have called Petrarch "the first humanist" or even "the first modern man," but very few people seem to have a clear answer when asked how and when Petrarch decisively parted from medieval ways. No doubt, his knowledge of antiquity constantly grew over the years. But was the outlook on life and history that distinguished him from his predecessors the result of a gradual process which continued throughout his life? Should we assume that he only very slowly moved away from the traditions of the Middle Ages and that, as a consequence, he was more detached from medieval values towards the end of his life than he had been during his younger years?

To the modern student, who likes to think in terms of historical continuity, a gradual separation from medieval traditions seems to be the natural assumption and, in fact, this has been taken for granted in much of the writing on Petrarch. But there is another side to this matter, a side which, strangely enough, is often neglected, even though it is closely intertwined with one of the historical priorities with which he is credited: that he was the first modern writer to leave penetrating autobiographical glimpses of his own development. In addition to his correspondence, it is especially the information found in his *De secreto conflictu curarum suarum*—his *Secretum*, "The Secret Book on the conflict of his restless strivings"—that allows us to see his life through his own eyes. This self-analysis and confession has often been called a counterpart to Augustine's *Confessions*; it certainly tries to be a close parallel to the writing of the church father in its objectives and *forma mentis* [mental approach]. Augustine's aim had been to clarify what we conceive to be his passage from classical, pre-Christian antiquity to a world formed by many of the elements characteristic of medieval thought; he had tried to understand and overcome the sinfulness of a life filled with literary and other solely secular ambitions. . . .

"Petrarch and the Discovery of Human Nature," by Hans Baron from "Petrarch: His Inner Struggle and the Humanistic Discovery of Man's Nature," in *Florilegium Historiale: Essays Presented to Wallace K. Ferguson*, ed. by J. G. Rowe and W. H. Stockdale, pp. 19, 26–46. Copyright © 1971 University of Toronto Press. Reprinted by permission of the publisher.

A review of the intellectual world of Petrarch's youth must begin with a description of his vision of ancient Rome. Here, doubtless, was his first deviation from medieval ways.

Among the authentic letters from the early period of Petrarch's life is one—written a few years before his ascent of Mont Ventoux—in which Pompey is reprimanded for having allowed Caesar to escape after his defeat at Dyrrachium. Pompey's failure to destroy Caesar, so the letter argues, caused all the subsequent evils that befell Rome: the slaughter of so many citizens, the death of Cato which brought Roman *libertas* [liberty] to an end, and, indirectly, all the misery of the world down to the present day.

It would be difficult, or even impossible, to find any comparable judgment in the whole of medieval writing. For, as the founder of the divinely appointed, universal empire in which the Middle Ages believed, Caesar had a secure and central place in the historical views of medieval writers. Why did young Petrarch dare to judge differently? His motive did not stem from any republican convictions. Already at the time when his implied criticism of Caesar was written, Petrarch had begun to dream of a strong saviour, a tyrant-monarch who could bring peace to Italy—a hope which in later years was replaced by republican ideals only during the brief episode of Cola di Rienzo's Roman revolution. But when contemplating ancient Rome, Petrarch, from the very first, felt magnetically attracted by the *virtus Romana* [Roman virtue] of the republican period.

In another early letter we read: though many great men have been of the opinion that those states are the happiest which are governed by one just ruler, it cannot be denied that the Roman state grew much more under the rule of many citizens than under that of a single head. It seems, therefore, the letter concludes, that the authorities and historical *experientia* [experience] contradict one another.

The use of the word *experientia* is remarkable in this context. Petrarch liked to contrast the superiority of *experientia* gained in actual life with the bookishness of mere studies; the relation he had formed to the history of republican Rome must have had for him the immediacy of one of those experiences in his life that made him revolt against medieval authority and precedent. He followed this historical *experientia* when, in 1339 during his first stay in the Vaucluse, he drew a picture of ancient Rome in the first books of his *Africa*, the epic which he wrote as a *poeta historicus* [poet-historian], as he put it in his coronation oration.

The crucial aspect of the new conception of ancient Rome in the *Africa* is a shift of attention away from those events that had been dearest to medieval writers. For the author of the *Africa*, the struggle between Scipio Africanus the Elder and Hannibal, and the final victory of the *virtus* of republican Rome in the battle with Carthage at Zama, have replaced in significance Caesar's foundation of the imperial monarchy and the rule of the Emperor Augustus under whom Christ was born. In the *Africa*, the story of Roman liberty begins with the exclusion of Tarquinius Superbus, the last king, from the Ciceronian heaven of the great Romans and with his banishment to the inferno, while the author notes that Tarquinius' tyranny was not futile historically because it caused the ardent desire for liberty to grow in Roman hearts. Lucrezia and the elder Brutus appear as Roman heroes of that period; with them "the freedom of our era begins"—the freedom of Scipio's days. In a dream of Scipio's, the later course of Roman history unfolds itself in a striking historical panorama. For the time of the republic the spotlight falls on Pompey, whereas Caesar is harshly criticized: he, the greatest of conquerors, could have been the happiest of men, had he known how to limit his passion for power; but "the wretched man could not," overwhelmed as he was by the ambition "to lay claim to all power for one ruler, thereby setting an evil example for others." He plundered the public treasury; he imposed new orders on the helpless senate; "he turned his ever-victorious hands against the flesh and blood of his own commonwealth and stained his triumphs over foreign enemies with the blood of citizens."

One is again struck by the boldness with which what the Middle Ages considered the landmarks of history are here overthrown. Petrarch was of course not the first to learn from ancient sources—Sallustius, Lucanus, and certain passages of Cicero—that the Roman dominion over the world had been built up under the republic. But whereas almost every medieval writer had eventually judged the republican period to be a mere preparation for the imperial and Christian era, Petrarch, in the *Africa*, above all admires the state of mind—the psychological force—responsible for Rome's ascendancy: the *virtus Romana* under the republic. It is the normal human condition, we read in the epic, that only a very few men do not flinch from danger, pain, and death; but, by "one of the greatest of all miracles," Rome by the time of Scipio the Elder had succeeded in making that rare attitude a common occurrence: every army of Roman citizens showed a readiness *pro libertate tuenda/recta fronte mori* [to defend liberty and die for a just cause]. Here republican liberty has become an indispensable condition for the greatness of Rome, though what Petrarch admires is not so much the republic's free constitution as the dedication and military prowess of her citizens.

During the same years in which these new historical views appeared in the *Africa*, a distinct note of independence from traditional standards entered into various judgments of Petrarch on the way of life of his friends and on the values he cherished for himself. His comments on contemplation and the active life were at times the very opposite of his consistent praise of the *vita contemplativa* [contemplative life] in the decades after the *Secretum*, when he was working on his *De vita solitaria* [On the solitary life].

In 1339, Petrarch became personally acquainted with a French prince—Humbert, the lord of the Dauphiné—who did not wish to be a lord, for he valued more highly a solitary and even monastic life, and eventually resolved to cede the Dauphiné to the French king. To Petrarch in 1339, this intention appeared in an entirely negative light. Anyone could see, so he wrote to the Dauphin, that a decisive conflagration was about to break out between France and England (it was the time of the beginning of the Hundred Years' War). Was not the land of every prince in Europe in danger of being drawn into the whirlpool of events? In such a time a man had to prove his virtue and make himself worthy of a good name. Countless examples from antiquity preached persistence in one's task and warned against shirking hard work. "Return to your responsibility!" When the world trembles, it is not the time to wish for sleep!

The tone as well as the content of this admonition make it unlike anything later written by the author of the *De vita solitaria*; and the same tone is found in Petrarch's reaction to a similar situation, which aroused his feelings still more strongly. A Genoese friend destined for a political career had decided after long consideration to enter a monastery. As long as we are young, Petrarch told him, we should live for our *patria* [fatherland]. You are not born for yourself; your country has a right to make her demands on you, as Plato teaches; and does not Cicero, in his *Somnium Scipionis* [*Dream of Scipio*], say that a heavenly reward awaits those who have helped to preserve and strengthen their country, and that nothing is more agreeable to God than a life spent in the *civitas* [city]? The step contemplated by his friend should not be taken before "a man's longings and passions have abated with increasing age." Do not believe, says the Petrarch of the 1330s, that this advice is contradicted by the preference of many philosophers and church fathers for the *vita contemplativa*. Does not even Plotinus teach "that man can attain felicity not only through the virtues of purification and those of the mind already purified, but also along the path of the *politicae virtutes* [political virtues]? And although in the gospels Mary Magdalene is said to have chosen the best part, is not Martha also praised?"

But what, then, of Petrarch himself? It will perhaps be said that the hermit of the Vaucluse did not heed the advice he gave to his friends. Yet, when at that time he spoke about the life of a writer and poet, the values which he extolled were very different from the ideals he was to defend six or seven years later, when the *De vita solitaria* was conceived. When, in 1341, he interrupted his Alpine retreat to be crowned as a poet on the Roman Capitol, the oration he gave on that occasion reveals quite strikingly his innermost thoughts. At this most impressive moment of his life, standing on the height of the Capitoline hill, dressed in a purple cloak, a gift of King Robert of Anjou, the poet laureate began his oration by quoting from Virgil's *Georgics*: "But a sweet longing urges me upward over the lonely slopes of Parnassus." This reference to a poet's impulses he then turned into the general psychological comment that "without loving effort, profound joy, and rapture" no work of the spirit will reach its goal.

What followed was an oration not merely on the poet's thirst for glory, but on the right and necessity of human passion. His argument was based on the fourth book of Cicero's *Tusculanae disputationes*, the same work which for many centuries had been among the most influential sources of that Stoic doctrine which in the name of reason calls for the suppression of all *affectiones* [emotions] and passions. In the nineteenth chapter of the fourth book of the *Tusculans*, one of the doctrines refuted by Cicero is the belief that *affectiones* might work as a positive force, as spurs to virtue and action. Anger, Cicero reports, is thought by the Peripatetic school to stimulate fortitude. Themistocles' unique gifts and energies are believed to have developed because envy of the glory of Miltiades did not allow him to rest; and some have argued that without a "burning longing" philosophy would not have advanced, and the earth would not have been explored by eager travellers.

To the author of the *Tusculanae disputationes* all this had been partial or false teaching, interesting merely because it revealed the innate longing of all men for immortal fame and, therefore, provided an argument to prove the existence of immortality. To Petrarch, in 1341, the examples referred to in the *Tusculans* bore evidence of the justification and necessity of great passion and of the striving after glory. They show, says Petrarch in his oration, that even among sages and philosophers hardly anyone will be found who is not spurred on by thirst for glory. Many great minds have admitted this motivation. Did not Cicero himself say that no man is willing to make a great effort and face danger "unless he may hope for glory as a kind of reward?" and did not Ovid express the opinion that "excellence grows when it is praised" and that "the thought of glory is a powerful spur"? Was Virgil not convinced that *amor patriae* [love for one's country] and an immense desire for praise are strong aids to success? The conclusion, as the speaker on the Capitol is not ashamed to confess, is "that the desire for glory is innate not merely in ordinary men, but to the greatest degree in those who have wisdom and excellence."

Let us try to place the outlook of the young Petrarch in historical perspective. When we recall the themes and values that were to come to the fore in humanistic literature after 1400, especially in quattrocento Florence, the Petrarch of those pre-*Secretum* years may be called a harbinger of the quattrocento. We can describe the most creative trends of thought in early Renaissance Florence in terms very similar to those which have emerged from our analysis: a rediscovery of the *Respublica Romana* [Roman Republic] and a critique of the imperial monarchy; a positive and sympathetic attitude toward the *vita activa politica* [active political life]; and, finally, the rise of a new psychology, beginning with a fresh evaluation of passion and the desire for glory.

Yet, if the guiding ideas are similar, their scope and function were to be totally different two or three generations after Petrarch, when citizens of Renaissance city republics looked upon life in the *Respublica Romana* as a model for their own day and they themselves led lives of political commitment like citizens of Athens and Rome. For Petrarch there were few bridges from the new values and the inspiration he found in the Roman past to his own way of life. He was a secular cleric who had taken the minor vows, lived on prebends, and was in constant intellectual exchange with other clerics whose minds were formed as much by a common piety as by their common classical studies. In time he became suspicious of what Virgil, Ovid, and his own personal experience were teaching him—that a poet's passion can be a needed incentive. During the latter part of his life, after he had returned from papal Avignon and from his solitary refuge in the Alpine valley of the Vaucluse to Italy, he was to attach himself to the north Italian tyrant courts and eschew the life of a citizen in the city republic of his Florentine ancestors. Increasingly he came to feel, as Dante had, that peace for a divided and war-devastated Italy could be expected only from the rulers of the *Sacrum imperium* [Holy Roman Empire], the successors to Rome's imperial monarchy; eventually he found himself in close personal affiliation with Emperor Charles IV.

It must be apparent that from this world of Petrarch to the intellectual world of the quattrocento there could be no continuous evolution or direct transition. If the historical discoveries and newly affirmed values of the young Petrarch were to be fruitful in his own time, they had to be garbed in a way that could be understood and appreciated by his still half-medieval age. Once Petrarch had experienced his change of heart, it resulted in effect in a building of bridges and a striving for reconciliations, even if this caused an attenuation, and sometimes the loss, of his original thrust. The full historical significance of Petrarch's thinking, therefore, does not emerge until we are equally aware of these two basic facts: that from his earliest years he was original enough to play the decisive role in the creation of a new humanistic view of man, but that he also became aware before long of the wide gulf between the religious mood of his age and some of the values which he extolled and in the second half of his life worked ceaselessly on some kind of synthesis.

That this process included a frequent wavering, a never-ending *dissidium mentis* [mental conflict], is an observation of more than merely psychological import. However little Petrarch was as yet able to question medieval standards in principle, his vacillation and inner struggles were the result of his inability and unwillingness to give up the new attitudes and values, once he had made them his own. In order to understand the work he produced during the second half of his life, one must never forget that soon after the coronation of 1341 Saul became Paul and, consequently, often contradicted outright the bold assertions he had formerly made; but in spite of his retractions he never fully reverted to the traditional ways.

The ambivalent attitude toward his own innovations and discoveries started with the *Secretum*. As the "Secret book on the conflict of his restless strivings" indicates, almost immediately after his return from the loud celebrations on the Roman Capitol to the peaceful Alpine mountains and the valley of the Vaucluse, he began to reassess his life according to the choices described in Augustine's *Confessions*: between a brilliant career in letters, and a life of spiritual concentration leading to God. As he now saw it, unless he could overcome the longings and passions which had once already driven him away from his Alpine retreat to the turmoil of his coronation in Rome and to estrangement from his true self, he would be lost, as Augustine would have been lost had he not found the strength to renounce his ambitions. But almost simultaneously Petrarch also realized to what extent the very essence of his being was ingrained with those longings and passions. Out of this conflict emerged a searching account *de conflictu curarum suarum* [of his conflicting anxieties], which examined all his unruly passions one by one and allowed the reader to see that, although many of the trends of Petrarch's youth had been reversed—so many, indeed, that in the manuscripts the *Secretum* is often entitled *De contemptu mundi* [*On contempt for the world*]—some of the yearnings of his earlier years proved unyielding to the warnings attributed to Augustine.

What, then, were the *passiones* [passions] that had made Petrarch restless and did not allow him to elevate his thoughts? As Augustine's interrogations bring out, none of the ordinary vices of envy, anger, avarice, pride of body or of talent were so strong in Petrarch that they could be the latent cause of his lack of inner peace. But when his probing reaches the point where Augustine calls the two strongest emotions of Petrarch's past years, his love for Laura and his thirst for glory, "chains" to be thrown off, Petrarch's devoted obedience to his master comes to an end. "You want to deprive me of my most beautiful concern; you want to cast gloom upon the bright side of my soul," Petrarch complains: "it is the most noble kind of passion that you condemn." His love for Laura had made him turn away from lowly pleasures; it had spurred him on to his literary work and to his love of fame. Any virtue he may possess has become stronger through his love. Yet is not this love one of the emotions that have estranged him from God? In the end Petrarch admits: all reasoning that love of a human being may lead a man to love of God is a delusion, because this "reverses the natural order." The progress of man is from God to his creatures, not vice versa:

"There are few things in the world that make man forget God more quickly than an attachment to earthly beings."

There remains as the ultimate stronghold of Petrarch's defence (his "last sickness," as he makes Augustine call it) his "striving, beyond all rational measure, for glory and the immortality of his name." Petrarch admits that this desire exceeds due measure in him. "Nonetheless, nothing will succeed in turning my thoughts away from this desire." The truism of the philosophers that the earth, the only arena for our glory, is no more than a tiny speck of dust offers no help. "I do not want to become a god," Petrarch replies, "as a mortal man I am asking only for mortal goods." "To my mind, as long as we are on this earth we should aspire to a glory which we can hope to achieve . . . Of a higher kind of glory or honour we shall partake in the future, in heaven . . . Is it not a well-ordered course for men to look to earthly things above all while we are on earth, and leave eternal things to the existence to come?" But again Petrarch finally has to admit that, with arguments of this sort, he is treading a path on which many have lost their God and salvation. At last he listens humbly to his master's teachings—but only until Augustine draws from them the inescapable conclusion: if, then, you wish your mind to be unburdened and free for divine things, give up your unending work on the *Africa* and the biographies of the *De viris illustribus* [*Of illustrious men*], the fruits of your ambition; "be free again, be yourself entirely, and prepare for the day of your death!"

This is the climax, but also the turning point of the discussion. Petrarch shrinks back: "What, then, should I do? Should I interrupt and abandon my labours? . . . How can I calmly forsake a half-finished work on which I have spent so much time and effort!" "Should I not rather hurry on even more urgently than before in order to complete these works with God's help, so that subsequently, with a free mind, I shall be able to devote myself to higher things? . . . I certainly can see that it would be a safer journey if I devoted my life to the one thought that is needed and chose the direct way to salvation. But I feel unable to restrain the longings of my heart . . . I will engage in my work with double dedication, to turn to the greater task as soon as the first is completed." Even Augustine must acquiesce in the end. "May it so be," the dialogue concludes, "since it cannot be otherwise. Humbly I implore God . . . to guide your fumbling steps onto solid ground."

How strong these longings actually were we know from Petrarch's subsequent accounts of the course of his literary labours. The ambivalence which in the *Secretum* he discerns in his very devotion to his work would never cease to stir his conscience, as some of his later letters testify. After his return to Italy, when he made ambitious plans at Milan to resume his work on the many books he had begun in the Vaucluse, he begged an intimate friend not to mistake this programme for a product of vanity. "You know my heart, you understand that I would be ashamed rather than considering it a glory if at my age I had ambitions other than the care of my soul. But I am convinced that what I am aiming at is something that will also profit my soul." And in another letter of those years he further tried to fathom his *affectus* [emotion]. "I swear, neither ambition nor greed are driving me, but my [accustomed] labourious leisure and an insatiable thirst for letters, which, I foresee, will never leave me until my last breath." It was, indeed, near the end of his life that he put down the most moving apology for the passion which even his firm will to learn from Augustine had been unable to suppress. In the year before Petrarch's death, Boccaccio entreated his friend and master to allow himself to rest at that late hour of his life, and to leave something for younger men to do. The old man replied that he appreciated the affection that prompted the thought, but "I should surely die the sooner if I followed your advice. Continued work and exertion are the nourishment of my mind. The moment I began to relax and rest, I should cease to live . . . Do you not know that passage from Ecclesiasticus 'When man has finished his research he is but at the beginning, and when he rests then does he labour'? To me it seems as if I had but begun . . . If in the meanwhile the end, which certainly cannot be far off, should come, . . . I desire that death should find me reading and writing—or, if it pleases Christ, praying and in tears."

To return to the *Secretum*, it is important to realize that the outcome of its psychological search is not simply, as has often been asserted, recognition of the power of the human desire for glory. Attempts to vindicate *cupiditas gloriae* [desire for glory] were to continue through Petrarch's later life, as we will presently observe; but the major result of his self-interrogation in the *Secretum* is the discovery that not only this *affectus* but also another passion that contradicted the demand of Augustine and the Stoics for cool, philosophic disengagement from life had been a necessary incentive for his literary activities, and that this passion, the creative drive, was giving deeper meaning to his striving for "glory."

It is also essential to realize that these apologies for the ceaseless activity of intellectual labour are unmistakably by the same pen that, during the 1330s, had written praises of the *virtus Romana* in the *Africa*. In spite of all the changes brought about by Petrarch's crisis at the time of the *Secretum*, deep down in his heart there had survived an assent to the right and to the psychological necessity of creative passion.

This does not mean that profound changes had not occurred and that there had not been serious curtailments of the bold vision of life and history found in Petrarch's younger years. Even apart from the *De remediis utriusque fortunae* [*Remedies Against Both Kinds of Fortune*], the work of his old age, in which a bitterly pessimistic view of man's nature defied the values he had once upheld, one can point to many occasions on which the Petrarch of the 40s, 50s, and 60s reacted in accord with medieval traditions and came into open conflict with what, as a daring young humanist, he had previously said. Indeed, it is through such a comparison that the historical place of the *De vita solitaria*, the major document of Petrarch's later humanism, can be best understood.

Let us once more recall how the young humanist had evaluated life and its goals on different occasions. He had censured Humbert of the Dauphiné for giving up his princely position in order to lead a life of religious withdrawal. Petrarch, at that time, had insisted that in the gospels Martha was not despised when Mary Magdalene was praised, that Cicero's *Somnium Scipionis* calls the life in the *civitates* the most agreeable to God, and that Plotinus had taught that man can attain felicity not only through the spiritual virtues, but also through the *virtutes politicae*.

In the *De vita solitaria*, Pope Celestine V, who had given up the papal see in order to lead a hermit's life and who, in Dante's *Divina Commedia*, had been relegated to the circle of those *animae tristes* [sad souls] who had lived "without ignominy and without praise," is glorified as a saintly teacher of the solitary life. If others "were made apostles, saints, and friends of God" for giving-up lowly positions or secular kingdoms, how greatly must we admire the man who "scorned the papacy, than which there is no loftier station." This was, to be sure, the renunciation of a saintly soul, but Petrarch's evaluation of the event is couched in such secular and psychological terms that comparison with his youthful reaction to decisions by others to re- nounce worldly careers and enter monastic orders does not seem far-fetched. For the description of Celestine's abdication, in the De vita solitaria, reads like the story of the escape of a follower of Petrarch's solitary life from a golden prison. The former pope left his office "with good cheer and with signs of spiritual joy in his eyes . . . his freedom restored at last, looking not as if he had withdrawn his shoulder from a flat- tering burden, but his neck from the fatal axe. . . . In truth, he was returning from toil to rest, from insane disputations to divine intercourse; he was leaving the city and, in his imagination, was ascending . . . a mountain: rugged and steep, I admit, but from which he had a smooth path to heaven."

Elsewhere in the De vita solitaria the story of Martha and Mary is again recalled. Some people, Petrarch now says, stress the fact that Martha, who did not follow Mary's flight to a desert cave and spiritual solitude, "is nevertheless a saint." The author of the De vita solitaria replies: "I do not deny it, but surely Mary is much ho- lier." The deeper meaning of the story of the two sisters "leaves no room for doubt that the contemplative life was placed before the active life in Christ's judgment and should be preferred by his faithful whenever there is a choice." As for the recognition in ancient literature of the values of the vita politica [political life], the De vita solitaria gives the following reply to Aristotle's saying that only a beast or a god could live outside human society: he, Petrarch, wished, indeed, to become a "godlike man." And what else was to be learned from Plotinus but that the virtues of the vita politica are the lowest in the entire scale of human perfection? The higher virtues will be acquired by "those who leave the cities behind, live in leisure, and become true phi- losophers" as men who have conquered their passions.

This new love of contemplation deeply affects the second book of the De vita solitaria, which in its substance is a series of historical biographies. After a long pag- eant of saints, philosophers, and poets has demonstrated that all of them owed their best to the vita solitaria [solitary life], statesmen and citizens are made the objects of severe criticism. Those of this group who interest Petrarch as human beings are men in public careers on whom the conflict between the two ways of life has left a special mark. There is Augustus, who always longed to become free eventually of his exalted position and spend his old age as a private citizen, but could never bring himself to give up the splendours of his high office. His life testifies to the almost unsurmount- able obstacles that arise once a man has become enmeshed in the responsibilities of public life. He may, of course, have hesitated out of fear of dangers that might have menaced him in private life, or out of a sense of obligation toward the senate and the people. But, "perhaps he was troubled by a natural human weakness. For, to one standing at fortune's peak as lord and ruler of the world, the descent to the humble and lowly position he desired must have appeared extremely abrupt . . . and so he stuck to his place and never descended from it until his death."

Diocletian "did what Augustus had desired to do," thus setting the greatest and most moving example to the world. Precisely because he was the first Roman em-peror to demand ceremonial worship as a god, he finally "grew weary of the turbulent court and the costly encumbrance of troops of attendants and of general servility, suddenly changed his mind, and felt a strong desire to be alone, poor, and free and to escape by swimming from the sea of imperial cares into the heaven of a humbler life, naked like a pilot from a great shipwreck." It is the same gesture that had attracted Petrarch to Saint Celestine; Petrarch draws the parallel himself: "We admire Celes-tine, although that holy man did for the sake of an eternal life what the great sinner Diocletian had done for the sake of the . . . uncertain remainder of his old age, when out of longing for the utmost peace of mind he accepted the lot of a private citizen."

The two figures who stand at opposite poles, and in the condemnation or ap-proval of whom the central issue of the *De vita solitaria* comes to a head, are Cicero, the philosopher who chose the political life, and Scipio the elder, the statesman and general who returned to a life of leisure.

Petrarch's denunciation of Cicero, after he had come to know him as a Roman citizen and statesman, is a crucial clue to the changes in Petrarch's outlook on life. In 1345, not long after the *Secretum* crisis, he had his first opportunity to gain inti-mate knowledge of Cicero's personality, thanks to the discovery of one of the collec-tions of Cicero's correspondence, the *Epistolae ad Atticum* [*Letters to Atticus*]. As a result, he strongly disapproved of Cicero's conduct and way of life. His criticism al-lows us to see that by that time both his attitude toward the *Respublica Romana* [Roman Republic] and his evaluation of the active life had moved away from the persuasions of his youth, and that the two changes were inseparable. Gone was the admiration and sympathy for those who had made themselves champions of the *Respublica Romana* in the period of the civil wars, the breakdown of republican insti-tutions, and the rise of Caesar. During the 30s, as we have seen, this sympathy had been so strong that Petrarch had become convinced that the course of Roman his-tory would have changed for the better had Pompey, after his victory at Dyrrachium, annihilated Caesar and his army; and in the first books of the *Africa* Petrarch had bitterly condemned Caesar as the destroyer of the republic. In contrast, his reaction to the *Epistolae ad Atticum* in 1345 is based on the claim that if Cicero had been a truly wise man he would have "withdrawn from the civil wars once liberty was extin-guished and the Republic buried and mourned." Those times no longer called for freedom, but for Caesar's famed "clemency." The Ciceros and Catos ought to have been content to accept it. It is true that a few years later, during the late 40s, we find a certain resurgence of Petrarch's sympathies for Caesar's adversaries when he looked for a while with hope upon Cola di Rienzo's audacious efforts to re-establish a repub-lic in papal Rome. But after Rienzo's failure, he finally renounced his former scorn of Caesar and applause for the last defenders of the *Respublica Romana*. In the end he even resumed Augustine's reproof that the ultimate motive of Cato and Brutus had been their striving for empty glory.

At the heart of these changes in Petrarch's attitude after the *Secretum* crisis was his increasing trust in the *vita solitaria* [solitary life] as the supreme standard: the truly wise man, concerned with intellectual and spiritual matters, should not become en-snared in distracting political struggles, as had happened to the Roman defenders of the [Republic]. As early as 1345 Petrarch's major criticism of Cicero ran: "what I find lacking in your life is perseverance, a striving for quietude such as is becoming to a philosopher's profession." "Why did you involve yourself in so many contentions and useless quarrels and forsake the calm so becoming to your age, your position, and the vicissitudes of your life? What vain splendour of fame drove you . . . to a death unworthy of a sage? . . . Oh, how much more fitting it would have been had you, philosopher that you were, grown old in rural surroundings, . . . meditating upon eternal life, . . . and not aspiring to consular *fasces* [rank] and military triumphs . . . !"

According to the *De vita solitaria*, Cicero emerges in his life and work as an historic witness—a witness despite himself—to the truth that those engaged in the pursuits of the spirit must, as Plotinus teaches, shun distracting involvement in politics and the active life. When the breakdown of the republic sent Cicero, champion of the *vita activa politica* [active political life], into enforced leisure and he took advantage of it for his literary work, he did so unwillingly. But the new way of life proved its worth. "It transformed the greatest of orators into a great philosopher, and there is not a student who does not know how magnificently Latin studies were enriched by this circumstance." Cicero himself was forced to concede the beneficial influence of his new environment. Although he still "affirmed that the active life is more profitable to the state, which in a measure even I will not deny, he admitted that the retired life is safer and easier, less burdensome and vexatious than other modes of life, and therefore he not only sanctioned it for those who have some good reason for embracing it, but especially commended it to those who excel in intellect and learning." Cicero began to be reconciled to his retirement, in which he accomplished much more than he had been able to achieve in all the occupations of his busy life before the downfall of the republic. He learned in his solitude to be "sufficient unto himself. . . . It was solitude that caused this man's mind to open out; moreover—this is the strange and wonderful thing—it was a solitude obnoxious to him. What, one may think, would it not have accomplished had he desired it, or, how much should we not long for that which brings such great benefit even to one who is unwilling to endure it?"

The evident bias in such sentences notwithstanding, there is a keen, personal interest in this endeavour to grasp the meaning of Cicero's fate. One ventures to think that nothing like it had yet been seen before the time when Petrarch passed through the successive phases of his development and experienced the struggle of opposing values in his life as well as through the medium of his humanistic and historical imagination. The same thing may be said of his pictures of the real hero of the *De vita solitaria*, Scipio Africanus the Elder, and of the man who continued his work, his namesake, Scipio Africanus the Younger. As the incomparable representatives of the spirit which animated Rome before the coming of Caesar and the rise of imperial monarchy, these two historical figures kept open for Petrarch access to the world of the *Respublica Romana* [Roman Republic] even at the time when his appraisal of Caesar and of the last defenders of the republic had radically and irreversibly changed.

The two Africani who, for the author of the *Africa*, were the great military and political leaders of Rome, had been vividly pictured by Valerius Maximus in the *otium* [leisurely life] which, after their victories, they had led on their estates by the sea. Thanks to their twofold distinction, they could become the supreme models for the *De vita solitaria*. They alone among the great men of public affairs, so Petrarch thought, knew how to lead a perfect life with friends in nature when, after the exertions of the wars, they showed themselves to be "as much lovers of solitude as of virtue." "What a wonderful spectacle, transcending the pomp and sceptres of all kings, to see such men, saviours of the state, liberators of the citizens, defenders of Italy . . . , their task successfully performed, . . . their bodyguard left in Rome, . . . strolling alone, at leisure, . . . over the hills and along the shore, often picking up little shells or sea pebbles. . . ." What this happy solitude meant in the lives of the two great leaders, we know from Scipio the Elder's "magnificent dictum, worthy of a great and wise man": "that he was never less at leisure than in his leisure, and never less lonely than in his solitude."

The picture of the *otium* [leisure] of the two Scipios is the climax of the *De vita solitaria*. "The virtue of Scipio's aphorism," comments Petrarch, "is that it conveys in a few words what I have in mind. I mean . . . a leisure that is neither idle nor profitless. . . . I do not allow the intellect to lie fallow except that it may revive and become more fertile by a period of rest." He would, says Petrarch, "make this wonderful saying of the great general fully my own" and even sharpen its expression: "I would assert that I was always at leisure except in my leisure, always lonely except in my solitude."

Next to the criticism of Cicero, Petrarch's continued admiration for Scipio the Elder provides the best clue for understanding the extent and limit of the changes in his outlook and evaluations. In his youth, Scipio had been to him the symbol of the vigour and driving force in the political existence of Roman citizens. Even when the values of the *vita politica* [political life] had faded from Petrarch's own philosophy of life, his old vision of the *virtus* [virtue] of the *civis Romanus* [Roman citizen], still focused on Scipio, continued to mould and nourish the ideal of the ceaseless activity of the mind. This was one of the enduring links between the world of the young Petrarch and the world of the post-*Secretum* humanist. Along this road some of the ideas of the young pioneer were carried on in disguise, despite the profound changes in Petrarch's outlook.

The truth of this observation becomes evident when it is realized that in the image of Scipio still another element of Petrarch's early bold persuasions survived: the recognition that a desire for glory is necessary. But this compels us to step beyond the confines of the *De vita solitaria*.

As early as the *Africa*, Petrarch had associated Scipio with the ideas on glory so boldly proclaimed in his oration on the Roman Capitol. According to ancient accounts, Scipio, when being crowned after victory, had the poet Ennius, herald of his deeds, crowned with the same laurel. The *Africa* celebrates their close companionship and Ennius' role in the making of Scipio's glory.

Thanks to the preservation of three consecutive versions of Petrarch's *Life of Scipio*, one of the major biographies in his *De viris illustribus* [*Of famous men*], we can trace the continuance and ever stronger defence of the *gloriae cupiditas* [desire for glory] as a trait of Petrarch's image of Scipio from the early days of his work on the *Africa* through his later life. Although the philosophical doctrines increasingly upheld by Petrarch after the *Secretum* were bound to throw deep shadows over all *affectus* [emotion], each return of Petrarch to Scipio's biography produced a more elaborate and positive analysis of the *gloriae cupiditas*—perhaps just because only by making this one, crucial exception could Petrarch submit to the demand of "ataraxy" [emotional tranquility] and the repression of all passions that he conceded theoretically in most of his later works.

In the first version of the *Vita Scipionis* [*Life of Scipio*], written several years before the *Secretum*, passionate longing for glory is claimed to have been one of the springs of Scipio's greatness, and the claim is couched in terms very similar to the defence of the poet's irrepressible striving for fame in the coronation oration. In that first version of the *Vita Scipionis* one of the episodes from Scipio's life runs: As the historians tell us, Scipio recklessly exposed himself and the fate of Rome in a small, unarmed vessel, in order to reach the shores of Africa more quickly. That, says Petrarch, was certainly indefensible before the judgment seat of cool reason; yet "the boundless hope and ardour in the heart of one who strove for the highest goal took Scipio through all perils. It made him think of nothing but true glory and of the end of the war as he had conceived it."

In revising this account, at about the time the *Secretum* was written (to be exact, between 1341 and 1343), Petrarch must have felt provoked by the Augustinian reproach that the Romans' great deeds had been the result, not of the often praised *virtutes Romana* [Roman virtues] but rather of their *gloriae desiderium* [desire for glory]. Although this is true, Petrarch says in an insertion made at that time, one should not forget Cicero's observations that hardly any man would greatly exert himself or expose himself to danger if he did not expect glory as his reward, and that the *gloriae cupiditas* [desire for glory] has ineradicable roots in noble minds, and especially in those of great generals. Petrarch undoubtedly had in mind two passages of the *De officiis* (I, 19, 65 and I, 22, 74), yet he was actually turning a Ciceronian warning against the dangers of *cupiditas gloriae* [desire for glory] into acceptance of this desire—exactly as in his coronation oration he used the *Tusculans* to reconstruct and make his own the Peripatetic defence of passion that had been denounced in Cicero's discussion. What the Ciceronian phrase in the *De officiis* to which Petrarch alluded actually averred was that "greatness of the spirit places moral relevance . . . not in glory but in conduct. . . . Yet it is the loftiest spirits that are most easily tempted by a passion for glory to commit acts of injustice. But here we are on slippery ground, for scarcely a man will be found who, after taking hardship and danger upon himself, does not wish for glory as his natural reward." The Petrarch of the early 40s, then, who glossed over the unmistakable moral disapproval in Cicero's words, using them unconcernedly in the defence of Scipio's *gloriae cupiditas*, was, on this one score at least, in spite of all his Augustinian leanings, still the man who on the Roman Capitol had delivered the oration on the creative passions of the poet. . . .

It has seemed best to describe the changes which took place in Petrarch's life by basing our understanding of his views of man and history partly on the observation of his literary and historical imagination. Indeed, since he was not a philosopher concerned primarily with the clarity and consistency of his definitions of ethical maxims, he cannot be fully comprehended unless the picture of his humanistic outlook is made to include the biographical and autobiographical imagery of his works—his changing representations of those whom he considered the great leaders of antiquity, as well as his own spiritual portrait, which he drew and redrew under the impress of successive experiences. If one gives this dimension of Petrarch's humanism due emphasis, as we have tried, and thus arrives at a clearer picture of the growth and retrenchment in his development, one also becomes better prepared to judge his place in the Weltanschauung [worldview] of the Renaissance. For, because of the fundamental differences in the various periods in his life, even a general estimate of the historical role of Petrarch's work must concentrate on the successive changes in his imagination and thought before one can attempt to define his place in the transition from the Middle Ages to the Renaissance.

The ideas of Petrarch's youth, as we have come to recognize, show a strong kinship with the outlook of the early quattrocento. Even for that phase of his life, however, the conventional notion of Petrarch as the "harbinger" or even "father" of Renaissance humanism proves to be too vague. Since Petrarch did not continue the trend of his early years beyond middle age, and since neither the *Africa* nor the coronation oration were among the works still widely read after 1400, we ought at least to add that the outlook of the young Petrarch on life and history was a prelude rather than the basic factor in the rise of the ideas of the quattrocento. The true historical relationship is that some of the key ideas that came to the fore after 1400, first in Florence and subsequently in many places in quattrocento Italy, had already been touched upon by Petrarch in his early years, but that they could not have gained currency and maturity had not Florentine citizens, living under unique political conditions around 1400, given humanism a changed place in the society of the Renaissance and on this different basis produced a new civic outlook and education. In other words, since Petrarch's early ideas, at the time of the conception of the *Africa*, had sprung from a rediscovery of the world of Roman citizens, the fruit could ripen only when citizens of Renaissance city states who, in their own lives, were near enough to the values and conditions of ancient citizens took over the intellectual work that Petrarch had left half done.

A second consideration must focus on the structure of Petrarch's humanism during the latter part of his life. One symbol of this period is Petrarch's Cicero: the quattrocento would base its ideals of conduct and culture on the same Cicero, Roman statesman and citizen, whom Petrarch during the second half of his life so bitterly denounced. No judgment of Petrarch's historical place is, therefore, adequate which does not take into account the fact that many of the ideas he held in his later years did not lead on to the world of the quattrocento. Petrarch's Scipio, on the other hand, reveals a different dimension of Petrarch's post-*Secretum* outlook. The impact of young Petrarch's psychological discoveries of the power of strong emotional drives had not been lost; besides the *gloriae cupiditas* [desire for glory], attributed to Scipio, one recalls Petrarch's inability to subordinate his passionate urge to do creative work to the demands of Augustinian and Stoic teaching. The observation that many *affectus* [emotions] are ambivalent—helpful to virtue, yet not justifiable in the light of the laws laid down by philosophy and religion—remained an integral part of the synthesis established with tradition in Petrarch's later years. We probably should look upon this synthesis as one of those powerful but, after the late trecento, soon abandoned efforts to accommodate the new with the old that are characteristic of the century of transition which had opened with Dante.

Petrarch's later—and more mature—writings are, however, not merely of interest as documents of the trecento struggles and efforts at conciliation. His *conflictus curarum suarum* [conflict of anxieties] transcends the level of late medieval doctrinal conflicts. In his hands, that *conflictus* [conflict] has developed into an analysis of human nature by an already truly humanistic mind; it is relevant beyond the disputes of Petrarch's century. There is something distinctly "modern" in his understanding of the necessity, fraught with inevitable tragic consequences, of Scipio's *desiderium gloriae* [desire for glory]—a grasp of the reality of life. In the realm of Petrarch's historical ideas, his return from the *Respublica Romana* [Roman Republic] to profound admiration of Caesar does not result in a mere revival of the medieval vision of the *Sacrum Imperium* [Holy Roman Empire]; it also opens the road to the modern discovery of Caesar's personality and greatness as a statesman and general. This interest in man as man and this deliverance from mere tradition are also obvious and have often been noted in the independence from conventional and ceremonial forms in Petrarch's relations with friends as well as with princes and emperors. Almost everywhere in his letters and works, even where the answers to his problems are still "medieval," the problems themselves are usually already those of the humanists of the Renaissance.

In other words: however indispensable it is to pursue the historical analysis of thought here proposed—to understand that the work of Petrarch in his youth, although a unique prelude to things to come, did not lead directly to the Renaissance ideas of the quattrocento, and that his own final view of life represents one of the great semi-medieval syntheses characteristic of the trecento—nonetheless there is also some lasting truth in the old claim that Petrarch with his basic human traits and sensitivity to new values was "the first modern man."

DOCUMENTS

In 1337 Francesco Petrarca, still a young scholar in his early thirties, set down a short list of his favorite books. Those books, listed in the first selection, establish the canon of early humanism. The works of Cicero in both philosophy and rhetoric head the list, followed by Seneca and Aristotle in Latin translation. Petrarch's reliance on second-rate Roman historians, such as Valerius Maximus, and the five "canonical poets"—Virgil, Horace, Ovid, Lucan, and Statius—of the medieval curriculum shows a rather conservative outlook. Petrarch does, however, list the historian of the Roman republic, Livy, whose manuscripts he studied and copied, before composing his own works on Rome, the epic *Africa*, and his lives of great men, *De viris illustribus*. Petrarch's most intriguing work is his *Secretum*, a series of imaginary dialogues between his young, sinful self and his later ego, represented by the great church father, Saint Augustine. Francesco is bound by the twin chains of love of Laura and desire for fame. In the selection included here (most of Book II of the *Secretum*) Francesco acknowledges his sinful state but because of his yearning for fame and glory in this world cannot commit himself to a life of monastic renunciation.

| Petrarch's Favorite Books, 1337

My especially prized books. To the others I usually resort not as a deserter but as a scout.

Cicero's [works]

Sixth Book of the *Republic*
Tusculan [Disputations]
On duties
Laelius on friendship
Cato Major on old age
On divination
Hortensius
On the nature of the gods
On the parodoxes [of the Stoics]

[Cicero's] Rhetorical [works]

On invention
Ad Herennium
On the orator
Invectives
common orations

Moral Philosophy

Aristotle's *Ethics*
Boethius's *Consolation [of Philosophy]*
Seneca
[Letter] to Nero
[Letter] to Lucillus
Remedies of fortune
Tragedies
On the tranquility of the mind
On consolation
On the brevity of life

Histories

Valerius [Maximus]
Livy
Justinus
Florus
Sallust
Suetonius

"Petrarch's Favorite Books, 1337," from B. L. Ullman *Studies in the Italian Renaissance* (Rome, 1973), pp. 116–119. Translated by Benjamin G. Kohl.

Festus
Eutropius

[Collections of] Exempla

[Macrobius] Saturnalia
A[ulus] Gellius

Poetics

Virgil
Lucan
Statius
Horace, especially the *Odes*
Juvenal
Ovid, especially the greater [work, that is, the *Metamorphoses*]

Grammar

Priscian
Papias
Donatus
Catholicon [of Johannes Balbus]

Dialectic

Tractatus [perhaps of Peter of Spain] and nothing more

Astrology

Sphere [of John of Sacrobosco]
Macrobius, but here is understood the more accessible of his treatises [referring to commentary on Cicero's *Dream of Scipio*]
Firmicus, and other commentaries

| Petrarch's Secret Inner Struggle, 1358

ST. AUGUSTINE Have we rested long enough?

FRANCESCO Yes, if you are ready.

ST. AUGUSTINE What is your frame of mind now? How confident do you feel? When a man is ill, hope is an important sign that he is getting well.

FRANCESCO There is no reason to look to myself for hope; God is my hope.

ST. AUGUSTINE Wisely spoken. Now back to the matter at hand. Many troubles lay clamorous siege on you, but you are unaware just how numerous and powerful

---

"Petrarch's Secret Inner Struggle" from Petrarch's *Secretum*, Book 2, ed. Davy A. Carozza and H. James Shey, American University Studies, Series XVII: *Classical Language and Literature*, Vol. 7, P. Lang Publications, 1989, pp. 65–83. Reprinted by permission of Verlag Peter Lang.

your enemies really are. This frequently happens to a man who sees his enemies at a distance and in close formation; he is contemptuous of their small number and is deceived. But when they draw closer and the battalions spread out more clearly in formation, their armaments glittering and flashing before his eyes, then he feels fear rise in him and he is sorry that he was not more cautious. I think the same thing is about to happen to you. When I have made you see all the evils which press upon and besiege you from all sides, you will feel ashamed at having taken this all so lightly and you will find it hardly surprising that your soul, beset by so many hostile forces, has been unable, so to speak, to break through enemy lines. You will see, then, how many opposing thoughts have overcome the beneficial meditation to which I am trying to bring you.

FRANCESCO   I am very much afraid. I have always recognized that I was in great danger, but now you tell me that I have grossly underestimated it and that compared to what they should be, my fears are nothing at all. What hope is left to me?

ST. AUGUSTINE   Despair is the ultimate evil, and most men give themselves to it prematurely. Therefore, I want you to know above all that there is nothing to despair about.

FRANCESCO   Yes, I knew that, but terror made me forget.

ST. AUGUSTINE   Now give me your complete attention as I recall the words of a poet most familiar to you.

> Behold what nations gather, what walled cities
> Shut their gates and sharpen the blade against
> You and your people

See what snares the world has set for you, what vanities flit about you, how many useless cares oppress you. First of all, consider the sin which caused those noble spirits to fall at the dawn of creation. You must take every precaution not to fall as they did. How many are the things that tempt your soul to perilous flights. You have great natural abilities, but they tire you out and make you forgetful of the weakness you so often experience. They crowd in and occupy your mind, until it can think of nothing else. And thus you become so proud, self-reliant, and self-satisfied that finally you hate your Creator. But even if your gifts are as great as you imagine them to be, they ought to have inspired you with a feeling of humility rather than pride, recalling that they all came to you through no merit of your own. Set aside for a moment the relationship of God and his Creatures. Even among men, servants will be more obedient to their master, if they see him display a generosity which they did not deserve. They strive, then, by their good services to comply with their master whose generosity they should have anticipated and merited by their actions.

Thus you can understand very easily how insignificant are the things you pride yourself on. You trust in your talent and in your wide reading; you pride yourself on your eloquence and take delight in the beauty of your mortal body. Yet you know in how many ways your talent often fails you and how many are the skills in which you are not a match for even the humblest of mankind. I can go further. You will find primitive and humble animals whose work you cannot imitate no matter how you try. Come, boast of your talent now.

As for reading, what is the use of that? Out of all that you have read, how much has really stayed in your mind? How much of it has taken root, so to speak, and produced mature fruit? Examine your heart carefully and you will find that the sum of your knowledge, when set in contrast to the vast extent of your ignorance, can be likened to a stream dried by the summer sun when compared with the Ocean. And yet what comfort is it to have even great knowledge, if after you have learned the dimensions of heaven and earth, the extent of the seas, the course of the stars, the properties of herbs and stones, and the mysteries of nature, you still do not have self-knowledge? What comfort is it if you know from your reading of the scriptures the right and upward path to virtue, but passion makes you swerve to the downward path? Or what use is it to know the deeds of illustrious men, if it makes no impact on your day-to-day life?

And what can I say about eloquence that you have not already admitted yourself? It is vain to have confidence in it. What does it matter that your audience perhaps approves of what you have said, if in your judgement it stands condemned? Although the applause of the audience may seem to be a considerable reward for the orator, how trivial is the roar of the crowd, if he cannot in his heart applaud himself. How can your oratory please others, if you yourself are not pleased with it? Therefore you were disappointed often enough in your expectations of glory from eloquence that you came to recognize how vain has been your pride in this windy nonsense. Tell me, what can be more childish, indeed more insane, than to be careless and lazy in all other matters, but waste time in the study of words and derive so much pleasure in speaking, while in your ignorance you never see your own reprehensible behavior? You are like those little birds they say take so much delight in their own singing that they sing themselves to death. And yet it often happened that in ordinary and everyday matters (to make it all the more embarrassing) you were unable to find proper words to speak of those things which you considered to be beneath the dignity of your style. Also, think how many things there are in the world which simply lack proper names; and there are many other things which do have names, but whose majesty cannot be described adequately in words by human eloquence without first experiencing them. How often have I heard you complaining and have seen you at a loss for words and angry because neither could your tongue nor your pen accurately express ideas which were so very dear and intelligible to you as you thought about them. What then is this eloquence, so limited and feeble, which can neither encompass all reality nor keep control of that which it has encompassed?

The Greeks criticize Latin because of the poverty of its vocabulary, and you Latins criticize Greek. Seneca thought the Greek vocabulary was the richer, but Cicero, in the introduction to *The Definitions of Good and Evil*, says, "I am completely baffled why people despise things Roman. This is not the place to discuss it, but I firmly believe and have often argued that the Latin language is not only not poor, as is commonly thought, but even richer than Greek." He says the same thing often both in other places and in the *Tusculan Disputations*: "Greek, the words in which you think you are rich are inadequate." This comes unhesitatingly from a man who knew he was the prince of Latin oratory and was bold enough to challenge Greece's supremacy in this literary endeavor. Against this set what Seneca, an admirer of the Greek language, wrote in his *Declamations*: "Whatever Roman eloquence has which can rival or surpass the arrogant Greeks is associated with Cicero." That is great praise and undoubtedly very true.

There is, then, as you see, a great controversy on the subject of primacy in Eloquence not only between us and the Greeks, but among our most learned writers themselves. We have in our camp those who favor the Greeks, just as the Greeks perhaps have some who favor us—at least some say Plutarch, the famous philosopher, favored our side.

And then, Seneca, a Roman, while according all due respect to Cicero because of the extraordinary charm of his style, in everything else thinks the Greeks were the best, though Cicero held the contrary opinion. If you really want my view, I say that both Seneca and Cicero were right in what they said about the limitations of both languages. But if this is true of these two famous countries, what can any place else hope for? Consider what faith you ought to put in your powers when you see the nation as a whole, of which you form a very small part, has such poor language resources. It will shame you to have spent so much time pursuing something which cannot be attained, and if it were attained would be utterly useless.

But I shall pass on to other things which have to be dealt with. Do you take pride in your physical attributes? "Do you not see the dangers that surround you"? What is there that pleases you about your body? Your strength and good health? Nothing is more precarious. Fatigue from trivial causes, the onset of various diseases, insect bites, a little draft, and many other things are all cause for alarm. Or maybe you are fascinated by your good looks and when you look in a mirror at your complexion and handsome face, you find something to admire, something which entrances and charms you. Are you not put on guard by the story of Narcissus? Does not an unflinching consideration of what vileness lies beneath the body's external form give you warning? No, content with superficial appearances, you look no further. Even if all the other signs failed to convince you that beauty wilts and fades, the very disquieting passage of time, which each day robs you of something, should have convinced you beyond doubt. I am sure you will not dare say it, but even if you thought you were impervious to aging, disease, and other things which alter appearance of the body, you ought not forget the thing which ultimately destroys everything and always remember this verse of the satirist, "Death alone proves how frail are the bodies of men."

These, unless I am mistaken, are the reasons that you are puffed up with pride, that prevent you from recognizing your low estate and keep you from meditation on death. And there are other reasons, which I intend now to pursue.

FRANCESCO Stop a while, I beg you. You are overwhelming me with such a weight of criticism that I am unable to rise to my defense.

ST. AUGUSTINE Speak up. I shall gladly yield the floor.

FRANCESCO I am astonished to hear you criticize me for things that I know very well never entered my mind. You say that I trusted in my intelligence, but the only sign that I have any intelligence at all is that I never put any trust in it. You say that I became proud of my reading of books, but along with some small measure of wisdom, they brought to me cause for much anxiety. You say that I sought glory from my oratory; but as you yourself said, no one ever got more angry than I that language was inadequate to my ideas. Unless you have it in mind to challenge me, you know that I have always been conscious of my own insignificance, and if by chance I ever thought I was something, this might have come about sometimes by comparing myself to the inadequacies of someone else. We are forced to acknowledge, as I often remarked in accord with Cicero's famous statement, that "we are not strong because of our strength, but because of the weakness of others." But even if I were abundantly endowed with the gifts you mention, what is so magnificent about them, that I should take pride in them? I am not so unthinking and frivolous that I would let myself be troubled by these unsubstantial things. Of little use are talent, knowledge, and eloquence, if they do not heal the disease that tears at my soul. I remember complaining of this very thing in a certain letter of mine.

And what you said (in all seriousness) about my physical advantages almost made me laugh. Do you really think that I put trust in my mortal, frail, little body, when I see each day time taking its toll? May God save me from that. There was a time in my youth, when I worried about my hair style and adorning my face, but this concern quickly passed with age, and I now know the truth of the statement of the Emperor Domitian. When writing to a friend about himself, he complained of the evanescence of beauty, saying "You can be sure that nothing is more pleasing than beauty and nothing so short-lived."

ST. AUGUSTINE I could say much against what you have just said, but I prefer that your own conscience inspire shame in you rather than anything I might say. I shall not press you, nor wring the truth out of you. I am a magnanimous inquisitor and will simply contradict you and ask that in the future you continue to avoid what you maintain you have always avoided. If ever you are tempted to become conceited over your appearance, just recall what your body, which now pleases you, will become; think how pathetic, foul, and hideous even to yourself it will become, if you could only see it then. Then recall often this maxim, "I was born for greater things than to be a slave of my body." It is utterly insane for men to neglect the most important part of themselves and pamper the body which they live in. If a man were for a short time locked up in a dark, dirty, disease-ridden prison, would he not (unless he were mad) keep himself as much as possible away from contact with the walls and dirt floor? And when it was time for his release, would he not listen intently for the footsteps of his deliverer? But if this stopped being a concern to him and instead he became immersed in the filth and horror of his surroundings, fearing to leave prison and eagerly turning his attention to painting and adorning the walls that imprison him in an attempt to make the place livable, would he not be rightly considered a miserable fool? Well, you poor humans know and love your prison; and although you are on the point of leaving it or being dragged out of it, you cling to it and worry about decorating what you ought to hate. As you yourself in your *Africa* made the father of great Scipio say, "We hate and fear bonds and chains we have known, the restraints on liberty. / We love what we have become—free." Well put indeed, if only you would apply to yourself what you apply to others. But there was one thing out of all you said a moment ago which you probably thought was most humble, but which seemed supremely arrogant to me and I cannot pretend otherwise.

FRANCESCO I am very sorry if I said anything arrogant; but if the soul judges a man's words and deeds, I can testify that I said nothing arrogant.

ST. AUGUSTINE It is a much more intolerable kind of pride to downgrade others than to exalt oneself more than one ought. I would have much preferred to see you exalt others and then put yourself above them than to see you reduce others to dust beneath your feet and then out of a refinement of pride take up a shield of humility made of contempt for others.

FRANCESCO Interpret my words anyway you want, but I do not think much of myself or others. I am grieved to say what experience has made me feel about the majority of men.

ST. AUGUSTINE It is very reasonable to despise oneself but to despise others is quite dangerous and useless. But let us proceed to the remaining points. Do you know what else leads you astray?

FRANCESCO Say whatever you wish, only do not accuse me of envy.

ST. AUGUSTINE I wish you had been as little affected by pride as you have by envy. As far as I can tell you are free of that sin, but there are certain other ones I will accuse you of.

FRANCESCO From now on no accusation will upset me. Tell me frankly what drives me off course.

ST. AUGUSTINE An appetite for things of this world.

FRANCESCO No, I do not accept that. I have never heard anything more absurd.

ST. AUGUSTINE Suddenly you are upset and have forgotten your own promise. Things are different when we are not talking about envy.

FRANCESCO No, but about avarice. I know no one less avaricious than I.

ST. AUGUSTINE You try hard to justify yourself, but believe me you are not so free of this fault as you think.

FRANCESCO You mean I am not free from the charge of avarice?

ST. AUGUSTINE No, and you are ambitious too.

FRANCESCO Press on! Redouble your efforts and play the role of accuser to the hilt. I am waiting to see what fresh wound you will inflict on me.

ST. AUGUSTINE You call the truth about yourself accusation and abuse. Juvenal was right when he said, "Anyone who speaks the truth will be an accuser." Equally true is this line from a comic poet, "Flattery makes friends, truth makes enemies." But tell me, what is the use of these preoccupations and worries that wear you out? Why is it necessary in so short a life to have such long-range hopes? "The short span of our life forbids us to have long-range hopes." You read such things often enough, but ignore them. You will say, I suppose, that you do it out of love for your friends and so find a fair name to put on your error. But what kind of madness is it to declare war on yourself and treat yourself as an enemy just to make friends with someone else?

FRANCESCO I am not so selfish and inhuman as to be unconcerned about my friends, especially those whose virtue and merit have drawn me to them. For it is they whom I esteem, revere, love, and take pity on. On the other hand, I am not so generous that I would ruin myself for my friends. No, hardly that. What I want is enough to live on. And since you shoot darts at me from Horace, I shall shield myself with something taken from the same poet. What I want is "a supply of books and stores for one year so I do not have to worry from one hour to the next." And, as the same poet says, "I want to live out my old age with honor and enjoying my art." Because I dread the pitfalls of advanced old age, I am providing beforehand for this twofold wish and combine with my work for the Muses attention to household matters. But I do this only with such indifference that it is evident that I descend to such necessities because I am forced to.

ST. AUGUSTINE I see how deeply these pretexts, which you use to excuse your folly, have taken root in your heart. Why is it that you have not also taken to heart the words of the satirist,

> Why do you torture yourself to gather wealth
> When it is sheer lunacy and madness
> To live like a beggar so you may die rich?

You do it because you think it is a great thing to die in a purple shroud, to be buried in a marble monument, and to leave to your survivors a dispute over a rich inheritance. You desire, therefore, the wealth by which these things are gotten. It is wasted labor, believe me, and senseless as well. If you observe human nature in general, you see that it is content with little. In your own case, there is scarcely anyone who needs fewer things than you to get along on, if a common error were not leading you astray. The poet was referring to the habits of ordinary people or perhaps his own when he said, "The earth gives sparse sustenance; I pick cornel-cherries and / The grass plucked out by the roots feeds me." But you, unlike the poet, should confess that there is nothing more pleasant and attractive than such fare, if you live by your own standards and not those of the mad crowd. Why then do you torment yourself? If you judge yourself according to nature's requirements, you have long been rich. If you judge by what people think, you will never be rich, and there will always be something missing, and in pursuit of it you will be swept over bottomless chasms of desire.

Do you recall with what delight you once wandered far into the country and listened to the murmur of the swirling streams as you lay on a bed of grass? At another time, you would sit on a mountain top and with unobstructed view you would gaze at the fields stretched out below. At other times, you would sleep peacefully in a patch of shade in a sunny valley and revel in the silence. Never at a loss for something to do, you were always deep in meditation and, with the Muses for companions, you were never alone. And as you returned at sunset to your little house, like the old man in Vergil who "to his way of thinking matched the wealth of kings and returning late / Set his table with food from the garden," do you not think that of all men you were by far the richest and most fortunate?

FRANCESCO Ah! I recall now and I sigh with regret at the memory of that time.

ST. AUGUSTINE Why do you sigh? What was it, do you suppose, that caused all these problems? Your soul, of course, which was ashamed to obey the laws of its own nature and thought that it was a slave only because it had not broken the chains that held it. Even now it drags you along like a runaway horse and unless you rein yourself in, you will rush to your destruction. Ever since you began to weary of your fruit trees and simple clothes, and the association of country folk became distasteful to you, you have through the urging of your avarice plunged into the uproar of the city, where the look on your face and your words tell how happily and peacefully you are living. What unhappiness have you not seen there. Obstinate in the face of sad experience, yet you stay on, perhaps held fast by the bonds of your sins. And perhaps God is pleased that just as once you spent your childhood under a harsh schoolmaster, you now live out a miserable old age in the same way, though now your own master. Certainly I saw that you were not affected by avarice and ambition when as a young man you gave promise of great things to come. But now you are a changed man, and the nearer you approach the end of your journey, the more concerned you are for travelling provisions. I can see no other course but that on the day of your death, which perhaps is near and certainly cannot be far off, you will be lying half-dead, poring over your account book, still thirsting for gold. For whatever increases as each day passes must in the end have grown to gigantic proportions.

FRANCESCO Well, if I look ahead to the poverty of old age and provide for when I can no longer work, what is so reprehensible about that?

ST. AUGUSTINE Ah, what absurd anxiety and tragic neglect, to worry about a situation you may never be in and certainly one you will be in for a very short time and yet to be oblivious to a situation which you must necessarily be in and one which you can never get out of. But such is your deplorable habit, to worry about transitory things and neglect eternal things.

As for your delusion about providing a shield against old age, I think the phrase in Vergil got stuck in your mind about "the ant fearing a destitute old age." And so you adopted the ant as a model, understandably enough because as the satirist says, "Some learned from the ant to fear cold and famine." But if you do not renounce instruction from ants, you will find that there is nothing more dismal and absurd than to burden yourself with worry about poverty, fearing that sometime you might have to suffer it.

Well, then, am I saying that you should be poor? Not at all. One should not hope for it, but bear it with courage, if Fortune, who turns human affairs upside down, reduces you to it. I think moderation should be sought in every situation. I do not, therefore, restrict you to the views of those who say, "Bread and water are enough to live on; with these none is poor, and whoever restricts his desires to these things will rival the happiness of Jove himself." I do not think a man should limit himself to bread and water. Such views are as extreme as they are tiresome and odious to hear. And so, to adjust to your weakness, I do not advise you to empty yourself of all natural desires, but to restrain them.

What you possessed was sufficient for all necessities, if only you had been satisfied with them. But as it is, you have brought on the poverty you suffer. The accumulation of goods is the accumulation of stress and worry. That has been proved so many times that we need not argue it again. It is a strange delusion and a tragic blindness that causes the human soul, whose nature is so noble and which is begotten above, to neglect heavenly riches and to dote on the metals of earth. Think carefully, I beg you, and focus the eyes of your mind lest the brilliance of gleaming gold bedazzle them. As often as you are drawn by the hooks of avarice and you are pulled away from your lofty meditations to these base ones, do you not realize that you have plunged headlong from heaven to earth and that from the bosom of the stars you have been plunged into a bottomless pit?

FRANCESCO I do know, and there are no words to express what I have suffered in the fall.

ST. AUGUSTINE Why are you not afraid of a danger you have experienced so often? And when you have reached a higher life, why do you not hold on more tightly?

FRANCESCO I do try, but my human needs unsettle me, and I am torn away unwillingly. I think that it was with good reason the poets of old dedicated the twin peaks of Parnassus to two gods. They wanted to beg from Apollo, whom they called the god of intelligence, inner resources for the mind, and from Bacchus, a supply of things for the body. Not only does the teaching of experience incline me to this way of thinking, but also the frequent testimony of learned men whom I need not quote. Thus, while the polytheism of the ancients is ridiculous, nevertheless this opinion of the poets has a lot of sense in it. If I beg for these two things from the one God from whom all good comes, I do not think I am being unreasonable, unless it seems otherwise to you.

ST. AUGUSTINE No, I think you are right, but what angers me is that you divide your time so unevenly. There was a time when you devoted your whole life to honorable pursuits; if you were forced to spend time on other things, you considered it wasted time. But now whatever energy is left over from your avaricious passion, that is what you give to honorable pursuits. Everyone would like to reach old age, which so changes a man's priorities. But what limit or end will you impose on yourself? Set a goal for yourself and when you have reached it, stop and breathe a while. You are aware that this sentiment was spoken by a man, but that is has the force of an oracular saying—"The greedy man is always in need; fix a definite limit to your desire." What limit to your avarice will you set?

FRANCESCO My goal is not to be in need and not to have more than I need. I do not want to control others nor do I want to be under their control.

ST. AUGUSTINE You will have to put off your humanity and become God, if your goal is not to be in need. Do you not know that of all creatures man stands in most need?

FRANCESCO I have heard that quite often, but I should like you to refresh my memory.

ST. AUGUSTINE Just look at him—born naked and unformed amid wailing and tears, comforted by a little milk, trembling and crawling, in need of another's help, fed and clothed by dumb beasts, his body weak, his mind restless, beset by all kinds of diseases, subject to all kinds of passions, lacking in wisdom, fluctuating between sadness and joy, unable to master his will, unable to control his appetite; he is ignorant of what is good for him and in what proportion, and does not know what is the proper measure of food and drink; he is forced with great labor to find food which is so readily available to other animals; benumbed by sleep, distended with food, stupefied by drink, exhausted by lack of sleep, famished by hunger, parched by thirst; greedy and timid, disgusted at what he has, bemoaning his losses, anxious alike about the past, present, and future; proud amid his miseries and aware of his frailty, lowlier than the vilest worm. His life is short, his days uncertain, his fate inevitable, since death may take him in a thousand different ways.

FRANCESCO You have heaped up such a mass of misery and destitution that I am sorry I was ever born.

ST. AUGUSTINE Yet in spite of such weakness and destitution in man's condition, you go on dreaming of riches and power such as emperors and kings never fully enjoyed.

FRANCESCO Who made use of these words? Who ever mentioned riches and power?

ST. AUGUSTINE You might as well have, for what greater wealth is there than to lack nothing? What greater power is there than not to be under anyone's control?

Certainly the kings and lords of the earth whom you think so rich need countless things. And the generals of armies are subservient to those they seem to control; surrounded by their armed legions, they ought to fear the soldiers who cause their leaders to be feared. Then stop hoping for the impossible and content yourself with your human lot; learn how to live in need and how to have more than you need, to command and to obey. Do not by living your life according to your own ideas try to cast off the yoke of Fortune to which kings submit. You will know you are free of the yoke at last, when you have renounced all your human passions and have yielded completely to the rule of virtue. From that time on, you will be free, subject to no man, and finally a king, truly powerful and completely happy.

FRANCESCO I now regret what I stated and I desire to desire nothing, but I am swept along by bad habit and I am always aware of some unfulfilled need in my heart.

ST. AUGUSTINE To keep to our subject, this is the very thing which keeps you from a contemplation of death. All involved in earthy concerns, you do not lift your eyes to higher things. If you trust me at all, you will cast these concerns off like so much dead weight upon the soul. And it will not be hard to do, if only you adjust yourself to your human nature and let yourself be ruled by it rather than the ravings of the common crowd.

FRANCESCO Indeed, I shall do so willingly. But I have long been waiting to hear what you had begun to say about ambition.

ST. AUGUSTINE Why do you ask me what you can explain yourself? Examine your heart; you will find that ambition is not the least of your faults.

FRANCESCO It did me no good, then, to have fled the cities whenever I could, to have despised association with people and involvement in public affairs, to have sought out the retreats in the woods and the silent countryside, and to have ex-pressed my hatred for vain honors, if I am still accused of ambition.

ST. AUGUSTINE You mortals give up on many things, not because you despise them, but because [you] despair of being able to get them. Hope and desire goad each other on, so that when the one grows cold, the other dies down; but when the one grows warm, the other boils up again.

FRANCESCO Tell me, why should I not hope? Was I lacking in any good accom-plishment?

ST. AUGUSTINE I am not now talking of your accomplishments, but certainly you did not have the kind by which men advance themselves in today's world. I mean skill at cultivating the powerful, flattery, deceit, promises, lies, pretense, and the ability to put up with all sort[s] of disagreeable and unseemly demands. Lack-ing these skills and others like them and supposing that your natural disposition would resist them, you turned to other pursuits. And in this you acted wisely and prudently. As Cicero says, "To contend with the gods, as the Giants did, is to go against nature."

FRANCESCO I will say farewell to great honors, if I have to get them in this way.

ST. AUGUSTINE Those are fine words, but you still have not convinced me of your innocence. You do not show your indifference to honors simply because you are afraid of the trouble of pursuing them. You are like a man who refuses to set out because he is afraid of the bother involved in travel and says that he did not want to see Rome anyway. In any case, you have not held back in your pursuit of honor, as you pretend to yourself and as you try to persuade me. You are not fooling any-one. I see quite clearly all your thoughts and actions. Your boasting of your flight from the cities and of your great desire for solitude is not an excuse but only an indication of a shifting of culpability. There are many ways to produce one result. Although you have not taken the way most commonly travelled, believe me, you are headed towards the same ambition you pretend to hate by a path off to the side. The leisure, the solitude, the elaborate indifference to human affairs, and those researches of yours lead you towards ambition, and their aim is self-glorification.

FRANCESCO You have pushed me into a corner from which I could extricate my-self; but because time is short and must be apportioned to many topics, let us pro-ceed, if there is no objection.

ST. AUGUSTINE Follow me, then, as I advance. I make no mention of gluttony. You have never shown any proclivity for it, although on occasion you cater to the tastes of friends and allow rather a grand cuisine at your table. But I am not alarmed by that, for each time the influence of the country reasserts itself over you, all the attraction for such pleasures disappears. When temptation is removed, I have noticed with pleasure that your life surpasses that of your friends and others in sobriety and temperance.

I shall pass over anger as well. Although you get angry more often than you should, you control your emotions, thanks to your naturally good temperament and recollection of Horace's advice, "Anger is a brief madness; control your pas-sion. If you do not control it, / It will control you. Curb and master it."

FRANCESCO I confess that I have been helped by this piece of poetry and by words to this effect in the philosophers, but above all by recalling how short life is. It is sheer folly to use up the few days we spend with our fellow men in hating and trying to do them harm. Soon enough that last day will come which extinguishes these flames in the hearts of man, puts an end to our hatred. And if we wish for nothing worse than death for our enemy, our wicked prayer will be answered. Why, then, should anyone want to hasten one's own or another's death? Why lose the best part of a very short time? When the days allotted for honest joys of the present and for planning for the future are hardly long enough, though they were used with the utmost economy, what good is there to take them away from their proper and necessary uses and turn them into times of sadness and death for our-selves and others? So far, when I have been strongly tempted by anger, this thought has prevented me from falling completely under its power and has helped me to recover, if I did fall. However, I have not been able to entirely escape the strong winds of anger.

ST. AUGUSTINE But since I do not fear that the wind of this anger will ship-wreck you or others, I quite agree that you content yourself with the moderate view of the Peripatetics in this matter, even if you do not realize the promises of the Stoics, who vow they will pull out the diseases of the soul by the root. Leaving aside for the present these failings, I hasten to deal with others more dangerous than these and against which you must be much more on guard.

FRANCESCO Good God, is there something more dangerous still to come?

ST. AUGUSTINE How greatly are you influenced by lust?

FRANCESCO So much so, sometimes, that I am very sorry I was not born without feelings. I would rather be some senseless rock than to be troubled by so many urges of my body.

ST. AUGUSTINE That, then, is what especially turns you away from all thought of divine things. For what else does the sublime doctrine of Plato argue but that the soul must protect itself from the passions of the flesh and eradicate its fantasies so it may rise pure and unfettered to the contemplation of the mysteries of the divine, combining meditation on one's own mortality with that contemplation? You know what I am talking about; these doctrines are familiar to you from Plato's writings, the study of which I am told you undertook most eagerly not so long ago.

FRANCESCO I studied them, I confess, with great hopefulness and desire; but the novelty of a foreign language and the sudden departure of my teacher cut short my attempt. But the doctrine which you mention is familiar both from your writings and those of other Platonists.

ST. AUGUSTINE It does not matter under whose guidance you learned the truth, although the authority of a great master will often carry great weight.

FRANCESCO The authority of Plato especially influences me. Cicero's remark in the *Tusculan Disputations* concerning him has made a profound impression on me. "Even though Plato," he said, "were to offer no proof (notice what deference I have for him) the weight of his authority would break down my reservations." Often, as I reflect on his god-like genius, it seems to me unfair that Plato was required to give proofs, when the Pythagoreans let their leader off without proof. But, not to stray too far from the point, authority, reason, and experience have long so much commended this view of Plato's to me that I think that no man has ever said anything truer or more holy. Sometimes, with God's help, I have raised myself up, so that I recognized with infinite and unbelievable joy what was helping me then, and what had been the cause of my earlier fall. Now that I have fallen again by my own weight into my old unhappiness, I bitterly experience the failing that has been my undoing once again. I have told this so you do not think it strange that I say openly that I have personal knowledge of Plato's doctrine.

ST. AUGUSTINE I am not surprised. I was witness to your struggles and saw you fall and then rise up again. Now that you have fallen, I pity you and have decided to give you help.

FRANCESCO Thank you for your compassion; but what human help is left to me?

ST. AUGUSTINE None, but there is unlimited help from God. A man cannot be chaste, unless God grants it. First of all, you must ask this gift of him humbly and often with tears. He is not accustomed to deny a man who asks for things in the proper way.

FRANCESCO I have done that so often that I almost fear that I am being tiresome.

ST. AUGUSTINE But you have not prayed with enough humility or seriousness. You have always left room for your passions to make their entry; you always pray for a slow answer to your prayers. I speak from experience; the same thing happened to me. I would say: Give me chastity but not now; put it off a while; the time will soon come. My life is still vigorous; let it go its own way and obey its own laws. Later it would be shameful to return to the practices of youth. I will have to give them up when in the course of time I have become less inclined to them anyway and when satiety has taken away the fears of relapse. When you say this, do you not see that you wish for one thing, but pray for another?

FRANCESCO Why?

ST. AUGUSTINE Because a man whose prayer is for tomorrow forgets about it for today.

FRANCESCO I have often asked with tears for it today, hoping that after breaking out of the bonds of my passion and casting off my unhappiness, I would escape; and after enduring the storms of so many useless worries, I would, so to speak, swim into some safe port. But you know how often I have nonetheless suffered shipwreck among the same reefs and how often I will suffer it again, if I am bereft of help.

ST. AUGUSTINE Believe me, something was always missing from your prayer; otherwise that Supreme Giver would have granted your prayer or would have denied it to you only to encourage the perfection of virtue and to show you how weak you are, as He did in the case of The Apostle Paul.

FRANCESCO I do believe that, but I shall go on praying tirelessly, unashamedly, and undespairingly. Perhaps the Almighty, taking pity on my struggles, will hear my daily prayers and justify them Himself, just as He would not have denied His favor if they had been pure.

ST. AUGUSTINE Yes, that is good, but keep trying. Like someone knocked to the ground, raise yourself on an elbow and keep watching out for dangers that assail you so that you are not crushed by the sudden onslaught of some force as you lie there, and all the while beseech help from someone able to give it. Perhaps He will help you just when you thought that He was nowhere near. Always keep in mind the view of Plato we just mentioned, that nothing prevents one from knowing the divine so much as one's carnal appetites and inflamed desires. Think over this doctrine well. It is the most important part of my advice.

FURTHER READING

James Banker, "The Ars dictaminis and the Rhetorical Textbooks at the Bolognese University in the Fourteenth Century," Mediaevalia et Humanistica, n.s. 5 (1974), 153–168

Hans Baron, From Petrarch to Leonardo Bruni (1968)

_____, Petrarch's Secretum: Its Making and Its Meaning (1985)

Thomas G. Bergin, Petrarch (1970)

Morris Bishop, Petrarch and His World (1963)

Marjorie Boyle, Petrarch's Genius: Pentimento and Prophecy (1991)

Vittore Branca, Boccaccio: The Man and His Work (1976)

Charles T. Davis, Dante's Italy (1987)

John Larner, Culture and Society in Italy, 1290–1420 (1971)

Nicholas Mann, *Petrarch* (1984)

James J. Murphy, *Rhetoric in the Middle Ages* (1974)

W. D. Patt, "The Early *Ars dictaminis* as Response to a Changing Society," *Viator* 9 (1978), 80–93

Nicolai Rubinstein, "The Beginnings of Political Thought in Florence," *Journal of the Courtauld and Warburg Institutes* 5 (1942), 298–327

Quentin Skinner, *Foundations of Modern Political Thought*, vol. 1: *The Renaissance* (1978)

Charles Trinkaus, *The Poet as Philosopher: Petrarch and the Formation of Renaissance Consciousness* (1979)

B. L. Ullman, "Some Aspects of the Origins of Italian Humanism," in his *Studies in the Italian Renaissance*, 2d ed. (1973), 27–40.

M. Viroli, *From Politics to Reason of State* (1993)

Robert Weiss, *The Dawn of Humanism in Italy* (1947)

———, *The Renaissance Discovery of Classical Antiquity* (1969)

J. H. Whitfield, "Petrarch and the Birth of Culture," *Italian Studies* 38 (1983), 39–55

———, *Petrarch and the Renaissance* (1943)

Ernest H. Wilkins, *Life of Petrarch* (1961)

———, *Studies on Petrarch and Boccaccio* (1978)

Ronald G. Witt, "Medieval 'Ars Dictaminis' and the Beginnings of Humanism: A New Consruction of the Problem," *Renaissance Quarterly* 35 (1982), 1–35.

CHAPTER 9

Humanism Serves the State

Petrarch's revolution in the intellectual history of the West became permanent during the next generation (in the late fourteenth century) as republics, ecclesiastics, and secular princes came to appreciate the power that the new rhetoric could bring to political situations. Petrarch's success as a humanist—applying the lessons of ancient history and moral philosophy to the daily needs of Italian society—stirred the ambition of countless bright young men to pursue a career in letters. Among his closest followers were Coluccio Salutati (1331–1406) and Giovanni Conversini da Ravenna (1343–1408), who in the last quarter of the fourteenth century served as chancellor of the Florentine Republic and the Carrara regime in Padua, respectively. Indeed, rulers appreciated men of this stamp. For example, the Duke of Milan, Giangaleazzo Visconti, often remarked that a single letter of Salutati was worth a troop of a thousand horsemen in resolving a conflict. As the pen proved as powerful as the sword, humanists were showered with favors and drawn to the chanceries and councils of city-states, the service of lords and princes, and the courts of powerful prelates, including the pope himself.

In Florence, a number of humanist statesmen developed a special appreciation of Florentine culture and republican institutions that later historians, especially Hans Baron, have come to call "civic humanism." Coluccio Salutati put his considerable skill as a letter writer and orator in the service of the Florentine Republic in its wars with the ruler of Milan, Giangaleazzo Visconti, at the end of the Trecento. Fixing on the singularity of Florence as a defender of liberty and protector of its citizens, Salutati and his successor, Leonardo Bruni (1370–1444), created a new myth of Florence, in which they glorified the active life of Florentine citizens in the service of the state and praised the special beauty of the city, the grandeur of its past, and the justice of its current institutions. In contrast to the humanists of Florence and Rome, often provincials who rose to high office over the obstacles the ruling class set in the path of newcomers, humanists in Venice were almost always members of the city's patriciate. Thus, Venetian humanists typically treated in their works themes of the service of the ruling class to state and society. Humanists also entered the service of such rulers as the duke of Milan and the king of Naples, often creating favorable accounts of a dynasty's history and praising the deeds of a ruling lord. In the course of the fifteenth century, then, Italian humanism came to serve all sorts of states—republican and princely, secular and ecclesiastical.

Essays

Hans Baron has been one of this century's most influential scholars of Renaissance humanism and culture (see Chapter 8). In the course of studying and editing the writings of Leonardo Bruni, Baron evolved the concept of civic humanism to characterize the Florentine revival of the classical ideal of the active political life. In his most important work, *The Crisis of the Early Italian Renaissance: Civic Humanism and Republican Liberty in an Age of Classicism and Tyranny* (2 vols., 1955), Baron developed his famous thesis on how the military threat that Giangaleazzo Visconti posed toward Florence brought about the emergence of the new rhetorical culture that praised the city and its republican heritage. Visconti's opportune death in 1402 ended the threat of Milanese expansion, but Florentine humanists now were thoroughly committed to praising the active life of the committed citizen and viewing Florence as the defender of the liberties of all Italians.

The first selection is an English version of the preface to an Italian edition of the *Crisis*, in which Baron replied to his critics, stressing the novelty of praise of the active life and the accuracy of his interpretation of key works of civic humanism, such as Bruni's *Laudatio Florentinae Urbis*. At the same time, Baron insists that his interpretation gives full treatment of the competing humanist outlook coming from the princely courts.

In the second selection, Albert Rabil, Jr., Distinguished Teaching Professor of Humanities at the College of the State University of New York at Old Westbury, interprets Baron's contributions and the validity of civic humanism within the context of contemporary historiography of the Renaissance.

Margaret King, professor of history at Brooklyn College and long-time executive director of the Renaissance Society of America, next dissects the moral philosophy of a Venetian humanist, Giovanni Caldiera. Writing at the middle of the fifteenth century, Caldiera stressed the family and household as the basic unit of state and society, and the duty of Venetian patricians to rule their city and guide the lower classes. As we elaborate in Chapter 11, the household ruled by a dedicated wife became fundamental to the political thought of the Italian city-states. In this private sphere were raised and trained the future rulers of Venice, imbued with the ideal of service to the state. Thus, all members of society—women, tradesmen, workers—had a defined role in ensuring the success of the Venetian polity.

In Defense of Civic Humanism

Hans Baron

One component of Quattrocento thought described in the *Crisis* was a new appreciation of what in the fifteenth century was called the *vita activa* [active life] and *civilis* [civic]. Nothing quite like it is found in medieval city-states, because in the Middle Ages the *vita contemplativa* [contemplative life] of the monk, pregnant with religious meaning, took precedence over the admittedly indispensable active and civic life. In the society of the Renaissance after 1400, the *vita activa* [active life], with its driving passions, was increasingly respected as a precondition for the full realization of human nature; action and political engagement, therefore, seemed to represent the only truly humane way of life. After I had proposed in various essays that early Quattrocento thought in Florence was characterized by this emphasis on the *vita civilis* [civic life], Eugenio Garin pointed out, and rightly so, that a similar tendency prevailed in later fifteenth- and sixteenth-century philosophy and literature throughout Italy. But as the *Crisis* reminds us, for two or three generations it had been almost exclusively Florentine.

In order to appraise this no longer medieval Florentine train of thought, the *Crisis* viewed it together with the simultaneous rise of a new type of historical thinking. Again, a strong difference from the preceding medieval mode of thought became evident. In earlier generations the concept of ancient Rome, so important to Humanism, had not been free of the theological assumption that, in its dominance over the world, it represented the last of those universal empires through which Divine Providence had given human history an order unintelligible in merely secular and causal terms. It was this intrusion of theology into history and politics which had caused Trecento thinkers, including Dante, Petrarch, and even Salutati, to ignore the lessons of experience and look upon the German emperors as the predestined restorers of peace. Soon after 1400, in contrast, a conception of history came into being by means of which the *Imperium Romanum* [Roman Empire] of Antiquity came to be viewed in a more modern light. The empire, it was now believed, had indeed come to an end when the Roman people lost its natural strength, and it was followed by new states, the Italian heirs to those independent regions and city-states which had flourished on the peninsula before Roman domination. Among the new medieval states were independent republics in which free men once again participated in self-rule and whose cultural and political promise was equal to that of the ancient *Respublica Romana* [Roman Republic] and the city-states of Etruria and Greece.

Both these lines of thought—esteem for the *vita activa* [active life] and the new perspective of history—unmistakably reflect a changed social and political environment after 1400. When I began my research on Florentine Quattrocento Humanism in the 1920s, the transition from the Trecento to the Quattrocento was still commonly explained in terms of a growing knowledge of ancient literature or of a gradual unfolding of Trecento ideas. Scholars had scarcely begun to make serious use of the fact that whereas the Trecento still conceived of a universal Christian empire as the counterpart to the universal Church, after 1400 new views concerning the political articulation or unity of the Italian peninsula emerged. This change was of no concern to the early twentieth-century historians of the Weltanschauung [worldview] of the Renaissance—Dilthey, Cassirer, Croce, and Gentile—who in their respective appraisals of the period all found sufficient explanation in the Burckhardtian view that the rising ideas of the Quattrocento were a result of the increasing intellectual and ethical "autonomy" of the individual.

The observations I made during the years when the *Crisis* was in preparation did not essentially follow Burckhardt, nor did they confirm the overwhelming impact of tyranny on Renaissance thought and culture assumed by him. It is true of most of the

Florentine Quattrocento ideas presented in the *Crisis* that they brought to greater maturity opinions which, in the hierarchically ordered outlook of the Middle Ages, had been considered valid only on a lower level, where they were not in the focus of observation and interest. The *vita activa* [active life] had its place in the medieval outlook, but since religious contemplation was set on a higher plane, there was no access to the later argument—so central to Quattrocento humanists—that virtue must be constantly tested and practiced and that contemplative withdrawal causes human nature to fragment. By the same token, the beginnings of a causal approach to historical phenomena had existed throughout the Middle Ages, but they had remained beginnings, because in the higher reaches where events became truly meaningful to medieval thinkers, history showed the hand of God and was not principally the work of man and a manifestation of his nature. Clearly, only when conditions emerged in which the actuality of life refuted the belief in a hierarchy of governments culminating in the Roman Empire could there finally develop an awareness that the rules of natural growth and decay applied even to Rome and that Rome could therefore be used as a model for modern states.

Why did these attitudes emerge during the first decades of the Quattrocento? The answers given in the *Crisis* again point to the changing socio-political background. Historical and political forces could at last be imagined as moving on one level when, about 1400, the purely secular hope or fear that large parts of the peninsula would be pacified through conquest by one of the powerful Italian monarchies—Milan or Naples—began to supplant the half-mystical dream of pacification by the ruler of the divinely ordained empire. Moreover, the importance of different forms of states could now be better recognized: monarchy might offer a more rational kind of government for a large state, but the city-state republic generated more political and cultural vitality, because its citizens could take an active, responsible part in communal life.

A second answer given in the *Crisis* also has to do with the influence of background changes: the same decades around 1400 saw the building of a Florentine region-state stretching from the Tuscan coast to the Apennines. This unexpected side effect of resistance to the territorial expansion of Milan made Florence and Florentine citizenship so important that historical comparisons of Florence with Athens and Rome finally became meaningful. When Florentine historians began to look upon their city as the protagonist of independence among the surviving Italian city-states, they also began to regard the freedom of the *Respublica Romana* [Roman Republic] and the autocracy of the Roman imperial monarchy as political alternatives. At that juncture the long, successful rivalry of the Etruscan city-state republics with early Rome was discovered; the constitutions of ancient and modern city-states alike were analyzed to determine what they contributed to freedom or to power. History became comparative and secular, and the vital foundations were laid for the later thought of Machiavelli and Guicciardini.

The chapters in the *Crisis* on Florentine resistance to Milan and Naples should be compared with Burckhardt's description of the Renaissance state. His view of the period, based as it was on the belief that the tyrant states and princely courts afforded fullest scope to the emancipated individual, ignored the fact that after 1400 city-state republics no less than tyrant states reached the stage where the experiences of generations were finally manifested in stated principles and conscious thought. If it is true that autocratic principalities could claim a more effective administration and the ability to fulfill the mission of bringing unity and peace to the peninsula once attributed to the empire, it is also true that city-state citizens had become aware of a mission of their own: to keep alive the values and traditions of the medieval communes and also, through the medium of civic Humanism, the heritage of the *libertas* [liberty] of ancient city-state republics. In short, the outcome of Burckhardt's insistence on the effects of tyranny was that only half the story of the humanistic outlook and the sociopolitical challenges after 1400 was usually told.

It is one of the unstated premises of the *Crisis* that Burckhardt's view of the Renaissance, though valid as far as it goes, needs to be complemented by approaches which may not be in easy harmony with his stress on tyranny and individualism, and it is this need that largely determined the structure of my book. It gathered together a body of evidence from formerly neglected sources showing that the cultural and political role of the city-state republic was not as fully played out after 1400 as Burckhardt thought. The *Crisis* attempted to give this source material its due place and urged the need for a multidimensional approach to the Quattrocento. Nevertheless, its introduction expressly states that "an estimate of the bearing of these findings on our total view of the Italian Renaissance is not the burden" of the book; it was hoped, rather, that "readers will pose this wider problem to themselves."

Even today, many years later, the time may not have come for a final weighing of the accumulated evidence. Although the strong impact of the city-state ideal of the *vita activa politica* [active political life] on the literature of the fifteenth and sixteenth centuries has become increasingly evident, we perhaps do not yet have enough information to judge the extent to which Humanism was permanently altered by that early Florentine Renaissance ideal. It is quite possible that the face of the period will change still further as our view of Quattrocento life and thought broadens.

It was not my intention in the *Crisis* to pronounce former scholarship wrong, but merely too narrow. In particular, I did not attempt to deny that from its medieval beginnings until the late Renaissance, Humanism was steeped in the rhetorical tradition of Antiquity; nor did I intend to minimize the part played by the birth of humanistic philology in the transition from medieval to modern thought. The decisive question, rather, was whether rhetoric and the new philology were the only essential, or even the foremost, humanistic contributions to the making of the modern mind; whether Humanism could have played its fundamental role in the fifteenth and sixteenth centuries if it had not also offered a new vision of man's nature and of history, a new estimate of human values. The *Crisis* tried to show that Florentine humanists of the Quattrocento not only were continuers of the rhetorical tradition and pioneering contributors to the new philology but also originated the philosophy of the active political life and a secularized conception of history and culture, the two leitmotifs of the school of thought analyzed in the *Crisis*. As is stressed in its epilogue, it cannot be claimed that every humanist of the fifteenth and sixteenth centuries shared this particular outlook; but neither can it be said that rhetoric and philology were the only important aspects of Humanism in that time. Although the later structure of Humanism is rarely mentioned in the *Crisis*, because its focus is entirely on the early Quattrocento, the picture presented there should be evaluated with a view to the total history of Humanism.

As many recent studies have disclosed, emphasis on the *vita activa* and *civilis* [active and civic life] and the secularization of historical conceptions were to reappear whenever Humanism became a trend in the remaining Italian city-state republics—as late as the sixteenth century in Genoa and Lucca and even later in Venice, where we still encounter a pattern of civic Humanism toward the very end of the Renaissance, about 1600, as has been pointed out by William Bouwsma. North of the Alps, where a politically oriented Humanism comparable to the civic Humanism of the Italian city-state republics appeared less frequently and was more limited in scope, other humanistic schools of thought confirm that Renaissance Humanism cannot be characterized in terms of rhetorical motivation and the new philology alone, or even preponderantly. As an example, wherever Humanism coincided with new inventions in the mechanical arts, in which the moderns definitely surpassed the ancients, the humanistic propensity for the active life assumed yet another dimension: a view of man as *homo faber* (the craftsman and inventor), the greatest proponent of which was the early sixteenth-century humanist Luis Vives. There were other, differently structured, humanistic trends in the later Renaissance. For many humanists of the sixteenth century there could be no proper outlook on life without freedom from dogmatism. The disputatious obstinacy of scholars and their claims to authority were feared as threats to true culture, which required a large measure of skepticism and even agnosticism. One need only recall Montaigne to be aware of the immense contribution made by this strain of humanistic thought to the modern world. In Montaigne's work, agnosticism stops short of the Catholic tradition; it has entered into a union—in typically sixteenth-century fashion—with religious fideism. But the humanistic rejection of philosophic dogmatism also lessened the dominance of dogma in religion. There is no need to elaborate the fact that this type of humanistic outlook, which appeared in the work and school of Erasmus, was one of the most significant and widespread developments in modern Western thought, rivaled in its influence perhaps only by civic-political Humanism. In none of these cases was the thinking of the truly great humanists shaped primarily by rhetoric or philology.

I do not doubt that the history of Renaissance Humanism will ultimately have to be presented in terms of a comparative phenomenology of the aforementioned (and possibly other) humanistic outlooks on life and the successive views of man, history, and politics. When I wrote the *Crisis* I hoped that a fuller understanding of the type of humanistic outlook encountered in early Renaissance Florence might prove effective in expanding Renaissance Humanism beyond its "rhetorical" and "philological" dimensions into a more complex phenomenon.

A misinterpretation of the attempt in the *Crisis* to bring the background of early Humanism into sharper focus led some of my critics to charge that the book is overly partial to Florence. To some, the *Crisis* is apparently a descendant of that questionable branch of historiography which carried forward the parochial struggles of the cities and regions of earlier Italian history.

This could hardly be more contrary to the objectives of the *Crisis*, which aimed on the basis of neglected sources to reestablish an historical balance. The fact is that, even before Burckhardt, a one-sided emphasis had been placed on the courts of princes and tyrants. In the historiography of the Enlightenment these courts, as early counterparts of the court of Louis XIV, already seemed to overshadow everything else in the fifteenth and sixteenth centuries. Even Quattrocento Florence—"the Florence of the Medici"—was regarded as a Renaissance principality. In his reconstruction of the history of the Italian city-state republics of the Middle Ages, shortly after 1800, Simonde de Sismondi, the republican-minded historian of Rousseau's school, was convinced that by the end of the Trecento, time had run out for the republics. He believed that republican liberty was dead and that only princes still counted in Italy. With the establishment in the mid-nineteenth century of an Italian monarchy, the expansionist policy of the strongest of these princes, the Visconti of Milan, was often viewed as a harbinger or forerunner of the later achievements of the House of Savoy.

The first lesson taught by the sources on which the *Crisis* is based was that the Florentine war of ideas carried on against the Visconti in the name of liberty and with the ancient city-state republics constantly in mind, was not merely a matter of propaganda. Private and public utterances during the wars with Milan show a rapid growth of Florentine political self-awareness. The new political and historical ideas make their appearance more or less simultaneously in personal *ricordi* [diaries] and letters, in the memoranda of Florentine officeholders and the minutes of city councils, in literary writings and, last but not least, in Florentine chronicles and humanistic histories, which were not composed by paid and supervised writers.

In the *Crisis*, I would claim, equal attention is given to the manifestations of the new spirit in Florentine literature and to the voices heard in the camps of the Visconti and the kings of Naples. There, too, especially among the followers of the Visconti in northern Italy, firm and representative political convictions were coming to the fore after 1400. In the *Crisis*, in fact, respect for the superior efficiency of tyrannical autocracy was traced, for the first time, in the writings of such north Italian humanists of the early Renaissance as Giovanni Conversino, Uberto Decembrio, and Pier Candido Decembrio. Thus in the *Crisis* a hearing is given to both sides, and the conclusion is drawn that the ideas of both republics and principalities have to be taken more seriously than had hitherto been the case. In the final analysis, the political struggles of the early Renaissance were not mere quarrels between local neighbors equal in the pettiness of their aims, as is often taken for granted; rather, the encounters of the time involved basic principles and persuasions. The triumph of the *principatus* [principate] in the so-called age of the principalities was not a foregone conclusion. On the contrary, an historic choice had to be made between two potential systems: a single monarchy for large parts of the peninsula or an equilibrium between regional states, in which independence and republican life could continue. To analyze the impact of this background on Renaissance thought without bias toward either side is one of the tasks of the *Crisis*. . . .

It is true nevertheless that the emphasis in the *Crisis* is on Florence and Florentine achievements. There are two reasons for this. In the first place, since modern historiography had so long stressed the principality, the balance could be righted only by presenting the overshadowed, and even ignored, role of the Florentine republic in full detail. For this purpose, considerable space is allocated in the *Crisis* to a reconstruction of the conduct of Florentine citizens during the ordeal of the wars and to the exploration of Florentine literary documents connected with the struggle. Most of the chapters in my book thus undertake spadework rather than a comprehensive reconstruction of the early Quattrocento.

Secondly, it is not the principal intention of the Crisis to weigh the significance of ideas as political weapons; the book is primarily intended to determine the impact of ideas, in a crucial period of war, on the nascent Weltanschauung of the Quattrocento Renaissance. From this point of view, its major finding is that Florentine writers in Bruni's time prepared the way for Machiavelli and Guicciardini, much more incisively than has been thought, not only through their literary influence on later Florentines but also because they moved away so rapidly from the medieval aspects of the Trecento, forming conceptions of history and politics that were in accord with much of the thought of the next few centuries.

If we compare this new intellectual climate of early Renaissance Florence with what contemporary humanists at north Italian tyrant courts and in the Visconti camp thought about history and politics or about the life of scholars and citizens under the efficient autocratic governments of princely states, we find that there, too, considerable strides away from Trecento thought were made about 1400. The writings of early Quattrocento north Italian authors like Giovanni Conversino in Padua and the elder and younger Decembrios in Milan, present themselves as guides ranging from idealized descriptions of enforced vocational instruction for adolescents in a strictly supervised society to realistic reports on the progress of order, hygiene, and city planning. In this matter, too, the Crisis was the first book to draw attention to some of the crucial texts. But how insignificant were these often utopian modes of thought in tyrant states when compared with the truly modern concepts of life and history that emerged in Florence at the same time! It is, indeed, their disproportionate historical significance that ultimately justifies the dominant position allotted to Florence in the Crisis. The reader must be judge of whether the conclusions reached in the course of my discussion of the opposing trends are convincing. But even if my conclusions should occasionally be not quite fair, it would be owing to my estimation of what were the most creative and relevant elements in the growth of Quattrocento thought, not to any pro-Florentine bias.

The Significance of Civic Humanism

ALBERT RABIL, JR.

Hans Baron has made the question of civic humanism the central preoccupation of his scholarly career. Although his interpretation is similar to [Eugenio] Garin's, it involves a thesis much more sharply defined. And it is Baron's formulation that has been so widely discussed in the interpretation of Renaissance humanism during the past generation.

Baron begins with two important assumptions. First, as he says, "we have learnt to interpret the coming of the early Renaissance also as a fundamental transformation in *Weltanschauung* [worldview]." This view, articulated in a general way by Wilhelm Dilthey, reinforces Burckhardt's contention that there is a fundamental discontinuity between the Middle Ages and the Renaissance. Something must therefore account for it. Second, as Vasari long ago recognized, there were two Renaissances in art, but only the second of them, in early Quattrocento Florence, established the new Renaissance *Weltanschauung*. But if the Renaissance really began in Florence at the beginning of the Quattrocento there must be some connection between this beginning and humanism.

Baron discovered the connection in "civic humanism," which appears in his earliest writings in German and English. In his edition of Bruni's works in 1928 he argued that from Salutati to Ficino humanists in Florence were identified with the wealthy ruling families, shared their interests, and developed a positive evaluation of social activity. Such a development was only possible in a republic; humanists who patronized the courts of despots were contemptuous of the business enterprises of the Florentine burgher and extolled the life of leisure. Thus civic humanism cannot be separated from Florence's republican political tradition, for it could have developed in no other environment.

The actual transition he traces in two articles published in English in 1938. In one, entitled "Franciscan Poverty and Civic Wealth as Factors in the Rise of Humanistic Thought," he demonstrates that in the thought of all Trecento humanists—above all in Petrarch, but also in his Florentine disciples—the attitude toward wealth and the active political life is ambivalent. Petrarch extolled poverty when he lived at Vaucluse but not after he moved to the court of Milan. Petrarch cites Cicero and Seneca in whose writings the Stoic wise man eschews riches in favor of a life of solitude and independence, and he finds these views echoed in writer after writer. Such an attitude was out of step with the feeling of the Florentine citizens, who could not be reconciled to a humanism of this kind. In fact a new view emerged in1415 in Francesco Barbaro's treatise *On Wifely Duties*, "the first time that we meet with expressions of the genuine civic spirit in humanistic literature." In it he de-

"The Significance of Civic Humanism" by Albert Rabil, Jr. from "The Significance of 'Civic Humanism' in the Interpretation of the Italian Renaissance" from *Renaissance Humanism: Foundations, Forms, and Legacy*, Vol. 1, ed. by Albert Rabil, Jr., University of Pennsylvania Press, 1988, pp. 144–151. Reprinted by permission of the publisher.

scribes possessions as useful for many purposes, especially for our descendants. Shortly afterward, Bruni's apology for wealth rediscovered the civic character of Aristotle's *Politics* and the positive evaluation of wealth in Aristotle's *Ethics*. Humanists in Florence and elsewhere began to echo these views, to rediscover Xenophon's *Oeconomicus*—the most kindly disposed of all classical works toward the acquisition of wealth—and to discover more positive attitudes in Seneca and Cicero as well.

In another article, "Cicero and the Roman Civic Spirit in the Middle Ages and the Early Renaissance," Baron examines still another side of the attitude toward Cicero that helps to mark the transition. In the Middle Ages Cicero was seen as the Stoic sage removed from the world (corroborated by the medieval view of Cicero's attitude toward wealth), a perspective affirmed in part by Petrarch, who was repelled by his discovery (in 1345 in the *Letters to Atticus*) of Cicero the political figure. The civic humanists of the early Quattrocento, by contrast, found in Cicero's combination of literary and political activity a view of him congenial to themselves.

Baron thus established his thesis that the transformation we call the Renaissance that occurred in early Quattrocento Florence applied not only to the history of art but also to the humanist movement. But the question remains: What caused the transformation? Why was there suddenly a new appreciation for the positive values of wealth and of Cicero the philosopher-statesman? Whence arose civic humanism? In his major work on the subject, published in 1955, Baron ascribed the cause to [be] Florence's conflict with Milan, culminating in a war fought between 1400 and 1402 in which Florence avoided Milanese conquest.

The possibility of conquest by Milan posed a threat to Florentine autonomy almost continually after 1350. Milan was ruled by Ghibellines, men who had been appointed by the emperors and who made themselves tyrants when Hohenstaufen rule came to an end (1254 in Germany, 1266 in Sicily). The leading force against the Ghibellines was the papacy, now in exile at Avignon, allied with Guelf (bourgeois) cities like Florence. More often than not (though not consistently) Florence saw itself as a defender of the church and supporter of its policies. In 1377, however, the papacy, preparing to return to Rome from its extended exile at Avignon, sent legates ahead to assert strong leadership (in effect tyrannies) in the areas surrounding Rome. Florence soon found itself at the head of a central-Italian league fighting in the "War of the Eight Saints" against the dangers of attack from the papal state. The outcome of this war was to strengthen the tendency of the Florentines to regard themselves as the leaders of the free city-states.

During the 1380s Milan continued to expand southward and to incorporate smaller city-states into its orbit of power. Neither Rome nor Venice would aid Florence but were content to let Florence bear the burden of opposition to Milan. Florence did so—between 1390 and 1392 and again between 1397 and 1398. The latter struggle ended in a treaty that did not, however, guarantee the safety of the city-states allied with Florence, and within two years Milan had annexed them all. In 1400, therefore, Florence was isolated; only Bologna stood as a buffer between Milan and Florence. With a sense of desperation, Florence hired a mercenary army of German knights, led by Rupert of the Palatinate, the newly elected pretender to the imperial throne. The Visconti, however, defeated Rupert in October 1401, before he could make his way very far into Italy. Milan was now at the height of its power, and Florence seemed doomed. In the spring of 1402 (when the armies could once again campaign), the Milanese entered Bologna. By June nothing lay between the Milanese army and Florence. The Florentines expected to see the enemy before the gates any day. Yet the signal for attack was not given, probably because the Visconti had defeated its other enemies by a show of might and by propaganda, waiting for treachery and defection to undermine a city. But the moment came and went. For the plague erupted in northern Italy, carrying off the Milanese tyrant, Giangaleazzo Visconti, on 3 September. Milanese expansion was altogether halted, at least for a time, by his death.

The Florentines "credited their almost miraculous salvation more to the brave stand which they alone had made than to the sudden removal of the tyrant from the scene." The fact that Florence had met the crisis alone was decisive for the climate of that city. "When the crisis had passed, the real issue of the Florentine–Milanese contest stood revealed: out of the struggle had come the decision that the road was to remain open to the civic freedom and the system of independent states which became a part of the culture of the Italian Renaissance."

The effects of this event on the humanists were immediate and decisive. In a *History of Florence, 1380–1406*, written in 1407, Gregorio Dati asserted that "all the freedom of Italy lay in the hands of the Florentines alone, that every other power had deserted them." To the humanists, Florence had become the city of freedom. This view is nowhere more evident than in Leonardo Bruni's *Panegyric to the City of Florence* (which Baron dates 1403–4 rather than, as previously believed, 1400) and his second *Dialogue to Peter Paul Vergerius* (which Baron dates 1405 rather than 1401). In the latter he raised for the first time questions about Dante's interpretation of Caesar and his assassins Brutus and Cassius. Dante had placed Caesar in limbo and his assassins in the depths of hell. Now Dante had long been the pride of Florence, but his monarchical views were contrary to the republican sentiments of those who had just lived through a crisis threatening their liberty. Bruni sought a solution that would both exalt republican sentiments and save Dante. He argued that Dante had used historical figures only to serve the ends of his poetical imagination without actually taking sides with Caesar's tyranny against the last defenders of civic freedom in Rome. This new republican view of Dante had been unknown during the Trecento. So congenial was it to the feeling of the humanists that it was repeated by humanists throughout the century.

Bruni also argued in dialogue 2 that the republic had given rise to men of great talent in many fields but that "after the republic had been subjected to the power of one man, those brilliant minds vanished as Cornelius Tacitus says." This judgment was new, both because no one had consistently maintained it in the past and because it rested on a new historian, Tacitus, who had only recently been rediscovered through the manuscript at Monte Cassino brought to Florence by Boccaccio. In Tacitus himself the judgment quoted by Bruni had been a secondary one, for he had accepted the imperial monarchy as a historical necessity and, indeed, became a guide for monarchical publicists in the sixteenth and seventeenth centuries. Bruni selected a facet of Tacitus congenial to his new point of view.

In his *Panegyric* Bruni maintained further, following the lead of Salutati, that

Florence had been founded during the days of the Roman Republic, before the corruption of the empire had set in. It was the Roman army under Sulla in the first century B.C. that founded Florence. By the time Bruni came to write his history of Florence some years later, he added to his arsenal of reasons for Florence's establishment during the Roman Republic the discovery of the part the Etruscan city-states played in pre-Roman times. Thus Florence had originally been a city with free blood running in its veins. To the argument that Vergil, Horace, and other great writers lived during the reign of Augustus, Bruni replied that they had been raised under the Republic. (Poggio was to make the same reply to Guarino during the next generation in the same dispute.) Finally, the freedom of these city-states was stifled by the Roman Empire and reemerged after its fall. Thus the resurgence of Florence in contemporary times has its roots in the earlier energy of the city in republican Rome. Machiavelli developed this conception of Bruni's that a wealth of human energies had been stifled by the Roman Empire but came to the fore again with the rise of free city-republics. Not until the triumph of monarchic absolutism in the latter part of the sixteenth century was this republican interpretation of Roman history in Florence challenged.

Baron argues further that this change in political preference from monarchy to republic involved at the same time a deeper underlying change in intellectual vision (part 4), in other words, that the humanism that emerged in Florence could only have emerged under the conditions of a free city-state. Not only so, but this new civic humanism became determinative for the whole of humanism during the Quattrocento (part 5): the essence of Italian humanism in general during the Quattrocento was Florentine civic humanism.

In order to appreciate these larger claims, the nature of the change in consciousness must first be explored. Baron sees it preeminently in Bruni's *Dialogues*. In dialogue 1 Bruni argues, through Niccolò Niccoli, that classical learning is dead in his own time (Salutati excepted) and that this fact is reflected in the myriad deficiencies of the "three crowns of Florence," Dante, Petrarch, and Boccaccio. Dialogue 2 rehabilitates the three Florentine writers and asserts that far from being dead, learning is everywhere being revived. The reversal of historical judgment is profound. Instead of seeing the classical past as something to which the present can never measure up, it is regarded as something to be equaled and surpassed. In other words, the classical ideal is no longer to be viewed only as an intellectual tradition but is fused with civic aspirations. Civic humanism is the result of this fusion.

Baron finds evidence of this new civic humanism in the transformation of humanist attitudes toward the vernacular. In 1435 a debate took place between Bruni, Biondo, and other humanists working in the Roman curia, which was exiled at the time in Florence. Biondo argued that the Italian vernacular had been created by a fusion of Latin with the languages of the Germanic invaders of the Roman Empire. Bruni opposed Biondo's view, contending that there had always existed both a popular and a learned way of speaking and that popular speech was the Italian vernacular, even in the days of Terence and Cicero. Biondo's theory is the more historically correct and was judged so even by his contemporaries. But Bruni may not have been affirming a rigid classicism that finds no value in the vernacular, as previous interpreters have largely maintained. Indeed, in Biondo's account of the debate itself, it is evident that he regarded the vernacular as inferior. Bruni instead may have been attributing a higher value to the vernacular, and so giving a higher status to popular culture. This interpretation is suggested more strongly by his *Life of Dante* written during the following year (1436) in which he asserted that *every* language has its own perfection, even its own way of speaking scientifically, thus explicitly placing the vernacular on a level with Latin and Greek. This judgment coincides with the earliest use of the vernacular as a literary language by humanists in the 1430s, notably by Palmieri and Alberti. After Bruni, one finds in Alberti, Lorenzo de' Medici, and Cristoforo Landino affirmations of the equality of the vernacular with the classical languages. This alliance indicates a new type of classicism, one "willing to employ the ancient model as a guide in building a new literature with a new language in a new nation."

The fusion between the civic spirit and Christianity is evident in a different way. In the Trecento there had been a tendency to fuse pagan and Christian literature. The tendency is evident in Petrarch and Boccaccio; Petrarch had argued that the pagan poets were really monotheists and Boccaccio that they were the first theologians. Salutati did not at first accept this position, apologizing in a letter of 1378 for reading pagan poets in spite of their errors. But in the late 1390s he developed the earlier position of his predecessors, maintaining that the pagan poets were genuine seekers after piety. Thereafter he used this idea as a key to interpreting classical mythology. He did not, for all that, identify pagan gods with Christian saints. But a number of humanists were led to make this identification. Francesco da Fiano, for example, a Roman humanist writing at the turn of the century, argued in his enthusiasm for antiquity, that even theologically there was little difference between paganism and Christianity. Salutati was drawn back from this tendency by the emergence of civic humanism. In other words, civic humanism arrested the movement of humanism toward paganism and brought it closer to Christianity. No longer glorifying classical culture as an ideal, humanists were free to use their classicism in the interest of elevating their own culture without confusing the two.

As one would expect, civic humanists assumed different attitudes toward their own world. Both Petrarch and Boccaccio extolled the ideal of the aloofness of the sage and expressed contempt for marriage and civic responsibility. In his *Life of Dante* Boccaccio viewed Dante's family life and his worries about administration of the city-state as the causes of his unhappiness. This attitude persisted among a number of Quattrocento humanists. The most outstanding example among many who could be cited is Niccolò Niccoli, Bruni's spokesman in his *Dialogues*. He sought neither marriage nor public office, but lived solely for his studies, as his eulogists said after his death. Baron characterizes him as "the type of citizen turned socially irresponsible man of letters," and cites in this connection Niccoli's opposition to Florentine efforts to resist tyranny. A purely scholarly attitude that seeks to avoid identification with civic life—exemplified chiefly in marriage and service to the state—was a strong tendency among *literati* [men of letters] which the emergence of civic humanism in Florence short-circuited.

These new attitudes, Baron believes, were not confined to Florence. When, in the 1420s, Milanese expansion once again brought Florence into conflict with the Visconti, Florence was badly defeated on the battlefield and was saved from being overrun only by the intervention of Venice. Venetian humanists, deeply influenced by Florentine civic humanism after 1402, spoke of themselves as protectors of Italy's liberty. Their hope for permanent cooperation between the "free peoples" of Italy became an inspiring political ideal among Venetians as well as among Florentines. Other, smaller city-states were subsequently added to this alliance. Genoa broke away from Milan in 1435–36 and joined Florence and Venice. Lucca followed suit in 1438. All four were then joined in an alliance of the "free peoples" of Italy. It was in this atmosphere that the Florentine Poggio Bracciolini (in 1435) and the Venetian Pietro del Monte (in 1440) defended the "Respublica Romana" against Caesar.

The high point of this republican sentiment was reached in the late 1440s. In 1447 the last Visconti died and the Milanese proclaimed a "Respublica Ambrosiana." Because of its lack of republican tradition, Milan was unable to establish a firm republican regime. Instead, in the ensuing chaos, Venice was persuaded to take over some of the smaller city-states formerly under Milan. This event led Milan to turn once again to dictatorship, this time to the Sforzas. The ensuing Treaty of Lodi pitted Florence in an alliance with Milan against Venice and Naples. The absence of a republican tradition in Milan halted the progress of republicanism and hence also of civic humanism. Neoplatonism replaced humanism as the dominant thought current in Florence. But by then the civic spirit had left its place of birth and had spread throughout Italy. Baron summarizes this period as follows:

> Humanism, as molded by the Florentine crisis, produced a pattern of conduct and thought which was not to remain limited to Florentine humanists. From that time on there would exist a kind of Humanism which endeavored to educate a man as a member of his society and state; a Humanism which refused to follow the medieval precedent of looking upon the Rome of the emperors as the divinely guided preparation for a Christian "Holy Empire" and the center of all interest in the ancient world; a Humanism which sought to learn from antiquity by looking upon it not melancholically as a golden age never again to be realized, but as an exemplary parallel to the present, encouraging the moderns to seek to rival antiquity in their vernacular languages and literatures and in many other fields. Whereas such an approach to the past and to the present had nowhere been found before 1400, it became inseparable from the growth of Humanism during the Renaissance.

These qualities of civic humanism became the chief contributions of humanism to the subsequent development of the West. Baron continues, "Renaissance Humanism would by no means occupy the place in the growth of the modern world that is rightly attributed to it had those traits ever disappeared again after they had emerged from the early-Quattrocento crisis." For "although this type of socially engaged, historically-minded, and increasingly vernacular Humanism far from exhausts the rich variety of the humanistic movements of the Renaissance, in many respects it was the salt in the humanistic contribution to the rise of the modern world."

To state this point in the strongest possible way, Baron wants to maintain that without civic humanism, which grew on Florentine soil—and could only have grown in a republican atmosphere—the western world would not now have as part of its heritage political pluralism in both thought and form, an orientation toward the future rather than toward the past, or vernacular literatures. It is in these senses, rather than in "the discovery of the world and of man," as Burckhardt would have it, that the Italian Renaissance represents the birth of the modern world.

There have been a number of critical responses to the idea of civic humanism in the form in which Baron states it. One kind of critique raises questions about the adequacy of his methodology. Others, focusing on his conclusions, arrive at various judgments. One critic denies the existence of civic humanism altogether. Others believe that Baron has effectively demonstrated the existence of a civic humanism but that many of the larger conclusions he wishes to draw from his demonstration are not warranted. Still others, accepting the establishment of a Florentine civic humanism, raise the question—as Florentine historians—whether alternative explanations do not clarify or augment the theory in important respects.

The Moral Philosophy of a Venetian Humanist, Giovanni Caldiera

MARGARET L. KING

Like some of his more famous humanist contemporaries, . . . [Giovanni] Caldiera praises virtues which are essentially civic; but unlike them, he simultaneously maintains a traditional system of moral norms. This "double standard" in Caldiera's ethical outlook may be deliberate. His rather archaic system of personal ethics is so designed, it seems, at least in part because it serves a specific purpose: to mute the problems of personal existence that might interfere with the functioning of an ideal community. Caldiera does not simply defend a civic ideal, but enforces it by defeating potentially competitive ideals of individual freedom and self-determination. Were such personal issues to become strident, the harmony of the whole, the cohesion of the community, would be disturbed. Venice is better served, he must feel, by the thinner and stereotypic psychology of late medieval Christianity than by the unruly new one already being articulated by some other humanist thinkers. This same model of human psychology reappears in Caldiera's analysis of the family, where it is the appropriate foundation for a domestic system characterized by authority and control.

Caldiera's *De iconomia*, though certainly influenced by Aristotle's *Politics* and the pseudo-Aristotelian *Oeconomica*, employs a narrow meaning of the term "economy." Where Aristotle had widened the scope of the science of economics, Caldiera adheres to its original strict sense of domestic administration, excluding most matters of finance and trade, and focusing upon the definition of the members of the family and their respective duties and functions. The elements of the family are the father (*paterfamilias* or *iconomus*), the wife, children, servants, and domesticated animals.

"The Moral Philosophy of a Venetian Humanist, Giovanni Caldiera" by Margaret L. King from "Personal, Domestic and Republican Virtues in the Moral Philosophy of Giovanni Caldiera," *Renaissance Quarterly* 28 (1975), pp. 549–562. Reprinted by permission of the publisher.

The family is a social system, in miniature, each member of which plays an appropriate and indispensable role, as do the separate members of a healthy body: "Hence if any of these fail in health the whole body sickens, yet more or less depending whether any more principal part is affected. The economy, similarly, or any domestic system, should have its principal and less principal parts. And indeed all should be sound, for if any one part is weak, they all perish, and the entire household is destroyed." Of this perfect domestic coordination, the *paterfamilias* is likened to the head. His vigor rests in his intellect, or in prudence. He is required to be just and temperate, diligent in the acquisition of wealth, kind to his wife, dutiful and mild to his children, and merciful to his servants, whom he should keep amply supplied with food and clothing, and to his chattels: "Likewise horses, cows, donkeys, birds, and other animals and inanimate things inhabiting the house demand their just right and portion." Women, the second in dignity of the family members, must be utterly obedient to their husbands, sober, constant, and prudent. They follow their husbands' model with regard to the rule of the household, and nourish their children and instruct them in good morals. Children are to be reverent and obedient to their parents, from whom they obtain being, nourishment, reputation, and the privilege of citizenship. Servants, finally, must be always busy and prompt, and above all, loyal.

Detailing in this way the various obligations of the family members, Caldiera views the family as a perfectly equilibrated system comprised of clearly articulated and seemingly inalterable personal relationships. A more dispiriting contrast to his contemporary Leon Battista Alberti's portrayal of family life, shifting and energetic, constantly in peril of bankruptcy or dissolution but constantly in search of new experiences, could scarcely by found. The scheme of family relationships described by Caldiera is static and mechanistic, almost untouched by the observation of actual domestic existence, and equally sterile of the understanding of individual psychological phenomena that derive from reflection of the kind that we have come to expect from Quattrocento figures who deal with themes of human content. Caldiera writes as a moralist, depicting an ideal functional system by imposing moral categories upon social reality, and not as an observer or as a critic.

Caldiera's schematization of family structure, however, is not without an element of real social content. The pattern of family organization that emerges from his writings is patently aristocratic. It is a family so affluent that its breadwinner's just pursuit of wealth is not only encouraged, but moderated; in which the abundance of spiced foods and wines must be shunned for the sake of health; in which the *paterfamilias* must consider it among his duties to give his wife valuable jewels, which are not only beautiful in themselves but also bring honor upon the household. The family's wealth and status is further indicated by the presence of servants and domestic animals, and by the care taken for the education of the children in the seven liberal and mechanical arts. Finally, the impressive construction of the house, the family's physical shell, as described by Caldiera, reveals that he is concerned only with families of substance. Their houses, located in the best neighborhoods and built with "zealous genius and the greatest and most excellent artistry," are equipped with broad portals and luminous inner courtyards. But extravagant display should be avoided, the author cautions, reminding a proud nobility of its civic responsibility:

Homes should not be built by citizens according to the abundance of their wealth, but for the sake of the dignity of the city, and according to the merits of the persons. For magnificence is fitting in the erection of churches, cities, and fortresses. What is truly appropriate to the houses of citizens is utility and not splendor. Those which are constructed with worked marbles and artful stones, likewise with gold, and painted with colors, seem to be utterly alien to both civility and the dignity of the citizens. And the householder should rather make himself worthy of admiration because of the virtue by which he excels than because of the sumptuous home by which he has desired to be conspicuous. Not the house but virtue makes men immortal and equal to the gods.

Clearly, the pattern of family organization set forth by Caldiera is an aristocratic one, pertaining to the nobility and not to the *popolo* [common people] of Venice. Also aristocratic are the political attitudes that are implied by his descriptions of certain aspects of family existence, especially the role of the father, class stratification within the household, and the subjugation of women.

The father, Caldiera states, is to have absolute rule in the household. Just as the architect is the one supremely necessary ruler or principle of the construction of the material house, the *paterfamilias* is the one necessary ruler or principle of the household, alone having the experience of virtuous life, the knowledge of good morals, and the prudence necessary to provide for the future. Every "economy," therefore, requires a single ruler. In this requirement, the domestic household resembles the rest of nature, for in nature, too, all things are subjected to one first principle of their kind: efficient or mobile things are traced to a first cause; forms are resolved into one principal form; all matter is subordinate to one material essence. Thus there is one God, who is the first agent, the first form, the first end, to whom all things are subordinated either efficiently or materially. In the city, there is one prince by whom all things are ruled. In the home, necessarily, there is one *paterfamilias*, who is supreme among the members of the family.

Thus for Caldiera, the authority of a single ruler within any system, domestic, political, or natural, exists by universal right. From the assertion of the absolute primacy of the father in the family to that of the doge in the city of Venice is a short distance, easily traversed.

Along with the necessity of absolute rule in any group, small or large, Caldiera accepts the inevitability and permanence of social class distinction. His hierarchical vision of family structure is compatible with assumptions of class stratification. Just as there are understood to be various concentrations of virtue and power in the different categories of family members, there are assumed to be diverse concentrations of moral qualities and mental capacity in different social categories. Caldiera's pursuit of the hierarchical model is relentless. Coolly he follows the chain of being downward, from father, wife, and child, through the servant class and into the category of nonhuman and even inanimate existence: "Servants are not merely instruments in homes, but animate instruments, whence by themselves and when they obey their superiors they are capable of supplying all the needs of the household. . . . Besides servants there are also other animate instruments serving the home, such as the ox, the ass, and the horse. Many instruments also besides these necessarily and instrumentally serve the household, which are directed by these same human domestic servants."

While servants are seen as a necessarily inferior class, useful to the functioning of the household if perfectly obedient, but in nature only slightly more elevated than chattel or household implements, children, their immediate superiors in the family hierarchy, are understood as having the capacity of assuming a higher rank and dignity. Parents, Caldiera urges, should occasionally allow worthy children to direct the household, including, of course, the servants, so that by practicing this form of leadership, like princes whose sons practice kingship so as to be fit for succession, they may become habituated to ruling and make themselves worthy of their elders.

Just as Caldiera unquestioningly accepts the inferior social condition of servants as inherent in the nature of things, and the justice of the dynastic succession of children to their fathers in the exercise of authority, he will later be seen to accept implicitly the class divisions within Venetian society, and the innate right of an oligarchy to perpetuate itself.

Women, like servants, constitute a class by nature inferior to that of the male ruler of the family. Whereas the husband's role is moral and intellectual, the woman's is biological. Superior in the family hierarchy to children, if only by reason of the latter's immaturity, the woman is subordinate to the *paterfamilias*, and must obey him. Wifely virtue consists in "unanimity" to the will of the husband. Caldiera's statement of woman's subordinate role in the family is followed by an exposition of the different categories of women in society. Matrimony is the first and most important of the conditions of women in society. Chaste and monogamous marriage, unknown to the ancient Hebrews or the Romans, was instituted by Christ. While Christian law (easily confused by our author with the words of Christ) commands chaste marriage, there are compelling natural reasons for marital chastity as well. Since the purpose of sexual intercourse is procreation, and the universe requires a perpetual replenishment of the human species, a mode of marriage must be established which best serves this purpose. Clearly, Caldiera argues, too frequent and promiscuous intercourse, which exhausts the finite quantity of sperm that men possess, would render them sterile. Therefore, both men and women should be chaste; marital chastity is an even more serious requirement of women, however, upon whom the responsibility for pure dynastic succession rests. Adultery is so to be feared that in the past many laws were instituted to prevent women from falling into adultery; thus wine was once forbidden to Roman women, so that by drinking only water, they would never be excited to illicit adventures. Laws have also been made to enforce the obedience of women to their husbands. For women, "since they have weak counsel restrained by no natural law, and incline easily to pleasurable things, quickly, unwisely, and impudently fall into the most evil deeds." When that rare woman is found, therefore, who excels in the virtues of prudence, justice, temperance, and constancy, " . . . in the whole orb of the earth and in all centuries she shall be remembered with perpetual glory."

A woman's duty in marriage is to conform her will perfectly to her husband's. For this reason, a virgin wife, more easily molded to the character of her husband, is desirable. Virgins therefore should be preferred to widows, Caldiera (himself married to a widow) argues. For widows' bodies, which have known other embraces, are polluted, and their souls, which have known the heat of passion, are still more polluted. In advising marital chastity and praising the virtue of virginity, Caldiera's motives appear to be pragmatic: he seems not so deeply concerned for the ideal of purity in itself, or the quality of the marital relationship, as for the tractability of the wife in a family scheme where obedience to the will of the *paterfamilias* is a fundamental theme, or for the legitimacy of offspring in an aristocratic society where purity of descent was a determinant of social status.

After describing the state of matrimony, Caldiera describes alternative conditions of women in society. First are the virgin women or widows who are gathered together in convents obedient to one continent, prudent, and holy ruler, and who desire to know and serve nothing but God. Some of these religious orders are particularly strict, constituted by holy women requiring nothing in life but the service of God: " . . . so that dead to the world, they are believed to live solely for God and for holiness." A second state of womanhood outside of marriage is that of young virgins before they become wives. They are to be trained in domestic tasks and virtues, and are most greatly prized if they excel in prudence. Widows comprise a third group of women not in a state of matrimony. Fourth are women servants, whose duty is obedience to their households. They should be under the supervision of wives rather than husbands, so that no suspicion arises concerning their relationship with the master of the family. The fifth category is that of prostitutes, of whom there was a flourishing population in Venice, and whom Caldiera roundly condemns.

Caldiera's contempt for the illicit sexual practices of women of all social classes would be sufficient indication of his skeptical view of women. A low valuation of women is also implied in his definition of the different conditions of women in society largely by sexual role rather than by social function. While throughout Caldiera's works men are distinguished into social classes by their particular functions in the total Venetian process—political rulership, intellectual assistance in political functions, economic leadership, and manual labor—women are distinguished by their sexual status or behavior—virginal, married, celibate, postmarital, or sexually promiscuous. Caldiera's relegation of women to a social category inferior to and essentially distinct from that occupied by men, together with his assertion of the unquestioned authority of the *paterfamilias*, and his acceptance of class stratification as natural and invariable constitute attitudes consistent with the advocacy of an authoritarian state and society. Indeed, these social attitudes are not merely consistent with such political views, but are seen by the author himself as having an explicitly political reference. Political values thoroughly permeate Caldiera's exposition of the science of domestic administration. Far from unconscious of the similarity of his domestic and political views, he argues eloquently the parallelism of the family and the state. "And just as every economy resembles a polity, so also the home is in the likeness of the city." The family is a cell, containing on a microscopic scale the genetic material determining the existence of the political body, not only because its structures are similar to those of the state, but because it is an instrument of socialization: the virtues to which children are habituated in their youth are displayed by them when adult, and the behavior learned in the family assures appropriate civic behavior in the future. The attitudes that Caldiera expresses, therefore, in his analysis of the family unit, may be expected to be transferred to the state, when he turns his attention to the larger group. An authoritarian state is founded on an authoritarian family.

In writing the De virtutibus, Caldiera had as his object the systematization of a modern moral science, by which men could learn to become virtuous. Similarly, the object of the De iconomia was the creation of an economic, or domestic, science, detailing how the ideal family institution should be formed. The De praestantia venetae politiae [On the Excellence of the Venetian State] is written, it seems, with a different purpose. The author does not create a science of politics, nor does he guide the creation of an ideal political system, but he describes a political system that had already, in his view, achieved the furthest limits of excellence. Caldiera's systematic exposition of the excellence of Venice in the seven mechanical arts, the seven liberal arts, and the seven virtues closes with a survey of Venetian government councils and a eulogy of the institution of the dogado [Dogeship]. Thus interlacing objective descriptions of Venetian life and achievements with a triadic system of timeless philosophical and theological categories, Caldiera mythologizes Venice, lending her real civic existence the tonalities of perfection. This imposition of the ideal upon the real is most conspicuous in Caldiera's discussion of Venice's excellence in the first three of the seven virtues, and in his description of the Venetian government, upon which sections of the De praestantia the following analysis will focus.

Merely personal virtues, performed for the sake of one's own soul, are brushed aside as Caldiera opens Book IV of the De praestantia. Virtue is only profoundly virtuous when it has a republican, or civic, or social, reference. No one can be considered virtuous unless he behaves virtuously toward the republic. Those citizens are more highly regarded who perform things which are useful to the republic than those which are distant from its needs. Men who live a private life are not so just or prudent as those who lead a civic life. Indeed, no one should be considered meritorious, unless his merits have been referred to the republic. Only those men are considered worthy before God, the Stoics said, who had served and profited the republic; " . . . for which they awarded themselves also the title of patrician, and after their deaths moreover would be made divine." A moralist in the De virtutibus, but now a spokesman for the Venetian republic, Caldiera changes guise as the object of the virtues hallowed by tradition which he so frequently enumerates becomes not God but the State.

In his exposition of the republican aspect of the three theological virtues, Caldiera creates a trinity of republican values. Devotion to the republic is related to devotion to God in his discussion of faith, the first of these three virtues. "Just as a man is constrained to preserve inviolate faith toward God, and so to compel his intellect to the belief in all things which are of God, so also he should show a similar faith in the republic, which merits all our talents, and from which we hope to have all merits and all supreme rewards." Faith in the republic gives rise to a number of different fidelities, so that anyone who excels in civic virtue also easily fulfills these other responsibilities. Devotion must be shown to parents and familiars, to citizens, and rulers, and all others who are raised to the principal magistracies of the city. The citizens of Venice, whose "civility" cannot be doubted, bear such great benevolence toward the republic that they spare no labors, no expense, not even their lives for its protection. "Whence, just as we hope to see at a future time God through faith, so equally do we judge that we are not satisfied, unless we have manifestly embraced the supreme felicity of the republic. Thus the immortal life of heaven and fulfilled republican existence are made rhetorically to converge. "Whereby the mutual faith existing among its members renders the republic immortal." Without faith, moreover, all republican activities would languish. Trade would decline, and public and private laws would lose their dignity. Faith in the republic, therefore, is treasured more than life itself, so that if men of any order have abandoned it, they are believed to have become utterly inhuman.

In this richly suggestive discussion of faith, the republic is made a second deity. Civic existence is likened to immortality. The application of the language of religion to political institutions dignifies the city, in an age which was still an age of faith, beyond all proportion. By this association of civic loyalty with religious faith, the republic is made absolute. The civic ideal could not be more firmly advocated: yet the uncompromising pronouncement of that ideal suggests that a stronger imperative is intended by Caldiera than that urged by the "civic humanists."

The parallelism between religious and republican values is continued, although it is less powerfully stated, in the discussion of the other two theological virtues, charity and hope. Charity consists in love of God, and toward the neighbor on account of God. But this charity is to be extended to citizens and to the republic. For the republic seeks the benevolence of the citizens, and they consider themselves to be obligated to the republic. Responsibility is owed toward the republic—indeed it is demanded by a "most worthy kind of coercion"—which results in the perfect conjunction of the citizens in love.

The *scuole*, charitable institutions of a type general in Italy but which developed a unique importance in Venice, are presented as exemplifying the kind of charity existing among the citizens of Venice. In their *scuole*, the men of Venice are held together like loving brothers, under one ruler, so that their lives are made secure. If they fall into poverty, they are assisted by the others and given riches and honors. There are four chief confederations of the citizens. Other *scuole* celebrate a particular saint, and all its members are joined in their devotion to him. Some are unified by the profession of one art, which community comprises the more conventional guild. These are the institutions which bind the men of Venice in civility and charity. They are also related by ties of class into charitable communities. Most loving of all are the nobles, who are considered noble because of their social background, their marriages, their magistracies, their ruling of the republic. As rulers, they coerce those delinquent in love toward the republic with public laws. Men of inferior social orders are also united in love. Even foreigners residing within the city, although they had come from other more dissident cities, are rendered pacific by the morals of the city of Venice, and learn to behave virtuously. The citizens are thus joined together lovingly in subgroups: in the institutions of the *scuole* and guilds; and according to class. The purpose of republican charity is the same as that of republican faith: to cement the obedience of the citizen to the city, and to maintain harmony.

Just as the force of love binds together the Venetian population in peaceful harmony, its absence, according to Caldiera, produces civil rebellion. The laziness, self-indulgence, and rebelliousness of their citizens have ruined many cities, and their many civil wars have led to the exile of now one and now another group of citizens.

Cities which cannot command the love of their citizens are destroyed: ". . . where-fore their fortresses fall, likewise their towers and walls as well, likewise the homes constructed with the greatest artistry are utterly dissolved and perish; likewise the men are incapable of erecting them again. The exiled, thus displaced by civic ruin, flow to Venice "from all parts of the world" and find a safe domicile.

Having earlier associated faith in God with faith in the republic, and Christian charity with the mutual love of the citizens, Caldiera proceeds to associate the Chris-tian hope for beatitude, the third of the theological virtues, with the striving for republican honors. Princes and citizens, many historical examples show, have risked danger and death in order to serve the republic. None would have performed these deeds if they did not have some hope of future rewards, just as none would be virtu-ous if they did not hope for eternal beatitude on account of their merits and the grace of God. There has never been a city which inspires hope as great as does Venice, which rewards the well-meriting citizens in an infinity of ways. "Just as God shows Himself infinitely generous to those with a good hope, so also citizens in every polity are granted excellent rewards for their merits." It quickly appears, however, that while the republic may reward all according to their merits, both merits and rewards are firmly determined by class lines. Caldiera takes this opportunity, under the rubric of republican "hope," to expound his perception of the Venetian class system, in an unknowing but ironically appropriate mimicry of the doctrine of predestination: for just as, in the Christian universe, some are born to salvation and some to damnation, some are born, in Venice, to rule, and some to serve.

DOCUMENTS

The first selection presents the rousing conclusion to Coluccio Salutati's invective against the Milanese chancellor, Antonio Loschi, at the height of the struggle in 1400 between Florence and the duke of Milan, Giangaleazzo Visconti. Replying to Loschi's criticism of Florence, Salutati gave exaggerated praise of Florence and stressed Florence's claims to unique greatness as a defender of liberty. Beginning a tradition of the civic humanists' unstinting praise of Florence, Salutati's peroration is very similar to the con-clusion to the *Laudatio* that Bruni wrote a few years later. The second selection is a chap-ter from Venetian humanist Francesco Barbaro's treatise *On Marriage*, written in 1416 as a wedding gift for the Florentine patrician, Lorenzo de' Medici. The excerpt stresses the "naturalness" of marriage and the need for the male rulers of Italian cities to marry virtu-ous women of their own class who will produce offspring worthy of governing in the future. Barbaro anticipated many of the themes of the family and household as a bedrock of society that Giovanni Caldiera wrote about in detail several decades later. The third selection is an excerpt from Leonardo Bruni's funeral oration praising the Florentine aris-tocrat Palla Strozzi for his service to state, society, and culture.

Coluccio Salutati's Invective Against Antonio Loschi, 1400

So that [neighboring peoples] would not be throttled by tyranny or despoiled of their ancient dignity, our city has snatched or rescued them from the hands of tyrants and constituted and established them subjects of the Florentines. Thus, these peoples have either been born with us in liberty or brought by us to the sweetness of freedom from the bitter constraints of slavery. For who can want to shake off their yoke when they don't have one? How can they desire to come under the tyrannical yoke of your lord [Giangaleazzo Visconti], as you seem to think, when they live with the sweet check of freedom, which is to live obedient to the laws to which all of us are subject? But I am not going to dwell on those many events that have made me so sad. For I have been saddened that so many peoples, cities and towns have been oppressed under the rule of your lord and subjected to his savage tyranny. And indeed I do marvel that God with infinite patience and benignity has borne this for such a long time. But I perceive that you (and I am really persuaded of this) take such great delight in this slavery, that you would not be able to live without a lord, and that you would not know how to function under the sweet permissiveness of freedom. To obey the laws, which rule all according to the same just dictates of equity, is for you a burdensome yoke and horrible slavery. But rather to obey a tyrant, who rules all according to his own arbitrary will, is for you the highest freedom and an inestimable honor. For this reason you believe that the part of the Florentine citizenry which resides in the towns and fields outside the walls of the city, who enjoy freedoms you could never imagine, desires instead of being subjects of our city lives of slavery under your master. Such an attitude now is and, I hope, will always be considered the height of folly and madness for those whose greatest glory is to be called Florentines—because they are our people by birth, by right, and by the gift of fate. For what can it mean to be a Florentine, except to be a Roman citizen, and, as a result, a free man and not a slave? For to be of the Roman stock and nation is to partake of that divine gift that is called freedom. And indeed that is so essential that anyone who lacks freedom cannot reasonably be called a Roman or, especially, a Florentine citizen. And who would ever want to lose that gift, that glorious name, except one who cares nothing about losing freedom and becoming a slave?

Believe me, we are much more disposed to defend and assert our freedom than you are accustomed to support a most base slavery with your cowardice and pusillanimity, which is greater than the whole world has ever seen. I have said "accustomed," not "disposed," so that I do not seem, as you do, to judge rashly the motives hidden in the hearts of others. Perhaps someday and somehow there will return in your breast the ancient values so that there will be aroused at some point in you the Italian spirit, if you are not really descendants of the Vinili, that is, of the Lombards. Perhaps someday you will be able to have the rigor of mind so that you will justly call

---

"Coluccio Salutati's Invective Against Antonio Loschi, 1400," from E. Garin ed. *Prosatori latini del Quattrocento* (Milan, Riccardi, 1952), pp. 31–37. Translated by Benjamin G. Kohl.

yourselves free and Roman citizens, and you will be able, with God's help, . . . to hate tyrants, and abominate as something horrible even the mildest servitude. But, to return to us, since our mind is firm, our powers are supplied, and the ability is present, we are resolved to come to the defense of our frontiers without the slightest hesitation. Now you have submitted that you do not see that we have enough men to oppose the four squadrons of cavalry, which, as you say, have been armed against us. But we will be able to resist because we are conscious that in battle courage will serve as walls, we are conscious that victory is not the result of the size of the army but is in the hands of God, and we know that justice is on our side. Here we recall what you deny—that we are of Roman stock, and we read that our ancestors have often resisted the overwhelming force of enemies, and with a few troops have not only defended their homeland, but have even won an unthinkable victory.

I do not believe that my Antonio Loschi, who has seen Florence, or anyone else who has actually seen this flourishing city, no matter who he might be, if he weren't a total fool, would be able to deny that it was the true flower of Italy and its most choice part. What city, not only in Italy but in the whole world, is more secure in its walls, prouder in its palaces, better decorated with churches, more beautiful in its houses, more splendid in porticoes, more spacious in its squares, has broader streets, greater people, more glorious citizens, more inexhaustible riches, more fertile fields, a more pleasing site, healthier climate, cleaner appearance, greater number of wells, sweeter water, more industrious guilds, and is more admirable in all respects? What city has richer villages, more powerful towns, more numerous municipalities, and more abundant farms? What city without a seaport imports and exports so many goods? Where is merchandise better, the variety of goods more plentiful, the merchants livelier in shrewdness and acumen? Where are men more outstanding? And I shall pass over an infinite number of things so you won't think I'm becoming tedious—where else are they so illustrious in affairs, so valiant in arms, so powerful in just lordship, and so famous? Where do Dante, Petrarch, and Boccaccio come from? Tell me, I beg you, you most vile beast, to what place and people would you be able to assign primacy in Italy if the Florentines and Florence can be called the dregs of Italy? Would to God that if the glory of the Florentine Republic were to remain in its present liberty and power, the rest of Italy could so improve that when compared to the others, the Florentines would see themselves as the dregs of Italy. But since in this corruptible world such grandeur is surely impossible, you should be ashamed, you dirtiest of the very dirty, your dung and vomit of the Lombards, or rather of the Longobards, to call Florence, the true and unique honor of Italy, the dregs of Italy.

| Francesco Barbaro Defines Marriage, 1416

Before I begin to speak concerning the selection and duties of a wife, I want to say a few words first concerning marriage itself. Moreover, I should like, first of all, to define here just what marriage is, so that from the beginning it is understood from the thinking of the most learned men, concerning which all our discussion will take its departure. For thus aware of the main point of the entire topic, we will be able to judge more correctly and more readily concerning other matters.

Therefore, it has been held that the marriage of man and wife is instituted for the perpetual coupling for procreating children or for the lawful avoidance of fornication. On this question there are, of course, many, diverse opinions; and just which ones are true could be debated and discussed for a long time. But most persuasive for me are the opinions of great pagans as well as Christian thinkers which because they are generally in agreement seem worthy of acceptance. Indeed to ensure that their city would be filled with the freeborn, the Romans instituted a fine, that was to be paid in bronze coins, against anyone who lived out his life as a bachelor. The Romans wanted their citizens to follow nature itself, which has instilled in every species of living creature the appetite for intercourse that results in procreation and the belief that its well-being is contained in caring for those who are born. Indeed the inclination for procreation has been observed also in beasts, inasmuch as we see in all birds (not to speak at length about other types of animals) the instinct for nesting. In this matter birds are obviously similar to [human] couples, given also to procreating and feeding their young. In this way, just as food nourishes the body, so the human race and animals are perpetuated. Lycurgus, under whose cherished laws the great state of the Spartans flourished, was disturbed by neglect [of this rule] and branded with ignominity those who reached the age of thirty-seven without having taken a wife. And he prohibited from frequenting the palaestra and gymnasium those who had not yet reached the state of marriage. Thus spurred to avoid this disgrace and to gain of crown of nobility the men of Sparta populated and honored their city with children. For that reason, no one criticized the rude remark made to Dercyllidas, a famous general in the honorable estate of old age, who had never sired any children for Sparta. Thus, one of the young Spartans refused to give up his place to him in the theatre, saying "You, Dercyllidas, have sired no children; you should make room for me."

It is certain that legitimate marriage is appropriate in order to have children born in an honorable estate, important for educating them and best for eventually making them useful citizens, from whom a great city will be more valued in justice to its friends and more terrifying in military valor to its enemies. For that great teacher experience has established well the fact that those who are conceived illegitimately in uncontrolled love-making often turn out to be inferior and infamous and are much more prone to immorality. The light of paternal glory does not permit the well-born to be mediocre; they understand that the image of their parents is more of

From Francesco Barbaro, *De re uxoria*, ed. A. Gnesotto, *Atti e Memorie della R. Accademia di scienze, lettere ed arti di Padova*, n. s. 32 (1915), pp. 28–32. Translated by Benjamin G. Kohl.

a burden than an honor unless they prove themselves by their own virtue worthy of the dignity and greatness of their ancestors. For surely they cannot be unaware that the expectation that they will be in a certain measure the bearers of the virtues of the lineage trains all eyes on them. Thus, we can praise those who are born noble as the walls of the city. When someone wanted to know from Agesilaus why Sparta lacked walls, he replied that the gods are the best walls; thus our city-state was already well furnished with walls. To the same question he also responded that the city need not be preserved and defended with timber and bricks, but with the virtues of its gods, penates, altars, hearths, kinsmen, spouses, and children. For what is more agreeable than to decide together all things, even while spared the concerns of the household? What is better than to have a modest wife, a companion in good times and bad, a spouse and a friend? To whom you can confide your most private thoughts regarding your business? To whom you can entrust your tiny common offspring? Whose sweetness and company will soothe all your cares and woes? Whom do you love so much that you think a part of your own life depends on her well-being? Cato the Censor considered that a wife was worthy of such worship and veneration that he affirmed that whoever laid hands on his wife, whom he should venerate just as though she were the image of the gods, was guilty of a foul and despicable act. We also understand that he was wont to assert that it seemed to him that it was much more difficult to be a good husband than a good senator. With this bond Adusius reconciled the factious Carians; with this necessity Cyrus brought the most warlike Chaldeans to peace with their neighbors. In ancient Rome in a single day, marriage changed the Sabines from enemies to citizens. Marriage also soothed the estranged attitudes of Pompey and Caesar. And it is even more incredible to note that Alexander with marriage joined Asia and Europe which could not be joined even by the most ambitious bridge.

There will be no end if I were to recall to mind how many philosophers, historians, poets, kings, leaders of cities (whom we could parade forth from literary monuments just as from the Trojan horse) have praised this necessity, this affection, this piety. But these opinions are already well known, so I shall be very brief, especially since in obvious matters it is not at all necessary to adduce numerous witnesses. Still Christian principles should not be passed over in silence because they are so filled with such dignity and merit that their authority can be grasped without much discussion. The institution of marriage established as a sacrament, by faith and for children, is thus readily commended, so that it was first ordered and later conceded. That marriage is worthy of approval our Lord Christ confirmed in the Gospel; not only did he forbid a wife to be put away and also he came as a guest to a wedding feast. On these matters it is thus to be understood that there are, in my judgment, some goods which are goods in themselves, and others which are not to be sought for themselves alone. We seek wisdom, friendship, well-being as goods in themselves, but we seek others—skills, learning, knowledge, marriage, sexual intercourse, food, drink, sleep—which are necessary for these higher goods. Therefore, we hold that marriage is good both as a source of offspring and for the companionship of the sexes, which nature has commended to us in a wonderful way. Otherwise the dignity of marriage would no longer be allowed among old people, especially if they had lost their offspring or if they had given up hope of having any, because procreating children is worthy of great praise; thus the honor of propagating children compensates for the baseness of sexual lust. Therefore, husband and wife are joined by law, by consent, and by necessity, so that their union can never be put asunder even by [physical] separation.

Now I realize that there are some who will immediately raise objection to my views and who would criticize the difficult behavior of Xanthippe [Socrates' proverbially nasty wife] and would take delight in the cleverness of a certain Spartan, who was criticized when he had taken an extraordinarily small wife, responded with that old and wise proverb, that if you have to accept an evil, you should choose the smallest. To such matters one could have responded with the anecdote of Socrates. When he took Euthydemus home from the palaestra so that he might provide him with the most sacred right of hospitality and goodwill, Xanthippe went into a frightful rage and upset the dinner table. Since Socrates understood that his guest was deeply troubled at this, he said: "Keep up your good spirits; we have often suffered far worse offenses from barnyard animals, from whom we only get eggs, poultry, and other trifles, which are much less than we get from a wife." To this add the speech of that very respectable man, the Censor Metellus Numidicus, in which, when he was urging the obligation of taking a wife, uttered these memorable words: "If we could get on without wives, Romans, we would all avoid the annoyance, but since nature has ordained that we can neither live very comfortably with them nor at all without them, it seems that they should be chosen for our lasting well-being rather than for the pleasure of the moment."

But we have spoken enough of defining marriage, since it has been treated very fully by many learned men. Thus, what we have considered especially important, we have collected here. Now we proceed to the choice of a wife, which we find has never been treated briefly and systematically by our predecessors. We will discuss various aspects briefly, and at the same time, we will forewarn you never to enter into a marriage no matter how excellent, unless you first take into account the will of your father. For this we have the example of Cyrus, who, when he was invited to Cyazeres to take an outstanding wife furnished with an enormous dowry, demanded that before he could say whether he wanted her he had to lay the matter before his own parents.

Leonardo Bruni's Funeral Oration for Nanni Strozzi, 1427

This is an exceptional funeral oration because it is appropriate neither to weep or lament. For we should be sorry for those who die having accomplished nothing which might bring comfort to those left behind. The life of this man was most enviable and his death was most glorious. We would be ungrateful to mourn a man who

"Oration On Palla Strozzi" by Leonardo Bruni from *The Humanities, Cultural Roots and Continuities*, Vol. 1, by Mary Ann Witt, et al., D.C. Heath and Company, 1980, pp. 224–226. Reprinted by permission of the publisher.

lived and died enjoying such a wealth of advantages. But in explaining the nature of his good fortune we must acknowledge that a good many things, the most important ones, were his by a kind of divinely ordained destiny. His first claim to fame is conferred on him because of his country's merit. For the homeland is the first and chief basis of human happiness and more worthy of our veneration than even our own parents. If we begin therefore by praising the motherland, we will be starting in the right order.

He was born in the most spacious and greatest of cities, wide-ruling and endowed with the mightiest power, without question the foremost of all the Etruscan cities. Indeed, it is second to none of the cities of Italy either in origin, wealth, or size. The two most noble and outstanding races of people in Italy cooperated in its foundation, that is, the Tuscans, the former lords of Italy, and the Romans, who acquired domination of the whole world through their virtue and their military prowess. For our city was a Roman colony integrated with the native Tuscan population. The Tuscans had been the chief people of Italy and supreme both in authority and wealth. Before the foundation of the Roman empire their power was so great that they had the seas on both sides of Italy under their control and governed the whole length of the country from the Alps to the Straits of Sicily for many centuries. Finally, this one people diffused the worship of the immortal gods as well as learning and letters throughout Italy. Other peoples of Italy borrowed their symbols of war and peace. As for the power of the Romans, their excellence, virtue, glory, magnanimity, wisdom and the size of their empire, it is better to say nothing than to have said only a few words.

What city, therefore, can be more excellent, more noble? What descended from more glorious antecedents? Which one of the most powerful cities is able to be compared with our own on these grounds? Our fathers, moreover, are worthy of commendation because inheriting this city in their turn, they so established and governed it that they were in no way inferior to their own fathers in virtue. Sustained by the most sacred laws, the state was ruled by them with such wisdom that they served as an example of good moral behavior for other peoples and had no need to take others as their model. With constant vigilance they either conserved their authority and power or even increased it with the result that in the memory of man this city has always been the foremost in Tuscany.

Worthy of praise as well are those who are its present-day citizens. They have augmented the power received from their predecessors even more by adding Pisa and a number of other great cities to their empire through their virtue and valor in arms. But there is not time here to recall wars, battles, and feats of arms. This is extensive material indeed, and such things demand the labor and attention of not one day but many years. However, at this point with the discussion of external affairs either laid aside or already considered, let us stop to view and investigate in some detail the very body, so to speak, of the city.

Our form of governing the state aims at achieving liberty and equality for each and every citizen. Because it is equal in all respects, it is called a popular government. We tremble before no lord nor are we dominated by the power of a few. All enjoy the same liberty, governed only by law and free from fear of individuals. Everyone has the same hope of attaining honors and of improving his condition provided he is industrious, has talent and a good sober way of life. For our city requires virtue and honesty in its citizens. It considers anyone with these qualities to be noble enough to govern the state. The pride and haughtiness of the powerful are so hated that the city has passed more numerous and stringent laws against this kind of men than against anything else. As a result it has conquered the proud, as if binding them with un-breakable chains of the law, forcing them to bow their necks and to humble them-selves to a moderate status. The result is that it is considered a benefit to transfer from the great families into the ranks of the common people.

This is true liberty and equality in a city: to fear the power of no one nor dread injury from them; to experience equality of law among the citizens and the same opportunity of ruling the state. These advantages cannot be had where one man rules or a few. For those who espouse kingly rule seem to imagine a degree of virtue in a king which they admit no man ever had. Has there ever been a king who did all of those things which are accomplished in a state on behalf of the people? Was there ever one who wanted nothing for himself except the empty glory of the name? Thus it is that praise of monarchy is like a thing false and shadowy, not clear and solid. Both good and evil people, says the historian, are suspected by kings. The virtue of another is always frightening to them. Nor is it much different under the rule of a few.

Thus the popular remains the only legitimate form of governing the state. In a popular government are found true liberty and equity for all citizens; in it the desires for virtue can thrive without suspicion. This capacity for a free people to attain hon-ors and this ability to pursue one's goals serve in a marvelous way to excite men's talents. For with the hope of honors extended, men raise themselves and surge up-ward; excluded they become lifeless. Since in our state men have this hope and the opportunity is offered, no wonder that talents and industry abound so exceedingly. Indeed our city has such a numerous multitude of citizens that, in addition to the countless population living in the homeland, an infinite number are diffused throughout the world. . . . There is no place in the world so remote or out of the way where some Florentine does not live. . . . Wherefore, if the whole multitude of our absent citizens variously diffused throughout the world be joined to those present in the city, an absolutely infinite and innumerable multitude would result, which no city in Italy could match. Our citizens excel so greatly in talents and intelligence that few equal them and none surpass them. They have vivacity and industry and alacrity and agility in acting with a greatness of spirit equal to all challenges.

We thrive not only in governing the republic, in domestic arts, and in engaging in business everywhere, but we are also distinguished for military glory. For our an-cestors splendidly fought many wars on the dusty battlefield, overcoming all neigh-boring people with their military prowess. They shattered a thousand enemy battle wedges and set up almost innumerable trophies. Besides our city has furnished gener-als to the most powerful kings and produced skillful leaders of military science.

What now shall I say about literature and scholarship in which all concede that Florence is the chief and most splendid leader? Nor am I now speaking about those popular arts executed for money—although in these as well our people are foremost. But I am speaking about those more civilized and lofty studies which are considered more excellent and worthy of everlasting immortal glory. For who is able to name a poet in our generation or in the last one who is not Florentine? Who but our citizens recalled this skill at eloquence, already lost, to light, to practical use, and to life? Who but they understood Latin literature, already abject, prostrate and almost dead, and raised it up, restored and reclaimed it from destruction? Camillus is rightly said to be the founder of the city of Rome, not because he established it at the beginning, but because he restored it when it was defeated and occupied by the enemy. For the same reason, should our city not merit being proclaimed the parent of the Latin language, which a short time ago it found lost and cast down, and which it restored to its brilliance and dignity? Furthermore, just as we attribute to Triptolemus, who first produced wheat, whatever has grown since, so whatever literature and culti- vated learning takes root anywhere ought to be credited to our city. Now the knowl- edge of Greek literature, which had decayed in Italy for more than seven hundred years, has been revived and restored by our city. Now we are able to confront the greatest philosophers, the admirable orators, and other men of outstanding learning, not through the obscurity of clumsy interpretations but face to face. Finally, these humanities [studia humanitatis] most excellent and of highest value, especially rele- vant for human beings, necessary both for private and public life, adorned with a knowledge of letters worthy of free men, have originated in our city and are now thriving throughout Italy. The city enjoys such resources and wealth that I fear to arouse jealousy by referring to its inexhaustible supply of money. This is demon- strated by the long Milanese war waged at an almost incredible cost, in which we spent over 3,500,000 florins. Now at the end of the war men are more prompt in paying their taxes than they were at the beginning of the war. As if miraculously, the abundance of money seems to increase in the city daily.

Therefore, the man we praise belonged by birth to this most noble, laudably established, most populous, spirited, rich and glorious homeland. By the will of the immortal gods he (Strozzi) achieved in this way at the very beginning the greatest part of his happiness. . . . In this regard he could not have been more fortunate than he was in fact.

FURTHER READING

Hans Baron, The Crisis of the Early Italian Renaissance, rev. ed. (1966)
_____, Humanistic and Political Literature in Florence and Venice at the Beginning of the Quat- trocento (1955)
_____, In Search of Civic Humanism: Essays on the Transition from Medieval to Modern Thought, 2 vols. (1988)
J. H. Bentley, Politics and Culture in Renaissance Naples (1989)
Allison Brown, Bartolomeo Scala, 1430–1497, Chancellor of Florence (1979)
Eugenio Garin, Italian Humanism: Philosophy and Civic Life in the Renaissance, trans. P. Munz (1958)
Gordon Griffiths et al., eds., The Humanism of Leonardo Bruni: Selected Texts (1987)
George Holmes, The Florentine Enlightenment, 1400–50, rev. ed. (1990)
Gary Ianziti, Humanist Historiography under the Sforzas: Politics and Propaganda in Fifteenth- Century Milan (1988)

Stephanie H. Jed, *Chaste Thinking: The Rape of Lucretia and the Birth of Humanism* (1989)

Margaret L. King, *Venetian Humanism in an Age of Patrician Dominance* (1986)

_____ and Albert Rabil, Jr., eds., *Her Immaculate Hand: Selected Works by and About the Women Humanists of Quattrocento Italy*, 2d ed. (1992)

Benjamin G. Kohl and Ronald G. Witt, eds., *The Earthly Republic* (1978), pp. 121–228. For Bruni's *Panegyric to the City of Florence* and Francesco Barbaro's *On Wifely Duties*

George McClure, *Sorrow and Consolation in Italian Humanism* (1991)

John McManamon, *Funeral Oratory and the Cultural Ideals of Italian Humanism* (1989)

Lauro Martines, *The Social World of the Florentine Humanists, 1390–1460* (1963)

Albert Rabil, Jr., ed., *Knowledge, Goodness and Power: The Debate over Nobility Among Quattrocento Italian Humanists* (1991)

Diana Robin, *Filelfo in Milan* (1991)

J. E. Seigel, "'Civic Humanism' or Ciceronian Rhetoric? The Culture of Petrarch and Bruni," *Past and Present*, 34 (1966), 3–48

_____, *Rhetoric and Philosophy in Renaissance Humanism* (1968)

David Thompson and A. F. Nagel, eds., *The Three Crowns of Florence: Humanist Assessments of Dante, Petrarca and Boccaccio* (1972)

B. L. Ullman, *The Humanism of Coluccio Salutati* (1963)

Ronald G. Witt, *Hercules at the Crossroads: The Life, Works, and Thought of Coluccio Salutati* (1983)

CHAPTER **10**

Schools of Humanism

S ince antiquity the term *humanitas* has had a dual meaning: the
notion of kindness and civility—a basic humaneness—and also the
concept of literary culture—an appreciation of literature, history,
philosophy and aesthetics, and the ability to communicate in elegant
Latin prose. In this second sense of the "humanities," Renaissance
humanism became the dominant educational ideal of Renaissance
courts and cities. Conceived as the study of Latin literature and Roman
antiquity, enhanced by improved knowledge of classical text and
history, early humanism adapted the teaching of ancient literature and
philosophy, especially Roman Stoicism, popularized in the works of
Cicero and Seneca, to the needs of the urban, lay, and literate society of
north and central Italian cities.

At the turn of the fifteenth century, Pier Paolo Vergerio's *De
ingenuis moribus (On the noble manners of young men)*, which is the
first document here, redefined the liberal arts as the educational ideal
for the Renaissance statesman, scholar, and gentleman. For him the
foundation of education in the humanities lay in grammar and rhetoric,
shaped by the power of reasoning provided by logic. History provided
knowledge of past human action, moral philosophy a guide to right
conduct in this life, and poetry the key to knowledge of divine and
inspired truth. These disciplines, based on the study of texts from
antiquity and early Christianity, became the basis for the new learning
in the private boarding schools of northern Italy and in most European
universities.

As humanism matured in the course of the fifteenth century, it had
to come to terms with the relation of Christianity to ancient culture and
the use of novel rhetorical forms, such as the dialogue, panegyric
(formal praise), and invective (formal denunciation). Discoveries of many
ancient Latin texts and increasing knowledge of ancient Greek language
and literature greatly expanded the canon of Renaissance humanism.
Relying on Plato and Aristotle, as well as the great Greek historians,
moralists, and dramatists, humanists became much more cosmopolitan
and provided a new secular vision that challenged late medieval
scholastic and religious thought.

Essays

The dean of Renaissance studies in the United States in the second half of the twentieth century has been Paul Oskar Kristeller. Born in Berlin and educated in Germany and Italy, Kristeller taught the history of philosophy at Columbia University in New York beginning in the 1940s. His seminal essay, the first selection below, identifies humanism with a well-defined cycle of studies, known later in the fifteenth century as the *studia humanitatis*. Kristeller shows that Renaissance humanism was characterized more by the study of rhetoric and the persuasive use of language than by philosophy and coexisted with other forms of inquiry, including scholasticism and professional studies, such as law and medicine. In the second essay, Charles Trinkaus, who taught at Sarah Lawrence College and the University of Michigan, attempts to define post-Petrarchan humanism. He examines the relationship between pagan and early Christian culture and clearly contrasts the Florentine school of social and ethical humanism represented by Bruni and Poggio with the deeper philosophical inquiry of Lorenzo Valla. Kristeller provides an overview of humanism as an educational program, whereas Trinkaus sees dissidence within humanism arising from various intellectual concerns and commitments.

Humanism and Scholasticism in the Italian Renaissance

Paul Oskar Kristeller

The most characteristic and most pervasive aspect of the Italian Renaissance in the field of learning is the humanistic movement. I need hardly say that the term "humanism," when applied to the Italian Renaissance, does not imply all the vague and confused notions that are now commonly associated with it. Only a few traces of these may be found in the Renaissance. By humanism we mean merely the general tendency of the age to attach the greatest importance to classical studies, and to consider classical antiquity as the common standard and model by which to guide all cultural activities. It will be our task to understand the meaning and origin of this humanistic movement which is commonly associated with the name of Petrarch.

Among modern historians we encounter mainly two interpretations of Italian humanism. The first interpretation considers the humanistic movement merely as the rise of classical scholarship accomplished during the period of the Renaissance. This view which has been held by most historians of classical scholarship is not very popular at present. The revival of classical studies certainly does not impress an age such as ours which has practically abandoned classical education, and it is easy to praise the classical learning of the Middle Ages, in a time which, except for a tiny

Excerpt from "Humanism and Scholasticism in the Italian Renaissance" by Paul O. Kristeller from *Renaissance Thought and Its Sources*, edited by Michael Mooney. Copyright © 1981 Columbia University Press, New York. Reprinted with permission of the publisher.

number of specialists, knows much less of classical antiquity than did the Middle Ages. Moreover, in a period such as the present, which has much less regard for learning than for practical achievements and for "creative" writing and "original" thinking, a mere change of orientation, or even an increase of knowledge, in the field of learning does not seem to possess any historical significance. However, the situation in the Renaissance was quite different, and the increase in, and emphasis on, classical learning had a tremendous importance.

There are indeed several historical facts which support the interpretation of the humanistic movement as a rise in classical scholarship. The humanists were classical scholars and contributed to the rise of classical studies. In the field of Latin studies, they rediscovered a number of important texts that had been hardly read during the Middle Ages. Also in the case of Latin authors commonly known during the Middle Ages, the humanists made them better known, through their numerous manuscript copies and printed editions, through their grammatical and antiquarian studies, through their commentaries, and through the development and application of philological and historical criticism.

Even more striking was the impulse given by the humanists to the study of Greek. In spite of the political, commercial, and ecclesiastic relations with the Byzantine Empire, during the Middle Ages the number of persons in Western Europe who knew the Greek language was comparatively small, and practically none of them was interested in, or familiar with, Greek classical literature. There was almost no teaching of Greek in Western schools and universities, and almost no Greek manuscripts in Western libraries. In the twelfth and thirteenth centuries, a great number of Greek texts were translated into Latin, either directly or through intermediary Arabic translations, but this activity was almost entirely confined to the fields of mathematics, astronomy, astrology, medicine, and Aristotelian philosophy.

During the Renaissance, this situation rapidly changed. The study of Greek classical literature which had been cultivated in the Byzantine Empire throughout the later Middle Ages, after the middle of the fourteenth century began to spread in the West, both through Byzantine scholars who went to Western Europe for a temporary or permanent stay, and through Italian scholars who went to Constantinople in quest of Greek classical learning. As a result, Greek language and literature acquired a recognized place in the curriculum of Western schools and universities, a place which they did not lose until the present century. A large number of Greek manuscripts was brought from the East to Western libraries, and these manuscripts have formed the basis of most of our editions of the Greek classics. At a later stage, the humanists published printed editions of Greek authors, wrote commentaries on them, and extended their antiquarian and grammatical studies as well as their methods of philological and historical criticism to Greek literature.

No less important, although now less appreciated, were the numerous Latin translations from the Greek due to the humanists of the Renaissance. Almost the whole of Greek poetry, oratory, historiography, theology, and non-Aristotelian philosophy was thus translated for the first time, whereas the medieval translations of Aristotle and of Greek scientific writers were replaced by new humanistic translations. These Latin translations of the Renaissance were the basis for most of the vernacular translations of the Greek classics, and they were much more widely read than were the original Greek texts. For in spite of its remarkable increase, the study of Greek even in the Renaissance never attained the same general importance as did the study of Latin which was rooted in the medieval tradition of the West. Nevertheless, it remains a remarkable fact that the study of the Greek classics was taken over by the humanists of Western Europe at the very time when it was affected in the East by the decline and fall of the Byzantine Empire.

If we care to remember these impressive facts, we certainly cannot deny that the Italian humanists were the ancestors of modern philologists and historians. Even a historian of science can afford to despise them only if he chooses to remember that science is the subject of his study, but to forget that the method he is applying to this subject is that of history. However, the activity of the Italian humanists was not limited to classical scholarship, and hence the theory which interprets the humanistic movement merely as a rise in classical scholarship is not altogether satisfactory. This theory fails to explain the ideal of eloquence persistently set forth in the writings of the humanists, and it fails to account for the enormous literature of treatises, of letters, of speeches, and of poems produced by the humanists.

These writings are far more numerous than the contributions of the humanists to classical scholarship, and they cannot be explained as a necessary consequence of their classical studies. A modern classical scholar is not supposed to write a Latin poem in praise of his city, to welcome a distinguished foreign visitor with a Latin speech, or to write a political manifesto for his government. This aspect of the activity of the humanists is often dismissed with a slighting remark about their vanity or their fancy for speech-making. I do not deny that they were vain and loved to make speeches, but I am inclined to offer a different explanation for this side of their activity. The humanists were not classical scholars who for personal reasons had a craving for eloquence, but, vice versa, they were professional rhetoricians, heirs and successors of the medieval rhetoricians, who developed the belief, then new and modern, that the best way to achieve eloquence was to imitate classical models, and who thus were driven to study the classics and to found classical philology. Their rhetorical ideals and achievements may not correspond to our taste, but they were the starting point and moving force of their activity, and their classical learning was incidental to it.

The other current interpretation of Italian humanism, which is prevalent among historians of philosophy and also accepted by many other scholars, is more ambitious, but in my opinion less sound. This interpretation considers humanism as the new philosophy of the Renaissance, which arose in opposition to scholasticism, the old philosophy of the Middle Ages. Of course, there is the well known fact that several famous humanists, such as Petrarch, Valla, Erasmus, and Vives, were violent critics of medieval learning and tended to replace it by classical learning. Moreover, the humanists certainly had ideals of learning, education, and life that differed from medieval modes of thinking. They wrote treatises on moral, educational, political, and religious questions which in tone and content differ from the average medieval treatises on similar subjects. Yet this interpretation of humanism as a new philosophy fails to account for a number of obvious facts. On one hand, we notice a stubborn survival of scholastic philosophy throughout the Italian Renaissance, an inconvenient fact that is usually explained by the intellectual inertia of the respective philosophers whom almost nobody has read for centuries and whose number, problems and literary production are entirely unknown to most historians. On the other, most of the works of the humanists have nothing to do with philosophy even in the vaguest possible sense of the term. Even their treatises on philosophical subjects, if we care to read them, appear in most cases rather superficial and inconclusive if compared with the works of ancient or medieval philosophers, a fact that may be indifferent to a general historian, but which cannot be overlooked by a historian of philosophy.

I think there has been a tendency, in the light of later developments, and under the influence of a modern aversion to scholasticism, to exaggerate the opposition of the humanists to scholasticism, and to assign to them an importance in the history of scientific and philosophical thought which they neither could nor did attain. The reaction against this tendency has been inevitable, but it has been equally wrong. Those scholars who read the treatises of the humanists and noticed their comparative emptiness of scientific and philosophical thought came to the conclusion that the humanists were bad scientists and philosophers who did not live up to their own claims or to those of their modern advocates. I should like to suggest that the Italian humanists on the whole were neither good nor bad philosophers, but no philosophers at all.

The humanistic movement did not originate in the field of philosophical or scientific studies, but it arose in that of grammatical and rhetorical studies. The humanists continued the medieval tradition in these fields, as represented, for example, by the *ars dictaminis* [the medieval art of letter-writing—see Chapter 8] and the *ars arengandi* [the art of oratory], but they gave it a new direction toward classical standards and classical studies, possibly under the impact of influences received from France after the middle of the thirteenth century. This new development of the field was followed by an enormous growth, both in the quantity and in the quality, of its teaching and its literary production. As a result of this growth, the claims of the humanists for their field of study also increased considerably. They claimed, and temporarily attained, a decided predominance of their field in elementary and secondary education, and a much larger share for it in professional and university education. This development in the field of grammatical and rhetorical studies finally affected the other branches of learning, but it did not displace them. After the middle of the fifteenth century, we find an increasing number of professional jurists, physicians, mathematicians, philosophers, and theologians who cultivated humanistic studies along with their own particular fields of study. Consequently, a humanistic influence began to appear in all these other sciences. It appears in the studied elegance of literary expression, in the increasing use made of classical source materials, in the greater knowledge of history and of critical methods, and also sometimes in an emphasis on new problems. This influence of humanism on the other sciences certainly was important, but it did not affect the content or substance of the medieval traditions in those sciences. For the humanists, being amateurs in those other fields, had nothing to offer that could replace their traditional content and subject matter. . . .

. . . When we inquire of the humanists, it is often asserted that they were freelance writers who came to form an entirely new class in Renaissance society. This

statement is valid, although with some qualification, for a very small number of outstanding humanists like Petrarch, Boccaccio, and Erasmus. However, these are exceptions, and the vast majority of humanists exercised either of two professions, and
sometimes both of them. They were either secretaries of princes or cities, or they
were teachers of grammar and rhetoric at universities or at secondary schools. The
opinion so often repeated by historians that the humanistic movement originated
outside the schools and universities is a myth which cannot be supported by factual
evidence. Moreover, as chancellors and as teachers, the humanists, far from representing a new class, were the professional heirs and successors of the medieval rhetoricians, the so-called *dictatores,* who also made their career exactly in these same
two professions. The humanist Coluccio Salutati occupied exactly the same place in
the society and culture of his time as did the *dictator* Petrus de Vineis one hundred
and fifty years before. Nevertheless there was a significant difference between them.
The style of writing used by Salutati is quite different from that of Petrus de Vineis
or of Rolandinus Passagerii. Moreover, the study and imitation of the classics which
was of little or no importance to the medieval *dictatores* has become the major concern for Salutati. Finally, whereas the medieval *dictatores* attained considerable importance in politics and in administration, the humanists, through their classical
learning, acquired for their class a much greater cultural and social prestige. Thus the
humanists did not invent a new field of learning or a new professional activity, but
they introduced a new, classicist style into the traditions of medieval Italian rhetoric.
To blame them for not having invented rhetorical studies would be like blaming
Giotto for not having been the inventor of painting.

The same result is confirmed by an examination of the literary production of the
humanists if we try to trace the medieval antecedents of the types of literature cultivated by the humanists. If we leave aside the editions and translations of the humanists, their classical interests are chiefly represented by their numerous commentaries
on ancient authors and by a number of antiquarian and miscellaneous treatises. Theoretical works on grammar and rhetoric, mostly composed for the school, are quite
frequent, and even more numerous is the literature of humanist historiography. Dialogues and treatises on questions of moral philosophy, education, politics, and religion have attracted most of the attention of modern historians, but represent a comparatively small proportion of humanistic literature. By far the largest part of that
literature, although relatively neglected and partly unpublished, consists of the
poems, the speeches, and the letters of the humanists.

If we look for the medieval antecedents of these various types of humanistic
literature, we are led back in many cases to the Italian grammarians and rhetoricians
of the later Middle Ages. This is most obvious for the theoretical treatises on grammar and rhetoric. Less generally recognized, but almost equally obvious is the link
between humanist epistolography and medieval *ars dictaminis.* The style of writing is
different, to be sure, and the medieval term *dictamen* was no longer used during the
Renaissance, yet the literary and political function of the letter was basically the
same, and the ability to write a correct and elegant Latin letter was still a major aim
of school instruction in the Renaissance as it had been in the Middle Ages.

The same link between humanists and medieval Italian rhetoricians which we
notice in the field of epistolography may be found also in the field of oratory. Most

historians of rhetoric give the impression that medieval rhetoric was exclusively con-cerned with letter-writing and preaching, represented by the *ars dictaminis* and the somewhat younger *ars praedicandi* [the medieval art of preaching], and that there was no secular eloquence in the Middle Ages. On the other hand, most historians of Renaissance humanism believe that the large output of humanist oratory, although of a somewhat dubious value, was an innovation of the Renaissance due to the effort of the humanists to revive ancient oratory and also to their vain fancy for speech-making. Only in recent years have a few scholars begun to realize that there was a considerable amount of secular eloquence in the Middle Ages, especially in Italy. I do not hesitate to conclude that the eloquence of the humanists was the continua-tion of the medieval *ars arengandi* just as their epistolography continued the tradition of the *ars dictaminis*. It is true, in taking up a type of literary production developed by their medieval predecessors, the humanists modified its style according to their own taste and classicist standards. Yet the practice of speech-making was no invention of the humanists, of course, since it is hardly absent from any human society, and since in medieval Italy it can be traced back at least to the eleventh century.

Even the theory of secular speech, represented by rules and instructions as well as by model speeches, appears in Italy at least as early as the thirteenth century. Indeed practically all types of humanist oratory have their antecedents in this medi-eval literature: wedding and funeral speeches, academic speeches, political speeches by officials or ambassadors, decorative speeches on solemn occasions, and finally ju-dicial speeches. Some of these types, to be sure, had their classical models, but others, for example, academic speeches delivered at the beginning of the year or of a partic-ular course or upon conferring or receiving a degree, had no classical antecedents whatsoever, and all these types of oratory were rooted in very specific customs and institutions of medieval Italy. The humanists invented hardly any of these types of speech, but they merely applied their standards of style and elegance to a previously existing form of literary expression and thus satisfied a demand, both practical and artistic, of the society of their time. Modern scholars are apt to speak contemptuously of this humanistic oratory, denouncing its empty rhetoric and its lack of "deep thoughts." Yet the humanists merely intended to speak well, according to their taste and to the occasion, and it still remains to be seen whether they were less successful in that respect than their medieval predecessors or their modern successors. Being pieces of "empty rhetoric," their speeches provide us with an amazing amount of information about the personal and intellectual life of their time.

In their historiography, the humanists succeeded the medieval chroniclers, yet they differ from them both in their merits and in their deficiencies. Humanist historiography is characterized by the rhetorical concern for elegant Latin and by the application of philological criticism to the source materials of history. In both re-spects, they are the predecessors of modern historians. To combine the requirements of a good style and those of careful research was as rare and difficult then as it is at present. However, the link between history and rhetoric that seems to be so typical of the Renaissance was apparently a medieval heritage. Not only was the teaching of history in the medieval schools subordinate to that of grammar and rhetoric, but we also find quite a few medieval historiographers and chronists who were professional grammarians and rhetoricians. Even the Renaissance custom of princes and cities appointing official historiographers to write their history seems to have had a few antecedents in medieval Italy.

Most of the philosophical treatises and dialogues of the humanists are really nothing but moral tracts, and many of them deal with subject matters also treated in the moralistic literature of the Middle Ages. There are, to be sure, significant differences in style, treatment, sources, and solutions. However, the common features of the topics and literary patterns should not be overlooked either. A thorough comparative study of medieval and Renaissance moral treatises has not yet been made so far as I am aware, but in a few specific cases the connection has been pointed out. Again it should be added that the very link between rhetoric and moral philosophy which became so apparent in the Renaissance had its antecedents in the Middle Ages. Medieval rhetoric, no less than ancient rhetoric, was continually quoting and inculcating moral sentences that interested the authors and their readers for the content as well as for their form. Moreover, there are at least a few cases in which medieval rhetoricians wrote treatises on topics of moral philosophy, or argued about the same moral questions that were to exercise the minds and pens of their successors, the Renaissance humanists. . . .

. . . The humanists did not live outside the schools and universities, but were closely connected with them. The chairs commonly held by the humanists were those of grammar and rhetoric, that is, the same that had been occupied by their medieval predecessors, the *dictatores*. Thus it is in the history of the universities and schools and of their chairs that the connection of the humanists with medieval rhetoric becomes most apparent. However, under the influence of humanism, these chairs underwent a change which affected their name as well as their content and pretenses. About the beginning of the fourteenth century poetry appears as a special teaching subject at Italian universities. After that time, the teaching of grammar was considered primarily as the task of elementary instructors, whereas the humanists proper held the more advanced chairs of poetry and of eloquence. For eloquence was the equivalent of prose writing as well as of speech. The teaching of poetry and of eloquence was theoretical and practical at the same time, for the humanist professor instructed his pupils in verse-making and in speech-making both through rules and through models. Since classical Latin authors were considered as the chief models for imitation, the reading of these authors was inseparably connected with the theoretical and practical teaching of poetry and of eloquence.

Thus we may understand why the humanists of the fourteenth and fifteenth centuries chose to call their field of study poetry and why they were often styled poets even though they composed no works that would qualify them as poets in the modern sense. Also the coronation of poets in the Renaissance must be understood against this background. It had been originally understood as a kind of academic degree, and it was granted not merely for original poetic compositions, but also for the competent study of classical poets.

History was not taught as a separate subject, but formed a part of the study of rhetoric and poetry since the ancient historians were among the prose writers commonly studied in school. Moral philosophy was always the subject of a separate chair and was commonly studied from the *Ethics* and *Politics* of Aristotle. However, after the beginning of the fifteenth century, the chair of moral philosophy was often held by the humanists, usually in combination with that of rhetoric and poetry. This combination reflects the expansion of humanistic learning into the field of moral philosophy. The chairs of Greek language and literature which were an innovation of the fourteenth century were also commonly held by humanists. This teaching was not as closely tied up with the practical concern for writing verses, speeches, or letters as was the study of Latin, and it was therefore more strictly scholarly and philological. On the other hand, since the fifteenth century we find several cases where humanist teachers of Greek offered courses on Greek texts of philosophy and science and thus invaded the territory of the rivaling fields.

Later on the fields of study cultivated by the humanists were given a new and even more ambitious name. Taking up certain expressions found in Cicero and Gellius, the humanists as early as the fourteenth century began to call their field of learning the humane studies or the studies befitting a human being (studia humanitatis, studia humaniora). The new name certainly implies a new claim and program, but it covered a content that had existed long before and that had been designated by the more modest names of grammar, rhetoric, and poetry. Although some modern scholars were not aware of this fact, the humanists certainly were, and we have several contemporary testimonies showing that the studia humanitatis were considered as the equivalent of grammar, rhetoric, poetry, history, and moral philosophy.

These statements also prove another point that has been confused by most modern historians: the humanists, at least in Italy or before the sixteenth century, did not claim that they were substituting a new encyclopaedia of learning for the medieval one, and they were aware of the fact that their field of study occupied a well defined and limited place within the system of contemporary learning. To be sure, they tended to emphasize the importance of their field in comparison with the other sciences and to encroach upon the latter's territory, but on the whole they did not deny the existence or validity of these other sciences. This well defined place of the studia humanitatis is reflected in the new term humanista which apparently was coined during the latter half of the fifteenth century and became increasingly popular during the sixteenth century. The term seems to have originated in the slang of university students and gradually penetrated into official usage. It was coined after the model of such medieval terms as legista, jurista, canonista, and artista [law professor, Roman law professor, canon law professor, and liberal arts teacher], and it designated the professional teacher of the studia humanitatis. The term humanista in this limited sense thus was coined during the Renaissance, whereas the term humanism was first used by nineteenth century historians. If I am not mistaken, the new term humanism reflects the modern and false conception that Renaissance humanism was a basically new philosophical movement, and under the influence of this notion the old term humanist has also been misunderstood as designating the representative of a new Weltanschauung [worldview]. The old term humanista, on the other hand, reflects the more modest, but correct, contemporary view that the humanists were the teachers and representatives of a certain branch of learning which at that time was expanding and in vogue, but well limited in its subject matter. Humanism thus did not represent the sum total of learning in the Italian Renaissance.

If we care to look beyond the field of the humanities into the other fields of learning as they were cultivated during the Italian Renaissance, that is, into jurisprudence, medicine, theology, mathematics, and natural philosophy, what we find is evidently a continuation of medieval learning and may hence very well be called scholasticism. Since the term has been subject to controversy, I should like to say that I do not attach any unfavorable connotation to the term *scholasticism*. As its characteristic, I do not consider any particular doctrine, but rather a specific method, that is, the type of logical argument represented by the form of the *Questio* [inquiry]. It is well known that the content of scholastic philosophy, since the thirteenth century, was largely based on the writings of Aristotle, and that the development of this philosophy, since the twelfth century, was closely connected with the schools and universities of France and England, especially with the universities of Paris and of Oxford. The place of Italy is, however, less known in the history and development of scholastic philosophy. Several Italians are found among the most famous philosophers and theologians of the twelfth and thirteenth centuries, but practically all of them did their studying and teaching in France. Whereas Italy had flourishing schools of rhetoric, of jurisprudence, and of medicine during the twelfth and early thirteenth century, she had no native center of philosophical studies during the same period. After 1220 the new mendicant orders established schools of theology and philosophy in many Italian cities, but unlike those in France and England, these schools of the friars for a long time had no links with the Italian universities. Regular faculties of theology were not established at the Italian universities before the middle of the fourteenth century, and even after that period, the university teaching of theology continued to be spotty and irregular.

Aristotelian philosophy, although not entirely unknown at Salerno toward the end of the twelfth century, made its regular appearance at the Italian universities after the middle of the thirteenth century and in close connection with the teaching of medicine. I think it is safe to assume that Aristotelian philosophy was then imported from France as were the study of classical authors and many other forms of intellectual activity. After the beginning of the fourteenth century, this Italian Aristotelianism assumed a more definite shape. The teaching of logic and natural philosophy became a well established part of the university curriculum and even spread to some of the secondary schools. An increasing number of commentaries and questions on the works of Aristotle reflect this teaching tradition, and numerous systematic treatises on philosophical subjects show the same general trend and background. During the fourteenth and fifteenth centuries, further influences were received from Paris in the field of natural philosophy and from Oxford in the field of logic; and from the latter part of the fourteenth century on we can trace an unbroken tradition of Italian Aristotelianism which continued through the fifteenth and sixteenth century and far into the seventeenth century.

The common notion that scholasticism as an old philosophy was superseded by the new philosophy of humanism is thus again disproved by plain facts. For Italian scholasticism originated toward the end of the thirteenth century, that is, about the same time as did Italian humanism, and both traditions developed side by side throughout the period of the Renaissance and even thereafter.

However, the two traditions had their locus and center in two different sectors of learning: humanism in the field of grammar, rhetoric, and poetry and to some extent in moral philosophy, scholasticism in the fields of logic and of natural philosophy. Everybody knows the eloquent attacks launched by Petrarch and Bruni against the logicians of their time, and it is generally believed that these attacks represent a vigorous new movement rebelling against an old entrenched habit of thought. Yet actually the English method of dialectic was quite as novel at the Italian schools of that time as were the humanistic studies advocated by Petrarch and Bruni, and the humanistic attack was as much a matter of departmental rivalry as it was a clash of opposite ideas or philosophies. Bruni is even hinting at one point that he is not speaking quite in earnest. Such controversies, interesting as they are, were mere episodes in a long period of peaceful coexistence between humanism and scholasticism. Actually the humanists quarreled as much among each other as they did with the scholastics. Moreover, it would be quite wrong to consider these controversies as serious battles for basic principles whereas many of them were meant to be merely personal feuds, intellectual tournaments, or rhetorical exercises. Finally, any attempt to reduce these controversies to one issue must fail since the discussions were concerned with many diverse and overlapping issues. Therefore, we should no longer be surprised that Italian Aristotelianism quietly and forcefully survived the attacks of Petrarch and his humanist successors.

But the Aristotelianism of the Renaissance did not remain untouched by the new influence of humanism. Philosophers began to make abundant use of the Greek text and of the new Latin translations of Aristotle, of his ancient commentators, and of other Greek thinkers. The revival of ancient philosophies that came in the wake of the humanistic movement, especially the revival of Platonism and of Stoicism, left a strong impact upon the Aristotelian philosophers of the Renaissance. Yet in spite of these significant modifications, Renaissance Aristotelianism continued the medieval scholastic tradition without any visible break. It preserved a firm hold on the university chairs of logic, natural philosophy, and metaphysics, whereas even the humanist professors of moral philosophy continued to base their lectures on Aristotle. The literary activity of these Aristotelian philosophers is embodied in a large number of commentaries, questions, and treatises. This literature is difficult of access and arduous to read, but rich in philosophical problems and doctrines. It represents the bulk and kernel of the philosophical thought of the period, but it has been badly neglected by modern historians. Scholars hostile to the Middle Ages considered this literature an unfortunate survival of medieval traditions that may be safely disregarded, whereas the true modern spirit of the Renaissance is expressed in the literature of the humanists. Medievalists, on the other hand, have largely concentrated on the earlier phases of scholastic philosophy and gladly sacrificed the later scholastics to the criticism of the humanists and their modern followers, a tendency that has been further accentuated by the recent habit of identifying scholasticism with Thomism. . . .

Thus we may conclude that the humanism and the scholasticism of the Renaissance arose in medieval Italy about the same time, that is, about the end of the thirteenth century, and that they coexisted and developed all the way through and beyond the Renaissance period as different branches of learning. Their controversy, much less persistent and violent than usually represented, is merely a phase in the battle of the arts, not a struggle for existence. We may compare it to the debates of the arts in medieval literature, to the rivaling claims of medicine and of law at the universities, or to the claims advanced by Leonardo in his *Paragone* [comparison] for the superiority of painting over the other arts. Humanism certainly had a tendency to influence the other sciences and to expand at their expense, but all kinds of adjustments and combinations between humanism and scholasticism were possible and were successfully accomplished. It is only after the Renaissance, through the rise of modern science and modern philosophy, that Aristotelianism was gradually displaced, whereas humanism became gradually detached from its rhetorical background and evolved into modern philology and history.

Thus humanism and scholasticism both occupy an important place in the civilization of the Italian Renaissance, yet neither represents a unified picture, nor do both together constitute the whole of Renaissance civilization. Just as humanism and scholasticism coexisted as different branches of culture, there were besides them other important, and perhaps even more important branches. I am thinking of the developments in the fine arts, in vernacular literature, in the mathematical sciences, and in religion and theology. Many misunderstandings have resulted from the attempts to interpret or to criticize humanism and scholasticism in the light of these other developments. Too many historians have tried to play up the fine arts, or vernacular poetry, or science, or religion against the "learning of the schools." These attempts must be rejected. The religious and theological problems of the Protestant and Catholic Reformation were hardly related to the issues discussed in the philosophical literature of the same time, and supporters and enemies of humanistic learning and of Aristotelian philosophy were found among the followers of both religious parties. The development of vernacular poetry in Italy was not opposed or delayed by the humanists, as most historians of literature complain. Some humanists stressed the superiority of Latin, to be sure, but few if any of them seriously thought of abolishing the *volgare* [vernacular] in speech or writing. On the other hand, many humanists are found among the advocates of the *volgare*, and a great number of authors continued to write in both languages. Again, modern historians have tried to interpret as a struggle for existence what in fact was merely a rivalry between different forms of expression.

The admirable development of the fine arts which is the chief glory of the Italian Renaissance did not spring from any exaggerated notions about the creative genius of the artist or about his role in society and culture. Such notions are the product of the Romantic movement and its eighteenth-century forerunners, and they were largely foreign to the Italian Renaissance. Renaissance artists were primarily craftsmen, and they often became scientists, not because their superior genius anticipated the modern destinies of science, but because certain branches of scientific knowledge, such as anatomy, perspective, or mechanics, were considered as a necessary requirement in the development of their craft. If some of these artist-scientists were able to make considerable contributions to science, this does not mean that they were completely independent or contemptuous of the science and learning available in their time.

Finally, mathematics and astronomy made remarkable progress during the sixteenth century and assumed increasing importance in their practical applications, in the literature of the time, and in the curriculum of the schools and universities. If this development did not immediately affect philosophy, this was due not to the stupidity or inertia of contemporary philosophers, but to the fact that physics or natural philosophy was considered as a part of philosophy and that there was almost no traditional link between the mathematical sciences and philosophy. Galileo was a professional student and teacher of mathematics and astronomy, not of philosophy. His claim that physics should be based on mathematics rather than on logic was not merely a novel idea as far as it went, but it revolutionized the very conceptions on which the curriculum of the schools and universities was based. It is hence quite understandable that he was opposed by the Aristotelian physicists of his time who considered his method as an invasion of their traditional domain by the mathematicians. On the other hand, there is no evidence that Galileo met with any serious resistance within his own field of mathematics and astronomy in which the main chairs were soon occupied by his pupils. If we want to understand and to judge these developments we must know the issues and the professional traditions of the later Middle Ages and of the Renaissance.

Modern scholarship has been far too much influenced by all kinds of prejudices, against the use of Latin, against scholasticism, against the medieval church, and also by the unwarranted effort to read later developments, such as the German Reformation, or French libertinism, or nineteenth-century liberalism or nationalism, back into the Renaissance. The only way to understand the Renaissance is a direct and, possibly, an objective study of the original sources. We have no real justification to take sides in the controversies of the Renaissance, and to play up humanism against scholasticism, or scholasticism against humanism, or modern science against both of them. Instead of trying to reduce everything to one or two issues, which is the privilege and curse of political controversy, we should try to develop a kind of historical pluralism. It is easy to praise everything in the past which happens to resemble certain favorite ideas of our own time, or to ridicule and minimize everything that disagrees with them. This method is neither fair nor helpful for an adequate understanding of the past. It is equally easy to indulge in a sort of worship of success, and to dismiss defeated and refuted ideas with a shrugging of the shoulders, but just as in political history, this method does justice neither to the vanquished nor to the victors. Instead of blaming each century for not having anticipated the achievements of the next, intellectual history must patiently register the errors of the past as well as its truths. Complete objectivity may be impossible to achieve, but it should remain the permanent aim and standard of the historian as well as of the philosopher and scientist.

Antiquity Versus Modernity

CHARLES TRINKAUS

The controversy over the relative merits of antiquity and modernity was an obvious and prominent feature of the literature of the Renaissance period. How could it not be so when the very notion of "renaissance," paradigmatically articulated by Petrarch, asserted the greatness of ancient culture but also declared it not inimitable and the suitable model for the golden age which either had already dawned or was just about to dawn? Therein lies the inextricable ambiguity of the conflict; both sides were asserting the superiority or the potential superiority of "the present age" but in different terms. The Ancients claimed the distant past would remedy the ills of the modern world, meaning by the latter the recent past. The Moderns held that all the desirable values of antiquity were already present and had been augmented in such a way as to make them even more worthy in the modern times.

Certainly more was involved than these formal alternatives, though it has been ably argued by Robert Black in a recent analysis that the quarrel was not much more than a rhetorical topos meant to praise or denigrate. But at least, according to Black, there was some progress over medieval partisanship in that the rhetorical humanists of the Renaissance had a more specific notion of historical circumstance. Hans Baron . . . stressed the seriousness of the argument and saw the first endorsement of modern political, cultural, and intellectual values as coming in Renaissance Italy, not Cartesian France. Baron, in harmony with his well-known theory of the rise of civic humanism, saw a transformation in attitude from the pessimistic down-playing of their own age, as pitifully unable to achieve the heights or noble conditions of antiquity, into an optimistic self-admiration of Florentine civic achievements after the providential death of Giangaleazzo Visconti.

A related but somewhat different scenario will be outlined in this paper. The cast of characters is the same, but the motives and viewpoints are not. I would follow Eugenio Garin and Cesare Vasoli in seeing the early humanists—especially Petrarch and Salutati—as engaging in a sharp polemic against the scholastic dialecticians and natural philosophers, presumably the group of late medieval thinkers loosely designated as the *via moderna* [modern mode], though it needs to be much more precisely differentiated and individualized. The early humanists were unquestionably "ancients" in their appeal to Cicero and Plato (as they knew him by reputation only), to Augustine and other ancient Christian writers, whom they regarded as superior to contemporary schoolmen. The latter they knew only distantly or whimsically spoke of as inhabiting the islands of Britain and Sicily, but some they knew more directly. Salutati corresponded with Pietro degli Alboini da Mantova and surely knew Biagio dei Pelacani when he held a chair at the Studium in Florence.

This emphasis on a distance between humanism and scholasticism, or more

"Antiquity Versus Modernity" by Charles Trinkaus from *Journal of the History of Ideas*, Vol. 47 (1987), pp. 11–21. Reprinted by permission of The Johns Hopkins University Press, Baltimore/London.

specifically between rhetoricians and dialecticians, should not be exaggerated, however. As Garin has pointed out, the humanists were not opposed to philosophy as such but rather very specifically to the formalism of the new logic. This seemed to them to make the technique of arguing more important than the substantive issues, moral and religious, that were at stake. Positions supposedly taken by natural philosophers interpreting Aristotle, either directly or following Averroës's commentaries, seen as affirming the eternity of the world, denying the creation, and questioning individual immortality, were also viewed with apprehension. As for the ancients, Petrarch made it clear not only that he would reject anything that was un-Christian (which might be regarded as an apologetic disclaimer) but that he regarded Cicero as having a wrong and inverted view of the powers to be ascribed to men and those possessed by the gods. For Cicero, as for Seneca, man had control over his own moral behavior but had fortune and the gods to thank for his material well-being. Petrarch held that Cicero and the ancients had come far in their admiration of virtue but added that salvation and a charitable life depended on divine grace, whereas man's worldly condition was more possibly within his own control. Sin and lust were the only things that were truly man's before man gained knowledge of the Advent of Christ, a knowledge denied to Cicero and the other ancients. "And so where Cicero's and his companions' swift mind was stuck our slow mind gradually progresses thanks to Him by whom both the progress of the mind and the plainness of the road are given."

In this thought lies the basis for the transformation of at least some of the humanists from ancients into moderns. But not all. As we shall see, Poggio Bracciolini, Leonardo Bruni, and a number of humanists up to and including the Ciceronians of the sixteenth century clung to antiquity. But this transformation, which we shall argue occurred in such influential figures as Coluccio Salutati, Lorenzo Valla, and Erasmus (not forgetting Petrarch), was subtle and complex. The issues were complicated, and it would be difficult for any of the humanists not, on some issue and some occasion, to be an ancient, and on other issues and occasions a modern.

What was the situation of the humanists in relation on the one hand to the intellectual, religious, and moral traditions which were then functional and influential and on the other hand to the kinds of impact events and institutions were then making on individual thought, motivation, and behavior? As I see it, they could and did take opposing or qualitatively varying positions on the following four basic issues: (1) historical consciousness and periodization, (2) the relation of the Christian religion to ancient culture, (3) the viability and appropriateness of Christian ethics in the contemporary world of urban Italian society, and (4) the role of rhetoric, poetry, and other types of written expression in the consideration of moral, religious, political, and philosophical questions. I believe these issues are fundamental not only for identifying the contrasting positions within the humanist movement but also for understanding the general historical significance of humanism.

Despite the number of very fruitful studies of humanist historical writing and historical consciousness in recent years, the question of the ways in which history was conceived by humanists remains complex. Study of the impact of rhetoric and philological language study on historical thought such as that by Nancy Struever, Donald Kelley, Sarah Stever Gravelle, and others has shown a growing awareness of cultural relativism at least in the concepts and values of men living in historically, geographically, and religiously separated cultures. At the same time both Christianity and the stereotyped notions of antiquity paradigmatically identified in such dominating figures as Aristotle or Cicero fostered the belief or attitude that there was one eternally right way of living, feeling, thinking, and acting, and many false or wrong or maliciously destructive ones. It should be recognized that neither of these modes of historical consciousness achieved full expression but that statements symptomatic of either or of both can be found with great frequency. I am convinced that something of both types could exist together in the thinking and writing of many humanists; at least I have encountered it in a considerable number of those I have studied. There is no such thing as conceptual purity or consistency in humanist thought. But there are definite types and crystallizations towards one or another of these two poles, and a humanist's historical periodization would be influenced by this as well as by his view of antiquity in comparison with the intervening Christian or "barbarian" centuries and with modernity or the present age.

The second issue identified as the relation of the Christian religion to ancient culture could either be resolved in absolute terms of rightness or wrongness or be seen in the more relativistic terms which considered antiquity as the *praeparatio evangelii* [forerunner of Christianity]. In a certain sense it had to be the latter for most humanists, but an important differentiation occurred. What element of ancient culture, if any, might be regarded as acceptable to a modern Christian? Could it be Aristotelianism or Platonism or Stoic thought? Or could it be the poetry of Homer, Vergil, Horace, Ovid, and others properly read? In one battle over this question the early humanists Petrarch, Boccaccio, and Salutati clearly sided with the poets against their critics. But a more important issue emerged within this larger one. Could ancient philosophy and religion in any sense at all be of value to a modern Christian? As we shall see, Petrarch and Salutati gave a qualified "No," as did Erasmus, but Lorenzo Valla's "No" was emphatic.

The third issue of the viability of Christian ethics is closely related. If virtue is not the goal of life, as Petrarch, Salutati, and Valla all held, then classical ethics and the Christian life are irrelevant to each other. Secular moral behavior, it was strongly argued by Salutati and even more so by Valla, was egocentrically motivated. Only divine grace, replacing the pursuit of worldly goals with the goal of salvation in the individual, could bring about truly charitable behavior.

The fourth issue, that of the role of the disciplines, is also related to the first three in that rhetoric, poetry, and the visual arts became aids to piety, while classical philosophy cannot and must not be of aid to the Christian. On the other hand the liberal and visual arts can come to be regarded as the only acceptable secular mode of thought and expression for mankind, with dialectic subordinated to rhetoric and metaphysics and dialectical theology regarded as delusory, if not heretical, modes of thought, since they do not acknowledge their basically linguistic and rhetorical nature. Again it was Lorenzo Valla who arrived at this extreme position (as later Ramus, Nizolius, and others). But there were other humanists who accepted the legitimacy of scholastic thought and learning provided its practitioners improved their style of writing and translated their Greek texts with more eloquence and polish. Better still they could use (as eventually some did use) the translations of ancient philosophers made by the humanists.

One can see most of these issues laid out in the famous polemic of Poggio against Valla and in Valla's *Antidota* to these charges. In Poggio's first *Oration on Valla* of 1452 he expresses his outrage at many of Valla's positions, but particularly maddening was Valla's criticisms of the verbal usage of classical writers, such as Priscian, Donatus, Servius, Pompeius Festus, Nonius Marcellus, Aulus Gellius, Marcus Varro, Aristotle, Boethius, Augustine, Jerome, and Lactantius—proceeding from the lesser ones to the greater. Worst of all, Valla "prefers himself to Cicero in elegance." Moreover, he commits heresy and religious deviation in his employment of Augustine, Jerome, and Lactantius and in his attempt to correct the Vulgate by comparing it with manuscripts of the Greek New Testament. He is charged with philosophical error for his treatment of Aristotle, Boethius, and Albertus Magnus. Indeed, Valla's criticism of both the metaphysical theology of high scholasticism and of the late medieval dialecticians was radical. His attempted reduction of metaphysics to grammatical categories placed him in his opposition to the use of ancient philosophy in theology beyond the contemporary scholastic adherents of a so-called *via moderna* [modern mode], who still adhered to Aristotelian metaphysics in the secular sciences.

Poggio's sympathies were not only with the ancients but also with the classical scholastics of the so-called *via antiqua* [ancient mode], especially Thomas Aquinas. Poggio's anger toward Valla, however, is greatest for his employment of a historical conception of language and his readiness to criticize the deficiencies of even the greatest classical authors. "See how great is the blindness and insanity of this monster. The propriety, the force, the meaning, the construction of Latin words is established, not so much by reason, as by the authority of ancient writers. If this is taken away, the foundations and maintenance of the Latin language necessarily will perish. For usage was always the master of Latin speech, and this is contained only in the books and writings of the ancient authors. This mad critic, having removed the authority of all the superior writers, inserts a new meaning into words, introduces a new manner of writing, a practice of such great presumption that he attributes to himself alone more authority than to all the rest.

Poggio employs the word *usus*, meaning usage, linguistic practice, something that was central to Valla's historical conception of language. But Poggio transforms its meaning into *autoritas*, or authority, and in so doing aligns himself with a classicist point of view opposed to Valla's modernist one. It should be clear that, without denying Valla's own great admiration for the classical authors, I am recognizing at the same time his readiness to treat them historically. As we shall see below, his selectivity in admiring the ancients was confined to the arts, particularly Quintilian's analysis of the modes of utilizing the linguistic arts which Valla would try to use in the service of Christian faith.

But Valla was not alone, and his major predecessor was Salutati. In the last year of his life (1405/6) Salutati chose to answer two attacks from seemingly opposite quarters: Giovanni Dominici for his *Lucula noctis*, which attacked Salutati for giving preeminence to the will over the intellect and for finding religious value in classical poetry, and Poggio Bracciolini for asserting that he was wrong to consider Petrarch the equal or even the superior to ancient writers, particularly Cicero. Salutati's reply to Dominici is a defense of the necessity of employing the liberal arts in order to understand scripture and to defend one's faith. His reply to Poggio was contained in two letters of 17 December 1405 and of 26 March 1406, the fortieth day before his death on May 4th. In the first (his reply to Dominici) he was speaking as a defender of antiquity, but antiquity utilized as an instrument in the service of Christ. In the second he spoke explicitly as a "modern" asserting the superiority not only of Petrarch but of all Christians over the ancients.

Salutati defended Petrarch both for his wisdom and for his eloquence. Petrarch's wisdom derived from his Christianity but was evident in his letters and in his treatises: *The Life of Solitude, The Retirement of the Religious*, and (most important to Salutati) the *Secretum*, which weighed the influence of a deeply meditated experience of life against the superficiality of the mouthing of platitudes in the scholastic classrooms. "How much, moreover, of morality did that Florentine Petrarch add to the Cordovan and our Arpinate? He who reads his little books will see and, weighing everything in his deeper mind, he will admit that Seneca, equalled by him in his thoughts, is exceeded by him in beauty of expression, and that Cicero, though richer in store of language and weightier in gravity, is without contention lesser in invention." If Poggio can forget the hate and prestige of the ancients, "believe me you would not be such an inequitable and disapproving estimator of your own age. You should see and rejoice that these our two centuries in which we fall come forth in no mediocre way, so that, though they may be lesser than a few [of the ancients], you can and ought to affirm that in manifest reason they are more celebrated than very many. . . . Now please say, why do you prefer those ancients to the moderns whom you so despise? Give us one, even the smallest reason, besides the smoke of glory and the opinion of antiquity, why we ought to place those vanquished and dated men ahead of the later and more recent."

Poggio's two letters are not extant, but we can reconstruct his point of view from Salutati's direct quotations of them. It seems to have been the automatic assumption that any ancient writer would be superior to one of his own age. Against this Salutati asserts that "even the less than moderately learned of our time go ahead of the pagans Cicero and Varro and all Romans, Aristotle, Plato, and all Greece by the benefits and teaching of the Christian faith." To this he adds the specific beliefs of Christians which place pagans in error: "We are not suspended from that unknown and impossible eternity of the world, which cannot be, yet leads them to argue that the souls of mortals are corruptible. . . . Nor are we hanging upon that error concerning divinity by which they wish God to be infinite in duration and to act with infinite power, but only according to a certain natural necessity, which is servile, and not by the choice of his own will, which, as is fitting to that majesty, is free and regal. Moreover, they wish that God know or see nothing outside of Himself." We do not determine the end of human action to be pleasure, as the Epicureans, or virtue, as the Stoics, or the integrity of human society, as Cicero, or the meditation and contempt of death, as Seneca, or speculation, as Aristotle, or any other opinion of the human mind. "But we believe man's end to be that comprehension of the blessed object by which, having ourselves become blessed, we shall perpetually enjoy beatitude." Not only does Poggio anticipate his arguments against Valla of forty-six years later, but Salutati sets forth the same argument that Valla defended in his *De vero falsoque bono*. "By knowledge of this," says Salutati, "and of those things by which this is achieved, which are in some ways infinite, we Christians excel all the Gentiles."

Poggio's own views, as we know them, were shifting and complicated. He also had little faith in the ideals of classical moralists but seems in his attacks on Salutati and Valla to affirm a superiority both of classical literary expression and of philosophy and even of the legitimacy of supporting or developing a Christian theology within a Stoic or an Aristotelian framework, however doubtful he may have been personally. It has been argued by Hans Baron that his associate at the time of these letters to Salutati at the papal curia, Leonardo Bruni, persuaded Poggio to be more accepting of Petrarch's importance. Salutati in his second letter neither believed in Poggio's sincerity nor thought his statements went far enough. I would agree here with Salutati and not with Baron's claim that they thus became "moderns" as evidenced in the second book of Bruni's *Dialogi ad Petrum Istrum*. Bruni himself seems to have argued in his *De studiis et litteris* that classical morals were universally applicable. Arguing with a critic of the reading of the classics, a certain "severe one" who refused to read the poets, Bruni says, "But Plato and Aristotle read them, and if you would put yourself above them, I could in no way tolerate it. Do you think you discover something which they did not see? 'I am a Christian,' he says. But did they perchance live according to their own customs? As if true virtue and gravity of morals were not the same then as they are now!" This suggests that for Bruni, on the level of secular existence at least, no important historical changes occur, a view which contrasts with that of Salutati and Valla, who thought that fundamental differences of morality and knowledge were the historical consequences of the coming of Christianity.

As Salutati argued in his first letter and Valla later said, ". . . as much as our theologians are victorious over the Gentiles in the knowledge of truth, so much they conquer ours, not in the learning and majesty of speaking, which is puerile without knowledge of truth, but in that aspect which Horace calls, 'verses lacking substance and sonorous trivialities.'" The ancients knew they spoke falsely because they had not yet penetrated to the depths of truth. They were industrious in pursuing what they were able and desired to know, and studious of those things they were able to know by nature as well as of eloquence. Their understanding, Salutati declares, was limited to the liberal arts: "Hence with quite marvellous thoroughness they examined into arithmetic, geometry and music, grammar, logic, and, what we are disputing, rhetoric almost to perfection, and into astronomy itself as far as they were able to follow it by conjectures. However, they were unable to comprehend in any way and scarcely to touch upon natural science and metaphysics and, what transcends all, theology." . . .

This declaration by Salutati of the intellectual failure of the ancients in all but the liberal arts was paralleled by the later statement of Valla in the prologue to book four of his *Elegantiae*. The Christian theologian should not pretend that he ought not to speak eloquently just because the pagans did. Rather he should seek to embellish the house of God. "Not the language of the Gentiles, not grammar, not rhetoric, not dialectic and the other arts are to be condemned, for the Apostles wrote in Greek; but the dogmas, the religions, the false opinions of the action of virtues through which we ascend to heaven. The other arts are placed in the middle of things where one can use them well or evilly. Therefore I pray, let us strive to attain to that, or at least come close to where those luminaries of our religion [i.e., the Apostles and Church Fathers] arrived."

Thus, just as Salutati insisted in his reply to Giovanni Dominici that the liberal arts and the *studia humanitatis* [Humanities] were essential for religious understanding—"The *studia humanitatis* and the *studia divinitatis* [Theology] are so connected that true and complete knowledge of neither can be had without the other"—so he urged upon Poggio the duty to devote his great facility in writing to refuting those who deny the truths of the Christian faith today. "I do not wish [to argue] that our writers surpass the Gentiles because they are Christians, but because, as we see, in these very writings in which they deal concerning life and morals, they without doubt dispute far more rationally and better and more perfectly than do the Gentiles." This the moderns can do, for to them "has come the perfection and truth of the doctrines of humanity."

Erasmus at the end of his *Ciceronianus* argued in similar vein that "For this reason the disciplines are acquired, for this philosophy is studied, for this eloquence is learned: so that we may understand Christ, that we may celebrate the glory of Christ. This is the purpose of all erudition and eloquence."

There was then a continuing debate among the humanists from the time of Petrarch to that of Erasmus over the proper use of ancient culture: whether it was to be venerated and imitated as the all-time highest and classical model or whether it was to be stripped of its philosophical and religious content, but its instruments of learning, that is, the arts, were to be taken over and utilized in the service of Christianity and humanity. On each of the four issues delineated above the humanists differed along consistent lines. Both parties were in their own sense ancients and both in their differing ways moderns. Both considered themselves true Christians and true students of the humanities. Moreover, whether or not they were aware of it, the line of their division echoed and paralleled that of scholastic thought after the Condemnations of 1277.

DOCUMENTS

At the beginning of the fifteenth century, Pier Paolo Vergerio, as tutor in the Carrara court at Padua, defined humanism as a system of education for the sons of the ruling classes of Italian cities, stressing instruction in grammar and rhetoric, informed by the study of history, moral philosophy, and poetry. In the first document, addressed to Ubertino, the son of Francesco Carrara, Vergerio sets out the new learning that was to become the humanities in Western education. In the second document (from 1438), the churchman Tommaso Parentucelli, later Pope Nicholas V, draws up the list of books for Cosimo de' Medici's library in Florence, defining the *studia humanitatis* as five disciplines: grammar, rhetoric, history, moral philosophy, and poetry. The list contains the set texts of the Greek and Roman classics for the study of the humanities in the West; many of the authors will be familiar to today's students of the classics and ancient history. The third document is the preface to Lorenzo Valla's work on how to write elegant Latin. Here Valla defines his task as recovering classical Latin usage and purity from the barbarians,

while arguing that purified, classical Latin is the proper medium for instruction and expression in all the art and sciences.

| Pier Paolo Vergerio on Liberal Learning, 1403

We call those studies *liberal* which are worthy of a free man; those studies by
which we attain and practise virtue and wisdom; that education which calls
forth, trains and develops those highest gifts of body and of mind which ennoble
men, and which are rightly judged to rank next in dignity to virtue only. For to a
vulgar temper gain and pleasure are the one aim of existence, to a lofty nature, moral
worth and fame. It is, then, of the highest importance that even from infancy this
aim, this effort, should constantly be kept alive in growing minds. For I may affirm
with fullest conviction that we shall not have attained wisdom in our later years
unless in our earliest we have sincerely entered on its search. Nor may we for a moment admit, with the unthinking crowd, that those who give early promise fail in
subsequent fulfillment. This may, partly from physical causes, happen in exceptional
cases. But there is no doubt that nature has endowed some children with so keen, so
ready an intelligence, that without serious effort they attain to a notable power of
reasoning and conversing upon grave and lofty subjects, and by aid of right guidance
and sound learning reach in manhood the highest distinction. On the other hand,
children of modest powers demand even more attention, that their natural defects
may be supplied by art. But all alike must in those early years, . . . whilst the mind is
supple, be inured to the toil and effort of learning. Not that education, in the broad
sense, is exclusively the concern of youth. Did not Cato think it honourable to learn
Greek in later life? Did not Socrates, greatest of philosophers, compel his aged fingers
to the lute?

Our youth of to-day, it is to be feared, is backward to learn; studies are accounted
irksome. Boys hardly weaned begin to claim their own way, at a time when every art
should be employed to bring them under control and attract them to grave studies.
The Master must judge how far he can rely upon emulation, rewards, encourage-
ment; how far he must have recourse to sterner measures. Too much leniency is
objectionable; so also is too great severity, for we must avoid all that terrifies a boy.
In certain temperaments—those in which a dark complexion denotes a quiet but
strong personality—restraint must be cautiously applied. Boys of this type are mostly
highly gifted and can bear a gentle hand. Not seldom it happens that a finely tempered nature is thwarted by circumstances, such as poverty at home, which compels
a promising youth to forsake learning for trade: though, on the other hand, poverty
is less dangerous to lofty instincts than great wealth. Or again, parents encourage
their sons to follow a career traditional in their family, which may divert them from
liberal studies: and the customary pursuits of the city in which we dwell exercise a

"Pier Paolo Vergerio Defines Liberal Learning, 1403," from W. H. Woodward ed. *Vittorino da Feltre and
Other Humanist Educators* (Cambridge, England: Cambridge University Press, 1897), pp. 102–109.

decided influence on our choice. So that we may say that a perfectly unbiased decision in these matters is seldom possible, except to certain select natures, who by favour of the gods, as the poets have it, are unconsciously brought to choose the right path in life. The myth of Hercules, who, in the solitude of his wanderings, learned to accept the strenuous life and to reject the way of self-indulgence, and so attain the highest, is the significant setting of this profound truth. For us it is the best that can befall, that either the circumstances of our life, or the guidance and exhortations of those in charge of us, should mould our natures whilst they are still plastic.

In your own case, Ubertinus, you had before you the choice of training in Arms or in Letters. Either holds a place of distinction amongst the pursuits which appeal to men of noble spirit; either leads to fame and honour in the world. It would have been natural that you, the scion of a House ennobled by its prowess in arms, should have been content to accept your father's permission to devote yourself wholly to that discipline. But to your great credit you elected to become proficient in both alike: to add to the career of arms traditional in your family, an equal success in that other great discipline of mind and character, the study of Literature.

There was courage in your choice. For we cannot deny that there is still a horde—as I must call them—of people who, like Licinius the Emperor, denounce learning and the Arts as a danger to the State and hateful in themselves. In reality the very opposite is the truth. However, as we look back upon history we cannot deny that learning by no means expels wickedness, but may be indeed an additional instrument for evil in the hands of the corrupt. To a man of virtuous instincts knowledge is a help and an adornment; to a Claudius or a Nero it was a means of refinement in cruelty or in folly. On the other hand, your grandfather, Jacopo da Carrara, who, though a patron of learning, was not himself versed in Letters, died regretting that opportunity of acquiring a knowledge of higher studies had not been given him in youth; which sh[o]ws us that, although we may in old age long for it, only in early years can we be sure of attaining that learning which we desire. So that it is no light motive to youthful diligence that we thereby provide ourselves with precious advantages against on-coming age, a spring of interest for a leisured life, a recreation for a busy one. Consider the necessity of the literary art to one immersed in reading and speculation; and its importance to one absorbed in affairs. To be able to speak and write with elegance is no slight advantage in negotiation, whether in public or private concerns. Especially in administration of the State, when intervals of rest and privacy are accorded to a prince, how must he value those means of occupying them wisely which the knowledge of literature affords to him! Think of Domitian: son of Vespasian though he was, and brother of Titus, he was driven to occupy his leisure by *killing flies!* What a warning is here conveyed of the critical judgments which posterity passes upon Princes! They live in a light in which nothing can long remain hid. Contrast with this the saying of Scipio: "Never am I less idle, less solitary, than when to outward seeming I am doing nothing or am alone": evidence of a noble temper, worthy to be placed beside that recorded practice of Cato, who, amid the tedious business of the Senate, could withdraw himself from outward distractions and find himself truly alone in the companionship of his books.

Indeed the power which good books have of diverting our thoughts from unworthy or distressing themes is another support to my argument for the study of letters.

Add to this their helpfulness on those occasions when we find ourselves alone, without companions and without preoccupations—what can we do better than gather our books around us? In them we see unfolded before us vast stores of knowledge, for our delight, it may be, or for our inspiration. In them are contained the records of the great achievements of men; the wonders of Nature; the works of Providence in the past, the key to her secrets of the future. And, most important of all, this Knowledge is not liable to decay. With a picture, an inscription, a coin, books share a kind of immortality. In all these memory is, as it were, made permanent; although, in its freedom from accidental risks, Literature surpasses every other form of record.

Literature indeed exhibits not facts alone, but thoughts, and their expression. Provided such thoughts be worthy, and worthily expressed, we feel assured that they will not die: although I do not think that thoughts without style will be likely to attract much notice or secure a sure survival. What greater charm can life offer than this power of making the past, the present, and even the future, our own by means of literature? How bright a household is the family of books! we may cry, with Cicero. In their company is no noise, no greed, no self-will: at a word they speak to you, at a word they are still: to all our requests their response is ever ready and to the point. Books indeed are a higher—a wider, more tenacious—memory, a store-house which is the common property of us all.

I attach great weight to the duty of handing down this priceless treasure to our sons unimpaired by any carelessness on our part. How many are the gaps which the ignorance of past ages has wilfully caused in the long and noble roll of writers! Books—in part or in their entirety—have been allowed to perish. What remains of others is often sorely corrupt, mutilated, or imperfect. It is hard that no slight portion of the history of Rome is only to be known through the labours of one writing in the Greek language: it is still worse that this same noble tongue, once well nigh the daily speech of our race, as familiar as the Latin language itself, is on the point of perishing even amongst its own sons, and to us Italians is already utterly lost, unless we except one or two who in our time are tardily endeavouring to rescue something—if it be only a mere echo of it—from oblivion.

We come now to the consideration of the various subjects which may rightly be included under the name of "Liberal Studies." Amongst these I accord the first place to History, on grounds both of its attractiveness and of its utility, qualities which appeal equally to the scholar and to the statesman. Next in importance ranks Moral Philosophy, which indeed is, in a peculiar sense, a "Liberal Art," in that its purpose is to teach men the secret of true freedom. History, then, gives us the concrete examples of the precepts inculcated by philosophy. The one sh[o]ws what men should do, the other what men have said and done in the past, and what practical lessons we may draw therefrom for the present day. I would indicate as the third main branch of study, Eloquence, which indeed holds a place of distinction amongst the refined Arts. By philosophy we learn the essential truth of things, which by eloquence we so exhibit in orderly adornment as to bring conviction to differing minds. And history provides the light of experience—a cumulative wisdom fit to supplement the force of reason and the persuasion of eloquence. For we allow that soundness of judgment, wisdom of speech, integrity of conduct are the marks of a truly liberal temper.

We are told that the Greeks devised for their sons a course of training in four subjects: letters, gymnastic, music and drawing. Now, of these drawing has no place amongst our liberal studies; except in so far as it is identical with writing (which is in reality one side of the art of Drawing), it belongs to the Painter's profession: the Greeks, as an art-loving people, attached to it an exceptional value.

The Art of Letters, however, rests upon a different footing. It is a study adapted to all times and to all circumstances, to the investigation of fresh knowledge or to the re-casting and application of old. Hence the importance of grammar and of the rules of composition must be recognised at the outset, as the foundation on which the whole study of Literature must rest: and closely associated with these rudiments, the art of Disputation or Logical argument. The function of this is to enable us to discern fallacy from truth in discussion. Logic, indeed, as setting forth the true method of learning, is the guide to the acquisition of knowledge in whatever subject. Rhetoric comes next, and is strictly speaking the formal study by which we attain the art of eloquence; which, as we have just stated, takes the third place amongst the studies specially important in public life. It is now, indeed, fallen from its old renown and is well nigh a lost art. In the Law-Court, in the Council, in the popular Assembly, in exposition, in persuasion, in debate, eloquence finds no place now-a-days: speed, brevity, homeliness are the only qualities desired. Oratory, in which our forefathers gained so great glory for themselves and for their language, is despised: but our youth, if they would earn the repute of true education, must emulate their ancestors in this accomplishment.

After Eloquence we place Poetry and the Poetic Art, which though not without their value in daily life and as an aid to oratory, have nevertheless their main concern for the leisure side of existence.

As to Music, the Greeks refused the title of "Educated" to anyone who could not sing or play. Socrates set an example to the Athenian youth, by himself learning to play in his old age; urging the pursuit of music not as a sensuous indulgence, but as an aid to the inner harmony of the soul. In so far as it is taught as a healthy recreation for the moral and spiritual nature, music is a truly liberal art, and, both as regards its theory and its practice, should find a place in education.

Arithmetic, which treats of the properties of numbers, Geometry, which treats of the properties of dimensions, lines, surfaces, and solid bodies, are weighty studies because they possess a peculiar element of certainty. The science of the Stars, their motions, magnitudes and distances, lifts us into the clear calm of the upper air. There we may contemplate the fixed stars, or the conjunctions of the planets, and predict the eclipses of the sun and the moon. The knowledge of Nature—animate and inanimate—the laws and the properties of things in heaven and in earth, their causes, mutations and effects, especially the explanation of their wonders (as they are popularly supposed) by the unravelling of their causes—this is a most delightful, and at the same time most profitable, study for youth. With these may be joined investigations concerning the weights of bodies, and those relative to the subject which mathematicians call "Perspective."

I may here glance for a moment at the three great professional Disciplines: Medicine, Law, Theology. Medicine, which is applied science, has undoubtedly much that makes it attractive to a student. But it cannot be described as a Liberal study. Law, which is based upon moral philosophy, is undoubtedly held in high respect.

Regarding Law as a subject of study, such respect is entirely deserved: but Law as practised becomes a mere trade. Theology, on the other hand, treats of themes removed from our senses, and attainable only by pure intelligence.

The principal "Disciplines" have now been reviewed. It must not be supposed that a liberal education requires acquaintance with them all: for a thorough mastery of even one of them might fairly be the achievement of a lifetime. Most of us, too, must learn to be content with modest capacity as with modest fortune. Perhaps we do wisely to pursue that study which we find most suited to our intelligence and our tastes, though it is true that we cannot rightly understand one subject unless we can perceive its relation to the rest. The choice of studies will depend to some extent upon the character of individual minds. For whilst one boy seizes rapidly the point of which he is in search and states it ably, another, working far more slowly, has yet the sounder judgment and so detects the weak spot in his rival's conclusions. The former, perhaps, will succeed in poetry, or in the abstract sciences; the latter in real studies and practical pursuits. Or a boy may be apt in thinking, but slow in expressing himself; to him the study of Rhetoric and Logic will be of much value. Where the power of talk alone is remarkable I hardly know what advice to give. Some minds are strong on the side of memory: these should be apt for history. But it is of importance to remember that in comparison with intelligence memory is of little worth, though intelligence without memory is, so far as education is concerned, of none at all. For we are not able to give evidence that we know a thing unless we can reproduce it.

Again, some minds have peculiar power in dealing with abstract truths, but are defective on the side of the particular and the concrete, and so make good progress in mathematics and in metaphysic. Those of just opposite temper are apt in Natural Science and in practical affairs. And the natural bent should be recognized and followed in education. Let the boy of limited capacity work only at that subject in which he sh[o]ws he can attain some result.

Tommaso Parentucelli Defines Humanistic Study, 1438

Moreover, concerning the Humanities (*studia humanitatis*), which include grammar, rhetoric, history, poetics and moral [philosophy], I think that you already know very well what are the best authors. Still if I were forming a library and could not have all the authors, I should especially want to have these included.

[Grammar]

Priscian, everything that he has written.
Donatus, and any other early author who seems to be worth reading.

"An Ideal Library of the studia humanitatis, 1438," from G. Sforza ed. *La patria, la famiglia e la giovinezza di Niccolò V* (Lucca, 1884), pp. 480–481. Translated by Benjamin G. Kohl.

Varro's work on the origins of the Latin language.
Nonnus Marcellus.
Pompeius Sextus.

[Rhetoric]

All the works of Cicero, because everything he wrote is important.
Quintilian's on the education of the orator, and on causes.

[Moral Philosophy]

All the works of Seneca, because he was a most learned man.
The books on natural history by Pliny Secundus.
The books on medicine by Cornelius Celsus.
Macrobius on the dream of Scipio and the *Saturnalia*.
Martianus Capella on the marriage of Philology.
All the works of Apuleius of Madaura.
A. Gellius's *Attic Nights*.
Columella on agriculture.
Cato on rural matters.
Vitruvius on Architecture.
Vegetius on military matters.
Laertes Diogenes on the sects of philosophers.

[Poetry]

All the works of Virgil.
Servius's commentary on Virgil.
Donatus's commentary on Virgil.
Ovid's *Metamorphoses* and *Fasti*.
Statius's *Thebaid* and *Achilleid*.
All the works of Horace, since all of them are outstanding.
I also judge that Lucan should be added.

[History]

Sallust's works on the Cataline and Jugurthine wars.
[Caesar's] commentaries on the Gallic, Civil and Alexandrine wars.
Suetonius on the twelve caesars.
Aelius Spartianus and Lampridius on the later caesars.
The lives of illustrious men translated from Plutarch, since much history is contained there.
And whatever I judge still ought to be added to history.

| Lorenzo Valla on the Elegance of Latin, 1448

When, as often happens, I compare the accomplishments of our forebears with those of other kingdoms and nations, it seems to me that our compatriots [the ancient Romans] excelled all others not only in the extent of their dominions but also in the diffusion of their language. To be sure, the Persians, Medes, Assyrians, Greeks and many other peoples possessed vast territories for a long time, and although each of these states was inferior in extent to the Roman Empire, still several of these empires lasted longer than Rome's. But none of them was able to spread its language as our [Romans] did. In addition to all of Italy and that part which was called Great Greece and Sicily where Greek was spoken, the Roman language was in a short time spread to almost all of western and northern [Europe] and not a small part of Africa. Called Latin from Latium where Rome was located, this famous and even regal language soon reached all the provinces of Rome, offering to all mortals there the best means of spreading its people. Indeed Latin soon became the most illustrious and attractive means for spreading the power of the Empire. Now those who increase the empire are usually much honored and come to be called emperors, but those who have conferred benefits on all humanity are celebrated with praise worthy not of men but of the gods, because they have not just bestowed glory and grandeur on their own city but have contributed to the welfare and advantage of the entire human race.

Thus, though our forebears [the Romans] surpassed other nations in military prowess and many other matters, they surpassed themselves in the extension of the Latin language, and almost leaving behind their heavenly empire, they attained heaven as the consorts of the gods. If you consider that Ceres probably discovered grain, Bacchus wine and Minerva the olive, and that many other benefits of this sort were bestowed by one or another of the gods, is it any less important to be granted to many peoples the use of Latin tongue, an outstanding and indeed almost divine gift? For this is food, not for the body, but for the soul. Now this language is used to instruct all nations and all peoples in those arts, which are called liberal: it is used to guide them in the best legal system; it will open to them the way of all wisdom; it will even free them from being called barbarians. Therefore, must not any clear-sighted judge of human affairs prefer those who have become illustrious through the cultivation of literature to those given to waging destructive wars? Men will call the latter activity imperial, but the former must indeed justly be named divine. For these did not limit themselves to merely increasing the power and dominion of the Roman people (as is appropriate to human beings); they contributed to the welfare of the whole world (as is the province of the gods). Now the more foreigners came under our dominion, the more they lost their own sovereignty and considered themselves deprived of their former liberty—which they judged, and justly perhaps, a very bitter thing. On the other hand, they understood they were not diminished by using the Latin language but, in a certain sense, enriched by it—just as discovering wine does

"Lorenzo Valla Identifies Latin Elegance, 1448," from E. Garin ed. *Prosatori latini del Quattrocento* (Naples, 1952), pp. 595–601. Translated by Benjamin G. Kohl.

not make you abandon the use of water, nor silk the use of wool and linen, nor does the possession of gold make you reject the use of other metals—no, this is a good added to other goods. Just as a gem mounted on a gold ring does not diminish but indeed embellishes it, so our speech, added to the vernaculars, increases rather than reduces their splendor. Now Latin does not obtain its dominion through arms, warfare and bloodshed, but with benefits, love and concord.

And these matters, insofar as they can be surmised by conjecture, are, in my opinion, the reasons for their success. First, our forebears cultivated incredibly every sort of study, so that, unless someone was outstanding in the study of literature, he did not seem to excel in military affairs, and this attitude was an important inducement for others to emulate. Next, they clearly offered important rewards to those who professed literature. Finally, they persuaded the citizens of the provinces to speak the language of the Romans in the provinces as well as in Rome. But I have discoursed enough on this subject—indeed I do not want to go on too much, comparing the Latin language with the Roman Empire. For a long time now, nations and peoples have rejected the Empire—as a hateful burden—while they have thought of Latin as sweeter than any nectar, finer than any silk, and more precious than any gold and gems—and they jealously guard it like some god sent down from Heaven.

Therefore, great is the puissance of the Latin language, surely greater is its magic—foreigners, barbarians, even enemies [of Rome] have guarded it as something sacred and holy down through the centuries. Thus, rather than grieve the Romans ought to rejoice, indeed to glory, in the fact that Latin is heard spoken throughout the entire world. We have lost Rome, we have lost power and dominion, not from our own faults but through the ravages of time. But yet through this most splendid lordship [of language] we continue to rule, even now, in a great part of the world. Our language reigns in Italy, in Gaul, in Spain, Germany, Pannonia, Dalmatia, Illyria, and in many other nations. For wherever the Roman Empire used to hold sway, there the language of Rome dominates. Now the Greeks boast a great deal about the wealth of their own language. But one single and (as they would have it) impoverished language is worth more than their five (and as they would have it) very rich languages. Just as many nations have only one law, they have only the language of Rome; only Greece has—and is proud of it—not one but many languages, rather like a commonwealth divided into several factions. Many foreign nations are as one with us in using Latin, but the Greeks cannot come to agreement among themselves, and even less can they hope to convince others to use their languages. Among them, authors use various dialects: Attic, Aeolic, Ionic, Doric, and *koine* [the common speech].

Among us, that is, among many nations, everyone uses Latin, and a language that embraces all the disciplines worthy of a free man; but among the Greeks, these disciplines are taught in several tongues. Who does not realize that when the [Latin] language flourishes, all subjects and disciplines flourish and that when it declines, they too decline? For who were the greatest philosophers, the greatest orators, the greatest jurists, and, finally, the greatest authors, if it were not those who were most adept at speaking well [in Latin]? But pain stops me from discoursing further on this subject and moves me to tears and exasperation when I consider from what great heights the faculty for using Latin well has fallen. For what devotée of literature, what lover of the public good could restrain his tears when he perceives that the Latin language has fallen to the same low estate as Rome did when it was sacked long ago by the Gauls? All was burned, ruined and destroyed so that even the citadel on the Capitoline scarcely survived.

Since then for many centuries, not only was no one able to speak Latin, but in fact, no one even knew how to read Latin. Lovers of wisdom did not study the philosophers, rhetoricians did not study the orators, courtroom lawyers did not study the jurists—there were no competent students of the ancient texts. With the fall of the Roman Empire it was no longer proper to know or speak Latin; thus, it happened that the ancient splendor of the Latin language was covered with rust and mould. Learned men have advanced many various theories as to why this happened—I do not approve or disapprove of any of these. Indeed I have not dared to say anything about this subject. Even more will I not speculate on the reason why those arts— such as painting, sculpture, and architecture, which stand very near to the liberal arts and for a long time had also been in decline, so that they seemed to be almost as moribund as literature was—have been aroused to new life and now flourish greatly both because of [the] skill of our craftsmen and the patronage of cultured men. However, the more we can leave behind those earlier ages, when no learned men were to be found, the more we ought to rejoice in our own age, when, if I allow myself to exaggerate a bit, I think that we can claim that we are on verge of restoring to life the language (though not the dominion) of Rome, and all the disciplines associated with its study. Therefore, given my love of our homeland, rather than for all humanity, and given the magnitude of the task, I wish to exhort and call upon, as from a place on high, all those lovers of eloquence to sound—as they say—the battle cry.

For how long, O Quirites—thus I call the true lovers and cultivators of the Latin languages, only these are the true Quirites, the rest are mere foreigners—how long, I say, O Quirites, will you permit our City, which I do not call the capital of the Empire but the mother of Letters, to be occupied by the Gauls? That is, how long will you allow the Latin language to be oppressed by the barbarians? How long with harsh and almost impious gazes will you allow the language to be profaned? Will it be until perhaps not even the foundations remain? It's true that one of you writes history, but he lives outside Rome at Veii; another translates works from Greek, but he resides at Ardea. Others compose speeches and poetry; these truly defend the Capitoline and its citadel. Indeed these are important undertakings, worthy of not indifferent praise, but alone they will not drive out the enemy; they will not liberate the homeland. What we must do is imitate Camillus, Camillus who, as Virgil says, "brought back the victory banner to our homeland" [Aeneid 6.815] and gave it back its freedom. His military prowess was so superior to the others that without his deeds, the defenders on the Capitoline and at Ardea and Veii could not have been saved.

In the same way, at the present time, other authors may derive some profit from one who would compose a treatise "On the Latin Language." Thus, insofar as I am able, I hope to imitate Camillus and take him as my model. With whatever poor power I may possess, I shall assemble an army that, at the first opportunity, I shall lead to take the field against the enemy. Thus, I beg you, join me in the fight, in this most honorable and excellent struggle—not just so that we can recover our homeland from the enemy, but also so that in the reconquest it will become obvious to all that we have matched the valor of Camillus. Indeed, it will be very difficult to equal the accomplishments of that man, who was, in my opinion, the greatest of all Roman leaders and was justly called, after Romulus, the second founder of Rome. Therefore, many of us should collaborate in this endeavor so that, working together, we can accomplish what he did all by himself. Still anyone who accomplishes great work in this enterprise will truly and justly be viewed and praised as a new Camillus. For my part, I can only affirm that you should not expect me to carry out all of this great task, since I have assumed the hardest part of the work and taken on its most demanding aspects, so that others may be eager to assume the work that remains. For this reason, my books will contain almost nothing that other authors—insofar as they survive—have treated. And now let us proceed to the beginning of our work.

FURTHER READING

John F. D'Amico, *Renaissance Humanism in Papal Rome* (1983)
Eric Cochrane, *Historians and Historiography of the Italian Renaissance* (1980)
Brian P. Copenhaver and Charles Schmitt, *Renaissance Philosophy* (1992)
Arthur Field, *The Origin of the Platonic Academy in Florence* (1988)
Eugenio Garin, *Italian Humanism*, trans. P. Munz (1958)
_____, *Portraits from the Quattrocento* (1972)
Anthony Grafton and Lisa Jardine, *From Humanism to the Humanities: Education and the Liberal Arts in Fifteenth- and Sixteenth-Century Europe* (1986)
Paul Grendler, *Schooling in Renaissance Italy: Literacy and Learning, 1300–1600* (1989)
James Hankins, *Plato in the Renaissance* (1990)
Benjamin G. Kohl, "The Changing Concept of the *Studia Humanitatis* in the Early Renaissance," *Renaissance Studies* 6 (1992), 185–209
Paul Oskar Kristeller, *Eight Philosophers of the Italian Renaissance* (1964)
_____, *Renaissance Thought and Its Sources* (1979)
_____, *Renaissance Thought II* (1970)
David Marsh, "Grammar, Method and Polemic in Lorenzo Valla's *Elegantiae*," *Rinascimento* 19 (1975), 91–116
John Monfasani, *George of Trebizond* (1976)
John W. O'Malley, *Praise and Blame in Renaissance Rome* (1979)
Rudolf Pfeiffer, *History of Classical Scholarship from 1300 to 1850* (1976)
Albert Rabil, Jr., ed. *Renaissance Humanism: Foundations, Forms and Legacy*, 3 vols. (1988)
Eugene Rice, *The Renaissance Idea of Wisdom* (1957)
Charles Schmitt, *Aristotle and the Renaissance* (1983)
Nancy Struever, *The Language of History in the Renaissance* (1970)
_____, *Theory as Practice: Ethical Inquiry in the Renaissance* (1992)
Charles Trinkaus, *In Our Image and Likeness: Humanity and Divinity in Italian Humanist Thought*, 2 vols. (1970)
_____, *The Scope of Renaissance Humanism* (1983)
Robert Weiss, *The Spread of Italian Humanism* (1964)

PART V

Urban Society and Culture

Mantegna, *The Gonzaga Family* (1474). Detail of
a fresco in a small room in the Ducal Palace in
Mantua, probably painted to celebrate a
Gonzaga marriage.

CHAPTER **1 1**

Marriage and Gender

M embership in the political elite of Renaissance cities was
usually determined by belonging to a local, established,
wealthy family. The marriage of a young, upper-class man and
woman represented an alliance between two families that was of
fundamental importance to the ruling elite, as well as to the private
fortunes of the families themselves. The two families exchanged a large
amount of property (usually cash and movable wealth, such as clothing,
furniture, and other liquid assets) and forged strong, new kinship ties
that would eventually radiate outward to aunts, uncles, cousins, and
beyond, and they looked forward to offspring who would perpetuate
and might even elevate their families' position in society.

Most families measured their position in terms of wealth, political
influence, and social prominence. These qualities, along with the family
name, were transmitted directly from father to son and on down the
male line, according to a partrilineal pattern of descent. When a young
woman married, she moved both physically and symbolically from the
house of her father to the house of her husband. From then on her
primary allegiance was theoretically to her husband's family and to her
sons. In practice, however, the woman maintained close ties to the
family she had been born into, and the concrete expression of these ties
was the legal status of her dowry. While a woman's husband was alive,
he was permitted to use the income from the dowry as he wished, but if
he died, his heirs were required by law to return the dowry intact to his
widow. She then owned the property in her dowry outright and could
dispose of it as she wished. A widow who was still young might choose
to remarry, thus transferring the dowry to another family; an older
woman might choose to live out her days as a widow, probably with
one of her children, enjoying the power and influence conferred upon
her by owning property.

Over the course of the fifteenth and sixteenth centuries, the cost of
a respectable dowry grew to enormous size, both in absolute terms and
as a proportion of the total family patrimony that it represented, largely
the result of the competition for social position and prestige so
characteristic of Italian urban society. This growth had two important
consequences for women. Increasingly, families could not afford
dowries for more than one or two daughters, and the only respectable

alternative to marriage for upper-class women was joining a convent. As a result, convents filled up with women denied the chance to lead a secular life yet with little interest in the religious life. Second, as the size of dowries increased, so did the power and influence of the women who were lucky enough to receive them. Indeed, wealthy women clearly recognized the advantages of a larger dowry, and their wills are filled with contributions to the dowries of their female relatives.

Essays

Because the sources available for the study of the private lives of elite men and women are so much more abundant than for other classes most scholarship on gender in the Renaissance has been confined to the upper class (one notable exception is Judith Brown's article on working-class women in Chapter 3). The two essays that follow offer nearly opposite views of women's position in the patrilineal society of Renaissance Italy. Christiane Klapisch-Zuber (see Chapter 4) of the École des Hautes Études en Sciences Sociales in Paris, based on extensive study of Florentine diaries (*ricordanze* see representative excerpts in Chapters 3 and 4), argues that women were insignificant players in the marriage alliance, which was arranged by two groups of men: on the one hand her father, uncles, brothers, and other relatives (her "agnatic" kin), and on the other, her husband and his family (her "cognatic" kin). Indeed, women were so powerless that, if widowed, their father and brothers could force them to remarry, thus using the family property contained in the woman's dowry to forge new kinship ties for their own political and social advantage. A woman in such a position would, nevertheless, be accused of being a "cruel mother" because she was forbidden to bring children from a first marriage (one patriline) to live with her and a second husband (another patriline). Stanley Chojnacki, who teaches at the University of North Carolina, pioneered the study of gender, politics, and society in his work on the fifteenth-century Venetian patriciate. In the essay reprinted here, based largely on studying men and women's wills, he argues that ties of affection between husband and wife, clearly expressed in those documents, complicated their more traditional loyalties to family and patriline. He then suggests that the increasing size of dowries, and hence the increasing importance of attracting the favor of wealthy women, led to changes in the gender identity—the range of social and emotional behavior considered appropriate for one's gender—of both men and women. As women thus gained influence, social relations changed as well, away from traditional lineage concerns toward more flexible, affective ties of personal loyalty.

Maternity, Widowhood, and Dowry in Florence

CHRISTIANE KLAPISCH-ZUBER

In Florence, men *were* and *made* the "houses." The word *casa* designates, in the fourteenth and fifteenth centuries, the material house, the lodging of a domestic unit, and it is in this sense that many documents of a fiscal, legal, or private nature use the term. But it also stands for an entire agnatic kinship group. The *casa* in this case designates all ancestors and living members of a lineage, all those in whose veins the same blood ran, who bore the same name, and who claimed a common ancestor—an eponymic hero whose identity the group had inherited.

"Houses" were made by men. Kinship was determined by men, and the male branching of genealogies drawn up by contemporaries shows how little importance was given, after one or two generations, to kinship through women. Estates also passed from one generation to another through men. Among the goods that men transmitted jealously, excluding women from ownership as far as they could, was the material house, which they "made" also, in the sense that they built it, enlarged it, and filled it with children who bore their name. The Florence of the early Renaissance, the Florence of the great merchants and the first humanists, was not a tenderly feminine city. Family structures and the framework of economic, legal, and political life remained under the control of level-headed males, bastions of solidarity, and family values were inspired by a severely masculine ideal.

In these *case*, in the sense of both [the] physical and the symbolic house, women were passing guests. To contemporary eyes, their movements in relation to the *case* determined their social personality more truly than the lineage group from which they came. It was by means of their physical "entrances" and "exits" into and out of the "house" that their families of origin or of alliance evaluated the contribution of women to the greatness of the *casa*. The marriage that brought a woman out of the paternal house and lineage, the widowhood that often led to her return, these incessant comings and goings of wives between *case* introduced a truly indeterminate quality in the ways they were designated: since reference to a male was necessary, a woman was spoken of in relation to her father or her husband, even when they were dead. It is clear that the mere reference to the name of the lineage into which she was born or into which she married situated a woman much more clearly than the place where she was living at the moment. Women, then, were not permanent elements in the lineage. Memory of them was short. An important woman, a benefactress for her kin, for example, would eventually be known under her own name and brought to people's attention; but the family chronicler or the amateur genealogist would feel obliged to explain *why*, since the process fit so poorly within their definition of kinship. . . .

The determination of a woman's identity thus depended on her movements in relation to the "houses" of men. The corollary was that upper-class Florentines found females who remained in their house of birth just as intolerable as females who lived independently. "Honorable" marriages were what regulated the entries and exits of the wives, and the normal state, the state that guaranteed the honor of the women and the "houses," could be no other than the married state. Any woman alone was suspect. An unmarried woman was considered incapable of living alone or in the absence of masculine protection without falling into sin. Even if she were a recluse and lived a holy life, even if she retired to a room on the upper floor of the paternal house, she placed the family honor in jeopardy by the mere fact of her celibacy. The convent was the only way out, although terrible doubts about the security of the cloister continued to torment her parents. Among the "best people," therefore, families did not include females over twenty years of age who were not married.

The widow's solitude was hardly less suspect. Although the Church advised the widow with a penchant for chastity not to remarry and to practice the related virtues of *mater et virgo* [mother and virgin], secular society did not set much store by her chances of remaining chaste. The problem of where the widow was to live became crucial in such a case, for she was a threat to the honor not only of one family but of two. Given that a wife must live where her father or her husband lived (since they were the guarantors of her good conduct and her social identity), where should a wife be when she lost her husband?

ON THE DWELLING PLACE AND THE VIRTUE OF DOWERED WIDOWS

Theoretically, a widow had some choice in the matter. She could live in her husband's family, by her children's side; she could live independently without remarrying, but near her children; or, finally, she could remarry and leave the first family that had received her. But in practice a widow, if young, was barred from the second option and found herself subjected to contradictory pressures that prevented her from quietly choosing between the other two possibilities. Young widows were in fact the target of a whole set of forces struggling fiercely for control of their bodies and their fortunes.

The statistics of the *catasto* (tax survey: see Chapter 3 documents) show that widows in 1427 were much more numerous in the general population than widowers (13.6 percent and 2.4 percent, respectively). In Florence these percentages doubled (25 percent and 4 percent). Widowers tended to be older men (14 percent of the age classes of 70 years old and older were widowers), for men remarried promptly up to a late age. Definitive widowhood came much earlier for women: at 40—that is, at an age at which they might still give children to their new husband—18 percent of Florentine women appear in the census as widows, and at 50, nearly 45 percent do so. Furthermore, according to the statistics on couples drawn from family diaries, two-thirds of the women who became widows before 20 found a new husband, one-third of those widowed between 20 and 29, but only 11 percent of those widowed between 30 and 39—when their numbers grow. We might conclude that after 40 they no longer had much chance of remarrying, while from 75 to 100 percent of all men up to 60 years of age took another wife. Even if they hoped for remarriage, then, widows' liberty of choice was singularly limited by their age. . . .

Since it is strikingly obvious that a widow's ability to live alone or simply to head the household of her minor children was correlated to her wealth, we need to raise questions concerning the processes that tied her fate to that of the family estate. By processes I mean legal mechanisms as well as individual and collective behavior that affected the widow or motivated her decisions.

It was of course the dowry that tangled the threads of a woman's fate. In principle, the dowered goods that a wife brought her husband were attached to her for life: they had the double function of providing for the expenses of the household and, when the household dissolved at the husband's death, of providing for the surviving wife. Since she could not inherit her father's estate, which went to her brothers, a woman looked to her dowry to assure her subsistence: she could "keep her estate and her honor" before transmitting to her children, male and female, the dowry she had received at marriage. This lovely scheme was unfortunately often belied by the facts. Every widowhood threatened the economic equilibrium the domestic group had achieved during the father's lifetime. If the widow was 40 years old or older, the difficulty of finding her a new husband discouraged her own parents from intervening. It was up to her husband's heirs to persuade her to remain with them and not to "leave with her dowry" to live independently. What is more, her husband would do his utmost, on his deathbed, to encourage her to give up any such idea. He would agree to assure her a lifetime income and supplementary advantages, over and above the income from her own estate, if she would remain under his roof, and he would make his heirs swear to show her all consideration and to consult her in the management of the holdings in which her dowry would continue to be sunk. All of this was not unique to Florence, or to Italy. Clearly, well-off Florentines did succeed in dissuading their wives from flying with their own wings, since there were very few rich and elderly widows who lived independently. If a widow, however, did not get along with her husband's heirs and preferred her freedom, she had no claims other than to her dowry. The suits initiated by widows to regain their dowry show that the heirs did not always see matters her way. In the fifteenth century, however, widows had the law and judicial institutions on their side: if they were not discouraged from the start, they ended up by taking back what they had brought to their marriage.

Finally, if the heirs—who were not always her own children—did not want to keep her under their roof or give her back her dowry, the Florentine widow could fall back on the *tornata*, a right of refuge in her family of birth. It was the obligation of her close kin or their heirs to receive her and assure her board and lodging. . . .

These arrangements attest to an anxiety among men—who were deeply committed to maintaining the honor of their "house"—at the thought that a woman of their kin might not be included in a familial group. Even when old, a widow represented a threat to the reputation of good families. Since she had tasted the pleasures of the flesh, she was considered prone, like the hideous merry widow portrayed in Boccaccio's *Corbaccio*, to fall into debauchery. If the heirs let their material interests pass before defense of their honor, the widow's kin, their allied family, felt sufficient responsibility toward her to take her back under their charge—not always without recriminations. Piero di Bernardo Masi, a coppersmith, gave solemn instructions to his progeny, in 1512, to take all precautions to avoid what had happened to his own father and to get guarantees for the dowries they gave their daughters. For fifteen years—until she died—his father had had to maintain at his own expense a sister whose husband had left her penniless.

In this game, a married woman embodied stakes that were fully revealed only if she was widowed young. Early widowhood revived the claims of the widow's family of birth on the goods brought as a dowry. As these were irrevocably attached, by law, to the physical person of the woman for the duration of her life, widowhood forced her own kin to use her as a pawn by making her "come out" of her husband's family. When she remarried, her family could join a new circle of affines. By the remarriage of a widow of their blood, Florentines affirmed that they had never totally relin-quished control over the dowries that they had given their daughters or their sisters. At the same time, they claimed a perpetual right to the women's bodies and their fertility. Marriage alliance did not obliterate blood kinship; it did not signify a defin-itive break between the wife and her family of origin. When the widow returned to her family of birth and once again became part of its matrimonial strategies, the family took back cards it had already played, with every intention of making the most of a second deal of social prestige bought by the conclusion of a new alliance.

As soon as the husband had been buried and the funeral ceremonies had ended, the wife's kin came to claim her if she was young. They brought her back to their own house: such is "the custom of Florence," Paolo Sassetti says in 1395, and a con-temporary asserts that it was less than honorable for the widow to leave before the ceremony, but that it was understood as proper and accepted by all that she do so immediately afterward. The right of families of birth to take back their widows was stronger than the desires the deceased had expressed in his will. The Sassetti "ex-tracted" (the verb *trarre* is used) a sister in 1389, a niece of this same Paolo, and they remarried her promptly, even though she had "three little boys of very young age," for whom her husband had named her guardian and of whose inheritance she had been named coadministrator. But, Paolo Sassetti says, "as we had to remarry M[adonn]a Isabetta, she could not, and we did not want her to, take on this guard-ianship, and she renounced it 7 December 1389." The maternal uncles then took over responsibility for their sister's sons.

THE WIDOW'S DEFECTION
AND THE ABANDONMENT OF CHILDREN

A departure like Madonna Isabetta's constituted a double threat: to the children of the couple broken up by the death of the father, and to the children of a previous marriage. If their mother or their stepmother left them abruptly for a second mar-riage, their economic situation underwent a much more brutal shock than when an aged widow demanded her dowry in order to retire where it suited her. The heirs could put many an obstacle in the way of an older widow, for she would find less support from her own kin than if they had decided to remarry her. Remarriage was an honorable objective—so honorable, in fact, that long delays in the restitution of the dowry were frowned upon. For this reason testators who left minor children and a young widow made every effort to stave off the danger by including many dissuasive stipulations. . . .

"Give a thought, reader," writes one hard-pressed guardian, "of the expenses that have fallen to me in order to satisfy the widows so that they will not abandon their children, especially Neri's widow, who was 25 years old." The remarriage of a widow cast the shadow of a second threat: the abandonment of the children. In fact, the children belonged to the lineage of their father. Thus, boys all their life and girls until their marriage resided with their agnatic kin. Statistics on households, like the daily events chronicled in family journals, show that children rarely stayed for long periods with their maternal kin. If the latter did take them in, they were paid for the children's keep, or they took on management of the children's estates, since children had no rights to goods that belonged to a lineage not their own. Children who followed their remarried mother were even rarer. The documentation shows that arrangements permitting a widow to establish the children of her first marriage (also with payment of their keep) under the roof of the second husband were usually provisional. Although the stepmother was a very familiar figure in Florentine households, the stepfather was practically unknown.

When a widow left a house in order to remarry, she left with her dowry but without her children. In 1427, many of the tax declarations deplore the abandonment of orphans whose mother had "left the family, taking away her dowry," leaving her husband's heirs in the charge of guardians and of paternal kin. The Florentine family journals, too, overflow in the fourteenth and fifteenth centuries with such situations, brutally initiated by the departure of a widow. The paternal kin had to take charge of orphans "of whom it can be said that they are orphaned on both the father's and the mother's side," one Florentine orphan reiterates, "since it can well be said of those who still have a mother that they have none, given the way she has treated them and abandoned them." Giovanni di Niccolaio Niccolini left four orphaned children in 1417, and his uncle Lapo notes bitterly that the widow "left the house [with her dowry of 900 *fiorini*] and left her children on the straw, with nothing." When Bartolo di Strozza Rucellai's mother remarried, he threw himself, with his brothers, on the mercy of the tax officials, declaring, "See what a state we are in, without a father and, one could also say, without a mother, having no one else on earth, abandoned by everyone."

Young widows would certainly have to have had singular tenacity and a good deal of courage to resist the contradictory pressures of their two families. . . . Often, widows really did want to remarry. Nevertheless, what contemporary reports emphasize above all is the irresolution of widows, and they leave an impression of widows' abject submission to the demands of their kin. Widows had few legal weapons, their whole upbringing had inculcated docility in them, and only in exceptional circumstances could they avoid remarriage if their relatives had decided in favor of it. The widow of Barna di Valorino Ciurianni, to the immense displeasure of her stepsons, "leaves the house with her dowry" the minute her husband was in the ground, probably with remarriage in mind, since she was young. In spite of her promises to Barna and the advantages assured her in his will, she left her twelve-year-old son in the charge of his half brothers.

Manno di Cambio Petrucci's narration, in 1430, of the days following the death of his father, who was carried off by the plague, offers a striking example of the anguish to which a widow could be subjected when her brothers wanted her to remarry. We see her here at the age of thirty-four torn between her aunt—probably sent by her family—and her children and stepchildren, who beg her to remain with them. "Madonna Simona," Manno, the eldest of her stepchildren implores her, "your own children are here. We will treat them as our brothers and you, Madonna Simona, as our mother. Alas! our mother, I beg of you and throw myself at your mercy, for you know our situation. Left without father or mother, if you do not come to our aid we will go headlong into ruin." The widow, however, bowed to her family's wishes: "I will do what my family decides," she says, and Manno adds, "for Madonna Pipa, her aunt, had done her job well overnight." It is a poignant tale, and one in which the children's dismay at the threat of being abandoned is expressed in protestations of respect and fidelity. The children avoid frankly broaching the question of what was most at stake in the conflict, however: the dowry that they might have to give back. Manno admits as much once the break was irreversible: "If Madonna Simona had agreed to remain with us, we would not have had to sell our things at half their price, wasting our substance so that we could give her back some of her dowry."

"GOOD MOTHERS" AND "CRUEL MOTHERS"

. . . The "cruel mother" was the woman who left her young children, but it was above all the mother who "left with her dowry." There is no better evidence of this than this same Giovanni Morelli, who lived a good part of his childhood and adolescence in his stepfather's house, brought up by the very mother whom he nevertheless accuses of having "abandoned" him. The abandonment was economic as much as affective, and what abandoned children complained of explicitly was the financial implications of their mother's remarriage. The mother who deserted the roof under which her children lived placed the interests of her own lineage and her own family above her children's interests, and that is why she was stigmatized. The clearest reproaches on the part of children or children's guardians rarely dwell on anything other than this consequence of remarriage.

The positive image, that of the "good mother," shows a contrario, the range of functions that the "cruel mother" who left to remarry failed to fulfill. There is truly no "good mother" who is not "both mother and father." This is the widow who refuses to remarry, no matter how young she might be, "in spite of the objurgations of her entire family," "so as not to abandon her children," "in order not to lead them to ruin," and who is both "a father and a mother for her children." Just like the father, she assured, by her stability, a transmission that was first and foremost a transmission of material goods, without which there was no family. "Remaining," "staying," "living with" her children, bequeathing them the wealth that was theirs—such was the primary paternal obligation in a system of residence and transmission of patrimony organized by patrilineal filiation. The virtues of an exceptional mother are from this point of view all manly virtues.

The widow qualified as a "good mother" was also one who devoted herself to the upbringing of her children with firmness and discipline. Perhaps she could not compete with the father on the terrain of pedagogy. She could not offer a boy all the models of behavior that a father offered his sons, and her inexperience in public and political life constituted a vexing handicap. Her culture was often limited, and worse yet, she was unable to transmit to her sons the values and the spiritual heritage of the lineage, to talk to them of "what happened to their ancestors and of their actions, of those from whom they had received gifts and services and those by whom they had been badly used, of who was their friend in need and, conversely, the vendettas they had engaged in and of recompenses given to those to whom they were obliged." A uniquely maternal upbringing had lacunae and was necessarily incomplete. Nevertheless, if undertaken with constancy and rigor, it could be comparable to the education administered by a father. When widowhood precluded other choices, the "good mother" was an acceptable substitute for the father. The "love" she bore her orphaned children took its full value from its masculine connotations.

Conversely, the bad mother, the "cruel mother," violated the values and the interests of her children's lineage when she showed too much docility toward her family of birth. In this she demonstrated the traditional vices of woman in exaggerated form. "Inconstant," "light," "flighty," she swings from one family to the other, she "forgets" her children and the husband she has just buried to seek pleasure in the bed of a second husband; she shifts shamelessly between the rigid structures of the contending masculine lineages. There is no doubt that the growing misogyny and mistrust of women at the dawn of the Renaissance were reinforced by structural contradictions that made it difficult to combine dotal system with patrilinearity. Among jurists, moralists, and those who reflected on the family, stereotypes presented woman as avid and capricious, eager to appropriate male inheritances for herself or other women, without pity for her children, whom she abandoned the moment she was widowed; a creature inconstant in her family loyalties, of immoderate attachments and inordinate sexuality, insatiable, and a menace to the peace and honor of families. In short, a creature intent on destroying the "houses" that men had constructed. . . .

Few contemporaries grasped the reasons for these tensions and tried to look beyond their lineage-inspired and antifeminist prejudices. One, however, puts a fine defense of remarried widows into the mouth of a young Florentine. In the *Paradiso degli Alberti*, written around 1425 by Giovanni Gherardi of Prato, a courtly discussion arises among a group of people of polite society. The problem posed is whether paternal love or maternal love is the better. One young man argues heatedly that mothers are not worth much since, contrary to fathers, they abandon their children. In any event, as they are inferior beings, their love could not possibly be as "perfect" as that of men. One young woman "of great wit and of most noble manners" is then charged by the women to respond to him. She cleverly turns his arguments against him by placing herself in his logic: since women are less "perfect" than men, they must obey men and follow them; and "since [women] cannot take their children, nor keep them with them, and they cannot remain alone without harm, especially if they are young, nor remain without masculine protection, it is almost perforce that mothers see themselves constrained to choose the best compromise. But it is not to be doubted that they think constantly of their children and remain strongly attached to them in spite of this separation."

In this demonstration the young woman throws back to her male interlocutor the very contradictions in which he—along with the whole society of his time—let himself be trapped. For how could the "honor" and the "status" of a lineage be increased by taking back a woman and her dowry in order to give them elsewhere, without offending the honor and the standing of the family to which she had given children? How could such a family reassert its rights over the person and the wealth of a woman without depriving another family of those rights? How could the separation of mother and child be avoided when the mother's identity was always borrowed and the child could belong only to his paternal kin? How could a woman be reproached for her docility before men when society denied her economic and legal autonomy?

But the young woman's words go farther. When she evokes the mother's attachment to her children—an attachment that the males of her time either failed to express, rejected, or sublimated into "paternal love," according to whether they stood on one side or the other of the dowry fence—our clever Florentine exposes the mechanisms by which a society that manipulated woman and the wealth attached to her attempted to prove its own innocence by reinforcing the image of the insensitive and destructive female.

Wives and Husbands in Late Medieval Venice

STANLEY CHOJNACKI

In December 1445 Valerio Zeno and Vittoria Vitturi, a Venetian patrician husband and wife, summoned a notary to draw up their wills. In his will, written December 2, Valerio designated Vittoria as his sole executor and, acknowledging his obligation to return her dowry of twenty-four hundred ducats to her, instructed that she was to inherit all his other goods as well, whether she remarried or not. He made a point of underscoring this intention, anticipating "impediments or opposition" to Vittoria's inheritance from his agnatic kinsmen, who would be reluctant to see his property escape them, especially if Vittoria should remarry (as, in the event, she did, twice). Still, that he favored his wife over kin did not signal alienation from his lineage, for he asked to be buried "in our tomb of Ca' Zeno at SS. Giovanni e Paolo." In her will nineteen days later, Vittoria reciprocated by making Valerio her sole executor and universal heir [the heir to the estate after all specific bequests have been fulfilled]—except for one other bequest, a four-hundred-ducat dowry contribution to a daughter of Valerio's late brother, Basilio Zeno. This generous bequest surprisingly shows Vittoria more beneficent toward her husband's kin than he himself was and indeed more than she was to her own natal family, which then included one brother

From Stanley Chojnacki, "The Power of Love: Wives and Husbands in Late Medieval Venice," from *Women and Power in the Middle Ages*, ed. Mary Erler and Maryanne Kowaleski, pp. 126–140. Copyright © 1988 The University of Georgia Press. Reprinted by permission of the publisher.

with a son just entering adulthood. Yet although like Valerio she favored her spouse over her kinsmen in tangible bequests, also like him she wanted to be buried "in the tomb where my father, *Dominus* Andrea [Vitturi], and my mother are buried."

The wills of Valerio and Vittoria Zeno, fairly typical examples of the genre, expose the rich complexity of social relations among married patricians in late medieval Venice. They show married people's enduring loyalty to family and lineage of origin, expressed here in the symbolically weighty choice of burial sites, but they also show deep trust and generosity between husband and wife. Such strong bonds between spouses had the potential to subvert other, older loyalties, notably those to the natal clan. The Zeno wills, and others like them, however, reveal that married patricians did not always face a sharp either/or choice between natal and marital family. Rather, they inhabited a dense interwoven thicket of social and psychological relationships, through which they navigated in a variety of ways, limited by the constraints of individual circumstance but also following the urgings of individual desires. Family and lineage ties were important, as was calculation of personal interest, but affection also figured in married people's choices in bestowing loyalty and largesse. In the following pages I make an initial foray into the uncharted realm of affection between spouses, with special concern for its place in patricians' overall social orientation. I pay particular attention to husbands' regard for their wives, for there are signs that husbandly affection deepened in the fifteenth century. This development appears to have been influenced by an increase in the status and power of women in patrician society. At the same time, it contributed toward expanding still further women's influence—economic, social, and cultural.

On the whole, the literature on marriage among the late medieval and Renaissance Italian elites has tended to emphasize, properly and profitably, its alliance aspect, viewing marriage as an instrument of family and lineage strategy, a means of promoting the family's status and advancing its interests. . . . Such family-centered concerns were manifestly important, but emphasis on alliances can give the impression that marriage had little to do with the personalities or even identities of the spouses, who figure in this picture chiefly as instruments of family interest, especially the teenaged brides (grooms, in contrast, often took part in marriage negotiation). When we stress alliances, too, we take a perspective that shows all parties—contracting families, spouses, even children—operating chiefly, if not solely, from calculated interest.

Although marriage was an important vehicle of patricians' family and individual interest, attention to alliances did not necessarily preclude intense relations between spouses. Indeed, it would be surprising if close bonds did not often develop. As instruments of family strategy, spouses might be drawn to each other by mutual sympathy. For that matter, family strategy encouraged good relations between the two joined links as a guarantee of the alliance's enduring success. Over the course of years and decades of proximity and intimacy, during which the contours of their families were constantly being reshaped and their shared experiences accumulating in scope and complexity, husbands and wives could develop feelings of companionship, loyalty, and affection for one another. A full picture of marriage must consequently consider husband-wife relations over time. The interfamilial dimension is important, but so are the years after the bride and groom were thrown willy-nilly into connubial bliss by the interests of their families, the long postnuptial period when spouses had the opportunity to forge a relationship of their own.

Special attention should be given the experience of wives over the uxorial cycle, the long evolution that saw them change, in many cases, from terror-stricken child brides into mature wives and mothers and finally into widows who often commanded formidable resources. Because each of these phases has its own dense and busy reality, distinct from those of other phases, no one moment in the wifely experience captures its essence. Nor can a "typical" wife be found. Different women went through the uxorial cycle in different ways. Some had many children, some had few or none. Some kept close ties to their natal families; others forged warm affinal associations. Some built relationships of loyal tenderness with their husbands; others suffered through marriages marked by strain and alienation. Some predeceased their husbands; others lived into long widowhoods and, like Vittoria Vitturi Zeno, contracted second and even third marriages.

Sparse documentation makes it difficult to reconstruct married persons' concerns and sentiments in detail, but one type of source offers abundant insights into the attitudes of patricians at moments of social and economic assessment. The source is wills. Wills, or testaments, allow us to observe women, and men as well, confronting the last things, taking careful stock of the contents of their lives, and expressing their ultimate preferences and hopes. Because the concerns of Venetian testators emerge with remarkable clarity from the thick undergrowth of formulas that often mark wills, these documents are a rich mine of information about husbands' and wives' opinions of each other. Accordingly, the principal documentation in this essay is a group of 361 wills drawn up between 1290 and 1520 by patricians with living spouses.

Fourteenth- and fifteenth-century wills reflect changing attitudes during the period. We must be wary of assigning neat dates or precise causes to attitudes and especially of devising too clear-cut a chronology of sentiment. Whether historical conditions trigger new kinds of emotional relationships among people is a hugely delicate and complex question and a controversial one. Nevertheless, evidence is strong that the fifteenth century saw the emergence among Venetian patricians of a higher regard for women and a deepening of husband-wife affection. These tendencies appear tied to certain general developments in patrician marriage during the period.

In his will, Valerio Zeno acknowledged the large dowry of 2,400 ducats that his wife Vittoria had brought to their marriage. He declared that half of it had come in the form of real estate which he treated as his own while he was alive but which should be returned to her at his death. Vittoria's family, the Vitturis, had thus considered her marriage to Valerio worth a substantial investment of movable and immovable Vitturi wealth. As Vittoria's will showed, such marriage portions could take permanent flight from the wife's lineage. Had Valerio outlived his wife, her bequest to him would have given him the real estate her family had put into her dowry. The construction of patrician marriages on big and growing dowries is a phenomenon that Venice shared with other Italian cities during this period. One of the strongest reasons for it in Venice was the growing importance of marriage in patrician family strategy and a consequent willingness to invest heavily in it. This emphasis on marriage increased women's influence in patrician society by increasing their wealth. This is a vast, many-sided question, but the main points can be stated briefly.

Contributing strongly to women's enhanced power in patrician society were major changes in the nature of the patriciate during the decades around 1400. Briefly, members of the class became at this time more dependent on government support for their economic well-being and more jealous of their status and the prestige and privileges it brought them. The two tendencies led to the erection in the early fifteenth century of a barricade of exclusivist legislation around the ruling class. The officially enforced patrician self-consciousness set a higher premium on the choice of marriage partners, specifically on the prestige and influence of brides' and grooms' families. Already in the early fifteenth century, Venetian legislators were raising the status requirements for patrician wives, and the patrician humanist Francesco Barbaro was attaching at least as much importance to a mother's birth as to that of a father in the breeding of worthy patricians. In these circumstances, matchmaking was a serious business indeed.

The currency of matchmaking was dowries, which climbed steadily throughout the period, as families invested ever larger portions of their substance in marriages that brought prestige and cemented valued friendships. So important to family strategy were advantageous marriages that in the fifteenth century girls' dowries sometimes outstripped their brothers' patrimonies—something occasionally noted by will-writing parents, such as the father who excluded his married daughter because she had already received "much more than all her brothers will get." By the sixteenth century the impact of the dowry on male-female relations had reached such a point that legislators were blaming Venice's declining commercial enterprise on the tendency of husbands to live off their wives' dowries.

Still, for all the dowry's importance as a tool of family strategy, in the end it belonged to the daughter whom it accompanied to marriage. It was in fact her "patrimonium," to be returned to her or transferred to her chosen heirs at the end of the marriage. For this reason a testating father would bid his married daughters to "be well content with their dowries and have no reason for complaint" when they were denied further bequests. Yet although some fathers (and mothers) were concerned about the deep bite that dowries were taking out of family wealth, others compounded the effect by leaving additional bequests to their already dowered daughters. These contrasting attitudes alert us to the variety of patrician family situations and the broad range of personal choice open to individuals. They also signal that fathers benefited their daughters in a number of ways over and above dowry provision—benefits that added further to women's disposable wealth. This wealth, rising pari passu with dowry levels, gave married women formidable new power in their social relations. For one thing, they were now in a position to help their own daughters meet the rising dowry standards—in the process contributing to their further rise. They could extend their largesse to others as well, however. The result of the swelling of married women's actual and potential benefactions was to exalt their importance and influence within their social worlds. A wife's or widow's family and kin had compelling practical reason[s] to keep in her good graces by showing her every affectionate consideration.

These circumstances magnified the influence of married women on those near them, notably their husbands. The material expression of a wife's regard could now literally change her husband's life—as no doubt Valerio Zeno's life would have changed if, instead of bequeathing him her twenty-four-hundred-ducat dowry, his wife, Vittoria, had exercised her legal right to have him restore it to her estate, for the benefit of other kin. Some wives followed Vittoria in selecting their husbands as prime beneficiary. Others made different choices, however, and favored natal kin, so that they returned the dowry to the family from which it had come in the first place. It was the capacity to dispose of their wealth as they liked—on the basis of calculation but also of inclination—as much as the wealth itself, that gave married women their potent new presence in patrician society. A constellation of potential beneficiaries, most prominent among them fathers hoping that their daughters would return at least some of the dowry wealth to their natal families and husbands desirous of lodging it permanently in their own family, was anxious to earn the favor of these increasingly rich benefactresses. The parental bequests to already married daughters, mentioned above, were probably stimulated at least in part by the desire to retain the daughters' continued benevolence and the economic generosity in which it might find expression.

The heightened importance of women affected men in a variety of ways. One was in their attitude toward women's fashions in clothing. This complex subject, on which I can touch only glancingly here, involves important aspects not only of women's economic autonomy but also of individual psychology and the relations between private and collective interests as well. Female fashion, like male fashion, grew increasingly splendid in the fifteenth century and elicited ambivalent responses. Public concern centered on costly attire that proponents of sumptuary legislation saw as unproductive waste, an attitude fully displayed in the preambles to the sumptuary laws that increased in the fifteenth century. These express endless agonizing over women's "excessive expenditures on wicked and impractical [inutilem]" apparel that "consumes their husbands and sons" or, again, leads to the "ruin of their husbands and fathers." Many individual men shared this concern, their votes passing the laws, but others took pride in their handsomely decked-out womenfolk, even encouraging their expenditures. In the sixteenth century, we are informed, family and friends saw brides-to-be display their elaborate trousseaux at betrothal parties, and husbands themselves engaged tailors and mercers to clothe their brides in up-to-date splendor.

Yet the wearing of sumptuous clothing may also have been a way for women with wealth but few opportunities for productive economic (let alone political) outlets to make a gesture of self-assertion. In a culture which narrowly limited women's activities in the public sphere, heavy spending on lavish dress could be viewed as doubly assertive, calling visual attention to individual identity and demonstrating the autonomous possession of wealth. That it might be detrimental to men may have been incidental—or for some it may have been a gesture, with available means, protesting institutional or individual male domination. The significance of female fashion in male-dominated societies is a rich subject, with the erotic as well as the sumptuous aspects touching relations between men and women at several different levels. Whether women wore splendid attire to attract or to challenge men (or without regard to men at all), whether men took pride in their wives' appearance or were sexually or economically threatened by its public display, whether expenditures on dress were regarded as wasteful or as investments in status—these questions deserve extended consideration. Although the answers are incomplete at present, the Venetian legislation makes it clear that women were spending money on fashion, that men were thought to be suffering as a result, and that neither government nor private male society was able to curb these expenditures.

Women's wealth and their autonomy in using it—even in ways that were potentially harmful for men—made women formidable figures. This power inspired a complex variety of responses. Here we venture into psychological waters ill charted in the sources and the literature. The first fruits of research, however, strongly suggest that the increase in married women's wealth led the menfolk to take their mates more seriously and to court their favor more assiduously. This development in turn seems to have produced a deeper bond between spouses, with implications for the whole patrician culture and specifically for the articulation of both male and female gender identity.

The new regard that women gained found varied expression. One form was an increased tendency in the fifteenth century for husbands to name their wives as executors (*commissari*) of their wills. . . .

Practically speaking, these appointments made good sense in the fifteenth century. Well-dowered wives would acquire substantial personal wealth upon becoming widows; as noted, many also had other wealth, from legacies not encumbered with dowry restrictions, to enjoy during their marriage. The practical skills or expert help they used managing their own resources might fruitfully be applied to the benefit of their husbands' estates and especially to that of their common offspring. A family-conscious patrician had every reason to deepen his widow's involvement—and possibly that of her wealth and her brothers—in his sons' grooming for adulthood. To be sure, in entrusting his estate to his wife, a husband effectively removed it from the control of his agnatic kin. The short-term alienation, however, could be counterbalanced by the lineage's potential longer-term benefit from his sons' improved chances for a generous inheritance from their mother and also for the support of her natal familiars, especially the sons' maternal uncles. At any rate, a husband entrusting his estate to his wife's care was likely to be pretty sure of her benevolence toward their children and even (as with Valerio Zeno) toward his other kinsmen. Yet apart from these hardheaded reasons, that husbands placed their wealth in the care of their wives, alone or with others, signifies trust and a sense of shared interest, impulses that marital intimacy could easily blend into strong emotional attachment.

Another sign of men's personal regard for women can be found in fathers' attitudes toward their daughters' vocational preferences. We must tread cautiously here. Family interest weighed heavily on fathers, and marriage was one of the chief weapons in the arsenal of family strategy. An attractive, intelligent daughter and adequate dowry resources added up to a combination of family-enhancing assets a father would only reluctantly avoid using. Alternatively, scant dowry capital might make the convent unavoidable for the daughter. It was a rare father who would or could go against the perceived family interest to satisfy a daughter's choice of adult life. And indeed, most testating fathers left instructions about their daughters' futures with no regard for the girls' thoughts on the matter; the governing principle apparently was that as many daughters should marry as family resources permitted. Yet despite the powerful imperative of family economic and social needs and interests, we do find the occasional father giving weight in his will to his daughters' "intentions" or "desires" when providing for them. Such cases appear more frequently in the fifteenth century than in the fourteenth. . . .

. . . In the context of the present discussion, it is important to note that fathers' new solicitude for their daughters' preferences may have been encouraged by the example of their wives, who when writing their wills appear even more inclined to offer their daughters the choice between the convent and marriage. Indeed, an emerging maternal tendency to allow daughters complete freedom of vocational choice, including even lay spinsterhood, represented a challenge to traditional male conceptions of family honor, seen as threatened by unmarried daughters' exposure to secular temptation. I have seen no evidence that husbands permitted women to choose a single life, but the willingness of even a few of them to entertain their daughters' preferences in a choice between marriage and the convent may indicate that the increased importance that wives were gaining from their wealth was spilling over into influence on their husbands' cultural attitudes as well as on family strategy.

The more influential presence of women in the patrician family seems to have stimulated not only men's regard and solicitude but their affection as well. Affection arises from many things, and it would be simplistic to attribute it to the wealth or power of the loved one, even more so to assume that Venetian spouses had not loved one another before the rise in dowries. Nevertheless, men in fifteenth-century Venice were more eloquent than their grandfathers in expressing their affection for the women in their lives. Nowhere is the change more apparent than in the language of wills, in which terms of endearment became steadily more frequent and more elaborate during the fifteenth century. . . .

The new articulateness in affection did not belong only to husbands and wives but extended to other relations as well. We find in the Quattrocento, for example, a daughter called "dilectissima et dulcissima [most delightful and sweetest]," a son "mio fio dilectissimo [my most beloved son]" a "carissimum [dearest]" brother, and even—tellingly—"dilectissmos [most beloved]" brothers-in-law. Still, men had applied similar (though less effusive) terms to natal kinsmen in the previous century, too. The big change was their new application to wives. The new language of husbandly love is remarkable not just because of its warmth but because of its flexible variety, its individuality. Testators chose the exact terms they wanted, supplying their own nuances; superlatives, for example, seem to have been chosen expressly to convey an exceptionally close bond. Sometimes husbands used different terms in different passages of a single will, showing that each instance was an act of personal choice. The contrast with the narrow vocabulary and perfunctoriness of such usage in fourteenth-century wills could not be sharper.

The change owes much to increased literacy and verbal confidence, evident in the greater incidence of wills written not by notaries but by the testators themselves, in the vernacular—although Latin wills from the late Quattrocento also contain far more terms of affection than Latin wills of a century earlier. Especially noteworthy (and worthy of more systematic investigation) is the notion that women as well as men drafted their wills by hand more frequently in the fifteenth century than they had earlier. The personal language in these handwritten wills gives even more weight to their expressions of affection as well as showing women's increased control of language as a means of asserting themselves. While this new expressiveness in conveying marital affection suggests development in literacy and linguistic facility, however, it also shows that new feelings were stimulating a new articulateness. The language of affection was so widespread in wills of the later Quattrocento that it appears to have become a convention, raising the question of whether its use is a valid gauge of individual feeling behind the words—although even its adoption as a cultural convention would suggest that affection between spouses was becoming normative. There is also evidence, however, that the affectionate expressions in fifteenth-century wills were not empty formulas.

The wills reveal still more about sentiment in the testators' descriptions of the relationships that they reward or ignore in their bequests. It is telling, for example, to read a man's instruction that his wife and children not come to his funeral "to avoid compounding their pain" at losing him. However much pain his death actually did cause them, such bereavement at least seemed to him likely or at least natural, and his instruction a touching last thoughtful gesture to his loved ones. Another testating husband declared that he wanted his wife to be aware of "the love I have always borne her." Disarmingly candid was Jacopo Morosini, who in 1448 praised "Cristina, *mia molier charissma* [my dearest wife], to whom I am altogether too obliged, for her admirable conduct, and also for all the cash—over and above her dowry—that I have received from her family." In gratitude he made her his universal heir. Such expressions of sentiment, rarely found in fourteenth-century wills, crop up regularly in the fifteenth, displaying a greater male concern with the feelings of wives and children and more openness about sentiment in general. . . .

The complexity and implications of husbands' affection are even more apparent in their bequests to their wives. Again, variety is the rule. Some husbands bequeathed nothing, some just their wife's dowry—although that was not really a bequest at all, for a widow's legal right to her dowry did not depend on any action by her husband. Indeed, her entitlement to its restitution was so strong that it took precedence over all other claims on her husband's estate. Nevertheless, a husband's acknowledgment of the dowry in his will helped his widow by supplying quick and sure documentation for the *vadimonium*, the legal action by which a widow (or her successors) established the fact and amount of her dowry, thus taking the indispensable first step toward the *diiudicatum*, or dowry-recovery procedure. Men, however, characteristically went beyond the dowry in providing for their wives, adding a few hundred ducats, a life annuity, very frequently food and lodging, and sometimes, like Valerio Zeno or Jacopo Morosini, the entire estate. To be sure, motives of interest were not absent from these husbandly bequests. Generous bequests to wives, like their selection as testamentary executors, could stimulate wifely reciprocity, to the benefit of the husband's family and lineage. Moreover, husbands normally made bequests to their wives conditional on the latters' willingness to renounce remarriage and stay with the children. Will-writing husbands were considerate of their wives, but they also thought hard about their children's reduced prospects of inheritance from a remarried mother.

Yet tender feelings are unmistakably evident in husbands' bequests. Even child-less husbands sometimes offered economic inducements for their widows to forgo remarriage; Donato Arimondo did so, and so did his uncle, Marino. Marino, who was very generous to his wife as long as she remained a widow, instructed his kinsmen to treat her "as if she were my own self." Disturbed at the prospect that their wives might desert their memories for other husbands, these men made it worth the wives' while to preserve in death the lifelong marital bond, in Marino's case forged forty-five years earlier, in Donato's, thirty-seven. Yet others, including Valerio Zeno, be-nevolently encouraged, or at least accepted, their wives' remarriage, explicitly grant-ing the wives benefits whether they married again or not. All these gestures show husbands committed to caring for their companions of many years. The variety in their approaches, however—acknowledging the dowry or not, making outright be-quests or not, encouraging widowly celibacy or cheerfully contemplating their wives' remarriage—shows men acting individually, tailoring their bequests to the distinc-tive qualities of their personal marital relationships. This male behavior can be seen as one of the transforming cultural effects of women's changed place in patrician society. Men did not abandon lineage loyalty in their affection for their wives; on the contrary, one form taken by husbandly love was the association of their wives with the lineage, its fortunes, and its symbols. Indeed, for success, marriage strategies, on which families staked large chunks of their resources, hoping for benefits from mat-rimonial alliances, required at least tolerable relations between spouses. Neverthe-less, the testimony of fifteenth-century patrician wills reveals a new element in men's social orientation, rooted in a new respect and affection for their wives, that was now taking an influential place alongside lineage loyalties. . . .

Yet calculations of interest, personal and lineage, alone did not determine these men's choices. The new husbandly attitude is also evident in terms of changed emo-tional relations between the sexes. Indeed, the validation that women's wealth gave to the sentimental ties that connected men to them—validation from the material standpoint of the lineage—enabled men to complement the lineage-based discipline that had traditionally dictated their social behavior with more personal kinds of loy-alty. Thanks to the enhanced importance of marriage in patrician society and the increased stature it gave to well-dowered women, husbands could more closely ap-proach the freer, less circumscribed, less lineage-determined orientation of women, in which individual responses to the contingencies of personal relationships, re-sponses such as gratitude, respect, and affection, were allowed wider scope. Men could respond more fully, more reciprocally, to their wives' personal gestures and in their wills appear to have been more inclined to do so. Maddaluzza da Canal made her husband her universal heir, in the event of childlessness, as a reward for his "ex-cellent companionship." Maddaluzza had her dowry and no particular economic ax to grind; she simply wanted to show her pleasure in her husband's company. The same kindly affection probably led Lucrezia Priuli in 1503 to bequeath her husband Sebastiano a dwelling and one thousand ducats in state securities, along with in-structions that, as with Valerio Zeno's strictures about his wife Vittoria's legacy, Sebastiano was not to be subjected to "any molestation" in enjoying his legacy from her.

When well-dowered wives voluntarily bestowed their affection in these ways, their husbands were now able and willing to respond in kind. Marco Loredan, for example, in 1441 admonished his kin not to be surprised that he was making his wife his sole executor and universal heir, for he was obliged to her more than to "any [other] creature in the world" for her ministrations, costly to her own health, during his protracted illness—ministrations that he likened more to the labors of a slave than to the attentions of a wife. Less touching but still full of tender gratitude is the statement of another Loredan, Francesco, who after allocating his wife's dowry repayment, regretted that "I lack the capital to give her what she merits for all her benefits to me." These cases and others like them illustrate how, gradually and always within the limits of family and lineage obligations, men, under the influence of their wives, were now enriching their social culture with a new responsiveness in word and deed to the claims of emotion.

The change in women's wealth and influence thus had a larger significance apart from the fact that men were more respectful and solicitous, and more affectionate and generous, toward women. Women, with their economic weight and their traditionally less lineage-encumbered model of social relationships, were also providing a pattern for male culture and a stimulus toward modifying it and making it more flexible. Women's gender identity was changing with the growth in the power and influence of the wifely state, but men's gender identity was being transformed, too, as male society's changing attitudes toward marriage and wives modified husbandhood. In apportioning bequests in response to personal as well as lineage urgings—in choosing interment with a wife rather than a father, in respecting the convent or marriage preferences of a "dulcissima e charissima" daughter, in thoughtfully apportioning bequests to brothers, nephews, sons, daughters, and also the "dilectissima consorte"—in carving out a structure of bequests that reflected the peculiarities of individual social geographies and the diverse loyalties they evoked, men were modifying their social personages under the influence of their formidable, substantial wives and in a manner more congruent with female patterns of social relations.

Three principal results of women's influence are apparent. One was to perpetuate and enlarge women's influence still further, as the men in their families courted them with ever larger bequests, gifts, and dowry settlements. This swelling of female wealth alarmed patrician legislators as a group, but individual patricians continued to find, in the importance of marriage in patrician relations, compelling reason to assemble large dowries for their daughters. Once under way, the transfer of family resources into female hands was carried along by its own momentum. The second result followed. With so much invested in marriages, patrician families sought to gain more from them. In consequence patterns of social relations altered throughout the patriciate. Lineage remained the principal framework of social orientation, but the desire to capitalize on the investment in marriage led to greater emphasis on affinal ties and the support and prestige they could offer. In this dense blending of kinship and marital association, the mediating role of propertied women, objects of both natal and marital kinsmen's interest, had large and growing significance.

Third and most important, women's large and growing share of patrician wealth and the influence it brought could find expression in an approach to social relations less restricted by lineage obligations than that of men. It is ironic that the heavily patriarchal structure of Venetian lineage patterns made women freer of enforceable lineage discipline. A man was bound to his lineage by an array of legal constraints and economic inducements. A woman, at least a married woman, shared in two lineages and thus was bound tightly to neither except by moral ties which themselves pulled in two directions. In this freer female social space, personal loyalties and sentiments and tangible expressions of them took their place alongside the defined patterns of lineage loyalty and the more adjustable but no less strategically rooted expectations of marriage alliances. Women were the chief proponents of this more individualized approach to social relations, but their impact, on patrician society generally and especially on their own husbands, stimulated a response in kind.

Husbands were obliged, by self-interest and lineage interest—and specifically by the centrality in family strategy of favorable marriage alliances—to pay more attention to their well-dowered wives (and daughters). To do so they had to devote greater efforts to gaining and keeping the women's tangible favor. Women's favor, however, owing to their position outside the strict confines of kinship discipline, responded more to personal loyalties than to family or lineage loyalties and thus had to be earned in personal ways, so that men had a powerful inducement to adapt their male culture to the affective culture of women. This tendency, offered here only as a hypothesis, needs further study, as do a host of related questions—such as the coincidence of increased women's wealth and a rising marriage age, the patriciate's remarkable sociability in the sixteenth century, and the frank sensuality of Venetian art and social behavior in that century. Even at this early point, however, there is reason to believe that changes in the relations between the sexes, in the function and nature of marriage, and, fundamentally, in the status and influence of women had a powerful transforming effect on the culture of Renaissance Venice.

DOCUMENTS

Wills and dowry agreements are two of the richest sources for the study of gender in the Renaissance. The last will and testament of Fina Buzzacarini, the wife of the Francesco il Vecchio da Carrara, the Lord of Padua, was dictated on her deathbed in 1378. Fina was an extremely wealthy woman who had inherited property from her father's family. Her chief interests centered on artistic patronage of churches and convents, providing dowries for the young ladies-in-waiting as her miniature court and for the young women of her rural villages, and ensuring that her three daughters received inheritances equal to their station as consorts of dukes and counts in central Europe. Her wishes at her death reflected the concerns of her life: religious benefaction, the welfare of offspring and friends, and the prosperity of her villagers and servants. The second document, a dowry agreement from fifteenth-century Verona, was drawn up in the presence of a notary, several witnesses, the betrothed couple, and their male kin. In formal legal language, it describes the property transaction itself, which is made between the bridegroom and his father and the bride's father and then records the simple exchange of vows and rings between the bride and groom. As was customary, a priest did not officiate at the transfer of the dowry. Elaborate wedding festivities would have followed in the homes of both the bride and groom. The third document is a short story from Giovan Francesco Straparola's *Entertaining Nights*, a popular collection of tales first published in 1550. Straparola created a literary frame for his collection by saying that the stories were recently told over the course of thirteen nights by a group of noble men and women gathered in a Venetian palace. Filled with telling contemporary detail, this story of the lovers Nerino and Genobbia plays on themes of love and deceit, by both men and women, that were typical of Italian Renaissance short stories.

Last Will and Testament of Fina da Carrara, 1378

In the name of Christ, Amen. In the 1378th year of His Nativity, the first indiction, on Wednesday, the 22nd of September, at Padua in the palace-residence of the testatrix Fina written below in her grand chamber above the garden, that is, in the chamber called "Of the Four Virtues," in the presence of the following honorable and prudent men: Ser Francesco Turchetto, son of the late lord Antonio Turchetto, Paduan citizen residing in contrada Duomo, treasurer of the below-written magnificent lord; Jacopino, son of the late Niccolò Gafarello of contrada San Niccolò of Padua; Manfredino, son of the late lord Alberto Conti, factor of the aforesaid magnificent lord of Padua, citizen and resident of Padua in contrada Santa Cecilia; Ser Luca, son of the late Judge Pietro da Casale, citizen and resident of Padua in contrada San Leparenzi; Simeone, son of the late lord Pietropaolo degli Statuti, of contrada Stra Maggiore of Padua; Antonio, son of the late Ser Domenigino de Giuniciato of contrada San Niccolò of Padua; and Baldasera, son of the late Ser Giovanni da Monselice, of the aforesaid contrada San Niccolò—all witnesses called by the testatrix, along with others.

Because the condition of the present life has an unstable status and those which are now visible beings tend visibly to nonbeing, thus, each person ought to engage in beneficial meditation, so that on the last days of the pilgrimage of this life, he can come to make a testamentary disposition, because nothing in the present life is more certain than death, and nothing more uncertain than the hour of death. In recognition of this fact each mortal ought to be anxious in the disposition of his affairs, lest his affairs be overturned in a fleeting moment, because the greater is one's dignity, honor, and sublime status in this life, the more one must be aware of the deceits and sins of mortal men.

Therefore, the illustrious and magnificent Lady Fina da Carrara, consort of the magnificent and powerful Lord Francesco da Carrara, daughter of the late outstanding and respected knight, Lord Pataro Buzzacarini, of celebrated memory, honorable citizen of Padua, wishing, on prudent advice, to hasten to put an end to human perplexity and uncertainty by making a disposition of her property, and wanting to demonstrate at the end of her life, the wisdom that she had all through her life, and by the grace of God, sound in mind and of good memory, of unclouded intellect and of

From "Last Will of Fina da Carrara, née Buzzacarini, 1378," Archivio di Stato, Padua, Archivio notarile, reg. 35, fols. 95–98v, from B. G. Kohl ed. "Giusto de' Menabuoi e il mecenatismo artistico in Padova," in *Giusto de' Menabuoi nel battistero di Padova* (Trieste: LINT, 1990), pp. 24–26. Translated by Benjamin G. Kohl.

perfect disposition, though sick in body, fearing that she may die intestate and wishing to provide for the salvation of her own soul, now makes her testament orally and without writing in this fashion.

First of all, if it should happen that she were to depart from this world, she commends her own soul to her Creator, Almighty God, and for salvation in all His heavenly court.

Next she elects for the burial of her body the Major Church or Duomo of Padua, in the place called the Chapel of Saint John the Baptist, which today is called the Baptistery.

Item, she wants, orders, and bequeaths that in the aforesaid Chapel or Baptistery there is made for her body an honorable tomb according to her station, taking into consideration the status of the aforesaid magnificent Lord, and of her magnificent son, Francesco [Junior] da Carrara, with attention and respect [to the wishes of] the said testatrix.

Item, she wishes and bequeaths that the said Chapel of Saint John the Baptist or Baptistery by the aforesaid magnificent Lord, her consort, and by the executor written below from the property of the said magnificent Lady testatrix and according to her station, just as it will be pleasing and acceptable to the same magnificent lord, her executor named below.

Item, she wishes, orders, bequeaths, and ordains that for celebrating Masses and Divine Offices in the aforesaid Chapel her executor should appoint two priests, who, and likewise with their successors, should have forever and perpetually each year the income of the aforesaid endowment bestowed on this Chapel, so that these priests are held and ought to sing and say Masses and Prayers for the soul of the same magnificent Lady, the testatrix, and for her [soul] raise prayers to Jesus Christ on high. The same priests are also held and must in the . . . Chapel always and continually celebrate Masses and Divine Offices.

Item, she bequeaths to the aforesaid Chapel, solely for decorating and adorning the Chapel and the altars existing in it, all her silver and all her clothing which the said testatrix will have had in her possession at the time of her death.

Item, she bequeaths, wishes, orders, and ordains that the produce, rents, and income of all her possessions on Via Nuova in the suburbs of Padua should be allotted, placed, and distributed for the execution and in execution of the legacy bequeathed to her by the late noble and venerable man of blessed memory, Lord Salione Buzzacarini, her paternal uncle, in his last will and testament, just as it is plainly stated in the same testament. And because the income of the said possession amounts to more than the sum of the legacy of Lord Salione, the said testatrix wishes and orders that all that there is in excess of the aforesaid legacy should be distributed by her executor given below to fulfilling another legacy, that one which is especially appointed and established by her in that manner, namely, that the prior of the Dominicans of Padua, whoever he now is and will be in the future, will be her executor on the matter, that will become clear below, and should have every year for the remunerations of his labors £8. Indeed all above this should be divided every year, forever and in perpetuity, between two nuns of the convent of San Benedetto of Padua, whoever they are now and will be, so that each of these [nuns] every year is held and ought to say a [complete] Psalter for the soul of the said testatrix. And to ensure the execution of this legacy she precisely and specifically appoints, requires, and wishes the religious and venerable Lady Abbess of San Benedetto of Padua, whoever she now is and in the future will be, and the religious man, Lord Prior of the convent of Sant'Agostino of the Dominicans of Padua, whoever he now is and in the future will be. Moreover, the magnificent Lady testatrix wants and orders that if the income of her said possession on Via Nuova, because of bad weather or any other misfortune, should not suffice in any year for the execution of the legacy of the said Lord Salione, then and in that case, she orders that her said executors should pay for the execution of the legacy of said Lord Salione from other properties of the said Lady testatrix, burdening her [principal] heir given below, so that her aforesaid executors ought and must give and transfer from other goods of the inheritance of the said testatrix whatever and all that is required for the complete payment of the said legacy [of uncle Salione].

Item, she bequeaths to [unnamed] wife of the nobleman Ubertino Arsendi 400 golden ducats for her dowry, for her own soul.

Item, she bequeaths to [unnamed] minor daughter of Pietro Capodivacca £1,000 for her dowry, for her own soul.

Item, she bequeaths to Caterina, daughter of Gerardo Tergola, £1,000 for her dowry and a robe from the said testatrix, for her own soul.

Item, she bequeaths to Anastasia, daughter of Ser Lucchese of Pisa, for her dowry £600 and the clothes she has on her back and other clothes that Anastasia has for her use.

Item, she bequeaths to Margherita, granddaughter of the late Paolo Dotti and the daughter of Antonio da Giudecca, £1,000 for her dowry, and all her goods that Margherita now has in her possession, and when the marriage takes place she should have a dress or robe, for her own soul.

Item, she bequeaths to Caterina, daughter of the late Marchiano Festucci, £600 for her dowry as well as the goods she had been given for her use, for her own soul.

Item, she bequeaths to Caterina Zabarella, a house [in place unnamed] which yields a certain rent, and £200 in addition to the aforesaid house, and also robes, belts, and clothing that she had been given for her use, for her own soul.

Item, she bequeaths to Pulzeta £200 and her clothes, for the soul of the said testatrix.

Item, she bequeaths to two nuns of the Costabile family, one in the convent of San Benedetto in Padua, the other in the convent of Sant' Agata in Padua, £200 for each of them, for her own soul.

Item, she bequeaths to Domenico, son of the late Jacopino, steward of her estate at Bellaguarda, £400 as a dowry for marrying his daughter, and this sum should not be included in the accounts of those properties that he oversees and manages in the aforesaid estate, nor can he be compelled or forced to render accounting for this [dowry], since she [Fina] acted well and legally, since it was for her own soul.

Item, she bequeaths to Antonio her steward for estate as Noventa £400 for marrying his daughters, for her own soul, and this sum should not be included in the accounts of the affairs and overseeing done by him in the said estate, nor can he be compelled or forced to render accounts for this sum, because she did rightly.

Item, she bequeaths to a chapel in the Church of San Benedetto of Padua, which is called San Lodovico, in its endowment, the incomes of the possession of the said testatrix located in the neighborhood of Santo Spirito of Padua, for her own soul.

Item, she bequeaths to the commune of Brugine £200 for the satisfaction of any unpaid debts she may have incurred there.

Item, she bequeaths to the commune of Arzercavalli £200 for the same reason.

Item, she bequeaths to the commune of Noventa £200 for the same reason.

Item, she bequeaths to Margherita da Carrara, who lives in the same home or court with the said testatrix, £100 and clothing, for her [Margherita's] soul.

Item, she bequeaths to Dorotea, daughter of the late Antonio Pavanello, £200 for her dowry, for her own soul.

Item, she bequeaths to Bartolomeo Celegino, son of the late Francesco Peruzzo, £400, for her own soul.

Item, she bequeaths for celebrating Masses and saying prayers for her own soul £1,000, to be distributed by her executor named below or on his orders, wherever he pleases and sees fit.

Item, she orders and wishes that this legacy above should be executed and fulfilled according to the income and with respect to the quantity of the income that her universal heir shall have and enjoy from the possessions and property inherited from the same testatrix.

Item, she bequeaths to the illustrious and lofty princess and lady Gigliola, Duchess of Saxony, and the magnificent and outstanding lady Caterina, Countess of Veglia, her daughters and the daughters of the aforesaid magnificent lord, her consort, Lord Francesco da Carrara, for use during their lifetime the house that the said testatrix inherited from the late aforesaid Lord Salione [Buzzacarini], with all its outbuildings and properties, located in Padua in contrada Sant'Urbano, which is bounded on two sides by a public street, on a third side by [the property of] the outstanding knight Arcoano Buzzacarini, and on a fourth side by the same Arcoano, and perhaps there are other truer boundaries. This [house is theirs] in the event that one or both of them should come to reside in Padua, should it happen, God forbid, that one or both of their consorts should die. And if one of the said daughters should die, the right of inheritance should fall on the other surviving [daughter], coming to reside in Padua. Indeed if both of the parties were to die, the legacy and all its rights ought freely to devolve upon her universal heir.

Item, the said magnificent Lady testatrix bequeaths to her aforesaid two daughters, Gigliola and Caterina, 6,000 gold ducats each, which, the same testatrix orders and wishes that immediately after her death, her universal heir ought to use to purchase two properties, each equivalent in value to 6,000 ducats, which ought to be appointed and assigned to these same daughters for their use. And the income, produce, and any rents from these properties ought, from the day of the death of the said testatrix, continually to be paid out for the use and benefit of the said ladies. The execution of this legacy falls upon her universal heir, and further the said magnificent Lady testatrix wants and orders that if one or the other of her daughters should die, without any surviving offspring, that the deceased daughter may bequeath as she wishes up to but no more than 3,000 ducats or its equivalent. But the other half should come to her universal heir. And if indeed at the time of the death of one or the other or both of her daughters, there are offspring, either sons or daughters, from the decedent, then the whole legacy ought to be paid to the sons or daughters of the deceased daughter or daughters. And in this matter she instructs and orders her [other] heirs to be quiet and content.

Item, she bequeaths to the magnificent Lady Lieta da Carrara, her daughter and the daughter of her husband, the aforementioned magnificent Lord Francesco da Carrara, her house with garden near San Michele of Padua and located in the contrada San Michele, which is half-timbered with a second story and covered with a tile roof, with all its outbuildings and properties, and which is bounded on the front by a public street, on the back by the public street of Borgo Paglia, on one side by the city walls, and on the other side, partly by the property of the Church of San Michele, partly by Matteo Conte of Bragaledo, partly by the weaver Jacopo da Montagnana, and partly by the mason Bartuccio, and perhaps there are other truer boundaries.

Item, she bequeaths to the said magnificent Lady Lieta, her daughter, 6,000 golden ducats which the same magnificent testatrix orders and wishes immediately after her death to be used to purchase possessions, equivalent in value to the sum of 6,000 ducats, appointing and assigning the same [properties] to her daughter Lieta for her use. And the execution of this legacy falls upon her universal heir. The same magnificent Lady testatrix wants and orders that if the same magnificent Lady Lieta, her daughter, should die without offspring, she may bequeath, from this present legacy, to whomever she wishes up to but not more than 3,000 ducats. And the other half indeed should devolve upon her universal heir. If indeed at the time of the death of the same magnificent Lady Lieta, there exist from her either male or female offspring, this same legacy ought freely to come to these children. And in this matter, she orders and instructs her [other] heirs to be quiet and content.

Item, she wishes and orders that from the property of the said testatrix her universal heir ought to pay out and bestow the following gifts in this manner: Caterina, nurse of the aforesaid magnificent Lady Lieta, and Fontana, Margherita, and Pasqua [her servants] should have the clothes on their backs and all that they need for food and lodging as long as they shall live.

Item, she bequeaths to the outstanding knight, Arcoano Buzzacarini, her brother, the large house where the noble knight Lord Boscarino Buzzacarini resides, and two other little houses covered with tile roofs, which pertain to the large house, bordering the same large house on the street from the angle of the said large house, abuts the church of Sant' Urbano, with all their outbuildings and properties. Now this large house is surrounded by walls, with a second story and tile roof, with court and well and with two wooden sheds with tile roofs, located in Padua in contrada Parenzi or Sant' Urbano, and is bounded on two sides by a public street, on another side by said Lord Arcoano, and another side by said magnificent Lady testatrix, and is also bounded by the said Lord Arcoano, by the property of San Lazzaro and that of the Dominicans of Padua, and perhaps there are other truer boundaries.

Item, she bequeaths to the church of San Michele of Padua annually in perpetuity £60 that the same testatrix orders [the church] ought to have as income from the rental of certain properties located near her house at San Michele, so that the priest of San Michele, whoever he now is and will be in the future, is required to say prayers and celebrate Masses and to pray to God for her own soul.

Item, she bequeaths for any unknown misdeeds, if indeed she ever committed such, £1,000, which the said testatrix wants to be used and distributed as a dowry for marrying a [certain] daughter of the nobleman Giovanni da Monfumo. And if that daughter should die before she is married, then the said sum should devolve on another daughter of the said Giovanni for her dowry. If indeed both of them were to die unmarried, that the said £1,000 should be given as part of the dowry from another impoverished noble lady-in-waiting, for her own soul. The said testatrix wants and orders that the said £1,000 can and must, in no way, come into the hands of the Lord Bishop of Padua.

Finally, all other real estate and movable property and all rights and actions whatsoever belonging and pertaining to the said testatrix with any title or right, and wherever they are located, found and situated, should come to her son, the magnificent and outstanding Lord Francesco [Junior] da Carrara, and son of the aforesaid magnificent and powerful lord, her consort, Lord Francesco da Carrara, whom she makes, orders, institutes, and wishes to be her universal heir.

Moreover, as her executor and administrator of this her last will and testament, she appoints, orders, ordains, and wishes to be the magnificent and powerful Lord Francesco da Carrara, Lord of Padua, her consort, attributing, giving, and conceding to the same magnificent lord, her executor, full license, authority, power, and permission, to give and alienate whatever is required of her property, real and movable, for the perfect and complete payment, satisfaction, and execution of all her legacies written above. And the same illustrious and magnificent Lady Fina da Carrara, testatrix, says and decrees that this is her last will and testament, and she praises and approves this as her last will and testament and says that she is pleased with it. And if she has made any other testament at any other time, that [will] is henceforth revoked, annulled, and invalidated, and she now orders that this [new will] should have forever force and validity. And this her present testament may be altered by the law of codicil and any other last will, and gift because of death, and in any other way, form, mode, or law, and such [changes] can be and are to be seen as valid and efficacious and holding now and in the future.

I, Bandino Brazzi, son of the notary Angelo di Bandino, citizen of and resident in the city of Padua, in the quarter of the Duomo, and the neighborhood and contrada of Santa Lucia, by imperial authority notary and ordinary judge, and scribe for the aforesaid magnificent Lord of Padua, was present, as requested, at all that was done and said by the aforesaid magnificent Lady testatrix, and I have written it in good faith and redacted it in public form, under my customary sign and signature.

| A Fifteenth-Century Dowry from Verona, 1422

In the name of Christ, Amen. In the year 1422, Friday, the 26 June, in the contrada of Mercatonovo of Verona, in the home of Federico de' Zaccari, in the presence of the outstanding Doctor of Laws Bartolomeo de Carpo, the son of Silvestro; Giacomo qd. Bartolomeo Curto, notary, both of Pigna; Lapo qd. Andrea del Bene, of S. Michele alla Porta; Michele, a notary, qd. Master Giacomo de Farfuzzola, of Isola Sotto; Giacomo qd. Bonmartino della Verità of San Zenone Oratorio; Facino, son of the outstanding Knight Guidotto de Monteselice, of Chiavica; Antonio, son of Zanino da Campo of Sant'Eufemia, Luchino qd. Gianfrancesco de Cesena of San Fermo, gathered here and sworn by the undersigned notary.*

Outstanding and Prudent Gentleman Federico qd. Lord Nicolai da Zaccari of Mercatonovo, wishing to bestow a dowry on his legitimate and natural daughter, Outstanding and Honest Lady Maddalena, the betrothed of Bartolomeo della Verità, with title and name of the same dowry to his daughter, in that place, in the presence of the witnesses and of me the notary, gave and counted out to Noble Gabriele qd. Giacomo Verità and to Bartolomeo his son, betrothed of the said Maddalena, here present, receiving six hundred gold ducats of just weight and measure. And Gabriel and his son confessed that they have been paid this quantity of money in ducats [and the Verità father and son declare themselves fully satisfied and paid in full]. And in the present instrument, with his consent and permission, the Verità [father and son], in the name of a marriage gift [*donatio propter nuptias*], invest the said lady Maddalena, the betrothed here present, with so many goods and property in the present and future, wherever existing, which would be equal to the value of the said dowry. Both parties then pledge to fulfill their obligations of the dowry and the marriage gift according to the laws and statutes of Verona, and obligate their heirs and guarantors (*fideiussores*) to uphold their pledge.

The said Gabriele and Bartolomeo his son, the betrothed, and each of them mutually and completely obligating themselves promised with all their other rights and making solemn stipulation for themselves and their heirs, to the said Federico and his daughter, the betrothed of the said Bartolomeo, present and here receiving the dowry for themselves and their heirs, that they will pay back and restore the same [dowry] to Lady Maddelena and her heirs, or to whomever the law and circumstance may require, and in any event, the said dowry and marriage gift are to be given, paid back, and restored according to the form of the [common] law and the statutes of the commune of Verona. And this is to be paid in cash, or movables, or in real estate, or in whatever kind of goods, in present and future, by the said Gabriele or by his son, to the said Lady Maddalena and her heirs, or to whomever events will require or the law dictate should receive the dowry and marriage gift described above, because thus has been the agreement between the said parties.

The aforesaid Bartolomeo, the betrothed, and his father, also present, swore

---

"A Fifteenth-Century Dowry," Archivio di Stato, Verona, Archivio Notarile, Pergamene Verità, terza serie, busta 4, perg. 221, 26 June 1422. Translated by Alison A. Smith.

*The abbreviation "qd." (for quondam) means "son of the late . . . ".

before me, the notary, that he is younger than twenty-five years but older than twenty-two, upon his oath freely taken in full knowledge he has sworn thus with his hand placed on God's Holy Gospels to fulfill and inviolately to observe all and everything of the contract, and in no way overturning it, because of his minority or any other reason.

And in the presence of witnesses and me, the notary, having invoked divine aid, the aforesaid person, Maddalena, was questioned by the judge, Bartolomeo da Carpo, if she wanted to take Bartolomeo as her husband, according to the requirements of solemn matrimony, and she responded, saying: "Yes, I will." And then Bartolomeo was asked if he wanted to take Maddalena as his wife, and he responded, saying: "Yes, I will." And after these questions and answers, Bartolomeo had two gold rings, and with affection took and married his wife, and she likewise married him, each placing a ring on the third finger of the right hand.

I Battista, son of Bartolomeo de Cendratis of Chiavica in Verona, public notary, testify to the above and sign this instrument.

I Agostino Montagna, son of Niccolò Montagna of S.Benedetto, in Verona, public notary, witness and sign this instrument.

I A Tale of Love and Deceit in Padua, 1550

IV

NERINO, SON OF KING GALLESE OF PORTUGAL, IN LOVE WITH GENOBBIA, THE WIFE OF DOCTOR RAIMONDO BRUNELLO THE PHYSICIAN, OBTAINS HER LOVE AND TAKES HER TO PORTUGAL; AND DOCTOR RAIMONDO DIES OF GRIEF.

There are many men, delightful ladies, who because they have spent a long time in the study of fine writings, think they know many things, and then turn out to know little or nothing. And while men like these think they are crossing themselves on the forehead, they poke out their own eyes, as happened to a doctor very learned in his art who, thinking to fool another, was to his own grave harm ignominiously fooled, as you will fully understand through the present fable, which I intend to tell you.

Gallese, king of Portugal, had a son named Nerino; and he brought him up in such a manner that, until he came to his eighteenth year of age, he was unable to see any woman other than his mother and the nurse who took care of him. When Nerino had come then to the age of adulthood, the king decided to send him to study in Padua so that he might learn his Latin letters and the Italian language and manners. And as he had decided, so he did. Now while the young Nerino was in Padua,

From Giovan Francesco Straparola, *Entertaining Nights*, ed. and trans. Janet Levarie Smarr, *Italian Renaissance Tales*, pp. 182–188, Solaris Press, Inc., Rochester, MI, 1983.

having made friends with many students who daily courted him, it happened that among them was a medical doctor named Doctor Raimondo Brunello the physician; and often talking together about different things, they began, as is the manner of young men, to talk about the beauty of women; and some said one thing and some another. But Nerino, because he had previously seen no woman except his mother and his nurse, said spiritedly that to his judgment no woman in the world could be found more beautiful, more lovely, and better dressed than his mother. And although many women were shown to him, he considered them all as garbage in comparison to his mother. Doctor Raimondo, who had as wife one of the prettiest women that nature ever made, entering into this idle chatter said, "Lord Nerino, I have seen a lady of such beauty that if you saw her perhaps you would not consider her less but instead more beautiful than your mother."

Nerino replied to him that he couldn't believe she was as pretty as his mother, but that he would like very much to see her.

To him Doctor Raimondo said, "If you would like to see her, I offer to show her to you."

"This," replied Nerino, "will please me very much, and I will be obliged to you."

Then said Doctor Raimondo, "Since you wish to see her, come tomorrow morning to the cathedral; and I promise you will see her."

And going home, he said to his wife, "Tomorrow rise early from bed, and arrange your hair, and make yourself beautiful and dress very elegantly, because I want you to go at the hour of high Mass to hear the service in the cathedral." Genobbia, such was the name of Doctor Raimondo's wife, not being in the habit of going now here and now there but for the most part staying at home to sew and embroider, was much surprised at this; but because he wished it so and it was his desire, she did it, and dressed up smartly and adorned herself so that she seemed not a lady but rather a goddess.

When Genobbia was gone to the sacred temple, as her husband had bidden her, Nerino, son of the king, came into the church; and seeing Genobbia, he judged her within himself most beautiful. After the fair Genobbia left, Doctor Raimondo arrived and, coming up to Nerino, said, "Now what do you think of that lady who just left the church? Do you think she has any rival? Is she more beautiful than your mother?"

"Truly," said Nerino, "she's a beauty; and nature couldn't make a more beautiful woman. But tell me, please, whose wife is she and where does she live?" Doctor Raimondo did not reply to this because he did not want to tell him.

Then said Nerino, "Doctor Raimondo, my friend, if you don't want to tell me who she is and where she lives, at least satisfy me in this, that I may see her another time."

"Gladly," answered Doctor Raimondo, "tomorrow come here to church, and I will arrange for you to see her as today."

And going home, Doctor Raimondo said to his wife, "Genobbia, make yourself ready for tomorrow morning, because I want you to go to Mass in the cathedral; and if ever you made yourself beautiful and dressed splendidly, see that you do it tomorrow." Genobbia was much surprised at this as before. But because her husband's command was important, she did all that he bid. Come morning, Genobbia, richly dressed and much more adorned than usual, went to church. And not long after came Nerino, who, seeing her extremely beautiful, was inflamed with such love for her as ever man felt for any woman. And when Doctor Raimondo arrived, Nerino begged him to tell who she was that looked so beautiful to his eyes. But Doctor Raimondo, pretending to be in a hurry because of his business, refused to say anything to him at the time; but leaving the young man to fry in his own grease, he went away delighted.

Thereupon Nerino, somewhat kindled with anger because of the small regard that Doctor Raimondo had shown him, said to himself, "You don't want me to know who she is and where she lives; but I will find out despite you." And leaving church, he waited until the beautiful lady also came out of church; and bowing to her, with modest manners and a happy face he accompanied her home.

Having thus learned clearly in which house she lived, he began to woo her; nor did a day go by without his passing ten times in front of her house. And desiring to speak with her, he tried to imagine by what way he could keep safe the lady's honor, while he himself obtained his aim. And having considered and reconsidered without finding any remedy that would help him, still he mused on until it occurred to him to obtain the friendship of an old woman who had her house across the street from Genobbia's. And having given her certain small presents and sealed a close friendship, he secretly went into her house. The house of this old woman had a window which looked into a room of Genobbia's house, and from it he could at his leisure see her go up and down through her house; but he did not want to reveal himself lest he give her cause for not letting him see her any more. So then, as Nerino was spending every day in this secret gazing, unable to resist the hot flame which burned his heart, he decided within himself to write her a letter and throw it into her house at a time when it seemed her husband was not at home. And so he threw it to her. And he did this a number of times. But Genobbia, without even reading it, nor thinking twice about it, threw it into the fire and burned it. And after she had done this many times, she thought she might just once open and see what was contained in it. And opening it, and seeing that the author was Nerino, son of the king of Portugal, ardently in love with her, she thought it over a bit; but then considering the sad life her husband gave her, she made good cheer and began to show Nerino a glad face; and having arranged things well, she brought him into the house. And the young man recounted the supreme love which he bore her, and the torments which he felt for her at every hour, and similarly the manner in which he had fallen in love with her. And she, who was beautiful, pleasant, and compassionate did not deny him her love.

So then, both of them being joined in reciprocal love and in the midst of amorous conversation, here came Doctor Raimondo knocking at the door. Genobbia, hearing it, made Nerino lie down on her bed and stay there with the bed-curtains pulled shut until her husband left. The husband, entering the house and taking a few things of his, left without noticing anything. And so did Nerino. On the following day, as Nerino was strolling in the Piazza, by chance he passed Doctor Raimondo, to whom Nerino made a sign that he wanted to speak with him; and coming up to him, he said, "Sir, don't I have a bit of good news to tell you!"

"What's that?" said Doctor Raimondo.

"Don't I know," said Nerino, "the house of that beautiful lady? And haven't I had delightful conversations with her? And because her husband came home, she hid me in her bed and pulled the curtains so that he couldn't see me, and he left immediately."

Said Doctor Raimondo. "Is this possible?"

Replied Nerino, "It is possible, and it's true; and I have never seen a more merry nor a more gracious lady than she; if perchance, Sir, you go to her house, commend me to her, praying her to keep me in her good graces."

Doctor Raimondo promised him to do so and parted from him in a bad mood. But first he said to Nerino, "Will you go there again?"

To whom Nerino replied, "What do you think!" And going home, Doctor Raimondo decided not to say anything to his wife but rather to wait for a time when he could find them together.

The following day Nerino returned to Genobbia; and while they were in the midst of amorous pleasures and delightful conversation, home came the husband. But she at once hid Nerino in a chest, on top of which she put many clothes that she was cleaning so that they wouldn't get moth-eaten. The husband, pretending to look for certain things of his, turned the house upside down and even looked on her bed; and finding nothing, he left with a calmer mind and went about his practice. And Nerino similarly departed. And encountering Doctor Raimondo again, he said to him.

"Sir Doctor, did I not return to that gentlewoman? But envious fortune disrupted all my pleasure; for her husband arrived and disturbed everything."

"And what did you do?" said Doctor Raimondo.

"She," answered Nerino, "opened a chest and put me in it; and on top of the chest she put many clothes that she was taking care of so they would not get moth-eaten. And he, turning the bed upside down and every which way and finding nothing, left." How tormenting this was to Doctor Raimondo, he can imagine who has experienced love.

Nerino had given Genobbia a pretty and precious ring in the gold setting of which were carved his crest and name; and when day came and Doctor Raimondo was gone about his practice, Nerino was brought into the house by the lady; and as he lay with her in pleasure and sweet conversation, here came the husband back home. But Genobbia, naughty girl, perceiving his arrival, immediately opened a large letter cabinet that was in her room and hid Nerino in it. And Doctor Raimondo, entering the house, pretending to look for certain things of his, turned the room upside down; and finding nothing, neither in the bed, nor in the chests, quite bewildered, he took a brand and set fire to all four corners of the room with a determined intent to burn down the room and everything in it. Already the walls and beams were beginning to burn when Genobbia turning to her husband said, "What does this mean, husband? Have you perhaps gone crazy? If you want to burn down the house, burn it as you wish; but by my faith don't burn that letter cabinet which holds the documents pertaining to my dowry," and calling for four strong porters, she had them carry the cabinet out of the house and set it in the house of her neighbor the old woman; and Nerino opened it secretly, so that no one noticed, and went home. Out of his wits, Doctor Raimondo still stood there to see whether any-one was coming out whom he didn't like; but he saw nothing except the intolerable smoke and hot fire that was burning up the house. Already the neighbors had come running to extinguish the fire; and they worked at it until they put it out.

The next day Nerino, going towards Prato della Valle, ran into Doctor Raimondo, and greeting him, said, "Doctor, my friend, don't I have something to tell you that will amuse you greatly?"

"What's that?" replied Doctor Raimondo.

"I have escaped," said Nerino, "the most fearful danger that ever a living man escaped. I went to that gentlewoman's house; and as I was with her in pleasant con-versation, her husband arrived; who, after he had turned the house upside down, set fire to it in all four corners of the room, and burned everything that was in the room."

"And you," said Doctor Raimondo, "where were you?"

"I," answered Nerino, "was hidden in the letter cabinet that she sent out of the house."

Hearing this and recognizing that what he was telling was true, Doctor Raimondo felt like dying from grief and passion; but still he did not dare reveal him-self because he wanted to catch them in the act. And he said, "Sir Nerino, will you ever go back there again?"

To whom Nerino answered, "Having escaped the fire, what more do I have to fear?" Now putting these matters aside, Doctor Raimondo asked Nerino to deign to come the next day and dine with him; and the young man gladly accepted the invitation.

The following day, Doctor Raimondo invited all his relatives and the relatives of his wife and prepared a splendid and sumptuous dinner, not in the house which was half burned out but elsewhere; and he ordered his wife to come too, but she was not to sit at the table but stay hidden and prepare whatever was necessary. So then, when all the relatives and the young Nerino had assembled, they were placed at the table; and Doctor Raimondo with his blockheaded science tried to get Nerino drunk so that he could then do what he had in mind. Therefore after Doctor Raimondo had many times brought him a glass full of wicked wine, and Nerino had drunk it down every time, Doctor Raimondo said, "Say, Lord Nerino, tell these relatives of ours some little story good for a laugh."

The poor young Nerino, not knowing that Genobbia was Doctor Raimondo's wife began to tell them his story, holding back, however, the names of all the characters.

It happened that a servant went to the room where Genobbia was and said to her, "My lady, if you were hidden in a corner, you would hear the best story that you ever heard in your life; come, I pray you." And going into a corner, she recognized that it was the voice of Nerino her lover and that the story he was telling was about her.

And the lady, prudent and wise, took the diamond that Nerino had given her and, putting it in a silver cup full of a delicious drink, said to the servant, "Take this cup and give it to Nerino, and tell him to drink it so that afterwards he'll talk better."

The servant, taking the cup, carried it to the table; and as Nerino wanted something to drink the servant said, "Take this cup, lord, for afterwards you will talk better."

And he, taking the cup, drank down all the wine; and seeing and recognizing the diamond that was in it, he let it slip into his mouth; and pretending to clean his mouth, he slipped it out and put it on his finger. And realizing that the beautiful lady about whom he was talking was the wife of Doctor Raimondo, he did not want to go on any further; and being urged on by Doctor Raimondo and by the relatives to continue the story he had begun, he replied, "Oh yes, oh yes! The rooster crowed, I ceased to snore, and in the day I heard no more." Hearing this the relatives of Doctor Raimondo, who had first believed that everything Nerino told them about the wife was true, treated both of them as big drunks.

After several days Nerino met Doctor Raimondo, and pretending not to know that he was Genobbia's husband, he told him that he was about to leave in a few days because his father had written him to return to his kingdom. Doctor Raimondo in reply wished him a speedy journey. Nerino, having made secret arrangements with Genobbia, ran off with her and took her to Portugal, where with supreme joy they lived a long time. And Doctor Raimondo, going home and not finding his wife, died a few days later of despair.

FURTHER READING

Gene Brucker, *Giovanni and Lusanna, Love and Marriage in Renaissance Florence* (1986)

James Casey, *The History of the Family* (1989)

Stanley Chojnacki, "Dowries and Kinsmen in Fifteenth-Century Venice," *Journal of Interdisciplinary History*, 5 (1975), 671–700

———, "Kinship Ties and Young Patricians in Fifteenth-Century Venice," *American Historical Review*, 91 (1986), 791–810

———, "Marriage Legislation and Patrician Society in Fifteenth-Century Venice," in *Law, Customs, and the Social Fabric in Medieval Europe: Essays in Honor of Bryce Lyon*, ed. B. Bachrach and D. Nicholas (1990), 163–184

———, "Patrician Women in Early Renaissance Venice," *Studies in the Renaissance*, 21 (1974), 176–203

Margaret W. Ferguson, Maureen Quilligan, and Nancy Vickers, eds., *Rewriting the Renaissance: The Discourses of Sexual Difference in Early Modern Europe* (1986)

David Herlihy, *Medieval Households* (1985)

Diane Owen Hughes, "Representing the Family: Portraits and Purposes in Early Modern Italy," *Journal of Interdisciplinary History*, 17 (1986), 7–38

F. W. Kent, *Household and Lineage in Renaissance Florence* (1977)

Margaret L. King, *Women of the Renaissance* (1991)

Julius Kirshner, *Pursuing Honor While Avoiding Sin: The Monte delle Doti of Florence* (1978)

——— and Anthony Molho, "The Dowry Fund and the Marriage Market in Early Quattrocento Florence," *Journal of Modern History*, 50 (1978), 403–38

Christiane Klapisch-Zuber, *Women, Family and Ritual in Renaissance Italy* (1985)

Thomas Kuehn, *Law, Family and Women: Toward a Legal Anthropology in Renaissance Italy* (1992)

Ian Maclean, *The Renaissance Notion of Woman* (1980)

Anthony Molho, *Marriage Alliance in Late Medieval Florence* (1994)

J. B. Ross, "The Middle Class Child in Urban Italy," in *The History of Childhood*, ed. Lloyd de Mause (1974), 183–228

Guido Ruggiero, *The Boundaries of Eros: Sex Crime and Sexuality in Renaissance Venice* (1985)

Richard Trexler, *Children in Renaissance Florence* (1992)

———, *Women in Renaissance Florence* (1992)

Merry E. Wiesner, *Women and Gender in Early Modern Europe* (1993)

CHAPTER **12**

Conspicuous Consumption

The phrase "Italian Renaissance" immediately conjures up images of glorious art and architecture in most people's minds. Indeed, the idea that artistic style has a history was born in the sixteenth century when men like Giorgio Vasari (Florentine painter and architect who wrote the most famous biographies of Renaissance artists) began to chronicle their extraordinary artistic heritage. This artistic renaissance was largely caused by a huge increase in the demand for decorative art, which was fueled by public and private building programs carried out on a massive scale throughout the cities of northern and central Italy. This chapter examines the social and economic forces behind all this artistic production, from the point of view of both the consumer, or patron, who paid for it, and that of the craftsman, or artist, who produced it.

The intense competition for wealth, power, and prestige in the cities of Renaissance Italy (see discussion of urban society in Chapters 2–4) fostered spectacular conspicuous consumption. Living in such close proximity to each other, wealthy families, and those who wished to appear wealthier than they were, devised ever more elaborate ways to decorate their homes, churches, and public buildings. Men and women dressed in the latest fashions, artistic styles changed rapidly, and ritual expressions of family status, such as weddings, funerals, and banquets, became increasingly complex and expensive. At the height of Renaissance society, princes and prelates courted the greatest painters and architects, offering them grand artistic opportunities as well as stipends and security.

During the Middle Ages, painters, sculptors, and architects had been considered little more than highly skilled craftsmen. The wealthy cities of Renaissance Italy, however, not only encouraged the development of artistic talent but also rewarded the finest artists by recognizing their special artistic genius that set them apart from all other craftsmen. To please their patrons, Renaissance artists executed increasingly sophisticated compositions based on mythological and allegorical texts, which let them claim a new intellectual status. Botticelli, Mantegna, Michelangelo, Titian, and scores of others achieved much higher intellectual and social status than artists ever had before—and charged ever higher prices for their work. The Renaissance thus gave birth to our modern notion of the artist—an independent, temperamental genius worthy of special treatment and, often, great respect.

ESSAYS

Richard Goldthwaite of The Johns Hopkins University explains in the first essay how the massive building projects of the Renaissance fostered unprecedented growth in the decorative arts sector of the economy, which encompassed the production of colorful tin-glazed pottery and elaborately carved furniture as well as the majestic altarpieces and frescoes of Michelangelo and Raphael. Artists increasingly developed strategies to distinguish themselves from lesser artisans in an attempt to boost their intellectual, economic, and social status. Diane Owen Hughes, a professor at the University of Michigan and a historian of late-medieval Genoa and, more recently, of Renaissance women, examines the nearly universal phenomenon of sumptuary legislation in Italian cities. City governments worried that wealthy families—and hence the ruling class—would become impoverished by excessive conspicuous consumption and so tried to curb citizens' ability to display their wealth by imposing limits on dress, jewelry, lavish banquets, funeral rites, and so forth. Ironically, the city councillors themselves were often among the worst offenders, and all sumptuary legislation, even though it was revised regularly, tended to be ignored. These laws reveal much about attitudes toward public morality, the female body, social relations, and the powerful symbolism of dress.

The Building of Renaissance Florence

RICHARD A. GOLDTHWAITE

In Florence the construction of homes and family chapels on a larger scale and in greater quantity, and the new life-style implicit in this development, generated demand for more objects for the decoration and furnishing of these places—gold, silver, and metal utensils; wood, terracotta, and stone sculpture; bronze statuettes and medallions; and, certainly not least of all, pictures (to which must be added picture-frames, now needed to accommodate painting to a function so new as to revolutionize the art itself)—in short, the entire range of the interior decorative arts. Dress, too, was affected by the new life-style played out in the palaces of the rich, becoming more elaborate and more technically demanding in its tailoring to fit the body more closely (reflecting the fascination of artists with the human form). Perhaps this extravagance was partly a result of the freedom the patrician could now find from the sumptuary laws (and more subtle kinds of social censure) by withdrawing from public places into the vast new spaces of his private world.

Before the fourteenth century the decorative arts in Tuscany hardly penetrated the domestic world; by the fifteenth century a considerable variety of objects was being produced to fill up the vastly enlarged residential spaces. Perhaps it would be more correct to say that the domestic world had come into its own by the fifteenth century as both a physical place and a set of values, and that palaces were simply the most grandiose statement of this new fact of life. This new world, at any rate, needed

Text by R. A. Goldthwaite from *The Building of Renaissance Florence*, pp. 400–407, 412–419. The Johns Hopkins University Press, Baltimore/London, 1981. Reprinted by permission of the publisher.

to be filled up, whether the palace of a patrician or the humbler abode of a prosperous artisan, and the rush into the marketplace created a huge new demand for the decorative arts, thus stimulating what was perhaps the most dynamic sector of the economy of Renaissance Florence. And, needless to say, the secularization of art is tied to this process of its domestication.

In this domestic world of the arts demand arose for two basic household items— furniture and glazed pottery—that is of particular note for the economic activity it generated and for the subsequent history of European taste. The furniture industry was not new on the European scene, but it has its first full chapter as a minor art in fifteenth-century Florence. Earlier household furniture consisted mostly of nondescript stools, tables, and, above all, chests of all sizes. Forms were starkly simple, decoration was minimal, and items like chests were usually portable and multifunctional. In the fifteenth century, however, chairs, tables, beds, cabinets, and chests evolved into new forms, and the variety of their decoration introduced a new taste for furniture that soon spread throughout Italy and all Europe.

The cost of furnishings was no object to some of these rich Florentines, who were prepared to pay the equivalent of what a skilled worker earned in a year for a bed or a chest or even an altar picture-frame. . . . Local craftsmen could turn out items that were major works of art, something worthy of the household of a prince. Lorenzo the Magnificent had no qualms about presenting a bed as a gift to the sultan of Egypt; Benedetto da Maiano made one for King Ferrante of Naples, and his brother Giuliano made at least two for other Neapolitan noblemen. During the siege of Florence [1512] that unscrupulous proto-art dealer, Giovanbattista della Palla, eyed the famous bedroom in the Borgherini palace while the owner was out of town, in the hope of making a deal to get the city fathers to give the entire ensemble of furnishings as a gift to no one less than Francis I; but he had not counted on the stout resistance of the lady of the household, who, anything but flattered, had strong ideas about her matrimonial bed becoming an object of mere commerce, even if among governments and kings.

The colorful tin-glazed pottery—*maiolica*—that covered the ever-expanding shelf and table spaces inside palaces was another distinctively new art form to appear in the domestic world, and Florence enjoys a certain preeminence in its history because the domestic world was so highly developed there. Maiolica is one of the glories of the Italian Renaissance. Inspired by the importations from the Islamic world (much of it by way of Spain), Italians—above all, Florentines—much enlarged the possibilities of this craft once they undertook their own production. Their imaginative elaboration of shapes and decoration, not to mention their perfection of pottery techniques (which in the later sixteenth century brought the Florentines almost to the point of inventing porcelain), went much beyond the relatively restricted range of Islamic production. Florentines filled their homes with these things. With prices low enough to bring it within reach of much of the population, large quantities of maiolica turn up in the inventories even of modest artisans, and it was sold in shops throughout the remote territories of the Florentine state. Some merchants took their own pottery with them when they went to live in backward northern Europe, which was still eating off pewter and wooden dishes. Northern Europeans must have found this pottery strikingly beautiful, to judge from the number of these objects that show up in Flemish painting—many more than can be found in the corpus of Florentine painting. It was not until the late sixteenth century that the North began to catch up with Italian taste and manners in the matter of tableware of this kind.

The success of pottery in the local market points up another feature of this expanding decorative arts sector of the economy: the production of items inexpensive enough to be within the reach of customers well below the level of great palace-dwellers. By resorting to materials of lower cost in order to make cheaper products, artisans set new productive forces to work in a wider market. Is this not the significance, for example, of Luca Della Robbia's move away from marble sculpture and his development of the technique of making glazed terracotta pieces, which could be produced more quickly and certainly more cheaply than marble pieces? The extraordinary quantity of Madonna reliefs made of such inexpensive materials as clay, stucco, and cartapesta, and then gilded, painted, or glazed attests the kind of market that had opened up in Florence; it is significant that production of such items was not to be found elsewhere in Italy. . . . Likewise, the abandonment of expensive ultramarine and gold leaf in painting, more than just a matter of change in taste, meant that more men could afford a painting. Most, of course, bought Madonnas, which are ubiquitous on the household inventories of the fifteenth century, even of artisans. Neri di Bicci sold one (for lb.15) to a stonecutter, Giuliano Sandrini, and another (lb.13 s.6) to the foreman at Santo Spirito, Giovanni di Mariano—just to mention two customers of this productive shop who worked in the building trades. Vasari mentions sales made by painters like Andrea del Sarto and Pontormo to mercers, joiners, tailors, and others of similar economic status.

The expansion of the decorative arts sector of the economy is self-evident in the totality of all its production that survives today, so much more impressive in its range and its quality for this one small city than for any other place in Europe at the time, be it one of the other great Italian cities or a large northern European territorial kingdom. . . .

The success of the decorative arts sector did not mean much expansionist growth in the economy. Increased activity of the artisan industries in no significant way expanded Florence's economic frontiers abroad, however much it boosted the city's prestige as an art center. Although probably no city in all Europe was so well known for the variety and quality of its luxury crafts, we can hardly talk about an export industry, at least in the fifteenth century. Francesco di Marco Datini, the merchant of Prato, occasionally sold inexpensive panel paintings abroad, and in the accounts of other great import-export firms of the fifteenth century, such as Strozzi and Cambini, major works of decorative art turn up—terracotta, furniture, gold and silver objects, jewelry, clothwork, pictures—that were sent off to the papal court, to the king in Naples, to princes in northern Europe, and even to the sultan in Egypt. The value of such objects, however, was utterly insignificant within the total international operations of these firms.

Moreover, no large investors can be turned up who had any interest in developing this sector of the local economy, although more than one Florentine took advantage of the market opportunities abroad to turn a profit in the commerce of products in this category—like Netto di Bartolomeo, who declared in his Catasto report of 1427 investments in manufactures of drinking glasses in Ferrara and Bologna; and like Baldassare Ubriachi, who spent much of his life traveling across all of Europe supplying the market with carved ivory- and bonework, which (toward the end of his life, around 1406, when he was in exile) he had manufactured in his own house in Venice. Later the grand dukes, anticipating mercantilist policy, attempted to de-velop some of Florence's luxury crafts for the export market, but failed; beyond its traditionally strong cloth industries Florence was never able to promote a significant second line of luxury products for export, as Venice had, for instance, with glass, jewelry, books, embroidery, lace, and soap. Rather than export works of art Floren-tine artists themselves went abroad, almost in droves, and found work all over Italy—the point hardly need be driven home by illustrating how the Renaissance of art in most of the regional centers of Italy goes back to the arrival of Florentine artists on the local scene. Florentine artists' travel abroad to work, however, had no signif-icant effect on the city's balance of payments.

Nevertheless, this sector did help the balance of payments to the extent that production successfully met the enormous increase in internal demand that might otherwise have damaged the balance by having recourse to foreign markets. Indeed, growth of local crafts probably cut into imports from abroad. Whereas in the four-teenth century all kinds of luxury products were imported for local consumption, from Flemish cloths to the variety of expensive merchandise for which the Levant was famous throughout the Middle Ages, by the end of the fifteenth century (to judge from merchants' accounts and household inventories of the wealthy) the range of such imports had contracted considerably. Items made of raw materials not readily available to Florentine craftsmen continued to come—furs from Russia, pewterware from England, glass from Venice, an occasional tapestry (no longer other kinds of cloth) from Flanders, small rugs and Damascene metalwork from the East—but for the most part . . . Florentine merchants scattered all across Europe from Flanders to Egypt brought their profits home in gold because, quite simply, there was little they wanted to buy in any of those places.

In a market where a locally produced piece of furniture or a good picture might cost from 10 to 50 florins and a fine example of Chinese celadon a mere 2 or 3 florins, the criterion for selection was obviously more a matter of taste than rarity, and, in fact, the shrinking of the market for luxury imports at a time when the demand for luxury goods in general was surging reveals just how much the emergence of taste, or fashion, can have significant repercussions in an economy. For example, Florence had long imported Near Eastern ceramics and Hispano-moresque pottery, but in the fifteenth century its demand for these items became much more particular and selec-tive, and by the sixteenth century imports were reduced to a trickle—and, indeed, there is evidence that Florence had turned the tables and was exporting its own wares to Egypt. Most interesting in the history of this trade is the articulation of a definite taste as, on the one hand, Florentines became more and more selective and, on the other, the local producers of maiolica used those same criteria as inspiration for their own production in their attempt to give the customer what he wanted. Likewise, in numerous fifteenth-century inventories metalwork is described as "alla domaschina [in the style of Damascus]" and glass as "alla veneziana [in the Venetian style]"—objects made in Florence to compete with the imported product.

Little is known about the minor arts in Florence, despite an extraordinary abundance of documentation and numerous surviving examples of that production too often stacked away in museum storehouses. As an index to the history of taste they deserve more attention than they have as yet received from students of the so-called "finer" arts. For the economic historian the history of taste is an important part of the history of demand, and until it is written we cannot have a full understanding of the development of one of the most vigorous sectors of the economy of Renaissance Italy.

THE QUALITY OF ECONOMIC EFFORTS

The acquisitive instinct that lay behind the new demand of the rich has intricate psychological roots. In part, if the enlargement of interior private space created many more possibilities for the acquisition of the new objects now being manufactured in greater variety and number to fill it up, this inflated private world may also have generated pressures on men to sustain their increasing social isolation by surrounding themselves with more objects. In part, too, for men whose spending habits betray that liberated sense of individual private wealth, . . . the possession of objects can assume such a psychological significance that the disposition to spend could be aroused even more by the very existence of more objects. Whatever the psychological state underlying acquisitiveness, the greatest success of this sector of the Florentine economy was the ability of the producer to arouse this acquisitive instinct of the rich, thereby generating even further demand for his production.

The quality of the economic efforts of some of these producers is, therefore, not irrelevant to the success of the sector as a whole. In organizing themselves to operate a business, artisans were not unaware of how their rich clients did things in the wider world of capitalist enterprise. They used the formal partnership contract to gain greater flexibility from the pooling of resources and talents so that they were able to increase the number of commissions and lessen the risks of going it alone. Artisan partnerships could have the formal features typical of Florentine business practice— written, renewable, pacts of specific duration, fixed capital, and carefully kept written records. The painter Jacopo d'Antonio had a shop where a wide range of work was undertaken. . . . It was in the marketplace where the artisan enhanced his status, where in selling his wares to customers and seeking new ways to get them to buy more he conditioned public taste to the point that, eventually, he was able to sell himself and everything he stood for as something special. In the sixteenth century he clinched his case with intellectual claims as well, but until that time, ironically, the sense of progress in craftsmanship that he exploited in the marketplace had worked as a countervailing force against the notion of the exalted genius and dignity of the artist and helped stave off that eventual victory of the higher over the so-called minor arts. In the fifteenth century the drive for virtuosity still precluded much of a distinction between artisan and artist.

In short, the decorative arts sector of the economy had built into it the capability of maintaining and even increasing demand for its production. The number and variety of objects aroused the acquisitive instinct in man and sharpened his taste for quality and fashionableness; with variables like these at play as forces stimulating demand the artisan could become more aggressive in the marketplace. His initiative was an important new element in the growth of this sector, and the effect was especially far-ranging in this economy because of the diffusion of demand throughout a large segment of the population. In societies where wealthy consumers constituted a more coalescent group around a single dominating authority, as in almost all aristocratic societies later in the Renaissance and throughout the early modern period with the rise of princely courts, consumers were less independent and their taste more subject to the dictates of court fashions and to the canons of quasi-official artistic authority. In these places, although the structure and level of demand may otherwise have been comparable to the situation in Florence, the nature of demand kept the producer more constricted in his ability to take the initiative in the marketplace.

SOCIAL QUALITY OF THE ECONOMY

. . . If on the one hand the opportunities that opened up to [artisans] were determined by the level, structure, and nature of demand, on the other their ability to seize those opportunities very much depended on the freedom to develop their talents. In Florence the opportunities were all the greater because the artisan's movement in the marketplace was not largely restricted by social structures—by guilds, by class hierarchy, by large-scale capitalist industrial organization, or by highly personal patronage systems. Perhaps in no other city in Europe at the time was the artisan less confined by these traditional barriers.

Take the guild, one of the most fundamental institutions that shaped the structure of artisan society in medieval Europe. The late thirteenth-century reorganization of the guilds into great conglomerates for purposes of political consolidation threatened the solidarity and exclusiveness of single crafts and precluded the kind of corporate parochialism found elsewhere. The eventual result was the extinction of the protective and collective spirit of medieval guild corporatism. The city's leading master masons, for example, did not control the Maestri [officers of the guild], and they could not direct guild policy to assure their domination of construction activity. The industry was therefore much less exclusive than in most places in northern Europe, where artisan dynasties perpetuated themselves through institutional arrangements. Family craft traditions among Florentine masons, as among all artisan groups in preindustrial society, were strong, but among the leaders of the craft there is remarkably little family continuity. . . .

Furthermore, talent was not confined to narrow guild categories. On the contrary, the economic system encouraged multiple expression, with the result that the arts and crafts encouraged one another, expanding knowledge in a way that is hardly irrelevant to increased productivity. As Bernard Berenson so wisely observed, comparing Michelangelo, Leonardo, Pollaiuolo, and other Florentine painters with Venetian artists: "Forget that they were painters, they remain great sculptors; forget they were sculptors, and they still remain architects, poets, and even men of science." Berenson goes on to say that the range of these Florentines' genius could not be contained by the usual categories, but it is more correct to say that in Florence the usual categories were not sanctioned in economic and social institutions like the guilds. The artisan was free to choose his own forms of expression, and versatility as a craftsman was his notable, if not characteristic, endowment as a Florentine.

This versatility is nowhere more striking than among goldsmiths, who left the mark of their identity on so much Renaissance art. Throughout the Middle Ages the goldsmith was considered the aristocrat of artisans because of the materials he worked with and because of his stature as one who could be entrusted with them. Moreover, the peculiar nature of European demand for his work challenged him to develop his talents in virtuoso performances. In the monastic isolation of the early Middle Ages the goldsmith decorated display manuscripts with gold leaf and proba-bly did some of the painting of miniatures therein. His production of shrines, reli-quaries, and liturgical utensils took him also into architectural design. He was a de-signer, an engraver, a modeler, a caster of metal, a jeweler, an enameler, and by logical extension of these talents he had potential as a sculptor. All these skills flour-ished among the goldsmiths of Florence with the development of their craft in the fourteenth century, and it is a commonplace in the art history of Florence that many of the city's most talented and versatile artists came out of the goldsmith's shop.

The extraordinary versatility and virtuosity of the goldsmith is epitomized by Ghiberti, whose life illustrates how Florentine goldsmiths realized the full potential of their talent and developed their skills beyond the traditional confines of their craft. As a craftsman with a keen appreciation and knowledge of the drawings of earlier Trecento painters, Ghiberti himself made designs for painters and makers of stained glass. Some of the best painters of the next generation—Uccello, Benozzo Gozzoli, and (possibly) Masolino—came out of his workshop. As a modeler in wax and clay he did work for both painters and sculptors. As a metalworker he made his mark in the history of bronze sculpture as one of the great virtuosos of all time with the Doors of Paradise and the first life-size free-standing statutes since antiquity, and the tradition of his foundry was carried down by his son and grandson, especially in the area of munitions. As one who knew something about architectural design he submitted proposals for vaulting the cathedral, and although the final solution was not his (as he asserted) he nevertheless served for a while as foreman of that proj-ect—until he was edged out by another goldsmith. Ghiberti, in short, embodied the many-faceted talent of the master goldsmith brought to full fruition with enormous implications for the course of Renaissance art.

Goldsmiths were bound to flourish in a city that made up its favorable balance of payments with gold imports and where gold was put to industrial use. Although their artistic versatility was inherent in their craft and therefore not altogether unique to Florence, their mobility into the other arts was made easier here than elsewhere by the absence of rigid guild barriers. Goldsmiths did not have their own guild but were incorporated instead in the Arte di Por Santa Maria, which was dom-inated by silk manufacturers. Their corporate ties were no stronger than for any other craft group in the Florentine system of guild conglomerates. The easy entry into the craft has already been remarked, and by the same token other guilds did not block them from developing their talents in any direction they wished. It was not until late in his career (1426) that Ghiberti became a member of the Maestri. Many goldsmiths joined the painters' confraternity of San Luca but not the guild to which they belonged. . . .

If artisans were not held back by corporate guild ties, neither were they, like cloth workers, subordinated to an industrial process controlled by capitalists with an eye on foreign markets; nor were they caught up in the web of personal relations so characteristic of courtly patronage in more established aristocratic societies. Artisans were independent economic agents operating on their own in a marketplace where demand was widely diffused, and the considerable entrepreneurial skill with which they refined the terms of their economic existence has been amply illustrated in the careers of many. . . . Even the modest stonecutters formalized the conditions of their employment by drawing up complex schedules of task rates, submitting bids for jobs (sometimes written and sealed), and entering into contracts. . . .

As artisans became more aggressive in the marketplace, the more skilled of them were able to claim an added value for individual talent, and this became an increasingly important variable in the determination of prices, which were usually fixed—often by arbitration—only after the completion of work. The art market was never altogether freed from the commission nexus, and retail trade did not develop to the extent that it could sustain the kind of luxury shops that later grew up in London and Paris. Nevertheless, many of these artisan shops probably had ready-made "art" for sale over the counter. Already in the late fourteenth century the local market was well enough developed that at least one wool merchant made some extra money on the side by buying and selling pictures.

Craftsmen operated in a marketplace where social structures were loose, where relations were fluid, where the cash nexus dominated, and where contracts were protected by impersonal legal authority. Hence, they were all the less inhibited in seeking to improve their skills and enlarge their imagination. This initiative, above all their claim to *scientia*, or knowledge, as Erwin Panofsky pointed out, gave expression to the emerging self-consciousness of artistic inventiveness so characteristic of the Renaissance, a self-awareness that sharpened competition among them. Who will ever be able to assess the importance of the competitive instinct on the artistic genius—on Donatello, who fearfully locked his workshop door at the cathedral lest someone see what he was doing; on Ghiberti, who never could admit that the cupola of the cathedral was Brunelleschi's invention and not his own, and who must have shuddered in rage as he worked on the baptistry doors in the growing shadow of that cupola; on Brunelleschi, who was so hesitant to commit his ideas for decorative detail to paper or to plastic models for his workers lest they be stolen, who was indignant when Donatello was allowed to decorate the sacristy at San Lorenzo, and who in a fit of anger destroyed his model for the Medici palace when it was rejected for someone else's? Competition may be just an aspect of artistic temperament (and these instances of it just the age's myth about its artists), but there can be no denying that the terms of competition were much expanded in Florence with the increase in options, with the specialization of skills, and above all with the greater challenge for the artist to demonstrate his knowledge. Competitions were the normal way in Italy to proceed with commissions for great public projects, and because Florence had somewhat more public art than other places, its artists scrambled all the more to get them. Their competition, however, was not limited to these conditions. It was no wonder to Vasari that talented provincial painters (for example, Lorenzo Costa) did not quite teach the highest standards, since they did not live in places where the competition demanded top performance. The competitive drive was a distinct trait of Florentine artists, and it may have been nothing more than good business sense.

It is important to add to all this that the considerable expansion of the artisan's ambitions and his rising stature as a virtuoso craftsman were not accompanied by a comparable enlargement of his hopes to improve his economic status. After the Black Death Florentine workers of all kinds, both skilled and unskilled, enjoyed a period of prosperity that lasted into the sixteenth century, until the inflation we associate with the price revolution began to cut into their earnings. An artisan could realistically hope to build up a modest estate consisting of a furnished house in town and a piece of land in the countryside, and given the economic structure of pre-industrial society, such opportunities were probably sufficient to fire up motivation throughout a wide segment of the population. More substantial wealth, however, lay beyond the reach of all but the most enterprising—and the luckiest—for although wage rates were high the structure of wages was remarkably rigid; with limited investment possibilities open to the man of modest means he could hardly build up a patrimony qualifying him for entry into the ranks of even the lower patriciate.

Artisans who sold their wares rather than working directly for wages or salary could do somewhat better. The value of their work—for example, a painting or a sculpture—was generally estimated on the basis of costs of materials and labor at the going rates, with added value for originality or artistic quality. That variable, however, was never a major component of the final price. . . . No architect in the fifteenth century was paid so much for his ideas as incorporated in plans or models that he did not have to work as a craftsman or construction supervisor in order to make a living. Evaluations made of contemporary works of art, for example on the Medici inventories, make little allowance for artistic quality. Moreover, the artisan-entrepreneur could do little to increase the margin of profit of his business by organizational or technological improvements in the production process, and economies of scale were possible only to a limited extent. The largesse of a great princely patron could, of course, change the artisan's economic situation dramatically, but for that kind of windfall the Florentine artisan had to go abroad—until the establishment of the Medicean duchy in the sixteenth century. Only from a prince could Cellini have made the 200 percent profit he earned on his enormous investment in making the Perseus—a sum roughly equivalent to what it took Ghiberti twenty years to earn working on the Doors of Paradise (and his earnings accounted for no more than a quarter of the total cost).

Nevertheless, however much an artisan's social ambitions were confined by economic structures, his mobility was not blocked by a rigid hierarchical social structure. Not many artisans could realistically look forward to a social climb into the upper class; it is doubtful that any of them really had such hopes, and those whose families eventually made it probably arrived there by routes that lay outside the artisan shop. Yet mobility was possible in a society as fluid as that of Florence. Two of Taddeo Gaddi's sons continued in their father's and grandfather's craft as painters, but their brother Zanobi (who died in 1400) somehow went into business, ending up as a merchant in Venice and the chief correspondent there of Francesco di Marco Datini. In the 1427 Catasto two of Zanobi's sons show up as wealthy wool producers, and a century later their descendants included one of the biggest Florentine bankers at the papal court. The Rosselli, one of the most numerous fifteenth-century families of second-rate painters and masons, who took their name from a forebearer, a mason called Redhead, in the sixteenth century moved into the upper ranges of society, where they are still firmly implanted today with patents of nobility. . . .

The pretentious claims of Michelangelo about his family's social status and the obsessive social-climbing of Baccio Bandinelli are symptomatic of the mobility in Florentine society; such social ambitions would have made no sense, for instance, in Titian's Venice. Although a lot of nonsense has been written about how far up the social ladder artists were able to move in the Renaissance, the dissolution of the confining corporate and hierarchical structure of traditional Europe did leave society more fluid, and so incentive and motivation became more prominent in the economic world of the artisan.

Artists, furthermore, enjoyed a definite status in the eyes of their contemporaries, however it has eluded modern observers with their neat categories of sociological analysis. We have already remarked how they gained this recognition by successfully conditioning Florentines to an appreciation of their work. They are included among famous citizens of their times who brought fame to the city, and possession of the works of specific artists gave a man like Giovanni Rucellai considerable pride. The triple portrait of Taddeo, Zanobi, and Agnolo Gaddi (in the Uffizi) expresses already in the fourteenth century the new dignity painters could feel even though represented as artisans. They were certainly literate—most artisans in Florence were—and a surprising number of them, from Ghiberti to Vasari, could claim considerable literary and even scholarly accomplishment. Hence the way was open for them to enter the world of the intellectual if not the patrician. Ghiberti, Brunelleschi, Donatello, and Luca Della Robbia were friends of that first great patrician bibliophile and collector of antiquities, Niccolò Niccoli, and of the humanist Alberti. Michelozzo's sons studied with Ficino; Bernardo Rossellino's son took a degree in law and taught for awhile at the University of Pisa; Bernardo Rosselli's son studied medicine and set up practice in Florence. This intellectual status, however, did not bring the artist the usual advantages the modern historian associates with social climbing—"strategic" marriage, political office, access to good investments and wealth.

Sumptuary Law and Social Relations in Renaissance Italy

DIANE OWEN HUGHES

History has proved that all sumptuary laws have been everywhere, after a brief time, abolished, evaded or ignored. Vanity will always invent more ways of distinguishing itself than the laws are able to forbid.

Voltaire's dismissal, written when sumptuary laws were on the wane in his own country, prompts the question, why, then, were they enacted? We do not have to wait until the eighteenth century to find reference to their futility. The concept of legislating against consumption was ridiculed almost from its inception, often by those who favoured controlling it. Franco Sacchetti, writing in Florence during the first century of its legislative activity against consumption, went further even than Voltaire to suggest that the law itself promoted what it sought to control. As the defeated enforcement officer in one of his *Trecentonovelle* [Three Hundred Tales] explains to his superiors, legal insistence on restraint bred linguistic and stylistic invention:

> My lords, all the days of my life have I studied to learn the rules of the law, and now, when I did believe myself to know somewhat, I find that I know nothing. For when, obeying the orders that you gave me, I went out to seek the forbidden ornaments of your women, they met me with arguments the like of which are not to be found in any book of laws; and some of these I will repeat to you. There comes a woman with the peak of her hood fringed out and twisted round her head. My notary says, "Tell me your name, for you have a peak with fringes." The good woman takes this peak, which is fastened round her head with a pin, and, holding it in her hand, she declares that it is a wreath. Then going further, he finds one wearing many buttons in front of her dress, and he says to her, "You are not allowed to wear these buttons." But she answers, "Yes, Messer, but I may, for these are not buttons but studs, and if you do not believe me, look, they have no loops, and moreover there are no buttonholes." Then the notary goes to another who is wearing ermine and says, "Now what can she say to this? You are wearing ermine." And he prepares to write down her name. But the woman answers, "Do not write me down, for this is not ermine, it is the fur of a suckling." Says the notary, "What is this suckling?" and the woman replies, "It is an animal."

The laws themselves tried to respond to this inventiveness of language and style: by the fifteenth century, the outlawing of expensive buttons involved the listing of *bottoni, maspilli,* and *pianetti*; of headdresses, *berretti, cuffie, balzi, cappuci* and *selli*; of head ornaments, *cerchielli, ghirlande, corone, fruscoli, guazzeroni, frenelli* and *vespaii*. When the Venetian Senate in 1443 forbade women to wear dresses cut from cloth of

"Sumptuary Law and Social Relations in Renaissance Italy," by Diane Owen Hughes in John Bossy, ed. *Disputes and Settlements.* Reprinted by permission of Diane Owen Hughes.

gold or silver, they and their tailors began to use it to line sleeves, which were slashed or lengthened to let it show. . . .

If legislators recognized a certain defeat in their innumerable preambles lamenting that their statutes were not observed, their usual solution was not to abandon but to increase their legislative activity. . . .

Most cities turned their sporadic medieval legislation into formal Renaissance codes, which were endlessly amended in response to criticism and fashion. It has been calculated that the Italian cities produced eighty-three substantial sumptuary laws in the fifteenth century and more than double that number in each of the following two centuries. . . .

What provoked such legislative zeal? . . .

Historians have tended, with Voltaire, to mock sumptuary legislation and, by implication, its legislators. At the best their impulses are labelled paternalistic, a term for which it is hard to find a definition without pejorative overtones. This label does not do justice to the fanaticism of legislating zeal within Italian Renaissance cities, nor does it explain the developmental aspects of the legislation. Finally, it obscures the fundamental question of why some societies—but not others—develop a passion to legislate against consumption. These questions lie at the centre of this [essay].

I

. . . The aristocratic governments of other developing medieval cities do not seem to have issued sumptuary laws. They first appear, in the middle of the thirteenth century, in communes which had admitted the "popolo [non-nobles]" in at least a partial way into the government. . . .

The limitation of numbers at weddings and funerals, if a form of sumptuary control, also served as a control on noble gatherings and a means, as Heers has suggested, of weakening the power of those noble "clans" that had dominated the cities' early political life. In Bologna, for example, a proclamation of 1276, repeated in the statutes of 1289, deprived mourning of its focus for manifestations of family power. Weeping at or striking the doors of the dead was forbidden, bells might be rung only at the place and time of burial, and a death might not be announced through the city. Those in attendance were limited to ten men and eight priests and the mourners at home, to male relatives within the fifth degree and women within the third. If torches were forbidden, candles limited, and shrouds regulated, the proclamation as a whole seems less dedicated to sumptuary than social control. Early clothing regulations also have an anti-aristocratic flavour. Siena's early reduction of trains on women's dresses, if it saved cloth, also censored an aristocratic style, one which by a later law of 1277 was completely forbidden to servants; and the outlawing of golden, jewel-bedecked crowns had similar overtones. . . .

The sumptuary law, seen in this way as a curb on aristocratic display, becomes a symbol of republican virtue. Savonarola's reformed city comes to mind as perhaps the most fervent mating of sumptuary controls with republicanism; and the memory outlived a generation of Medici rule: one of the first acts of the re-established

Florentine Republic in 1527 was the publication of a new sumptuary law. Despots also sought to control consumption, of course, but with less enthusiasm. One of the least active cities in legislating against extravagance was Milan, whose first sumptuary code seems to have been that issued by Gian Galeazzo in 1396 after his assumption of the title of duke of Milan. The law was re-issued virtually untouched in its 1480 edition. . . .

The earliest sumptuary laws offered no economic explanations. When, in the last half of the fourteenth century, the custom of preambles [formal introductions to the legislation] began, we find some differences of approach between the maritime trading cities and the more artisanal cities of the interior. Both Venice and Genoa emphasized investment: "our state has become less strong because money that should navigate and multiply . . . lies dead, converted into vanities," said a Venetian law of 1360; "a great quantity of money which is kept dead and wrapped up in clothing and jewels, converted into trade might bring great returns and profits," began the Genoese law of 1449. The cities of the interior expressed the need for restraint in almost exclusively moral terms. The Bolognese laws of 1398 and 1401 were issued so "that the state might be strengthened by good and honest customs and those pleasing to God." That of Siena in 1412 indicated a clearer sense that "it is necessary to provide for a restraint of superfluous outlays from the purses of citizens, the rich as well as the poor, for the conservation and utility and honour of the Commune," but later preambles became even more general and moralistic. The Pistoia legislation of 1558 also referred to the ruin of citizens, which led to urban decline, but the legislators were thinking in the personal and often strictly demographic terms that became common throughout Renaissance Italy.

Economic protectionism can be detected in some laws from about the middle of the fifteenth century. The government of Siena began to back a local silk industry in 1438, and by 1440 the commune had decided to fine and brand anyone who removed a silkworker from the city. While in its total banning of silk garments (except for one pair of sleeves) in 1433, the *Consiglio Generale* [General Council] seems not to have considered the effects on Siena's *setaiuoli* [silk manufacturers], who were necessarily doing business with silk acquired elsewhere, its legislation of 1460 was protective of the new and still fragile industry. It allowed Sienese women a few silken garments as long as they had been made from cloth manufactured in the city. Milan began in the seventeenth century, after its prosperous silk industry had dramatically declined, to issue protectionist legislation. Protectionist attempts are, however, both late and sporadic. They should not encourage us to believe that protectionism was generally an object or provocation of the law.

Nor do the sumptuary laws show a developed economic interest in bullion. Gold and silver, along with pearls and certain furs, form a privileged list of restricted items throughout the whole period of sumptuary control. The Sienese legislation of 1277–82 had allowed to women only one unadorned garland of silver for their heads, which was to weigh no more than two ounces. In Bologna in 1289 circlets for the head made of silver and gold were outlawed, as was almost every other ornament made of the precious metals. The fourteenth- and fifteenth-century allowance in many Italian cities of three gold rings became, like the single strand of pearls, a cliché of both law and contemporary portraiture. The restrictions were real, and the fines could be steep—in Siena £100 (or about one-half the average dowry of the period) for exceeding the two-ounce limit. But the level of concern seems to have borne no relation to the shifting price or availability of precious metals. . . . In Genoa, where the fluctuations in the gold market were probably better understood than elsewhere, a law of 1449 allowing women up to £1,000 of gold and silver jewellery—far more than Siena and many other inland cities permitted their wives and daughters—was left essentially unchanged for more than half a century of increased availability of gold; and the new law of 1512 seems, without comment, to have reduced this allowance. It is true that three merchants whose wives wore golden chains worth 25 florins apiece in contravention of the law were hauled before a magistrate in 1453, but they escaped conviction by arguing that since the jewellery had been hidden by their clothes, it had not set a bad example. Public morality, not money, was the magistrate's concern.

II

The church came at sumptuary legislation through the same moralistic door. Suspicious of an economy whose health lay in expansion, dependent on the use and manipulation of money, churchmen worried not about the economic consequences of the withdrawal of wealth from productive enterprise, but about the personal and social consequences of the victory of *luxuria*. If civic governments spoke of public and private ruin, the church spoke of corruption. The friars, confessors of the medieval Italian cities, looked to sumptuary legislation as a weapon in the war against sin. . . . St. Thomas had allowed that female display, even if it enhanced natural beauty, was usually not a sin so long as it was employed in pursuit of a husband; it was, in any case, venial, not mortal. The Franciscan Orpheus de Cancellariis rejected this argument. The sin was mortal, he argued, not only because it was in contempt of God, but because, by threatening to ruin the fathers or husbands who supplied the wherewithal for their finery, women were a peril to others. And when their dress or habits were provocative; when, for example, they bared their shoulders or even their breasts, they became a public scandal. Orpheus admitted that the measure of extravagance was tied to fortune and that a woman could wear rich clothes without evil intention, but such expenses became a mortal sin if the clothes were unsuited to her station or would impoverish her and hence reverse her station. San Bernardino of Siena went even further to set the question of extravagant dress in the context of social charity, condemning extravagant trousseaux as extracted from the blood of the poor. . . .

Renewed episcopal activity under the influence of a strong papacy probably stimulated sumptuary legislation throughout Italy in this period. In some places, the church assumed full or substantial responsibility for the promulgation of the law. Citizens seem to have found episcopal legislation particularly hard to bear, both because of its severity and because of its penalty—excommunication. When Ginevra Sforza married Sante Bentivoglio in 1454, clothed with twelve attendants in gold brocade, a cloth the sumptuary law of Cardinal Bessarion had just denied to all Bolognese women, the church of San Petronio closed its doors to the bridal party. It went on to San Giacomo, where the friars married the couple, but some of the party suffered excommunication for flouting the law. . . .

It would be wrong to see sumptuary legislation as a simple response to ecclesiastical demands. Initially the aims of the church and those of city governments seem to have differed. Cardinal Latino, whose limitation of trains was in line with contemporary urban legislation, also ruled that women must cover their heads, an ordinance which, according to Salimbene—if no lover of women, an admirer of their abilities—encouraged the production of silken veils woven with gold, "which all the more encouraged lust in the eye of the beholder." But this concern for female modesty did not find its way into contemporary civic codes, which on the contrary began to restrict first the sumptuousness of female head coverings and then the anonymity they might provide. Yet ecclesiastical attempts to control seductiveness in female dress (and deportment) do seem to have made headway throughout Italy in the course of the fifteenth and sixteenth centuries. The Piacenzan chronicler De Mussis was commenting as early as 1388 on "shameful dresses . . . called *ciprianae* . . . which . . . have such a large neck that the breasts show: and it looks as if the said breasts want to burst from the bosom." But only one commune, Perugia, whose legislation already reflected the influence of ecclesiastics, had acted (in 1342) to control *décolletage* "beneath the collarbone." Milan, where the Dominican Galvano Fiamma had disapproved in the first half of the fourteenth century of the bare throats and necks of its women, seems to have waited for almost a century before legislating against such exposure, and then only in the mildest way: low-cut necklines were allowed as long as the shoulder bones were covered in some other way. The law encouraged women to resort to those shoulder covers of transparent silk mousseline (often embroidered with gold) which formed a part of many contemporary trousseaux. It was only at the end of the fifteenth century that Milan, in legislation of 1498, outlawed necklines lower than one finger—placed sideways, as they took care to specify—from the collar-bone.

By then a movement to cover female flesh was under way. Florence had already, in a law of 1456, forbidden any "baring of the throat and neck" although in 1464 the government had relented and allowed a *décolletage* of about three centimetres from the collar-bone in front and twice that amount from the neckbone behind, measures which, as portraits of the period show, were not rigidly observed. Savonarola, however, made of *décolletage* a major issue, insisting on a two-finger measure. Like the Franciscan Orpheus de Cancellariis, who reminded his readers that the baring of shoulders and breasts, by making the woman a public scandal, brought style to the level of mortal sin, Savonarola inquired whether such display was the sign of an honest woman. By the sixteenth century, Venice and even Genoa, whose women had a reputation for daring display, had begun to regulate the amount of flesh they might expose. A Genoese law of 1506 insisted on lower hemlines, while one of 1511–12 decreed that women must cover completely their shoulders and the "two bones before the throat," regulations that neighbouring Savona copied in 1531. A Venetian law of 1562 ruled more liberally, and certainly more realistically, that camisoles or other coverings of the shoulder must be "so closed in front that the breast is covered." Whatever the details of the legislation, they had become persuaded that such rules were necessary to ensure "la honestà muliebre [honest wife]." . . .

The growing association in Italian cities of *décolletage* with shame should be seen in the context of a larger change in the direction of the law. Early sumptuary legislation can be divided fairly evenly into laws concerning clothes (often those of men as well as women), weddings and funerals. Although the expenses involved in the ceremonies and feasts accompanying marriage and burial rose steadily with their further elaboration and although new and extravagant customs surrounding parturition and baptism ate into household budgets, legislation directed against ceremony declined significantly in the fifteenth century in relation to that directed against clothing, particularly the clothing of women. While some of this can be accounted for by legislators' attempts to counter rapid changes in style or evasions in the law, like those Sacchetti relates, that alone cannot explain the change, which the preambles to the laws enshrine. The preambles to the Venetian sumptuary laws of 22 May and 9 June 1334 locate in both sexes the extravagance they intend to attack, but that of 1360 mentions only "vanities" which are directed towards "brides and other women and ladies." Most fifteenth-century preambles state explicitly that women are the ruin of men. . . .

. . . In Bologna, Cardinal Bessarion's law did provoke a female protest—from Sante Bentivoglio's learned and beautiful lover, Nicolosa Sanuti, whom Sabadino degli Arienti described on a hillside wearing a gown of purple silk and a rose-coloured cloak lined with the finest ermine. She might have heard of events a year earlier in Siena, where the Emperor Frederick III had stopped with his fiancée Leonora of Portugal on the way to their coronation and marriage in Rome. Battista Petrucci, the daughter of a professor of rhetoric, had given a Latin recitation so appreciated by the couple that they asked her to select a reward. She chose release from all sumptuary regulations, a request which the city government reluctantly conceded. Sanuti, however, argued not only for herself but for all the women of Bologna.

TABLE 1   A Comparison of Sumptuary Restrictions
in Three Cities

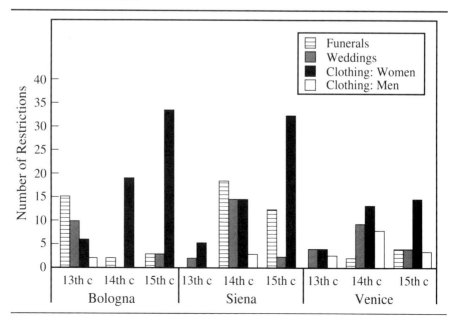

Her elegant oration reminded the cardinal that although Roman women had been limited in their use of gold and precious cloth during the rigours of the Second Punic War, freedom in finery was restored to them after the crisis had passed. That law, imposed by conditions of war, might be understandable, but it was hard to excuse the Bolognese restrictions, devised to feed the avarice of husbands who put money before dignity. They showed no concern for the domestic disruptions which would be a certain consequence of their restrictions, an argument that some Paduan nobles would use at the beginning of the next century in an attempt to defeat that city's sumptuary controls over women. The histories of women of the ancient world as well as the lives of many women of her own day proved, she argued, that feminine abilities could equal those of men: many resembled that "Amesia, whom, since she bore a manly spirit beneath a female form, they called Androgynos." Individual women of Bologna could rise, like some of their Greek and Roman predecessors, to heroic action; and collectively, she reminded the cardinal, they had within them the power of the Sabines—to save a civilization from demographic ruin. Women deserved freedom of choice in clothes because it was to clothes that they had been reduced. If one conceded (as surely the cardinal would) that "as patricians from the people, so should remarkable women differ from the obscure," then, she concluded, the sumptuary restrictions should be lifted. "Magistracies are not conceded to women; they do not strive for priesthoods, triumphs, the spoils of war, because these are considered the honours of men. Ornament and apparel, because they are our insignia of worth, we cannot suffer to be taken from us."

In a letter to her lover on the eve of his marriage to Ginevra Sforza, a despairing Nicolosa Sanuti recanted. But she had been right. Clothes were women's insignia, and the legislators knew it. They knew, too, that men had become implicated in them: they designed and made them, their money bought them, their status was reflected in them. In 1343 the rich women of Florence lined up before a notary to register the clothes they owned which were in contravention of the recently promulgated sumptuary law, which allowed that such clothes might continue to be worn as long as they were taxed and marked with a special lead seal bearing the Florentine lily on one side and a cross on the other. The clothes, recorded in an extant register, show that same restless variety as the laws designed to control them: dresses (usually of silk) take the form of sleeved and sleeveless underdresses and overdresses, often accompanied by cloaks and mantles, in various hues of red, blue and green, sometimes striped or pierced with white or contrasting colours, trimmed with fabric embroidered or woven with crowns, stars, rosettes, butterflies, birds and dragons. But from such sumptuous riot some order emerges. Lady Guerriera, the wife of Jacopo di Antonio de Albizis, and her sisters-in-law Nera and Piera all registered gowns and matching tunics of green samite (a heavy silk often interwoven with gold). The same Guerriera and Nera registered mantles of white cloth embroidered with vines and grapes of blood-red and lined in cloth of shimmering white. Their clothes appear just after those of their mother-in-law Joanna, who distinguished herself from them in counterpoint: a cloak of purple to their white and blood-red; a dress of scarlet with silken crowns, which reflected the green of the gowns of her daughters-in-law only in its lining. Dinga, the daughter of Sandro Altovito, and Lisabetta, the daughter of Gentile Altovito, came together to register their identical and elaborate tunics, which were divided into two spheres of red, then checked with silk, and trimmed with yet another fabric. Relationships can be as easily guessed from the clothing lists as from the names. Nor are we dealing here with simple thrift—some cloth and a tailor for all the women of a household. Lady Ginevra, the wife of Agnolo di Giani de Albizis, probably a distant relative of Joanna and her daughters-in-law, who lived in another district of the city, had earlier registered the single piece of her clothing which was in contravention of the law and on which she chose to pay the tax—a mantle of white cloth embroidered with vines and blood-red grapes, lined in cloth of shimmering white. Those brilliant and distinctive cloaks must have become Albizi insignia. Even the limited view of wardrobe that this register of outlawed clothes gives us provides a glimpse of a society that described itself through clothes. Is it any wonder that the ordering of dress became for legislators a metaphorical way of talking about social distinction, a way of ordering human relations?

III

Fashion, in its delicate balancing of "the desire for imitation and differentiation," signifies, as Simmel observed, "the form of the social process." Unlike more hierarchical societies, whose rules repressed such a process, or poorer ones, whose poverty forbade it, the urban society of medieval Italy measured progress in terms of its dynamic. . . . But sumptuary law of the thirteenth and fourteenth centuries sought to restrain, not to re-order. . . . Most of the others regulated yardage, material and ornament. If this reflected the realities of dress, which was of simple cut, depending for its effect on the quality and amount of material and on accompanying ornament, it also reflected a society more attuned to excess than disorder.

By the middle of the fifteenth century, however, as women's costume, with the extraordinary development of ruffs, bodices and detachable sleeves, became a series of interchangeable parts, fashion and change became a new target of the law. It sought to regulate the rapidly shifting parts of an unstable whole, which even Cesare Vecellio, in his popular book on fashion, found hard to grasp. In Venice on the eve of the crisis of the League of Cambrai the Senate debated fashions in sleeves. The debate had begun in 1503 when the legislators outlawed "manege a comedo," those great leg-of-mutton sleeves which Lotto's subjects so favoured for their portraits and which the Senate found "an ugly fashion" requiring three or more *brachia* [armlengths] of cloth of gold or silk for their execution. By October 1504 the senators recognized that that "dishonest fashion that is not appropriate to women" had been replaced by "another fashion, larger and uglier than the first," and they decided to ban all sleeves wider than one third of a *brachia* at any point. Within a year, they were outlawing "certain fashions and new apparel, both offensive and dishonest, which were never before used in this city"—namely, sleeves cut of many pieces of fabric of diverse colours. On 4 January 1507, the Senate complained that sleeves of the *investidure* had grown larger every time the matter had been legislated about. "And if [women] are granted the right to put six *brachia* [into the sleeves], in a few months they will grow to an even larger size, so that they can be called not sleeves of the *investidure* but sleeves of the gown itself and it will become necessary to concede more." They repeated the former limits and restricted the sleeves of the gown, the so-called "manege ducali [ducal sleeves]," to 32 *brachia* of silk or 28 of serge or another non-silken fabric. In the difficult summer of 1509, the doge spoke before the *Maggior Consiglio* [Great Council] and accounted for Venice's decline by the inordinate length of its sleeves. The concern for expense is, of course, ever present: every extra *brachia* was a drain on the individual, and the point of the doge's speech was to encourage Venetian nobles to pay their state debts. But in the eyes of Renaissance legislators, fashion changes bred worse than excess or extravagance, they bred disorder. . . .

. . . Useful splendour was one thing, fashion another. Under the rule of fashion, clothing lost both its real function and its emblematic significance. Shoes that impeded walking, robes and accessories that confused or concealed rather than expressed identity—such perversions were the sign of a profoundly disordered society. The Milanese friar Pietro Casola remarked on the similarity between the Chinese custom of binding women's feet to make them smaller and the Venetian one of wearing shoes on platforms so that "they appear giants." If such shoes kept feet from the mire, the legislators knew that women really wore them because "through the height of the shoes gowns can be made much longer." The resulting "enormous and excessive expenses" were to be lamented, but the chief concern of the laws enacted against them was functional: these shoes, like bound feet, impeded walking to such an extent that, according to Casola, some women "are only kept upright by the support of slaves." Legislation against veils, which seems to have begun in Siena in 1343 and had little economic purpose, was concerned with the freedom from proper identification that such veils accorded their wearers. Officials of the commune were empowered to demand, on encountering a veiled woman, the name of her father and husband, her "terzo," "popolo" and "contrada" [the area and specific neighborhood she lived in]. This let them discover the names of those responsible for paying the fine if her clothing was in contravention of the sumptuary law but, more importantly, it restored an identity which clothes were meant to convey, not obscure. The perversion of purpose of the shoes and clothing perverted the wearer and society itself. . . .

The difference between *meretrix* [prostitute] and *matrona* [matron] stands at the heart of sumptuary distinction. Zaleucus' suggestion that only prostitutes be permitted rich dress as a means of shaming the virtuous into simplicity was taken up in the laws of some Italian cities: Siena allowed them not only platform shoes but also the dresses of cloth of gold and clothes painted or embroidered with trees, fruits, flowers and animals which it denied to other women; Brescia devised similar allowances. In other cities, prostitutes were assigned more humiliating marks of distinction: in Venice, yellow scarves; in Milan, a cloak of common fustian, whose colour—white in the original law of 1412—was changed to black in the new sumptuary code of 1498. In most places prostitutes were increasingly segregated. In Genoa, for example, a city that did not identify them by either rich clothing or humiliating marks, a series of laws began at the end of the fourteenth century to confine prostitutes to a special district. This made it easier for communal officials to stand at the bordello door and collect the new tax imposed in 1418; but fiscal purposes were secondary. Prostitutes were considered such outsiders in Ferrara by the end of the fifteenth century that responsibility for them was assigned to the same officials who collected the taxes on imported goods. . . .

. . . Nevertheless, at least part of the law's purpose was more positive than contemporary preaching and moralizing might seem to suggest. It sought to reconcile a woman's dual legal personality, as the daughter of one lineage and wife in another. The moment of reconciliation was marriage, when men's honour and position were most publicly displayed through their women, particularly through brides in whom the honour and position of the two houses merged. The bride, at that moment, dowered and arrayed in a trousseau, stood poised between the two sumptuary states—between childhood, when to a greater or lesser extent she might be indulged, and matronhood, when she would be struck by the full force of the sumptuary law. . . .

Although when she married, a trousseau pushed the Genoese bride towards sumptuary adulthood, the law demanded three further years of partial restraint when she could not receive from either her own family or her husband's any more than one silk dress, which could not, in any case, be dyed a fine red, and when all garments of silk pile were denied her. Three years from the day she crossed the threshold of her husband's house (the so-called *transductio*), she came of sumptuary age. Within this long period, the daughter was separated from her father's largesse, which was restored only on the day of her marriage, as trousseau; on this she had to live and dress while she was integrated into her new home. By the end of that period, it might well be understood that she would produce an heir and so move physically as well as legally from the status of *sponsa* [bride] to that of *matrona* [matron]. The period of greatest sumptuary restraint and special sumptuary status thus coincided with those years when her sexuality (and hence the honour of the man who was her legal guardian) was most at risk: when sexually mature, she had no husband; when married, she had borne no child.

No city found such distinctions totally satisfactory. By the beginning of the following century, Genoa had decided to allow girls to wear until they were taken into marriage golden headdresses that the law would deny them as wives. The new approach may have been made necessary by the growing inability of fathers to arrange unaided the marriages of their daughters. Every city had come to feel by the fifteenth century that the institution of marriage itself had become a source of social disorder, from which fathers and daughters, not husbands, suffered most. . . .

If demographic evidence suggests that men were marrying later and less frequently and that the convents were becoming fuller, the sumptuary evidence suggests that women who did marry were felt to have the whip hand over husbands whose livelihood seemed more and more to depend on their dowries. It is no wonder that such men lashed out at the changing fashions of their wives, which not only ate into the estate but also seemed to signify their loss of control. . . .

Women were an object of fear, their power sufficient to ruin cities. Yet there was a gulf between most of the urban legislation and the ecclesiastical ranting of contemporary Isaiahs who sought to "smite with a scab the crown of the head of the daughters of Zion" because they "are haughty, and walk with stretched forth necks and wanton eyes, walking and mincing as they go, and making a tinkling with their feet." For it was issued by men who were fully implicated in female folly. They lived off the condemned dowries, they paid for the forbidden dresses, whose splendour reflected their status, and they generally appeared in court and paid the fines demanded for contravention of the law by their women. In talking about women, their dress and deportment, men were talking about themselves and about their often conflicting roles as fathers and husbands. But they did not just talk, they acted.

We must distinguish between *enforcement,* which failed, and *legislating,* which achieved objects of its own. The doge Andrea Gritti, on the way to the ceremonies marking his coronation in 1523, was being ostentatious in sending home a female relative to change out of her outlawed dress of cloth of gold; just as the earlier wedding festivities of a Corner and Loredan in the city in 1512 when "the women [were] obedient to the ordinance [because] they feared the *provedadori* [Commissioners] would condemn them," are remembered for that concern. Where prosecutions were undertaken, appeal and influence often let the guilty escape. And, of course, one could simply take the fines as a kind of luxury tax, an experiment which had been tried as early as 1299 in Florence and which finds a place in the Genoese and Sienese legislation of the fifteenth century—*pagar le pompe* [paying for luxuries] as the Venetians said. The process of legislating had better success. The endless codes attest to it. So does the sense of development within them of, for example, the relations between fathers and daughters, husbands and wives.

It is striking in a society whose single most important transfer of personal assets had arguably become a woman's dowry (which even in marriage she continued to own) that so much legislation was designed to keep women from wearing their wealth. This infuriated women rich in their own right, as Nicolosa Sanuti's oration shows. Some communes came to allow women to display their dotal worth, "since all should not be equal to all," as the Genoese put it when they established jewellery limits based on the value of the dowry a woman took into her marriage. But the wealth which determined what a woman might wear was always paternal wealth— what she had received as her father's daughter. When Siena toyed with this system, in 1424, it limited the gifts husbands might give to their wives at marriage and established the limit as a percentage of the dowry. This system stressed patrilineal distinctions at a time when rising dowries were exaggerating them. If hungry husbands were the villains of sumptuary laws which set limits on dowries, the wealth they gained did not keep the wives who brought them from being distinguished, ever more clearly, as their fathers' daughters. . . .

. . . Renaissance legislators tried to create order at those points in social organization where structure was ambivalent, particularly where social ideology was in conflict with many social practices. Their society had an ideology of orders but was in practice governed by money, which could alter position and rank. Clothes were a visible sign of this conflict: a better tax position would probably have let Messer Lorenzo's wife clothe herself in cloth of gold. Their society had a patrilineal ideology but was governed in everyday life by a confusion of cognatic, patrilineal and conjugal arrangements. This had the effect of splintering women's social identity, while giving them, as status-bearers of their fathers' lineage and their husbands', a position of increasing dominance within the household. High dowries and accompanying marital gifts were a sign of this, diminishing fathers and the economic strength of the patrimony, and at the same time diminishing the power of husbands in the home. These structural inconsistencies, for which there was no real cure, created social tensions which the legislation sought to remedy and which the *process* of legislating may have eased. They became clearly visible in Italian cities in the thirteenth century, as men who rose through money became politically significant and assumed political power and as urban governments, freed from aristocratic control, began in a concerted way to attack lineal bonds and organization. It is not a coincidence that this was when the sumptuary legislation began.

Italian sumptuary legislation was, among other things, an approach to easing tensions caused by structural problems of a local social nature. Though it resembled the legislation of the northern monarchies, and even more closely that of German and Swiss cities, it was far less hierarchical than the one and far more anti-feminist than both. But Europe did in a sense form a sumptuary whole, expressing its frustration over social problems it could not fully solve through legislative control over their outward signs. These signs can be controlled by formal, often religious means in societies where orders attain the rigidity of caste, and they are generally allowed as more legitimate expressions of identity in a society ordered by class. In Renaissance Italy, a society that dreamed of orders while facing the daily consequences of class fluidity, they had to be controlled by legislation.

DOCUMENTS

In the first and second documents two painters record the contracts for commissions they have received and then note when the work of art was finished and paid for. Neri di Bicci was a successful, though second-rate, painter in mid-fifteenth-century Florence, and Paolo Farinati was a well-known artist who lived and worked in the provincial city of Verona toward the end of the sixteenth century. Both men kept track of all their commissions and other commercial transactions in journals, somewhat like the *ricordanze* kept by so many Florentine merchants. The journals (which are among the very few artists' journals that have survived) reveal that they were sensible businessmen who were willing to do a wide variety of work in order to satisfy their customers and keep their workshops busy. Note that they do not arrive at the final price to be paid for their work in the same way: Neri agrees to wait until he finishes the altarpiece in order to negotiate the price, but Farinati sets the fee for his frescoes as he begins. This difference reflects important changes in the valuation of painting that occurred in the century separating the two men, as well as Farinati's higher status and local renown. Farinati's house, for example, is sufficiently elegant to serve as a model for some of the work he does for his customers.

The next document is an inventory of an aristocratic household in mid–sixteenth century Verona and typical of its time in the organization of its rooms and furnishings. This is not an especially lavish establishment; no clothing and only one painting is listed, perhaps because such valuables were removed by the heirs or the executor before the inventory was taken. Nevertheless, the many bedcoverings, tapestries, rugs, napkins, and other textiles were quite valuable in their own right. Three examples of sumptuary legislation from Venice, which attempted to control the costs of weddings, regulate women's dress, and limit the size of banquets, complete the section.

Neri di Bicci Paints an Altarpiece for Geri Bartoli, 1455

Today, 18 January 1455, on Monday:
I record that several days ago I undertook to paint for Geri Bartoli, merchant in Calimala Street, in the classical manner, with a *predella* panel below, fluted columns on the sides, and architrave, frieze and large foliated cornice above, of [. . .] yards wide and [. . .] yards high, in which I am to paint a Madonna in the center; on the right St. Andrew and St. James; on the left St. John the Baptist and St. Anthony; and in the panel below five half-figures as he desires and his coat-of-arms on the side; fine gold is to be applied on the front parts and fine ultramarine blue for the Madonna and all well executed all at my expense for gold, blue and every other thing which is needed to paint said altarpiece and he has given me the frame and when I will have furnished said altarpiece we must set a price and thus I agreed with him today and today I had the central panel of the frame of said altarpiece.

[Next entry:] I delivered said altarpiece to above-named Geri on the 13th of July 1456 and I set a price with him and he must give me thirty florins as agreed. Made this day, 5 August, with above-named Geri in this volume on p. 26. [Also] in Volume D [his account book] on p. 16.

Paolo Farinati Decorates Bastiani's House with Frescoes, 1586–1587

[First entry:] On 12 May 1586 I, Paolo, made an agreement with the magnificent Knight Verità and Sir Zanieronimo Bastiani, the son-in-law of the said Knight, to paint the frieze in the Great Hall of the said Sir Zanieronimo: in which frieze there will be the story of Esther in eight parts, in fresco. And I am obliged to build and take down the scaffolding and plaster as necessary; and in gratitude for my painting, they are obliged to give me ninety ducats . . . ; and this [agreement] can be found with me, Paolo, in a contract for ninety ducats signed by the magnificent knight Verità. The frieze was begun on 14 April 1587 and was finished by 20 June.
[Farinati records that the final payment was made by Bastiani on August 31 1587.]

[Second entry:] On the 2 of September 1586 I, Paolo, made a deal with the said

From Neri di Bicci, Le ricordanze, 1455, Bruno Santi, ed., (Pisa, 1976), no. 95. Translated by Alison A. Smith.
From Paolo Farinati, Giornale (1573–1606), Lionello Puppi, ed. (Florence, 1968). Translated by Alison A. Smith.

Zanieronimo di Bastiani to paint the frieze in his bedroom above the cornices; which frieze should resemble bronze, like that in the ground-floor room of Count Mario Bevilacqua; and also to paint the cornices to resemble carved stone; and to put in a few ornaments in the frieze. In addition, I am to paint the walls in the dining room, from the ceiling to the floor in fresco, just as it is in my own home; and he wants me to do the scaffolding and the plastering. And for the above pictures they are obliged to give me forty ducats, as is written in the contract signed by him, and in my possession.

The painting of the walls and the columns of the dining room of Zanieronimo were finished on 6 October 1586.

On the 24 October 1586, I painted and gilded an ornament on a canopy, for one ducat. And also put some gilding on the bronze frieze, for one ducat.

[Farinati notes that final payment was made for the work on 6 November 1586.]

| An Aristocratic Home in Verona, 1568

Recorded on Friday, May 7, 1568, by the notary Gregorio Albertini in the contrada of Ferraboi in Verona.

Inventory of all the movable goods of the estate of the Magnificent Giulio Verità, deceased, contained in his house in the contrada of Ferraboi and made at the request of the widows Anna Bevilacqua de Lazise and her daughter Lucrezia, widow of Giulio, both guardians and executrixes of Giulio's estate, and his children, Carlo, Marco Antonio, Pietro Francesco, Giulio Cesare, all minors. [The fifth child, Giulia, is not mentioned here.]

First, in the Great Hall of the house were paid to the Magnificent Count Paolo Sesso (in payment of a debt) the sum of 100 gold crowns and 100 gold ducats contained in a box, in the presence of two Venetian officials.

Repayment of several outstanding debts with silk merchants and with a baker.

Lady Anna admits to having a box containing 41 gold ducats in the villa in Concamarise, which belong to Giulio's heirs.

In the Great Hall were to be found the following items:

8 walnut chairs
3 walnut benches
1 walnut chest of drawers
1 large table with stools
1 large bench
Fireplace equipment

"Household Inventory of Giulio Verità and Lucrezia Bevilacqua-Lazise, 1562," Archivio di Stato, Verona, Fondo Malaspina-Verità, busta 215, processo 2296. Translated by Alison A. Smith.

In the painted room adjoining the Great Hall:

9 new rugs, and 8 old rugs for chests
3 rugs for tables: one large one for the table in the Great Hall and the other two
four meters long; a cloth for the chest in the Great Hall
5 brocade tapestries: 3 large ones and 2 with coats of arms to hang on either side
of the fireplace in the Great Hall
1 quilt made of yellow velvet brocade
1 bedspread of yellow satin with the arms of the Verità and Bevilacqua-Lazise
entwined; a matching coverlet for the cradle with the same arms
1 bed canopy with a gray border, with matching quilt and bedspread
1 old quilt of green silk
1 new quilt of yellow satin filled with black silk
2 coverlets, one new and yellow, the other old and white
6 more coverlets, one painted in the Venetian style
54 sheets, new or somewhat used
18 very thin linen sheets
5 walnut chests carved with the Verità coat of arms
1 walnut bed carved to match the chests
1 bed and wool mattress
2 lengths of cloth to make a quilt
26 cushions of different kinds, both old and new

In the room next to the kitchen:

1 walnut bed with columns
1 bed with 2 covers, one white and one blue
1 wheeled cradle with a new yellow coverlet
3 chests painted with the Verità coat of arms, containing the following: 17 tablecloths, including 4 for the table in the Great Hall; 15 kitchen tablecloths; 18
kitchen towels; 46 old napkins and 50 new embroidered ones
4 cushions covered in gilt leather
2 walnut chairs and 2 benches
1 walnut chest of drawers
1 pine table
Fireplace equipment

In the kitchen:

15 large tin plates
30 medium tin plates
7 small tin plates
34 tin bowls
26 small bowls
1 olive oil can
3 brass basins
4 candlesticks
1 brass bedwarmer

Assorted cooking equipment
A bench, a table, and an old chest of drawers

In the room for the female servants:

1 cot and cradle
1 bed with quilt

In the room next to the study:

1 carved walnut bed
1 new yellow bedspread
3 carved walnut chests with the Verità coat of arms
1 small round walnut table
Fireplace equipment

In the study:

Benches on the walls for sitting
1 small cupboard

In the ground floor room where the tutor is teaching the children:

1 carved walnut bed with columns
2 bedcovers, one multicolored, one blue
6 walnut chests carved with the Verità coat of arms
4 chairs and a bench
Fireplace equipment
1 sacred picture [*ancona*] with gilt frame
1 map of the world
1 table

In the room for the male servants:

1 pine bed with mattress and blue bedcover
1 bench

In the stable:

1 new woolen mattress
1 heavy woolen cloak
2 old saddles

In the cellar:

7 large barrels (for carrying on a cart)
2 large wine casks, part of which was for drinking and part for sale

Under the portico, in the courtyard:

1 large wine vat

Sumptuary Legislation in Venice, 1360–1512

THE SENATE LIMITS THE VALUE OF WEDDING GIFTS, DRESSES, ORNAMENTS, AND LUXURIES GENERALLY, 1360

Because the beginning of all wisdom and the foundation of any government is the fear of God, and because it is well known that in our city more than any other part of the world, there are many vanities and inordinate expenses, especially concerning weddings and other matters concerning wives and ladies, all of which certainly offends God greatly. Morever, these illicit and depraved expenditures cause our state to be less powerful than it should be, because money which ought to be used in trade and to increase from time to time, now lies useless, because it had been diverted for these vanities and expenses. And in addition, since it has been seen and is seen that God had preserved us from many adversities and difficulties in the past, so we wish to recognize and correct our defects so that we will be preserved and defended by His mercy and piety in the future. Therefore, it is decreed, invoking the love of Christ, from whom comes every perfect gift, that concerning these vanities and expenses it should be provided as follows: no bride may receive, beyond her dowry including a trousseau and other gifts, more than 40 lire di grossi. Any person giving a dowry of 30 lire di grossi and upwards must present himself before the Avvocatori di Comune and swear to observe the law. Any notary drawing up a will must remind the testator that it is illegal to bequeath to his daughters more than the value named. No husband, at the time of marriage or within four years after, may give his wife dresses or jewels exceeding the value of thirty lire di grossi. Costly furs, such as ermine, are to be denied to men under twenty-five years old. The maximum value of a girdle is fixed at twenty-five ducats for a man, twenty ducats for a woman. The clothes and jewels of an unmarried woman must not exceed thirty lire di grossi in value, of a married woman seventy lire di grossi.

THE SENATE ALLOWS WOMEN TO WEAR HEAD COVERINGS ONLY FOR RELIGIOUS PURPOSES, 1443

Whereas, for some time, an abominable fashion has been introduced among our ladies and other females of every condition, who go about with the head and faces covered, contrary to the ancient and good custom, under which dishonest mode various dishonest acts have been and every day are committed, against the honour of God and of our dominion. . . . It is decreed that for the future no lady or other woman or girl, of any condition whatsoever, may go abroad with the head and face covered beyond what has been the custom, by land or by water, except those ladies and other good persons who desire to hear mass, and sermons, and divine service, and attend confession. To such it is conceded, when they enter any church for the said reasons, to remain covered as it shall please them. Further, all ladies and other

From Margaret Newett ed. "The Sumptuary Laws of Venice in the Fourteenth and Fifteenth Centuries," in *Historical Essays*, eds. T. F. Tout and James Tait (Manchester, at the University Press, 1907), pp. 245–248, at pp. 249–250.

females may be covered to the earliest communions in their parish churches, or in the convent churches near, but only on Sundays and the prescribed festivals, and they may return home covered.

THE SENATE LIMITS THE SIZE OF BANQUETS IN VENICE, 1512

Waiters and cooks who serve at any feast are compelled, the waiters under fine of twenty ducats, and the cooks under fine of ten ducats and four months' imprisonment, to come to the office of the Provveditori sopra le Pompe and declare the time and place of any banquet for which they have been engaged, in order that our office may be sent to inspect, and find out if in any respect the law will be violated. And the waiters, under the aforesaid penalty, are under obligation to lead the officers through the halls and smaller rooms, in order that they may perform their duty. And if any person of the house where they happen to be, or any other person, should interfere with our officers, and hinder them from doing their duties, or should molest them in any way by making use of injurious epithets, or throwing bread or oranges at their heads, as certain presumptuous persons have done, or should be guilty of any insolent act, it will be the duty of the waiters to leave the house immediately, and not to wait or be present at the banquet, under the aforesaid penalty. And nevertheless they shall have their salary, as if they had served.

FURTHER READING

Michael Baxandall, *Painting and Experience in Fifteenth-Century Italy* (1972)
Peter Burke, *The Italian Renaissance: Culture and Society in Italy* (1972)
D. S. Chambers, ed., *Patrons and Artists in the Italian Renaissance* (1970)
Samuel K. Cohn, *Death and Property in Siena, 1205–1800* (1988)
Georges Duby, ed., *A History of Private Life, II* (1988) Essays by Charles de la Roncière and Philippe Braunstein on housing.
Richard Goldthwaite, *Private Wealth in Renaissance Florence* (1968)
_____, *Wealth and the Demand for Art in Italy, 1300–1600* (1993)
Richard J. Goy, *House of Gold: Building a Palace in Medieval Venice* (1992)
Diane Owen Hughes, "Earrings for Circumcision: Distinction and Purification in the Italian Renaissance City," in *Persons in Groups: Social Behavior as Identity Formation in Medieval and Renaissance Europe*, ed. R. Trexler (1985)
F. W. Kent and P. Simon, eds., *Patronage, Art and Society in Renaissance Italy* (1987)
Guy Lytle and S. Oregl, eds., *Patronage in the Renaissance* (1981)
M. Newett, "The Sumptuary Laws of Venice in the Fourteenth and Fifteenth Centuries," in *Historical Essays*, eds. T. F. Tout and James Tait (1907), 248–278.
John White, *Art and Architecture in Italy, 1250–1400*, 3rd ed. (1993)

Photo Essay

The Ca'd'Oro, a sumptuous palace on the Grand Canal built for a Venetian noble family in the early fifteenth century. (Alinari/Art Resource, New York)

The building of the Strozzi Palace, an imposing
patrician palace in Florence, was begun in 1489.
(Scala/Art Resource, New York)

Gozzoli, "The Medici in Procession," detail of his
Adoration of the Magi (c. 1459), a fresco in the
Medici palace in Florence. (Alinari/Art Resource,
New York)

Pisanello, portrait medal (c. 1445) of Sigismondo
Malatesta, the powerful prince of Rimini.
(Alinari/Art Resource, New York)

Palladio, Villa Rotonda (begun c. 1567), near
Vicenza. One of many villas designed by Palladio
and others and built by noble families on their
farms on the Venetian mainland. They combined
classical forms in new ways to accommodate the
needs of these urban aristocrats seeking
temporary relief from the stresses of city life.
(Alinari/Art Resource, New York)

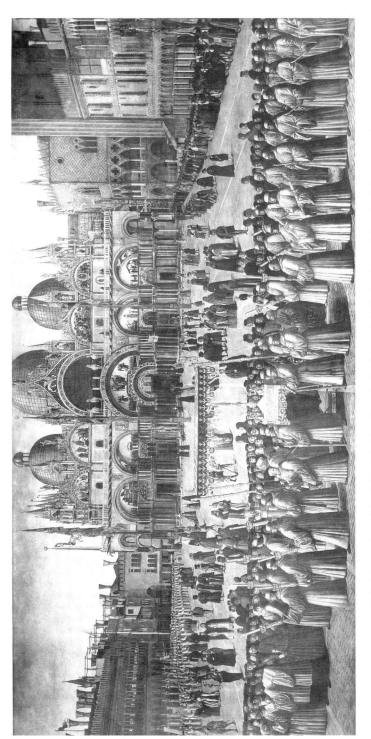

Bellini, *Procession of the Relic of the True Cross in San Marco* (1496). A solemn civic and religious procession around Venice's central square, the location of supreme political and religious authority. (Alinari/Art Resource, New York)

Anonymous, *The Burning of Girolamo
Savonarola* (c. 1500). The Florentine Republic
reasserted its control over the city when it
burned this charismatic religious leader at the
stake in the Piazza della Signoria, the civic center
of the city. (Alinari/Art Resource, New York)

Carpaccio, *The Dream of St. Ursula* (c. 1490). A
Venetian painting showing an elegantly
furnished bedroom. (Alinari/Art Resource,
New York)

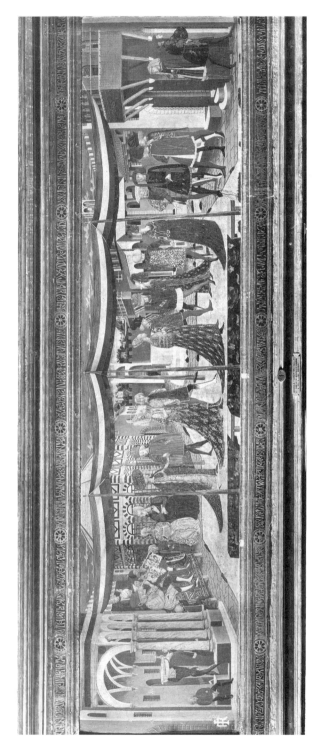

Anonymous, *Wedding Procession* (15th century). An elaborately carved wedding chest containing the bride's trousseau would usually accompany the bride to her new home. Paintings of contemporary scenes often decorated the sides of the chest. (Alinari/Art Resource)

10

memorant. Si sine uxoribus   O R O .
quirites esse possemus. omes ea
molestia caretem? Si quia ita
natura tradidit. ut nec cū illis
satis cōmode. nec sine illis ullo
modo uiuere possimus. saluti
perie potuis q breui uoluptati
consulendū uidetur. Si hec sa
tis de coniugio. qa adoctissimis
uiris sint tractata uberius. ut
aut maxime nota cōplecterem.
hec ipa collegimus. Nuc ptis vxo
rias qs amatorib, nostris nulq
in ordine digestas inuenim?.
qi sb uno aspectu positas breuit
exponemus. si pus q ingredia
mur hunc locum. qualis uxor
delior debeat instituerimus.
M odo id pmouerim? nulla tanta
nuptiar, excellentia ptingere debe

Manuscript page from Francesco Barbaro's *De re uxoria* (c. 1440), displaying the rounded, legible forms of humanist handwriting. (The Pierpoint Morgan Library, New York. B.38, f.10r.)

The Studiolo (late 15th century) at the Ducal Palace in Urbino. Inlaid and carved wood depicting classical images, books, scientific instruments, and other emblems of intellectual life decorate the walls of this intimate study for the Duke. (Alinari/Art Resource, New York)

Michelangelo, Facade of St. Peter's (c. 1547) in
Rome. Part of the vast project to rebuild and
enlarge the Vatican sponsored by the
Renaissance Papacy, Michelangelo's design is
one of the greatest examples of High
Renaissance architecture. (Alinari/Art Resource,
New York)

CHAPTER **13**

Spirituality and Ritual

Notwithstanding the powerful secular outlook developed by many Renaissance Italians, expressed in their enthusiasm for the classical tradition, civic virtue, sumptuous fashions, and luxurious entertainments, theirs was a profoundly Christian age. The volatile, competitive world of Italian cities fostered new levels of spiritual anxiety, especially among the laboring classes, that challenged the established church.

The growth of lay piety dates back to the thirteenth century and was closely tied to the founding of the mendicant orders, the Franciscans and the Dominicans. The rapidly growing ranks of preaching friars in cities fostered a new spirituality but also discontent with the organized church. Confraternities, or lay brotherhoods devoted to pious and charitable acts, sprang up all over Italy. These organizations, often associated with a parish church, provided fellowship, charitable assistance, and a much-needed sense of communal identity to their members, as well as a focus for their intense piety.

By the fifteenth century, confraternities played important civic roles as well, building chapels, providing dowries for indigent girls, sponsoring funerals for their members, and, above all, participating in elaborate ceremonies and processions that punctuated the religious calendar. Municipal authorities eagerly promoted civic rituals that could include—and thus control—these lay spiritual organizations. Civic and religious ritual were also closely intertwined, because holy images and devotional objects both supported the civic order and were sustained by public devotion. On religious holidays, huge, solemn processions of city councillors, other civic leaders, the bishop, parish priests, and representatives from all the confraternities and monastic orders unified the city in a single, powerful demonstration of ritual devotion. These rituals provided an ideal opportunity for both civic and religious authorities to manipulate the images of state power and religious authority they wished to convey to their urban audience. By studying these images, as well as the ritual behavior associated with them, historians can explore the spiritual world of Renaissance Italians.

Essays

Until recently, scholars have almost completely neglected the history of religious spirituality in Renaissance Italy, partly because the glorious, secular aspects of the age are so compelling, and partly because the fifteenth and early sixteenth centuries fall between two periods of great religious intensity in Italy that have been studied in greater detail: the rise of lay piety in the late Middle Ages, followed by the Protestant and Catholic Reformations. Now that historians have begun inquiry about the urban poor and working class in Renaissance Italy, religious rituals and institutions are providing valuable insights into the historical experience of ordinary people.

Richard Trexler, a historian at the University of Binghamton, pioneered the study of ritual, popular piety, and urban life in fifteenth-century Florence. In the first selection, he demonstrates how the "power of the sacred," especially sacred objects—an altar, a vessel containing the body of Christ (the Host), a holy image, a relic—closely relates to the power of pageantry. His analysis of processions through the streets of Florence shows how a "civic religion" united the city. Just as civic authorities used the power of sacred objects to augment their own power, so did dishonor to a powerful saint threaten the civic order.

The second essay, by Edward Muir, who is on the faculty of Northwestern University, describes civic pageantry in sixteenth-century Venice. All important processions and civic displays were focused on the Piazza San Marco, the large square in front of the Basilica of St. Mark and adjacent to the seat of government (see photo essay section). Muir describes how the increasingly authoritarian regime organized this pageantry to convey specific messages that enhanced the prestige of the state. One consistent theme, "the story Venetians told themselves about themselves," emphasized the stability, seamless unity and serenity of the state and the ruling class. By invoking this "Myth of Venice," the city articulated its own special relationship with its patron saints, as well as God, in order to guard its independence.

Ritual Behavior in Renaissance Florence

Richard Trexler

In pre-reformation Europe public religious ritual afforded an avenue to religious experience for the majority of men. The present essay will examine the setting for such behavior in late medieval and Renaissance Florence. It is intended to be less a description of behavior than an analysis of the nature of the sacrality of place, objects, and time upon which the religious ceremonies of an urban center rested during periods of stability. The article is in a sense a study of civic religion, for it finds that the Florentines perceived the sacred as a union of the cosmic and the particular. What was sacred? When? Where? And how did the Florentines utilize the power of the sacred?

From Richard Trexler, "Ritual Behavior in Renaissance Florence: The Setting," *Medievalia et Humanistica*, new ser. 4 (1973), 125–144. Reprinted with permission from the Medieval and Renaissance Society.

I

There was no holy land in Florence. The city's perimeter of walls and gates was lustrated, and nunneries were to be found near most entrances to the city. But within this enclosed space, there were only holy relics, images, and persons. Nunneries, churches, and government buildings were revered as houses for these sacred objects. The Florentines altered their behavior as they approached the narrow confines of power: the altar, cloister, and throne.

Within the city these three buildings were the fixed locations of ritual behavior important to the whole of society. All were covered by laws prohibiting gambling and whoring, as well as drinking in the ambient. Blasphemy was prohibited to protect their inhabitants. All three had some right of asylum or immunity attached to them. Sacrilege within them sullied not the ground, but the sacred presences.

Nunneries were peculiar in that they stood apart from society. Secular patrons might support the nuns and compete to affix familial coats of arms to monastery walls. Nunneries created merit-making opportunities for laymen, who received prayers in return. Yet laymen afforded this help in order to keep the houses apart from the world, and not to absorb them into it. The constant ritual sacrifices performed in these sanctuaries were thought to guarantee the continuity of public life. These were the city's holy enclaves. Monastic life was a stable rite of passage, a generational or biological phase converted into a durable social entity. The women's sacrality was located in their ritual activity more than in their persons or nunneries. Utility to the commune depended on their ceremony being carried out in seclusion.

Churches on the contrary were public places, the departure and terminal point of most manifestations of public unity. A wide range of activities was carried out there, including preaching, meetings of public commissions, and the sale of religious objects. But none of these activities was limited to churches. Fundamentally, the church was a shrine containing powerful objects near altars. One did not so much "go to church" as "go to see the body of Christ" or of some other sacred personality. Indeed, the word "altar" was used interchangeably with "church" or "chapel." The church's main business was the articulation of social and transcendental order. Through participation in sacrifice, men bound themselves to various saints and to each other in the presence of the saint. From the solemnization of an international treaty "over the host," "over the altar," "over the relic," or "over the bible," to the simple promise of the individual to his image-saint, the church served as a nexus of obligations, patronage, contract.

The dignity of a church depended upon the number and quality of its relics, images, and *ex votos*. All major churches kept lists, and visitors mentioned relics first in describing a church. The honor of the Florentine government required that the store of sacred objects in the cathedral and in the church of its Protector, St. John the Baptist, be superior to those of any lesser church. The value attached to these objects did not, however, transfer itself to the physical area of the church. The main occasions for their demonstration were in fact outside the church, when they were carried in procession through the city. Inside or out, it was proximity to the holy object which modified behavior.

Before the construction of the city hall, the priors of Florence had met in churches and had used their altars as the backdrop and seal of their executive actions. The new city palace (started 1298) articulated the location and fledgling independence of the communal power, but it heightened rather than eliminated the need for an altar of submission, communion, and contract. The city hall had to be partly church. The sacramentals of political power, the myriad of flags, the high towers, seals, chairs, and batons, functioned in one sense to "frame" the exercisers of powers, to define and limit communal power without extinguishing it. The raised platform added to the building in the 1320s gave the effect of an altar, and it commonly served as such during festive occasions, with mass, displays of relics, and sermons making it the main outdoor shrine of Florence. Upon these steps each successive Signoria took its oath or "sacrament" of office in full view of the *popolo*. On the rare occasions when civic turmoil made it necessary to solemnize this contract out of the people's view, chroniclers of local events recorded such privacy as never having happened before. These altar-steps were also the stage where the subjects of Florence displayed their annual signs of submission to the public authority. . . .

Within the confines of these three places, the behavior of Florentines took on a ritual nature distinguishable from the forms of the marketplace. The meeting halls of the religious confraternities, private homes, and hospitals were not areas associated with socially significant ritual behavior. Unlike the *palazzo* or the church, they were not on the processional route. Unlike the monastery, the special prayers and cultic activity of their inhabitants were not sought out during crisis. It was primarily these places' lack of power objects which accounted for their inconsequential ritual position in the city.

The city was a unified whole. No boundary procession marked off its sectors, and no administrative subdivision of the city had its own divinity or saint, its own particular sacrality. The standard processional route in Florence was a *via sacra* only when the processional day and its activity were underway. This route was intended to touch most of the signal buildings of the city. If for political reasons a sector of the city was purposely omitted, the insult consisted in depriving it of the presence of the sacred objects in the procession. One of the purposes of the procession was, in fact, to *de*sacralize the public areas of the city. By concentrating offerings and obeisance to the sacred objects in the procession, the populace marked itself off in the passage of the processional group from the world of the holy; the procession once past, the areas of the city returned to an unconsecrated state.

II

The common charisma of nun, city governor, and the religious object properly speaking, is more significant as a social fact than their obvious differences. All three demanded and received a formalized behavior. No sacrality was perceived as resident only in its own material, but rather as mediated and heightened by patronage. Ritual behavior was provoked by the combined authority of heaven and earth. Originally and persistently, chapels and churches in the city belonged to certain families which had built them, posted their arms upon them, and installed their relatives in them as priests and clerics. Relics were imported. Previously passive images started to perform miracles. In order to increase their resources, families obtained indulgences for those who visited their churches. It was a fortunate family indeed which possessed such a piece when it first showed signs of holiness. Otherwise, an object which began to gain attention would be purchased by the families for installation in their churches. The result was that every significant holy object had patronal associations. The *tavola* of Impruneta was the Buondelmonte's, a nunnery was associated with the Adimari, a relic of the cross was the Pazzis', and so on. This consorterial association with valuable religious objects penetrated deeply into Florentine life. The new bishop on first entering the city afforded the chance for an ostentatious display by his family and those of the *vicedomini* of the see. The Cerchi enhanced their fortune by housing a saintly recluse in their palace. The Palagi and the Soderini patronized holy persons. The Ruspi possessed renowned relics. The list could be extended. But the point is made: possession of valuable religious objects was one of the most important signs of honor and dignity.

The developing commune had to compete with this tradition, increasing its own dignity by acquiring communal relics and images, combating the accumulation of sacred objects by family groups. When the Medici in the 1420s and 1430s started to inflate the number of dignitaries in their parish church of S. Lorenzo, it was a sign that the family sought to challenge the charisma of the commune. Determined that no single family should exceed its honor, the commune responded by increasing the dignity of the cathedral. In time-honored fashion, the commune also took under its protection many of the religious entities in the dominion and city, and as part of the contract, it obtained a promise from the religious that only the communal herald would be posted on the building or near a shrine.

This rivalry to bestow terrestrial authority upon the sacred had important implications for the social perception of holiness. Relics, first of all, were an important agent in particularly solemn contracts, protecting and patronizing agreements. Matteo Villani told how the prior of the Dominican friary in Florence, seeing his church tower repeatedly struck by lightning, removed the images from the tower and replaced them with relics, apparently a superior protective agency. The power of the relic was personal. When one received a relic into the city, one took in part of the saint himself. These saints aided civic and cosmological continuity; images, on the other hand, enabled the city to bend and change bad fortune, heal ruptured contracts between it and the cosmos. . . .

Most miracles in Florence which achieved publicity were associated with images. Two of the great Madonnas were fixed and could not be borne about, while several others were portable. The figures were charismatic because they *saw*, and dozens of minor miracles resulted from the image having viewed something pleasing or displeasing. Their public utility consequently depended on their being given sight only when and where something edifying was to be viewed, namely a ritual activity sanctioned by public authority. Veiled and unveiled, dressed and disrobed, given gifts, struck and caressed, carried under the baldachin of her patron(s), the image was encouraged to cause patterned behavior rather than incalculable acts. The value of image or relic depended on the value set upon it by a patron. Patronage determined what was institutionally holy just as surely as it bestowed fame upon an artist. By vouching for value, patronage prevented idolatry, and this clarity as to what was venerable contributed to the articulation of social bonds.

This dual personality of the object of religious devotion, incorporating the charisma of the saint and of the patron, was one of the prime facets of the Florentine perception of the holy. In passing the gates into the city, the indiscriminate, anarchic holy was transformed into a cult instrument. The same may be said of the host, the living God himself. Feared precisely because of its unitary charismatic power, it was accompanied with the marks of authentification. Decorated and engraved hosts were displayed in homes. In the church a special architectural enclosure was developed for it which, often enough, bore the herald of the donor. The altar cloths beneath the sacrifice of the host were donated by testators and fitted out with coats of arms. In Corpus Christi processions, the living God was surrounded with the safer files of the civic order. Nearness to the host in procession was a mark of signal prestige. The coats of arms of recognized civic and familial authority hung from the baldachin under which the host was carried in its precious monstrum. A main reason for these accompanying paraphernalia was a desire of the group or individual involved to partake of the sacred power of the host. Here again, the sacred was perceived as an amalgam of charismas.

Ex votos are the clearest expression of this mixture; these relics of promises and contracts kept were separated from the image or relic they accompanied. As authentication of the power of a relic or image, ex votos increased the devotion of the visitor even though they were neither flesh nor clothing of a saint. The more striking their size and quality, the more honored the church. Indeed, in 1502 life-sized votive figures in the Servite church were jokingly said to be "adored" in a manner usually reserved to the cult object. Ex votos became part of the total reaction to the sacred object. Like secondary relics, they partook of the sacrality of the holy objects themselves by their nearness to them. Yet unlike them, the votives were nothing apart from the ambient of the sacred object. They were profane. In civic revolutions one of the first actions of a victorious faction was to remove and destroy votive representations of the defeated politicians, a sign of disrespect designed to diminish the influence of the vanquished with the populace and with the sacred object.

Patrons used sacred objects to increase their authority over the whole. Conversely, the fame of an object once sacralized ennobled the patron. The relation between them may seem to have its origins in the power of the family or government which valued the sacred objects. It was not the object which ennobled the family, but familial and social power which ennobled a cold, material instrument. Before the scientific revolution, however, holy power was conceived to exist beyond social or familial force. It resided in those objects and persons which could massively affect the whole body of humans.

The urban religious experience, then, is one of a holiness captured, veiled, framed, and manipulated. The logical but unstated object of public urban religious ritual was to create a continuity which would make the miraculous unnecessary. Holiness was liturgical. Cult objects did not lose their sacrality in the process of manipulation, but rather increased it. The power enclosed in a church was activated through contact and manipulation by priests or devotees. Those many objects in a church which were efficacious only for individuals were open to view, but framed by flowers, ex votos, and the like. Objects of communal power were veiled, and their activity was closely supervised. The political powers enclosed in the church were restrained by being surrounded by frames or houses of precious stones. Individual devotion and submission to these objects were accomplished while the veil covered the object. Its unveiled display was a sociopolitical, even cosmological act done only on certain days, only to certain persons, and only when the commune contracted or supplicated in the process of manifesting the power and the unity of the republic. Indiscriminate and repeated unveiling of social and divine power by random individuals decreased the devotion of the people and therewith the social efficacy of the object. The less dignified the viewer of the unmasked image, the less devotion it could command. Those whose faces were recklessly shown to the masses could cause crowds, disorders, scandal, incalculable crowd actions. The objects in a church were meant to be predictable. They were a resource of power which when exposed acted to bind men together, not tear them apart. It would be unjustified to say that the signs of public authority *became* the relic, even though contemporaries often failed to distinguish. Yet the accompaniment of relics, images, and hosts cannot easily be distinguished from the objects themselves as causes of ritual behavior.

Spontaneously drawn or etched images (a cross, an IHS [abbreviation for Jesus]) were akin to the objects used by the magicians. Manipulated only by creator and private utilizer, these unframed objects were essentially uncontrollable. Such random creations and drawings created outlets for power without the authentication which would simultaneously engender devotion while rendering the images of positive value. Outdoor images or symbols thus had to be enshrined, fitted out with candles, frames, and altars; they became objects with constitutional authority. They bore the authoritative marks of the politically accepted division of labor; they had been blessed by the priest, fitted out with indulgences by the pontifical authorities, and adored by respected groups or individuals. Spontaneity had been harnessed, and the objects now radiated the power of the political order. Their desecration meant the defilement of that order. To hurl mud at a corner shrine meant not only to curse the figure represented, but as well the altar and frame of social authority.

Among secular individuals, only the communal power affected the whole and can thus be included under the category of sacred objects. Like the image, the Signoria had to be kept concealed from sight as much as possible, for constant viewing of the civic authority would diminish its charisma. Again, the days on which the Signoria entered office were among those feasts on which, according to law, the population should behave better. Most important, the city's industry was shut down, and debts were suspended on the days the priors took office for the same reason they were curtailed when a particular saint was festively honored: so that the people of the city could accompany such venerable objects. The analogy has already been drawn between fetching the Signoria from the palace during procession and solemnly proceeding to a church along the processional route to incorporate its main relic to the parade. In all these forms the populace saw its government accompanied and exalted in the same fashion as its more strictly religious objects.

The Signoria was exalted not as a priest, but as a holy object. With the nuns excluded from manifestations of public religiosity, the priors of Florence functioned as sacred but lay monks whose holiness was in their activity. They had acceded to their office (short-term in Florence) through ceremonies resembling rites of passage. In this liminal state they offered the city to its protective powers in a manner not unlike the nuns, who also recommended the commune to the divine power through their activity.

Here the analogy to the monastic life ends, and the fundamental distinction between the power of the Signoria and that of other objects appears. The power of the church was manipulated, while that of the nunneries was continually formalized. The public power within the city hall was basically incalculable and intended to be so. Within their palace—which they could not leave except for ceremonial purposes—the city priors in defending the whole were expected to punish in an anormative, wondrous fashion those who violated accepted norms. The chroniclers narrate these horrible punishments as if proving the solidity of the commune by the terrible vengeance visited upon those who stepped outside. The penalties of the Italian municipalities were creatively frightening, for executive violence of an imaginative nature was one of the instruments for retaining the whole. The public officer, unlike other cult objects, exercised a continual power often beyond control, power without mask or veil: ceremonial spontaneity. The public power was, so to speak, the solemn magician whose power, if not his person, was always exposed to the public view. The paraphernalia accompanying that power were meant to limit it and heighten it, but never to extinguish this flame of authority. The commune, said the Florentine merchant-historian Dati, was an authority which did not die. Machiavelli realized that in order to perpetuate authority, *terribilità, ferocità,* incalculability had to be the portion of the Prince alone.

III

. . . Like place and objects, time's power was interpenetrated with divine and earthly authority. Renaissance Florentines continued to keep time by saints' days. They assumed almost without question the idea that time was civic-minded, and that its normal rhythms had to respond to communal authority and private utility.

Segments of time were sacred to certain powers. Most commonly, a day was associated with the saint whose feast was being celebrated. But mixed with the influence of the saint was the moral configuration of the stellar sphere, which exerted either a malevolent or friendly influence upon the city. While morally and temporally at variance with each other, the fixed liturgical calendar of the saints and the shifting rhythms of astral events were in ritual melded together. Florentines often scheduled military and other governmental actions to coincide with both conjunctions and saints' days thought to be friendly to the public weal. In one case, a clerical astrologer of the commune scheduled the dates of religious processions. In another, three days of solemn clerical processions preceded the astrologically determined time of the consignment of authority to a military leader. Priests and laymen stood in the service of the Christian saints, but their movements were geared to those of the planets as well. . . .

Collective ritual aimed at the same goals for the political groups which

participated in common ceremonies. It is in the nature of the city especially to manipulate the power of time and objects to reasonable ends. The city pits its concentrations of political authority against the chaotic sacrality which hovers above and
outside it, and which threatens to appear within the walls itself in the varied social
and familial groups which threaten its unity. Human experience proved how subject
cities were to the incalculable. Civic and diplomatic order were not truly natural.
They required the genius of men applied to the infinity of the sacred to make them
so. To Machiavelli's mind, human ability was tested by man's capacity to defeat and
"acculturate" fate, to use the interstices of freedom between the fields of implacable
and mysterious force. Was it not this principle which led the astrologers to attune
processions to the conjunctions of the heavens? Certainly in the Middle Ages as well
as during the Renaissance, processions were timed astrologically, and saintly geniuses were intermingled with astral personalities and forces to predict, explain, and
manipulate events.

All students of the Renaissance know how preoccupied contemporaries were
with astrological calculations. Scarcely a battle could be fought, a cornerstone laid,
a military baton consigned without the consultation of an astrologer. Such cere-
monialization of auspicious time had to include the organization of the political and
social body in public manifestations of religion. This was especially true in a republic
such as Florence, where sovereignty was public, and was constituted in the processional parts. The procession in the republic reflected a potent order which that of a
principate could not. Certainly Machiavelli, like all other observers of the processions of the Savonarolan period, must have been impressed by their discipline and
solidarity. It is interesting to speculate that the young chancellor may have had them
in mind when he went about organizing the civic militia which was to be the salvation of his beloved republic. Yet the value of such ruminations is limited. Like
Machiavelli, we must turn repeatedly to the principles underlying the actions of the
men who determined social, political, and military policy.

In a universe of intelligences, one cannot be sure of the true meaning of any act,
the real nature of any moment. The festive calendar of the commune helped to clarify the ambiguity of individual and communal actions. Like most men of the age,
Florentines believed that their actions might mean something *in specie aeternitatis* [in
the long run]. The Florentine historian Goro Dati described how, when spring came,
the thoughts of the Florentines turned to games, dances, and a long preparation
for the feast of their patron, St. John. It seemed, he said, that they had nothing else
to do but feast and make merry. He understood no better than we just why certain
points on the calendar were associated with group behavior which deviated from
social and divine norms. What did Dati mean, for example, when he described how
wedding banquets were postponed until the feast of the patron "so as to do honor to
the feast"? An examination of communal laws and institutions relating to time will
help to answer this question. . . .

Calendrical feasts achieved group solidarity in urban Florence through behavioral deviations toward both ends of a continuum from dance to procession. Two
examples from the Florentine tradition may serve as illustrations. A confraternity
anniversary mass for its dead was attended by all the brothers. After solemnly attending divine services, they participated in a fraternal meal which was all other than

solemn. Mass and meal, the propitiative and assertive aspects of the affair, were viewed as equal parts of the total honor paid the deceased. The same extremities can be observed in the feast days celebrated in Florence. Foot and horse races, singing, buffoonery, and floats balanced the solemn offering to the saint and the procession of the clergy with their relics, images, and crucifixes. Both were in honor of the saint.

Legal norms were not for all days; behavior depended on time. This was a fundamental principle of communal law, and not just a datum of special experience. Sumptuary laws were not enforced during celebrations. Prohibited games were legal on some days of the year. And, what might seem oddest in a city so dedicated to merchandising, debts were suspended during several feast days. It was a commonplace that people behaved worst on feast days and that ease was conducive to sin. Some felt that the fewer feasts there were the better. Still, the principles of such deviant behavior were rooted in a calendar of behavior sanctioned by the communal law itself.

Thus, prohibited activities which might lead to sin or which were sinful on occasion were relaxed. On the other hand, the solemnity of the feasts caused the commune to suspend activities such as usury which were licensed in everyday life although they were in violation of divine law. Sinful activities per se were forbidden. The exchange tables of the usurers and pawnbrokers were closed, but also removed from the public—and divine—view. The feast displayed opulence without the workaday sin which had produced it. . . .

Through games and sacrifices the Lord becomes a friend. Expected behavioral deviancy, time's possession by particular sacred forces, and the teleological homogeneity of events in time are all attempts to reduce the sacred to an order which then can be subjected to manipulation.

Yet this is not enough. After all, the simplest agricultural communities have organized time to use it. In the city the sacred was subjected to a process of political authentification which left its mark on the citizen's perception of the holy. Far from the rural wood where unsuspected power resided, the city afforded a perception of the holy which, though seen as a unity, was in fact an amalgam of social and divine power. In turn, each city compartmentalized its sacred time in accordance with its own history and traditions.

Several aspects of the political impress upon sacred time have already been mentioned. The days on which the Signoria entered office were included among the sacred feasts upon which "men should conduct themselves more modestly." The populace was released from work and debt collection on those days so that they could accompany the Signoria, just as on other days they accompanied the relics and images of the commune. The festive calendar was dotted with recollections of events in the communal past. Yet the best way to determine the nature of the communal impact upon time is to find how often and why celebrations of feasts were stopped.

The answer is, quite often. Ritual activities were commonly postponed or canceled. Moreover, our sources reveal little anxiety at these departures from the ordinary. The chroniclers regularly record when St. John's Day was not at all or only partly celebrated, yet they give no indication that such postponement was a matter of great concern. When the baton could not be bestowed upon a Florentine mercenary captain at the moment the communal astrologers had planned, the Signoria assured those responsible that they should not be concerned by the situation. Clearly, time was no more exempt from social authentification than object.

The most common reason for postponements or cancellations was a disunity of the city which under public circumstances might precipitate disorders. The danger that a gathering might display the weakness of the public authority was, however, only one part of a larger whole. For public scandal would not have pleased the honored saint. The power of a saint was in part measured by the devotion shown him. Disorder was in some sense a demonstration of divine weakness as well as a challenge to divine and temporal authority. . . .

A second reason for failing to hold festive activities on the correct day was that through a postponement the participation in and audience to the celebration could be increased. In 1289 a delay of some days permitted the victorious Florentine troops near Arezzo to return and participate. In 1402 the celebration of St. John was held off until the French ambassadors arrived to see it. During the Council of Florence the date was again modified so that a greater number of visiting prelates could view it. The more Florentines participating, the greater the honor paid the saint. The more foreigners who saw the power, unity, and opulence of Florence on display, the more imposing the honor accruing to the patron and the commune.

Government did suppress or postpone celebrations which might not redound to the greatest honor of the saint and the commune. Timely celebration increased the power of solicitation only when the commune was stable, and only if the maximum publicity could be achieved. The liturgical calendar obeyed a communal dynamics.

Still, the yearning for festival imposed limits on the government's ability to postpone or suppress a public manifestation of power and unity. And the political authority had to be sure that its motivations in postponing these events were credible. Neglect of the saint was no more readily condoned than the needless suppression of festive joviality. The Dominican rigorist Savonarola had to learn this the hard way. For him, the traditional horse races, masks, and spinning firewheels so much a part of the Florentine festival were little more than the devil's handwork, and were suppressed. Yet by 1497 he had to yield to popular pressures, and the rollicking of the Florentines was again offered to their saints. Savonarola failed for many reasons, not the least of which was his inability to convince the Florentines that his opposition to the buffoon was based on genuine spirituality. To some of his opponents, his reasons were more sinister:

> He wants to impede our divine and annual ceremonies and triumphs and feasts and praises and illuminations, which reach to the feet and soles of the glorious God. . . . He hopes that our patron and benefactor St. John the Baptist and the other saints, deprived of their accustomed honors, will, justly, turn against us, and then ruin will follow.

The cosmology behind these words is eminently local. Social and political welfare depended upon honoring the time and the person of saintly benefactors, while ruin followed the neglect of the city and the political and familial traditions which had hallowed the patrons. Savonarola promised a New Jerusalem. Florentines chose to retain a religion impregnated with local values, and a political and social life suffused with sacred meaning.

Art and Pageantry in Renaissance Venice

Edward Muir

During the sixteenth century members of the Venetian ruling class witnessed a number of events that could only lead them to question the efficacy of their traditional values. The results of this questioning and re-evaluating included a greater division within the patriciate, a more rigid authoritarianism, an abandonment of trade by the nobility in favor of investments in land, and an anxiety to display a noble lifestyle through conspicuous consumption. News of two events arrived in Venice in 1499, precipitating the malaise: one report lamented that the Turks had defeated the Venetian fleet at Zonchio and the other, a letter from Alexandria, warned that three ships under the Portuguese flag had arrived in Aden and Calicut in search of spices. With the naval defeat the Venetians lost their claims to many Greek and Albanian cities, vital to the eastern trade of *La Serenissima* [the More Serene Republic, Venice] and, according to Frederic Lane, Venice's leaders henceforth abandoned their commitment to naval supremacy. Although it was a century or more before Venice experienced a permanent economic loss as a result of the Portuguese adventure, the startling news that it had been outmaneuvered in the campaign to secure the lucrative pepper trade did not buttress domestic confidence in the shipping business. But events much closer to home triggered the deepest paroxysm of insecurity. On May 14, 1509, the combined forces of France, Spain, the Empire, the papacy, and various Italian states under the banner of the League of Cambrai routed the entire Venetian army at Agnadello. Soon most of Venice's mainland domain from Brescia to Padua declared for the enemy, and Venice prepared for a siege that never came. Divisions within the league and seven years of war saved Venice and returned most of its former territories, but many Venetians would never recapture the faith that *La Serenissima* could rule a great empire or be the mistress of the seas, however much the gigantic statues of Mars and Neptune on the stairs of the Ducal Palace might proclaim the contrary. . . .

The continuing insecurity of the Venetian patriciate was . . . manifest in the transfer of many families' investments from trade to land. Although Venetian nobles had owned mainland estates from as early as the fourteenth century, the War of the League of Cambrai seems to mark the beginning of their increased acquisition of such holdings. . . .

Besides living on great estates, nobles were supposed to be generous and open-handed, as the saying went, *spendere largamente*. As if in almost desperate compensation for their mercantile heritage and despite ingrained habits of personal frugality, many patricians in the middle and late sixteenth century spent reckless sums on buildings, tombs, entertainments, and other ostentatious items. Contemporaries believed that conspicuous consumption grew as the patriciate retreated from maritime

From Edward Muir, "Images of Power: Art and Pageantry in Renaissance Venice," *American Historical Review* 84 (1979): pp. 30–52 passim. Reprinted by permission of the American Historical Association.

commerce; foreigners were often amazed at the glittering displays they witnessed, and more than one family's slide from wealth to ignominy was blamed on an unreasonable pursuit of pomp. There were repeated and apparently futile attempts on the part of the government to limit the amounts the nobles might expend on wedding banquets and pearl necklaces for their daughters; the Great Council even established a special agency, the *Magistrato alle Pompe*, to monitor private consumption. The notion that expensive self- indulgence would eat away at the patrimony of the ruling class apparently worried the older, sober men who sat in the inner councils of the state. Yet that same government, as much as it condemned such extravagance for private purposes, enthusiastically encouraged opulent array when it could advance the dignity of the state. Private expenditure to add luster to the republic was approved, indeed invited, and the rulers took pains to keep the grandeur of the state commensurate with the higher standards of the new fashion by advocating, as well, public support of commissions to magnify Venice.

In the years after the War of the League of Cambrai, the person most directly concerned with elevating the *nobiltà* of the republic was Doge Andrea Gritti (1523–38). A polyglot who spoke French, Latin, Greek, and Turkish and a man who behaved in the grand manner of a tyrant, Gritti personally instigated a number of artistic projects. The legal restrictions imposed on the doges after the death of Agostino Barbarigo constrained any ambitions Gritti may have had for self-aggrandizement; so he devoted himself to refashioning the traditional image of Venice into a more contemporary one. In doing so, he employed some of the best artists of his time.

In 1527, over the opposition of the procurators, Gritti supported the appointment of Adrian Willaert as the *maestro di cappella* [master of musical performance] for San Marco, thus making Venice one of Europe's great musical centers. After the Sack of Rome in that same year, Gritti welcomed to Venice the architect, Jacopo Sansovino, and the poet, Pietro Aretino, both of whom served the city for the rest of their lives. In his concern for improving churches, Gritti was the chief advocate of rebuilding San Francesco della Vigna and enriched the high altar in San Marco with tapestries ordered from Brussels. But the most significant achievements of his reign were his efforts to bring order and harmony to the great ceremonial spaces of the city, the Piazza San Marco and the Piazzetta of the Ducal Palace, and to reorganize the state ceremonies themselves. During Gritti's reign, Sansovino made frequent attempts to remove the squalid wooden stalls around the columns at the entrance to the Piazzetta and to tear down the illegal shacks of the butchers and salami sellers who had infested both ritual spaces. In league with the procurators who had the actual jurisdiction over the area, Gritti sought to separate the commercial and political centers of Venice, freeing the government of nobles from the taint of commerce.

The centerpiece of the architectural reorganization of the republic's ceremonial space was the reconstruction of the "Loggetta." Standing opposite the Foscari arch at the intersection of the Piazza and the Piazzetta and complementing the great stairs where the doges were crowned, the Loggetta has been called "the most complete surviving visual representation of . . . the Venetian view of their own state as the perfect republic." In the last year of Gritti's dogeship the procurators commissioned

Sansovino to rebuild the Loggetta to serve as a place for patricians to meet to discuss politics or conduct business with governmental officials and as an office for the procurators to use during the Sunday meetings of the Great Council. Sansovino's designs show, however, a far greater interest on the part of the patrons in propagandistic display than in utility, for the Loggetta is quite small. The iconographic program used classical mythology and allegory to translate the traditional political imagery of Venice into Renaissance terminology. On the upper level three reliefs express the city's imperial claims: "Venice" symbolized by Justice sits in the middle flanked by personifications of the mainland rivers, representing the cities of the *terra firma* domain; on either side Venus as queen of Cyprus and Jupiter as king of Crete signify the pillars of Venice's maritime empire. Beneath these, four bronze statuettes of Pallas Minerva, Mercury, Apollo, and Peace represent respectively wisdom, eloquence, liberty under the law, and the state of Venice's relations with other cities. With the completion of the Loggetta and Sansovino's Library and Mint across from the Ducal Palace, Venice gained a monumental center worthy of its claim to be a "New Rome" and a classical iconography to express its virtues.

Just as he was concerned with the music, decorations, and architecture of the governmental center, Doge Gritti was active in reforming the public ceremonies so they might reflect the full dignity of the state. Under the two previous doges, Leonardo Loredan and Antonio Grimani, the government eliminated several of the ritual vestiges of the greater powers the doges had wielded in the early centuries, but Gritti was the more thorough reformer. His greatest change was the alteration of roles played by the senators and other magistrates at the festivities of Giovedì Grasso, the culminating holiday of Carnival. In the past, the doge and Signoria had witnessed the formal condemnation and decapitation of a bull and twelve pigs in the Piazzetta in memory of the defeat of a twelfth-century rebel patriarch of Aquileia and his Friulian allies. After the gruesome punishment of the symbolic captives, the doge and dignitaries retired to the Ducal Palace where they watched septuagenarian senators, brandishing clubs, smash miniature wooden models of the Friulian castles destroyed after the Venetian victory. Thinking the ceremony too undignified for the times, Gritti eliminated it altogether, retaining only a bull-baiting to entertain the crowds, and he and his successors called for more "noble" entertainments, such as comedies, ballets, masquerades, fireworks, and pageants.

Within the context of shifts in social values toward a more noble lifestyle, an oligarchical concern for authority, and the spread of classical motifs in the visual arts, Venetian pageantry blossomed, an exotic flower grafted onto a hardy ceremonial tradition. Always known for the great pomp of its rituals and processions, by the last half of the sixteenth century the very name of Venice conjured up a vision of extravagant spectacles. . . .

To the historian the most obvious attribute of Venetian pageantry is its overwhelmingly political character. An art form created for a particular liturgical, diplomatic, or governmental occasion, pageantry revealed how its patrons wished an issue to be understood; through pageantry, for instance, an ideal vision of the political world might be used to mask the unseemly reality of a specific event. In sixteenth-century Italy and Europe, pageantry, though transitory, became a major art form that taxed the ingenuity of some of the greatest painters, sculptors, architects, composers, and poets of the Renaissance. . . . In Venice, although relatively obscure artists were often employed to design public pageants, on occasion Titian, Carpaccio, Tintoretto, and Palladio employed their talents to create floats, *macchine* [floating stages], allegorical scenes, and triumphal arches. Willaert and Gabrieli composed music for some of these occasions, Aretino contributed verse, and leading humanists usually drew up the programs and planned their iconography. In great water processions, regattas of decorated barges were rowed up the Grand Canal or across the lagoon to celebrate the annual Marriage of the Sea on Ascension Day, the visits of foreign princes, or special events like the coronation of a dogaressa. All such pageants, however, began or ended with a procession on foot around Piazza San Marco and a visit to the basilica, as one has seen, the ceremonial and liturgical stage devoted to the presentation of the ideals of the Venetian republic. Pageantry was not an independent activity but one rooted in the great cycle of rituals conducted by the government. Indeed, both pageantry and the decorations of San Marco and the Ducal Palace illustrated the political ideas that underlay the ceremonies of state.

As was the case for all publicly commissioned works of art, the planning of pageantry was a matter of government policy. Patricians, appointed to special committees for important occasions, often invented the programs themselves or at least approved what someone else drew up, and magistrates at the highest levels of government including members of the Council of Ten, the Collegio of the Senate, and the procurators made direct policy decisions with regard to the occasions for and even to the detailed subject matter in pageantry devices. . . . A ducal chancellor regularly acted as master of ceremonies to handle organizational details, and the guilds, *scuole grandi* (lay confraternities), parishes, and monasteries that actually built the tableaux were required to participate in the procession under pain of a stiff fine. Until 1565 the *compagnie delle calze*—groups of young nobles formed to sponsor banquets, comedies and festivals for their own entertainment and for the glory of the republic—usually planned and even financed pageants as training for higher responsibilities. To design and execute their contributions to public festivities, the companies appointed each year a poet, an architect, and a painter. The ruling nobility not only took their own processions seriously but were deeply interested in accounts of foreign spectacles, seeing in them clues to possible shifts in policy and using them as a catalogue of the political ideas current in distant courts. Although pageants often displayed governmental magnificence for its own sake and were reminiscent of the *circenses* [circuses] with which imperial Romans entertained and controlled the crowd, they were more than that. Their planners used them to explicate specific and frequently quite sophisticated political ideas.

In comparison with the other arts, pageantry appeared late in the artistic development of Renaissance Venice. In the context of this study, pageantry refers to all of the artistic elements created for a particular ceremonial occasion, including triumphal arches, pageant stages, display booths, decorated floats and barges rowed on the lagoon and canals, and tableaux vivants set up on platforms and carried in procession around Piazza San Marco. The portable tableaux became the characteristic device for pageantry in Venice, seen far more frequently than floating *macchine* or fixed stages. Before the sixteenth century, tableaux employing either live actors or groups of wooden or plaster statues were rare. Proto-tableaux were at first appendages to the ducal processions and for centuries displayed only the insignia of the doge or a relic, miraculous painting, or statue of a saint.

To emphasize the untouchable holiness of sacred objects and to compete for attention with the rich white, black, scarlet, and vermillion robes of the noble participants, the canons and *scuole grandi* members carried ever larger, more gilded and bejewelled reliquaries, which eventually required four or more men to support them. People in the procession began to use portable platforms *(solari)* on which they carried their reliquaries and statues of saints, sometimes made for the occasion. When the little dramas that could be told with groups of statues or actors took over as the primary visual elements in the processions, tableaux had reached their maturity. Even though there are numerous descriptions of brilliant processions in the fifteenth century, the visual domination of tableaux over the other elements of the procession does not seem to have been common before the first decade of the sixteenth century. This is not to say, however, that the processions held before the development of tableaux were without political impact. Besides the elaborate rankings of noble officials and the imperial bearing of the doge, the very orderliness and solemnity of the processions impressed foreigners as unparalleled, and processions were often read as a commentary on the harmony of Venetian society. . . .

The earliest tableaux in Venice took their peculiar shapes from the longstanding Venetian tradition of turning art and religious themes to political ends. At a procession formed in 1511 during the War of the League of Cambrai, religious motifs were used to defend Venice's interests in the latest diplomatic alignment of powers with and against the republic. The members of the Scuola Grande di San Rocco built a tableau with statues depicting Justice, Saint Roch, Saint Mark, and a woman dressed as Venice holding a dove representing the Holy Spirit; they were accompanied by two kings on horseback, the kings of Spain and England, who had recently joined the Venetian cause, and by a ship with a sign reading "nolite timere, cessavit ventus [don't be afraid, the wind has ceased]." Venice's remaining enemy, the king of France, faced a flaming ball, representing *Amor Dei* [Love of God], and beside him stood the pope with a placard questioning why France had denied the true faith. To oppose Venice was clearly to become God's enemy. Religious images continued to dominate Venetian pageantry tableaux for several decades. The signing of a new league in 1526 was celebrated with a procession of tableaux that compared the doge to Joshua and represented each of the alliance's members as under the guidance of the divine. Even as late as 1532, pageants still borrowed imagery exclusively from the Christian tradition and concentrated as much on the display of precious objects as on creating dramatic scenes on *solari*. At one procession that year the Scuola Grande di San Rocco, by then famous for its tableaux vivants, built three *solari* to carry some of its members acting out scenes from the Old Testament, but it also brought to the procession a *solaro* adorned solely with silver liturgical objects and had sixty-six members walk in the procession carrying silverplate in their hands. The show of material riches was still dominant, and less valued was ingenuity in creating allegorical scenes. While the image of Venice as the "New Rome" and classical allusions in the other arts had been gaining favor in Venice for some time, pageantry and tab-leaux were still closely tied to the liturgical elements of the procession. Jupiter and Venus had not yet joined Mark and Mary on the ceremonial stage.

Perhaps fostered by the Venetians' anxious quest for *nobiltà* and Gritti's cam-paign for monuments and ceremonies more suited to an empire, a major shift in the iconography of pageantry came in 1542. In March 1541 a group of twelve young nobles organized a new *compagnia delle calze* [company of young nobles] called the *Sempiterni*. From the very first they commissioned artists of the premier rank to cre-ate the company's festive decorations; for the first initiation party in Campo Santo Stefano, Titian designed a grand *apparato* or stage. For Carnival in the following February the *Sempiterni* hired Pietro Aretino to write a comedy for them to produce. To design a floating stage on which to perform the play, Aretino sent for his young compatriot from Arezzo, Giorgio Vasari, who built a barge complete with architec-tural elements, sculptures, and paintings that represented the rivers, lakes, and is-lands of the Venetian domain. Before this, the *compagnie delle calze* comedies had always been performed on a modest stage set up in a palace courtyard that had been decorated with tapestries, streamers, and silverplate to create a festive mood. Juergen Schulz has pointed to Vasari's Carnival *apparato* as the source for the adoption in Venice of the elaborate stylistic motifs popular in central Italy, especially in the dra-matic productions of the Medici court. Although the Venetians did not entirely abandon their own largely religious iconography, Venetians of the 1540s and after increasingly accepted pageantry in which neoclassical motifs were properly trans-formed to serve Venetian ends. The mythical gods of antiquity joined the saints as symbols of the state, decoration that was merely sumptuous yielded to ingenious de-sign, straightforward messages became complicated allegories, and carefully planned propaganda supplanted simple allusions to the divine guidance of the rulership.

Concurrently, the annual number of state processions that provided the oppor-tunity for pageantry increased markedly in the late sixteenth century, and to this increase one music historian has credited the extensive use in Venice of polychoral music, a form well suited for outdoor ceremonies. Significantly, the stylistic and iconographical transformation reveals more than a change in taste. The young no-bles who had joined the *compagnie delle calze* during the 1540s and sponsored the introduction of the new themes eventually became senators. By the 1570s they had entered the councils of power, and the government officially endorsed the use of the classical style for state pageantry. By this time the allusions to antiquity seldom served the ends of an ambitious doge, as had the staircase in the courtyard of the Ducal Palace for Agostino Barbarigo, but polished the noble image of the patriciate and proclaimed the authority of the government. The new pageantry revealed a po-litical ethic that emphasized obedience rather than communal responsibility, and, despite the apparent resurgence of opposition to the oligarchy in the 1580s and the appearance of discourses on republican government by patricians such as Paolo Paruta, the public image of *La Serenissima* grew ever less republican, ever more au-thoritarian.

The last three decades of the sixteenth century became the great age of Venetian pageantry. The magnificence of the antique style appealed to the ruling elite, who were concerned with projecting an image of strength and majesty both at home and abroad in the face of renewed external threats to Venice's imperial reputation, beginning with the loss of Cyprus to the Turks in 1573. This calamity was followed by a devastating plague in 1575–77 that killed over one-third of the population and by the fires of 1574 and 1577 that destroyed the council chambers of the Ducal Palace. All of these events brought into question the conception of Venice as a city favored by God. The patricians in charge of planning responded by developing two artistic themes. In one, Venice's steadfast Catholic orthodoxy was contrasted to the machinations of the insidious heretics and powerful infidels who menaced Europe, and, in the other, Venice's situation was compared to Imperial Rome's struggle to rally forces against the barbarians. The themes were pointedly self-serving: without the Venetians would not all Europe fall to the sword of the Turk or to the perversions of the Protestants? . . .

. . . When Henry III of France visited Venice in 1574 on his way to be crowned Most Christian King after spending an unhappy year as the king of Poland, the entertainments in his honor were the most expensive and spectacular of the Venetian Renaissance. From the triumphal arch to the sugar sculptures served as dessert at the state banquets, the decorations had a consistent theme of courting French favor at the expense of the Spanish. A committee of nobles, including two already well known for their humanistic interests and their patronage of Palladio, planned the decorations, coordinating the diplomatic intentions of the state with the proper Neoclassical allusions. The major creation for the visit was a wooden triumphal arch built on the Lido by Palladio and decorated by Veronese and Tintoretto in imitation of the arch of Septimius Severus in Rome; on it the escutcheons of Venice and France were paired under statues of Victory and Peace, and around the arch were paintings of battles that Henry had won against the Huguenots. Classical images served an overall scheme that had strong military and religious tones: Venice was the natural partner of France because the city was the bulwark against the heathen Turk, just as the French kings were the stalwart protectors of the Catholic cause against the heretics.

The late sixteenth century's greater enthusiasm and appreciation for the dramatic as opposed to the merely spectacular was also marked in pageantry. The visit in 1585 of some Japanese nobles, newly converted to Christianity by Jesuit missionaries, offered a consummate opportunity for didactic drama. The Collegio postponed the procession scheduled for Saint Mark's Day (June 25) to coincide with the festival of Saints Peter and Paul three days later and ordered that the usual midsummer frolics and games be suspended so the city could prepare a properly spiritual and devout holiday for the guests. Built to tell "as in a theater" the sacred history of the Old and New Testaments and the trials of the saints and martyrs, three hundred *solari* were accompanied by an unprecedented display of reliquaries, jewels, and silver liturgical objects. The six *scuole grandi*, the Dominicans and Franciscans, and other religious orders created tableaux vivants instructing the Japanese about Christian truths and, inevitably, about Venice's special place in the divine plan. There were the usual personifications of Venice as a queen surrounded by the virtues and legions of saints, but there were also attempts to explain complex subjects, such as the local legend of Saint Mark's gift of his episcopal ring to a Venetian fisherman, Solomon's demonstration of his wisdom and wealth to the queen of Sheba, and the baptism of Constantine and his subsequent charity to the poor. . . .

The last illustration of particularly effective pageantry is drawn from the most famous event in the history of the "political reputation" of Venice. The very decline of the republican ideals in practice may have corresponded with a reassertion of them in theory, and it was this theoretical defense of republican values more than the realities of Venetian political life that garnered for *La Serenissima* its European reputation as the ideal living republic. Venice's reputation for the "defense of republican liberty," as William J. Bouwsma has called it, was immensely strengthened, particularly in Protestant countries, by its adamant resistance to papal interference in Venetian domestic affairs. The conflict between Venice and the papacy reached its highest pitch when Pope Paul V put Venice under interdict from 1606 to 1607, and Venice's most famous and long-lasting defense dates from this event, eloquently expressed in the writings of Paolo Sarpi, a Servite friar, who argued passionately against the supposed desire of the pope to establish a universal monarchy. The government, for its part, wanted to show the world that it had the complete loyalty of its subjects even on religious issues by carrying on the celebration of the liturgy in defiance of the interdict.

Thus, the Corpus Christi procession of 1606 provided the opportunity for a demonstration of popular resistance to the interdict and a display of antipapal propaganda through pageantry, a manifestation so wonderfully successful that the sympathetic English ambassador, Sir Henry Wotton, called it "the most sumptuous procession that ever had been seen here," and the Jesuit spy, Giacomo Lambertengo, derided it as a "spettacolo miserabile [miserable spectacle]." The congregations of secular priests, most of the orders of the regulars, and the *scuole grandi* participated in the procession—the latter contributing numerous tableaux that, according to the official euphemism of the day, had "some scenes which alluded to the reasonable claims of the republic against the pope." In particular, the tableaux proclaimed the distinctions between sacred and secular authority on which the Venetians built their case. On one *solaro* an actor dressed as Christ stood above a Latin motto quoting Mark 12:17: "Render unto Caesar that which is Caesar's and unto God what is God's"; and, on another, Christ reminded his Apostles that their priesthood did not allow them to usurp the authority of kings who properly ruled over the temporal affairs of mankind. The most pointed reference to the follies of the pope was a collapsing church ("chiesa cadente") supported by the Venetian doge assisted by Saint Dominic and Saint Francis. On either side of the church, other friars held up broad swords, emblazoned with the motto, "VIVA IL DOSE."

The procession was a diplomatic coup. Some nine days earlier at Pentecost, when the Signoria had walked in the procession unaccompanied by any foreign ambassadors, rumors spread that Venice had been abandoned by its friends. To the delight of the crowds, both the French and the Imperial ambassadors made a belated appearance on Corpus Christi Day. Ambassador Wotton saw exactly what was going on: "The reasons of this extraordinary solemnity were two as I conceive it. First, to contain the people in good order with superstition, the foolish band of obedience. Secondly, to let the pope know (who wanteth not intelligencers) that notwithstanding his interdict, they had friars enough and other clergymen to furnish out the day." Apparently, the procession achieved these ends and helped to turn the diplomatic tide in Venice's favor.

In the course of the sixteenth century, pageantry had thus evolved into a signal art form and a public mirror meant to reflect images of political power. It had not superseded the other arts as a political device, but its pliable and adaptive form appealed to those trained to rule others. In pageantry the elite of Venice had a superior means of exploiting Machiavelli's dictum that to most men appearances mattered more than realities.

In all of the examples discussed, the arts disclosed political ideas by making analogies. Through symbolism and allegory the arts elevated a political idea—however self-serving, prevaricating, or mean—to a transcendent plane: doges resembled saints, the gods directed the fortune of war or diplomacy, and Venice itself was the epitome of the theological, political, and classical virtues. Although the images changed and pagan deities joined Christian saints in the city's pantheon, the analogical process remained the same. This form of reasoning was not unusual, for much of Renaissance political thought, even when crafted by the finest minds, depended on metaphors—the "King's Two Bodies," the "Ship of State," or the "Marriage of the Sea," for example—to unveil in human terms the implications of a given principle or abstraction. It is certain that many people took these comparisons seriously, but it is much more difficult to tell to what degree such a habit of thought influenced ordinary political perceptions and decisions. In any historical period and for any one person, it is probably impossible to determine the exact balance of ideology, belief, and objectivity in motivating a particular action. In Venice, however, it seems that ideology always played a considerable role among supporters and opponents of the regime; in the major Renaissance protests against the dictatorial habits of the oligarchs, opposition was always phrased as "restoration" of a traditional balance of responsibilities and privileges to all patricians, and the most tired clichés of the established order were used by the protesters to argue against that very order.

Perhaps the most important attribute of political imagery in the arts was its persuasive power. Visual images cajoled belief by simplifying and distorting political issues, by ignoring objectionable facts, and by juxtaposing symbols that connected ideas that may not have had any relationship in logic or reality. Herbert M. Atherton has found a similar persuasive tendency in eighteenth-century political prints, and other instances of politics so translated into art can surely be traced to the present day. But for Renaissance Venetians, art was not just a gloss on public issues nor a mere reinforcement of status discriminations and hierarchical rank; rather, the arts provided a commentary upon the whole political and social order and specifically upon the nature of class distinctions, noble privilege, and sacred inherited institutions. If the art in Venice can be reduced to anything so simple as a "function," then its function was interpretive: it was a Venetian reading of Venetian experience, a story they told themselves about themselves.

The relationship between patronage of the arts and political power is a less elusive problem: the richest men in the highest ranks of power preserved exclusive control over all political ideas in the arts. Only nuances of disagreement about political images in the arts, such as how to depict the powers of the doge, ever emanated from within this tight circle of men who rotated the important offices among themselves. The poorer nobles, the few privileged *cittadini* [citizens], and the disenfranchised masses were mute. Art may have once been the common tongue of the people, as Berenson believed, but a small group of powerful men chose what was to be said, and in the sixteenth century they increasingly chose a language that only an educated few could fully understand: what did fishmongers and gondoliers know of Jupiter, Mars, and Latin epigrams?

This elitism is not surprising. Anthropologists have shown that in many traditional societies village strongmen dominate over the most popular and universally accepted phenomena. For Western society Morse Peckham has noted that the "high arts" have always been associated with and have validated the centers of power. The modern illusion that artists must be honest with themselves and only serve, to borrow a phrase from Danton, "Truth—truth in all her rugged harshness" ignores the harshest truth, that artists survive only at the will of their patrons, customers, and audiences, and the powerful who sponsor the high arts have seldom been interested in truth for its own sake. The bohemian individual had no place in Renaissance Venice, and, with the exceptions of a few doges, the arts did not extol the uniqueness of the self, supporting personal oppositions to an inherited social role, as believed by those who equate the Renaissance with individualism, but protected the claims of society on the individual and offered an explanation for the existing order.

There were, of course, some changes in the political use of art in sixteenth-century Venice. The rise of pageantry, the acceptance of the antique style and iconography, and the interest in ingenious allegories that followed in the century after the War of the League of Cambrai reveal, if not a direct correspondence to the elite's quest for *nobiltà*, at least the emergence of a culture less accessible to the common Venetians than the old Venetian world of religious myth and communal civic values preached from every pulpit and in every ceremony. It is also clear that the interest in classical culture did not correspond in any way to the triumph of "bourgeois capitalism" but more likely to its rejection as a dominant value. Lastly, these changes in Venetian state art may express a new sensitivity among the patricians to the notion that they could use the apparatus of the state to impose their own values and cultural proclivities on the entire society. This notion is, of course, a rudiment of what many historians call "modernization." What apparently governed the artistic transformation in Venice, then, was not so much an empirically verifiable change in economic or social conditions as it was the patricians' perceptions of a change. Had the worldview the patricians inherited so colored reality that they could see things in no other way? Very little of their heroic, mythic past was evident in the reality of sixteenth-century Venice. That they felt insecure as a consequence was only natural. From their ancestors, however, they had also inherited a remedy for insecurity—myth-making. For them the manipulation of ever more brilliant images of power remained part of the pursuit of power itself.

DOCUMENTS

In the first document, Savonarola's last few years in Florence before he was burned at the stake in 1498 are described by Francesco Guicciardini in his *History of Florence* (1509). A Dominican friar and charismatic preacher in the Church of San Marco, Savonarola achieved extraordinary power in Florence after the expulsion of Piero de' Medici in 1494. With the restoration of republican rule in 1494, Savonarola gave valuable support to the faction in power, criticized the established church, and tried to persuade the Florentines to renounce their sinful luxuries and repent. Eventually he was excommunicated and burned as a heretic, with the full cooperation of the Florentine government. Guicciardini's *History* is a perceptive narrative of the turbulent history of his beloved city from the age of Lorenzo the Magnificent, based on shrewd observation and careful research. Guicciardini is often mentioned with Machiavelli as one of the giant intellects of his age. Indeed what he admires most about Savonarola's success is his political savvy and rhetorical skill.

In the second document, the Englishman Sir Richard Guildford describes two Venetian processions, for the feast of the Ascension and for Corpus Christi, that he witnessed on his way to the Holy Land in 1506. He was struck by their size, splendor, and solemnity, and he marveled at the great variety of Venetians participating in the pageantry: representatives from all the confraternities, great and small, and people from all social classes and neighborhoods of the city.

Francesco Guicciardini Describes Savonarola's Impact On Florence, 1494–1498

The attitude of the Florentines [toward greater piety] was reinforced by the sermons of Brother Jerome [Savonarola], who, after the expulsion of Piero [de' Medici], and the establishment of the Great Council, continued to preach in Santa Reparata to larger audiences than any preacher had ever had. Openly saying that he had been sent by God to announce future events, he often made statements about the future of the Christian religion in general and of our city in particular. The necessary renewal and reformation of the Church toward a better life would be accomplished not by temporal blessings and happiness but by scourges and tribulation. Before that, Italy would first be struck down and tormented by famine, plague, and war; several armies of foreign barbarians would invade it and skin it to the bone. The governments of Italy would have to change, for neither their counsel nor wealth nor force would suffice to resist this onslaught. Our own city would have to suffer many troubles and be reduced to the extreme danger of losing everything. Nevertheless, because God had chosen it as the place where these great events were to be prophesied, and because the light of the Church's renewal would shine from here to the rest of the world, the city would not perish; in fact, even if all our possessions were lost, the city would be saved. Finally, reduced by these scourges to true and simple Christianity, Florence would recover Pisa and whatever else it had lost. This would take place not through any human means or agency, but by the hand of God, at a time no one foresaw, and in a manner that everyone would clearly recognize as divine intervention. Florence would also acquire many places that were never hers before; she would become more prosperous, more glorious, and more powerful than she had ever been. The popular government and the Great Council, being the work of God,

Text with abridgements from *The History of Florence* by Francesco Guicciardini, translated by Mario Domandi, pp. 115–117, 126, 136–148. Copyright © 1970 by Mario Domandi. Reprinted by permission of HarperCollins Publishers, Inc.

should not be changed; in fact, anyone who opposed them would meet with a bad end. These prophecies would be fulfilled so soon, he added, that anyone who heard these sermons would witness them if he lived out the natural course of his life. He gave many other details concerning both the spiritual and the temporal persecutions still to be suffered; but I shall omit them because they are irrelevant here, and because they are clearly set forth in his sermons, which are available in print.

This sort of preaching brought him the hatred of the pope, for in predicting the renewal of the Church he openly detested and flailed the behavior and habits of the clergy. The Venetians and the duke of Milan also hated him because they thought he favored the French and had caused the city to refuse to join the league. Furthermore, his sermons aroused dissension in the city and brought him the hostility of many citizens, who opposed him either because they naturally disbelieved these things, or because they did not like the popular government he so warmly favored and maintained. Some others opposed him because they had more faith in the Franciscans and the other religious orders than in the brothers of San Marco, who were enjoying such great popularity. He was also opposed by many depraved men, who were unhappy because his detestation of sodomy and other sins and games had very much restricted their way of life. All together they rose fiercely against him, persecuting him publicly and opposing his works whenever they could. . . .

On the other hand, many citizens strongly supported him and approved of his works. Some of them were quite naturally led by their good nature and by their religious inclinations to have faith in him. They believed that his works were good and that his predictions were being realized every day. Some others, evil men of bad reputation, supported him only to acquire a good name and a cloak of holiness with which to hide their actions. Others, generally considered decorous men, seeing that his side was stronger, supported him in order to gain easier access to office, greater public favor, and reputation. . . . Since his persecutors were hated and in bad odor, whereas his supporters were accepted and well liked, the latter group got far more honors and offices in the city than the others. From these positions of power his supporters prevented Florence from joining the league; for they believed, among other things, that the rulers of Italy were headed for ruin, just as Brother Jerome had predicted. Great dissension and strong hatreds were born among the citizens, and in many families brothers, fathers, and sons disagreed on matters concerning Brother Jerome. Another fundamental division was that all those who supported the friar were on the French side, whereas those who opposed him wanted to come to terms with the league. . . .

. . . On the morning of Ascension Day, Brother Jerome was preaching in Santa Reparata when a great uproar spread throughout the city, for which no cause could be found later except suspicion. The shouting was very loud, and he was obviously very frightened. Unable to finish his sermon, he returned to San Marco accompanied by many armed citizens, among whom was Giovan Battista Ridolfi carrying over his shoulder a weapon mounted on a pole.

But the dissension among the citizens did not cease; in fact it grew worse every day. Then, in the month of June, Pope Alexander had his excommunication of the friar published in Florence, alleging that he had publicly preached heretical doctrine and that he had subsequently been summoned but had failed to appear. It is believed that the pope was willing enough to do this of his own accord, but the instigation of the friar's enemies in Florence made him even more eager. To prove the friar's innocence, a petition was started in San Marco and signed by many citizens, all of whom affirmed that he was a true and good Catholic. About five hundred signed, including just about every known member of his party. Since he abstained from preaching on account of the excommunication, and since his enemies were satisfied, the discord seemed to be subsiding a little. . . .

. . . Brother Jerome broke the silence imposed by the excommunication in June [1497] and began preaching again in Santa Reparata. He had continued to celebrate mass in San Marco to show he did not fear the excommunication; now, seeing his influence on the wane, and having a favorable Signoria and gonfalonier in office, he made his decision to preach again, asserting with many and spurious reasons that he was obliged neither to observe nor to fear his excommunication. His decision resuscitated those evil humors and divisions that had died down somewhat while he was not preaching. When the pope heard of his disobedience he was furious. Urged on by many of our priests and citizens, he sent a brief commanding that no one go hear him under pain of excommunication. Brother Jerome's audience dwindled, and when the chapter of Santa Reparata made it clear it did not want him to preach there, he withdrew to San Marco to avoid scandal. While he was preaching there the new Signoria for March and April was elected, with Piero Popoleschi as gonfalonier. It was one in which the friar had little influence, although his supporters Lanfredino Lanfredini and Alessandro di Papi degli Alessandri were Priors. Letters came from the pope warmly urging the Signoria to prohibit his preaching. A large committee met to discuss the matter; and after many arguments, the great majority finally advised that he stop preaching. The Signoria commanded and he obeyed, leaving Brother Domenico da Pescia to preach in his place in San Marco, and other friars to preach in other churches.

His enemies were much stronger than in the past, for several reasons: first, because it is the habit of people to turn coat after they have favored one cause for a while, even if there be no reason for it; then there was the excommunication, which had alienated many of his followers and made enemies of all those middle-of-the-roaders who considered it a very serious and unseemly thing for good Christians to disobey the orders of the pope. And finally the leaders of the friar's opponents had organized a group called the *Compagnacci*. These spirited, brave, and well-armed young aristocrats would often meet and dine together. And because they were young, well-armed men of good families, everyone was afraid of them. Paolantonio Soderini, a passionate supporter of the friar, had his son Tommaso join them, just to be safe in case they should win out. . . .

1498: There followed the year 1498, a year filled with very grave and varied events, started by the fall of Brother Jerome. When he had stopped preaching at the command of the Signoria, his persecutors both lay and cleric seemed to let up somewhat; but then a small incident caused a complete change in everything. At San Marco there was a Dominican named Brother Domenico da Pescia, a simple man reputed to be of good life. Imitating Brother Jerome's style of predicting future events, Brother Domenico had said from the pulpit in Santa Reparata about two years earlier that whenever it became necessary to prove the truth of the friars' words, they would raise a man from the dead, and would also walk through fire un-scathed, by the grace of God. Brother Jerome had repeated this later, but nothing more was said about it until this time. A certain Brother Francesco, a member of the Observantist branch of the Franciscan Order, was preaching in Santa Croce. He detested Brother Jerome and all his works; and he now began saying in his sermons that to demonstrate how false those statements were, he would be happy to have a fire made in the Piazza della Signoria and walk into it himself, so long as Brother Jerome did the same. He said he was sure he would burn, but that Brother Jerome would burn too. That would prove there was no truth in him, for he said many times that he would come forth from the fire unscathed. When Brother Domenico, who was preaching in Brother Jerome's place, heard about this, he accepted the challenge from the pulpit, offering to take on the ordeal himself in place of the friar.

This prospect pleased many citizens of both parties, for they hoped finally to see an end to these feuds and at long last have done with all this uncertainty. They began discussions with both preachers for the purpose of bringing about this trial. After many meetings, all the brothers agreed to have a fire made, into which would walk a Dominican chosen by Brother Jerome, and a Franciscan to be chosen by his superiors. When the date was fixed, Brother Jerome got permission from the Signoria to preach; and in San Marco he preached on the great importance of miracles, saying they were not used except when necessary, and when reason and experience did not suffice. Since the truth of the Christian faith was proved in an infinite number of ways, and since the truth of his predictions had been so effectively and rationally shown that anyone not hardened in evil ways could easily see it, he had not had recourse to miracles only because he did not want to tempt God. Nevertheless, now that he had been provoked, he gladly accepted, and he assured everyone that when the friars walked into the fire, the Dominican would walk out alive and unscathed and the other would burn. If that did not happen, let them then say openly that he had preached falsehood. He added that not only his own friars, but anyone who entered the fire in defense of this truth would be safe. He asked them whether, for the sake of such great work ordained by God, they would not go into the fire if nec-essary; and almost everyone answered with a loud yes. What an amazing thing! Without doubt, very many would have done it had he asked them.

Finally, on the designated day, which was on the [seventh] of April, the Satur-day before Palm Sunday, a platform filled with great heaps of wood was erected in the middle of Piazza della Signoria. The Franciscan friars came at the designated hour and went over to the loggia of the Signoria; then came the friars of San Marco, many of them in their most formal robes, singing the psalm *Exurgat Dominus et dissipentur inimici eius* [Psalm 67. Let the Lord arise, and let his enemies be scattered.]. With them was Brother Jerome, holding the body of Christ in his hand, and behind him some friars and many laymen reverently carrying lighted torches. Their arrival was so full of devotion and showed so clearly that they were coming to the trial with great courage, that it not only reassured their partisans but also completely frightened their enemies.

When they too had entered the loggia, where they were separated from the Franciscans by a fence, there arose some difficulty concerning the clothing Brother Domenico da Pescia was to wear, for the Franciscans feared some sort of enchantment or spell. Since they could not agree, the Signoria sent two citizens for each side to iron out their differences: messer Francesco Gualterotti, Giovan Battista Ridolfi, Tommaso Antinori, and Piero degli Alberti. When they finally came close to a settlement that seemed acceptable to both sides, they took the leaders of the friars to the palace, where they settled their differences, stipulated the terms, and then left to get the trial started. Just then the Franciscans heard that Brother Domenico intended to enter the fire with the body of Christ in his hand. They objected very strongly, saying that if the Host burned, it would be a grave scandal and danger to the faith of Christ. On the other side, Brother Jerome insisted that he carry it. After long argument, with each side persisting in its position, no agreement could be reached, so they all went home without even lighting the wood.

Brother Jerome immediately mounted the pulpit, to argue that the fault lay with the Franciscans and that his side had won; but many people nevertheless believed that this difficulty about the body of Christ was only a subterfuge. That day many of his friends turned from him, and the great majority of the people became very hostile. The next day saw his deluded supporters abused by the people, while his enemies were emboldened by the support of the populace, by the backing of the armed *Compagnacci*, and by the fact that a Signoria sympathetic to them sat in the palace. It happened that on that day, after dinner, a friar from San Marco was to preach in Santa Reparata. A great tumult arose, apparently by accident, and quickly spread throughout the city, as is apt to happen when men are excited and minds full of fear and suspicion. The friar's enemies and the *Compagnacci* took up arms and turned the people toward San Marco, which was filled with many of his supporters who were at vespers. They began to defend the convent with stones and arms, as though it were besieged. . . .

. . . After a few hours they finally forced their way into San Marco, and took Brother Jerome, Brother Domenico, and Brother Silvestro [Maruffi] da Firenze prisoners to the palace. Though Brother Silvestro did not preach, he was a confidant of Brother Jerome and was believed to know his every secret.

After this victory arms were put aside, and the power and prestige of government were transferred to the friar's enemies, who now went about securing their position. Since they had little faith in the Eight and the Ten, who were reputed to be *Piagnoni* (as the friar's supporters were called), they convened the Great Council and elected a new Ten and Eight, made up entirely of men trusted by those in power. . . .

About twenty citizens were assigned to examine Brother Jerome and his colleagues, all of them his fierce enemies. Without the pope's permission, they gave him a taste of the rack; and then after a few days they ordered a trial. They reported to the Great Council the statement they said they had got out of him, signed by the vicars of Florence and Fiesole and by some of the leading friars of San Marco. The document had been read to Brother Jerome in their presence, and when he was asked if its contents were true, he answered that they were. In brief, the most important conclusions were these: that the things he had predicted were not from God, revelation, or any divine source, but were of his own invention, without the participation of any layman or friar; that he had done it out of pride and ambition, and that it had been his intention to have a council of the Christian princes called to depose the pope and reform the Church; that if he had been offered the papacy he would have accepted;

nevertheless, that he wanted far more to carry out this great work than to become pope, because even a man of little worth can become pope, but only an excellent man could be the leader and author of such a reform. . . .

Then the new Signoria was elected. . . . During their term the commissaries arrived from Rome, again examined Brother Jerome and the others, and finally condemned all three to be burned at the stake. On the [twenty-third] of May, they were first degraded, then hanged and burned in the Piazza della Signoria, in the presence of far more people than were generally at his sermons. It was deemed an astonishing thing that none of them, not even Brother Jerome, should have used the occasion to make a public statement, either to accuse or excuse himself.

That was the shameful end of Savonarola. It will not be out of order to speak at some length of his qualities, for neither in our age nor in those of our fathers and forefathers was there ever seen a monk endowed with so many virtues, or one who enjoyed so much reputation and authority. Even his enemies admit that he was learned in many subjects, especially in philosophy, which he knew very well and used so skillfully for his purposes that one would have thought he had invented it. He was so well versed in sacred scripture that many people believe we would have to go back several centuries to find his equal. His judgment was very profound not only in matters of erudition, but in worldly affairs as well. In my opinion, his sermons demonstrate clearly that he knew very well the principles that govern this world. Endowed with these qualities, and with an eloquence that was neither artificial nor forced but natural and easy, his sermons were by far the greatest of his age. It was marvelous to see what audiences and what reputation he kept, for he preached for many years not only during Lent, but on many of the holidays as well. Moreover, he was in a city full of subtle and fastidious minds, where even excellent preachers came to be considered boring after one Lenten season, or at most two. These virtues were so clear and manifest in him that they are recognized not only by his supporters and followers, but by his enemies as well.

But questions and differences of opinion arise concerning the goodness of his life. It should be noted that if he had any vice at all, it was only simulation, caused by ambition and pride. Those who observed his life and habits for a long time found not the slightest trace of avarice, lust, or of any other form of cupidity or frailty. On the contrary, they found evidence of a most devout life, full of charity, full of prayers, full of observance not of the externals but of the very heart of the divine cult. Although his detractors searched industriously during the investigation, they could not find even the slightest moral defect in him. The work he did in promoting decent behavior was holy and marvelous; nor had there ever been as much goodness and religion in Florence as there was in his time. After his death they disappeared, showing that whatever virtue there was had been introduced and maintained by him. In his time, people no longer gambled in public and were even afraid to do it at home. The taverns that used to cater to wayward and vice-ridden youth were closed; sodomy was suppressed and decried. A great many women gave up their shameful and lascivious clothing. Nearly all boys were made to give up their many shameful practices, and brought back to a holy and decent way of life. Under his direction, Brother Domenico organized them into companies, and they went to church, wore their hair short, and would hurl stones and insults at lecherous men, gamblers, and women who wore lascivious clothing. At carnival, a day generally celebrated with a thousand iniquities, they first held a religious procession full of devotion; then they would go about collecting dice, cards, make-up, shameful books and pictures, and then would burn them all in the Piazza della Signoria. Older men turned toward religion, mass, vespers, and sermons, and went to confession and communion often. At carnival time a great number of people went to confession; alms and charity were distributed in abundance. Every day the friar urged men to abandon pomp and vanity, and to return to the simplicity of religion and the Christian life. . . .

. . . Because the results of his works were so good, and because several of his prophecies were fulfilled, many people continued to believe for a long time that he was truly sent by God and that he was a true prophet, despite the excommunication, the trial, and his death. For my part I am in doubt, and have no firm opinion on the matter. I shall reserve my judgment for a future time, if I live that long; for time clears up everything. But I do believe this: if he was good, we have seen a great prophet in our time; if he was bad, we have seen a great man. For, apart from his erudition, we must admit that if he was able to fool the public for so many years on so important a matter, without ever being caught in a lie, he must have had great judgment, talent, and power of invention.

Sir Richard Guildford Describes Two Processions in Venice, 1506

The richness, the sumptuous buildings and religious houses and the establishments of their justices and councils, with all other things that makes a city glorious, in Venice surpasses all other places that I ever saw. And especially at two feasts where we were present. The one was upon Ascension Day, when the Doge, with great triumph and solemnity, with all the Signoria [high government officials], went in their Triumphal Ark, which is a type of Galley of strange construction and stately wonder, and so rowed out into the [Adriatic] sea with the presence of their Patriarch, and there espoused the sea with a ring. The words of espousal be: "In sign of the true and perpetual dominion [of the sea]." And therewith the Doge let fall the ring into the sea. The procession and ceremonies [of this event] were too long to write.

The other feast was on Corpus Christi Day, where was the most solemn procession that ever I saw. There went pageants of the old law and the new, joining together the figures of the blessed sacrament in such numbers and so apt and convenient for that feast that it would make any man joyous to see it. And beyond that it was a great marvel to see the great number of religious folks and of schools, that we call brotherhoods or fellowships, with their devises, which all bore lights [candles] of wondrous goodly fashion, and between every [one] of the pageants went little

From *The Pylgrymage of Sir Richard Guylforde to the Holy Land, A. D. 1506*, ed. Sir Henry Ellis, Camden Society, Vol. 51 (London, 1851), pp. 8–9. Spelling is modernized.

children of both kinds, gloriously and richly dressed, bearing in their hands in rich cups or other vessels some pleasant flowers or other well smelling or rich stuff, dressed as angels to adorn the said procession. The form and manner thereof exceeded all other that ever I saw so much that I cannot write it. The Doge sat in Saint Mark's Church in right high estate, with all the Signoria, and all the pilgrims were present. The Doge thus sitting, the said procession came by him, and began to pass by at about seven o'clock, and it was past twelve o'clock when the said procession had come once about, passing by as fast as they might go but one time. There was great honor done to the pilgrims, for we all most and least went all there next to the Doge in the said procession, before all the lords and other estates, also holding in our hands candles of wax, of the freshest forming, given unto us by the ministers of the said procession.

FURTHER READING

James R. Banker, *Death in the Community: Memorialization and Confraternities in an Italian Commune in the Late Middle Ages* (1988)

Rudolph M. Bell and Donald Weinstein, *Saints and Society: The Two Worlds of Western Christianity, 1000–1700* (1985)

C. F. Black, *Italian Confraternities in the Sixteenth Century* (1989)

Daniel Bornstein, *The Bianchi of 1399: Popular Devotion in Late Medieval Italy* (1993)

William Bowsky, *Piety and Property in Medieval Florence: A House in San Lorenzo* (1990)

Judith Brown, *Immodest Acts: The Life of a Lesbian Nun in Renaissance Italy* (1986)

Patricia Fortini Brown, *Venetian Narrative Painting in the Age of Carpaccio* (1988)

Rona Goffen, *Piety and Patronage in Renaissance Venice* (1986)

Denys Hay, *The Church in Italy in the Fifteenth Century* (1977)

John Henderson, *Piety and Charity in Late Medieval Florence* (1994)

Craig Monson, ed., *The Crannied Wall: Women, Religion, and the Arts in Early Modern Europe* (1992)

Edward Muir, *Civic Ritual in Renaissance Venice* (1982)

Iris Origo, *The World of San Bernardino* (1962)

Brian Pullan, *Rich and Poor in Renaissance Venice: Social Institutions of a Catholic State, to 1620* (1971)

Marjorie Reeves, ed., *Prophetic Rome in the High Renaissance Period* (1992)

Richard Trexler, *Public Life in Renaissance Florence* (1981)

Charles Trinkaus and H. A. Oberman, eds., *The Pursuit of Holiness in Late Medieval and Renaissance Religion* (1974)

Timothy Verdon and John Henderson, eds., *Christianity and the Renaissance* (1990)

Donald Weinstein, *Savonarola and Florence* (1970)

Ronald Weissman, *Ritual Brotherhood in Renaissance Florence* (1982)

CHAPTER **14**

The End of the Renaissance?

C hanges in the attitudes of Renaissance humanists and in the
structure of political society in the sixteenth century are often
held as heralding the "end" of the Renaissance. There is always
debate about the boundaries of historical periods, and in this case, too,
the nature of the changes, and even the causes of the changes, are not
clearly understood. A neat, all-encompassing synthesis assessing the
many developments in economic and social organization, politics,
intellectual life, and artistic styles of the later Renaissance does not
yet—and may never—exist.

During the first decades of the sixteenth century, when Italy
became the battleground for foreign armies (See Chapter 7), republics
and principalities alike relied increasingly on diplomatic negotiation in
favor of military operations to defend and preserve their liberty. Great
value was placed on servants of the state with sufficient intelligence,
appropriate education, and social stature to carry out delicate
diplomatic maneuvers. Concurrently, the consolidation of territorial
states encouraged the development of central administrations, thought
to minimize the danger of faction and personal interest to internal
stability. These two related developments caused the corps of public
officials paid directly by the central authority to grow in both numbers
and power. A professional mentality began to develop within their
ranks, characterized by a new importance of political office, and the
separation of the public, official duties of a civil servant from the private
sphere.

Humanistic education, which stressed the power of letters over
arms, merit over birth, reason over tradition, and, above all, the political
effectiveness of learning, contributed to the development of the new
ethos (See Chapter 9). Writers grew in demand for their professional
skills as bureaucrats as well as their literary skills; their presence in a
princely court lent it prestige, and their public, highly visible, and
politically powerful roles contributed to that prestige. Their attachment
to a court depended less on ties of personal obligation to a prince than
on political and financial opportunities. Within the framework of
constantly shifting alliances, ambitious courtiers exercised their freedom
to move from one court to another. The increasingly cosmopolitan
nature of the courtly milieu facilitated this movement, which
encouraged the diffusion of a new literary culture throughout Italy.

Evidence for the changing position of the courtier, the new

functions of the writer in the service of a prince, and the growing power of the civil service can be found in the proliferation of treatises discussing aristocratic and administrative conduct, of which Castiglione's *Courtier* was the most famous and influential. Historians tend to view these works as the expression of an increasingly exclusive aristocratic elite wishing to remove themselves from the rest of society and thereby to secure their political and social superiority. Nevertheless, these authors were addressing issues that they, as public servants and political actors in an increasingly complicated world, perceived to be of critical importance to themselves and to their readers. The elaboration of modes of conduct, intended to minimize friction within administrative hierarchies (and princely courts) and tied to the notion of service to the prince and, by extension, to the state, met very practical demands.

The increasingly authoritarian governments of Venice, Florence, Rome, Milan, and smaller principalities encouraged an "aristocratization" of society, that is, a clear articulation of aristocratic status based on wealth and learning as well as birth. Wealthy families increasingly shifted their investments from commerce to agriculture, thus apparently disengaging themselves from the life of the city. The ultimate expression of this trend was the proliferation of elegant country villas where weary noblemen and women could escape from the stresses of urban life to enjoy nature. Due in part to the republican bias of some of the finest Renaissance scholarship, historians relate this aristocratization of society to Italy's loss of political liberty and to the "end" of the Renaissance in the sixteenth century.

Recent evidence unearthed by social and economic historians shows that the story of aristocratization in the sixteenth century is not that simple, however. In the first place, the shift of investments from commerce to land was almost certainly a shrewd response to market conditions that maximized profit as it minimized risks. Second, the same nobles who eagerly built villas still spent most of the year in their urban palaces, because their political and social lives continued to center on the city. Their writings about the delights of villa life, although no doubt genuine, were also in imitation of the ancient Romans. Finally, the process of aristocratization itself had begun much earlier and was part of a broader European trend culminating in the formation of early modern elites.

By the middle of the sixteenth century, the sophisticated, urbane Italians responsible for the Renaissance were living in a much bigger world. The invasions of their peninsula by French and Imperial armies had culminated in the Sack of Rome in 1527. The Protestant Reformation had caused the permanent division of Christendom, and the papacy's response—the Counter-Reformation—created a more oppressively religious society. Much of northern Europe was torn apart by religious warfare, and the Turkish armies continued to threaten from the East. The commercial hub of Europe was slowly shifting from Italy and the Mediterranean to cities on the Atlantic and the North Sea. And perhaps most important, the audacious explorers of the globe, themselves imbued with a restless curiosity that was kindled by the spirit of Renaissance humanism, had vastly enlarged the boundaries of the known world.

Essays

William J. Bouwsma, an intellectual historian at the University of California at Berkeley, discusses the problem of the "later Renaissance" in the first essay. He notes an important change in humanists' attitude toward rhetoric, beginning in the middle of the fifteenth century. Whereas the earlier humanists placed rhetoric at the very center of human existence, providing the essential bond of human community, later humanists began to separate rhetorical form from content. Rhetoric became a literary embellishment, an ornament of aristocratic status, and no longer concerned with the power of communication. Bouwsma concludes that it was this later version of Italian humanism, not the earlier, more radical civic humanism, that was adopted so enthusiastically by northern intellectuals.

In the second essay, Carlo Dionisotti, a literary scholar at the University of London, examines the careers of men of letters during the first half of the sixteenth century. That so many of the finest writers and intellectuals were clerics he relates to the supreme importance of the papacy in the international political arena, which was enhanced by one of the most sophisticated and elaborate administrations in Italy. Although similar mechanisms for advancement certainly existed for laymen in princely courts, Dionisotti argues that men of letters in the early to mid-sixteenth century could most effectively realize all of their political ambitions by entering the service of the pope and aspiring to the cardinalate.

Changing Assumptions in Later Renaissance Culture

WILLIAM J. BOUWSMA

The familiar notion of a "later" Renaissance immediately presents itself as an innocent effort at chronological arrangement, as a convenience for determining relationships in time. But of course it is much more. It calls upon us to distinguish the differing characteristics of successive moments, to trace a process of development from inception to maturity and possibly on to decline; and it introduces the complicated problem of the relations between Italy and the Northern Renaissance. It is thus closely connected with one of the most fruitful tendencies in all aspects of modern Renaissance scholarship: the effort to distinguish stages in a larger movement which, without such analysis, is filled with an ambiguity that makes useful discussion almost impossible. This tendency is perhaps nowhere more apparent than in the study of Renaissance humanism, a subject which, though by no means their only significant expression, brings into unusually clear relief the assumptions underlying what was most novel and creative in Renaissance culture. By the same token concentration on humanism is a convenient way to deal with the inner development of Renaissance culture.

The most persuasive attempts to work out the stages in the evolution of Renaissance humanism have concentrated on particular places, as, for example, the work of Baron on Florence, of Branca on Venice, or of Spitz on Germany. Such efforts have proved remarkably useful, but by their very nature they can be no more than

From William J. Bouwsma, "Changing Assumptions in Later Renaissance Culture," *Viator* 7 (1976), reprinted in his *Usable Past: Essays in European Cultural History*, pp. 74–92. Copyright © 1990 The Regents of the University of California. Reprinted by permission of the publisher.

suggestive about the development of humanism as a general phenomenon of Renaissance Italy or even of Renaissance Europe, responsive to more than local influences. In addition, what has so far been said on this subject is not very helpful for the problem of the later Renaissance. Students of humanism have been concerned chiefly with its earlier, formative stages, as though, once the movement were well established, its full story had been told. Here, as elsewhere in Renaissance scholarship, we can perhaps sense a reluctance to deal with the notions of maturation and then of decay, decline, and end. Back of this may lurk the old idea of the Renaissance as the beginning of the modern age—which, by definition, must still be with us.

I should like to approach the problem of the later Renaissance, then, by calling attention first to changing attitudes towards rhetoric, now generally recognized as the core of Renaissance humanism. The Renaissance humanist was first of all a rhetorician, concerned to perfect in himself and others the art of speaking and writing well. From this standpoint his interest in the classics was secondary and at any rate hardly a novelty; we are now fully aware of the deep classicism of medieval culture. What was significant in the Renaissance humanist was not his classical interests but the novelty of his preferences within the classical heritage. For him the most important classical writers were the Latin orators, the supreme teachers, by both precept and example, of the rhetorical art. It is now clear, therefore, that humanism must be understood initially as a movement in the history of education which proposed to substitute, for the philosophers beloved by the dialecticians, a new group of classical authors, the orators, and then their allies, the ancient poets, historians, and moralists, as the center of a new curriculum, the *studia humanitatis* [the Humanities].

For some scholars this conception of humanism makes it appear less serious. The reason is, perhaps, that in our own culture rhetoric is popularly regarded as an ambiguous art, and we try to protect ourselves from those who abuse it by attaching to it the adjective "mere," though the need for such protection suggests a fear hardly consistent with the adjective itself. The phrase "mere rhetoric" implies that a rhetorician is at best only a frivolous and minor artist who does no more than decorate serious content with ultimately superfluous adornments; at worst he is a seducer. Back of the phrase "mere rhetoric" also lies, perhaps, a quasi-metaphysical assumption that form is distinguishable from substance, a conception that betrays the persistent influence of one important strand of ancient thought on the Western mind. But it seems to me the very essence of Renaissance humanism, insofar as it differed from the humanism of the Middle Ages, that it rejected this distinction. It took rhetoric seriously because it recognized that the forms of thought are part of thought itself, that verbal meaning is a complex entity, like the human organism, which also cannot survive dissection. . . .

And there is a further profound implication of this position, which Valla, the deepest mind among the earlier humanists, did much to elucidate. Since the forms of thought can at any rate be perceived as historically determined, the indivisibility of form and content suggests that all intellectual activity is relative to its times. So Renaissance rhetoric opened the way to a denial of absolutes in favor of a novel cultural relativism. Man, for the rhetorician, not man as a species but man in a particular time and place, becomes the measure of all things, a conception that suggests a further element in the lineage of rhetoric, and also brings out the irony in the familiar humanist designation of the schoolmen as "sophists."

Thus there was nothing frivolous in the cult of rhetoric in the Renaissance, or at least in the early Renaissance in Italy. Nor was there anything trivial about its practical uses. As the art of effective communication, rhetoric was not only the instrument of divine revelation but also the essential bond of human community, and therefore of supreme value for an increasingly complex society struggling to develop more effective patterns of communal life. Enthusiasm for rhetoric was most intense among townsmen responsible for welding the inchoate mass of individuals thrown together within the urban walls into a genuine community. Rhetoric thus provided a natural foundation for the new urban culture of the Renaissance, and it operated at every level of human interaction, both private and public. Businessmen had to communicate persuasively with their customers, suppliers, and associates; lawyers had to argue conflicts of interest in the courts; citizens conversed and corresponded with their friends on personal matters or sought the agreement of their peers on questions of public policy; rulers had to maintain the support of their subjects; governments corresponded with each other, sent out embassies, courted foreign opinion.

Rhetoric, therefore, because it gave form to every subject of human concern and made it communicable, was not on the periphery but at the very center of human existence. Accordingly a rhetorician could only be a generalist, and a rhetorical education became, in the Renaissance, the first truly general education in European history. A Florentine statute at the end of the fourteenth century, even before Poggio's discovery of Quintilian, justified the appointment of a public teacher of rhetoric on the ground that "the art of rhetoric is not only the instrument of persuasion for all the sciences but also the greatest ornament of public life," and that it "embraces the precepts for advocating or opposing anything we wish." Rhetoric brought into focus all knowledge and all experience.

This elevation of rhetoric also had other major ideological implications; thus if, as Kristeller has shown, it had no explicit philosophical substance, it had considerable significance, as he also recognized, for philosophy in a larger sense. Above all the new rhetorical culture rested on a novel conception of man. Rejecting the abstract man of classical anthropology with its separate, hierarchically distinguished faculties, rhetoric accepted and appealed to man as it encountered him in the individual moments of his existence. Man was no longer merely a rational animal but an infinitely complex being, a dynamic and unpredictable bundle of psychic energies, simultaneously sensual, passionate, intellectual, and spiritual; like the rhetoric he used, a mysterious unity. If his nature could be defined at all, he was a social and verbal animal who needed to share with others the whole range of his experience. As Leon Battista Alberti's Uncle Lionardo remarked, "Nature, the best of builders, not only made man to live exposed in the midst of others, but also seems to have imposed on him a certain necessity to communicate and reveal to his fellows by speech and other means all his passions and feelings."

But this position not only subverted the old hierarchy of the human personality; it also eroded the gradations of status in society corresponding to it. The broader function of speech meant that communication should not primarily serve the intellectual needs of the few but the general needs of many. The first requirement of speech was that it be commonly understood. Petrarch, himself no lover of crowds, pointed to this perception early in the history of the movement. "The strongest argument for genius and learning is clarity," he declared. "What a man understands clearly he can clearly express, and thus he can pour over into the mind of a hearer what he has in the innermost chamber of his mind." Castiglione's Count Lodovico was only repeating an old humanist cliché when he urged the Courtier to employ "words which are still used by the common people." Language was the common property of men.

The tendency in rhetoric to break down the old barriers and divisions previously seen as inherent in the nature of man, society, and the cosmos itself, points to a further aspect of its deeper significance. Rhetoric was uniquely suited to reflect a world whose order was tending to escape objective comprehension. Its malleability, its adaptability to the nuances of experience, allowed it to mold itself flexibly around the infinitely varied and constantly shifting particularities of life, and at the same time it encouraged the conviction that reality could not be grasped by the fixed and general categories of rational and systematic thought. Rhetoric was agnostic in regard to general propositions; from its standpoint man could not hope to penetrate to the ultimate order of things but only make particular sense of his immediate experience. But the result was that rhetorical expression could be supremely creative, as language could not be if it aimed only to reflect an absolute and static reality. Language itself was a human creation, a point on which Valla rebuked the schoolmen, who, as though forgetting Genesis 2:19, seemed to believe that God Himself had invented words.

The apparently neutral rhetorical doctrine of decorum concealed another set of striking implications. Decorum meant simply that effective communication required the adaptation of a speaker's discourse to his subject and above all to his audience: to its special characteristics, its immediate circumstances of time and place, its mood, and the purpose of the speaker. It too suggests that language seeks man out as he is from moment to moment and addresses him not as the representative of a species, in the timeless language of absolute truth, but as an individual. When Petrarch declared, "I am an individual and would like to be wholly and completely an individual," he was thus expressing one of the deepest impulses underlying Renaissance rhetoric. At the same time, decorum pointed to an attitude of complete flexibility in confronting the infinite variety of life.

Step by step, then, the humanists of earlier Renaissance Italy developed this new vision of man who, with all the resources of his personality, engages fully with the total range of experience. We can trace their progress most vividly in their growing recognition of the role of the passions and the will in the human personality, which advanced into prominence as the intellect receded. . . .

Closely associated with the passions was the will, which translates the impulses of the passions into action. For in this new vision of man the will was no longer merely the servant of reason; it had replaced reason, in Nancy Struever's phrase, as the "executive power" of the personality. The quality of man's existence thus depended now not on the adequacy of his reason but on the strength and freedom of his will. For Salutati the will was a faculty "whose force . . . is so great and its hegemony over the other powers of the soul so large that even though the instruments of the senses receive the images of sensible things, the effect of such reception scarcely proceeds further without the commands of the will." The will represented the active power of the soul.

Thus its primacy pointed, finally, to a revised conception of the existence best suited to man in this life. Since man was no longer an intellectual being, he could no longer hope to fulfill himself through contemplation but only through active engagement with the demands of life, especially in society. Even the ambivalent Petrarch, though frequently lamenting the interruption of his repose, sometimes admitted that a life free from choice and struggle is unsuited to human nature, and his successors were steadily clearer on this issue. Alberti's dying father emphasized the point in his parting message to his sons. "Adversities are the material of which character is built," he declared. "Whose unshakeable spirit, constant mind, energetic intelligence, indefatigable industry and art can show its full merit in favorable and quiet situations?" Uncle Lionardo said this less solemnly: "Young men should not be allowed to remain inactive. Let girls sit and grow lazy."

I do not mean to offer the line of thought I have traced here as a balanced description of earlier Renaissance humanism; Petrarch's equivocations are also significant, and they were never fully overcome by his successors. I have simply tried to offer a brief sketch of the radical novelties implicit in the movement, in the hope that they may help us to assess the quality of the later Renaissance. For, beginning about the middle of the fifteenth century, humanism began subtly to change. The impulses we have just reviewed were still at work and capable of further development, as we are reminded by such figures as Machiavelli, Pomponazzi, and Guicciardini. Yet even in writers in whom we can still discern the earlier attitudes, the novelties of the earlier Renaissance were often being modified.

Once again we may conveniently begin with the problem of rhetoric, towards which attitudes were changing. We still can find, to be sure, enthusiastic celebrations of the power of words. . . .

Yet even among the champions of eloquence one is aware of a growing sense of its limits. This is evident in a tendency, once again, to see eloquence as the mere embellishment of truth. Rhetoric no longer seemed to give access to the solid realities of life, which once more appeared to have some absolute and independent existence; and the relationship between eloquence and knowledge, form and content, once thought an indissoluble marriage, began to look like a passing affair.

This is particularly evident in the attitude of later humanists to the Gospel, which for Valla had been, in the fullest sense, rhetorical communication. Now such a view hardly seemed serious; as ultimate truth, the Gospel could not be dependent on the contingencies of eloquence, and rhetoric could only be of incidental help for its communication. . . .

A natural accompaniment of this separation of the form from the content of verbal expression was a growing emphasis on the value of literary refinement for its own sake, or at most for the esthetic satisfaction it could provide. Thus Castiglione's discussion of language in the *Courtier* suggests more concern with the propriety of language than with its deeper powers of communication. He devotes much attention to this subject, indeed, but the effect is largely to trivialize what had earlier been of profound human importance. There is no concern with virtue or duty in Count Lodovico's vision of the Courtier's literary education. He reviews the old curriculum; the Courtier is to acquaint himself with both the Greek and Latin classics "because of the abundance and variety of things that are so divinely written therein," and he is to pay particular attention to the poets, orators and historians. But the count's explanation lacks the old high seriousness: "besides the personal satisfaction he [the Courtier] will take in this, in this way he will never want for pleasant entertainment with the ladies, who are usually fond of such things." The humanities will, to be sure, also "make him fluent, and . . . bold and self-confident in speaking with everyone." But this contribution to the personal effectiveness of the Courtier seems something of an afterthought; after all, as the count remarks, arms are the chief profession of the Courtier, and all his other accomplishments are only "ornaments thereto." The Courtier is a specialist. Another of Castiglione's interlocutors drives the point deeper. For Federico Fregoso the Courtier "should be one who is never at a loss for things to say that are good and well-suited to those with whom he is speaking, he should know how to sweeten and refresh the minds of his hearers, and move them discreetly to gaiety and laughter with amusing witticisms and pleasantries, so that, without ever producing tedium or satiety, he may continually give pleasure."

One can observe of this ideal that at least it does not discriminate against women. Indeed it seems particularly suited to women; the old curriculum of the rhetoricians here provides a culture for aristocratic ladies, but for men chiefly when they are in the company of ladies. By sixteenth-century standards nothing better illustrates the low estate to which the *studia humanitatis* had fallen. And decorum, which in the earlier Renaissance meant primarily the appropriateness of language to its audience or the intentions of the speaker, tended now to mean appropriateness to the speaker's status in life, and eventually what was appropriate to the upper classes. It was no longer the vehicle of a flexible attitude to existence but simply a virtue of the drawing room. Ficino, to be sure, defined decorum more grandly, but only to elevate it altogether above ordinary human life. "Decorum," he declared, "is God Himself, from whom and through whom all decorous things come to being."

But Ficino's conception was exceptional and perhaps only inadvertently applicable to rhetoric. In general rhetoric tended now to be seen as little more than embellishment and thus relatively frivolous; and so it became in some circles a kind of play, a source of pleasure and a form of self-display, but therefore for serious men an object of suspicion, as a distraction from the naked apprehension of truth. . . .

This divorce between eloquence and wisdom was, of course, nowhere more pronounced than among the Florentine Platonists. Ficino, concerned with truth, was troubled by the rhetorical enterprise. Pico distinguished sharply between truth and eloquence, which he thought likely only to obscure, distort, and taint truth. From their perspective the authentic task of language is simply to describe objective reality, and the fact that the majority of men lack the capacity to understand philosophical discourse suggested not the limitations but the distinction of philosophy. "What if," Pico wrote in defense of philosophers, "we are commonly held to be dull, rude, uncultured? To us this is a glory and no cause for contempt. We have not written for the many. . . . We are not unlike the ancients who by their riddles and by the masks of their fables made the uninitiate shun the mysteries; and we have been wont by fright to drive them from our feasts, which they could not but pollute with their far more repulsive verbal inventions."

One result of this sentiment was a return to abstraction; another, more widespread but perhaps equally remote from daily life, was a new type of communication, both verbally and in the plastic arts, through a variety of cryptic devices: riddles, allegory, hints. This notion of communication was as applicable to reading as to writing; and it meant, among other things, a recovery of medieval ways of studying the classics, the discovery in ancient texts not simply of a noble but human communication from the past but of hidden insights into a perennial and ultimate truth. Landino made the point in his commentary on Horace's *Art of Poetry*: "When [poetry] most appears to be narrating something most humble and ignoble or to be singing a little fable to delight idle ears, at that very time it is writing in a secret way the most excellent things of all, which are drawn forth from the fountain of the gods." Erasmus, for all his evangelical impulses, preferred the allegorical to the literal meaning of the Scriptures.

But the familiar classics, already too widely known, were insufficiently esoteric to satisfy the longing for an exclusive wisdom by which aristocrats of the spirit could raise themselves above the corrupt and vulgar masses. The result was a turn to less accessible writings in Greek, Hebrew, and eventually other Semitic languages, to the Orphic hymns, the Hermetic corpus, the cabala. As Pico observed, the canonical scriptures could only meet the needs of "tailors, cooks, butchers, shepherds, servants, maids," persons whose "dim and owlish eyes could not bear the light." For superior souls some further revelation was required. Nor were such conceptions confined to a fringe of intellectual extremists. The eminently respectable General of the Augustinian Friars, Giles of Viterbo, one of the most influential figures at the Curia, shared Pico's conviction that the Gospel of Christ required cabalistic explication. We may also note in these interests the disappearance of the incipient cultural relativism of the earlier Renaissance.

In this new atmosphere classicism itself became increasingly academic. No longer an inspiration for the active life, it developed into a new and often less serious form of the contemplative life; a humanist was now less likely to be an orator than a philologist or a man of letters. The leading humanists of the later fifteenth century were men like Poliziano, who discovered the esthetic virtues of the Latin silver age; Merula, who edited texts and standardized spelling; and Ermolao Barbaro, who restored the Greek text of Aristotle. We continue to call these men humanists, but it is sometimes hard to see them as more than superficially like Petrarch, Salutati, Bruni, or Valla. They loved the classics, they knew them better than their predecessors, and they wrote better Latin. But earlier humanism, with its high seriousness about the tasks of rhetoric, had rebelled against the detachment of literature from life, the style from the substance of communication. Barbaro, Pico, and sometimes even Poliziano and Erasmus look increasingly like professional intellectuals.

But, as this account of the fate of rhetoric in the later Renaissance has at various points already suggested, these changing attitudes to language and communication were accompanied by, and gave expression to, a deeper set of cultural changes. If rhetoric in the earlier sense of the art of touching men in their hearts and so stimulating them to action was now declining, the reason was that man himself was increasingly perceived, once again, as essentially an intellectual being. Since intellect is a faculty man shares with other men, man was also beginning to lose some of his passionate individuality. And since the object of intellect is the general and rational order of reality itself, the decline of rhetoric signified too the recovery, albeit under somewhat new forms, of the old sense of the cosmos as a unity organized according to fixed patterns, accessible to the mind, which dictate the norms of man's individual and social existence. The attitudes of the earlier Renaissance, it is well to repeat, by no means disappeared. But a major shift in the intellectual climate seems to me unmistakable.

At the center of the change was a decline of the secular principle underlying the culture of the earlier Renaissance: the sense, to cite the typically Renaissance sentiment of a seventeenth-century Englishman, that man lives in divided and distinguished worlds, each of which operates in accordance with principles of its own. The movement of thought was now towards synthesis rather than analysis; men preferred the One to the many, simplicity to complexity. Thus if, in describing the assumptions of earlier Renaissance culture, we must begin with its anthropology, in dealing with those of the later Renaissance we must start with its cosmic vision. We are back in a world of thought in which the imagery of divine activity and human existence is once again cosmological. Colet recalls Dante in his description of "the uniting and all-powerful rays of Christ . . . streaming as it were from the Sun of Truth, which gather and draw together towards themselves and towards unity, those who are in a state of multiplicity." The aged Erasmus hinted at something very like the naturalism repudiated by earlier humanists in his explanation of man's yearning for rest:

> Why is it that even in inanimate things you may see that each and every one is drawn to its own peculiar abode? As soon as a rock dropped from a height hits the earth, it comes to rest. How eagerly a flame is attracted to its own place! What is this which sometimes rocks the earth so hard it dislodges mountains and stones except the north wind struggling to break through to the place where it was born? Thus it is that a bladder full of air, when forcibly pressed down into water, springs back up. Now the human spirit is a flammable thing which, though hindered by this absurd little body of clay, still does not rest until it mounts up to the seat of its beginning. By nature, indeed, all men hunt for repose; they seek something in which the spirit can rest.

This impulse to imbed man once again in the objective order of the cosmos, from which earlier humanism had freed him, explains the popularity now of the notion of man as microcosm, a conception whose prominence in the later Renaissance hardly requires illustration. It is also closely related to the revival of various forms of occultism, both esoteric and popular, which sought, in Pico's words, to "wed earth to heaven." It nourished too the ideal of harmony (though this could be expressed in human as well as absolute terms) and above all the revival of the conception of hierarchy, which was, for Ficino, almost synonymous with order itself. . . . Thus we are once again back in a single holy order of reality whose principles are mandatory in every aspect of existence. It is true, of course, that something of the earlier Renaissance persists in the uses of hierarchy by the Neoplatonists. Ficino's hierarchy is not simply a static structure but a system for the transmission of vital influences; and Pico sought to protect human freedom by allowing man the liberty to ascend or descend "the universal chain of Being" and so freely to shape himself. But what is most significant here, it seems to me, is not the impulses retained from the earlier Renaissance but the overwhelming presence of the hierarchy itself. For Pico man ought clearly to rise rather than to descend on the ladder of being; its existence prescribes the uses of human freedom.

But it is above all in the application of these conceptions to the understanding of man that we can best see the difference from the earlier Renaissance. Once again the human personality was conceived not as a dynamic unity but, reflecting the structure of the cosmos, as a set of distinct and graded faculties, properly ruled by reason, the soul, or the spirit; the terminology varied from thinker to thinker, depending somewhat on whether he wrote under Aristotelian, Stoic, or Platonic influence. . . .

But the sovereignty of the highest part of man meant that the essence of man was once again seen to reside in his intellect, or, as sometimes in Ficino, something above the intellect, but always a high and separate faculty. Thus for Castiglione's Bembo (we may compare him with Petrarch or Valla on the point) knowledge is prior to love, for, "according to the definition of ancient sages, love is nothing but a certain desire to enjoy beauty; and, as our desire is only for things that are known, knowledge must precede desire, which by nature turns to the good but in itself is blind and does not know the good." This intellectual vision of man was also accompanied by a remarkable optimism; it agreed with the classical traditions by which it was nourished that to know the good is to do the good. Thus Erasmus remarked that it is fitting "for all to recognize the motions of the mind, then to know none of them to be so violent but that they can either be restrained by reason or redirected to virtue." This, he continued, "is the sole way to happiness: first, know yourself; second, do not submit anything to the passions, but all things to the judgment of reason." In his colloquy *The Wooer and the Maiden*, the maiden Maria tells her lover, a bit pompously, "What emotions decide is temporary; rational choices generally please forever"; and her young man rather surprisingly agrees in what might be taken also, however, as a bit of Erasmian irony: "Indeed you philosophize very well, so I'm resolved to take your advice." Obviously the will remains an important element in this conception; every exhortation to choose the way of reason implies both its existence and its power. But the will is no longer at the center of the human personality; it has been reduced to servitude: if virtuous, to reason; if vicious, to the passions. Much of the educational thought of the later Renaissance rests on this conception.

Inevitably now the passions, identified with either the body or the lowest part of the soul, once again presented themselves rather as a problem than as a resource for good as well as evil. Even Erasmus, although a bit ambivalent, did not give them much praise. Indeed he applauded his own poems for their *lack* of passion: "There is not a single storm in them," he wrote, "no mountain torrent overflowing its banks, no exaggeration whatever." He preferred the poetry that seemed most like prose and disliked the choruses in Greek drama because of their violent emotionality. . . .

Nor is there much question, for the later Renaissance, of the vileness of the body, which was once again, as with Ficino, an "earthly prison" and the "dark dwelling" of the soul. Ficino excluded the body from his definition of man. "Man," he asserted, "is the soul itself. . . . Everything that a man is said to do, his soul does itself; the body merely suffers it to be done; wherefore man is soul alone, and the body of man must be its instrument." Erasmus could make the point lightly, as when his lovers agree that the soul is a willing prisoner of the body, "like a little bird in a cage." But at times he was in deadly earnest. "If there is any evil in the mind," he wrote in his *Education of a Christian Prince*, "it springs from infection and contact with the body, which is subject to the passions. Any good that the body possesses is drawn from the mind as from a fountain. How unbelievable it would be and *how contrary to nature*, if ills should spread from the mind down into the body, and the health of the body be corrupted by the vicious habits of the mind." Again we are reminded of the dependence of human existence on the larger order of nature. Vives was more vio-lent: "Our souls carry the heavy burden of bodies with great misery and pain; because of bodies, souls are confined to the narrow limits of this earth, where all filth and smut seem to converge." In this insistence on the separation and even antagonism between the higher and lower parts of man, between the rational soul or the spirit and the body and its passions, we can discern a significant counterpart to the distinc-tion between the substance and form of verbal discourse, or between its rational con-tent and its rhetorical embellishment, the soul and body of thought. . . .

This new tendency in the idea of man also helps to explain the revival of the contemplative ideal and the recovery of interest in philosophy. Pico was typical. "I have always been so desirous, so enamored of [philosophy]," he wrote, "that I have relinquished all interest in affairs private and public, and given myself over entirely to leisure for contemplation." Giles of Viterbo oddly thought of Jesus as a man who avoided cities, market places, and the company of men; "the happy man," he wrote a friend, "is he who, conscious of how short life is, lives for himself, apart from the tumult of human affairs." Even Castiglione's Ottaviano, confronted with the stock problem whether the active or contemplative life is to be preferred by a prince, could only offer the unlikely suggestion that "princes ought to lead both kinds of life, but more especially the contemplative," which ought to be "the goal of the active as peace is of war and as repose is of toil." The persistent longing of Erasmus for peace devoted to study is not only a personal taste but the ideal of a generation, and the peace movement among the intellectuals of his time was no more simply a response to the political situation than was Dante's *De monarchia*. . . .

Again, I must emphasize, there was here no absolute change, no total repudia-tion of the ideals of the earlier Renaissance. Yet it seems clear that a profound shift was under way, which calls for some explanation. Part of the explanation is probably to be found in a kind of dynamic within humanism itself. When men first sought to enlarge their powers of verbal expression by imitating the classics, they discov-ered not only the principles of classical expression but also new and undreamt-of potentialities within themselves. But as classical philology was more and more fully explored and objectively mastered, it could be submitted to general rules; and classi-cism became no longer liberating but confining. The feeling for propriety in the use of language was also nourished by the printing press, another major development of this period, which standardized every aspect of verbal expression and, as printed books poured off the presses by the millions, imposed its norms on a growing literate public. Yet, even if we do not look beyond humanism itself, I think we can see a deeper impulse at work, pushing the movement in the same direction. For implicit in the culture of the rhetoricians, with its rejection of an objective cosmic order by which man could take his bearings, was not only liberation but also the danger of total anarchy and disorientation. From the beginning the more sensitive among the humanists had been aware of this problem and had tried to solve it by calling for the union of eloquence with wisdom. But there was no necessary reason, in the absence of an objective order accessible to philosophy, or of spiritual guidance supplied by faith, for such an alliance; and in fact the earlier humanists were themselves not only exuberant about the newly discovered freedom and creativity of the individual but also increasingly anxious about the uses men were likely to make of these gifts. Petrarch allowed Augustine to reproach Franciscus for glorying in his eloquence; Salutati was troubled by the fact that many orators were not good men; Poggio was increasingly depressed that rhetoric seemed rather a tool for the abuse than for the strengthening of human community. Thus, in spite of its attacks on philosophy, even early humanism recognized the need for something more than the power of rhetoric. From this standpoint the later Renaissance seems to have been seeking to supply a defect in the culture of the earlier Renaissance. At the same time we must ask whether this defect was not in fact a necessary element in its identity.

Yet I think that we must finally look beyond humanism itself to developments in the larger social and political world. We may point immediately to the deterioration of conditions in Italy. Centuries of internal conflict within the towns of Italy had produced, by the middle decades of the fifteenth century, a climate of intolerable insecurity; and this was aggravated by the long period of large-scale warfare and destruction initiated by the French invasion of 1494, which effectively destroyed the freedom of the Italian states. Order, not freedom, was the most urgent need of this new age; society became more rigidly stratified and governments more authoritarian; all change appeared increasingly terrifying. And in the same period too the papacy, at last fully recovered from the conciliar ordeal, was reasserting the authority of the medieval vision of reality. The general proposition that all things are part of a single holy order of reality at once objective, intelligible, hierarchically organized, and ruled from above was, under these conditions, not entirely anachronistic. It provided relief from the immediate and pressing dangers of the times. Its conception of government also bolstered the authority of princes, with whom the papacy was now prepared to come to terms by concordats. In Italy, with the exception of Venice, princes were everywhere in the ascendancy; and, whatever their particular differences with the pope, princes found the new hierarchical vision of order congenial. Under these conditions rhetoric lost much of its public utility; social solidarity and social order were no longer created from below, by persuasion, but imposed from above, by force; and intellectuals, their own social roles reduced, were increasingly contemptuous of the masses, who corresponded socially to the doubtful passions of the body politic. By the same token the art of speaking well became a badge of social distinction, the peculiar property of a social and political aristocracy gathered in princely courts. And the image of man, which at least since Plato had been closely correlated with the image of society, once again reflected the perception of the general order of things.

This account of the changing assumptions of later Renaissance culture is obviously not a sufficient or balanced description of the later Renaissance. Just as, along with its novelties, the culture of the earlier Renaissance preserved some residues of medieval culture, itself not entirely homogeneous, much from the earlier

Renaissance survived in the later fifteenth and sixteenth centuries, often in uneasy tension with the tendencies I have described. And it is at this point in the argument that we must take cognizance of the relationship between the Italian Renaissance and cultural developments in other areas. The fact that Germans, Frenchmen, Spaniards, and Englishmen were nourished by Italian movements of thought largely in the period of this retreat from earlier novelties is worth some reflection. Thus it may be that the regressive tendencies in later Renaissance culture made Italian modes of thought more congenial than they would otherwise have been to Europeans elsewhere, who might have been put off by the less veiled novelties of earlier humanism. The modification of earlier Renaissance culture, as it was transposed from the urban republics of its birth into the milieu of the princely courts, doubtless also assisted its adaptation to the aristocratic circles of the northern monarchies, though these changes had a more ambiguous meaning for the free cities of the Empire, now under growing pressure from territorial princes.

But, as I have from time to time emphasized, the more vital impulses of the earlier Renaissance had not altogether disappeared from the culture of the later Renaissance even in Italy, however much they had been compromised; and these too were known beyond the Alps, where they nourished, if they did not precisely cause, the novelties in what, for all the ambiguities in the term, is conventionally described as the "Northern Renaissance." Northern Europeans, however equivocal their feelings about Italy, regularly admired her Renaissance achievement as a break with the medieval past; and the deepest assumptions of earlier humanist culture found theological expression in the Protestant Reformation. Thus if the earlier Renaissance was an Italian affair, and the attitudes of the later Renaissance found expression, as the examples cited here reveal, in both Italy and the North, the later Renaissance seems to have had a very different significance outside of Italy, where it presents itself rather as the beginning of a new phase in cultural history than as the decline of a movement already well established. In the North, therefore, and perhaps most conspicuously in England, we can discern with increasing clarity much the same sense of the potentialities of human freedom, the same restless and creative exploration of the possibilities of individual existence as in earlier Renaissance Italy. And this too requires explanation.

The major cause for the continuation of the vital impulses of the Renaissance in Northern Europe after the first decades of the sixteenth century is to be found, I think, in its political pluralism. This, together with geographical and spiritual distance from Rome, the symbol and champion of universalism, posed an insuperable obstacle to the full recovery of any conception of a single, holy, and cosmic order. On this point the distinction between Catholicism and Protestantism is largely irrelevant. France and Spain, the piety of Philip II notwithstanding, resisted papal influence as successfully as England or the Elector of Saxony; all together represented the secular principle of divided and distinguished realms that made any conception of a unified hierarchy embedded in an objective structure of reality ultimately implausible. And political particularity provided a foundation for the development of national cultures which, because of their secularity, also gave room for the same kind of personal individuality that had characterized the earlier Renaissance in Italy. Nowhere is this development more apparent than in the emergence of the great vernacular literatures, in which Northern Europeans discovered for themselves the creative and liberating power of language, much as the rhetoricians of Italy had begun to do two centuries before.

Clerics and Laymen in Italian Literature

CARLO DIONISOTTI

The debate about the relationship between church and state has been rekindled in postwar Italy. If by "state" we mean lay society, . . . I think that it is possible and necessary to discuss church and state with reference to our writers: not only their contributions, in emotions and ideas, to the history of the debate but also, and above all, for their positions on both sides, ecclesiastical and lay, and for the parts played by both sides in the development of Italian culture. . . .

I will examine three generations of writers from the first half of the sixteenth century, although each had its own characteristics: the generation that greeted the dawn of the sixteenth century as adults, with a fifteenth-century education, and participated fully in the momentous events of the first three decades; the generation born around the turn of the sixteenth century, who grew up during the difficult years but reached their prime after the crisis; and finally the generation that was not directly affected by the years of crisis and reached literary adulthood during the great, expansive period of Italian literature, from 1540 to 1550.

It is doubtless arbitrary to confuse more than one generation in a single picture, . . . but, on the other hand, there was a rare continuity and agreement in literary work in the first half of the sixteenth century, creating the possibility that old, young, and very young could proceed together. This naturally implies and confirms diversity among them, . . . but the young were more precocious and able than the old, in a process that accelerated progressively. The final, crowning example of this, just after 1550, was the youth of Tasso.

In my view, about one hundred writers from these fifty years can represent with sufficient accuracy the conditions of that era. . . . To these men, therefore, who found themselves living and writing during the first half of the sixteenth century, we can ask, among other questions, the following: Were they clerics or laymen, and of what sort? If they were clerics, did they belong to the secular or regular clergy? Were they cardinals, bishops, or merely endowed with benefices without any pastoral duties? We should also ask if they had family of their own, because clerics occasionally succumbed to "human fragility" and produced children, legitimated them, and lived

From Carlo Dionisotti, "Clerics and Laymen in Italian Literature of the Early Sixteenth Century," from "Chierici e laici nella letteratura italiana del primo Cinquecento," in *Problemi di vita religiosa in Italia nel Cinquecento* (Padua, 1960), pp. 167–185, reprinted in Dionisotti, *Geografia e storia della letteratura italiana* (Turin: Einaudi, 1967), pp. 47–73 passim. Translated by Alison A. Smith.

very similarly to laymen. Among these, however, we do not lack evidence of a strong repugnance for conjugal life as an impediment to the free exercise of genius. For efficiency's sake, we will simply inquire into the public situations, known by their contemporaries, of the men of letters of the early sixteenth century. Out of about one hundred writers, one-half were laymen who lived on family wealth or their own labor without any economic dependence on the church. Of the other half, about twenty were cardinals or bishops, a dozen belonged to religious orders (some of which . . . are already included in the preceding category of cardinals and bishops), and about twenty lived off ecclesiastical benefices, performing whatever duties and obligations they required.

One dozen writers belonging to religious orders is not many, and it is noteworthy that most of them either fled from or refused to adhere to the discipline of the orders they originally belonged to. . . . This suggests a crisis in discipline and morale, as well as a greater openness within the religious orders to nonsacred literature. Among this small group of writers belonging to religious orders, two subgroups can be identified: those who rebelled against monastic discipline and those who were promoted to bishoprics on the basis of their literary merits rather than on the recommendation of their original order. This analysis reveals the singular fact that out of one hundred writers, twenty were cardinals and bishops. It is a high proportion, and the literary quality of the group is high. The bishops include [Bandello], Castiglione, Colucci, Della Casa, [Zaccaria Ferreri], Giovio, Guidiccioni, Minturno, Musuro, Palladio, Piccolomini and Tolomei, and [Vida]. . . . Where did these writer bishops and cardinals come from? Certainly not from the clergy with pastoral duties. Most came from the many clerics who, not being priests, held ecclesiastical benefices, and lived as laymen, even if they were not lay. One conspicuous example of this was Ludovico Ariosto, who, in his *Satires*, was a faithful witness to the ambiguous position between the lay and ecclesiastical state in which our writers from this period found themselves, and of the economic and moral problems that the situation created.

The case of Ariosto is that of a man of minor nobility. This was the class that during the preceding century had found its natural function in the service of the greater and lesser Italian principalities. An example is Ariosto's own father. When the son found himself having to assume responsibility for his family, times had already changed. Castiglione laughed, as if at a half-wit, at his associate who bravely continued to identify himself as a councillor to the duchy of Milan, when a duke of Milan no longer existed. Many large and small principalities, beginning with the two largest, Naples and Milan, had disappeared or were about to. Those surviving were put on the defensive and weakened by the crisis. In such conditions, dependent relationships became fewer in number, riskier, and more servile. On the other hand, it was a culture ever more aware of its wealth and its worth, increasingly reluctant to adventure, improvise, take risks. The crisis that enveloped all of Italy between the fifteenth and sixteenth centuries, and which Italian culture experienced as a national crisis, embittered and worsened provincial and municipal enmities and revealed the weakness of the system. The culture escaped from narrow provincial and municipal isolation, which was both insecure and humiliating, and sought shelter, foundation, and inspiration at the center. Even the two great Florentine laymen, Machiavelli and Guicciardini, found the spark of their masterpieces when political experience in their city became, because of the Medicean papacy, central to Italian political experience of the national crisis. From this point on, Machiavelli, in his enforced leisure, leaped beyond the actual events to the utopia of the prince, from the repeated attempt of a lay principality to graft itself onto the trunk of papal politics. His relationship with Florence remained close and indissoluble, because that was his language and his life; but he never repaired the break of 1512, and therefore Florence recedes into the background in his *Storie*, leaving the present and the future to utopia, and the unchanging laws of politics.

[For Guicciardini] there remained a fundamental repugnance toward the ecclesiastical state, shared by his father, his family, and his environment. In fact, that repugnance had deep roots in Florence. The two great laymen, Machiavelli and Guicciardini, lead and represent a group. Out of about fifty laymen, one-quarter are Florentine and one-third Tuscan. (If we were one century earlier, in the first half of the fifteenth century, when Florentine and Tuscan literature were dominant, this would not be unusual.) But in the first half of the sixteenth century, the percentage is high and shows that Florentine lay society was more open, wealthier, and, notwithstanding the political upheaval before Cosimo's regime, more confident and stable.

Wealth, confidence, and stability thrived in Venice, but here immediately one notices the rigidity of a closed society, the difficulty of a normal relationship between this society and the new literature of the first half of the sixteenth century. In this literature, the lay Venetian patriciate is barely represented. . . . Although foreigners living in Venice enjoyed an intellectual marketplace that was the freest and most productive anywhere in Italy (as the history of publishing shows), those who were directly involved in government felt control and pressure from above that imposed insuperable limits on their creativity. . . .

One cannot survey Venetian literature in this period without discussing Pietro Bembo. Behind him, in the person of his father, is the fifteenth-century tradition of high culture together with high political responsibility—lay culture and responsibility, that is; in Venice, the clergy did not interfere with the politics of the state. Also behind Bembo there had been a decisive break with that tradition in the work of the man who best represented it—Ermolao Barbaro—who in spite of the Venetian government exchanged the clothes of an ambassador for those of the patriarch of Aquileia and therefore died in exile and disgrace. This break was repeated with Bembo, as it would be in the future with Contarini. These breaks with the past were made by mature men, not hot-headed youths. In 1500, Bembo was still planning an ambassadorial career, to be a lay magistrate of the Venetian republic. Shortly after, however, he abandoned Venice, seeking his fortune in the courts of Ferrara and Urbino. A Venetian patrician could naturally be a guest at a court, but it was unthinkable that he should become a courtier. Bembo was pursuing ecclesiastical honors in the princely courts; the road he took in the middle of his life brought him to the cardinalate at the age of seventy. The greatness and authority of this man made him at once unique and influential. It is enough to consider the group to which Bembo belonged as a young man. They were five young Venetians, of equal nobility and nearly the same age, as close friends as they could be at that age, and remarkable for their talent and dedication to study: Bembo himself, Trifon Gabriele, Tommaso

Giustinian, Vincenzo Querini, Niccolò Tiepolo. Of the five, only one, the least tal-
ented, had a family and pursued the lay career available to him in Venice. Trifon
Gabriele lived an austere, secluded life supported by ecclesiastical benefices.
Tommaso Giustinian became Brother Paul, a Camaldolese hermit, and persuaded
Querini, who had begun a brilliant career as an ambassador, to join him. Brother
Pietro Querini's early death in 1514 prevented him from being appointed cardinal.
We are not facing here a set of statistics about individual lives but rather a crisis of
an entire generation in a particular environment. Without doubt, this was an envi-
ronment that was as narrow and closed as it was socially elevated.

In the fifteenth century, society honored many humanists who did not have
noble titles and created honorable offices for needy laymen not only in the chancel-
ries but also, and especially, in the schools. The figure of the humanist, in the technical sense of the word, of the master of Latin and Greek letters, is a central figure in
the picture of fifteenth-century literature, and it is nearly always a layman. There are
certainly exceptions and Poliziano is a significant example. But they were exceptions, and in the latter half of the fifteenth century there developed a lay scholarly
tradition that stayed alive into the sixteenth century. . . . In minor as well as major
centers, the lay humanist, demoted to pedant, receded into the humble shadow of
the school as an end unto itself, which neither offered nor supported a literary career.
The only ones who were saved were the few great technicians of philology, who
extended the prestige of Italian pedagogy into the second half of the sixteenth century in the great university schools. After the crisis of the early sixteenth century,
there was a reform of the grammar schools under the direction of the new religious
orders. . . .

The brief investigations we have made until now are sufficient to call attention
to a characteristic aspect of the crisis that Italian culture went through during the
first half of the sixteenth century. To conclude, I wish to say something about two
works that can be viewed as two very different literary interpretations of the aristocratic society of the age—that is, the aristocracy of birth and of talent: The De Cardinalatu of Paolo Cortese and The Courtier of Baldesar Castiglione. As the titles indicate, one deals with an ecclesiastical aristocracy, the other with a lay aristocracy, and
only a few years separate their publication. The De Cardinalatu was published in
1510, posthumously, but apparently the author was feverishly completing it up to the
last days of his life. The Courtier was published in 1528, after a long wait, but it was
essentially finished by 1518 and was inspired by and supported by a situation that
predated 1510. The two works meet, therefore, in one point, conclusive for one,
initial for the other. Moreover, they enjoyed two very different fortunes. The Courtier
became a classic, known to all, and the De Cardinalatu, never reprinted and known
only to a few scholars, has until now been mined for anecdotes and scholarly details
rather than read as a work with its own message. Thus the fame of the author is based
on his earlier works. . . . We know that he was working on a draft of a treatise "on the
prince" in 1504, which was intended to instruct a prince, following him through his
entire life, from his childhood to old age, in those disciplines that were most useful
for each age. Probably after 1504, following a suggestion of the cardinal Ascanio
Sforza but certainly also because of a change in the direction of his thought, Cortese
radically changed his work: The prince was replaced by the cardinal, and he replaced
the instruction through time with a more spatial illustration of what the life of a

cardinal could and should be, in its various aspects both sacred and profane. Of the three books into which the *De Cardinalatu* is divided, the first, "ethics and contemplation," discusses the cardinal's solitary intellectual life and deals with moral virtues, science, rhetoric, philosophy, and canon law. The second book, "economics," represents the cardinal in his private life and deals with sources of income, the household, family, friendships, diet, physical health, passions to avoid, the audiences that the cardinal must give to people of all ages, conditions and nationalities, the language that he must use and all of the proprieties and adornments of this language, such as the use of anecdotes, proverbs, and metaphors in discussion, and finally almsgiving and other financial transactions. The third book is political, and represents the cardinal in the exercise of official functions: in the consistory, in the conclave, in the various congregations and offices, in the face of both routine and extraordinary affairs of the church: simony, heresy, and schism.

Before Cortese, the cardinalate already had a juridical literature and after him would follow antiquarian discussions of the origins of the institution. Cortese's work, however, as one can see, was completely different. . . . The cardinal was for Cortese what the courtier was for Castiglione: an ideal figure of a man standing in the center of the picture of real, modern life, at the center of society and of the curia in the early sixteenth century. Why, one must ask oneself, did this early sixteenth-century life, investigated and described by Cortese in all its variety, profane as well as sacred, acquire the title *De Cardinalatu?* Why was the cardinal made the center and protagonist of this life? The point of departure for the work "on princes" that Cortese first intended to write was clear: It mirrored the historical moment in the Italian principate that the adventure of Cesare Borgia in a sense concluded. So did the decision not to write "on princes." In 1504 Cesare Borgia, who had become prince from his position as cardinal, had already been overtaken by events, and the cardinal Ascanio Sforza, survivor of his ruined house, could well suggest that Cortese change course. The pontificate of Julius II had already begun, and the church was becoming that which, for better or worse, it would remain for the first half of the sixteenth century: the center of Italian politics. It was necessarily a politics of warfare, about which Italian humanists felt a natural reserve. It is significant, however, that Cortese, while dedicating the work to Julius II, did not attempt to discuss the pope himself: The cardinal presumes that there is a pope, but he is not himself the pope. Just as significant was Castiglione's choice of the courtier, who also presumes that there is a prince but is not the prince. In both works, the protagonist is chosen, prudently, to represent the high aristocracy but not the highest point of society, law or ecclesiastical. There remained the fundamental difference between the two societies, and one thinks of the position of women in Castiglione's work and in the literature of the age. In 1510 the work of Cortese certainly could not be considered a sufficiently broad and faithful mirror of reality. The language itself, erudite Latin, linked the work to a previous age, whereas the vernacular Italian of Castiglione joined the new current of Italian literature. But the comparison of the two works does not end there.

We have already seen that Castiglione's work was published in 1528 even though its historical setting was 1507. In the interval, a little more than twenty years, Castiglione reviewed the work in two famous passages in the book: the dedicatory letter to Michel de Silva and the prologue to the fourth book, which should be read in inverse order. In the prologue, Castiglione defines the change between 1507

and 1516: the wonderful group in Urbino is dispersed, and some of the minor characters in the dialogue—Gaspare Pallavicino, Cesare Gonzaga, and Roberto da
Bari—have died young. But the pain of the dispersion and of premature death is
tempered by the successes of the survivors: Federico Fregoso has become archbishop
of Salerno, his brother Ottaviano is doge of Genoa, Ludovico Canossa is bishop of
Bayeux, Bibbiena is a cardinal, Bembo is secretary to Pope Leo X, and Giuliano de'
Medici is the duke of Nemours. All of these successes are directly or indirectly connected to the politics of the church in those years, from Julius II to Leo X, and in
those same years Castiglione and all the surviving characters in the dialogue have
left Urbino, most having relocated to Rome.

Moving on to the dedicatory letter, ten more years have passed, and Castiglione
lengthens the list of characters who have died: Alfonso Ariosto, Giuliano de' Medici, Bibbiena, Ottaviano Fregoso, the Duchess Elizabeth. Of the survivors he says
nothing. Let us try, then, to draw up a balance sheet of that which Castiglione said
and that which he decided not to say, and then that which his death prevented him
from saying. Among those characters of *The Courtier* who appear in the work to be
laymen, or at least without any ecclesiastical inclination, when we see them again in
1516, there are a cardinal (Bibbiena), two bishops (Fregoso and Canossa), and a
papal secretary (Bembo). . . . Also in 1516, both Bembo and Canossa were trying
with all their might to conquer the red hat (of the cardinal). It was an unfulfilled
ambition during the papacy of Leo X and Clement VII, and for Canossa, after the
Sack of Rome and the failure of his policies, a complete disappointment. At this
point, which coincides more or less with the publication of *The Courtier*, one should
verify the position of Castiglione himself. He too moved from Urbino to Rome in
1513 and remained there for most of the time, first as ambassador for the duke of
Urbino and then for the marquis of Mantua. He was in Rome in 1520 when his wife
of four years died in childbirth. By 1521, Castiglione too had become an ecclesiastic,
and in 1524 he joined the court in Rome, as papal nuncio to Spain in the service of
Clement VII. When not much older than fifty, he died in 1529, Castiglione, the
maker of *The Courtier* and one of the finest knights in the world, died not as a courtier and knight following his dukes but as a papal nuncio, with the bishop's cross on
his chest, certainly a candidate for the cardinalate. . . . And his *Courtier* had just
been published, with a dedication to Michel de Silva, bishop of Viseo, a Portuguese
in the Roman curia who had been conquered by humanistic culture and the elegant,
intellectual life of Italy. In other words, to look at *The Courtier* of Castiglione in the
process of its composition, a great deal seems to follow the *De Cardinalatu* of Cortese.
Just as, in historical reality, behind the fragile splendor of the Urbino court of
Guidobaldo was felt the power of Julius II's papacy, so behind the book that glorified
an ideal society of lay gentlemen there seems to be the darkening shadow of another
society, that of men dressed in the purple clothes of the curia. Still, until the death
of Castiglione, it remained nothing more than a shadow. This was because, even
though there was a visible tendency among the humanist aristocracy in the early
sixteenth century to aim for ecclesiastical benefices, bishoprics, and, if ambitious and
hopeful enough, the cardinalate, there was not yet a corresponding inclination by
the church to appoint humanists to the highest ecclesiastical positions. . . . Italian
humanists could not throw themselves into the politics of warfare being conducted
by the church, nor could the church, so employed, permit itself the luxury of ap-

pointing to its highest offices peaceful and decorative men unable to provide financial and political support.

After the failure of the church's politics in 1527 and the full declaration of the Protestant Reformation, the relationship between literature and the church changed. In 1534 Alessandro Farnese became Pope Paul III, succeeding Clement VII. Among the cardinals whom Paolo Cortese had known and befriended, no one was closer to him than the young Alessandro Farnese. And it is known what the College of Cardinals became under Paul III; the ideal that Paolo Cortese described in his book came close to becoming a reality. The survivors of Castiglione's *Courtier* entered the college one by one. Bembo joined in 1539, reappearing with Sadoleto, his colleague in the secretariat of Leo X: Jacopo Sadoleto and Pietro Bembo, echoing the lines of Ariosto who painted them together in the canvas of the *Furioso*, who before, in completely different clothes, knelt before the "sacred hem" of the Duchess Elizabeth of Urbino. Federico Fregoso joined in 1540, and in 1541, so did the bishop of Viseo, to whom the work was dedicated. One cannot help but think that, had they lived, both Castiglione and Paolo Cortese would have found themselves in that college, and there they would have entered into a dialogue very different from that of *The Courtier*. Their dialogue would also have been very different from the difficult and ambitious prose of the *De Cardinalatu*, nourished, however, by the diverse experience of both the works: the experience of a culture that during the crisis of the Italian states found refuge in the church and that in the crisis of the church carried the not-unimportant skills of persuasion and dialogue, of classical moderation and the continuity of thought and words through time.

Paul III died in 1549. Under his successors in the second half of the sixteenth century, the situation of Italian culture and relations between church and state changed yet again. One cannot talk of decadence in relation to the age of Tasso and then Galileo, an age of powerful Italian language and literature still predominant in Europe. In this period, as is well known, the distinction between ecclesiastics and laymen became clearer, and the control of the church much more stringent in discipline and dogma over everything that was written. But there did not occur a phenomenon of clericalization analogous to that of the earlier sixteenth century. On the contrary, laymen became the majority in the age of Tasso and Galileo. Without doubt the gentleman of this age was the heir of the "courtier," but with the support of a society more rigidly organized, inspired by a new mythology of the sovereign and the state, of politics and honor, finding in one's class and rank a sufficient identity.

To conclude, we should abandon the illusion that in the history of Italian literature, the lay tradition has deep, uninterrupted roots. Above all, one must accept the fact that this history was for many centuries inseparable from the active and responsible presence of the church.

DOCUMENTS

In the first document, Lodovico Almanni addresses the problem of how the Medici should gain effective control over Florence, having returned and overthrown the republican regime in 1512. Written in 1516, the treatise was probably directed to the pope (who at the time was Giovanni de' Medici), because Alamanni hoped for a position in the papal administration. He recommends that the current Lorenzo de' Medici (the grandson of Lorenzo the Magnificent) develop friends among the Florentines rather than suppress the rebellious factions using force. He argues that the citizens will prefer an orderly, strong, princely regime to a republic and that Lorenzo can no longer live as a private citizen as his grandfather did. Finally, he recommends that Lorenzo cultivate younger noblemen not yet accustomed to republican ways and train them to accept the ways of a princely court.

Giovanni Della Casa, remembered chiefly for his lyric poetry and the *Galateo*, a treatise on good manners, pursued an important career in the service of the papacy in the mid-sixteenth century. The opportunities and difficulties he encountered during his career reflect the new circumstances facing an ambitious, aristocratic young man in the 1520s. Born in 1503 to a minor but wealthy Florentine patrician family, he received a thorough humanistic education and some training in law and then further distinguished himself by learning Greek. He moved to Rome, joining a group of vigorous, irreverent young writers, and eventually became part of the administration of Pope Paul III in 1537. Della Casa's political advancement was closely related to his literary activity. His youthful friendships contributed to his literary development, introduced him to the skills and sociability necessary for effective diplomatic action, and provided a network of influential friends who served him well throughout his career. The death of Paul III shattered his hopes for the long-awaited appointment to the cardinalate, and he died in 1556, at the age of fifty-three. He wrote the *Galateo*, excerpted here, late in life, in order to instruct young gentlemen in the useful arts of living in a courtly entourage. Drawing on his personal experience, he devotes much of the treatise to the problem of conversation and friendship in the hierarchical world of a princely court, where honesty could easily be compromised by flattery. He makes practical recommendations for a world that could no longer conceive of political behavior within the framework of a republican ideal.

The last document is from one of many books on the pleasures of villa life that began to appear in northern Italy in the mid-sixteenth century. Agostino Gallo wrote a dialogue in which a villa owner (Avogadro) describes the days he spends at his villa to an aristocratic visitor (Ducco). A prominent theme in all of these books was the purity and tranquility of the countryside in contrast to the corruption, squalor, and filth of city life. Avogadro, in his description of urban stress, reveals a great deal about upper-class life in Renaissance cities.

Lodovico Alamanni on Establishing Princely Control in Florence, 1516

People will attribute the success of the older Lorenzo de' Medici [Lorenzo the Magnificent, the grandfather of the current ruler of Florence] to the fact that he adopted civilian dress and familiar manners, conducted affairs of state in his home, came to the city square every day to listen to anyone who wished to speak to him,

From Lodovico Alamanni, "Discourse on Florentines Accepting Medici Rule," ed. R. von Albertini, *Firenze dalla Repubblica al principato* (Turin: Einaudi, 1970), pp. 382–383, passim. Translated by Alison A. Smith.

was informal with the citizens, and behaved with them as though he were their brother rather than their superior, and for these reasons, the more they loved him, the more they were content, and the more they were loyal. Now it is no longer possible for His Excellency the Duke [Lorenzo] to do any of these things, because being in such a grand position, it would be improper for him to act like a private citizen, and thus it is foolish to think of going to meet him at home and expect that he open the door. This grand way of doing things is very useful to him, but it is completely unfamiliar to Florentines, and the citizens would never become accustomed to this willingly. . . . There is, however, an excellent solution to this and other problems.

The inability of the Duke to act like a private citizen is not in itself displeasing to the citizens, because it is useful to them: the larger the court he holds, the more he will let them go about their business. But they are accustomed to acting foolishly rather than loving real liberty, and in Florence they refuse to bow in reverence to anyone, even if someone merits it, except to their own magistrates, and to these they do so only reluctantly. And for this reason Florentines are completely unfamiliar with the ways of the courts, more so, I think, than nearly anyone else. Nonetheless, when they are away from Florence, they do not act so proudly. I think this derives from the principle that it seems completely inappropriate for them to remove their hat for someone; and this act of deference might become a habit, and from there, an instinct. But I believe, when they are away from their homeland and this way of doing things, they don't have much trouble talking to princes. This idea will never be removed from the minds of the elders, but they are the wise ones, which one need not fear, because they never take significant action. And young men can easily become unaccustomed from these habits and learn the customs of the courtier, if the prince wishes. To do this, the prince must appoint all the young men of our city, who are esteemed for their own qualities or for those of their father and their family, and to send first for one, then for another, and to ask them to come be with you, giving to each the job and support that is appropriate. No one would refuse, and as soon as they entered the prince's service he would have to get rid of the civil habits and reduce them to courtiers like all the others.

Galateo, A Treatise on Good Manners, 1551

GIOVANNI DELLA CASA

[1]

In as much as you are now just starting that journey that is this earthly life which I, as you can see, have for the most part completed, and because I love you as much as I do, I have taken it upon myself to show you (as someone who has had

---

Galateo, by Giovanni Della Casa, trans. by Konrad Eisenbichler and Kenneth R. Bartlett (Ottawa: Dovehouse Editions, 1990), pp. 3–7, 9–12, 15–17, 20–24, 53, 55–56. Reprinted by permission of the publisher.

experience) those places in which I fear you may easily either fail or fall, as you proceed through them, so that, if you follow my advice, you may stay on the right path towards the salvation of your soul as well as for the praise and honour of your distinguished and noble family. And since your tender age would not be capable of grasping more important or subtle teachings, I will save them for a more suitable time and start with what many others might perhaps consider frivolous, that is, how I believe one ought to behave when speaking or dealing with other people so as to be polite, pleasant, and well-mannered. If this is not a virtue, it is at least something very similar. And although liberality, courage, or generosity are without doubt far greater and more praiseworthy things than charm and manners, none the less, pleasant habits and decorous manners and words are perhaps no less useful to those who have them than a noble spirit and self-assurance are to others. This is so because everyone must deal with other men and speak to them every day; thus, good manners must also be practised many times daily, whereas justice, fortitude and the other greater and nobler virtues are called into service much more seldom. Generous and magnanimous persons are not called upon to put such virtues into practice on a daily basis; rather, no one could behave in this way very often. Similarly even men who are strong and courageous are rarely required to demonstrate their valour and virtue by their works. Thus, while the latter virtues easily surpass the former in greatness and weightiness, yet the qualities I speak of surpass the others in number and frequency. I could very easily, if it were appropriate, mention to you many men who, though not worthy of high praise in other things, nevertheless are or have been highly esteemed only by reason of their pleasant manner. Thus helped and sustained, they have attained high rank, leaving far behind those who were gifted with those nobler and more outstanding virtues which I mentioned earlier. And, just as pleasant and polite manners have the power to stimulate the benevolence of those with whom we live, rough and uncouth manners lead others to hate and disdain us. . . .

[2]

So that you may learn this lesson more easily, you must know that it will be to your advantage to temper and adapt your manners not according to your own choices but according to the pleasure of those with whom you are dealing and act accordingly. This you must do with moderation, for when someone delights too much in favouring someone else's wishes in conversation or in behaviour he appears to be more of a buffoon or a jester, or perhaps a flatterer, rather than a well-mannered gentleman. And, on the contrary, someone who does not give a thought to another's pleasure or displeasure is boorish, unmannered, and unattractive.

Therefore, our manners are considered pleasant when we take into consideration other people's pleasures and not our own. And if we try to distinguish between the things which generally please the majority of men and those which displease them we can easily discover what manners are to be shunned and what manners are to be selected for living in society.

Let us say, then, that every act which is disgusting to the senses, unappealing to human desire, and also every act that brings to mind unpleasant matters or whatever the intellect finds disgusting, is unpleasant and ought to be avoided.

[3]

Dirty, foul, repulsive or disgusting things are not to be done in the presence of others, nor should they even be mentioned. And not only is it unpleasant to do them or recall them, but it is also very bothersome to others even to bring them to mind with any kind of behaviour.

Therefore, it is an indecent habit practised by some people who, in full view of others, place their hands on whatever part of their body it pleases them. Similarly, it is not proper for a well-mannered gentleman to prepare to relieve his physical needs in the presence of others. Or, having taken care of his needs, to rearrange his clothing in their presence. And, in my opinion, when returning from nature's summons, he should not even wash his hands in front of decent company, because the reason for his washing implies something disgusting to their imaginations.

For the same reason it is not a proper habit when, as sometimes happens, one sees something disgusting on the road to turn to one's companions and point it out to them. Even less so should one offer something unpleasant to smell, as some insist on doing, placing it even under a companion's nose saying: "Now Sir, please smell how this stinks," when instead he should be saying: "Don't smell this because it stinks."

And just as these and similar actions disturb those senses which they affect, so grinding one's teeth, or whistling, or shrieking, or rubbing together rough stones, or scraping metal is unpleasant to the ear, and a man ought to abstain as much as possible from doing such things. Not only this, but he must avoid singing, especially solo, if his voice is out of tune and unharmonious. But few refrain from doing this; in fact it seems that whoever has the least natural talent for singing is the one who sings most often.

There are also some who cough or sneeze so loudly that they deafen everybody. And some who are so indiscreet in such actions that they spray those near them in the face.

You will also find the type who, when he yawns, howls and brays like an ass; or someone who opens his mouth wide as he begins to speak or carries on with his argument, producing thus a voice, or rather a noise, that a mute makes when he attempts to speak. And these vulgar manners are to be avoided because they are bothersome to the ear and to the eye.

Indeed, a well-mannered man ought to abstain from yawning too much because, besides the above-mentioned reasons, it seems that yawning is caused by boredom and regret, because whoever yawns would much rather be somewhere else and dislikes the company he is with, their conversation, and their activities. . . .

And when you have blown your nose you should not open your handkerchief and look inside, as if pearls or rubies might have descended from your brain. This is a disgusting habit which is not apt to make anyone love you, but rather, if someone loved you already, he is likely to stop there and then. . . .

[5]

. . . A well-mannered man must . . . take heed not to smear his fingers so much that his napkin is left soiled, for it is a disgusting thing to see. And even wiping one's fingers in the bread one is about to eat does not seem to be a polite habit.

The servants who wait on gentlemen's tables must not, under any circumstances, scratch their heads—or anything else—in front of their master when he is eating, nor place their hands on any part of the body which is kept covered, nor even appear to do so, as do some careless servants who hold them inside their shirt or keep them behind their backs hidden under their clothes. They must rather keep their hands in sight and out of suspicion, and keep them carefully washed and clean, with no sign of dirt anywhere upon them. . . .

[6]

You must know that men naturally desire different and varied things: some want to satisfy their wrath, some their gluttony, others their sexual desires, others their avarice, and still others some other appetite. When dealing with other men, however, it does not seem that one asks, or could ask or desire, any of the above-mentioned things, in as much as these appetites are not evident in their manners of behaviour or in their speech, but elsewhere. They therefore desire whatever can facilitate this act of social intercourse; and this appears to be kindness, honour, and pleasure, or some similar thing. For this reason one must not say or do anything which may give an indication that one holds the other person in little affection or harbours a low opinion of him. Thus, the habit of many people of falling asleep quite eagerly wherever a respectable group of persons is sitting in conversation appears to be impolite. By doing this, they show that they have a low opinion of the company and appreciate very little indeed both them and their discussion. Not to mention that whoever falls asleep, especially if he is in an uncomfortable position—which is inevitable—most of the time succumbs to the tendency to do something which is unpleasant to see or to hear. Very often he wakes up sweaty and slobbery.

For this same reason it appears to be a bothersome habit to get up where other persons are sitting in conversation and pace about the room. There are some who so fidget, writhe, stretch, and yawn, turning first to one side, then to the other, that it looks as if they have just caught the fever. These are obvious signs that they are unhappy with the company.

Those who occasionally pull a letter out of their pockets and read it act just as badly. Someone who pulls out his nail clippers and devotes himself to his manicure acts even worse, appearing to hold the company in no esteem at all and so tries to find some other amusement for himself in order to pass the time.

One must not indulge in the habits of some other men, such as humming to oneself, or tapping one's fingers, or moving one's leg to and fro, for they indicate that the person does not care for others.

In addition, one must not turn one's back to someone, nor hold one's leg so high that those parts covered up by clothing become visible, for these acts should not be done among persons one respects. However, it is true that if a gentleman did them among very close friends or in the presence of a friend of lower social rank he would show not arrogance but rather love and intimacy. . . .

[7]

Everyone must dress well according to his status and age, because if he does otherwise it seems that he disdains other people. For this reason the people of Padua used to take offence when a Venetian gentleman would go about their city in a plain over-coat as if he thought he was in the country. Not only should clothing be of fine material, but a man must also try to adapt himself as much as he can to the sartorial style of other citizens and let custom guide him, even though it may seem to him to be less comfortable and attractive than previous fashions. If everyone in your town wears his hair short, you should not wear it long; and where other citizens wear a beard, you should not be clean shaven, for this is a way of contradicting others, and such contradictions, in your dealings with others, should be avoided unless they are necessary, as I will tell you later. This, more than any other bad habit, renders us despicable to most other persons. . . .

[10]

It is also not appropriate, especially for men, to be overly sensitive and fastidious, for to deal in this way with other people is called not companionship but servitude. There certainly are some who are so sensitive and easily hurt that to live or to be with them is nothing more than finding oneself surrounded by many fine glass objects, for they fear every little blow, and so they must be treated and respected like fine crystal. If you are not quick or solicitous enough in greeting them, visiting them, answering them, or paying your respects to them, they become as distressed with you as another man would if you had mortally insulted him. If you do not grant them all of their titles correctly, bitter quarrels and deathly hatreds immediately ensue. "You called me Sir and not Lord. And why don't you call me Your Lordship? I, after all, do call you signor Such-and-such." Or, "I did not have my proper place at the table. And yesterday you did not deign to come visit me at home, as I had come to visit you the day before yesterday. These are not ways of dealing with someone such of my rank."

These people truly bring others to the point of not being able to suffer their presence, for they indulge immoderately in self-love, and being so pre-occupied with themselves they have little time available to love anyone else. Besides, as I said at the beginning, men expect from the company of others those pleasures which they themselves seek. To be with such fussy people whose friendship tears as easily as a thin veil is not, therefore, a benefit but a burden. For this reason such company is not pleasant, but is highly unpleasant. Such sensitivity and such fastidiousness are best left to women. . . .

[13]

... You will meet many men who lie without intent of malice or personal advantage or with no wish to do damage or bring shame upon anybody, but because they like lying, much as someone who drinks not because he is thirsty but because he likes wine. Others tell lies for their own aggrandisement, boasting, claiming great accomplishments or great knowledge for themselves.

It is also possible to keep silent and lie, and this is done with actions and deeds. You will see some of middle or lower rank do this when they bear themselves with great solemnity and behave pompously, speaking so rhetorically, or rather pontificating, eager to sit in judgement on anything and strutting about so much that it is a deadly nuisance just to watch them.

You will find some who, although they have no greater wealth than others, have so many gold chains around their necks and rings on their fingers and so many brooches on their hats and here and there on their clothing that it would not befit the Seigneur [Lord] of Castiglione himself. Their manners are full of affectation and self-importance arising first from arrogance and ultimately from vanity, and these must be avoided because they are unpleasant and unbefitting. Know that in many of the best cities it is forbidden by law that a wealthy man parade about attired much more gorgeously than a poor man, for it would seem that the poor are wronged when others, even in matters of appearance, show themselves to be superior to them. So one must diligently take care not to fall into these silly habits.

Nor should a man boast of his nobility, his titles, his riches, least of all his intelligence. Nor should he praise at length, as some do, his past deeds and accomplishments, nor those of his ancestors, for in so doing it seems that he wants either to challenge those present who show themselves to be or who aspire to be equally as noble, as well off, and as capable, or to overwhelm them if they are of lesser stature, even appearing to chastise them for their humble origins and their poverty. In both cases such behaviour displeases everybody. Thus, one should neither humble nor unduly exalt oneself. Instead, one should rather subtract something from one's merits than add something to them with words, for even the truth, if flaunted, is displeasing. You should know that those who humble themselves beyond measure in their speech and refuse all honours that are their obvious due show far greater arrogance in this than those who usurp these honours without real merit. ... As you can see, we have named ceremonies with a foreign word, as is done for things for which our own language does not have a name; for it is evident that our ancestors did not know these ceremonies and so could not give them a name. In my judgement, ceremonies are, because of their emptiness, very little removed from lies and dreams. Consequently, we can very easily treat them together and join them in our treatise, seeing that the occasion to speak of them has arisen.

According to what a good man has explained to me several times, those solemnities which the clergy uses towards God and sacred things during divine services at the altar are rightly called ceremonies. But when men first began to pay respect to each other in artificial, inappropriate ways, and to call each other Lord and Sir, bowing and bending and writhing as a sign of respect, and uncovering their heads, and giving themselves exquisite titles, and kissing each others' hands as if they were sacred like a priest's, someone who did not have a name for this new, silly habit called it a ceremony. I think it was done in mockery, just as drinking and carousing are often called in jest a "triumph." This habit is certainly not native to us but is foreign and barbarous, only recently brought into Italy from where I do not know. Our poor country, brought low and humiliated in fact and effect, grows and is honoured only in vain words and superficial titles.

If we consider the intention of those who use them, ceremonies are an empty show of honour and reverence towards the person to whom they are directed, consisting of appearances, words, titles, and salutations. I say vain because we appear to honour those whom we hold in no special reverence and those whom we sometimes hold in contempt. None the less, in order not to stray from the habit of others, we refer to them as "the most illustrious Sir So-and-so," and "the most excellent Lord Such-and-such." Similarly, we sometimes present ourselves to someone to whom we would rather do a disservice than a service as "your most devoted servant."

Ceremonies should then be seen not simply as lies, as I have said, but also as infamies and treacheries. But because the words and titles I have mentioned have lost their strength and have been worn down like iron by the constant use we make of them, one should not listen to them as seriously as one does to other words, nor interpret them literally. The truth of this is evident when in our daily experience we meet someone we have never seen before and for some reason we need to speak to him without knowing his actual rank. More often than not we would rather say too much than too little. Thus, we will call him "Sir" or "Gentleman" even if he is only a cobbler or a barber dressed decently enough. In the past titles used to be determined and distinguished by papal or imperial privilege, and these titles could not be withheld without insulting and injuring the bearer, nor, on the contrary, could they be granted without mockery to those who did not possess them. Similarly, nowadays, one must grant much more liberally these titles and other similar indications of honour because custom—far too powerful a lord—has greatly privileged the men of our times with them. This habit, then, so beautiful and becoming on the outside, is inside totally empty, and consists in appearances without substance and in words without meaning. This does not allow us, however, to change it. On the contrary, we are obliged to abide by it because it is a fault of the times, not of ourselves. Ceremony, however, must be carried out with moderation.

[15]

For this reason one should keep in mind that ceremonies are observed for three reasons: for profit, for vanity, or out of duty. Every lie told for one's own profit is a fraud, a sin, and a dishonest thing, for one never lies honestly. This is the sin committed by flatterers. These men appear to be our friends and pander to our wishes, whatever they may be, not for our good but for their own profit, not to please us but to deceive us. And, although this vice may appear to be a pleasant habit, none the less it is not fitting for a well-mannered man because it is in itself despicable and harmful, for it is not acceptable that one should give pleasure by causing harm. Because ceremonies are, as we have said, lies and false flatteries, whenever we use them for our own profit we behave as disloyal and evil men. Therefore, no ceremony is to be used for this purpose. . . .

[28]

Therefore, a man must not be content with doing what is good, but he must also seek to do it gracefully. Grace is nothing else but something akin to a light which shines from the appropriateness of things that are suitably ordered and arranged one with the other, and in relation to the whole. Without this measure, even that which is good will not be beautiful, and beauty will not be pleasing. Just as with food which, although it is wholesome and nutritious, will not please the guests if it has no taste or a bad taste, so it will sometimes be with a man's manners. Even if there is nothing harmful in them, they will appear silly or distasteful unless he flavours them with that certain sweetness which is called, as I believe, grace or charm.

For this reason alone, every vice must be in itself offensive to other people, for vices are such ugly and improper things that their unsuitability displeases and disturbs every sober and well-balanced spirit.

Therefore, it is most advisable for those who aspire to be well liked in dealing with other people to flee vices, especially the fouler ones such as lust, avarice, cruelty, and the like. Some of these vices are despicable, such as gluttony or drunkenness; some are filthy, such as being a lecher; some are evil, such as murder. Similarly, other vices are despised by people, some more than others, each for its own nature and quality. But, as I have shown you before, all vices in general, because they are disordered things, render a man unpleasant in the company of others. However, since I undertook to show you men's errors and not their sins, my present care must be to deal not with the nature of vice and virtue, but only with the proper and improper manners we use toward each other. . . .

It is therefore suitable for well-mannered persons to be mindful of this balance of which I have spoken in their walking, standing, sitting, movements, bearing, and in their dress, in their words, in their silence, in their repose, and in their actions. Thus, a man must not embellish himself like a woman, for his adornments will then contradict his person, as I see some men do, who put curls in their hair and beards with a curling iron, and who apply so much make-up to their faces, necks, and hands that it would be unsuitable for any young wench, even for a harlot who is more anxious to hawk her wares and sell them for a price.

One should not smell either foul or sweet, so that a gentleman does not smell like a beggar or a man like a common woman or a harlot. Still, I do not say that at your age certain simple fragrances made from distilled waters are not suitable.

For the reasons I have mentioned above, your clothes should be according to the custom of those like you in age and condition. We do not have the power to change customs as we see fit, for it is time that creates them and likewise it is time that destroys them. Everyone, however, may adapt the current fashion to his own need. For example, if your legs are very long and the fashion calls for short clothes, you could make your garments a little less short. If someone has very thin legs, or unduly fat ones, or perhaps crooked ones, he should not wear hose of bright or attractive colours so as not to invite others to gaze at his defect.

Your garments should not be extremely fancy or extremely ornate, so that no one can say that you are wearing Ganymede's hose, or that you have donned Cupid's doublet. But whatever clothes you are wearing should fit your body well and suit you, so that it does not look as if you are wearing someone else's clothing. And above all they must befit your condition, so that a priest does not look like a soldier, or the soldier like a jester. When Castruccio was in Rome with Louis the Bavarian and enjoyed the glory and pomp of being duke of Lucca and Pistoia, count of Palazzo, a senator of Rome, lord and master at the court of the aforementioned Bavarian, he had made, for his pleasure and ostentation, a cloak of crimson velvet which on the breast bore in golden letters the motto "It is as God wills" and on the back, in similar letters, "It shall be as God wills." I believe you will recognize that this cloak would have been more appropriate for Castruccio's trumpeter than for Castruccio himself. And, although kings are above the law, still I could not commend King Manfred for the fact that he always dressed in green.

We must therefore take care that our garments fit not only the body but also the status of the person who wears them. And, furthermore, they should be suitable to the place where we live. For as in other lands there are other weights and measures and yet one sells, buys, and trades in every country, so in different places there are different customs and yet in every land a man can behave and dress himself properly.

The feathers that Neapolitans and Spaniards wear on their hats, and their elaborate trimmings and embroideries, do not suit the apparel of serious men or the clothes of city-dwellers. Armour and chain-mail are even less suitable. So, what is perhaps suitable in Verona, in Venice may not do, for these men, so feathered, decorated, and armed are out of place in that venerable city of peace and orderliness. In fact, they appear like nettles and burrs among good and sweet garden greens, and for this reason are ill received in noble gatherings, because they are so out of keeping with them.

A noble man must not run in the street, nor hurry too much, for this is suitable for a groom and not for a gentleman. Besides, a man will tire himself out, sweat and pant for breath, all of which are unbecoming to men of quality. Nor, on the other hand, should one proceed as slowly or demurely as a woman or a bride does. Also, it is unsuitable to wiggle too much when walking. One should not let his arms dangle, nor swing them around, nor throw them about so that it looks like he is sowing seed in a field. Nor should one stare a man in the face as though there was something to marvel at.

There are some who, when walking, lift their feet high up, like a frightened horse, and it looks as if they are pulling their legs out of a bushel basket. Others stamp their feet so hard on the ground that they make almost as much noise as a cart. One man points out with one of his feet. Another man raises one leg more than the other. There are some men who bend over at every step to pull up their stockings, and some who wiggle their behinds and strut like peacocks. These things are unpleasant not because they are very appealing, rather quite the opposite.

If by chance your horse held his mouth open or showed his tongue, even though it would not reflect on its skills, it would affect its price very much and you would get very much less for it, not because this habit would make him less strong, but because it would make him less graceful. We also see that two equally well built and comfortable houses will not have the same price if one appears well proportioned and the other does not. Thus, if one appreciates grace in animals and even in things, which have no soul or feelings, how much more should one seek and appreciate it in men?

| The Advantages of Villa Life, 1553

CORNELIO DUCCO Messer Giovanni Battista, you have very kindly persuaded me to interrupt my journey so that you could honor me at your table; and since your friends have left us alone to amuse themselves in this shady garden, moved by my love I feel I must tell you how warmly I appreciate your courtesy. Not only have you given me the opportunity to see this place, which is truly worthy of a prince, with its sumptuous house, its charming garden, extensive pergola and large fish pond; you have also given me the chance to tell you how astonished many people in the city are who, knowing you to be a cultivated man, cannot help finding fault with you for abandoning them and coming to live on this little estate. Now, because I am extremely fond of you, I should love to hear the reasons that led you to this decision. And I want to know all the more because I am sure that you did it only after much thought, and not on impulse, as the others believe.

GIOVANNI BATTISTA AVOGADRO My dear Messer Cornelio, I know you have always had my good name at heart, so I can do no less than tell you frankly why I came to live here. I see that our companions are nearing the gate of the garden where they are going to take their accustomed siesta, so I shall be able to give you a full account. Let me say to begin with that if those who criticize me knew the reasons that persuaded me to settle here, they would not blame me at all. Instead, they would inscribe over my door those words which were justly written over the door of Cato the Censor when he gave up his high position in Rome in order to enjoy the remainder of his life quietly on his little farm: "Cato, you are truly fortunate since you alone know how to live in this world."

You know from long experience what my life was like before, and how everything went wrong for me because of bad company. When shame finally made me realize this, I decided to abandon that whole world and retire here, determined to live in as civilized a fashion as I could for the time that remained to me. The more I feel the joy of every hour, the more I think that just as my former life was a constant hell, the present one is like paradise. Here my neighbors are civilized, courteous and peaceable, and they love me far more than I deserve; indeed we share everything to

"The Advantages of Villa Life" from Agostino Gallo, "Le dieci giornate . . . della Villa," in James Ackerman, *The Villa: Form and Ideology in Country Houses*, pp. 124–133 passim. Copyright © 1990 by Princeton University Press. Reprinted by permission of Princeton University Press.

such a degree that our possessions belong more to our friends than to the people who own them.

We go hunting together, or birding; we talk, read, sing, make music, play games, or eat together, as you saw this morning. And if by chance a quarrel should break out, everybody else immediately makes an effort to smoothe it over, and we become friends again just as before.

COR. DUCCO I am as pleased to hear these reasons why you left the city and retired to this beautiful estate as I am gratified more than I can say to hear that you have kept a holy peace among you. . . .

GIO. BATT. AVOGADRO . . . Is there anyone who would not seek to enjoy that view which extends from the distant mountains in the north to the plain of Brescia, stretching out for miles, and on to other territories? It is an ideal place from which to admire and meditate on the effects of dawn and of sunlight, the beauty of the heavens, the pattern of the stars, the phases of the moon—the serene air, the lofty mountains, the bewitching hills, the fertile valleys, and the spaciousness of the slopes and countryside.

COR. DUCCO O blessed hill! It has belonged to the noble Apiana family for more than a century, and is now even more beloved, tended and embellished than ever before by the worthy judge and orator Messer Lanterio and his brothers.

GIO. BATT. AVOGADRO Another great advantage of living in a villa is that in the morning you can be fifteen or twenty miles on your way on horseback before they have even opened the gates at Brescia. And similarly in the evening, we can linger as long as we like, and no one is going to lock us out, as they invariably do in the city, as soon as it strikes ten o'clock.

Is there anything to compare with the freedom and ease that we enjoy? In the city you are expected to go about well-dressed and attended by servants, and to be full of a thousand courtesies, showing deference to all sorts of people whom you do not respect at all. I am not speaking of those who deserve it—I never mind showing my respect for them at all times—but I must admit that I do it very unwillingly in the case of others who are completely worthless but are so puffed up with pride that they take offense if you fail to pay homage to them as they think proper. Here, on the other hand, I can go out or stay at home, without servants, without a hat, without a cloak, dressed in any way I choose. In the city people look down on you if you do not behave as they do, but here nobody envies us or scoffs at us or criticizes us or tells us how we ought to live. These privileges are no less welcome to our ladies than to ourselves. They are much happier leading their own lives here and decorously enjoying themselves in precious freedom than being constrained by the kind of social conduct that is expected of a married woman in the city.

COR. DUCCO You should be grateful to them for behaving in this praiseworthy fashion. I know many women who are so involved with life in the city that they would never agree to leave it. They want to be able to go wherever they like at any time, they want to dress up in the latest fashions, make themselves beautiful and wear perfume. They go around, bursting with vanity, wishing to be admired and flattered by everyone that sees them, thinking of nothing but dashing here and there wherever their fancy takes them. They turn up wherever there is a dance, a comedy, a tragedy, a joust, a feast or a tournament. Otherwise they spend most of the day standing in their doorway or looking out of the window, as if they had lost either their wits or their sense of shame, and they are invariably a source of scandal all over the town. Things were not like this in the old days; it only started after the barbarians corrupted us with their bad ways—not just in this part of the country but everywhere throughout Italy.

GIO. BATT. AVOGADRO I would to God that women did not behave like that (those who do, I mean, for there are many others who are models of propriety). But this plague seems actually to be spreading all the time, thanks to blind husbands and foolish fathers who are really the ones to blame. The only way to stamp out this corruption in our society is to impose the full penalties of the law on these evil women. Every bad daughter should get death for a dowry, worms for clothes, and a tomb for a house. Unfaithful wives should have their eyes gouged out, their tongues cut out, and their hands chopped off—or rather they should be wiped off the earth altogether, burnt alive!

COR. DUCCO Please, I beg you, no more of such thoughts, which lead nowhere. Tell me more of the contentment that you enjoy here.

GIO. BATT. AVOGADRO Here at this villa you do not hear people slandered, as you often do under the loggia in the city, or in workshops or other places. I am not speaking now of vicious people, but of ordinary respectable men and women who have no hesitation in blackening the reputation of honest wives, chaste widows, well-brought-up girls and even nuns! And they seem to enjoy talking about sordid things, like the price and warehousing of grain, money-making, money-lending, swindles, and other shady deals.

People here are not ambitious, envious, proud or underhand; they are not disloyal, hot-tempered, vindictive or murderous; they are not cuckolded by their wives; still less will you find them acting as false witnesses, dishonest notaries, lying officials, false lawyers, unjust judges or devious legal clerks.

Here you are free from bawling streetsweepers and garbage collectors, jostling porters and wine-carriers, bawds and whores reeking of musk, crooks and sorcerers who ensnare you, soothsayers and diviners who tell your fortune, cheats and cutpurses who deceive you, mercenaries and swaggering soldiers who bully you, and hypocrites and confidence tricksters who swindle you.

Nor, finally, will you see here debtors languishing in jail, criminals dragged off by force, swindlers sent to the galleys, slanderers having their eyes put out, blasphemers having their tongues slit, malefactors being branded on the face, false witnesses having their hands cut off, murderers being beheaded, thieves being hanged by the neck, traitors being quartered, and assassins being tortured with pincers and flayed. These are sights that wring one's heart, and move one to pity and loathing and extreme horror—especially when, as sometimes happens, the main square of the city is turned into a human slaughterhouse.

COR. DUCCO I do beg you to stop talking about these unpleasant subjects, and to go back to the reason why you enjoy such a cheerful life here.

GIO. BATT. AVOGADRO Who would want to live anywhere but in the country? Here we have complete peace, real freedom, tranquil security and sweet repose. We can enjoy pure air, shady trees with their abundant fruit, clear water, and lovely valleys; we can make use of the fertile farmland and the productive vines, as well as appreciating the mountains and hills for the view, the woods for their charm, the fields for their spaciousness and the gardens for their beauty.

Another source of enjoyment is being able to watch the hard work of the farmers and the obedience of their teams, as they skillfully plow and sow the fields, and then the crops growing well and being harvested; and also to hear the songs of the peasants, the pipes of the shepherds, the rustic bagpipes of the cowherds, and the sweet singing of the birds. . . .

COR. DUCCO . . . Now tell me how you spend your time throughout the year.

GIO. BATT. AVOGADRO First of all, I usually get up at dawn, and these days I join my companions at that hour to go out hawking. We roam all over the countryside, crossing slopes, climbing cliffs, scrambling over banks and across vineyards, waterways, bushes, meadows, fields of millet, areas of scrubland, and other places. Sometimes we keep together, sometimes we separate, in order to catch as many partridges as we can. We keep this up until after the third hour. Then we come home and often we eat together, as you saw us doing this morning. Over the meal we talk about what we have discovered and caught, and the contrary and favorable things that happened to us, and other diverting topics, until it is time to rest and to attend to some necessary business. After that we often find ourselves getting together again to read, play cards or board games or chess, sing or play musical instruments, as you will see shortly when the ninth hour has struck. So we modestly while away this time until quite late, keeping out of the heat as much as we can at this time of year. After we have amused ourselves in this way, we walk in a group to visit this friend or that, to see the beauties of his flower and kitchen gardens, his ponds, or his fountains combined with pleasant retreats. There we sit and talk, not altogether seriously, in the open air. This evening I hope to show you similar things. I am sure you will enjoy them, and decide that for good breeding, sound administration and good manners this tiny estate is the equal of our city or any other place.

And what would you say if I told you that sometimes, at the same hour, we come across our ladies in the midst of their own amusements, strolling about the estate to see some of the charming sights I have mentioned, or chatting beside some pool or clear fountain? We greet them with proper ceremony and then we talk with them in a bantering way, mingling ingenious arguments with pleasantries and innocent jokes. Sometimes one of us sits down to play the lute or the viol or some other instrument of that sort. Then you see the wife taking her husband by the hand, the father his daughter, the son his mother, the daughter-in-law her father-in-law, the brother his sister, the uncle his niece, the grandfather the grandmother, and so on, until they are all dancing joyously and chastely. If only God would grant that all dancing today was of that sort we should avoid a great deal of the licentiousness and scandal that is now so widespread throughout Christendom! At the end of these pleasant excursions we accompany the ladies one by one with sweet conversation back to their rooms.

COR. DUCCO You describe these excursions so vividly that I am quite transported and hardly know whether I am seeing them in a dream or listening to you telling me about them. But I am sure that everything you have said is true.

GIO. BATT. AVOGADRO I assure you that what I have told you and what I am going to tell you is just the simple truth. I confess that I enjoy harmless tricks myself, but I would never be capable of devising one, let alone of playing it on you.

FURTHER READING

James S. Ackerman, *The Villa: Form and Ideology in Country Houses* (1990)

William J. Bouwsma, *Venice and the Defense of Republican Liberty* (1968)

John K. Brackett, *Criminal Justice and Crime in Late Renaissance Florence, 1537–1609* (1993)

Andre Chastel, *The Fall of Rome, 1527* (1983)

Eric Cochrane, *Florence in the Forgotten Centuries* (1973)

———, *Italy, 1530–1630*, ed. J. Kirshner (1986)

———, ed., *The Late Italian Renaissance* (1970)

Denis Cosgrove, *The Palladian Landscape: Geographical Change and Its Cultural Representations in Sixteenth-Century Italy* (1993)

Virginia Cox, *The Renaissance Dialogue: Literary Dialogue in Its Social and Political Contexts, Castiglione to Galileo* (1992)

Anthony M. Cummings, *The Politicized Muse: Music for Medici Festivals, 1512–1537* (1992)

Robert C. Davis, *The War of the Fists: Popular Culture and Public Violence in Late Renaissance Venice* (1994)

Elisabeth G. Gleason, *Gasparo Contarini: Venice, Rome, and Reform* (1993)

J. R. Hale, *England and the Italian Renaissance* (1963)

John Martin, *Venice's Hidden Enemies: Italian Heretics in a Renaissance City* (1993)

Edward Muir, *Mad Blood Stirring: Vendetta and Factions in Friuli During the Renaissance* (1993)

Laurie Nussdorfer, *Civic Politics in the Rome of Urban VIII* (1992)

Guido Ruggiero, *Binding Passions: Tales of Magic, Marriage and Power at the End of the Renaissance* (1993)

J. N. Stephens, *The Fall of the Florentine Republic, 1512–1530* (1983)

Fulvio Tomizza, *Heavenly Supper: The Story of Maria Janis*, trans. and ed. Anne J. Schutte (1991)